To John —
Special Bless

Diana Stone

Testimonials

Some names and addresses have been omitted at the request of the sender.

I connected with the book *The Lightbody Activation Manual* and fell in love with it. Wow....will share with a couple of friends who are into healing and crystal work. Please include me in your newsletter listing. Thanks so much. Seeking the light."
Alice E.

****

"I am looking forward to receiving the *Ascension Guidebook. I love the lightbody activations!* The energy is amazing. Thank you. I read the Crystal Triangle and was so touched by Duane's journey on the Big Island. I am a Reiki master. Yesterday I did my first 5th dimension LBA (lightbody activation) with my friend and afterward did a Reiki session…the energy is so beautiful. I am so grateful to all of you who journeyed to bring this to all of us. I could go on and on.
Blessed be,"
Melissa A.

****

I've been a big fan for several years now & first started with your brother Duane with the Ascension Activations. Read your books and with his guidance offered to do these sessions for several years. Followed them to a tee and felt them to be wondrously powerful. I was also one of the first to get the Galactic Activations. This was just after they were downloaded to Duane, I believe. Loved those too!
Thanking you from my heart for the significant work you two offer humanity!
Tina B.

****

A third reason you survive and keep coming back again is your terrific sense of humor. My true genetic family comes from the City of Odessa in Ukraine (formerly part of the USSR) -- it's the comedy capital of eastern Europe. I'm a believer in humor and I think it's genetic! You can be an honorary descendant from Odessa. You once said I was an honorary Aquarian (strategically placed Uranus against a BIG Capricorn stellium); thank God for Uranus. So I'm bequeathing honors back to you.
Carol Astrid
Colorado

****

Greetings to both of you! Your books have changed/saved my life. Thank you so much. I am eternally grateful.
John A. C.
Kansas City, MO

"I have your other books and DVD...and just loved the whole set!!!"

“Also as note to you and loved ones.... I programmed small sets of amethyst, jade and rose quartz with the intent of each to carry either the Madam Pele, Sea Turtle and Dolphin energies and set them up permanently around the room used for energy work. The intent of these crystals is to constantly provide "crystal triangular grid protection , but especially to be activated when doing healing work on others. This avoids my having to always set up and take down the formations... It's nice to know with "intent" it works wonderfully.”

S.M. Scarpone — Usui Reiki Master and Karuna Reiki Master,
GTA (Greater Toronto Area), Ontario, Canada.

****

I can wholeheartedly recommend Diana Stone. Her wisdom and insight have been part of my life for over twenty years. In these unpredictable times it is an incredible help to have someone with her expertise to help advise me.
Donna M.
Italy

****

“Just received the first activation from a friend, wow, so powerful!
Thank You for bringing this material into the Earth plane.
Much Divine Love and Light to You and Yours!”
Alix L.

****

Thank you for all you and your brother have given to the world and helping us to raise our vibrations for this Ascension Co-Creative process!! I am a light worker and have been assisting with Light Body Activations & DNA upgrades since I received the activations myself and then read your books several years ago!
I am so grateful for all your selfless gifts. In gratitude, love & more Light,
Victoria Simoneaux www.QuantumLifesource.com

****

Thank you Diana!
I have enjoyed your books and they have been keeping me up late at night these days (smiling) ...Thanks for your help. I am gathering my stones to do the activations
Sherry N.

****

I would like to thank you and to send gratitude to you and your unconditional sharing. Also, gratitude in assisting the people, the world and the universe as a whole.
Karen C.

"Just wanted to tell you how much I enjoyed your book. Very enlightening and interesting.

A friend introduced me to the lightbody activation process recently and I must say it was truly a wonderful experience. She had been activated to the lightbody energy and wanted to share the experience with others. It was truly amazing.

We were in the Colorado mountains at another friend's cabin when each of us received the lightbody activation. I had mine preformed in the beautiful mountain air amongst the pines and aspens at about 13,500 feet elevation. Wow, what an experience. My totem animal came to oversee the event, which made it even more of a powerful experience. Just as we were coming to the close of the activation a Red-tailed Hawk carne and hovered flapping his wings to let us know he was there, when he knew he had all of our attention he circled 3 times. This to me signified that this was truly a blessed event for me.

Since the activation I have experienced many wonderful events on a person level, as well as seen changes occurring for the better within my family. I thought you would like to know that you have another light worker and Reiki Master that appreciates your writings and positive energy work. Thank you!"
Blessings!
Maggie B.

****

"...I have your other books and DVD that your hubby sent and just loved the whole set!!!"
Suzie S.

****

"...I wanted you to know that I have started doing the lightbody activations with some people here on Crete in Greece. It's amazing how it does work! I feel very excited that we have this opportunity due to you and your brother. I am looking forward to your book, whenever it is ready ... It will be done just at the right moment!!! I do appreciate your work highly, thank you so much for being here!!!"
Friendly Greetings,
Eva J.

****

"...I sure hope you are doing well .!! We LOVE doing the activations. What a gift! Thanks for sharing. We appreciate you."
Christine B.

****

"Have been meaning to mention I got the book Crystal Triangle and used the method also on my father in his last days at Hospice. The SW made a comment about how I'd made the energy in the room so nice.... it helped us both thanks"
Fay M.

PLAYING THE ASCENSION GAME

Participation in games shifts our entire consciousness into right-brain intuition, opening the door to the vast resources of all knowledge and all solutions.

THE TECHNOLOGY OF
ASCENSION SERIES©

Book Three

Diana Stone

Coauthor of *The Lightbody Activation Manual*

Contributing author David Bills

By analyzing the fundamental protocols in this book, I am convinced that what is outlined here serves as a multi-dimensional primer for any soul preparing to shift into the next dimension. Maybe a spiritual traveler will discover this volume on a library shelf in Year 2051 and find its dog-eared pages just as relevant as it was for us who traveled on so long ago.

Crystal Triangle Publishing
Vancouver, Washington

Did you ever dream about coming to planet Earth to participate in the greatest spiritual adventure in the history of all humanity?

You did! You can! You are!

Cover design: Donald Hurd
Page Composition and book design: Donald Hurd

Crystal Triangle Publishing
12005 N.W. 14th Avenue
Vancouver, WA 98685
www.DianaStone.com

Printed in the United States of America
Library of Congress Control Number: 2012942322

ISBN-13: 978-0-9725745-5-6
ISBN-10: 0-9725745-5-7

Other Books by Diana Stone

The Lightbody Activation Manual

First Edition published February 2003
Second Edition published December 2003
Third Edition published November 2005

Llewellyn's New World Astrology Series

Edited by Noel Tyl

Published by Llewellyn Publications

Book 11 – Published 1993

How to Manage the Astrology of Crisis

Chapter "Root Causes of Mental Crisis"

Book 12 -- Published 1993

Exploring Consciousness in the Horoscope

Chapter "The Artistry of Imagination"

Book 15 – Published 1995

Communicating the Horoscope

Chapter "A Communication Model for Astrologers"

The United States Wheel of Destiny

Published 1976 by American Federation of Astrologers

Out of print – To be completely revised and published under the new title:

The Spiritual Destiny of America

The Astrological Signatures and Occult Foundations of the United States

Dedication

To Thomas
for his Patient Guidance
(I sure hope you are real)

AND

To my little family group who unhesitatingly supported me
no matter how wild and crazy (in order of appearance):
Utterly trustworthy confidant and brother, Duane Henkle
Ex-husband and soul mate, Rex Bills
Son and wing man, David Bills
Husband and soul contract mate, Don Hurd
Husband-in-law, Christopher Johnson

AND

"Mr. Lux"
The teacher who opened my eyes to myself
And who loved me madly

This book is also fiercely dedicated to the other lightworkers who stayed the course every step of the way with me. You know who you are. You were wounded, yet laughingly played the Game. You believed. You rode the horse backwards and we all yelled, "Yippee!"

ACKNOWLEDGEMENTS

This is the part of a book where you recognize the people who have helped and supported you throughout the process of writing the book and bringing it through to final publication. .

Since this is a book about playing a game, a game must have heroes and villains. I did not have heroes; I had SUPER HEROES. Each and every one played a role so critical to this book that I can honestly say that there would be no book without them. Otherwise, I truly would have derailed and ended up in the middle of nowhere, despairing how I ever got so far off track in successfully completing a lifetime of work, experience and wisdom—and most of all—my soul mission.

My husband, Don Hurd, literally sat at my elbow, solving the endless mysteries that exist deep in the bowels of a computer. He devoted endless hours to the front and back covers' progression through dozens of revisions. He was totally in charge of interactions with the printers and submission of the final copy for publication. Most of all, he unflaggingly held a powerful image of the book, even at the times when I lost faith in it myself. He is a Super Hero.

My friend and colleague, Christine "Kriss" Shellman, was my angel messenger girl. Throughout the years that this book was struggling through a long pregnancy, she was the eyes that spotted even the most obscure bits of information that were so crucial to fill in the holes, and just when I needed them. Without her input, the book would have resembled Swiss cheese. She is also a shaman, an astrologer, a soul sister and we share the same birthday. She is a Super Hero.

My son David Bills contributed key original articles that would have been impossible for me to fully articulate myself. He deserves recognition as a contributing author. However, his ultimate contribution was his continuing support and unshakable faith that I could complete the book. He opened the door to the gaming world, a world that is totally foreign to me. Also, he is the funniest person I ever knew. Besides that, I am still #1 on his telephone speed dial. How many mothers can say that? He is a Super Hero.

My long-time friend, Judy Child, put me in touch with Jane McGonigal. This was the most powerful connection that literally led to the title of this book and opened the door to finding my true message. There is no doubt that she was following the promptings of Spirit, and for listening, she goes in the Hall of Fame for Super Heroes. Her friend, Maureen, qualifies as a Super Hero because they are a matched set.

My brother Duane Henkle was the one person who was most inside my head because of our long journey together on this soul mission. His advice on matters both technical and spiritual were always the most succinct and cut through to the spring board that catapulted me forward by mighty leaps. His deep appreciation of typography speaks silently to the reader through a subliminal awareness of beauty, balance and ease of reading the text. He has always been my Super Hero.

Rex Bills is one of my soul mate relationships and has been unfailingly approving of everything I have done throughout every day of my adult life. He was a person who supported me through the many life crises that delayed this book and said it was okay right where I was at any given time. He is the one other person who introduced me to the on-going evolution of the gaming world as well. He is a super hero. And Christopher Johnson my husband-in-law who joined my entire family group instantly and without question was also my computer angel. He is a super hero.

I owe a huge debt of gratitude to Douglas Bloch and Robert Blaschke, both astrological colleagues and authors themselves. They are the ones who first suggested that we publish this series of books ourselves. They generously mentored Don and me through the steep learning curve of self-publishing. Thank you Douglas, and God rest your soul, Robert. You are Super Heroes.

To discover my soul sister, Jane McGonigal, was so much more than soul satisfying. Before I read her book *Reality Is Broken* and listened to her message, I thought I was just playing—and indeed I was! I failed to understand the role that gaming played in the ascension process and the Shift into a brave new world. Understanding her journey tore down all limiting boundaries and revealed my game and my own true self. She is my Super Hero.

We have all heard the expression, "They were there when I needed them." Dr. Elizabeth Carlson puts a name and a face on those words. My call to her on Friday at 7:00 A.M. in April 2010 spared me a trip to the psych ward. She continued to hold my hand—day or night—for the coming months. If not for that I would be languishing in a very bad place even yet. What makes her support even more Heroic is that she was wounded herself at the time. She is my Super Hero.

Rev. Judith McLean is the author of the Foreword. I was thrilled that she accepted. She gets extra Hero points because she not only agreed to do it, she said she was "honored and thrilled" to be asked. Considering the common bond that we share through similar work, we are colleagues and soul sisters.

I needed a fresh set of beta readers to plough through the manuscript, especially while I was coping with cataract surgery and could not see well for several weeks until I got my glasses fitted. Rex Bills and Christopher Johnson were willing to interrupt their retirement activities to diligently analyze everything with a critical eye. I appreciate their conscientious efforts, but not THAT conscientious. Only kidding. You are Super Heroes.

There are so many more Super Heroes. These are the ones who have written such wonderful letters of love, appreciation and support of my astrological, healing and writing endeavors through many years, letters that have often moved me to tears. Only a representative few are included in the testimonial pages at the front of the book. I want you to know that I keep a fat file of your letters. On a bad day, I pull them out and read them again. They instantly restore my soul. Thank you, all of you.

I believe without a single doubt that I am surrounded by those that exist in the unseen world around me. I feel your guidance and am impressed and amazed at your ability to steer me in the right direction. I thank you and count you among my Super Heroes as well. Now if you could only type...

TABLE OF CONTENTS

Judith Marie McLean, Ph.D.

Judith McLean, Ph.D.

Judith Marie McLean has worked in the field of healing for over thirty-two years. She has been a professional clinical and pastoral counselor, a health care provider and manager of a health care advocacy department. She has worked in many types of social and mental health venues. Her professional degrees include an M.S. in Pastoral Counseling from Loyola College of Baltimore, Maryland, and a Ph.D. in Philosophy from Stratford University, British Columbia, Canada. She was a licensed clinical professional counselor in both Maryland and Pennsylvania until her retirement in 2008.

Her spiritual healing work has been her life's passion and continuous avocation since her kundalini awakening in 1980. Her gifts of clairvoyance, clairsentience, psychometry and the art of moving and constructing with energy have helped her in personal healing practice and global spiritual work.

Judith resides in Waynesboro, Pennsylvania with her husband, Mark McLean. She has four boys and two stepchildren. Her life is currently very active with the artistic activities of quilting and gardening, writing and doing ascension healing work for the planet and Universe.

Her 2009 book *Ascension Journey: A Handbook for Healing Through the Dimensions* is a landmark contribution to the field of ascension literature. She describes her kundalini experiences, soul retrieval, earth cleansing, etheric healing, death and enlightenment, and offers both traditional viewpoints and her own experiences. Reviewers have given her book a 5-Star rating.

FOREWORD

By Judith M. McLean, Ph.D.

If you want to laugh your way through your ascension process, then be sure that Diana Stone's new book is your guide. Some people are blessed with a powerful sense of humor which Diana has mastered. What a gift to be able to laugh at one's self and experiences and allow the reader to ride the tide of glee as each personal situation is shared! This is the power of her new book, ***Playing the Ascension Game.*** Without the self-deprecating mirth and amusing anecdotes, this book would not be as inspiring as it is. Diana allows the reader to suspend judgment and roll along with one episode after another enjoying each moment. If you were born with Mercury in Capricorn like I was, you can appreciate why I write like an encyclopedia but Diana's Mercury in Aquarius allows merriment to roll one along from one concept to another.

The Universe laughed when I was born in the same birth sign as Diana's—only fourteen years later. We both share moons in Cancer and other Aquarian aspects. I'm sure the healers from the Age of Pisces would look askance at our Aquarian jargon and indeed, our talk of vortexes, portals, dimensions and ascension symptoms. They used rattles, drums, vision quests, and herbs while we are moving energy with our thoughts and dissipating spooks with blasts of force. Despite our age differences, the similarities in our work are astounding.

Would you believe that the two of us are from Iowa? Yes, we are from the land of corn, cows and hard, hard work. Despite our conservative Midwestern and religious upbringings, we both ended up to be alien walk-ins with kundalini rising. Maybe I should clarify here that being a "walk-in" can also mean that a higher vibrational aspect of oneself is brought into the physical vehicle at an auspicious and agreed upon time between the soul and body consciousness. So maybe the alien walk-in part is really just a dimensional self that exists in what we would consider to be an "alien" place. But, I'm sure our friends agree upon one thing—we are a little different.

Diana and I live a coast apart. She is in Vancouver, Washington, and I am in Pennsylvania. Spirit doesn't care where we live. It makes use of us beyond our 3-D environments in one location. We traverse the dimensions and can as easily work in Australia as in our own physical location. We both do our shamanic work with groups. Diana's spiritual group consists of family members and my spiritual group varies from time to time, but exists in other dimensions. We both have male spirit guides that have helped us since our beginning awakening, and who check in from time to time to make sure we are on a good course. We have both specialized in healing, spirit releasement, soul retrieval, earth cleansing, and now, most importantly, ascension work. We tend to share similar types of experiences, and we are both proficient at messing up computers and anything electrical. Oh, the frustration!

Diana has set some ultimate goals in presenting this book for you. She wants to help you prepare your physical body to tolerate higher frequencies fundamental to the 5th dimension. To do this, she makes clear that "doing the work" is of profound importance. Diana would have a snappy reply to one of my email correspondents who thought ascension sounded wonderful and wanted it all now. It just doesn't happen that way. While the pioneers in ascension work have forged a path to ascension, they did so with great cost to themselves, their bodies, and psyches. The ascension symptoms are varied and many. At times it feels as though one's mental capacities have been torpedoed. The nervous system is always in jeopardy for shamans, and the aches and pains could fill chapters alone. Then there is the risk for those pesky varmints who tend to gravitate to your light after you release them from someone else.

The work and pioneering that has taken generations to achieve will now take a shorter amount of time for this age of spiritual seekers and those following. However, the same cleansing of body, mind and soul must take place. **It is imperative!** As to pioneering souls, Diana has been among the first of those called "ascension" workers and to her we owe great gratitude. Her life challenges have been many as she worked as a human vehicle in which the higher vibrational energies could build new pathways. She was a guinea pig of sorts, and it's not easy being among the first who establish new ways. I am infinitely grateful for Diana's work and writing , and the impact she has made upon the spiritual field! Without her, we would still be shuffling Tarot cards and not graduating to direct information and telepathic exchanges from other dimensional beings.

Playing the Ascension Game is an apt name for the concepts that Diana is imparting. Along with the humor and thoughts of playfulness that come with the title, one is led into the "rules" of ascension and the work to be done. I am reminded of the cult favorite; ***The Matrix*** where there is a world oblivious to the fact it is not really real. We are very much like players in the Matrix and can only graduate if we are aware and understand the rules of ascension. Among the guidelines that Diana seeks to teach are the ones about reincarnation, DNA, synchronicity, making the subconscious conscious, cleansing the body, mind and soul, and about the Universe as a great Trickster. Diana's fun with stories of food and food fallacies show Spirit as its trickster best.

She is indeed a "top of the line" shaman and knows how to clear not only the subconscious of cobwebs but chase away the literal gremlins as well. One of the most important works a shamanic healer does is to prevent foreboding gloom from extinguishing the light. Darkness comes in forms of fear, depression, criticism, judgment, trauma, despair and from negative beings and entities. Our New Age community often thinks that all is love and light, but in this dualistic world there is always the polarity of darkness that needs to be understood, acknowledged and surmounted. A denial of the darkness (or shadow side as Jung would have called it) causes disassociation of parts of the soul. My own experience of facing my masculine violence of past lifetimes was extremely difficult. However, without doing this work, I would still have fragmented parts of the soul that were not brought into wholeness and healed.

The potential in confronting the shadow side is that often along with the negative traits there are powerful ones. In bringing the darkness back into the light, we bring the capable qualities as well. When we disassociate unwanted parts of ourselves, we can create quite ugly doppelganger beings. This can be the result from unwanted parts of oneself that have not been acknowledged, healed and brought into awareness. The shaman can see the unhealed demons within the client and knows that they need the ultimate love and acceptance that end the negativity. If one is prone to attracting mishaps and discord, a shaman can also determine if past karma is involved; a negative mindset; a miasm coming down genetic lines; or just being in the wrong place at the wrong time.

One of the most powerful chapters of the book, Chapter Seventeen on Ho'oponopono, a Hawaiian healing technique, teaches the reader how to do self-healing. Using this technique emphasizes the power of forgiveness, love and gratitude. No spiritual journey is successful without these traits and they are powerful enough to lead one into ascension without specific guidance. If we could live a loving, grateful and forgiving life on a constant basis, we would automatically be in the 5th dimensional consciousness and would move into ascension.

To end my foreword and tribute to Diana and her book, I would like to say that she has impacted my life in the most wonderful and powerful ways. She has been able to help me with her astrological skills and answer questions in times of need. Most of all, she has been a fellow shaman to whom I could turn and ask the question, "Am I crazy?" There aren't too many healers of our type around and to find a "soul sister" has been one of the Universe's greatest gifts to me. Particularly since I was led to one with a sense of humor!

INTRODUCTION

"It is games that give us something to do when there is nothing to do. We call games 'pastimes' and regard them as trifling fillers in the interstices of our lives. But they are much more important than that. They are clues to the future. And their serious cultivation is perhaps our only salvation."

Bernard Suits
philosopher

The following are all quotes from Dr. Jane McGonigal's
New York Times' bestseller book *Reality is Broken:
Why Games Make Us Better and How They Can Change the World*

Gaming can solve all of the world's problems

We can make any future we can imagine.

Only in a game is the impossible possible.

Gaming: The best hope for surviving the next century on this planet.

People speak of being in the real estate game, or the insurance game or "playing the stock market." It has become part of the English idiom. We object to people who play games in relationships. Also, we don't really trust "players." We frequently regard them as people who manipulate others.

My very earliest exposure to any serious idea of games was in the 1970s when I enrolled in a two-semester class offered for college credits on Transactional Analysis, a psychotherapy developed by Eric Berne. A main feature of the class was the analysis of Berne's best-selling book *Games People Play* (1964). Berne, a psychiatrist, defined a game in his method of therapy as "an ongoing series of complementary transactions progressing to a well-defined, probable outcome. A game was played to satisfy some hidden motivation."

Eric Berne once described himself as a "56-year-old teenager." He was also a keen poker player. A biography, published posthumously, was titled *Eric Berne: Master Gamesman* (1954). When I merged all of these influences together at that time, I developed an attitude towards games that they were either psychologically unhealthy and destructive or childish and immature.

The next major encounter with the idea of "the game" occurred in the early 80s when I launched a shamanic journey with my grown son, our first undertaken together, and introduced him to a mind-expanding drug (legal at that time) under the careful tutelage of our Spirit Teacher, Thomas. The transfer from a purely psychological genre to a shamanic setting represented a shift as wide as the Grand Canyon in my consciousness around games.

In Chapter Three of this book "The Ascension Game" I describe how The Game of Life emerged as a primary theme of my son and my shamanic travels together. We actually thought we invented it at the time. We were wrong! After a while, the idea of the game was all over the map: books, TV, the Internet, you name it. Everything was some sort of game. Coincidentally, a movie *Hunger Games* is breaking box office records at theatres all over the country as I write this (May 2012).

One afternoon, the stars lined up just right. With adrenaline pumping, the right name for this book shot into my consciousness. My best effort at the time *Countdown To Ascension And Beyond* was trashed as I threw my arms wide to embrace *Playing The Ascension Game*. It was love at first sight. I was ecstatic. Nothing thrills me more than to find just the right name for something, for anything. I harbor a strong belief that everything has its one and only right name just for it. You may call that a metaphysical belief or whatever, but it's my strong feeling about the subject—just so you understand what that meant to me. It wasn't just any old name. It was the right name. It was the *exactly* right name.

However, my *cause celebre* was short-lived. So what was this reversal of fortune: atop the mountain in one breath and Alice plunged to the bottom of the rabbit hole in the next? I was experiencing the angst of the unwelcome realization that "playing games" and "gamers" carried a strongly negative connotation for a great many people.

I called my brother to ask his advice about my real fears that many people would not "get" the title of my book, and what did he say? "I always think of gamers as people who play games in Las Vegas"—Omygod, my own brother! Not to be overly-melodramatic or anything, but I just couldn't sacrifice my perfect title on the altar of what were strongly-held attitudes about what my title may be implying. How could I turn the tables on the only-too-real misconceptions about gamers and gaming when the odds stacked against me exceeded the dollar slots? Days passed. Tears were shed. Paragraphs were written and shredded. More tears. Weeks passed. My mood plummeted to desperation and panic. I was stuck.

Is That The Cavalry Coming Over The Hill?

Then synchronicity served up Jane McGonigal's *New York Times'* bestseller book *Reality Is Broken: Why Games Make Us Better and How They Can Change The World.*

I was led to the only woman on the planet, a best-selling author, who actually lectures in public and on TV that the greatest hope for solving humanity's most serious problems is by playing games. Pretty laughable, eh? Obviously a crackpot? Think again! Miss McGonigal holds a Ph.D. from the University of California, Berkeley. Her theories are backed up by 10 years of solid research. I knew I had found a soul sister, and the book had found its soul.

In order to understand this book *Playing The Ascension Game* I must take you through yet one more layer of the meaning of games and gaming. First, I would like to quote some interesting statistics (as of 2011); I probably should say, "some shocking statistics." If you are a gamer, you may still be shocked. Guess who was also shocked; I was!

Originally, my goal was to pull out all the stops in a campaign directed at convincing potential readers that the title of my book did not refer to people playing the latest game to hit Las Vegas. After reading McGonigal's book, however, I realized that if my book was *not* connected to game consciousness in some manner, it would soon be well on its way to a detour to a certain death. I felt a wave of panic. It was a close call. What if I had caved in and relinquished the *exactly* right name!

Following are those statistics that changed my consciousness, the ones intended to change yours. I still appreciate a good joke even when the joke is on me.

- In the United States alone, there are 183 million active gamers (Individuals who play computer or video games on average 13 hours a week.)

- 40 percent of all gamers are women.

- There are now more than 6 million people in China who spend 22 hours a week gaming, the equivalent of a part-time job.
- 69 percent of heads of households play computer and video games.
- 97 percent of youth play computer or video games.
- One out of four gamers is over the age of 50.
- The average game player is 35 years old and has been playing for 12 years.
- Most gamers expect to be playing games for the rest of their lives.

Gamers Have Had Enough Of Reality

We are forced to take this growing trend seriously. In the United States, over half of the population already are gamers! However, some people have no interest in why this is happening. They are already certain they know what games are good for—wasting time, tuning out and losing out on real life. Perplexed parents, concerned politicians and bewildered teachers view with alarm the skyrocketing amount of time and money spent on games.
However, while these value judgments and moral debates over games continue over neighborhood back fences, company boardrooms, local classrooms or coffee breaks everywhere, this disdain is blinding naysayers to the most significant consideration of all. Something must be attracting more and more people of all ages everywhere into the game worlds.

It is my opinion that we should be much more concerned about why this is happening at all. Pure common sense is dictating what to me is the obvious; gaming must be satisfying some human need that contemporary reality is not. The following is a direct quote from McGonigal's book, which makes some critically important explanations about this exploding phenomenon:

> "The truth is this: In today's society, computer and video games are fulfilling genuine human needs that the real world is currently unable to satisfy. Games are providing rewards that reality is not. They are teaching and inspiring and engaging us in ways that reality is not. They are bringing us together in ways that reality is not. Collectively, the planet is now (2011) spending more than 3 billion hours a week gaming. We are starving and our games are feeding us."

The back cover notes on this groundbreaking book show how we can leverage the power of games to fix what is wrong with the real world—from social problems like depression and obesity to global issues like poverty and climate change—and introduces us to cutting-edge games that are already changing the business, education and nonprofit worlds. Gamers are not escapists who do not live a "real world" life. And how about this amazing prediction: Virtually every person on this planet will someday be a gamer!

Next, McGonigal's TED lecture was on TV, and I watched it. She started off her lecture by making certain statements that evoked titters from the audience. By the end of her talk she had them eating out of her hand. Do games really make us happy? Can games really solve the problems of the world?

Now I can peel back another layer and arrive at an updated definition of a game. In reality, excuse the pun, there is an infinite variety of games beyond the kind in which the player sits before a computer console. There are single-player games and games that run the continuum all the way to huge multi-player games. One may choose a five-second minigame, a ten-minute casual game, story-based games or ones with no story.

Compared with games, reality is hard to get into. Games motivate us to participate more fully in whatever we're doing. To participate wholeheartedly in something means to be self-motivated and self-directed, intensely interested and genuinely enthusiastic. If we're forced to do something, or if we do it halfheartedly, we're not really participating. If we don't care how it all turns out, we're not really participating. If we're passively waiting it out, we're not really participating.
And the less we fully participate in our everyday lives, the fewer opportunities we have to be happy. It's that plain and simple. The emotional and social rewards we really crave require active, enthusiastic, self-motivated participation. .

Diana, *The Inventor of Games* game

The very first germ of my innate game consciousness may well have seen its infancy in a Huna group I sponsored free to anyone who cared to attend. That would have been in the late 70s and early 80s. It was a class about the ancient Hawaiian system of healing followed by meditations and healing work. It was very informal. There are some further references to this group in various chapters. (You won't want to miss them!)

We met in an extra room in the same building in which I had my astrology office in the daytime. My office address in Portland, Oregon, was on Canyon Road. The class got a big kick out of it when I began referring to the group as the *Canyon Road Power and Light Company*. Would you believe that to this day (2012) I occasionally hear from someone who signs himself "an old-timer from the *Canyon Road Power and Light Company* group? It still cracks me up.

Hey, Wait! It Goes Farther Back Than That

Maybe there is a special gene in certain individual's DNA that naturally produces game consciousness. I just made that up, but if it were true I would have that gene for sure. I realized it came so natural to me that I almost didn't think to mention it at all. When my son was a little kid, I swore that he would not grow up to be a finicky eater. Secondly, neither would I demand that he eat food that he hated. I don't want to eat food that I hate, so why should he? I also thought it was wrong to force a child to "clean up his plate" when he is already full. I consider all of these things a form of child abuse. This did not mean that I thought he should dine on Hershey bars and pizza, however. With that said, I thought it was also a parent's responsibility to see that the kid ate a healthful diet. To accomplish all of these goals, I invented the Eat Your Vegetables game. This is how it worked. Feel free to adapt it to your own children's needs.

I categorized certain foods according to age group. It is a pretty safe bet that any kid will like ice cream. So ice cream fell into the one year old and above category. Beets on the other hand, fell into the five years old and above category. Whenever I served beets for dinner, I carefully served my husband and me. David was not allowed to have any until he was five years old. Of course, he wanted what we were having, but I made a very big deal about him not being five years old yet. I emphasized that he would hate beets if he ate them too young.

He had a sleepover with one of his little friends, and the mother served beets for dinner. Of course, he sneaked some beets. He had to shamefacedly admit that he had done this terrible thing and eaten beets bcfore he was five years old. Of course, I made a huge "I tried to tell you" lecture. When he was five years old, it came time to have beets. Of course, he loved them and even called Grandma long distance to report on this significant step toward manhood. So it went with other foods.

And More Games

My husband hid back inside a deep closet that we had and called David's name. It really did sound spooky. "Dad's turned invisible," I screamed, "because he ate too much lettuce again." Of course, from that day forward David devoured lettuce and then ran to the mirror to see if he was invisible yet. "Not yet," I would say. That is when we started serving lettuce for breakfast.

So, how did the Eat Your Vegetables game turn out? Despite my mother's misgivings that I was twisting David's consciousness beyond all normal expression, he enjoys all variety of foods, is extremely health conscious, and in his early 50s is also very healthy. By the way, the over-50 age group is allowed spirits of their choice, which turns out to be expensive Scotch in his case. This ends up costing me top dollar to keep my liquor cabinet stocked for when he comes to hang out for the evening. Perhaps there is some karma-balancing in there somewhere.

Let the Games Begin!

I published an e-newsletter beginning in 2002. It was intended to be an approximately 500-word piece on astrology. Instead, it became a cutting-edge publication on alternative spirituality, several pages long. It was not long before inventing the Games began. From what I have told you, it was inevitable.

I invented the first e-newsletter game *The Ready For Prime-Time Players*. This was successful in joining Prime-Timers together, individuals of like-mind and interests, in a virtual network. Games were a continuing theme of the newsletter. I just did not realize its significance at the time.

There was *Project Wake-Up!*, which was a name for what was essentially Metaphysics 101. Then came the *Unreasonable Fanatics Game*, *The Inter-Galactic Federation of Electrical Workers* came along and lastly, the *Mission: Impossible Game.*

More Messages From The Universe

The following is a direct quote from one of Dolores Cannon's series of books *The Convoluted Universe*. This message came through a deep hypnotic session Cannon conducted with a woman client. I trust Cannon's work as generally uncensored and reliable information as it comes directly from the subconscious of deeply hypnotized subjects. It is not channeled. See the quote below:

> "Her (the hypnotized woman) subconscious saw her doing wonderful things during the Shift, and in the next ten, twenty years she is going to have a big part to play in all of this." (Diana's note: and so will many of us!)

This communicates to me that December 21, 2012, is one of the most significant dates in human history. Nevertheless, it is still just one day in a long process that started years ago and will continue for many more years to come. The games have already begun.

Since ascension is a process already begun and promises to stretch many years past the 2012 date, we can expect to move toward a greatly changed future in baby steps. Each of the chapters of this book should be perceived as not a final word but a door ajar, a baby step, a threshold through which we gradually pass into an ever-evolving and greatly transformed future world.

The Chapters Are A Continuum

The chapter "Food For Thought," for example, takes you from chowing down on whatever tastes good, moves to the threshold of listening to what your body needs on any given day, all the way to living only on prana. Is that where our future is taking us in the 5th dimension? The chapter "Believing is Seeing" examines the ability to constantly remain flexible and open-minded, which may in the last analysis determine one's access to the next dimension of reality versus remaining stuck, repeatedly circling the turning wheel of the reincarnation/karmic cycles.

The chapter "Lets Get Physical" initially examines the present situation of humanity's disconnection from the physical body, and consequently, from all of Nature herself; then gradually escalates to a heightened communication, eventually with individual organs and cells. Can we imagine also a future in which direct communication with the plants and animals is as routine throughout the ascension game process as it was in the amazing Findhorn gardens in Scotland?

In the first two chapters Harmonic Concordance I and II, conducted under the guidance of our Spirit Teacher, Thomas, the shamanic group with whom I work was privy to his prediction that "everything would be revealed, all the way to the top." That prediction has come true as corruption all the way from the Catholic church to giant corporations to government agencies and others have come to light. At the same time, I was directed to "let it all hang out" when I wrote this book. Consequently, I included some subjects that I never intended to write about. I gulped a couple of times, but I did as he asked. This is to tantalize you with the mystery of revelations yet to come!

Games have rules. Most of the chapters in this book are for the purpose of placing a rule book in your hands for raising 3rd dimensional consciousness in order to increase individual frequency rates to eventually complement those of the higher dimensions. "Thou shalt not enter the Kingdom of Heaven dragging thy baggage behind thee." 2 Diana 4:1

In the Huna system that I mention elsewhere in the book, the Middle Self refers to the conscious mind. The Low Self (beLOW consciousness) refers to the subconscious. The subconscious, or unconscious, mind performs various duties, among which is controlling the involuntary nervous system that includes breathing, metabolism and other functions of which you are unaware, day or night. For our purposes here we are interested in the most amazing aspect of the subconscious: ***It is in communication with the Universe as a whole!*** What that means is that it is the ultimate information source and can provide answers to absolutely anything upon demand.

Wouldn't you like to know the answer to anything in the entire Universe? It says right up there that you can. So how have you been doing in acquiring the answers to *anything* you want to know? Maybe you need to check that out again: Wasn't it the *subconscious* that grants you access to anything in the Universe? So do you have to be asleep before you are operating at the subconscious level? Well, yes, that is one way. However, I don't hear you asking many questions while you are asleep. So what is the catch?

The first thing you must understand is the most powerful reality in the entire Universe: *Everything is connected.* (Oh, yeah, the same thing that the new theoretical physics is saying.) Everything is One. Therefore, if the subconscious has access to all knowledge, a way must be found to by-pass the conscious mind to connect with the Whole. Fortunately, a guy named David Hawkins popularized a long-known system that does exactly that, and you can learn it in five minutes. Consequently, you are going to fall in love with the chapter titled "Let's Get Physical."

When we play games we are in right brain reality. And when we are in right brain reality, we have access to everything in the Universe. So let the games continue and change the world.

PREFACE

There are certain topics that are best explained right from the beginning. Otherwise they grow into ghosts that haunt the reader's mind, unanswered questions constantly lurking from behind the lines. For example, everyone knows what a dimension is, don't they? At this time of shifting realities, the word *dimension* is bandied about as though there is some consensus about the meaning: the 3rd dimension, the 4th dimension, and the Holy Grail 5th dimension.

Dimensions are states of consciousness. They are not places like Minneapolis, Minnesota, or Miami, Florida. They are not marching in a row like little soldiers: 1,2,3; neither are they climbing the rungs of a ladder: 3,4,5. Consciousness vibrates at different frequencies. My consciousness in the 3rd dimension does not vibrate at the same frequency as it would in the 4th or the 5th. Your thoughts and feelings determine "where you vibe."

The BIG Question: What Happens on December 21, 2012?

Obviously, I have written and published this book BEFORE the December 21st date. Does that mean that everything will change on December 21, 2012, making this book passé? Maybe everyone will be hanging out in the 5th dimension after that. Who needs a guidebook for shifting to the 5th dimension then? In this book, I state several times that I do not know what will happen on that December date. But one thing I DO NOT believe will happen is that everyone on Earth will allegedly "ascend" on that date, and I have said so.

I believe that you may find copies of this book on your local bookseller's shelves on December 22 and far beyond.

What Happened To The 4th Dimension?

Another common question addresses the popular notion that we are presently living in the 3rd dimension but are aspiring to a leap into the 5th dimension. When I went to school, *four* followed three. What happened to the 4th dimension? Yes, we *are* headed for the 5th dimension. You did not read it wrong.

We do pass right through the 4th dimension on our way to the 5th. Everyone functions at a different level of consciousness. Some people are in either the lower or higher frequencies of the 4th dimension. It is where most people hang out when they die. You are still on the wheel of karma and reincarnation in the 4th dimension. The point to remember is to abandon linear thinking and just be aware that when in the ascension mode, we are headed for the *5th* dimension.

The End of the Mayan Calendar

Despite the many disclaimers that the December 21, 2012, date as the end of the Mayan calendar is something to fear, scary rumors persist that this is the end of the world. There is no truth to these preposterous claims. That date is merely the end of a long cycle. It is not apocryphal. As an astrologer, I can assure you that there are numerous long cycles, and each one ends only to start again just like this one will do. Cycles are circular.

I am 76 years old as I finish writing this. I figure I have already lived through six or seven "ends of the world." Sometime back in the 1960s, I seem to recall a couple hundred souls gathering on the banks of the Mississippi River to await the end of the world. What is wrong with this picture?

Okay, now that I have allayed your fears; let's get technical. (Don't worry, not THAT technical.) So what is the big deal about the Mayan calendar? The Mayan culture existed until about 830 A.D. Back then, they possessed none of the precision instruments that we would take for granted as necessary to calculate an accurate calendar system. However, their astronomical knowledge *exceeded* ours until very recent times.

They were amazing. They calculated the precise orbits of the planets in our solar system. Even more amazing, they calculated the orbits of stars in the galaxy as well. They catalogued major cosmic events going back to—believe it or not—a staggering 400 million years! Considering all of that, how hard could it be for them to toss off the calculations of a mere 26,000 year cycle, or the lesser 5,200 year cycle? The answer: not hard at all—child's play! Even I can do it. Well, I admit I cheat. I have a computer.

On December 21, 2012, the Mayan calendar resets to zero, and then, of course, starts over again. Don't make this hard. That is all there is to it. So what happens when these cycles end and new ones begin? Well, first of all, when we are dealing with such huge cycles, you don't really think things are going to change in the blink of an eye, do you? That defies common sense. There is overlap before and after. So let's look back to find a time in recent history when things began to change. You may not have been around then, but you have probably heard of the 1960s. Oh, man, you shoulda been there! Seriously, many things changed big time.

This Shift is real. It is a cosmic cycle that is slowly unfolding and increasing the frequency of consciousness on the planet—and the planet herself. 2012 simply marks a turning point when *homo sapiens* shift into wholeness and "transform into a kind of *homo holisticus*," in the words of Owen Waters in his book *The Shift.*

All of this is run-of-the-mill for astrologers who work with charts of individual clients, including me. I watch the cycles come and go in client's charts—some cycles are long and some are short. When a long cycle comes to a close, it starts over again in a different cycle or different astrological sign. Obviously, this marks a time of transition and change. It works the same for all of humanity when long cycles shift; we all share the influence. It is a long, impersonal cycle, not a personal cycle that is based on one individual's birth date.

The 26,000 year cycle—actually slightly less than that—comes from a technical measurement called *precession of the equinoxes.* You don't really want me to get into all that complicated stuff, trust me. What I have just explained should be enough to convince you that any talk about the end of world is fear-mongering. I've always wondered just what "the end of the world" means anyway. Does everything just blow up or what? Wouldn't that be one hell of a sight!

Ascension Is Not the Same as The Biblical Rapture

In the event that the ascension process is confused with biblical accounts of the rapture, let's be clear that they are not the same. When you read this book, all references to changing dimensions refer to ascension.

This Is Not A Channeled Book

Despite the many references in this book to my association with a Spirit Teacher and perhaps other unseen forces, don't get the idea that this is a channeled book. No way. What do you think of that blood that is oozing from every word?

PROLOGUE

Four Basic Activations

Begin with the 5th dimension lightbody activations.

- The lightbody is the physical body and surrounding energy field transformed with light that includes the emotional body closest to the physical body.
- Next out in the energy field is the mental body and
- Furthest out is the spiritual body.

We're not going to go to the 6th dimension or the 7th dimension, but we need to open up to those levels to access the information that's available from those dimensions.

The lightbody activation begins the process of activating 5th dimension energies, which transforms the body with light to a point that when we shift into the 5th dimension, we're off the reincarnation cycle. The lightbody doesn't die as the dense physical body does.

There cannot be disease in the lightbody. There's no disease in the 5th dimension. Kryon says that we can actually talk to the DNA. Also refer to the chapter "DNA from A to Z" and an article titled "Russian Discoveries."

Pele is the energy of new creation. Dolphin energy is the energy of the upper dimensions, the sky energy. Sea Turtle energy is the energy of Earth. Those three energies synergize to approximate the energy of the 5th dimension, which is why they're used to activate the 5th dimension lightbody. Healing and clearing can take place at a stronger and deeper level if the person's lightbody is activated beforehand.

The 6th dimension activation activates the high feminine energies. It is the Venus activation because Venus represents the high feminine energy. It's a prerequisite to anchor in the Christ energy.

There are additional charkas that are activated during the 6th dimension activation. Then all you need do on the 6th dimension activation is to place the Venus Cross of Light onto all of the eleven charkas.

A polished amethyst carries the feminine vibration and a black obsidian carries the masculine vibration.

For the 7th dimension activation you use the same four crystals.

The 7th dimension is the Quantum Christ Activation. At the quantum level, everything can be created through simple thought alone. Activate the Christ level to access the quantum level, so then through pure thought and intent you can activate the DNA.

The 7th dimension stands on its own. In the Christ dimension, there is no east-west polarity, not even masculine-feminine. They merge into Oneness, into Unity. Tap 3 times on the heart chakra. The energy field opens simultaneously. The quantum Christ energy of the 7th dimension then completely surrounds the body in a "Christ cloud" 100 feet in diameter.

The energy of the 5th dimension is spiritual wisdom, the energy of the 6thdimension is compassionate love of the Goddess, and the 7th dimension is unconditional love of the Christ. That describes the three energies: spiritual wisdom, compassionate love and unconditional love.

As the tsunami of these powerful transformational forces meets your present day consciousness, everything that is blocking it comes to the surface to be cleared. It's different for everybody. It depends what's going to surface in one way or another. And, in addition, solutions that never surfaced before will present themselves.

Now you've accessed all the dimensions that are accessible to us at this point. Even the Law of One people, which are a 6th dimension group-memory complex, said of the 8th dimension, "It's still the great mystery to us."

The quantum level has been accessed—that's the 7th dimension Christ level. That is the level that opens the door to the fourth activation, which is the 12-strand DNA activation. This involves the eight master cells of the body, located in the thymus. This is a very important step. Each one of the eight master cells is changed from two-strand DNA to twelve-strand DNA. As master cells, they can then change ALL of the cells in the body. This completes a necessary process whereby a human possessing an activated 12-strand DNA is poised to merge into a higher frequency and dimension.

In the *Great Shift*, a book by Kryon (Lee Carroll), there are questions and answers in the back. Somebody asked if there was one signature cell in the body, and he said "Yes, it's the Pineal gland." Refer to the chapter titled "Playing The God Game." You will then understand why this carried mind-bending significance.

The changes in the physical body will transform it into the ascension vehicle. This means that literally billions of changes must take place. The additional strands of DNA receive their instructions from the 5th, 6th and 7th dimensions, which were accessed by the activations. They receive the instructions from those dimensions.

Maintain the activation in this technique by meditating in the crystal layout for a minimum of one half hour a month—the more the better. That's what the guides recommended. Be thankful if people do that much!

PREAMBLE

In Heaven between incarnations I was kicking back with my buddies in the bar at Alpha-7. That is located on a little asteroid on the outskirts of the Arcturus Star System. We were knocking back industrial-strength drinks the likes of which were never known on Planet Earth, thank god! As the evening faded into early morning, we began to exhibit the false bravado often found at the bottom of a shot glass. Well, I guess I started to regale the crowd with some of my exploits. Okay, okay, maybe I wandered a little far afield on some of the details, but look at my uniform. Just how do you think I got these medals and ribbons anyway?

A bunch of glocadytes were just back from acting in the *Star Wars* films. (You saw them in the bar scenes.) So they got to talking about Planet Earth and some of the weird stuff going on there. That brought back memories of my experiences on Earth back in Atlantean days.

"Don't tell me they are still up to the same old crap there? We tried to save them back in Atlantis. We shared technology and activated lightbodies to take them into the 5th dimension. It was a total fiasco. Well, they just blew up the whole goddamned place; yeah! that's what they did. I'm tempted to go back there and kick butt. Next time would be a different story, believe me."

Well, about that time the glocadytes started taunting me and throwing around "Double-dog dare ya" and "Put your money where your mouth is." I don't mean to be racist, but those slimy reptiles always got under my skin as it was.

Well, the gist of it was that when I woke up the next morning with one bitch of a hangover, what do I see but some official looking papers under my favorite magnet on the fridge. It was a contract to incarnate on Earth and basically clean up the place and deliver it to the 5th dimension, lock, stock and barrel. I apparently signed it with a DNA sample, and in that Star System, this is irreversibly binding. So off to Earth it was, baby.

*

As a certified master Lightworker, a commitment is a commitment, so I set about mapping out Project Planet Earth in all seriousness, I can promise you. First, I consulted with my High Teacher/Advisers and God! They were not cool. No way were they giving their blessing on this one. It was too risky. I was forced to play the free will card. However, I really prefer only high stakes games anyway. Besides, I always had a hankering to take on those smart-ass glocadytes, once and for all. The bets were down, the game was on, and if I pulled it off, there were some extremely nasty consequences involved for the losers.

Now that I was sober, I at least comprehended that this was a job for a group of allies; going it alone was suicidal. Lets not get hysterical or anything, but there was an excess of silent beard-stroking, eyebrow-raising and blood-drained faces. The realization that this was a colossal mistake, and that the whole thing was utterly hopeless, suddenly seized me. Those nasty consequences that fell to the glocadytes when they lost the bet? I began to envision that as MY future instead. Oops!

With an eye on the astrological patterns and the Mayan calendar, the twenty-first-century rolled around and..........WE WERE READY.

We may look pretty pitiful as we nurse our wounds. We did not bank on the current DNA stocks to be quite so pathetic. Our physical bodies took a bad hit. We figured out some great healing therapies, but I'll be damned if the natives hadn't been taken over by a band of drug pushers. Some of them were even licensed!

As it turned out, the natives were brainwashed and downright hostile. Some of my healer buddies were captured and sent off to the nut house. By the time we got some of our people back, they just cried for their mommies all day.

I was going for enlightenment, but they mistook it for psychosis. In a weak moment, I wondered if they might be right and succumbed to drug therapy. I don't want to talk about it. It was my own damned fault anyway.

We put our money where our mouths were that night on Alpha-7. I speak for the whole group of us that took this on. I don't know who you are or where you are, but there is nothing the matter with you. It was a soul mission. AND MISSION ACCOMPLISHED! We won. Go home.

We will meet once again at the bar on Alpha-7. Suggestion? Don't wear the uniforms this time.

CHAPTER ONE

Harmonic Concordance

And where love and need are one,
And work is play for mortal stakes,
Is the deed ever really done
For Heaven and the future's sakes?

Robert Frost

A friend of mine from California was visiting me in my home in Vancouver, Washington, one pleasant August afternoon in 2003. It was somewhat in the spirit of two girlfriends at a slumber party that she asked me to do a psychic past life relationship investigation of a young man whom she was currently seeing. I was at ease as I closed my eyes. Past life counseling is one of several services I routinely provide for clients. I was expecting nothing out of the ordinary. However, that session turned out to be anything but ordinary! I would never have imagined then that this was to propel me headlong toward the revelations and life-changing events that eventually became the subject of this book.

I was somewhat startled by the unusually strong energies generated by the initial past life images accompanying this particular reading. I am accustomed to experiencing a range of sensations whenever I do psychic work, so it was not inordinately distracting at first. I could not say that about the next blast. My eyes flew open as I was forcefully squished into the back of my chair. Following that it felt as though a spinning vortex of energy had completely enveloped me. I thought I was joining Dorothy's tornadic exit from Kansas. It lasted only a few moments, but those few moments changed my life and nothing would ever be quite the same again.

I glanced around the room and everything had subtly changed. I was surveying the physical world clearly from an altered state of some sort. My world did not immediately return to normal as I expected. I was clear-headed enough to proceed with the matter at hand, however, so I passed it off to my friend as something of no consequence.

When my visitor left in the late afternoon and I was still unmistakably locked into an extremely altered state, I grew a bit uneasy. "When is this thing going to lift?" I thought to myself. I finally confided in my husband just how increasingly disorienting the experience was becoming. We both regularly do a great deal of shamanic work, consequently, altered states are nothing new to us. My distress was definitely something atypical this time. I suggested that we go out for dinner, thinking an excursion into the "real" world would dispel whatever this was.

The restaurant only heightened the obvious fact that the real world was something of which I definitely was not a part. I felt like I was looking at everything from some detached and distant vantage point. It was even mildly amusing at first. The first nervous thoughts about "What if this never lifts?" quickly dispelled anything humorous about the situation. After a week passed with no change in sight, nobody was laughing. It was sort of like never quite sobering up after a night on the town. I was beginning to fear that something was growing inside my head that should not be there.

But First: Introducing Other Players in My Game

You cannot fully understand the ramifications of this unfolding story unless you are aware that the central focus of my spiritual life involves a relationship and connection to three other people. This group very much defines us and transcends separate individual expression in many significant ways. There are powerful energetic links that bond us on multiple levels.

My little band of spiritual warriors, in order of appearance into my life journey, includes my brother, Duane Henkle, who of course, is coauthor of the *Lightbody Activation Manual, Book One* of this series and author of *The Ascension Guidebook, Book Two* of the series. For many years, Duane lived in Santa Fe, NM, but in 2006, he moved to Vancouver, WA, close to the rest of the group. Next is my husband, Don Hurd, whom I met in 1982. The fourth member is my son, David Bills, whom I met in a delivery room in Newport News, Virginia, in 1958. We are known as the 4Ds.

An increasingly powerful group consciousness was forged over many years of extremely intense work. It was master-minded by a rare individual, our Spirit Teacher, Thomas*. When Thomas first made his presence known to me , one of the first things he said was, "I am a teacher of groups." The import of that statement is unfolding into deeper and deeper meanings even yet. In fact, were it not for Thomas's guidance and the creation of a group mind, the 12-strand DNA Activation Method would never have made it to Planet Earth. We were each stretched beyond nearly intolerable limits to just barely land the thing as it was.

Throughout the formation phase of several years, individuals came and went from my group. After many adventures, the dust settled, leaving the four of us who function as

---

* So as not to interrupt the continuity of the events leading up to the revelations about DNA activation, additional information about Thomas and the creation of group mind will follow in later chapters. We also feel that we owe our readers some background explanations about working with discarnate teachers and other entities. For all you know, we may simply be wandering about in a mutual schizophrenic delusional system.

the core group. Others form an outer ring on the periphery, and while they do not participate directly when we work, they do provide an essential support and stabilizing presence. This means support embodied in clearly defined roles and does not refer to the people who "send energy" in a casual—albeit greatly appreciated—and unstructured manner.

Thomas describes their roles as integral to a structure that has traditionally existed as an aspect of shamanic groups since ancient times. It is important to understand that this is a prototype that exceeds merely personal or familial relationships.

Christopher Johnson and Rex Bills provide the essential structural and harmonizing influences respectively for the core group. They both clearly exhibit these archetypal patterns in all aspects of their lives. Rex Bills seems almost physiologically incapable of tolerating disharmony. He represents the astrological Libra archetype, the Balance. I was married to him for eighteen years. Throughout those eighteen years, we experienced our share of difficult times and losses, financial catastrophe, the many changes involved in spiritual awakening and the pain of a divorce. Yet, never once was there a single argument, angry outburst or even a raised voice. To this day, he is still the one who spreads oil on troubled waters.

The last to find his way into Thomas's group was Christopher Johnson, which was sometime after he left the priesthood. There never was any special recognition, any special invitation or any sort of initiation into the group. One day he wasn't there. The next day he was there. It was seamless and never discussed except to note his extraordinarily unflappable acceptance of the group at every level. Considering the metaphysical activities of the core group at that time (1992), only one with whom a soul contract had previously been forged could have possibly embraced us so comfortably. He is structure personified, the archetypical Stabilizer. It so contrasts with the wild and crazy core group energies, we may only guess what disintegration would surely follow if his support beams were kicked out from under us. It's good to know that we can absolutely rely on him to fix popcorn at the same time every Monday night,

Adventures with Thomas came to an end in 1993 when he left us to our own devices. We didn't know whether he left because we were ready to go it alone or whether he just gave up on us as a hopeless cause. If you were there, you would know a case could be made for both.

Coming full circle from the beginning energy blasts described earlier, something was definitely up! As is typical, it was soon apparent that this new altered state that I was experiencing was not to be mine alone for long.

Periodic Physical Symptoms Shared Simultaneously

We simultaneously reported heart irregularities. I was aware that at times my heart raced wildly. At other times there were 20-30 minutes of arrhythmia. Sometimes when I felt my pulse, there were no beats for several seconds. The scariest was the occasional searing stab of pain that streaked through the organ. I had new appreciation for how painful it must be to be knifed in the heart. If that particular pain had lasted for any length of time, it would have been really unbearable. I was not sure but what I might faint. There were moments where I decided that this was it, and a fatal heart attack was not far behind.

The only thing that stood between a consultation with a cardiologist and me was the report from both Duane and my son, David. They were experiencing the identical symptoms. David pulled his car over to the side of the road on several occasions, not certain as to whether he would lose consciousness or not when the symptoms were particularly intense. I took comfort that in all likelihood the three of us probably were not going to share mutual heart attacks. With some twinges of doubt, I decided to ride this horse a little farther to see where it was taking us. By now, we all were confident that something decidedly major was on the way.

2003: Thomas Returns!! Wow!

That thought was confirmed when Thomas returned. Yes, Thomas was back! He was fairly casual about the whole affair. No drum rolls. No celestial music. No running into a mad embrace of reunion. I, myself, was surprisingly casual about this really unexpected turn of events, now that I look back on it. Maybe it just took me some time to thaw out from shell shock. That is not to say that we were unaware of the profound implications of his return, however. We were each left with our own private thoughts and memories of the many wild adventures with the wily old trickster and could not help but wonder, “What now?” This was September of 2003.

That was your fast fly-by covering Thomas's first appearance (1980), the formation of a core group, an unsettling blast of energies in August 2003, Thomas's exit and reappearance (1992, 2003), the big eclipse in November 2003 and Duane's move to Vancouver in 2006. Are you left just a little breathless and disoriented? Okay, then, you know how it feels! This ship is capable of shifting gears. So take a breath. We are on cruise control. We are on our way to Harmonic Concordance!

Another Eclipse Signals Great Changes

I am a professional astrologer and as such was very aware, along with the astrological community at large, that a rare planetary configuration was forming, coincident with a powerful lunar eclipse on November 8, 2003. Six planets moved into an interlocking double-triangle relationship in their circular orbits, creating a six-pointed figure called the Star of David pattern. The powerful shifting of energies, the puzzling heart irregularities, Thomas's return and now the eclipse; it was obvious that the core group was gearing up for a major piece of work together, just as we had so many times before.

Harmonic Concordance Day—Nov. 8-9, 2003

Another astrologer announced through his Internet website posting that the eclipse day was also Harmonic Concordance Day and that lightbeings worldwide were gathering together to observe and ground the energies that would be streaming through newly opened portals to Earth for the first time. Now we knew. We initiated plans to meet at my house. We had no idea what specifically would happen, but there was no doubt that we were being prepared for whatever it was.

It was time to have some serious conversations with Thomas. Interacting with a Being that you can neither see nor hear with physical eyes and ears is not just a matter of retiring to the library, lighting up a good cigar and chatting over a glass of merlot. My channeling pipelines were a bit rusty because I had not communicated with Thomas for a good 10 years.

Telepathic Communication Systems

First, I want to make a distinction between psychic communications, usually referred to as channeling, versus mediumship. A medium allows an entity to literally take over the physical vehicle and communicate directly. Normally the medium is unaware of what transpires. Years ago, when I was first interested in matters metaphysical, I decided at the outset that no one was going to take over my body and use me as a mouthpiece, particularly if I could not hear what was going on. That was long before we had the word *channeling* in the psychic vocabulary. Channelers communicate telepathically, are completely conscious and recall everything that is said. They can be compared to interpreters who translate information from one language to another.

In our first book, *The Lightbody Activation Manual,* my brother recounted how he received the activation method from Pleiadians who were described as "walking in" and joining their energies with Duane's. When Duane left Hawaii, the one main Being who had joined with him, disconnected. I view this as a bit different from either channeling or acting as a medium. Nor was it the typical walk-in situation where there is a permanent soul exchange, discussed further in a later chapter. (Also see the book by Ruth Montgomery *Strangers* Among *Us.)*

My brother was still very much himself, yet, he was aware of the other presence and was somewhat discomfited by it. However, that particular method was used in this one very unique situation to enhance the communication between human and discarnate. The Pleiadian asked for permission to join energies to which Duane readily agreed. There was no coercion involved and should not be confused with possession.

There were many conversations with Thomas. When he introduced the subject of activating and changing DNA, you must keep in mind that this was news to us. We did not realize then that Harmonic Concordance Day would include retrieving a new method of DNA activation, or writing another book.

My typical caution and self-doubts about communicating accurately with Thomas went into overdrive. My group's position has always been to bring through the information as best we could and then wait to see what developed. As the Big Day approached, we still did not know if we would be receiving momentous revelations or just tossing back a couple of gin and tonics in good company.

Thomas seemed very interested in another subject that was perplexing to us. He referred to group mind. He wanted us to "think as one." He frequently reiterated his apparent keen interest in facilitating this among the four of us on the eclipse day. In fact, he went so far as to suggest that this was one of the important reasons for forming the group. We had no idea what this meant, so I am afraid we were a bit cavalier about the whole matter. He also revealed that he originally came to me to facilitate the Shift into the 5th dimension; it was where he was heading all along.

Back to 1983: Thomas Introduces Drugs

Before continuing on with Harmonic Concordance Day, there is something that you need to know. Today, the drug culture is all over the place: from peddlers in dark alleys to cocaine-sniffing among Hollywood's brightest and most famous stars and everything in-between. It is definitely a ho-hum subject even on The ENQUIRER'S front pages. However, for us, the back story was outright shocking.

Don, Duane and I are senior citizens. We are children of the Fifties. In high school days, nicotine and alcohol were the drugs of choice if we wanted to sneak around and be naughty, that is. The drug culture of today had not begun to cast so much as a shadow to us of what was on the horizon.

You cannot imagine my chagrin when, in 1983, Thomas announced that he wanted us to work with a particular mind-enhancing drug!

"Maybe this Thomas character is not who I think he is," I thought to myself. I was overwhelmed with trepidation and paranoia. My only comfort was in the knowledge that I had no way of getting my hands on any sort of drug, not even a bag of pot. My comfort was short-lived. The very next day, a long-time client and psychotherapist just happened by coincidence—how does he do that?—to drop by my office to share some literature about this drug and its amazing effectiveness in a therapeutic setting.

She also handed me the name of another counselor who could supply it to me. (So much for that.) I put up a big fuss, but I knew Thomas always wins in the end. I notified Don, and we made plans to go to the Oregon coast. We intended to take our first drug trip looking from our motel windows onto an unimpeded sweep of the Pacific Ocean. We also made out our wills. If we overdosed or went permanently mad, at least it was in a first-class setting.

Understandably, I debated whether or not to write in this book about the role of a mind-expanding drug in our training with Thomas for fear that it would be misunderstood. I will not be identifying the drug so as not to encourage others to use it without the strict protocols and the guidance of someone who knows what he or she is doing. We will refer to it only as The Pill. It is not an hallucinogen (not LSD).

I realized that the drug experience was an integral part of our story and discovered that mind-altering substances have been very much a part of traditional shamanism over many centuries and in all parts of the world—and still are. At the time we were working with it, it was a legal drug. Partially because of later abuses, it could no longer be quietly implemented and confined to therapy rooms, thus it is now illegal, unfortunately. The entire situation with this drug was somewhat schizophrenic for a time. It was legal to possess it, but not legal to make it or purchase it. As far as I know, it ended up strictly illegal and that is where it now stands in the eyes of law enforcement.

Thomas thought it was advisable to include this information about the appropriate use of substances along with warnings about their misuse. He correctly predicted the widespread increase in drug abuse so better to have a clear voice out there to forestall what was too often dangerous and reckless experimentation.

Obviously Don's and my maiden drug experience was not fatal nor did we go raving mad. Apparently our brain synapses were left intact as well, but you readers can judge for yourselves on that one. What we did experience then—and on many other successive trips—you could say was simply mind-blowing all right, but in a positive way. It is said that we actually use only a shockingly small percentage of our brains. I don't know to what extent our minds expanded on The Pill, but I can tell you that it takes you to a phenomenally different place —a place to which a friend of mine was about to discover.

Fast Forward: A Drug Trip Among Friends

I was mentoring a woman I met at the annual astrology conference in Seattle in 2000. Christine "Kriss" Shellman is an astrologer and shaman. She made regular trips to spend the day with me. I wrote about her in *Book One* of this trilogy. She was one of the very first to field-test the Crystal Triangle Lightbody method. (She and her group are busy testing the DNA activations at the time of this writing, and initial reports are dramatic.)

Thomas introduced the idea of taking The Pill in 1983, so by the time 2003 rolled around, we had 20 years' familiarity with it. However, when Thomas left in 1993, we had 10 years' experience under our belts albeit when he departed, we all but abandoned its use. Nevertheless, the whole thing was old hat, whichever way you looked at it.

Thomas Pulls a Rabbit Out of His Hat

When Kriss came for a visit in early October 2003, much of the day was spent talking about the influx of new energies and Thomas's return. Along about four o'clock, I thought I was hearing whisperings from Thomas that we do a session with Kriss—with The Pill! I struggled not to hear it. It was an outrageous suggestion. I had not used The Pill for some years by then and, furthermore, I didn't think Kriss would do it. Also, these trips stretch over many hours, and it seemed too late in the day to begin.

Even though Kriss would not be sitting with the 4Ds on November 8th, Thomas explained in earlier conversations that she was considered to be a peripheral member of our group. He was not making a casual offer when he agreed to engage in deep work with her. She was being cleared for take-off before she and her buddies participated in bringing in the energies on November 8th in Seattle.

Before long Kriss herself had an intuitive flash that Thomas wanted to work with her. That forced me in all good conscience to admit that I, too, had gotten the message. So there was nothing left to do but proceed. I was still pretty shocked that Kriss agreed so readily! We took a measured dose of The Pill in late afternoon.

Slowly and seamlessly our consciousness expanded over the next couple of hours. My husband, Don, sat with us for the entire time. He did not take the drug. It is typical to have a caretaker person available. Don is so sensitive that he gets a contact high just being in our presence under the drug. By 2003, we were sophisticated in our management of drug trips under Thomas's tutelage, of course.

I silently chuckled to myself at the look of delicious expectation on his face. He had seen the Thomas/Diana duo in action many times before. He relishes the glimpse of the realms from which the masters work with such easy facility. They engineer changes deep in the psyche over the space of a few hours. When Thomas worked with me in the early days, one session often triggered something to process over weeks or even months.

Tripping the Light Fantastic with Thomas

The basic agenda for Kriss was a load of fear, a long wide-ranging list of offenders. I wondered whatever had spawned such a bottomless pit of fear, capable of creating endless layer upon endless layer of scary monsters. I myself feared that it could lead to a serious heart problem. (It had!) Especially within the context of the insight from the drug, I clearly recognized the dark, dense colors that penetrated deeply through the emotional body into the cells.

However, the fear monster was in no way limited to Kriss. It is probably the primary problem in the mass consciousness. Nevertheless, in light of her role as a facilitator in her group, I could understand why Thomas wanted to clear it before Harmonic Concordance arrived on the day of the upcoming lunar eclipse.

Kriss had the typical periodic bouts of nausea and vomiting as the drug and personal issues surfaced. Don is a homeopathic physician and utilized homeopathic remedies as he followed the energies of nausea, fear or whatever else was the designated problem of the hour. He stood at the ready with the old, trusty, yellow plastic pail (that same bucket appears in a later chapter!) that has "Barf Bucket" crudely lettered on the side. It has been pressed into service for over 25 years. We store it in our garage. I experience a sickening wave of nausea if I catch even so much as a glimpse of the thing.

I don't know of anyone who absolutely detests nausea and vomiting as much as I do. It is not possible. I belong in the Guinness Book of World Records as the number one Loather of Nausea. That is, unfortunately, an inherent aspect of working with substances. For example, Native American peyote ceremonies are marked by severe physical reactions as well. In fact, shamanic work has traditionally been linked very closely to the physical vehicle and intense symptoms are not always pleasant. I expect a special reward in the hereafter to unwillingly suffer for humanity in this fashion.

I mention this in passing because some people are perplexed why my group and I must endure a certain level of physical discomfort—sometimes severe. Consciousness does not change and evolve separate from our physical bodies. This embraces the larger context of our work with the lightbody and DNA transformation. There is also a technology of the physical.

I just want to make the point here that we are not masochistic nor can the Teacher take it all away with the wave of his hand. We are dealing with complex evolutionary processes that embrace the full spectrum of the human experience. The primary reason for this book, after all, is to help clear the way for processing the ascension shift. The idea is to make it as easy as possible to work through the many changes that can be very trying.

At 11:00 p.m., Don gingerly shepherded Kriss out the front door and drove her to the motel to sleep it off. Coming down off the drug is not a stroll through the park, either. It depends on the issues that were part of the experience. The energies are controlled and strictly managed by the spiritual teacher. Distinctly personal material delivers an additional punch all its own, over and above the drug's influence alone.

Kriss turned out to be a real trouper from beginning to end. She eagerly cooperated with Thomas and was sensitive to the directions in which he was taking her. She certainly bore the marks of an awakened lightbeing who had already done a great deal of inner and outer work on the spiritual path. Her immediate response to her own inner guidance and total lack of resistance to her issues were extraordinary, to say the least.

Here Comes the Trip Through Hell

Don and Kriss had barely cleared our front step when a titanic wave of nausea engulfed me and sent me into spasms of dry heaves. I had been able to hold the energy until then. Through only the sheer force of will was I able to stumble to my bedroom. I was sick. God was I sick. I had the sinking realization that I was elected to do the honors and process Kriss's fears through my own body, a well-known practice among shaman.

Kriss deals with some health problems so I assumed that any Vesuvian eruption of a ton of fear—especially one cleared so rapidly—was possibly too overwhelming for her to handle. As the hours dragged by, I would very happily have elected for her to drop dead rather than endure one more minute of such horrific suffering myself. I suppose that cancels my karmic points. Don frantically gave me everything he could think of to abate my uninterrupted retching, all to no avail. He was resigned to just going to bed and enduring my loud moans until morning. It was several days before I completely laid claim to my wits and well-being once again.

How About a Little Sleight of Hand?

One of the things that we needed to do before our meeting on November 8th was to prepare The Pills. This drug was legal when we did our main work with it in the 1980s. Of course, we did not buy it at the corner drug store nor did we palm off cash to anonymous dealers in dark alleys. Don and I were never part of the drug culture and didn't have the slightest notion where to buy any kind of drugs. (As for my son, David, in his high school and college days, Mom isn't telling everything she knows.) This particular drug was widely used in conjunction with psychotherapy. When the hearings were held to determine its legal status, government officials were stunned when hundreds of therapists testified as to its amazing effectiveness.

Don's connections to the alternative healthcare community and mine as a long-time professional astrologer, put us in touch with a network of doctors and professional counselors. It apparently was not too hard for Thomas to "arrange" some contacts. Fortunately, we were able to acquire what we needed from sources that were trustworthy. Street drugs were too risky, even if we did know where to find them. We could not be totally certain that we weren't buying more than we bargained for. At first we were very apprehensive, I can tell you.

Later on, the legal status was cloudy. We were living in Portland, Oregon, in a state that is known as a maverick with definite ideas of its own. It was left to the individual states to decide how they wanted to handle it. As I said earlier, it came down to where it was not illegal to have possession in Oregon, but it was illegal to make or purchase it. We were left with a large amount of the loose material that we had acquired much earlier, which we encapsulated in varying dosages as needed. Our source was a friend—a naturopath whose daughter is a chemist. We at least did not have to worry about purity.

What we did have to worry about was our growing paranoia about it. I found out that paranoia* makes one very paranoid! I expected the knock at the door any day from a vice cop. During one of our more convoluted paranoid fits, Don decided that he would hide the drug in the house. By this time it was the early 90s, Thomas had left and we rarely used the drug anymore anyway.

In 1997, we moved to the north bank of the Columbia River across from Portland to Vancouver, Washington. That meant bringing the stash out of hiding before any movers found it. As it turned out, there was very little chance that the movers would find it or anyone else for that matter. Don could not remember where he hid it, and all searches were futile. We ransacked every square inch of the house repeatedly. In our frenzied searches we barely stopped short of prying the sheet rock off the walls. It was the kind of thing that haunted me even years later in the middle of the night, worrying whether anyone ever found that stuff.

---

* I don't want any misunderstanding here. It was not the effects of the drugs that created the paranoia. We managed to do that all by ourselves. You have to remember the climate back then. A home in our neighborhood had been raided by vice cops dressed in black and wearing no other recognizable clothing to identify who they were. They had the wrong house. One of the officers was shot and killed by the homeowner, thinking he was being invaded by thugs intent on god knows what. This resonated with other unfortunate incidents across the country and was creating an uneasy atmosphere of fear and uncertainty about the War on Drugs. The work we did with Thomas was extremely positive, even though difficult. We would not be doing the work we are today had it not been for those experiences. We understood that and willingly went along with the training.

One day early on when it first dawned on us that something big was afoot, David was at our house discussing with us the thorny problem of getting our hands on a supply of The Pill. By now, it was outright illegal, and all of our sources had long dried up. We devised some distasteful schemes that included, among other things, loitering about college campuses and seeing what we could lay our hands on. However, these schemes never materialized past excursions into the ridiculous, even for us.

Abracadabra!

As we talked, Don offered to make a pot of coffee. ***When he opened a frequently used cupboard for the coffee mugs, there, front and center, was unmistakably the long lost stash of The Pill!*** (That is how we came to have some on hand when we needed it for Kriss.) It appeared out of thin air. Apparently we were so paranoid about it that the Beings hid it where it REALLY wouldn't be found—in another dimension. If you have never seen anyone inhale continuously for twenty minutes, you should have seen me when I saw that bag of Pill supplies.

Whatever Happened to Telegrams?

One day in October preceding Harmonic Concordance, I noticed a nagging little pain high around my right rib cage. It was not long before the nagging little pain was seriously climbing the threshold ladder. It mushroomed into a full-blown eight-hour episode of such excruciating pain that I prayed to die. It easily rivaled childbirth. I wheezed and gasped for breath as my husband frantically administered homeopathics. It was a gallbladder attack. The only reason I did not call an ambulance and go to the emergency room was because I knew I could never tolerate being moved. God, was that pain horrific.

We Receive Our Orders

As an experienced shaman I understood that this was a message. Here I go again. It came in typical fashion—very physical, unmistakable and full of symbolic meaning. It was clearly an order from on high to prepare for Harmonic Concordance, everyone needed to do a liver-gallbladder cleanse. Soon, other channelers were announcing the same thing all over the Internet. Perhaps turning down the Pain Index next time would suffice.

It is always amazing to me the way in which so many lightworkers worldwide receive identical messages simultaneously. I received dozens of email messages in response to my newsletter. Fellow spiritual travelers validated my experience and also confirmed the advisability of preparatory physical cleanses. It is as if there is a cosmic radio, and all of us are dialed to the same station. However it happens, it is always a great confirmation that we are on the right track.

For a time I was very cranky about the painful way in which the need for cleanses was communicated to me, and I whined about the lot of the shaman in general. Regardless of how we received the message, it was increasingly obvious as the weeks passed that we were indeed preparing for a very big deal. Our entire group fortunately managed to administer cleanses and fine tune our diets fairly painlessly. We were ready to go 18 rounds.

The tension and anxiety that built up in the weeks preceding the Concordance Day was palpable. There were times when all of us thought we would jump out of our skins. We constantly pestered Thomas for information. He was mercifully patient and forthcoming, but we tortured ourselves about whether we were accurately interpreting what he said. We questioned everything over and over.

What was all this stuff about DNA for god's sake? We suffered moments of grave doubts that nothing would happen at all. Harmonic Concordance Day received wide publicity. This generated its share of skeptics and doubters to shake our confidence even further. (Since this book did not see the light of day until long after this initial chapter was written, I now look back years later while doing the final editing and realize how much has changed. Ascension is not in the future; it was in progress even then, I feel sure. I also believe that this Great Shift will continue, one way or the other, long after 2012 as well.)

Meanwhile, I had a busy astrological practice and healing ministry to deal with. The cockeyed energies that invaded earlier had not abated. All of us in the group, for that matter, were struggling many days to maintain even minimal functioning. Telephone calls flew back and forth.

Our Communication Systems Go Dead

Thomas told me from the time the energies first blasted me that things would never return to the way they were before, and I was beginning to believe every word of it. The final straw was one day when I sat down with Don to do some shamanic soul retrieval work, which we routinely did as part of our psychic healing with clients. I tuned in, but the circuits were not only interfered with a bit; they were now totally dead. I was shut down.

I railed at Thomas. We had serious commitments to people, many of whom desperately needed our services. I went on one of my rants, which were not entirely unfamiliar to Thomas throughout the years of our relationship. I demanded that he turn up the juice so I could get back to work that by this time was in a shambles. He said he could do that but he warned me about one thing.

Thomas Issues a Warning

Thomas was working with all of us to raise our vibratory frequencies so that we could meet the level of energies that would be required on Harmonic Concordance Day. This was the first time I sensed some glimmer of doubt that he wondered if we might not make it even at that. If he slowed my process now, it would be necessary to do a down-and-dirty fast jumpstart to another level later on. I would have to come up to speed to match the other members of my group. It would not be easy. "What the hell," I thought, "this is today. I'll worry about that when I get there." File that under the "famous last words" column.

The remainder of the days leading to Harmonic Concordance on November 8th crawled along in a morass of anticipation anxiety and fluctuating symptoms. The only relief from the intensity was to focus on work. Despite repeated messages from Thomas, we continued to brace ourselves in case nothing happened. It may seem strange that after all of our experiences that we would continue to harbor such misgivings. The rational mind will never accept as real the information from psychic sources. We regard it as not altogether negative. A healthy skepticism in this line of work aids discernment in picking through what is true or not. However legitimate the original information may be, I am still channeling it through my own individual consciousness where it is always susceptible to distortion.

I am writing this particular part of the book a year and eight months after Harmonic Concordance. To refresh my memory, I reviewed the video that we recorded that day. I came up with many excuses to avoid watching it. Just writing about it brings up the original energy. It is like wading through tar for every word.

Something Happened After All

Even if I were Hemingway, I couldn't adequately describe how excruciatingly horrific this event was. I could never find words that would allow you to come anywhere close to fathoming the suffering we endured in order to hang onto the energies. It was just beggaring description. Stick your fingers into a live light socket and leave them there for five hours and you may be getting close. Each second was an eternity in a nightmare. There is suffering beyond the physical. Now I know why we must prepare our lightbodies before we could ever tolerate the higher energies. It would be the most hellishingly cruel kind of torture to shift into the 5th dimension and find oneself trapped there if you weren't ready. That would truly be the real Hell.

The only comic relief was when our old Pleiadian buddies showed up. The one who originally joined with Duane began to join him again. Yet, Duane was in dual consciousness and was not yet quite aware that the Being was there. I asked the Pleiadian if he was going to give us some new information.

Duane, of course, assumed I was talking to him, to Duane himself. "Why do you expect me to bring in any new information? I don't have any information!" Duane bellowed. Then the Pleiadian commenced to speak, again through Duane. The more we conversed with the Pleiadian, the angrier Duane grew, vociferously assuring us that he did not know what we were talking about and besides, what was so damned funny. Throughout these journeys, Duane never sits down. He always paces back and forth and talks in a voice that a deaf person could hear. Soon the merge took effect and, when all was said and done, Duane was our super hero that day.

.

Duane Brings Through the DNA Activation

David was the first person to be given the DNA activation. He lay spread-eagled on the floor as Duane sat beside him and described the new method in a deep calm voice all the way through. I was lying helplessly in my recliner, moaning and gasping during this trip through Hell.

Duane stood beside my chair as he activated me. I could see that the physical and psychic toll on him was just about more than he could handle. Also, he had to stop for a minute each time, and I realized with concern that he could barely breathe. He asked me to activate him as we went, and I swear I don't know how I even raised my hand. You will remember that I had to be jumpstarted to the higher frequency at the last minute. I said I would worry about that when the time came? Well, that was the time.

We concluded our work about 6 P.M. the evening of the 8th—an eight-hour journey. Still very much under the effects of the drug and the other energies, I managed to drag off to bed where I just toughed it out for four days. It was an extremely painful crash landing, all descriptive words inadequate.

The passage of these intervening months, between that day and the present, gives me a different perspective now. I can look back and realize just what was given to humanity that day. What culminated on November 8th was begun with Harmonic Convergence back in 1987. I think it is important to put aside the doubts, the wild energies and the painful times to acknowledge that it is indeed true that we have the assistance of our space brothers and sisters—many of them—who are benevolently assisting Earth and Mankind in an ascension process that is very real.

A summary of the events of those hours includes other than just bringing in the activation methods on which most of the focus has been. Thomas had his own agenda as well. Earlier talk about forming a group mind among the four of us turned out to be legitimate. As the day progressed, there were some really mind-boggling manipulations of the energies that resulted in sudden shifts in consciousness from one person to another.

At one point, for example, Don appeared to be so atypically influenced by the drug that he could barely hold his head up. Thomas shifted the energy and immediately Don gave every appearance of assuming a completely normal demeanor. Conversely, ordinary consciousness could instantly convert into such overwhelming intensity that one could barely cope with it. I realized that I was grounding heavy energies for the group and especially for Duane so that he could do his job. Even at that, he could barely keep going. It became clear that if it were it not for the group connections, we never would have made it.

Important to Clear Memories of Past Catastrophes *

The first order of business was a complete surprise. Thomas asked us to clear our heart chakras of the grief over what we regarded as our failure in Atlantis to reach the critical mass necessary to shift into the higher dimensions back then. "I don't feel any grief over that," I thought. That was just before the knife-piercing pain hit my chest. I mention this because we are not the only ones still carrying that level of pain from the old days in Atlantis.* Since then I have heard reports that teachers in other workshops lead groups through identical clearings. Some readers may intuitively feel that they, too, resonate with this buried secret deep in the cellular memory of their heart chakras. We need to forgive ourselves and release it. (Duane tells this story in greater detail in the Epilogue later in this book.) In addition, there are deeply buried fears about impending natural catastrophes still lurking about.

I want to emphasize, at this point, how typical this sort of experience with Thomas has been over the years. We found out the wisdom of paying attention and listening closely. He does not rant and rave and dance on the table. We certainly did not grasp the full significance about residual fears around catastrophes. However, we did find evidence of it in some healing clients. Then, tons of printed material came from other channelers, shaman and healers. As I add this comment in July 2008, I understand so much more clearly how utterly significant it is.

Thomas led us through what he referred to as an uncloaking ceremony. Since then this also has assumed much greater significance than I reckoned at the time. Basically, he asked that we "take off our coats" and reveal who we are. Metaphysical belief systems and walking an alternative spiritual path are like medicines that do not go down very well among unenlightened family, friends and coworkers. Like many of you reading this, we kept our mouths shut. This book reveals things that normally would not have been included had it not been for Thomas's promptings.

---

* More information about this very subject has emerged in intervening months between the start of this book and its completion. The additional experiences we have encountered in healing work with others have been added in later chapters (see *Catastrophobia* by Barbara Hand Clow). Clearing the fears of impending catastrophe have been added to the list of clearings in Chapter Four.

Understatement of the Millennium!

He also intimated that the times ahead were ones where many more things would be revealed than our band's little secrets. "The truth will be revealed and that means all the way to the top," he predicted. I immediately took that to mean all the way to the White House. This predated the contentious elections and the questionable voting practices the following year in 2004. Thomas's understatements possibly belie the extent of the profound changes that will accompany the ascension process as it shifts gears into ever higher and more rapidly moving frequencies. We probably ain't seen nuthin' yet!

Once again Thomas called it right. From the perspective of July 2008, the veil is drawn back to reveal shocking dark truths ranging from presidential lies to long-standing corporation shenanigans. Even the scandalous revelations penetrated the religious community. It appears that it is necessary for the unbelievable corruption and nearly incomprehensible betrayal of our most sacred values to surface at last for all to see.

It is a continuing challenge for lightworkers not to give in to fear. In the end, the Light is always more powerful than the Dark. We are the victors who believed and embraced the promise of the New Era of peace and transformation for Earth and Humanity. This is all the more heroic because we transcended those fears to do it!

CHAPTER TWO

Harmonic Concordance II
October 14, 2004

An amazing revolution is coming to the world, one that is both disturbing and liberating.

Richard Zeitgeber
The Matrix (the movie)

My brother returned to Santa Fe immediately following Harmonic Concordance Day. There were many unanswered questions. I admit that I was more than a little relieved that it was he, not I, who had the job of figuring out just how this new 12-strand DNA activation was going to work with people. We really did not know much of anything about DNA.

That was November 2003. I am writing this in August of 2005. That gives you some idea about how long it took us to put it all together. I followed the stream of energy that originally catapulted me into another state of consciousness back in August of 2003. Thomas was right. I resigned myself to the reality that I was never going to return to my former state of "normal" consciousness.

Duane and I were the keynote speakers at the International Huna Conference in Cape Girardeau, Missouri, in July 2003. I lectured and Duane demonstrated how to do a 5th dimension lightbody activation based on our first book, *The Lightbody Activation Manual.* When it finally soaked in that we were actually writing a second book, we agreed to deliver the keynote address again the following year. This time the plan was to explain and demonstrate the 12-strand DNA Activation Method.

New Realities Slowly Sink In

As the months crawled toward the July 2004 conference date with no clear outline of our presentation, you can imagine our panic. The dilemma was solved with some shocking information. Duane was discussing the DNA activation with a friend in California, an experienced lecturer on healing and a variety of other metaphysical subjects, including DNA activation. The lady patiently listened as Duane laid out the details of what he had been up to. "Don't you know what you have here?" she demanded. By the time Duane hung up the phone, his concept of just what tiger we had by the proverbial tail blasted his consciousness.

This wasn't only a method for 12-strand DNA Activation. It was the formula for building the complete ascension vehicle for accessing the 5th dimension!

The next thing was for him to explain this entire matter to his sister. I was the designated lecturer for the fast-approaching July conference. It was my responsibility to give the background story and outline what Duane would be demonstrating. I probably will never completely understand what happened when Duane explained the whole thing during a five-hour phone conversation that lasted into the wee hours.

The Birth of a New Archetype

His patience was really superhuman. For some reason, I was completely unable to understand what he was telling me. It was as if I were brain dead. I was switched off. Duane repeated the methods over and over again. The only explanation we ever came up with was that I was mirroring how overwhelming it may be for some people, or the mass consciousness, to cope with understanding the larger context of ascension and the details of the method illustrated in this book.

Since then I lay claim to creating a new archetype: the Dumb Sister Archetype. We used it as a constant benchmark against which we measured the clarity of each new explanation. We hoped this alerted us to whenever we took for granted that any new idea was as obvious to everybody else as it was to someone with the familiarity of repeated use. Sure enough, the questions did come in proving that there was not always immediate understanding. Some people can be so stupid! Not you guys, of course. Since we don't have a bell that goes off every time some idiot does not get the obvious, we always have the Dumb Sister Archetype to fall back on.

This served as a constant check to be as clear as possible in our explanations and not take for granted that everyone immediately gets their arms around these new ideas. If you have a better explanation, write to me.

Harmonic Concordance II

I am an astrologer. If something is in the wind, I usually pick it up on the astrological airwaves first. In September 2004, word began to circulate on the Internet that a rare astrological configuration—a grand quintile* for you astrologers—was going to come along on October 14, again heralded by an eclipse on the same date. My shamanic radar was alerted. Could another big event come along on the heels of Harmonic Concordance I? Yes, it could and it did. The Earth was preparing to release even higher energies. It was not long before Harmonic Concordance II was announced and again worldwide observances were planned.

It was not long before my group and I were knocked out by the incoming energies. (Here we go again.) There were aches and pains, fatigue and brain fog. Some days we could not function at all. The telephone calls flew back and forth as we struggled to understand what it all meant, and even more to the point, what we were supposed to do. About 40 miles away in my own backyard, Mt. St. Helens awakened from her slumbering and was erupting once again. The Earth has her own version of cleansing. We decided we would take that as our cue to do the same. We were willing to do most anything to keep up with Big Momma as she changed frequencies.

The Astrological Indicators Were Amazing

An overview of the astrological timeline in October 2004 was remarkable. First, the horoscope for Harmonic Concordance II echoed a striking resonance with the horoscope for Harmonic Concordance I the previous November. The astrological line-up was extraordinarily rare during the month of October. The first grand quintile came together in the sky and initiated an incredible sequence beginning October 1. Astrologer Jill Whitman launched a computer search and apparently found this rare combination of planets almost completely absent throughout the past 2,500 years. Imagine the incredulity among the astrologers who tracked this with double takes when a SECOND one formed at the end of October on the 28th, again on the day of an eclipse!

---

* A quintile is the name for a relationship between two planets in which they are 72 degrees apart in the zodiacal circle of 360 degrees. A grand quintile is formed when five planets are spaced around the wheel, each at 72-degree intervals from the next. It is no accident that these alignments are forming five- and six-pointed stars composed of geometric shapes that imply different forms of consciousness. Sacred geometry is a subject much too huge to tackle here. Drunvalo Melchizedec's *Flower of Life,* Volumes I and II, are good sources if anyone wishes to explore the subject. They are listed in the bibliography.

At the mid-point on October 14 was Harmonic Concordance II, also coincident with a solar eclipse in 21 degrees of Libra, which conjoins the position of the great benefic fixed star, Spica. (Solar and lunar eclipses come in pairs and occur approximately two weeks apart at new and full moon periods.) The connection to Spica gave evidence that the Goddess was waltzing in with these energies. She represented the re-emergence of the Feminine. Venus, another aspect of the goddess, put on her own rare show as well.

That is another story, so we will leave with the point well-taken that powerful new themes from the Feminine principle will dramatically rebalance relationships and establish equality between the Feminine and Masculine, which by the way, is expressed in the DNA activations. From a variety of sources as well as our own, it came down the pipeline that Earth was opening a portal to the 6th dimension. That refers to the heart chakra, the body's psychic center for love and forgiveness. All of you have one.

Ceremony in the High Desert

Of course there was no question but what we would take time out for a special observance of Harmonic Concordance II on October 14th. It was an easy decision to head out for the high desert country in Central Oregon to the Warm Springs Indian Reservation, which was relatively isolated from civilization. We had visited many times before to recharge our batteries in the rarified energy there. The broad sweeping mesas and spectacular long views of the majestic volcanic mountains dotting the Ring of Fire Cascade Range created an atmosphere that cleared our heads and restored our souls.

The Lodge at Kah-Nee-Tah swallowed into the towering desert mesas appeared as indigenous to the landscape as the ancient rocky outcroppings. We entered the Lodge and searched out a quiet corner behind the free-standing megalithic stone fireplace that soared skyward at least 25 feet through the center of the main floor. Two huge logs, each nearly three feet in diameter, fed dancing flames that seemed alive for our ceremony. I just hoped that I would not do anything to attract unwanted attention. I think we had help from on High. The place was like a morgue; not a soul was around to cramp my style.

That day marked the first time my consciousness totally connected with the 6th and 7th dimensions. I made the breakthrough to the 6th dimension and saw beings outside a huge ornate gate. They were the Gatekeepers readying for the heart-chakra portal opening. At the 7th dimension I conversed at the soul level with each person in my group. I realized that I was passing old boundaries and savored the exploration of these other realities. It is beyond words to describe these journeys and their full impact. Let's just say that we thought it deserved a bottle of champagne at dinner.

Cow Consciousness Breaks the Moo-ed

We started home at deep twilight. The Warm Springs Indian Reservation is some distance from the main highway. There are free-ranging cattle, no fences nor any streetlights. We spotted cattle close by so wound along the narrow road about 20 miles an hour. What happened next gave me the shock of my life. Abruptly, the headlight on the driver's side illumined an unmistakable bovine head. Its eye locked onto mine, freezing an image in my mind forever. Don slammed on the brakes and whipped the steering wheel to the right. However, there was no mistaking the sickening thud as the car slammed into the animal's head.

The unfortunate critter did not run straight across in front of the car. Instead, it came from behind and angled forward alongside the car on the driver's side. That accounted for the fact that we could not see it coming. It was just a matter of a few inches that forestalled the real possibility of a much more catastrophic situation. I was raised in Midwestern farm country and sometimes drivers ended up with the beast coming through the windshield and sitting in their laps. Six months later you come out of the coma and wonder who you are, while the doctor holds up two fingers.

We were beside ourselves. It was too dark to see if the animal was dead or not. We prayed that it was out of its misery. We had no means to investigate or do anything about it if we had. Once we collected our wits somewhat, our attention turned to our car. We were aware that we were out in the middle of nowhere and if we could not drive the car, it would be a very complicated matter, to say the least. Visions of sleeping under the stars that night were mercifully short-circuited. The left headlight was torn up, wires and metal were hanging in a twisted knot, but by some miracle, it was still lit. The fender and bumper on the left side were caved in and the side rear view mirror was torn off.

We were able to drive to a little lone gas station at the edge of the reservation. We stopped and reported the accident to the Indian Reservation police. Don surveyed the twisted hood and other damage and decided we could risk the three-hour trip over the mountains back home. We drove very slowly and nervously in dead silence as the face of the animal and its staring eye lodged in our own inner eye throughout the trip—and remains to this day. I am sure the animal was killed, but every now and then I am tortured by irrational thoughts of the poor thing lying there suffering.

We got some incredulous stares from the group back home when we naively speculated aloud whether the incident might have some symbolic meaning. Here we were, two shaman doing ceremony, during an eclipse, on Harmonic Concordance Day II, on an Indian reservation, and we ask if it had any symbolic meaning? In the face of all of this, we conceded that we should take this seriously and get together for some shamanic journeying. David joined us. We lit the fireplace and invoked the Fire

Spirits. We usually do not observe much ritual ourselves, but this time I did some drumming that sent us deep into another reality.

The Goddesses Conduct Initiations

The Goddess, Isis, spoke through me. Long, curved bull horns growing from each side of her head distinguishes this particular aspect of the Goddess. The Bull is associated in mythology with the Sacred Feminine. Astrologically, the two eclipses that month were in Libra and Taurus, both ruled over by the planet, Venus, another aspect of the Goddess. The Isis mythology is interlinked with her husband, Osiris, and their son, Horus, all associated with the Sacred Bull religion.

This powerful Goddess led us through an initiation ceremony called Bathed in the Blood of the Bull, all images indigenous to religious rites in Egypt and other places throughout the ancient world. She reminded us that we had participated for real in that ceremony many lifetimes ago. There were later connections to the Blood of Christ in some of Christianity's most sacred rituals.

I recalled then an incredible example of synchronicity that occurred a short time before this. I watched a movie on television about two girls who were chosen to take part in this very same ceremony. I can only comment about this whole experience that each of us felt the blood of the slain bull running over our heads as very real that day.

The Western cultures have lost their connections to the ceremonies, rituals and initiation rites connected to the Ancient Mysteries. We were told that the animal that was struck sacrificed itself to awaken the memories of the ancient ceremony as a prelude to the emergence of spontaneous initiatory experiences within the mass consciousness. Many more people will raise their consciousness, but there are no formal ceremonies to legitimize it for them. Our experiences go onto the Earth grids making it available to the collective, a task we have done many times before. My only advice is that if you are really getting into this evolved consciousness business that you have good insurance and a cowcatcher on the front of your automobile!

No, Not Again

It may have been naïve of me, but I thought my adventures for October were over. What I failed to consider was that there was an eclipse and another grand quintile still coming into formation.

On the 26th of October, the day before the eclipse, an old familiar twinge bothered my right side. I implored the gods to spare me another gallbladder attack. They turned a deaf ear and before I knew it, I was beyond pain, reliving the horrific nightmare of the earlier one before Harmonic Concordance in November 2003. I moaned and barely gasped for breath until six o'clock the following morning.

I resolved to find other ways to be reminded that liver-gallbladder cleanses were once again called for all around. I informed my guides. Later in this book you will read about their nasty sense of humor when they did indeed figure out another way. (Chapter "Let's Get Physical) I have now adopted a regular regimen of liver and gallbladder cleanses to forestall any repetition of the ordeals. (Later chapters will identify specific resources for cleanses.)

When the pain subsided I was then greeted by a tornado of energies. I felt like a giant flat iron was pressing me down. It hurt; it really hurt. My husband, intending to do some Reiki healing to alleviate my discomfort, put his hands in my energy field and started as though he had been electrocuted. He said he never felt anything like it before. My energy field was wild and through the roof. I begged him to consult with Thomas. The Spirit Teacher told him that I was beginning to download the 7th dimension energies surging through me to ground them in conjunction with the Taurus-Scorpio eclipse.

A Bad Trip Through the Collective

The roller coaster ride continued its ups and downs when sometime in the early days of January 2004, I found myself mired in a particularly wretched energy. It was oppressive. My body hurt all over. Feelings of fear and powerlessness engulfed me in a black fog. I was reduced to lying almost paralyzed in my recliner, zoning out on mindless TV 15 hours a day, I seriously considered boarding the bus for the home in the country (with bars on the windows). A shock of insight saved me the trip. *I was hot-wired into the mass consciousness!*

I was bitterly disappointed that the collective was awash with such negativity. The overriding characteristic was denial, a pervasive blindness to the reality of things. Although sickeningly unpleasant, I was grateful for the insight into why people were acting out as they were. There are many scary things in the world, and many of our citizens feel frightened and powerless to do anything about them. It affected me to the extent that I began to doubt my own beliefs. There was so much fear; I just wanted to shut my eyes, and make it all go away. Thank god I had the tools to disconnect, once I realized what was going on.

I published an e-newsletter account of my troubling voyage through the landscape of the mass mind. There was a remarkably vigorous reaction from readers. Many lightworkers recognized the symptoms themselves as they bought into the messages of doom and gloom. The necessity of staying unwaveringly connected to the Light became starkly more essential than ever. No one trapped in the dark abyss can hope to shift into the higher dimensions. Lightworkers must transform their own inner worlds in sufficient numbers to reach critical mass to shift the collective or else the Ascension Express is going to pull out of the train station with a lot of empty seats.

The following comments are samples from readers who responded in living color to my story of checking out the mass consciousness. My hope is that this will reinforce how constantly vigilant and conscious we need to be to keep clear of the Siren Song of the collective. The test is whether or not we change-agents can unwaveringly maintain the vision of how we want things to be; a vision that must be more powerful than the fears and despair of so many people who lack the spiritual tools to understand that we are not powerless.

Readers' Comments:

> "Thanks for offering some explanation of the quagmire I have been in lately. It makes a great deal of sense."
>
> "You are not alone in what you have been through...I felt buried and overwhelmed...I felt mired in the terror. I couldn't shake it. I felt it was something I was receiving from 'outside.' When I read your newsletter it all made sense."
>
> "Thanks for reminding me I am not going insane."
>
> "Well, you hit it right on the money this time! You're right. It is fear. I just wanted to let you know that your sharing of your enlightened struggles is a definite light in the darkness. You keep me on track."
>
> "I can't get over it. You were describing blow by blow exactly what I was going through at exactly the same time. I can never thank you enough. Once again your shamanic self has taken the journey and brought back the message."

I am still contemplating whether the pain and suffering was worth it in the light of such grateful feedback and all. I would love to say with conviction that the pain and suffering was absolutely worth it to encourage fellow spiritual light seekers to hold the energies that bring transformation. The truth is: The jury is still out on that!

CHAPTER THREE

The Ascension Game

Many years ago before neither my son nor I had ever heard of ascension, we fell to talking about physical mortality. It came up in the conversation how he would feel when I died. He turned to me and said, "You know what, Mom? We aren't going to die. Someday I am going to turn to you and say, 'Time to get outta Dodge!'" As wildly improbable as that may have seemed, I believed him.

I remember very well when the idea of life as a game initially surfaced. It was the first time that David and I journeyed together using The Pill. In fact, it was the first time David ever used The Pill period. You can imagine that it was a process for a mom to introduce her grown son to a drug.

His wife at the time was not on the same page as I was as far as belief systems were concerned and that is putting it mildly! We waited until she was out of town on business. I sneaked over to his apartment, and we set off on a two-day trip. It is impossible to do justice to that wild and crazy roller coaster ride, presided over by Thomas, our Spirit Teacher, and the Trickster.

Unless you have experienced the Trickster archetype—also known as Coyote—up close and personal, you may as well forget about capturing on paper the energy of its utter genius for madness with meaning. These energies played with our heads. We were jolted past the boundaries of our belief systems. We laughed hysterically; we were mind-boggled. At one point we found ourselves moving toward other dimensions. When the lamps began to disappear—and I'm not kidding—we chickened out.

The Game of Life

At some point in the festivities, the idea that life is a game became a main theme of the journey. We took flight into our wildest imaginations and embraced the notion that the game had rules, players, winners and losers. We seized onto what we thought was a huge revelation of the Way Things Work, namely, that the winners of this present game won the right to set the rules for the next Game of Life.

For many years, we periodically entertained ourselves with the Game's various fantasy plot twists and brilliant strategies. For the longest time, we believed this was our very own inside joke. All one has to do now is search the Internet for references to life as a Game to discover that this is anything but our exclusive little secret. We obviously picked up an idea that was floating around in the ethers and is accessible to everyone.

Ever since I awakened to alternative spirituality and metaphysics in the 1960s, I have always asked lots of questions. I wanted to know the answer to all of life's mysteries. As the years went by, I discovered that some questions are answered right away, some questions probably never will be answered, and then there are the ones that I filed away in the back of my mind and, if I waited long enough, those answers would come eventually.

One big question haunted us after Duane returned from Hawaii in 1999. We didn't talk about it much, but it never went away. The question was, why us? This was not false modesty. Of all the lightworkers on Planet Earth, why would the Pleiadians single us out? The best we could ever come up with as an explanation was not very satisfying. We jokingly said it was simply because we would do it. But dammit, why us?

THE ASCENSION AFFAIR

The events that happened to eventually answer that question started back in 1991 and involved the four of us in the core group. We read a book *The Crystal Staircase,* one of the first books that talked about ascension. At the time, Duane was renting a house right on the Coast in Oceanside, Oregon.

David and I had driven over to spend the weekend and were sitting on the front deck discussing the book. As we walked back into the house, we had the most astonishing experience with telepathic communication, our first. It was just there. We both knew it. We both felt it.

The message passed between David and me that our group was to prepare to ascend immediately! It was one powerful message and confronted us with a tough decision. Did we hear that right? All four of us decided to take it seriously and see what happened. The only description for the events that ensued for months after that was a sort of controlled pandemonium.

First we wanted to be sure that this was a true directive. It became an obsession. There was session after session of the deepest meditations asking for confirmation. We called on Mary; we called on Jesus. We beseeched our guides to tell us if we were out of our minds.

Not one message ever came to indicate that we should stop or that we were off track. You need to understand that in those days we envisioned ascension-bound individuals as just disappearing when the time came. That mindset determined a lot of our actions. Obviously, if four of us just up and disappeared, critically important mundane affairs must be set in order.

This may seem totally preposterous at this point in time, but just accept that we were in that particular consciousness then. I turned over the deed to my house and changed bank accounts to my ex-husband. We wrote letters of explanation the best we could for those left behind.

We targeted August 14, 1991 for the big day. The thoughts of ascension were never far from our minds as we prepared over the ensuing months. One night we gathered together to take The Pill to see if it would provide more insight. It was one of the most powerful spiritual experiences of our lives. As we dropped deep into the influence of the drug, the message came through that we had to apply for ascension by "presenting our papers."

We had a rule in the group that we would never trust any entities until they had "presented their papers," attesting to who they were. We had many run-ins with the Dark side over the years. It behooved us to be sure with whom we were dealing. When I saw Jesus, I asked for his papers. I heard Duane loudly whisper, "Oh my god, she is asking Jesus for His papers!" I saw something that lives in my memory still and always will.

Apparently, Jesus was willing to follow protocol. First, I saw an explosion of light. Then images flashed by at supersonic speed. Jesus had papers all right. There were golden seals with mystical symbols and writings. There were ornate belts. It just went on and on until I said that I could accept that this was adequate.

What I really meant was, if the dizzying panorama flying by my inner eye did not halt immediately, I would throw up. We presented our papers of intention. David likes to say that his job was to manage the velvet ropes demarking the aisles as we filed by. (You have seen them in your bank.)

We expected a message any minute calling everything off. However, kites and balloons began to appear over and over again as the symbols of ascension. The synchronicities confirmed that we were on the right track. It was mind-boggling. People sent us notes and cards decorated with balloons. I saw TV documentaries on hot air balloons. Duane's house was right on the ocean. How many times does one see a lone balloon sailing over the ocean in full view of his deck? We all watched it float by. Some bawling kid who lost his balloon wasn't in our consciousness at the time. For us, it was straight from the gods.

In case we missed the signs, the trip to Duane's place for the big event was almost comical. As we pulled out of our driveway, the kid next door must have been a birthday boy. The local custom is to tie balloons to the celebrant's mailbox to mark the occasion. The grocery store across the street was not to be outdone. A towering hot air balloon, easily 50 feet tall, filled the parking lot to celebrate a grand opening!

Despite the signs, we continued with our deep meditations. We prayed and prayed to be turned aside from this venture if it were totally fanciful. Again, the signal never came to discontinue the mission. On the night before the big day, we gathered at Duane's house accompanied by our friends, Rex and Christopher. Christopher is an ex-Catholic priest. He agreed to do the "last supper." The spiritual energies were running high. We were in a solemn mood as the ceremony of bread and wine and prayers proceeded. Rex and Chris headed back to Portland with our car, wondering if they would ever hear from us again.

We had our stash of Pills, only this time we were directed to use a second drug. We had never done this before and admittedly were a bit jumpy. We took the plunge, nevertheless, and settled down to wait for them to take effect. Duane sat in the easy chair in front of the window. David sat alone on the couch on the opposite wall. Don sat in an easy chair at the other end of the couch. I sat at the table in the open dining area between the living room and the kitchen.

Time dragged on uneventfully. The drug pulled us in deeper and deeper. One hour passed. I don't remember how much longer it was before David said, "I think we are in a spaceship but don't realize it yet." I exploded out of my chair and stood in the center of the living room. "Spaceship my ass. We are in Duane's living room. We have been in Duane's living room, and we are going to continue to be in Duane's living room." I plunked myself down on the couch beside David and took his hand. Our energies were so heavy it is a wonder we did not sink into the ground.

David stood up and announced, "Well, I am going to go kill myself." Then after a well-timed pause he added, "No, I guess I will go read my book instead." He tromped off to his bedroom and read *The Lord of the Ring* in its entirety that day.

Duane went to bed, cocooning himself tightly in the sheets to sleep off the drug. Don and I slunk off to the downstairs guest room. All I remember after that is hugging the side of the bed to ride out the blast from the drug. It was just terrible. At 3:00 p.m. the next day the phone call to Rex was very much from the 3rd dimension.

We uneasily recalled the experience, frustrated by the absence of any explanation or resolution. What was that all about? How could we have misread the situation so completely? Furthermore, where were our guides? Why didn't they call a screeching halt to this nonsense? We about drove ourselves nuts trying to figure it out.

The best I ever came up with concerned the issue of over-dependence on guides. Right from the start, we understood the message loud and clear that true guides do not micromanage your life. Maybe the lesson meant that we needed to depend more on our own intuition. Also, I replayed the entire scenario, frame by frame, searching for evidence of the Trickster. I did not think that either explanation fit very well, but it was all I could hang my hat on at the time.

Thenceforth dubbed the Ascension Affair, this demonstrates that the high road of conscious spirituality presents many confounding twists and turns. The critical question is how to handle setbacks like this. To stay grounded, the best course is to avoid extreme reactions.

On the one hand, we could have abandoned everything associated with spirituality and just said to hell with it. I recall thinking that I should go back to school and learn the plumbing business. Another extreme ends up distrusting one's self and questioning every message after that, no matter what the source.

This is what we did do. For a while, we pulled in our horns and focused on our mundane life. After all, The Ascension Affair had taken our undivided attention for months on end. We did not allow it to shake our confidence. We did not think we were crazy. By placing it in perspective, it did not negate everything else we accomplished.

We fell back on the one guiding principle that has unerringly steered us through insoluble experiences like this in the past and would again in the future:

"One of the most dangerous threats to your spiritual journey is the need for explanations—the need to understand everything."

King Left Brain must abdicate its jealously guarded kingdom in the Land of Logic. Only the intuitive function has the "sense"—pun intended—to stand up and tune in. From the limited perspective of the 3rd dimension, the larger workings of the Universe stretch beyond my understanding. Yet, we went on to bring in the ascension lightbody work after that. Read on, however, and you will find out what big mistake we did make.

."

If You Wait Long Enough

Years later in 2002, I was working in my home office, which houses an extensive library. Bookcases from floor to ceiling cover each wall. One day Don was talking to me, standing with his back to a bookcase behind him on a wall behind the door to the room.

All of a sudden, the bookcase literally exploded off the wall. It had been there quietly for five years. A blizzard of books went flying through the air as though propelled by an invisible force. Dozens were tossed to the far side of the room. They barely cleared my desk and me as they zoomed by. The momentum was unearthly; I swear I barely escaped decapitation! We stood paralyzed as books thudded against the window.

However, maybe death by flying books is suitably exotic for a bookophile if death there was to be. The entire room was littered everywhere with hundreds of books.

When the bookcase came crashing down, it barely missed Don and came to rest dangerously close to my computer. It looked and sounded like we had been bombed. We were so shaken, we did not tackle the clean-up until the next day.

It was no mean task restoring the books to their rightful places. In fact, the organization of my library has never fully recovered. To this day, I wail in utter frustration, "Where is that damn book?" We had piles everywhere, sorted by subject. Impulsively, Don tossed a book onto my desk—just that one particular book. "You should be interested in this book." The subject matter was ascension. I impulsively opened it to a page, and this sentence caught my eye: **There are people who have already ascended, but they don't remember it.**

The Granddaddy Shock!

I thought the shock of remembrance was going to blow a hole in my brain. It was like dying and watching your life pass before your eyes in one single flash. It was as if a big monster hand smacked me upside the head. ***"We did ascend that day!" I screamed over and over again.*** The flood of memories halted any book sorting for the rest of that day.

This finally explained everything! It explained why the Pleiadians contacted us. It explained why no guidance from the other side warned us to stop the nonsense. Our petition to Jesus was real. We did cross over that day in Duane's living room! While we were in the other dimension that day, the entire mission came clear to all of us as one we had committed to at the soul level before any of us incarnated. That is why we were walk-ins. That is why the Pleiadians gave us the outline of the dimensional activations and the plan to reveal them to Duane.

Each of us had a role to play. And here is something interesting: we were first given the option to stay there or return and facilitate the Shift. They honored our free will. Actually, I was hesitant to sign off on my mission in case refusal resulted in some nasty karmic consequences. We all chose to return.

DIANA'S VISION

The Voices in the River

I actually was not as nonchalant about returning as this may sound. A vision years and years ago tipped me off that the day would come when I was offered the opportunity to get out of here but refused it. I privately thought to myself, "Don't count on that." When I say this was a vision, I mean a real in-the-daytime-living-color vision. This is what I saw. I should say, this is what I experienced, because it was so real.

It was night. A bitter cold rain was falling. I found myself swimming in the middle of a rain-swollen river. I could not see in the pitch black, but I could sense heavy objects like logs barely missing me as they lurched by. I was freezing cold. I could not see the far bank. I was exhausted. I could only pray that I made it without drowning or sustaining a fatal injury.

I reached the far bank, more dead than alive. I barely dragged my dog-tired body up the slippery, muddy slope. My fingers finally curled around a clump of grass and pulled me up onto solid ground with my last ounce of strength. I flopped belly down. I gasped deeply just to catch a breath. As I regained full consciousness, I rolled over on my back to thank my lucky stars to be alive. Only then was I startled out of my wits to see…HER!

It was the Goddess. She was very tall. Her white robes shimmered with a dim light. The energy was incredible. It was like being given the gift of life just to be in Her presence. She commanded me to stand. I do not know how I managed to stagger upright. She blessed me for making it across the river. She told me, "Mission accomplished!" I could go home.

Before I had the wits to get out of there, her upraised hand stopped me. A finger over her pursed mouth signaled me to shush and listen. I heard the rushing waters and then I heard the voices calling out in the night. She said, "Some of those souls will drown, one arm-length away from the bank of this river." She did not need to say more. I knew what *She* wanted me to do. I knew what *I* wanted to do. I also knew what I *probably* would do. Oh, s**t! I flopped down on the bank and extended my arm.

Now back to the story. When we 4Ds re-entered the 3rd dimension, the process of forgetting was the same as incarnating into a new life. We were unable to carry the memory back through the veil with us. Throughout the intervening years, I became increasingly psychically open compared to when we originally bi-located. "Someone" finally found the right time to blast the message through to me.

This explained why Duane so unhesitatingly pulled up stakes and packed himself off to Hawaii. Would he have so instantly responded unless something was resonating in the memory banks somewhere? That is why we became the receivers of directives from the Pleiadians on Harmonic Concordance. Once again, buried deep in consciousness somewhere, was a memory. We heard it all before. This confirmed once again my philosophy that if you wait long enough, the answers will come!

That nanosecond telepathic exchange between David and me could have so easily passed by as a whisper that wasn't there. It did not strike like a thunder clap. We caught this out of the corner of an eye just as it cleared the left field bleachers. I shudder to think how differently things would have turned out if we had missed it, and more than that, failed to act on it to its final conclusion. I'm glad David did not kill himself but read his book instead.

We have never revealed that we already shifted to the 5th dimension and back. I did not intend to include it in this book. We had an agreement with Thomas, however, to reveal everything. So here we are.

What was the big mistake that we made throughout The Ascension Affair ? ***Obviously, we did not believe our own experience!*** How much clearer could it have been? We also dismissed the abundance of confirmations every step of the way. We couldn't remember crossing over and coming back. That didn't mean that we had not done so. Also, it contradicted our skewed notion about people disappearing. We should have simply taken it at face value, regardless of whether it happened according to our preconceived ideas.

When you read about this and some of my other personal stories, plus those of my clients, I don't want to leave the wrong impression, either that the process is unbearably difficult or unrealistically blissful. It is not easy to spell out the general guidelines for preparing for ascension. That will depend on individual circumstances. One thing seems certain. If there isn't a powerful inner drive to sustain you, your ability to meet the challenges is greatly compromised. Conversely, if you committed to ascension this time around, the soul connection will most likely carry you through even the darkest of times.

THE PLANETARY GRIDS

The first time David ever took The Pill was the time with me in his apartment. Some time later, he embarked on his maiden voyage with Don and me together at our place. This was not the only first that night. It was also the first time I ever heard about earth grids. It certainly was not the last time. Afterwards, when we completed one of our adventures, Thomas said, "Put it on the grid." Here is how it all got started.

In the middle of the journey, David took off on a tangent to expound at length about grids surrounding the planet. No one can expound like David. When he takes off on something, you might as well just sit back and fasten your seat belt. It is a performance.

The next thing I knew we were embroiled in the most outrageous story about grids. His new job description was "Lineman for the County." He wore a hard hat. He furnished Don with a hard hat and engaged him in the grid work as well. Imaginary little neighborhood kids gathered around to watch them.

David was in his twenties. He hadn't traveled with Don and me before. I figured I'd give the kid the benefit of the doubt at first. We could sort this out later. After all, why discourage him?

David is a hysterically funny fellow, so at least we had a first-class stand-up comedy routine to "lighten" the energies. He further expounded on the evils of removing oil from the ground that same night. Disruption of one of her main circulatory systems greatly disturbed Mother Earth as well: The Truth according to David. I listened bemused at my progeny's wild imagination. After all, I set an extra place at the table for imaginary friends for this same kid.

Out Of The Mouths Of Babes

Not more than a couple of months later, I received Bob Longacre's newsletter. I knew him from crossing paths as lecturers at astrology conferences. I also recognized him as a powerful shaman and lightworker, a real heavyweight. What was the subject of the magazine that month? I was incredulous. An article about the earth grids and I'll be damned if that wasn't followed up with something about oil, almost exactly as David described.

Maybe if he hadn't acted like such a nut, I would have taken it seriously. Regardless, I ate the required amount of crow and when David expounds, I have learned to just bite my tongue and let him carry on. The Truth According to David dictates that the energy grids require periodic maintenance. For all I know, he is really doing something and besides, he's really funny. The Trickster possesses his soul and that trumps a mere mortal mother.

Planetary Grids: What are they?

What is the big deal about these so-called grids around the planet? Not only designated game players influence the grids, ***so does each and every one of us***! Furthermore, you may ***consciously*** participate in the formation and influence of the grids.

Grids are matrices that form an invisible network around the planet. The lines of latitude and longitude on a map are invisible in reality, and they are imaginary. Planetary grids may be invisible, but they are not imaginary. There is more than one grid, and each contains energy specific to it.

Before I delve into further technical explanations of grids, I will share my close encounter of the third kind with them up close and personal. I am grateful for having had this experience, but I would never want to repeat it! This happened long before the time when David introduced the idea of earth grids. Consequently, the word *grids* was not in my vocabulary nor did I entertain any notion of them at all. So when Thomas came sidling up to me with an innocent offer to open my crown chakra to see "what would happen," I had no reason to say no.

That is not to say that I had no reason to be somewhat wary, however. To place this in context, this took place in late 1984. Thomas had already initiated systematic work on the chakras several months earlier. So far, it had been quite an unpleasant experience. (I will write more about that in later chapters.) I trusted the value of doing this work so proceeded in spite of some very rough patches.

As I recall, I had romanticized the crown chakra in my mind as the superstar of the chakra system. (I also had a crush on Warren Beatty, and you can guess how that turned out.) Thomas found me engrossed in a good book in front of a warm fire in my den. Why not just kick back and give the crown chakra a whirl? When he told me that he planned to open it for just a second, I should have suspected it might be pretty intense.

I could not understand what was +the matter with Don as he leaned over me on the couch, pinning me down. Don likewise could not imagine what was the matter with me as I appeared to be experiencing some sort of seizure. Furthermore, how did I get on the couch? I was through playing crown chakra games with Thomas. I'm a fast learner.

When the next weekend rolled around, Thomas suggested that we give it another try. I said earlier that I trusted the work and proceeded in spite of some rough patches. That is not exactly true. We argued about it all afternoon. I finally relented and agreed to try again with the help of The Pill. This time I took refuge on the couch to begin with. This time the crown chakra was open for about 15 minutes. Again, it was an ordeal accompanied by uncontrollable violent shaking. On both occasions, two or three days were required for recovery.

When the third weekend came along, Thomas appeared once again. You must think I was out of my mind, but to make a long story short, I was cajoled into trying it again. Thomas's demeanor shifted. He asked me to take FIVE Pills. One Pill of 120 milligrams is a typical dose. The trip will last for about six hours at that dosage. Five Pills was a suicide attempt. I went into a rant and refused to do it. Finally we negotiated a deal whereby I would take two, wait for them to take effect, and then I would see the wisdom of taking the other three. I ended up taking the five.

Let me tell you that this requires absolute trust in the Teacher. If I did not wake up dead, I pictured myself in the back ward of the nearest mental health facility, singing nursery rhymes to myself from then through the next century. (Just a little reminder: this eventually will relate to earth grids.)

I sat on the couch. I can remember crossing my arms tightly around my abdomen, first rocking forward, and then slamming against the back of the couch as hard as I could. I did this over and over for seven hours. I am unable to come anywhere near to describing what this experience was really like.

The energies were intolerable. I demanded that Don play "Amazing Grace" on the organ. This somehow alleviated my terrible suffering. As you might imagine, he tired of this after several hours. The most terrifying, hysterical screaming, however, met any efforts to quit.

About halfway through, the uncontrollable shaking was so utterly exhausting me that Don felt he should do something to drain off some of the excess energies. He knelt down and grabbed hold of my feet. Don is a big man, and historically, was always the one in our group to handle the strongest .energies. He stiffened as though he had grabbed hold of a hot, downed power line.

I begged him to sing "Amazing Grace" over and over again. There must be something we don't know about the frequencies of that song. Anyway, between that and the contact high he got from me, we managed to get through it. Just now, at the very moment as I write about this, I have to stop to ask Don to sing that song again. I am feeling very drugged and nauseated just writing about it again after all these years.

This is what I remembered. My entire sense of self exploded out the top of my head. The awareness that I was an individual physical unit dissolved. I felt as though I were barreling through space at supersonic speed. Then the most amazing thing happened. ***I collided with a barrier***. I could not pass through it. It reminded me of a net, like a tennis net. I said aloud to Don, "Jesus put a net here."

I did not know about grids at that time, but I experienced one. It was the Christ Grid. I do not wholly understand why Thomas wanted me to have that experience. He usually has his reasons. I can say that, for me, grids are very real. Also, shortly after that, my group and I had some of our most powerful experiences.

As for my individual training with Thomas, my first inter-dimensional work began a few short months after that. Perhaps my outer space journey was the preparation for it. My terror that five Pills had inflicted permanent brain damage slowly dissipated. Seriously, I emphasize once more that even though mind-altering substances are traditionally associated with shamanic practices, they must always be used under the guidance of a trusted teacher or guide. By this time Thomas had already passed many tests, believe me!

You may think that knowledge of planetary grids originated with contemporary New Age channelings. Actually, Plato wrote extensively about his very complex theories concerning planetary grids. For a long time, this lost knowledge languished in oblivion. Today, extensive information is readily available to anyone via the Internet. Ah, the Internet! One cannot fail to appreciate the direct reflection of the spiritual grids onto the planet's worldwide communication network that resembles...a grid!

I don't want to get off on a tangent and end up writing a small book about planetary grids. What with the proliferation of information on the subject, it would be easy to do. So why am I writing about it? For one thing, Thomas would command after some of our adventures, "Now put it on the grid." I don't like to bandy about such phrases without explaining to the reader what they mean. I'm not saying that I appreciated what it meant at first myself. I didn't. I just assumed that by doing so, it somehow made the information accessible to everybody. Indeed that is exactly what it does mean. Furthermore, it also means that each person's thoughts, words and deeds are influencing the grids as well—yours and mine.

An Understanding of the Whole Picture is Empowering.

For another reason, humanity's evolving ascension consciousness, plus the planetary grids, and the systematic opening of portals and stargates, are all interrelated. To comprehend just how all of this fits together makes the remainder of this book more understandable. For myself, I found that this overview changed my consciousness. It was empowering to comprehend the whole picture.

When I undertook the serious study of astrology, there came a time when I realized that I should understand some of the technical aspects of the subject. When I comprehended the relationships in the solar system beyond some figures in the ephemeris,* I felt empowered when I understood and spoke the technical language. The same holds true for appreciating the nature of the great grid systems that organize and control the conscious evolutionary processes of ascension.

The grids reflect and regulate consciousness. The grid of light, or ascension, has evolved towards a more elaborate model, capable of regulating sophisticated and complex crystalline matrices more in accordance with the changes in DNA that we are experiencing. The entity, Kryon, adjusted the magnetic grid. Before the Crystal Grid was in place, it was necessary to leave the physical plane through death's doorway to ascend. We are now resonating to a higher vibratory level as we connect to the Crystal Grid.

---

* An *ephemeris* is a book of Tables listing the daily positions of the planets. Astrologers refer to it to calculate astrology charts.

FOUR PLANETARY GRIDS

The Gravitational Magnetic Grid

This one maintains our gravitational field around the Sun. It is shaped like a doughnut or toroid. Science knows about it. Its North Pole is associated with the Aurora Borealis light show. This grid is feminine and, of course, magnetic in its nature. Therefore, it is connected to the emotions.

The Telluric Grid

This grid is linked to the collective unconscious and is also feminine in nature. It manifests at the physical level along the geological faults. The energies are immense and are responsible for adjustments in the earth's crust. The huge earthquakes in Haiti and Chile, to name two, have aptly demonstrated just how immense these forces really are.

The Telluric Grid has been referred to as the circulatory system of Gaia (earth). This grid forms lattice-like lines created by disharmony and conflict. It's like wrinkles in our foreheads from worrying about the kids for twenty years. Wars, death and terrifying experiences leave an energetic footprint that draws conflict to the same geographical locations over and over again.

Ancient civilizations avoided building cities near these lines, just as we intuitively do not build our house over cemetery plots. The use of feng shui in Asian countries was partly to avoid inharmonious locations for dwellings and public buildings. Unfortunately, cities in the West rest atop fault lines as the ancient knowledge lay forgotten for centuries. I understand there is a new science of Geobiology, which quite deliberately heals these locations and dispels negative energies. I am not familiar with this particular specialty, but I cannot help but speculate about its similarity to shamanic practices of a like nature.

The Electric Grid or Technosphere

This grid is like a reservoir in which all of the human-created electrical energies are stored. Lines created by our civilization's use of electricity, microwaves, radio waves and television, form the Electric Grid. Its points of intersection are believed to be injurious to health if one stays near them for extended periods.

Also known as the Hartman Grid, it was named for German physicians who measured it to determine its effects on cancer patients. They found that it formed a rectangular lattice pattern normally about eight inches wide by seven or eight feet long but in some places greatly elongated.

I remember what was an unforgettable experience in a hotel hospitality suite at an astrology conference in San Diego in the late 70s. I was enjoying a conversation with a German astrologer whom I knew from previous conferences. Somehow the conversation turned to the subject of a lattice-like matrix overlaying the earth that was the subject of much interest in Germany. Of course at that time I knew nothing about grids.

Freddie, my friend, claimed that someone skilled in the art could dowse these lines. As it happened, my dad enjoyed a reputation as a local water dowser back in Benton County, Iowa. I grew up on a farm where it was common practice to dowse for water when someone needed a well. If you are connected to the Internet, log onto my website which includes a longer version about my experiences with dowsing. www.dianastone.com.

Dad taught me how to dowse, so almost before I realized what was up, I found myself walking back and forth across the room with a coat hangar, twisted into a forked dowsing rod. When dowsing, one sets the intent mentally. I pictured the lattice grid and to everyone's amazement, the coat hangar twisted violently downward at regular intervals all across the room.

Once when I had the occasion to lecture on astrology in Boise, Idaho, I visited the local astrologer, a friend of mine. He happened to be one of the amazed onlookers at my little dowsing demonstration in San Diego. He confided in me that he was quite ill and invited me to his house to dowse where the nodal points of the grid were. The intersecting lines at nodal points allegedly drain one's energy. I agreed.

I found his desk chair situated on a nodal point. He spent the remainder of the evening tearing up and rearranging his office. He told me later that he observed his cat and his dog; one of them always slept between the points and the other slept right on the nodes. I can't remember which was which. Nevertheless, I think of that every time I see one of my pets going around and around in circles before choosing the spot for a nap. I don't know personally what significance this may have, but I believe that our animals are aware of these energies and the way in which they are affected by them.

The Grid of Christ Consciousness or the Crystalline Grid.

This is the ascension grid. Plato knew about this one and wrote about it. Ancient civilizations knew of this and placed many monuments and religious sanctuaries along its lines. It is called the Christ consciousness because it is an aspect of the collective consciousness that recognizes itself as one Being. It is the grid on which is imprinted all the necessary information to experience the Christ consciousness.

The ley lines are the footprints on earth of this grid. Great concentrations of energy exist where these lines cross. Regarded as sacred or mystical sites, they draw people to them on special dates such as powerful eclipses, solstices and equinoxes, or the opening of stargates.

We must continually alter our vibratory level to connect to the Crystal Grid. When we say that we "connect" to a grid, it means that our personal frequency and the frequency of any particular grid are compatible. Increasing numbers of conscious and awakened individuals constantly change this grid. Consequently, I don't see any evidence that the journey to ascension means coasting along right where you are.

There are grids other than the ones I have written about here. There is an Axiatonal Grid to name one. This one connects the physical body to the earth's meridians, to the Crystal Grid and then to the Universal Grid above that.

How Many Grids Are There?

There are as many grids as there are manifesting intentions. Grids are created with a specific intention and function in mind. For starters, the Creator created cosmic grids that carry the intention to manifest the Creation. Interlaced and interwoven within a grand cosmic grid are various function-specific intentional grids. There are, for examples, Galactic Grids that outline the form and flow of each of the multitude of galaxies. Within each galactic grid are other grids that define and specify different functions and purposes.

Each star has its own solar system grid. Each planet has its own unique grid. You are familiar with the Gaia Grid. Each grid has its own consciousness and connections. To make this clearer, take the example of your precious human body. It is a grid defining its form, purpose and function. Within this human body grid (and it is further refined that each human has its own unique version of the species-specific prototype) are circulatory grids (your circulation system), your digestion grid, your structural support grid (bones and cartilage of your skeletal system), your nervous system grid that carries information through electrical and chemical interactions, etc.

What Is The Purpose Of A Grid?

A grid has as its function to hold something together, to hold something in form—to weave an intention and process to fulfill that intention into form. There are others forming as we evolve. The point I am making is that there is a relationship between ascension and the grids, There is a relationship between opening portals and the grids. Opening portals is for grounding new energies flooding into the planet.

Channelings from Archangel Michael suggest that it is our job to ground the energy into the Crystal Grids of the Earth. This serves to connect you to the planet **and make**

the energy available for the use by others, even those who are not yet awakened. (The energies can be grounded through the four elements—fire, earth, air and water—and are discussed in detail in the chapter "The Invisible Players.")

The Vibration of the Planet is Increasing

The question arises as to just how we can know if our "vibes" are compatible with ever-evolving grids. We know that many people are awakening, but that is fairly meaningless as far as any measurable barometer is concerned. I was excited to find this little clipping below (with no attribution) that gives further evidence about our planet's vibrational changes. What we intuitively suspected actually does translate to hard science:

> "The raising of the vibrational rate of the human being, and ultimately the raising of the vibration of planet earth, which has a scientific measure, is called 'Resonance.' This resonance has been measured by scientists at a rate of 7 Hertz since it was first noted in the early 1900s and actually measured in the 1960s. It is believed that this has been the standard rate of vibration for eons. ***Today it is now measuring 10 Hertz and moving towards 11 Hertz.*** Planet Earth and her inhabitants, humans, combined with their conscious awareness and new powerful gifts of Intention are now raising their energetic vibrational rate and moving together towards Ascension Status-—something never before seen on the planet."

The only way this makes any sense to me at all is that the 12-strand DNA activations are increasing our capacity to handle the higher frequencies. (Refer to *Book One* and *Two* of this trilogy for complete instructions.) The tired old two-strand 3rd dimension DNA is not going to cut the mustard in the higher frequencies. We don't let the baby poke pins in the light socket.

The Fundamental Principles of ALTERNATIVE SPIRITUALITY

On January 1, 2012, I mailed out a newsletter to my regular subscribers. The subject of that newsletter was an overview of the fundamental principles of Alternative Spirituality. The response was so overwhelming, I am including it as a reference guide in these shaded pages of this book.

Ultimate Truth is an elusive thing. It is never accomplished in one fell swoop. In the long run, every single one of these principles may well shatter into dust, blow away with the wind and be forgotten as though they never existed. But here we are today on this particular rung of the ladder of life. Everything may look different from the perspective of the next rung when we get there.

Reincarnation and the Soul

From New Newbies to Great Lightworkers beyond me, you simply are not going to cut it in alternative spirituality at this time without embracing the concept of reincarnation. That's for starters. It works like this. You are a soul that started out as a spark from the Creative Intelligence. You can call It God, that's allowed. Everybody then begins their own personal soul journey to someday evolve to the point where each one can reunite with God. To evolve, the soul may decide to incarnate as a human on Planet Earth.

Then there is this business of just what happens between lives. Forget Heaven and Hell. Organized religions use this ridiculous and gruesome idea for their own purposes, usually for control and to throw the fear of God into you, and as they say after that "follow the money." What really happens when you die is first to sort of float out of the physical body. Most people report from the other side that they are very nonchalant and detached about the whole procedure. Life goes on. What happens after that is different for each person, but there is no judge and jury, no matter how bad you were.

Spirit Guides and Master Teachers

The next thing you need to embrace is the idea that there are souls who are evolved beyond you, waaaay beyond you. Fortunately, they hang around to give advice. As a soul, you are granted free will on Planet Earth, and you can pretty much do any damn thing you want to. Well, okay, so you can't blow up the entire Universe; there are limits. The Guides and Teachers help you analyze your last life and plan the next one. I would caution any soul to follow their wise counsel. I am a shaman of long-standing, and one of my jobs is helping rebellious idiots undo the total mess they made of their lives after essentially telling their Teachers something considered very naughty that starts with *f* in the English language.

This business of analyzing your previous life sort of puts a different spin on just the two options of Heaven or Hell, now doesn't it? You are a good person; you are going to Heaven, end of story. Oh, *contraire*, mate. The soul and the forces of Light take this evolution business very seriously, I'm afraid. If you are indeed on the path of alternative spirituality, I am preaching to the choir. If not, this is how it goes.

These people who are awakened and enlightened tend their consciousness and monitor every action every single day. It is like a pair of glasses through which they look at *everything all the time*. It is like music always playing somewhere in the background.

Consciously evolving souls take responsibility for every single thing that happens to them. Doesn't sound too bad at first, but as you go along it develops into a very sophisticated system of constant self-therapy. Let's say you marry a guy who beats you up. What's so confusing about that? He's an s.o.b. and *you*, you are an innocent victim worthy of everybody's pity, therefore, you get to bitch about him for the rest of your life—post divorce.

On the other hand, lightworkers assume total responsibility for that s.o.b. in their lives and go looking into their *own* victim consciousness to examine how they attracted it to themselves in the first place, what the lessons are, and forgive the s.o.b. It may be interesting to stop for a moment to recall all those times when you weren't on your best behavior, times you wanted revenge, the hate you felt, how critical you were. How does that play in the viewing room after you die? As we like to say, the devil is in the details.

If you want to know more about life between lives, read Dr. Michael Newton's book *Journey of Souls* or any of Dolores Cannon's series of four books titled *The Convoluted Universe.* Another good little book is *Between Death and Life,* also by Cannon.

Additional Comments on Reincarnation

We just discussed incarnating on Earth. However, souls may have lives in other places. You don't *really* think we're alone in this vast Universe, do you? C'mon. That kind of thinking belongs in "the earth is flat" category. Furthermore, these other guys on other planets, or star systems, don't always look like we do. Did you see that *Star Wars* movie bar scene that was populated by some very strange types by our standards? Perhaps the writers of the movies are softening us up to meet them face to face one of these days. I won't guarantee it will happen, but just let us say that it might be good to start working on any problem with racism, transgender folks, and the like, right away. It is good practice for when a reptile comes to dinner.

You begin your soul journey as a lower life form and work your way through the mineral, plant, animal, and then human kingdoms (abbreviated list). You don't go backwards, meaning that once you achieve higher consciousness, you don't then incarnate as an ant or a camel, for example. I suppose you could if you were crazy enough to go backwards, but who wants to? However, there are exceptions to everything.

In past articles, I have referred to soul contracts. All this means is that when planning your next life, you forge agreements with other souls who then agree to play major roles in your next life drama. Brace yourself if you don't already know this, but you also choose your parents. Do with that what you will.

Once the outline of the life is cast, everyone shakes on it and takes the plunge. Each one of these relationships has a purpose, no matter how disastrous it may seem. However, if one of your traveling companions on the soul level falls so far behind you, evolutionarily speaking, that it retards your progress, eventually it may be time to kick them to the curb. That is allowed, even desirable.

Karma

I could easily get all wicky-wonky on this one, but I'll make it short and sweet. It is generally accepted to mean "what goes around, comes around." That expands somewhat to embrace actions you did in a past life that comes around and nips you on the behind in this life. Then there is good karma and bad karma. There is also the general view among metaphysicians that karma plays a role in mapping out one's next life because karma is cumulative. If you are not vigilant, the bad kind can build up by nasty proportions.

Ascension

Get on your snorkeling gear, because we are going to take the plunge into deeper waters. Humanity along with Mother Earth is in the process of an evolutionary leap into another, higher frequency, the 5th dimension. December 21, 2012, is a significant date in that process but by no means the sudden end in my opinion. Even though reams and reams of material are available on the subject, apparently nobody really knows what will happen on that day. My opinion? I don't know, either, but I absolutely believe that there is a Shift in progress that will continue in increments for a long time into the future. I further believe that it is our collective choices that determine what happens. No outside forces will do it for us.

The ascension date of December 21, 2012, corresponds with an astrological line-up with the center of our own galaxy, the Milky Way, which is itself marking a repeating cyclical occurrence. This time, however, humanity and Earth cycle off in tandem, reportedly the first time this has ever happened in any Universe. Those souls who have awakened to the ascension consciousness have not had an easy time of it all these years. And here's why.

Activating the Lightbody

To tolerate the higher frequencies, one must begin a process of transforming the usual *physical* body into the lightbody, which means transforming from a carbon-based body to a crystalline-based body. This involves changing our two-strand DNA vehicle into an activated 12-strand DNA vehicle. (In this book, I will write about the proof that some people have been found who have extra physical DNA activated.) The thing you most need to think about now if this is all new to you is the lightbody. People seem to have the most trouble understanding this particular piece. And the reason is that you *do not have to die in the usual way to go through the ascension process.*

Now is the time you need to change from your snorkeling gear into a full diving regalia to access deeper waters. What is this business about overcoming death itself? This is part of the story; freak out now so that we may move on. This event has been long anticipated. It coincides with the end of the Mayan calendar—merely the end of a cycle—and many other prophecies of native cultures worldwide.

To reiterate once again, the people who have successfully raised their physical frequency and activated their lightbody will shift, body and all, into another reality, another dimension of consciousness. They will never know physical death in the usual way. People will live very much longer, even for eternity if you understand that eternity is not a time; it is a dimension that you leave when and if you choose.

The good news is that in the new dimension there can be no sickness, no aging. New psychic abilities like telepathy, teleportation and much more will be the norm. The New Earth is the true paradise. Bad guys will revert to a place commensurate with their level of consciousness.

There you have the bare bones of reincarnation, karma and ascension. The most burning question is usually, "Am I going to ascend?" Just a hint to get you started: Stop judging others, forgive everyone who has hurt you and let go of fear.

Synchronicity

The technical, dictionary meaning of synchronicity is the simultaneous occurrence of events that appear significantly related, but have no discernible causal connection. The events appear unlikely to occur together by chance, but are experienced as occurring together in a meaningful manner. Philosophically and psychologically, this terminology was first used by the great psychiatrist, Carl Gustav Jung. I write about it as one of the most profound ways to connect with guidance from a higher source, call it your Higher Self, the Universe, or God; it matters little. Synchronicity represents a sign from this higher source. It can provide resolution of an unresolved issue in your life. Or it sometimes is confirmation of some question in your mind. Synchronicity demonstrates that you are connected to a powerful guiding principle in life that can and will communicate with you on a most personal level.

Alternative spirituality regards synchronicity as one of its core beliefs and encourages people to cultivate an ability to accept synchronous events as meaningful. There seems to be a dynamic at work whereby the more an individual embraces synchronous events as real and meaningful, the more synchronicity becomes a routine occurrence in everyday activities, both great and small. In fact, rather than simply waiting for examples of these meaningful coincidences to occur at random, one can ask for signs and be prepared to accept them when they come. I use this as a tool in my own life and have based important life decisions on the guidance from synchronicity's answer.

In the early 80s, I was suffering through the divorce from hell. I needed a lawyer. I needed a GOOD lawyer. I put the thought out to the Universe. It was a decision that was so critical, I asked for three signs. The first one came by way of a client who had her own version of a divorce from hell a few years earlier. She "happened" to call in for a consultation about that time and commented that she heard that I was going through a divorce. I did not ask, but she voluntarily suggested that I use the lawyer she had. I remember that she came off with the most outrageous divorce settlement in history. Sign number one.

Forget number two; it was the last sign that really put the frosting on the cake. As I parked my car in the parking lot behind my office building, I said to myself, "I want a huge, incredible, unmistakable sign." Just across the street, right at that moment, workers were putting up a new sign on the bill board advertising Alexander Cadillac auto dealership. The name of the lawyer was Tim Alexander. Did I take it seriously and hire him as my lawyer? You bet I did. Was he the best lawyer for me? He formerly prosecuted mafia criminals in Federal court, and was a good old boy from the South who believed in protecting the little lady. My ex-husband didn't have a chance. Synchronicity at work.

In the above example, I asked synchronicity for guidance. In the following story, you will see a little different version of synchronicity at work. Sometimes it just sneaks up and says boo!

In this book, some of the most powerful stories—also the funniest—concern synchronicity at work. You will read about the "Coffee Chronicles" and the "Cheetos Caper" in later chapters. They demonstrate how powerfully the Universe can broadcast a message, whereby an identical one is received by an entire group of people, all living in scattered locations from each other. It pays us all to listen and keep the faith.

CHAPTER FOUR

The Players

The more you expand into this awareness,
the more the Joy of playing enters giggles and laughter
the magic and miracles of your new world fill your days

Somewhere in all this playful exploring
you forget that the day is a dream place
for you to play.

In late 2002, I published the first *DIANA STONE'S FREE NEWSLETTER.* It was my intention to write about a variety of metaphysical subjects with an emphasis on short 500-word articles about astrology. The 500-word astrology articles somehow morphed into a six- to eight-page twice-monthly e-newsletter to become one of the voices for the dimensional Shift for thousands of readers all over the world. It drifted easily under the umbrella of The Ascension. Game. However, a game needs players.

This change of subject matter catapulted many readers into a world about which they were totally unfamiliar. However, many of these same readers wrote to tell me that they were intrigued in spite of the fact that they often did not understand what I was writing about. And I quote newsletter subscriber M.J. in Oregon, "I don't understand what the hell you are talking about most of the time, but I read it anyway—there is a little spark of enlightenment every now and then."

For those brave souls who stayed on board regardless, I created a special part of the newsletter and website for them. It is called **Project Wake-Up!** I did not want people who considered themselves babes in the woods when it came to metaphysics and alternative spirituality to feel left out. I also wanted to dispel any notions that one must be psychic, a healer or possess extensive esoteric knowledge in order to play. All you have to do is get in line. The box office is open and selling tickets.

The Ready for Prime-Time Players

So what about the target audience of advanced lightbeings who *did* understand everything that I was writing about? From this group, the overriding sentiment was how scattered about and cut off they felt from brothers and sisters sympathetic to the Path of Conscious Enlightenment. A repeated theme from correspondents was almost a desperate gratitude that my newsletters were confirming their reality, and that they were not crazy after all.

I am sure many readers will identify with the fact that even members of their own families often don't have a clue about what they're "into." I have close friends who would be shocked if they only knew what their kids were talking to me about in our private sessions. Since we can't all gather together in my living room, I was inspired one day to tie us together as a group mind.

That was the birth of the Ready for Prime-Time Players' game. A popular television show called *Saturday Night Live* introduced the actors as "not ready for prime time" (it aired at midnight), hence my idea for the name. I carefully synchronized the initial launch of the game with a propitious astrological time. Saturn began its passage through the sign Leo on July 17, 2004. That was the date on which the newsletter was published, explaining the game and inviting Players to sign on.

The Prime-Time Players' game was originally a somewhat humorous and lighthearted invitation to come play with me in my sandbox. Maybe it was a way for isolated lightbeings to feel part of a group, even if it were only in cyberspace. Of course, along with that, there was a commitment to changing one's inner life. A steady stream of magnificent letters from The Players shared stories of powerful spiritual labor pains. There was an unmistakable sense that our little group belonged to the provincial backwaters of mainstream society. We were contributing to the great forces of destiny by cleaning up our individual back yards.

At this point, I will slip in an odd little coincidence. (You know what I think about coincidences.) I was given to use the phrase, "Come play with me in my sandbox." One day my ex-husband, Rex, was visiting, and I happened to use that terminology about my sandbox in connection with this book. He just happens to be a gamer, so he said, "*Sandbox* is a gaming term. It is the kind of video game in which you do not have to follow a prescribed path but rather have the freedom to go anywhere in the game landscape." I just thought how interesting it is, and has been all along, that I seem to intuitively tune into the game consciousness.

There Is Also A Serious Side To Games!

Regular subscribers to *Diana Stone's Newsletter* appreciate that my signature humor helps the truth go down. Humor is what drives the Universe. God laughs. An on-going stream of communications bore unmistakable testimony to The Players' acute awareness of the serious side of spiritual business also—the labor pains of deep inner work on themselves.

The passage of time brought another group experience into being, one step beyond The Ready for Prime-Time Players' game. It is important to emphasize again that the focus for the Prime-Time Players was a commitment to tend to one's *inner* consciousness.

A Community of Light

The idea of a Community of Light was born. I was not about to organize a convention of lightworkers in a central location at some real hotel conference center. The only possible way to form a group was in cyber space. Again, I chose a propitious starting date. The summer solstice in 2009 launched The Inter-Galactic Federation of Electrical Workers, local union, #2012.

The Inter-Galactic Federation of Electrical Workers (IFEW) enjoyed the annual picnic. Again, the playfulness never diminished the universal theme of Oneness and Unity, which we all were striving for by loving and accepting our chapter mates unconditionally. The advantages are that there are no union dues and no meetings at the union hall on Friday night. That, of course, is in addition to the obvious rewards of our spiritual and energetic bond with our union mates. There is a standing open invitation for anyone to join.

Unity and Oneness

The idea is to connect to our group brothers and sisters in an attitude of unconditional love and acceptance, no matter what. Once we master that, and really feel it, we can move out into our world and make the same commitment to everyone. We clear the heart chakra of judgment, hate, anger and any other negativity toward anybody. Yes, there are bad guys. Some of the brothers and sisters suffer from imprisonment by the Dark. We may really hate what they act out. The difference is that we do not hate *them*.

There is an important difference in orientation of the two groups. The inner work was one thing. It ain't easy! However, neither is the work of the IFEW. This involves the *outer* life relationships to everything. It does not allow critical judgments about anything. Try that for a day. Try that for an hour.

Games Need Rules and Goals

As each one of the games was initiated, it was fleshed out with rules, lessons, mission statements and the like. And yes, the playfulness of every game was tied to these serious goals. Over and above that, something extraordinary was happening. Apparently, we were attracting players of the non-human kind as you will see.

Project Wake-Up! ala Metaphysics 101

Project Wake-Up! is basically Metaphysics 101. It is primarily information dedicated to explaining some of the most fundamental principles that experienced lightworkers collectively believe and live by. One of the first lessons for Metaphysics 101 was synchronicity. Of course, that is already included in the shaded pages in another part of the book. Therefore, no need to repeat it here. Following is the mission statement.

Mission Statement

Project Wake-Up! is a gentle guide for individuals who desire assistance in expanding conscious living and exploring alternative spirituality.
You do not have to pay dues.
You do not have to sign anything.
You may continue to attend the Methodist church.
No salesmen will call.
Your name won't be shared with any other mailing lists.
You do not have to tell your mother.

This story about the Buddha captured my attention. It seemed appropriate for beginners, so I included it in the mission statement:

> One of his students asked Buddha, "Are you the messiah?"
> "No," answered Buddha.
> "Then are you a healer?"
> "No," Buddha replied.
> "Then are you a teacher?" the student persisted.
> "No, I am not a teacher."
> "Then what are you?" asked the student, exasperated.
> "I am awake," Buddha replied.

Watching for Signs

Whereas synchronicity was the first lesson for 101-ers and since that has been covered, the second lesson was about signs and symbolic messages. Signs and symbols stand alone as one of the great guiding principles that all lightworkers would do well to cultivate. As promised, once a group formed to play a game there was no telling what or whom was magically attracted to get in on the action. All it will take to prove it is one little mouse tail, oops, I mean, "tale." Do read on!

A picture is said to be worth a thousand words. In my case, a story was worth a thousand words! Just remember to pay attention to the little things that are somehow askew just ever so slightly. From small things big things may come.

I am especially fond of this story because the Universe sent me a sign about an outcome that would number in *years* ahead, something that I would have no way of knowing about at the time. It was right. In fact, six long years have passed and I am just now, at the time of this writing, seeing the outcome of the sign that was sent from the Universe back then! You will have the rare privilege of a front row seat to see the story unfolded from beginning to end.

The following is a quote from an article that I ran in one of my e-newsletters way back at the end of 2005. Here it is:

> "I watch my life for any anomalous event because these aberrations—however big or small—as often as not carry some meaning and a message that is important. The last one was really gross. If you can figure out what it means, you will win a free consultation of your choice. Here is the story:
>
> 'I keep a tall, colored plastic cup on my desk to remind me to drink more water. Last week I found a DEAD MOUSE drowned in it. If that wasn't enough to gross anyone out for life, two days later I found a *second* dead mouse in my water cup (a different one, needless to say). Well, to be absolutely truthful, my husband actually spotted both mice before I did, sparing me the, "eek, eek, a dead mouse" trauma. The Universe was trying very hard to send me a message. I finally figured it out. Anyone want to take a guess?' "
>
> Later that month, I ran this message in the newsletter:
>
> "Roxanne Hallquist, a Portland, Oregon, astrologer, won the mouse contest. She nailed it. She wins a free consultation."

Not only was Roxanne a fellow professional astrologer, she was from the sister city across the river and a friend. When I called to schedule an appointment for her free consultation, she said, "Do you mean that you really are going to do it!" She was more excited than a layperson would have been. We professional astrologers very seldom treat ourselves to a consultation with another professional.

The Mystery Is Solved

So what did it mean to find a dead mouse in my water cup—not once, but twice? *I was writing a book when 2006 rolled around. And guess what? It was **this** book you hold in your hands right now.* Two thousand six was a year of constant disruption and distraction. I was terribly frustrated. I kept saying, "I am dead in the water."

The mouse, of course, referred to the computer mouse. If I had found one dead mouse, I would have expected that the mouse on my computer would lay idle for a long time, meaning the book project would be long delayed. But when I found *two* dead mousies, I knew it would not be a long time; it would be a ***very*** long time before the book was published. At this writing it is July 7, 2012, and despite seeing light at the end of the tunnel, the book is still not finished.

On the unlikely off chance that I might not notice dead mice in my water glass, our house was plagued by an invasion of mice as well. Or perhaps the Universe was just showing off. Anyway, we had to call an exterminator. Again, this was an exercise designed to call attention to the idea that life communicates to us if we just pay attention to any extraordinary signs that insinuate themselves into our everyday routines.

The question that remains in my mind is whether the Universe also meant that I *should* wait, or just that I would *have* to wait. Perhaps it was just cautioning me to be patient. This has caused me to stop and think about what has transpired in the interim.

There are parts of this book that obviously could not have been included had it not been for the countless delays. Many of those are parts of the book that lend it much greater power and would have been definitely much the lesser without them. The chapter "DNA From A to Z" is certainly a huge case in point. From time to time, something would come along that made the delays worth it, and I would say, "Well, that about wraps it up now." I soon learned never to say *never*!

It is entirely clear to me that if I had written this book any sooner, it would have been a catastrophe. I would have had to commit suicide. Well, maybe not suicide. Maybe I would just stick a pin in my eye—or finger.

The Last Word

Keep your eye out for the smallest things that may be a sign from the Universe. If you miss the small things, maybe a mouse will have to commit suicide to bring you a message. Come to think of it, I did find an ant in the bottom of my water cup. Come to think of it, I found a dead ant in the bottom of the water cup—twice! Do you suppose that meant something? .

I raced for one of my favorite books Ted Andrews's *Animal-Speak.* Below is a partial quote that was startlingly meaningful to me. It really does pay to remember over and over again that the Universe communicates with us individually, even utilizing the smallest of life's creatures to carry its message.

> "There are many types of ants, some of which are solitary...When by themselves, they display simple and uncomplicated behavior patterns...Predominately, there are three castes. (The first being) the queens who found new colonies...The queen ant has wings and the ability of flight until fertilized. Once she is fertilized, she pulls off her own wings, sacrificing her own flight for the newborn. The queen usually dies after twelve years. The cycle of twelve...will be significant...Ant teaches us that regardless of

> circumstances, if the effort is true, the rewards will follow—in the most beneficial time and manner...."

The confirmations from our animal totems can play a significant role in our lives. Staying alert to the animal world around us, and reading about individual ones in a book is not just a parlor game. I am always impressed how consulting information about my totem animal reveals fresh insights for a certain time period, and more than that provides the most soul-satisfying stamp of approval on current endeavors.

When the book talked about the queen ant pulling off her own wings, I was reminded how often I say, "My wings have been clipped," referring to the confines of a wheelchair. The queen performed that act for the sake of the baby ants. Well, my baby does not have multiple legs. It does not have legs at all; it has pages. My baby is a book. The last sentence and its referral to the phrase, "in the most beneficial time and manner" filled my heart. If I have not conquered the frantic feelings about finishing this book *on time*, that surely calmed my impatience.

The part about the queen's life span of 12 years did not scare me as a prediction of my own longevity. As an astrologer, I recognize 12 years as a Jupiter cycle. Jupiter in astrology-speak refers to the world of publishing. Right now, Jupiter has changed signs recently. It is passing through the sign of writers, Gemini. And Gemini is the career part of my own horoscope. I've been yelling, "Yippee!" ever since I read this. Maybe Oprah *will* call.

A last confirmation is one that I would have just as soon opted out of. You will recall that in conjunction with the mouse in the water glass, we also had an invasion of mice in the house. Once again, after noticing the dead ants at the bottom of my water cup, we were forced to call an exterminator once again, after living ant-free for many years. So, okay, I got the message already! These anomalies are different from what is discussed elsewhere in the book that involve the biggies like on-going marriage problems, for example. You need to become hard-wired to notice any aberrations popping up amidst the ordinary flow of your everyday life. This game attracts players of the non-human kind!

Ready For Prime-Time Players Revisited

So what is the mission statement for the Prime-Time Players? What are the rules? How do we play to win? What do we do next? The experience that answered those questions just has to be the wildest and craziest adventure yet, which by the way, blindsided all participants until well into the escapade itself. It proves that we game players in the 3rd dimension are a lesser reflection of a Higher Intelligence whose abilities for game playing has us totally out-classed.

Once a group was assembled that had game-playing on its mind, this apparently somehow opened the door for some Cosmic Hi-Jinks suitable only for group games. Read the following story, and you will see what I mean. My feeble imagination was trumped by whoever or whatever engineered this Granddaddy of all Ascension Games!

The Mission Statement

Let's start at the beginning. The Mission Statement for the Prime-Time Players was simple enough. There are few rules. That was the idea. Everyone willing to be a Prime-Time Player just needed to email his or her intention. There was just one thing everyone agreed to do everyday (when they remembered). This would serve as the connecting link.

1. Recite the community mantra every day (see below)
2. Play to win every day

A Community Mantra

I wanted everyone to recite exactly the same mantra every day, preferably on first awakening while still in the "twilight zone" and connected to the subconscious. That turned out to be a cosmic joke. Here's why. For the life of me, I could not come up with an appropriate mantra. I wrestled with a mental block the size of a boxcar. The joke was on me because as it turned out the obvious mantra was in *my very own book* that I myself cowrote *The Lightbody Activation Manual*!

One of the nine steps of the 5th dimension lightbody activation directs the receiver to repeat:

> **"I am the conscious master of every cell in my body. I fill each cell of my body with peace, joy and harmony."**

It is repeated three times. Each person may add anything else to the mantra that they wish. Each person also is free to use any other spiritual practice that they choose. As for me, I always add to that the following, "Each cell of my body is programmed for normal healthful functioning." The point is to deprogram every cell of old messages and reprogram them to align with the conscious self as master.

"Winning isn't everything; it is the only thing!"

Vince Lombardi

What does it mean to play to win every day? Never lose sight of what the Game is all about. It is about the victory of the Light over the Dark so that humanity and Earth may shift into a dimension of peace and enlightened consciousness. Every person counts. We must be the change we want to create. We must set the difficult course of clearing our hearts of all negativity. Hate, fear, anger, greed and other destructive attitudes are rife in the collective consciousness. It requires constant vigilance to create an opposing force.

Be alert to everything that enters your field of experience. If you encounter negativity in any form, the task is to track the energy to the inner source that has attracted it to you. It is too easy to blame. No one is required to like bad people or approve of the things they do. Stay aware that at the soul level, they have volunteered to hold the polarity of the Dark this time. They serve us by exposing our own dark corners, illuminating our psyches and moving us closer to the winner's column of the Ultimate Game, The Ascension Game.

Controlling the Vibrations of Food

The Ready for Prime-Time Players were given an additional assignment. They were asked to place their open hands with palms down about six to eight inches above any food before they ate and repeat several times, "I raise this food to my vibration. Every cell in my body uses this food for normal healthful functioning." The people who can feel the energies will sense a definite shift. If not, just go ahead and hold your hands over the food for a minute or so. Be discreet in restaurants. Other patrons may mistake you for a Christian praying. (Okay, lighten up. Joking, joking.)

Why did I choose this particular exercise for our group assignment? The answer also comes from the *Lightbody* book. One of the nine steps of the 5th dimension activation directs the cells to accustom themselves to prana, the life force energy. This is a life sustaining energy. The idea is that one eventually may sustain life at an optimum level on prana alone. By elevating the frequencies of food to match individual vibrations is a first step in the right direction. This practice also clears away any negative elements in the food you eat. Each lightworker was free to work this out and report in. I admit I did offer one piece of advice. In changing food to your own vibration, I suggested that one not start with rat poison.

What Game Is This?

As the games were introduced and more and more players joined in, we were engaging powerful forces about which we were completely unaware at the time.. Jane McGonigal's theories about gaming turned reality on its head. The title of her book is *Reality is Broken: Why Games Make Us Better and How They Can Change the World.* She went on to make some very bold claims, e.g., "Gaming can solve all of the world's problems," or "Gaming: The best hope for surviving the next century on this planet," or "Only in a game is the impossible possible." Were we all Players slipping through one of Reality's broken cracks?

.**Communication From God**

This may seem like an unusual subject to introduce the answer to that question. Bear with me. I didn't know where this was going either. What would you do if you were God, and you had to communicate to sleeping humanity in the 3rd dimension that the Shift of the Ages was imminent? There would also be the added responsibility to lay out some rules of engagement while you were at it. I can't speak to all of the tricks that God has up His-Her sleeve in every situation, but They put on a damned good performance for our little group.

When the God Game began, He escalated our consciousness that there was also a Her, the Goddess, through the archetypal energies of Venus in 2004. She was the star of the cosmic show by some very rare eclipses and other astrological events. Anyway, here goes the very long answer, so don't forget the original question. I underlined it just in case.

THE CHEETOS CAPER

You will recall that an assignment for the Prime-Time Players group was to change the vibration of their food. One day I received a most astounding letter from reader Jim who wrote to tell me that he had eaten nothing but Cheetos and macaroni for many years, and he is always in perfect health. I refer to the little crunchy snack, Cheetos, made by Frito-Lay, yes, those Cheetos. Jim says a mantra along with this regimen.

I published a newsletter as I was writing this book that referred to the Cheetos Caper. Many longtime readers are familiar with the story. In response, I received this update from Cheetos Jim on February 11, 2010. It appears that he is still going strong!

> "I laughed again at your comment about me and Cheetos. I am still doing fine on Cheetos. I am caregiving 60 hours a week."

It seemed inappropriate to remind Jim that most everyone considers Cheetos junk food. In light of the Players' commitment to raise all foods to their vibration, it seemed uncomfortably contradictory. It was easier just to pass by this message. I probably would never have given it another thought except for one thing that happened.

When the tsunamis hit Asia in December, 2005, my husband and I donned shamanic gear to assist just before it hit. Mother Earth was making one of her programmed ascension steps that day. We tuned in and experienced our own personal tsunamis. I doubled over with violent dry heaves—God! I hate that—every 15-30 minutes for a solid 24 hours. Throughout my miserable nightmare, I cared very little for Big Mama and her ascension plans.

Not Exactly Mom's Chicken Soup

After three wretched days of recovery, I weakly asked for something to eat. Be aware that Don is a retired chiropractor whose primary specialty was nutritional therapies in his private practice. He went to the store and brought back my recovery food, a large economy-size bag of Cheetos. When I expressed total incredulity in my loudest voice, his maddening nonchalance was absolutely unshakable. He seemed completely possessed by something that could not begin to grasp the utter lunacy of this Cheetos thing. Whatever happened to chicken soup?

Then I remembered reader Jim, the Cheetos and macaroni guy. I chowed down on Cheetos and macaroni. I was disgusted at how eagerly my wounded stomach welcomed the entire bag.

In the next newsletter, I told the story of reader Jim and Cheetos. What happened next was one of the most amazing scenarios to date. An avalanche—and I mean an avalanche—of emails came pouring in from every direction. Lightbeings had been eating Cheetos for months. There were stories of strange cravings. They were eating them by the bagful. They were eating them regularly. They did not think they should eat them. They ate them anyway.

Subscribers to my newsletter are not likely candidates for this sort of thing. As a group, most of them are very nutrition conscious. It was grossly out of character. Even they could not explain these impulses as this thing burgeoned by geometric progression month after month. However, this was just the beginning.

I wrote newsletters from my orange-stained computer keys. (Cheetos stain one's fingers orange.) Some days I just didn't get it all sucked off. I craved Cheetos. I loved Cheetos. I ate Cheetos every day and so did countless other lightbeings. People who did not consider themselves lightbeings were eating Cheetos. Some reportedly had eaten Cheetos for 30 years. Some people ate them from their lunchbox every day during their school years. Some had discovered them only recently as the little bags suddenly sent out a siren song at the check-out stand in the grocery store.

Eventually one asks, "Why are we eating Cheetos?" The whole gist of this caper was that there was this phenomenal simultaneous eruption in Cheetos consumption. Who was sending the message? Does it have something to do with jungle drums? By what avenue of communication were so many people receiving the same bizarre message? And why? I was as nonplussed at the phenomenon as anyone else was. I watched wide-eyed as letters from Cheetos-eaters everywhere regularly clogged my email.

Sex, Lies and Rock and Roll!

Remember what I have told you about belief systems? It is not the lack of knowledge that will most likely stop you on the path to enlightenment; it is a rigid, inflexible belief system that is perhaps the biggest block of all! Two of our readers playing the Unreasonable Fanatics Game have kindly offered to demonstrate how it works.

Letter #1

> "Diana I'm hoping that the views reflected in your last newsletter were just a lapse in judgment and not what you truly believe. Along with your *advice* comes a great responsibility. How can you possibly–and in good conscience–tell people to go and pig out? Isn't gluttony one of the seven deadly sins? Isn't gluttony part of what's got the people in this country entrenched deeper and deeper into sh*t (literally!).
>
> Greed and gluttony–do not make these ok for lightworkers Diana. You owe your readers an explanation."

Diana's comment: Usually I humor these people in the belief that they have a right to their point of view, even when it is this distorted. You can't change the minds of people like this. This time I gave her the courtesy of explaining the profound flaws in her grossly skewed conclusions. Not surprisingly, she did not throw herself prostrate at my feet and beg forgiveness for misunderstanding just about everything. (It gets worse!) Here is her next response:

Second Letter From Author of Letter #1

> "Diane [sic]–thank you for your response. However........I think there are some things you may be choosing to forget, like the companies that make the products you speak about eating. All are, without exception, corporate nightmares–not only do they test on animals but they also degrade and destroy our environment minute by minute. You are only addressing, in your limited view, the affects [sic] of the foods on the cells of our beings. (How wrong can one person be?) Are you not interested in addressing animal rights, environmental rights, social and international affects [sic], etc. etc. I would have thought that part of your claim to fame as a shaman would surely include the above."

Letter #2

> "Dear Ms Stone–you CANNOT possibly be serious!! Your latest newsletter is a disappointment because of its total untruth. It is ludicrous to even suggest that because of ascension symptoms, lightworkers can / should put junk into

their bodies. Shame on you for eating animal. You should know better.... and if you have cravings for things such as steak then may I suggest you learn to control yourself. Please be more responsible. There are plenty of people out there who just don't have enough discernment to know you're talking rubbish."

Diana's Answer

Hey, what a blast when these two letters arrived. It has been so many years since I played the Unreasonable Fanatics Game that I got such a rush you would not believe it. These kids are my neighbors down the street and are members of another ethnic background from me. In order to raise her daughter free of unreasonable prejudices, Mom made me play with them.

The first time I played the Unreasonable Fanatics Game was when I first started practicing astrology back in the Sixties. The Jehovah's Witnesses periodically came around and begged me to quit doing the work of the Devil. Since Mom made me play with the Fanatics, I already knew the rules of the Game, so every now and then I would go a round or two before getting back to reality.

I suggested they read selected Bible verses to see if that might loosen the Devil's grip on my soul. What they didn't know was that I grew up in a fairly fundamentalist church. (Mom wanted to be sure.) I was required to memorize a great portion of the Good Book. So it was I who selected the verses. (Are you aware of how much sex there is in the Bible?)

Lets see now, I think it is okay to include the autopsy at this point in order to do a reality check.. They are talking about Diana Stone who:

1. Has suffered a lapse in judgment
2. Doesn't truly believe what she writes in her own newsletter
3. Tells people to pig out
4. Supports gluttony. (We all know how bad that is. Thanks for the reminder.)
5. Apparently indirectly responsible for the entire USA mired in deep s**t.
6. Does not realize that greed and gluttony are not okay for lightworkers
7. Can't be serious
8. Writes newsletters that are TOTAL untruths
9. Recommends that people eat junk food
10. Should really know better
11. Blames Ascension symptoms as the reason lightworkers should put junk food in their bodies
12. Eats meat, which means "craves" meat
13. Eats meat, which obviously means she is out of control
14. Should get control of herself
15. Needs to be responsible

16. Is not aware of corporate abuses
17. Needs to be more aware that there are people out there who lack discernment. (I just have to tell you, this one is my favorite.)

Not Everybody Loves Me

I labeled these two as Players in the Unreasonable Fanatics Game. A constant theme of the newsletters emphasized the critical importance of one's belief system, one of the thorniest challenges on the road to ascension. That is exactly why I included these negative responses from two readers. It is a Technicolor demonstration of just how it works.

What you want to notice here is that everything they say is false or extremely skewed to their personal prejudices. People fanatically locked into these rigid systems are blinded to the actual reality around them. You can easily recognize that these two individuals are not living in the real world. Needless to say, I never told anyone to eat Cheetos. And it was ludicrous to suggest that I encouraged anyone to "pig out." Things really escalated until I was responsible for most of the ills of the civilized world! People who so grossly distort reality are mentally ill.

I find it incredibly ironic that I received this mission statement from Cheetos or Frito-lay, sent in by another reader. I laughed so hard I'm seriously concerned rupture-wise.

Letter submitted by Karen Alexander, One Of My Newsletter Readers:

> "GOD BLESS AMERICA Why is everyone so upset about Cheetos? They have a woman CEO and just look at their mission statement:"

Frito Lay's (they make Cheetos) Mission statement:

> "Understanding different cultures is a major advantage. In fact, we view diversity and inclusion as a key to our future. In our business, we advocate the development and the growth of minority and women suppliers. Our goal is to provide procurement, development and educational opportunities that will enable minority and women-owned businesses to excel as Frito-Lay suppliers and in America's free enterprise system. An integral part of our mission is a commitment to purchase from a supplier base representative of our employees, consumers, retail customers and communities. Therefore, we seek opportunities to give qualified minority and women suppliers a chance to succeed. It benefits PepsiCo, our business objectives and our communities. "

So What Did The Cheetos Message Mean?

What did we learn?

1. When a group of people INTENDS something, a higher source of Intelligence is triggered to provide information and guidance.
2. That Intelligence knows how to manipulate synchronicity to gain our attention right where we are.
3. We do not need any particular knowledge or psychic powers for the Intelligence to find a way to communicate with us.
4. There is often a trickster or outrageous quality about it. It is out of the ordinary.
5. Once we identify the message (eat Cheetos), many confirmations will follow: other people confirm it; we read it in a book, etc.
6. It has the effect of pushing us past the boundaries of our prevailing belief systems.

Watch for this in your personal life. If this succeeded in propelling a group of people to eating Cheetos, despite the fact that it violated their food sensibilities, then that same Intelligence is surely capable of communicating with us in other ways, if we just pay attention.

I do not feel so guilty about eating Cheetos now that we know the real energy behind them! Eating Cheetos is not the litmus test for an awakened consciousness. Some people reported eating other "bad" foods. Yes, God enjoys a sense of humor—just be thankful it wasn't liver.

If the Unreasonable Fanatics Players could have moved beyond their angry diatribe that served to block all awareness of reality and the truth, they would have discovered that Cheetos's manufacturers represented the antithesis of everything they hated. Frito Lay actually represents a change to enlightened consciousness in the corporate world.

A reminder that in more subtle ways many of us may have blind spots. Consciousness must be tended. The awakened travelers on the Path of Conscious Ascension must be alert and open-minded to the symbols and signs around them. That leads me to the rest of this story.

Love Thine Enemies

What it is that I needed to be aware of in this scenario? One of the most critically important rules in The Ascension Game calls for the recognition that EVERYTHING entering one's reality is attracted and magnetized by something *within one's own inner world*, however tenuous the connection. I asked myself this question: What were these two people mirroring to me?

I went digging around in my psyche and identified a subconscious pattern, the ramifications of which sent me reeling. Conscious recognition of this pattern was life-changing. (You don't need to know *everything* about my psyche.) Following that, the most interesting thing happened. My feelings unexpectedly shifted and I suddenly felt love for these two people. I didn't care if they changed their opinions or not. I'm being dead serious here. I wanted to invite them over for dinner. (I could serve Cheetos and steak.)

Understanding the Serious Side of the Games

Close analysis of the Cheetos Caper reveals a secret. Despite the wild and hilarious adventure, the entire episode could not be more profound. However playful it all may seem, a Game is still deadly serious. If you can understand the meaning of this story, you have discovered that benevolent gods know how to gain our attention and demonstrate the rules of the Game. Only one of Divine Intelligence could somehow impel a group of humans to eat Cheetos to demonstrate the point. Nevertheless, rigid fanatical beliefs skew and block true reality even from the Highest Intelligence itself.

One Last Souvenir

This last story has to be my favorite. My brother, Duane, visited me and we headed out for the Warm Springs Indian Reservation in the high desert country of Central Oregon for a little R&R. The main lodge was deserted as we settled into the easy chairs around the great fireplace.

One of the empty easy chairs was in my line of sight across the room. What I saw was absolutely mind bending. I could barely stammer or stutter. The two guys looked totally perplexed as I waved my arms wildly in the general direction of the chair. I swear to God, placed right in the center of the chair, was—***one single Cheetos.***

The packages in which Cheetos come have a picture of their trademark, a Cheetah, printed in color on the side of the bag. I said, “That looks like an animal dropping. Maybe the Cheetos Cheetah pooped in that chair.” Duane replied, "The Cheetos's Cheetah doesn’t poop. He takes a Sheet(o)." Hey, you can’t be spiritual all the time.

Hello God!

For most people the concept of God is probably fairly abstract, no matter how passionate the belief may be. The possibility that one may actually interact with God up close and personal is the profound message of the Cheetos Caper. When I spotted the one single Cheetos in that chair, there was an ever-so-brief glimpse of the Hand of God, carefully placing it with the playfulness and joy of a kid in Disneyland.

You need not read a thousand books nor attend endless classes and lectures to learn the rules of The Ascension Game. Light the lamp of intent. The Creative Intelligence will meet you at the intersection of your consciousness and your intention.

.

My e-newsletter became a focus through which the ambassadors of the Light could utilize a common snack to reveal the new rules. Maybe we could live on ***anything*** by changing its vibration. Ponder that for a minute.

The Answer to the Question

Circling back to the beginning of this discussion, remember the underlined question? Now we know that God is perfectly capable of sending us a message, by whatever means, and getting our attention. That is you. That is I. If it worked with Cheetos, it will work for ascension, don't you think?

You will not find the rules of The Ascension Game tacked to the front of the church door. One size does not fit all. Light your lamp of intent, and watch for your personal version of the Cheetos adventure. Your belief system must remain flexible to avoid the fanaticism that skews reality. The signs will be there. Be alert. Synchronicity will drop bread crumbs along the way to confirm and reconfirm any legitimate guidance.

It's Subtle, but…

There was a clue that occurred while the Cheetos business was in full swing. However, the implications are a big stretch. At that same time, Saddam Hussein was in custody awaiting trial. He is certainly universally regarded as a bad guy. One of his guards, in an interview on national television, curiously happened to mention that Hussein is addicted to Cheetos. If he does not get them every day, he is very cranky.

See the wink and the nudge? Hussein is apparently aware, at least on the soul level, that he agreed to hold the polarity of the Dark Side this time. It makes it easier for us not to hate when we know that his reprehensible behavior is just his role in this dimension.

And One More Game!

As I read through the past issues of my newsletters, I encountered the write-up of the starting date of yet another game. It is called the Mission: Impossible Game and was initiated in the fall of 2006. That predated my synchronistic discovery of Jane McGonigal's book *Reality is Broken* in 2012. I will quote what I wrote about the Mission: Impossible Game back in 2006:

> "**This is where we break the rules**. Here is where we are going to intend things that most people—especially the medical profession—say are impossible...Everything can be healed."

I'm sure you see how closely this mirrors Ms. McGonigal's revolutionary theories about game playing! The idea of the Mission: Impossible game has been expanded considerably to include *all aspects of life,* not just matters of health and healing. This proves to me once more that I am impinged from some higher source with cutting edge ideas well before they become common knowledge in the collective consciousness. This game is my favorite.

The Ascension Game

As time passed, I was stunned to realize that our innocent games were exact 3rd dimension reflections of the most evolved group minds from the highest dimensions assisting the ascension process. Furthermore, our role was critical to the success or failure of the mission to shift into higher realities, not only in 2012, but throughout a process beginning much earlier and extending far beyond! In fact, it was increasingly obvious that every one in any of the groups was there as the result of soul contracts.

Every word, every thought, every deed, every emotion and every interaction with anyone else by every single person on the planet directly affects the collective consciousness. ***There is only One Game. And everyone is a Player.***

CHAPTER FIVE

The Coffee Chronicles

I love coffee
I love tea
I love the java jive and it loves me.
Coffee and tea
And the jiving and me
A cup, a cup a cup, a cup, a cup…

"The Java Jive"
A song popular in the 1940s
Lyrics by Milton Drake
Music by Ben Oakland

Wake Up And Smell The Coffee

We rocked and rolled up to my February birthday, 2005. The Middle East remained the perennial hotspot on the planet. Environmental concerns pierced the mass consciousness a bit deeper. However, for newsletter subscribers, their morning coffee would never seem the same ever again! Was *something* up there communicating with us? And I mean waaaay up there!

Brace yourself: The coffee chronicles's journal entry concerns a legendary consciousness shift. It is a story about how God in Trickster clothing somehow manipulated a group of widely-scattered individuals into reaching for their morning "cuppa Joe"—in concert. Here we go again.

To appreciate fully the magnitude of that spiritual revelation of the Lord's mysterious ways, we must start at the beginning. As far as this book is concerned, the following account is titled *The Spiritual Traveler's Guidebook to the 5th Dimension.* (Copies available at the visitor's center.)

There is a good reason why this subject enjoys its position as a chapter unto itself. It is one thing to talk about tapping the inner guidance system that the great spiritual teachers claim is within us all. A quick look around generally reveals that not many of us have stopped by the visitor's center to pick up our copy of the handbook.

After all of our inner demons are slain; after all negative energies are cleared; after the chakras are all lined up in a row; there comes a time when we must dial into our channel on the airways to receive personal marching orders that guide every step of our way on the road to a new reality. "The Coffee Chronicles" unmistakably demonstrates just how that can happen. You will miss the point entirely, unless you understand that I hadn't the slightest notion that anything unusual was afoot on that birthday morning. Likewise, I was an innocent dupe until well after this scenario had played itself out.

"The Coffee Chronicles" Begin!

Two thousand and five rolled in, reminding me that my birthday was looming on February 4th—a time of reflection for me. I arose much earlier than usual that morning. I just wanted to loungbe around in my robe for a while. Two friends were dropping by around 1:00 p.m. that afternoon, so I had plenty of time to get dressed. We went to the family room, and I asked Don to make coffee. That was decidedly out of character. We never make coffee at home unless we have company for dinner. *The coffee chronicles had begun.*

I felt I had just made it past that first cup of coffee when all of a sudden it was noon. I was shocked and disoriented. That much time could not possibly have flown by. I hate those time warps. I was traveling far afield from my family room. Spirit teacher, Thomas, was leading the charge. Unbeknownst to me, I was into the fourth hour of channeling the most astonishing information. I panicked when I suddenly came to my senses and realized that company was due in less than an hour. Thomas wasn't finished. "I'll take care of them." I wanted to believe him.

Thomas was giving detailed instructions to Don about a complicated new healing modality. At this point, let me digress for a moment to fill in the back story that linked unexpectedly to the events unfolding there on my birthday. I am referring to a ceremony Duane did for me the previous November 2.

My group's (the 4Ds) home base is the star system Arcturus. Duane took me "home" to the Council on Arcturus and there a protracted healing ceremony, involving complex changes in my etheric body, was performed. I had made some unusual alterations in my invisible and physical bodies for this incarnation. This was in anticipation of the DNA changes I would be required to make later in life. I just took for granted that the work Duane did was all that was required at that point.

Fast forward again to February 2005. Apparently, it was not the end of the process after all. Thomas was apparently instructing Don as to the next step. He was directed to go into the etheric body and wire it to all the cells in my physical body. I guess he figured that only a detail-minded Virgo was up for this tedious exercise. As Don proceeded, I was thrown into violent shaking over my entire body. I thought I would shake my eye teeth out. Don was incredulous at my reactions. Here he was facilitating a healing technique he had never done before, and I was responding by all but tap dancing on the ceiling.

Trying Some New Healing Tricks

When things calmed down, Thomas suggested that Don use a new procedure he had also just been shown and apply it to a healing client with whom we were really struggling. We realized that this particular woman had flown in under the radar and was borderline schizophrenic, a condition we do not deal with in our healing work. We were just about ready to launch her.

We thought this was a strange choice of a client for Don's maiden voyage into the new system. She "just happened" to call us on the phone precisely at the moment Don had completed the work on her. It was a short conversation, almost businesslike. She thanked us for the fine work we had done for her in the past and reassured us that she could take care of the schizophrenia very well the rest of the way on her own! We never heard from her again, so we assume that she did what she said.

Thomas was true to his word. Our guests, Judy and Maureen, arrived two hours "late" and full of tales of unbelievable delays at every turn. These two friends were seasoned veterans of the strange and unusual, so they enjoyed a big laugh when they learned that their so-called delays were courtesy of Thomas.

The amenities were quickly by-passed in favor of settling down to work. They only too eagerly volunteered as guinea pigs for the hot new game in town. Don, under Thomas's close supervision, explored some deep issues with both ladies. There were tears and ah-ha's all around. It was clear that the new healing methods were laser-like in cutting quickly to the core of the deepest wounds.

By the time this particular episode drew to a close, I had racked up a total of more than eight hours of traveling with Thomas, zooming past previous boundaries and translating the information he gave me. Reentry was ugly. The next day was worse than any hangover from a night on the town. It took three days on the recliner before I could lay claim to anything resembling normal functioning.

Traveling on a Full Tank–Coffee!

Don and I seize upon St. Patrick's Day as an excuse to pig out on a big corned beef and cabbage dinner. This year 2005 was no exception. We feasted and watched a movie. At 10:30, I was tired, but once again, coffee sounded unusually appealing. Once again, I should have seen it coming. Once again, Thomas and I went off adventuring and this time our journey lasted until 2:30 a.m.

It was an incredible trip. With eyes squeezed tightly shut, I felt I was hurtling very fast through space to Somewhere Land. I could feel Thomas leading me past what I can only describe as walls or barriers. He repeated again that I was entering uncharted territory and breeching boundaries. However, the same old story of reentry requiring three days of recovery was getting old. (What was in that coffee?) While writing this, I think I smell the unmistakable aroma of cooked cabbage!

A Little Light Amid the Darkness

Before proceeding with more tales of woe, I will interject at this juncture a story that should flesh out a more balanced picture and broader overview of life in the strange lane. Lets go back to Harmonic Concordance on November 8, 2003. It so happens that Duane's birthday is November 9th. David offered to take Duane to breakfast the next morning to celebrate the occasion. I was lost in oblivion, of course, and at that point I did not care if Duane ever lived to celebrate another birthday.

Duane extolled the virtues of the breakfast he enjoyed that morning. He and David reported that the place served prime rib dinners each Friday and Saturday nights. They urged us to check it out. "The place" turned out to be a sports bar and grill about ten minutes from our house. We hadn't noticed it, despite passing it many times in going about our usual activities, and even if we had, Don and I rarely frequented bars. God, how things can change!

The Half-Time Bar and Grill is a very long, low rectangular building painted gray and is on a main suburban street, fit unobtrusively among private homes, some small businesses and our bank. It says on the front, "Open 24 hours." There are several pool tables at each end and a very long, impressive bar. We dropped in one Friday night, enjoyed a reasonably-priced prime rib dinner and a bottle of wine. There was a congenial atmosphere, and the place appeared to be a neighborhood hang out.

Now let me back up and share an inside joke we have in the group and the strange way it fits into the story. One of the long-running fantasies that we joke about is that when we are finished here on earth we will go home to a bar in our own star system, Alpha-7. If you saw the *Star Wars* movies, it resembles the bar shown there, populated by an assortment of alien creatures. (This is where the idea for the Preamble was hatched.)

As the story goes, we will swagger into Alpha 7 dressed in our uniforms, medals and other marks of greatness and announce, "We did EARTH!" Everyone will be struck dumb as we recount our great mission to Planet Earth. Duane has regaled us with occasional stand-up comedy routines performed for the imaginary denizens of Alpha-7.

Don and I became frequent visitors to the Half-Time Sports Bar and Grill, open 24 hours a day. We shared our find with friends who were not prone to frequenting bars, either, but took to the place as well. One evening, Don and I were enjoying prime rib night, and as I looked around, the energy of the place suddenly struck me. I turned to

Don and breathlessly announced, "This is Alpha-7!" And it has been Alpha-7 ever since.

Shortly after the baptism of Alpa-7, we invited a friend—who was privy to our inside joke—to join us for dinner. We learned from previous dining experiences there that the cooks ran out of prime rib fairly early, so we met at 5:30 p.m. Our dinners arrived at 9:00 p.m. No amount of cajoling received any more than perfunctory excuses from the servers that "it took a long time to dish up." I could have "dished up" faster than that blindfolded and with one arm tied behind my back. We concluded that all of this talk of Alph-7 had unwittingly sent us into another dimension that warped the time.

It was Valentine's Day that night and, if the truth be told, I am sure they were preparing another prime rib to serve the larger-than-expected crowd. Nonetheless, we agreed that we needed to be very guarded in any references to Alpha-7 just in case it really did catapult us into some weird time warp.

Then we discovered that the bartenders at Alpha-7 made the best coffee nudges in town—yes, COFFEE. Our fate was sealed. It wasn't unusual for our coffee nudge bar tab to exceed our dinner bill. If each of us drank three, you can see how this could add up. When Don and I came in the back way as usual, I could hear the girls behind the bar say, "Don and Diana just came in." There would be two coffee nudges waiting at our table.

Good to the Last Drop

Before we get so far afield that you forget, we were in the continuing saga of the Coffee Chronicles as read by all of my newsletter subscribers. The cosmic significance of this tale is lost unless you understand that this was a group experience. I regularly shared such adventures of mine with readers and received some interesting accounts of their own adventures in return. There was another episode on March 27th and off I went.

It was only too obvious that coffee was the rocket fuel for my spacecraft. It launched me into super space once again. This time Thomas took me slowly into the new realities, inch by inch. I returned slowly and with Thomas's coaching felt much more in control of the whole process.

Don was having a day of wild energies himself, so we decided to get out of the house. We went out to dinner and were just making small talk when, unexpectedly, I got the blast of energies, stronger than ever. It was all I could do to maintain my composure. (Why did I order coffee?) We arrived home at 9:30. I was still reeling. I was not a happy camper realizing that I was now apparently vulnerable to sneak attacks at any time. I reluctantly conceded that coffee in public places was probably not a good idea.

The next morning was a nightmare. I was experiencing intolerable physical pain over my entire body. I was on the edge of hysteria fearing I may never come out of it. Don reminded me of something that I did not want to hear. Several times before, Guidance came through loud and clear that in order to ground my energies after heavy traveling, it was sometimes imperative that I eat a meal of heavy food. I was trying to lose some weight and this ran very counter to my plans. I tried to ignore it. After three or four more days of the miseries, I succumbed and abandoned all thoughts of vegetable soup and salads. The void in my mid-section was calling for steak, potatoes, onion rings, chocolate cake and ice cream.

I relented and went to lunch. The waitress eyed me with a poorly disguised look of incredulity as I chowed down a meal fit for a field hand. I didn't know whether to be happy or sad that hearty food grounded the wildest energies in short order. Other lightworkers also confirmed the need to ground their energies with heavy meals, flying in the face of conventional ideas about diet. I sometimes wondered if I would even make it to the Shift because of arteries fatally clogged with t-bone steaks. (Check out the chapter "Food for Thought.)

At a point in 2008 as I was editing this book, a great deal of information about food and personal eating experiences had profoundly shifted my beliefs on the subject. Earlier New Age ideas had us all turning vegetarian and packing around little plastic bags of granola. You need not be a vegetarian to ascend. Each person is different. Protein from red meat is clearly a proper choice at times for many lightworkers, me included. All foods can be changed to your vibration. (Remember that?)

Meanwhile, packets of every persuasion of exotic coffees regularly arrived in the mail from readers of my newsletters who were following the Coffee Chronicles with avid interest. Even more unbelievable, at this writing, a total of hundreds of dollars in free gift cards to Starbuck's have accumulated. The franchise is the Northwest coffee giant largely responsible for fueling American's relatively new love affair with espresso, lattes and cappuccinos. Starbuck's became our second home as we lavished expensive coffee drinks on ourselves, guilt free.

Don't misunderstand my previous remarks about never home brewing coffee. I relish coffee but only a really great cup of coffee. I am a coffee snob. I also had long labored under the belief that coffee really is not good for you. I regarded relative abstinence as at least small evidence that I had some shred of discipline and the soul of a health food aficionado.

There Really is a Coffee Goddess

The burgeoning synchronicity generated by the little bean was not lost on me. It was incredible and certainly none more so than a conversation with a woman in my local area who called to order the *Lightbody* book. It came out as we talked that she worked at a branch of my favorite health food grocery store. She worked in the deli and was responsible for making the coffee drinks. I gasped silently, "I am talking to the coffee lady!"

She is a burrista par excellence. I was stunned by her declarations of undying passion for coffee. She told me it is her life. She had been devoted to studying every aspect of coffee for 15 years. It is her reason for being. She described in detail how coffee feels on different parts of the tongue to tell if the grind is right. She gave me hints about storing coffee (not in the refrigerator). I could not believe that such a person existed on the planet—the preeminent coffee devotee.

The sequence of hand movements used to prepare the coffee she regards as a kind of Tai Chi. She described how she deliberately creates a powerful healing energy field this way. Can you believe this? Many of her regular customers tell her that they do not really come for the coffee; they come to stand in the energy. I hope you appreciate how incredulous I was in the midst of all this business with coffee! Pay attention, because this was just the beginning.

I took her up on an offer to stop by her store for a coffee treat. I had a mocha latte with a little almond flavoring atop the whipped cream. It was ambrosia. The only thing that surpassed it was the woman herself. Her smile lit up the entire store. And if eyes are the windows to the soul, I was meeting the most delightful little elf that could instantly brighten the gloomiest day. What a great example of lighting a candle right where you are. I wasn't meeting the coffee lady; I was meeting the *Archetypal Coffee Goddess!*

I didn't know what kind of shenanigans Thomas was up to, but it was a hell of a lot better than The Pill. I was rolling along with this bizarre coffee madness as just another episode with Thomas and his wily Trickster ways. I chalked up these latest soirées as sort of a cute trick to show off that he could use coffee just as easily as The Pill to send me off into other dimensions. And he could, of course.

Keep Those Cards and Letters Coming, Folks!

As things unfolded, a nagging suspicion dogged my thoughts that this was leading to something far more serious. It was not long before these suspicions were confirmed. It was growing increasingly apparent that things were diverging into an unusual direction and unmistakably altering the face of this entire affair. Letters from readers trickled in, responding to the coffee chronicles, and I watched in shocked disbelief as the trickle swelled into a flood. The following sample letters from readers speak for themselves.

This first letter comes from a longtime client who recently moved to Italy. Here is what she had to say about all this coffee business:

"Here is a coffee quote for you from a book by Rollo May (famous psychologist) *Courage to Create.* It is attributed to Jules Henri Poincare, described as one of the great mathematicians of the late nineteenth- and -early twentieth centuries: 'For 15 days I strove to prove that there could not be any functions like those that I have since called Fuschian functions. I was then very ignorant; every day I seated myself at my work table, stayed an hour or two, tried a great number of combinations and reached no results. One evening, contrary to my custom, I drank black coffee and could not sleep. Ideas rose in crowds; I felt them collide until pairs interlocked, so to speak, making a stable combination. By the next morning I had established the existence of a class of Fuschian functions, those that come from the hyper-geometric series; I only had to write out the results, which took but a few hours.'" (What is in that coffee!)

And here are two more letters, just two of many!

"I went back to drinking coffee after a year's abstinence. Not just any brand but a special brand made here in town and has a cult following. **I found that it put me in this amazing state of clarity,** could virtually feel its chemistry working through my body. And then I would write and write and write"

"Thanks for letting us know we are not alone. Lord, I thought I was drinking too much coffee or something. Signed, Your fellow coffee Goddess."

Another Coffee Goddess…

"Dear Diana,
Thank you so much for clueing us in on what is going on. Geesh, it has been a weird past few days. I am so glad to know it is not just me and that others are feeling odd too. I have used all my grounding tricks that I can think of and it has not helped.
Thanks for the letting us know we are not alone!!
Lord, I was thinking I was drinking too much coffee or something!!
Many Blessings,
Your fellow coffee Goddess" (M.G.)

Some Heavyweights Weigh in

Edgar Cayce, America's most famous psychic, described coffee as a food classified as a bitter taste. According to Chinese medicine, the bitter foods are extremely important to the digestive process

I will end with the following letter that just left me breathless. What was happening? I was incredulous that no less than Rudolph Steiner himself weighed in on the subject way back at the turn of the twentieth-century:

> "In a lecture given in 1913 at The Hague, he elaborated on the deeper action of coffee as one that 'causes the human organism to lift its etheric body...out of the physical body, but in such a manner that the physical body is felt as a solid foundation for the etheric body...the physical body and etheric body become differentiated but in such a way that one feels the characteristics of the form of the physical body radiating into the etheric body.'"
>
> (from "Nutrition and Stimulants," Bio-Dynamic Literature, 1991.)

I remind you that this is exactly the process that was initiated when Duane began the work on my etheric body in November 2004 and continued with the coffee blast on my birthday the following February! Here is an example of the genius of the guides and spirit teachers in transmitting information to us that exists so far outside our belief systems and contradicts what we think we know.(I conclude from all of this that God does indeed have a sense of humor.) By whatever means could anything else possibly demonstrate the powerful workings of synchronicity, along with an amazing ability to anticipate the future while activating intuitive responses from a widely scattered group of folks enjoying their guilty pleasure in a favorite coffee shop.

I continued the coffee journeys with Thomas until I reached a point at which it was no longer necessary for Thomas to escort me in my travels to other dimensions. It was difficult at first. I eventually grew to tolerate the higher energies, however, and my earlier ordeals faded from my memory. I will never regard coffee quite the same again, needless to say. It taught me how to be a multidimensional being with a little help from my friends.

Each year, I was a lecturer at an astrology conference in Seattle over Memorial Day. Many of the people attending the conference received my e-newsletters. Would you care to wager a guess as to how many cups of coffee came my way? Pots of coffee were sent to my room. Starbuck's lattes arrived at the room first thing in the morning from anonymous donors. If I showed up at the lobby bar for a drink, numerous cups of coffee arrived instead, possibly sent by bar patrons sporting pussy-cat grins.

One of my astrology clients owns a bakery in Seattle. Not only did she show up with a thermos of coffee, but there was a huge assortment of pastries to go with it. I wondered if I would be diabetic by the time I got home. I was having a coffee orgy. I will share my favorite with you. Coffee is good, but how about coffee *and* chocolate *and* booze? Fill a mug with hot coffee. Add a packet of Swiss Miss cocoa mix. Then add a shot of Drambuie. It goes down very smoothly, even for breakfast (not that I would know this from first-hand experience).

My dear friend, Jae, died not long after she turned me on to this delightful drink recipe. Her life was worthwhile. She made a difference.

Knocking About the Dimensions

Now back to the 7th dimension: By this time I was navigating the different levels much easier, and the return voyages were free of the reentry misery that plagued me earlier. I was encountering difficulty with the 7th dimension, however. My brother told me that this was the level where the physical vehicle must be left behind. That barrier could be crossed only in consciousness. I found out just how tricky it is to divorce oneself from the body consciousness. One day I quit knocking myself senseless and slipped through the barrier.

There I met my Oversoul. This sort of event in one's spiritual life is not something that can ever be adequately described in words. I won't even try. All I can say is that I worked for nearly 40 years to reach this level and in that instant all of the pain, suffering and heroic efforts were worth it 10 times over, well, maybe not 10 times over. I raced for the phone to call Duane.

I briefly reiterated my journeys on coffee power over the past few months—saving the best for last, the account of reaching the Oversoul. I knew Duane would be as wildly excited as I was. He was wildly excited all right, but it was not quite what I expected. He began to shout over and over again, "YOU DID IT!! YOU DID IT!! BY GOD, SHE DID IT!! D.L., YOU DID IT! BY GOD!"

I was a little nonplussed at this unexpected reaction. It seemed just a little over the top. I interrupted this enthusiastic outburst on steroids to comment that while it is great to have such unbridled acknowledgement, this seemed somewhat excessive. "YOU DON'T GET IT! YOU DON'T KNOW WHAT YOU HAVE DONE. THIS IS INCREDIBLE!"

The ensuing conversation was conducted at top volume. Once I was able to translate what we were yelling about, the gist of it was that I had activated the DNA strands through the 10th strand and didn't even know it. In fact, Duane traced the levels that I traversed on coffee power, and they were a direct one-on-one correlation to each step that he used to activate people. "Do you realize that you took yourself up the DNA ladder on intuition alone?"

It was only too true that I was not conversant with the specific meanings of the activations with which Duane was so familiar by this time. In fact, I was surprisingly unfamiliar with the whole process. Yet, I heard Duane rattle off every detail of all the activations countless times. I hope you understand the purpose of the Dumb Sister archetype now!

I was deliberately blocked by my Higher Self from any intellectual or procedural understanding; rather, my mission was to find out whether or not—at a certain level of consciousness—it is possible to complete the journey solely on intuitive guidance systems alone.

If I could do it, it would go into the collective unconscious where anyone theoretically could access it him or herself. I did the whole thing blind. At the top of the ladder—surprise!—there was Duane waiting with the sheet of instructions I had unwittingly followed precisely. He had a "cat who ate the canary" grin on his face.. (What **WAS** in that coffee?)

Considering that I had already activated number 10, the logical next step, of course, was to activate the 11th. Now that we realized what was going on, it was decided that maybe it would be better if Duane did that activation for me, with Don standing by. They both were such mother hens about overseeing it, I began to fear that one of the things I missed about the instructions were that you disappear if there is the slightest deviation.

I tossed it up to universal guidance just when this next step would best take place. I was still caught up in exploring the powerful energies of the Oversoul, so for that reason felt it would be best to wait for a while. The Universe already had other plans as it turned out. Apparently, this entire ride was going to stay in character, which was that I did not really know what it was all about. Several days before that, I asked my son, David, to travel to a special chamber under the great pyramid and activate his codes.

David's Work in the Code Rooms

David first made references to codes and code rooms on our maiden shamanic journey together using The Pill. I had never heard of anything about them before then. This is evidently his mission because he has been involved with the code rooms ever since. Just so there is no misunderstanding, he does not go to Egypt physically, of course; he accesses the code rooms psychically and astrally. He doesn't get frequent flyer miles, but it is a lot faster.

Not just anyone is granted entrance to these areas. It is possible only if one has the code keys, which I do not. From time to time, David is guided to work in the code rooms. He refers to the place as the Command Center. We have always understood that it was somehow related to expanded physical functioning, but now that Duane has brought in the information about the codes in our DNA, we speculated that it was somehow related to that.

The subject of the codes that David is working with remains somewhat of a mystery. We don't always have the complete information about everything the guides and teachers direct us to do. You have seen how things somehow work out, for example, in the coffee chronicles. What seems innocent enough at first can suddenly take a left turn into completely unexpected territory. That is probably what will transpire before we have the whole code puzzle pieced together.

A SACRED CODE ACTIVATION

By David Bills

Diana Stone is my mother and the author of this book. It was she that first introduced me to metaphysical practices at the tender age of eight. Not surprisingly, I have actively participated in my family's shamanic journeys over the years. My mother requested that I briefly relate an account of the events just prior to a particularly important passage that she made to higher dimensions. I immediately agreed. No matter how far down the spiritual path one might travel, Mom is still Mom, and you have to do what she says!

Prior to this round of incarnations, each member of our group left behind a certain aspect of our consciousness stored in crystals located in higher dimensions. More specifically, the aspect left behind was a sequence of energetic "codes" that when activated would allow us to reconnect to the higher dimensions from whence we came. This subject alone and the reasons for leaving this knowledge behind are worthy of an entire book.

Suffice to say that we each elected to leave a certain aspect of our consciousness behind in a form that we could access later. It is like writing a special computer program available for when you need something to happen very precisely at a critical moment.

A **code activation** is the process of purposefully unlocking the codes and running the program.

As stand-up comedians say, "Timing is everything." This applies to the work that we do in a very significant way. Our groups' spirit teacher, Thomas, previously led us through a "group-mind" initiation. There were two apparent benefits to this procedure. First, whatever one perceives, the others perceive. Second, we find ourselves performing certain pieces of inner work synchronized for the proper time.

That is exactly how this event unfolded.

My mother stumbled across reading material dealing with code activations about two weeks prior to her journey. Since I have a penchant for this type of work, she suggested that I look into activating my codes. At the time, I didn't pay much attention to the idea, and threw it into the pot along with a thousand other things that I needed to do. (I read that, David. Signed, Mom.)

I awoke suddenly from a deep sleep at four a.m. in the morning of the day before my mother's journey. No one in the group, including myself, had received any advance notice of upcoming events. It was no good trying to get back to sleep. The idea of performing a code activation popped into my head.

There is a room directly beneath the Great Pyramid in Egypt where I perform most of my work. The room exists in the 4th dimension. I am able to transport my consciousness to this room to work on the grid and to conduct other kinds of energy work. This time I had arrived to perform something new to me—a code activation. Much of the work that I perform for the first time is under guidance or comes to me intuitively. No guides showed up to help, so I was on my own this time.

I had been in this particular room countless times, and now a door had manifested itself in a place where no door had appeared before. I opened the door and passed through a very long, low underground passage running straight as an arrow toward the Sphinx. At the end of the passage was the most remarkable door I had ever seen in my life.

The door stood about twelve feet tall and six feet across. It appeared to be made of solid gold. It was ornately carved with murals and many figures standing in bas-relief. The workmanship was unparalleled. At the top of the door was carved a large, open eye. It reminded me of the eye at the top of the pyramid on the reverse side of a one-dollar bill.

It occurred to me that this was the entrance to the Hall of Records. I remembered that Edgar Cayce spoke about this. This was turning out to be no ordinary journey. One does not just go strolling into the Hall of Records on a whim. I intuitively knew to stand in front of the door and let the eye see me. Inside my head a voice was saying that only certain individuals were permitted to pass through the door. I allowed the eye to scan my consciousness. I then sent a bright ray of light from my third eye to the eye in the door, and I could feel an exchange of information. The door opened and I was admitted.

If you have ever journeyed to a truly sacred place, then you know what it is like to stand in the Hall of Records. The cosmic silence was pervasive. The room was vast and filled with all kinds of objects, both familiar and unfamiliar. The voice in my head then firmly instructed me to quickly retrieve what I needed and get out. Apparently taking a casual stroll through the Hall of Records just isn't done.

A thin pedestal, standing waist high, was located fifty feet from the door. A perfectly formed clear crystal about the size of a baseball sat upon the pedestal. I knew to take this crystal and to leave immediately. That didn't stop me from taking a quick look out of the corner of my eye at the myriad of fascinating objects in the room. How I wanted to stay and explore! But I could sense that the voice in my head meant business, so I reluctantly followed its' instructions. The great, golden door silently closed and locked behind me after I exited the room.

I followed the passage back to the room under the Great Pyramid. A watermelon-sized crystal was now sitting on a pedestal in the middle of the room. It appeared to be constructed of the same material as the baseball-sized crystal I held in my hand. Next to the large crystal was a larger, horizontal slab of granite mounted on a pyramid-shaped stand.

I could see an opening at the top of the large crystal that was generous enough to perfectly admit the insertion of the smaller crystal. It was apparent how to proceed. I inserted the smaller crystal into the larger crystal and climbed up to lie on the slab. I was lying face-up. I could see the large crystal at my feet.

The small crystal began to glow softly. In a flash, the entire crystal was fully involved in an intense, white light. I could feel powerful energies flowing through my body and heavy pressure on my third eye. The actual code activation lasted about thirty seconds and ended abruptly. I came out of the meditation with every square inch of my body covered with gooseflesh.

In the hours that followed, my mother was taken on a uniquely powerful journey to higher dimensions. Since we had been initiated by Thomas and achieved group-mind, my mother's codes were activated at the same time as my own. The code activation allowed her to navigate successfully to her destination. As they say, timing is everything. End of Story

****

A Note of Confirmation

When David and I did that first journey together, I still look back in wonder at the information that came through. It was certainly of greater significance than either of us fully comprehended at the time. Over the years, as more information and new experiences presented themselves, we realized over and over again that we had already encountered just about everything at that earlier time.

When David, in his own inimitable fashion, dramatically presented a little scenario of some imaginary, so-called "watermelon crystals," I hadn't the slightest idea what he could possibly be talking about. It was only our first journey together, and with The Pill no less, and here he was babbling about watermelon crystals with whom he seemed to be on intimate terms.

When I asked him what they were, he seemed possessed of detailed knowledge of them. That is when he informed me with unhesitating confidence that these were the crystals in which we left "aspects" of ourselves back home. Each one of the 4Ds had their own individual crystal. I silently wondered where this kid was getting all of this information, but I let it go at that. In ensuing years, he made visits to the Control Room where the watermelon crystals supposedly resided. Occasionally, he traveled there to work on codes, which were as fully mystifying to me as all the rest of his gig.

Along the lines of my philosophy that if you wait long enough, you will find the answers to all mysteries; this was a long wait, but no exception. It was Year 2012 when I began reading all of Dolores Cannon's books in earnest. I read something in *Book Four* that sent me reeling. It was just a little snippet of a conversation with a woman who was in a deep hypnotic state. The woman was speaking about how she came from a place faraway in order to help Planet Earth. If I had not been reading carefully, I could have easily missed this altogether:

> **Dolores:** *What do you mean?*
> **Woman:** *The crystals were able to change the pink to where I was... The crystals were able to help me do this.*
> **Dolores:** *So all the energy went?*
> **Woman:** *No...*
> ***Dolores:*** *So only a portion, a part of you, went to Earth?*
> ***Woman:*** *Yes. I left my inner energy there...*

That is an edited copy of this woman telling Dolores that she had left a part of herself at some distant home. It was the first time I had ever heard of anyone else besides my son referring to such an arrangement. You can imagine that this was quite a stunning revelation. If she had said she left it stored in a watermelon crystal, I swear I would have fainted dead away.

Wrapping it Up

June 21st, 2005, was just another day as far as I was concerned. In an act of terminal naïveté, I arose early, went to the family room instead of my office and asked Don to make coffee. Captured in this completely out-to-lunch mentality, I also failed to connect the dots to the work that I had requested of David and was totally oblivious to the fact that he had done it less than 24 hours earlier. That probably accounted for my cavalier attitude when I off-handedly commented, "You know, I think this is Summer Solstice day. Maybe we should do something."

The conclusions to be drawn from this adventure teach some important dynamics about individual intuitive functioning in conjunction with a small tightly-connected group. First of all was my inexplicable inability to intellectually remember or understand the information about DNA activations. When I climbed the DNA ladder precisely following each step, it was accomplished without knowledge or memory. This was a simple demonstration engineered to prove it could be done.

Then there was the tricky timing bouncing around. David forgot about doing his code activation that I requested. Yet, he "just happened" to awaken the day before my journey. As he reported, he then went ahead with his adventure but unbeknownst to me, and, of course, I embarked on my adventure unbeknownst to him. (Are you keeping track here?) Solstice day on June 21st escaped my notice except for an off-hand remark to that effect. Yet both of us responded by "accident" to our own inner guidance.

Since we are also together as one consciousness, the timing fell into place with amazing precision. David acted as a surrogate for me when he activated his codes. It could not have fallen into place any better if it had been a military operation strategized by a 5-star general. This underscores once again that it is not necessarily the knowledge one possesses that opens the gates to higher functioning. The great portals to other dimensions open for those with intuitive inner guidance and unconditional love connections, or the heart connection.

I intuitively hit the target at which I did not even know I was aimed. This perhaps was the culmination of that time back in August 2003, when I was catapulted into a new energy from which I never returned. This was Solstice Day. This was *The* Day. David released the codes, a wormhole opened, and I embarked on a mission contracted by my soul before this lifetime. That journey, undertaken in the name of ordinary mortals, was logged onto the Earth grids. This laid the foundation for other just plain folks who may one day answer an uncharacteristic craving for a real great cup of coffee themselves.

One of the most remarkable aspects of the Coffee Chronicles occurred about six months after the peak of the coffee experience. A different message came to my attention—over and over again. *Coffee is good for you*!

THE COFFEE PAPERS

The "Grounds" for Drinking Coffee!

In my files, I have accumulated a thick stack of reports about coffee's beneficial effects on human beings. These are research findings from leading universities and institutions. It is not research conducted by Folger's. There are numerous newspaper and magazine articles reporting on this research.

Also, this information proliferates on the Internet. For those of you who are curious, it is an easy matter to Google the subject. I did just that myself a minute ago. I entered, "research on coffee's benefits" and 32,500,000 sites came up in 32 seconds. That's millions, folks.

When the Ink Spots sang, "I love the java jive and it loves me" in 1940, they could not have known how right they were. Coffee not only helps clear the mind and perk up the energy, it also provides more healthful antioxidants than any other food or beverage in the American diet, according to a study released Sunday (September 30, 2005). The findings by Joe A. Vinson, a chemistry professor at the University of Scranton...give a healthy boost to the warming beverage.

And here is information from a team of Japanese researchers reported in the Journal of the National Cancer Institute that people who drink coffee daily, or nearly every day, had half the liver cancer risk of those who never drink it. The protective effect occurred in people who drank one to two cups a day, and increased with three to four cups.

The following article turned up in my email October 11, 2005. It is titled "Coffee Perks" by Susan Yara:

> "It may be time to take coffee off the list of life's guilty pleasures. New studies indicate that moderate coffee drinkers can not only enjoy their morning java jolt, but they may also get significant health benefits in the process. ...Despite earlier beliefs that coffee has negative health effects, it is becoming increasingly clear that the opposite is in fact the case. Coffee consumption is now being linked to lowered occurrence of cases of certain cancers and chronic diseases. One study conducted by the Harvard University School of Public Health shows that the risk of developing Type II diabetes is lower among coffee drinkers. ...The problem is that there is this preconceived notion that coffee is bad...everyday there is more evidence that coffee is beneficial."

From Marcia, another newsletter subscriber, I received perhaps the most unusual information about the lowly bean:

"So, I'm browsing the perfume counter at Macy's and remembering the old advice never to sniff more than three scents at a time, because the olfactory sense goes on overload very quickly, and then you can't really tell the scents apart. However! A way around this limitation has been found. And what do you think they keep at the fragrance counter to "clear your head," as it were, and prepare your nose for a barrage of new information? Coffee beans! I kid you not. And it works, too!"

I just can't resist including the following article. It is from The *ENQUIRER*. This scandal rag's exposes of the rich and famous—and infamous—rest on very loosely corroborated facts. However, their medical reporters are outstanding. The information is cutting edge, beating the mainline media by months or years. Also, their reports are not shackled by the gag order that traditional medicine apparently exercises over its doctors and trade journals because many articles are definitely in the alternative health care column.

Here is the quote from The ENQUIRER, no less, in the January 11, 2010, issue:

"Here's some fresh-brewed news. Regular or decaffeinated coffee and tea can significantly cut the risk of developing Type 2 diabetes. An analysis of 18 different studies–involving nearly a half-million people–found that those who drank three or more cups of coffee a day had a 25 percent lower risk of developing diabetes...Those who drank more than three cups of decaf had about a one-third lower risk...the ...research team envisions doctors will one day advise their patients most at risk for diabetes to increase their coffee or tea consumption...."

So What Does it All Mean?

First of all, the powers-that-be addressed the myth about coffee's harmful effects *fully six months before the first research reports hit print.* This flew in the face of the prevailing notion at that time in history; coffee was a bad guy. Thankfully, I publish my newsletter. Any publication can serve as a conduit to broadcast a message to reach thousands of readers. In my case, consequently, I then receive the feedback here at Headquarters. Otherwise, we would miss the obvious big picture concerning the curious intuitive responses among a surprisingly noteworthy number of readers, confirming that they, as a group, were all on the receiving end of an identical message from on high. And furthermore;—even curiouser and curiouser—it was a message with which many disagreed but acted on anyway. *Drink coffee!*

It is now obvious that if "Someone" upstairs wants to grab our attention and send a message, It can certainly do it. In fact, it clearly did it—and did it by somehow manipulating god knows how many scattered people to drink coffee. When I reported on my coffee journeys, blow by blow, I was certainly oblivious to any such future ramifications as these.

Even though this whole adventure was humorous as hell, I think the profoundly significant implications are not lost on most people reading this. The subject at hand is about preparing for ascension. This was an object lesson. If (and these are big *ifs)* you will clear away irrational fears; learn to trust your intuition; maintain a flexible belief system; and accept synchronicity's signs, you can hear and respond to all of the guidance that you will ever personally require. Yes, God (or the Higher Consciousness) will anticipate your needs just as surely as It did in the "coffee chronicles" adventure. Let's not forget just how amazing this was!

As for any mass shift in consciousness, the idea that coffee is bad for you is dying a lingering death. Despite the fact that 80 percent of Americans drink coffee, and half drink it everyday, the prevailing notion that this is a bad thing drowns out the body's intuition to the contrary. If you are not hearing the true perks about coffee from your inner self, what is going to happen when you are tipped off that a tsunami is headed your direction? As for those of you who followed your nose to the nearest brew, perhaps you can sound the disaster warnings to those who are about to go swimming.

Coffee and Doughnuts

Speaking of synchronicity, I just cannot resist this perfect last ending to the "Coffee Chronicles." Ain't the Universe grand?

I required several months to recover from a hospital stay that included major abdominal surgery plus physical therapy to get me up and walking again with my walker. When you read about this next story, you will immediately recognize why I just *had* to put it in this chapter. Cute, eh?

Inevitably, there came the day after my long recovery when I had to face confronting my office to which I felt a certain resistance after such a protracted absence. To entice myself into the office, I decided I would be extremely motivated if I knew that coffee and doughnuts awaited me on my desk. I dreamt up a story to tell Don that this was Coffee and Doughnut Day in honor of everyone who died for their country in the name of coffee and doughnuts. To celebrate this patriotic observance, I asked husband to go to the store for coffee and doughnuts and leave them on my desk. He was only too happy to oblige. After all, these were American heroes we were talking about. (Some people will believe ANYTHING.)

As we watched the evening news together, I just about fell out of my chair. What did I see reported on the news but scenes of blocked off streets in Portland with hundreds of people milling around enjoying—what else?—coffee and doughnuts. My husband commented about how nice it was that Portland was observing Coffee and Doughnut

Day. If I had been eating doughnuts at the time, I surely would have choked to death. Talk about synchronicity at work! It follows me around like a street dog looking for a home.

I was just coming off my high over the whole coffee and doughnut affair, when I decided to try for National Pizza Day. I craved delivery pizza for dinner, so why not give it a shot? When I told my story about National Pizza Day, my husband went for it hook, line and sinker. Later that day, he ran some errands. When he came home, he was laughing his head off. He said, "I was listening to the car radio. You got it wrong. It isn't National Pizza Day. This is National Pizza *Month*." I just couldn't lose.

Wonder Woman is Wonder-ful

While I am on the subject, I just *have* to include the following story. You will understand why I just couldn't leave it out!

In July of 2007, I was rushed to the hospital suffering from massive internal hemorrhaging. Blood transfusions were administered as the doctors attempted to determine the bleeding site before performing surgery. I realized that I needed to keep my wits about me, considering what may lie ahead.

As a kid, Wonder Woman was my favorite cartoon character because her alter ego was named Diana. When I was still in the emergency room, I invoked the energy of Wonder Woman. I *was* Wonder Woman! The hospital staff must have sensed this image in my aura, because I was very quickly designated as "a real trouper." In fact, I was inexplicably unflappable throughout the entire ordeal.

The reason I like to share this story is two fold. First, when facing a difficult road ahead, it really does work to invoke whatever energies that match the situation the most–then become that! The second reason I love this story so much is that it is the wildest example of synchronicity I ever experienced. The way the hospital staff treated me–nurses and doctors alike–was unbelievable.

There was a contest on the special ward I was in. Each week the staff voted for the "star" patient of the week. I won in all of the three weeks that I was there. I am not sure by what criteria one was chosen star patient of the week, but whatever it was, no one else had a chance against Wonder Woman. Rumor had it that the nurses fought to be assigned to my room at every shift change.

After I was discharged, I required continued care at home for several months, as I already wrote as a prelude to Coffee and Doughnut Day, so I continued to invoke Wonder Woman. The most amazing thing happened! My son called me. He was so excited he could barely get the words out fast enough. **"The mayor has just announced on television that he has declared today 'Wonder Woman Day' in Portland!"** And sure enough it was. Life-size cut-outs of Wonder Woman stood on street corners all over the city. I am still WONDER-ing to this day if we were on some other planet!

I was definitely on a roll with synchronicity. Somehow I stumbled onto a zone of whatever I wanted to attract to myself, "something" was pairing me with it like drawing to a straight flush. My biggest mistake was not continuing while I was in the zone and things were flowing like magic. I regret to this day that I didn't try for National "Buy Your Wife Diamonds" Month.

ADDENDUM I

As you know, I have been writing this book in pieces over the years. I could not resist this little update that appeared in The ENQUIRER July 30, 2012. The article is by their medical reporters, who are excellent, Lisette Hilton and Laurie Miller. The title of the article is "Coffee for Heart Health." The research was done at the Beth Israel Deaconess Medical Center. These were the results of their study:

> "We found that moderate consumption, the equivalent of about two typical coffee shop beverages may actually protect against heart failure...Excessive consumption was considered equivalent to six coffee house cups per day."

After this article appeared in The ENQUIRER, it wasn't long before the news exploded onto the Internet. However, it was not so much that the health benefits were touted as it was its role in weight loss. A popular TV show hosted by Dr. Oz featured the weight loss benefits also.

To all coffee lovers, with love!

ADDENDUM II

Pass these articles in the Addendums to all your family and friends!

There seems to be no end to this subject! Obviously, "someone" upstairs had unmistakable insight about the benefits of coffee, plus the amazing ability to convince even the most anti-coffee diehards to brew up a cuppa java. Next came The ENQUIRER article about coffee and heart health. That is just the beginning according to a new study from the *National Institute of Health,* released in September 2012. While it is great news that coffee receives an undeniable heads up in connection with heart health, the latest research proves that coffee is what epidemiologists call "all cause mortality;" i.e., coffee drinking was associated with a markedly lower risk of dying from any reason at all—even injuries and accidents! Go figure. (Probably because you are more alert.)

First, you will need to get past deeply ingrained negative associations connected to coffee consumption. Smokers are often ravenous coffee drinkers as well. Other unhealthy images are of coffee used to recover from too much partying the night before. Also, there is the hefty additions of cream and sugar or the high-calorie coffee "milkshakes" contributing to the current obesity epidemic. Other unhealthy images are sleep-deprived individuals drinking coffee to stay awake. Certain religions group coffee along with nicotine and alcohol, implying that coffee drinkers are in the same poor health category as smokers and alcoholics. Also, those who successfully abstain from alcohol often switch to coffee. Finally, some people are sensitive to coffee and suffer from heartburn or jitters from caffeine consumption. These associations are hard to delete from our memory banks. However, if the truth will out, coffee drinking may rise to the conscious level of a healthy choice.

There is also the influence from individual messages in your household concerning coffee. In my case, my mother thought my brother and I should not drink coffee. All through our childhood, we were cautioned that it would "stunt your growth." Since I grew to just under five feet nine inches tall, it must have worked. Anyway, in my consciousness, coffee consumption for children was next door to tying off and shooting up.

In my home town, there was an occasional open house or special super sale at one of the local businesses. On these occasions, there was always free coffee and doughnuts. Once we were old enough, Mom allowed us to drop in and have one cup of coffee and a doughnut. I remember both of us feeling very grown up but also somewhat fearful of being arrested.

Believe it or Not: Read on!

Evidence is rapidly mounting that coffee drinking may add years to your life span. Numerous other studies demonstrate reduced risk of dying from *specific* diseases: a veritable laundry list of the nation's worst health problems, including vascular disease, cancer risk, stroke, diabetes, liver disease, and even Alzheimer's disease and other neurodegenerative disorders.

Coffee contains over 1,000 different natural compounds that favorably interact with cells. One compound in particular, chlorogenic acid, provides a multitude of these benefits. The full benefits of coffee consumption require drinking many cups a day, perhaps 12 in some cases. Standard processing destroys much of the beneficial polyphenols. Researchers have found a way to "super charge" coffee, dramatically increasing its benefits by more than 200 percent, while drinking less coffee. For those who cannot drink coffee, standardized chlorogenic acid capsules are becoming enormously popular. Consider taking 200 to 400 mg of the supplement before most meals. Use the capsules from green coffee concentrate.

Special warning

I have lately received information regarding the chlorogenic acid supplements. Apparently, some companies have jumped on the band wagon with inferior products that contain very little chlorogenic acid relative to what is the daily recommended daily allowances. Also, you want to investigate the quality of the green coffee beans. A good investigation via the Internet is recommended.

There are some contraindications that one should consider in some cases. Certain medications may not combine with caffeine consumption. Check with your doctor or pharmacist. If using this primarily for weight loss, check with your physician if you are on some other weight loss regimen. As with anything else concerning your health, use common sense.

I know that we are all used to hearing that something is first good for you, and then a few years later it is bad for you, or vice versa. Sometimes we don't know what to believe. However, I have read the research reports, and this definitely is information that is on solid ground. Regardless of the bad rap that America's favorite beverage has gotten in the past, we are passing up one of the most powerful protectors of our health on the planet if we can't take coffee consumption seriously.

For example, I think there is an epidemic of fear of contracting Alzheimer's disease. Many people tell me that if they temporarily forget someone's name, they admit that it crosses their mind that maybe it is the beginning of this dreaded disease. A study in the *Journal of Alzheimer's Disease* reports that drinking coffee may help at-risk adults over age 65 to fend off Alzheimer's disease due to the elevated blood caffeine levels.

Moderate daily caffeine/coffee intake throughout adulthood should appreciably protect against Alzheimer's later in life. As little as three coffees a day may ward off dementia. The scientists are careful to point out that coffee consumption will not completely protect people from Alzheimer's yet, firmly believe moderate coffee consumption can reduce a person's risk of Alzheimer's, or delay its onset. In my opinion, that surely is a painless way to increase peace of mind about you or your loved ones contracting this disease.

If you have any questions about the scientific research on the protective effects of coffee consumption, you may call a Life Extension Health Advisor at 1-866-864-3027.

ADDENDUM III

Warning: This one is About—ALCOHOL !

How would you like it, after a night of partying the night before, and then sobering up over coffee in the morning that you just prevented most of the major health problems that afflict mankind? Well, an exaggeration, but surprisingly, not by much! The previous article exposed the truth about coffee consumption. Now would you believe that the same startling turn-around concerns alcohol consumption? I know this is a chapter about coffee, but since there is no special place for discussing alcohol, I thought I might as well tack it on here. Life is looking up! Would someone please tell me if we ascended while I was not looking.

Once again, it is important to check out research reports because—believe me—they are not all created equal. I intend to tell you about the health benefits of the moderate consumption of alcohol. If there was only a single research study by a prominent whiskey distiller, one might be well-advised to discount the whole thing. However, when I was first alerted to some really unbelievable rumors about drinking, I went sleuthing for some reliable information. What I found was so overwhelming I am almost at a loss to know where to begin.

You need to take the following information seriously to take advantage of the most powerful health benefits on the planet. That's right, I'm talking about that "bad" stuff: wine, beer and distilled spirits. Alcohol, along with coffee, provides an unequaled one-two knock-out punch to "all causes mortality," or protection against all major diseases. Just think about it. In fact, the Harvard Medical School Guide to Healthy Eating, co-developed by scientists at the Harvard School of Public health and based on the best available scientific knowledge, actually includes drinking alcohol in their recommended food pyramid.

It has long been known in the medical field that alcohol may be beneficial in heart-related ailments. Not that this isn't great news in itself. That is America's number one killer. The radical shift in alcohol consumption in relation *to every other disease* is the shocker! A quick survey of research available on the Internet told me almost more than I wanted to know.

To make a long story short, the following is a list of diseases that are helped or prevented altogether by moderate alcohol consumption. Nothing is a 100 percent guarantee, of course, but I will accept the promise of a longer life span and any protection I can get against life's worst afflictions. Here is the surprising list as promised: generally better health, fewer heart attacks and strokes, arthritis, enlarged prostate, dementia (including Alzheimer's), several major cancers, diabetes, osteoporosis, gallbladder disease (gallstones), peripheral artery disease, hepatitis, macular degeneration, Parkinson's disease, stress, depression and even five strains of the common cold virus. Be aware that all of these are the result of individual research, many continuing over many years in heavily screened controlled studies.

I could cite endless studies, but it would bore you to death. If you are really interested, just Google it on the Internet. You will be shocked.

What is "Moderate" Consumption?

First, I re-emphasize that the benefits from the consumption of alcohol apply *only to moderate use.* That rules out heavy drinkers, no surprise there. It also rules out *abstainers* as well! The drinkers will attend your funerals; the percentages are definitively in their favor. Anyway, if you inquire as to just what moderation means, that's easy.

A Standard Alcoholic Drink:

- A 12-ounce can or bottle of regular beer
- A 5-ounce glass of dinner wine
- A shot (1½ ounces) of 80 proof liquor or spirits such as vodka, tequila, or rum either straight or in a mixed drink.

How many?

Medical researchers generally describe moderation as one to three drinks per day. Four or five drinks may be moderate for a large individual but excessive for a tiny person. The typical woman should generally consume 25-30 percent less than the average man. The National Institute on Alcohol Abuse and Alcoholism (NIAAA) describes moderate drinking as a man consuming four drinks on any given day with an average of 14 drinks per week. For women, it is consuming three drinks on any given day and an average of seven drinks per week. The research applied equally to all races and nationalities. It is definitely cheating to save up and drink all of your week's allowance on Saturday night.

Contraindications

Alcoholics should abstain from alcohol. Individuals who experience any adverse reactions should abstain without first seeking the opinion of their doctor.

Conclusion

Maybe we just played the Mission: Impossible Game.

CHAPTER SIX

Food for Thought

This little piggy went to market,

This little piggy stayed at home,

This little piggy had roast beef,

This little piggy had none.

And this little piggy went...

"Wee wee wee" all the way home.

Nursery Rhyme 1729

Pease Pudding Rhyme Poem

Pease pudding hot,
Pease pudding cold,
Pease pudding in the pot -
Nine days old.

Some like it hot,
Some like it cold,
Some like it in the pot -
Nine days old.

Food is the nemesis for a great many people on the planet. In the West, there is this continuing obsession with the body. Hey, I read The ENQUIRER. I even subscribe to it, so I know what's going on. Consequently, I know how much Kirstie Alley (actress) weighs this week, who has ugly cellulite and whose neuroses have dropped the scales to a dangerously low 89 pounds. The other half of the world is starving to death for real because they have no food. Clearly, there is something wrong with the global picture. In this chapter, however, I want to discuss the role food plays in your own *personal* transformation into your lightbody and your journey to ascension.

In the *Lightbody Activation Manual* which is *Book One* of THE TECHNOLOGY OF ASCENSION SERIES, there are illustrated directions for activating the lightbody. As time goes by it becomes increasingly apparent that there is more hidden wisdom in the activation technique than we ever suspected at first. One example involves Step Eight and is called "Activate Prana Flow." The spoken words that accompany the hand movements are "...prana is flowing into your entire body and all your cells. *You can live on this...*" (There is a further discussion of this elsewhere in other chapters also.)

That introduces the notion that once in your lightbody, you would require no food, just prana, or the life force energy. In preparing for ascension, you need to examine your relationship to eating and food, or even more to the point, developing an acute intuition that speaks to your dietary needs at any given time.

In Dolores Cannon's "Book Four" of her *Convoluted Universe* series, she writes about meeting a woman who approached her following a lecture. The woman claimed that she had not taken any food or water throughout her entire life. Yet, she appeared quite fit. There is every reason to believe that the woman was telling the truth. She is not unique in this respect. There are well-documented cases of people who have never eaten for decades. I have seen figures that estimate there are approximately 33,000 people worldwide who do not eat or drink.

If you don't mind a little humorous diversion, this story reminds me of something I saw in my organic, natural foods grocery store. The store features quotations painted high on the walls. For you older readers, you will remember W.C. Fields, a comedian whose signature persona featured regular imbibing of spirits of the liquid kind. This quote from him reads, "I once lived for two weeks only on food and water."

All joking aside, subsisting without food or water is very serious business. *Breathairianism* is the name given to a lifestyle that does not include eating. The philosophy underlying this practice is that humans can live on the air we breathe, or prana. Practitioners who successfully live for long periods without food or drink couple this with a strong devotion to the spiritual and consciousness-raising aspects of their lives. Those individuals who attempt to live without food but lack a strong spiritual commitment, can expect medical problems and even death.

On occasion, there may be perfectly good reasons for a short fast, however. Fasting for a specific health or cleansing regimen has benefited many patients but generally should be supervised by your medical advisor. Eclipses are also a very beneficial day to fast. Geographical areas in which the eclipse path actually travels is the most effective. Check the Internet for the dates, times and locations of yearly eclipses.

When you abstain from food on eclipse day, it supports the old outdated patterns in dissolving—thus making room for newer higher frequency patterns to form in their place. There are many good fasting regimens to choose from. Find one that you resonate with. If you are new to fasting, get the help and support of a spiritually involved ascension-aware health practitioner—especially if you have any medical conditions to consider.

True breathairianism is just one path on one's evolutionary journey. It obviously is at the far end of the spectrum in relationship to food. It is very likely that the road to ascension is advanced more from a strong spiritual commitment than achieving a healthful life without food. However, there is much more to consider when the subject is "What's for dinner?"

Visitors From Other Planets

As Earth progresses with her ascension process over many years to come, Beings from other planets that have never been on Earth before have incarnated here to participate in this unique time in history. I probably never would have pieced the following story together were it not for a healing case reported in our first book in this Series, *The Lightbody Activation Manual,* which concerned a healing client whose problems stemmed from imprints from another planet.

A close relative of mine gave birth to a daughter, Lindi. Despite her mother successfully breast feeding her other three children, Lindi was extremely agitated by any attempts to nurse her. As she graduated to solid food, the problem intensified. Every time the child was offered food, she screamed and grew hysterical. Fortunately, her mother handled the situation very calmly and patiently so that eventually Lindi would settle down and eat something.

One time when the girl was about three years old, her brother made a peanut butter and jelly sandwich and offered some to her. I was able to observe firsthand the hysterical fit and recognized raw fear in her eyes. I was totally perplexed and wondered if any explanation would ever present itself.

.As it turned out, after Lindi grew up, she and her husband lived in a city to which I regularly visited to teach astrology workshops and see clients for consultations. On these occasions, my husband and I invited Lindi and her husband to dinner. I had not seen Lindi since she was a little kid, so it was a treat for me to get acquainted with her as an adult.

Oddly enough, the dinner conversation turned to food and nutrition one evening, a subject in which she apparently had taken great interest. This, of course, reawakened those early memories of screaming Lindi. I learned also that her husband was the cook in their household. Then she said, most emphatically, "I just hate to eat. I wish I never had to eat again!"

As I like to believe: if you wait long enough you will get an answer to anything. It was only while preparing for this chapter that I realized the explanation jumped out at last! I was paging through our first book in this series and "just happened" onto Duane's healing case about the woman from another planet.

It is not unusual for "foreign" visitors to support the Earth firsthand throughout her process of ascension. This particular woman had never incarnated on Earth before and imprints, or memories, from her home planet caused some problems once she found herself in a physical body. My brother used crystals on this other woman to adjust specific patterns to solve that case. The woman lived relatively comfortably in her physical body afterwards.

I could not help but be reminded about some of my own healing clients who themselves were also from other planets and experiencing various maladjustments in the physical body. That finally sparked my curiosity about Lindi. You don't suppose...

I undertook a deep psychic investigation tracing her soul's journey and, sure enough, Lindi *was* from another star system. I could see no Earth incarnations in the stream of incarnations. An examination of this pattern in connection with food gave me my answer. From whence Lindi originated, they did not eat food. They existed in their lightbodies and lived on prana.

For them, eating dense food lowered their vibratory rate to a level that rendered them unable to tolerate the dimensional frequency in which they lived. Is it any mystery that she incarnated terrified of eating, when it was very possibly a life-threatening situation from where she originally came? Furthermore, even as an adult she claims that she would prefer never to eat again. I think it a perfect irony that she never prepares food at all and married a fellow who immediately laid claim to cooking duties himself.

My brother and I use crystals and shamanic healing to adjust off-planet imprints so that these volunteers who are here to help us may do so more comfortably. As for Lindi, she has adjusted to eating, but there are other earth frequencies that disturb her from time to time. Perhaps now that I have seen the light I can address these issues for her myself.

So Which Little Piggy Are You?

My newsletters generated heavy reader email responses whenever the subject even hinted that it was about food. We ate our Cheetos; we drank our coffee; and wondered what in hell happened to vegetables and granola. Emotional opinions poured in from every corner of the dinner table. As it turns out, the answer is vastly more complex than Betty Crocker and counting carbs.

If we play the Ascension Game, we'll need to toss out the old rule book. If ascension really is a game in progress, and one that will continue to cycle well past 2012; we may need to attune ourselves to fluctuating needs of the body on a somewhat regular basis. Automatically wiring into the food pyramid and mama's cookbook often merely obscure the promptings of spirit.

Anomalous events connected to two everyday items (Cheetos and coffee) on our grocer's shelves admittedly delivered some unbelievably powerful messages concerning our relationship to Spirit. The great philosophers would be hard-pressed to communicate what Spirit accomplished with a bag of Cheetos and a cup of coffee. However, these experiments were not intended to answer many other questions we may ask about food and diet and the ascension process.

As I survey my experiences with food along with my collection of literature on the subject, it is apparent that one size does not fit all. My conclusion is that eating certain foods and refraining from others is not the overriding determinate factor as to whether or not you can tolerate a higher frequency of consciousness. And while certain eating habits do not outright prevent ascension, they most certainly can make your journey much more difficult and painful.

The personal experience that is most painful to me concerns not my own food habits, but those of one of my dear friends, Helen, whom I have written about elsewhere in this book. I said that there were two taboo subjects with Helen. To simply breathe one single word about either of them would not jeopardize a long-term friendship; it would end it. Helen lived pretty much on junk food, and that was one of the taboo subjects.

We sometimes visited Helen in Seattle. We stayed with her in her apartment. One Sunday morning, we were sitting around in our robes drinking coffee. Helen turned to Don and asked him to channel Thomas. I could see that Don was somewhat taken aback as Helen was aware that we normally did not "just talk" to Thomas unless there was a specific reason.

I felt Don's reluctance to channel Thomas also, because of Helen's uncharacteristic light-hearted and somewhat frivolous demeanor. Despite his hesitation, Don tuned into the Thomas channel. Unpredictably, Thomas instantly came through with a no-nonsense lecture on—of all things—diet. There was no mistaking that this was directed to Helen by name, and he was cranky.

He basically issued a cease-and-desist order on all things chocolate. That wasn't all. A veritable litany of junk foods was added to the list. I had never heard Thomas speak in such an authoritarian manner before. He was as close to laying down the law as I had ever heard him. I remember that there were some fairly dire warnings about the consequences of not cleaning up her food act. I was utterly shocked at her reaction. Rather than outrage as I expected, she totally fluffed off the message with a remark that "Thomas was just being his old Trickster self." Is that what we call denial?

Sadly, Helen died in my arms during another one of our visits in June of 1991, the terrible year. She was in her early fifties. A year or so earlier, she developed cancer which rapidly developed into a terminal situation. We "just happened" to be visiting when she died of an apparent heart attack.

When the police came to conduct their investigation, I noticed that the cupboards were stuffed with bags of Hershey kisses, potato chips, Hostess cupcakes, Cracker Jacks, candy bars and evidently an entire cache of favorite goodies. I discovered the grocery receipt dated two days earlier for a total of $200. At least she could die happy.

I do not understand why Helen lived almost exclusively on junk food. More to the point it was she, not I, who rightly should have been motivated to probe deeper into a lifestyle pattern that most likely would have health consequences sooner or later, especially after Thomas's uncharacteristic intervention. Even though certain dietary habits could well be responsible for serious, even life-threatening health issues, it is the refusal to deal with our *consciousness* issues that block the road to ascension. Diet was the red flag, but consciousness was the reason.

I have a dark confession to make before I close the book on this story. I devoured a truckload of Helen's goodies before her dead body was even removed from the apartment. I am especially partial to Hershey kisses. One thing I can say about Helen: She had great taste when it came to junk food!

To Eat Meat, or Not to Eat Meat, That is the Question

Sorry, Shakespeare, I couldn't resist it. This meat-eating issue comes up as frequently as writers like me paraphrase the bard's famous query. Including meat in one's diet remains controversial. There are medical considerations, moral considerations, religious and spiritual considerations. At this point, it is pretty much a given that vegetarianism does not necessarily facilitate the ascension process in and of itself. Our concern is not with the morals or health considerations, however, but only whether or not eating meat—or any other food—actually short-circuits the ascension process. In general, eating meat slows our progress, but does not stop it—but read on.

There are always exceptions to every rule. If certain well-intentioned individuals force themselves onto a vegetarian diet for strictly spiritual reasons and, consequently, every meal is accompanied by heavy vibes of deprivation and sacrifice, these negative attitudes are far more likely to delay ascension goals more than any food ever would! Those people are far better off eating meat with feelings of gratitude. If eating meat is repugnant to you, or you are making the choice on moral grounds, for example; don't eat it.

There are several concerns that if taken into consideration will all but neutralize meat eating's influence. The first concern is that most birds, animals and fish in your market are loaded with toxins. The problem is not the meat itself. There are grocery outlets that advertise organic, farm grown products. If you are going to eat meat, stick with the natural foods. The influence on your ascension process will be all but irrelevant. However, there are other types of pollution that legitimately can be considered before that is precisely true.

The meat that arrives on your dinner plate has experienced a history before it ever makes it to your table. That history is varied, but whatever it is, the vibrations are imprinted on that animal, chicken or fish and are ingested along with protein and fats.

I grew up on a farm. We raised cattle and hogs for market. They were transported to a slaughterhouse in a nearby city. There came an opportunity for me to tour the facility one day. I do not want you to carry the same images that will haunt me for the rest of my life. Therefore, I will simply say that all animals are not slain in a humane manner. You very likely have no way of knowing where the food you eat came from or what imprinting it carries. For all you know, many people with very negative attitudes left their all too real energy signatures behind.

It is a simple matter to clear all negativity from meat, or any food. Meat is probably the most vulnerable to abuse. I don't think a tomato is terrorized by the knife in quite the same manner as the animal in the slaughterhouse. However, don't be too sure. Reread the chapter where there are instructions for clearing and transmuting negative energies from the food you eat (Chapter Four). These somewhat playful game instructions have a way of growing heavier all the time.

Native Ritual Revisited

There is an ancient custom of indigenous peoples that we would be well-served to emulate. These cultures depended on hunting animals for food and other survival needs. However, their relationship to the animal world is all but unknown in our Western countries. (In later chapters, there will be further discussion about connecting with all levels of Nature's kingdoms.)

In native cultures there is a contract between hunter and hunted. Nothing happens unless there is a choice involved. That idea applies to a very broad spectrum of circumstances in which it may appear that someone is victimized or abused. There is always a choice, but we'll examine this only in light of hunting. The animal's spirit knows full well that it is taking on a form to be sacrificed as its devotion to a higher form of life.

The clan or tribe's shaman or medicine people very likely performed traditional ceremonies the night before the hunters ever left. The shaman may well have journeyed in spirit and arranged the special circumstances with a specific animal. Once the animal was killed, certain rituals were usually performed right on the spot.

These of course varied, but the object was to express gratitude to the animal and its contribution to human life; afterwards that gratitude for what was received was passed to the Great Spirit. It is easy enough to take a moment before meals to silently express your own thanksgiving to the animal that once lived. If our consciousness embraces all sustenance from God, *we are blessed by what we eat and not cursed by it.*

As for the meat-eating issue, under whatever circumstances you choose, the worst that will happen is to somewhat retard your progress to ascension, but will never prevent it. There is more harm in torturing yourself in the belief that eating flesh is good or bad, than in eating meat itself.

I know that many readers have vigorous objections to eating meat under any circumstances and will undoubtedly take exception to this material. Frequently, these objections are based on health, medical, moral or religious grounds. Please be aware that there is no suggestion here that you should abandon those beliefs or any practices associated with them. This information on the subject of eating meat is intended only to comment on its relationship to ascension, nothing else.

Just What Are The New Rules of the Game?

Even though the food we do or do not eat doesn't determine our ascension status, the variety of the above situations makes it obvious that the subject is more complex than at first blush. Because the physical body is changing into a lightbody, there are new rules of the game. Consciousness is the key. Just how that plays out at the dinner table is our next consideration.

Vegetarian, meat eater, breathairian, Cheetos, chili dogs: you pays yer money; you makes yer choice. From the above stories, it becomes apparent that under the right circumstances, it doesn't make a damn bit of difference what you eat—or even if you eat at all! Therefore, it behooves us to identify what those "right" circumstances are and if they can ever overturn our long held, most cherished beliefs about food.

Do You Owe Your Body An Apology?

Let's start off by letting go of everything you have ever been told and believed about your body. Let go of how the body works and what is good or bad for it. Let go of all the metaphysical stuff. Let go of the belief that one food is good and another food is bad. You know that voice inside that tells you that you must be good and eat right to "purify your body and raise your vibration to ascend." You know that voice that cracks the whip of discipline and makes you feel guilty. That is a belief system; that's all.

Your body does not need a specific amount of calories for energy. You can junk the recommended daily allowances of vitamins, proteins and minerals that you find printed on food products everywhere. In fact, it is absolutely true that we can live without food or water altogether.

I am not suggesting that you should adopt this lifestyle or even aspire to it. I'm just demonstrating how an entrenched belief system can overpower reality. You don't mean to tell me that I can eat Twinkies all day? My teeth will rot out and I'll die. I believe it, so it will manifest fine. So that proves it. Pssst, it sure would be fun to eat Twinkies all day. (Remember Cheetos Jim?)

So what is this business about apologizing to your body? First be very aware that your body is conscious. It hears you. When I was engaged in my shamanic healing work, I talked to *other people's* bodies as a regular thing. Each body part has it own separate voice. I've had many intimate conversations with broken hearts. Your body knows what it wants and when it wants it, and it tells you. (Just like my cat!)

How would it feel if someone said, "You're too fat" or "You're too thin" or "You look terrible"? How would you feel if someone said, "You are so out of shape, I'm taking you to the gym three times a week."? Do you say those things to your body?

Every time you criticize your body, you are abusing your body. You are abusing your body when you eat what the body hates. It is abuse when you refuse to eat what the body wants. It's abuse to exercise when the body wants no part of it. Your body is extraordinarily intelligent. It is also very accommodating and forgiving and creates what you tell it. You say, "I'm too fat." You got it, pal.

The Rules Apply To Us Only If We Let Them

Your body knows what it wants. Furthermore, it communicates those wants to you very precisely through desire. If you are emotionally distressed, stressed out or bored to death, you probably can not listen to your body. Learn to stop for a moment, and check out your emotional state. Ask each part what it needs. Separate your mental-emotional self from your physical self. It is all about awareness, awareness of what part of you is hungry and for what.

Let's turn to someone who is an expert on rules about food and eating. St. Germain is one heck of an interesting fellow. He is a Master and his claim to fame is that he lived in his physical body for hundreds of years. He did not need food. That's not all. He never aged. I have seen movies about him. I can't guarantee their accuracy, but the story goes that he lived in Europe and after years in one place it began to be very weird that he never changed, hence prompting a move every so often.

Sarah Biermann, a channeler, has worked with St. Germain for years on the other side of the veil. He reports with a great deal of levity that the Ascended Masters regard humanity as so silly as they themselves enjoy their wine and cigars. He actually looks forward with joy to his next embodiment so he may once again enjoy the things we deny ourselves.

He was willing to introduce us to the real rules of the eating game. Welcome to the food-gasm. (The following material is only for those over eighteen.) This is the idea. When you eat something that your body *truly* desires, it should be so scrumptiously delicious, it is like an orgasm. When it stops being totally yummy, you quit eating it. Maybe that is one bite or the whole pie.

From an expanded state of consciousness, your body will always communicate its desires. Ask and it will answer. Some answers may seem crazy, but the body has its reasons. It will defeat the purpose if you are thinking how bad something is for you while you are eating it. We should celebrate with gratitude that we have a physical body at this fabulous time to be on Earth. We are in charge of creating our own reality!

If you can align your consciousness with the voice within, sometimes it might be a special diet that is the answer to stubborn health problems. In that case, the special knowledge required to manage the eating plan designed especially for your needs will exceed your own ability. In that case, the answer to your problem may well arrive in the form of a real person: the right doctor, the right nutritionist or whatever best serves you at the time.

Some personal experiences

As far back as 2005, it seemed that lightworkers were really struggling with food issues. My newsletter was generating a flood of responses to any articles about food. I myself was noticing a big change in my eating habits. I was born with the gene that governs canine appetites. It is a wonder that I did not eat my parents out of house and home throughout my teen years.

My basketball coach called my parents suggesting that I be tested for a tape worm because I ate so much but never gained weight. When boys asked me out, I actually negotiated what food we would get after the movies. I can't believe I did that. Furthermore, I can't believe they tolerated it. I must have been a babe then. I even wrote kid's class assignments for a hamburger and fries.

That is why it was so remarkable when my eating patterns changed dramatically. I ate very little food in a day. Sometimes I did not want to eat at all, but I made myself do it because I thought I should. My husband was right behind me when it came to chowing down, yet he suddenly also ate about half as much food as before. Even though we were very involved in ascension and the lightbody work, the consciousness that we would very likely experience unmistakable physical changes had not quite soaked in yet.

In looking back over communications with other lightworkers, I am convinced that some sort of shift was happening at that time. We were struggling with unseen forces and our own intractable belief systems. Vicki, one of my correspondents and casual acquaintances, wrote a very insightful article. She was editor of *Connexions,* an alternative newspaper in Portland, Oregon.

In the fall of 2005, Vicki wrote a response to one of my newsletter articles. I would like to include this quote from her letter which I believe is brilliantly insightful.

> "Diana, Another good newsletter with lots of food for thought!... (no pun intended?)...Your food guidance seems to correspond with the changing role of lightworkers. When lightworkers began building their inner bridge to Spirit through chakra meditations and energy clearings, Spirit guided us to become vegetarians and watch our consumption of processed foods. As lightworkers

now build the relational bridge between humanity's brothers and sisters, we are being guided to bulk up with meat and other products.

"...Lightworkers 'lightened up' and cleared themselves of old pain in order to take on this new task of embodying crystallized Source energy, so it's time to ground down into the body, using the body as a weight to anchor these higher crystallized energies...

"Last night I received an initiation prayer from the Goddess energy. After performing ceremony I was guided to drink coffee, which I seldom do. At 2:00 a.m. the energies peaked and I experienced the sensation of total weightlessness. I felt like my human body disappeared...I felt grateful that I had been guided to drink coffee and also to eat a turkey sandwich. Without that added 'weight' I felt like I could not have handled the energy flowing through me.

"I once considered myself a vegetarian, but I have now decided to think of myself as a spiritual flexitarian—someone who eats meat and other products when guided by Spirit. I became a vegetarian based on spiritual guidance, so being a flexitarian is no different."

What About Our Animal Friends?

Many of us animal lovers have concerns about our pets and the ascension process. Perhaps a cat in Duluth, Minnesota has a message for us. Dave Anderson, in an NBC news report, featured a story about this cat. He was a remarkable 36 years old. That is 250 in human years. Of course there is the perennial standard question in all cases of longevity, "To what do you attribute your extraordinarily long life?" Tabby's owner credited his cat's long life to exercise and a diet of cheese puffs.

As you move to the next chapter, "bodyspeak" introduces you to even deeper interactions with your physical self. The last chapter on ho'oponopono also deals with food issues and weight concerns.

One Final Thought

There truly is a lot to consider in making your own personal choices about food. Probably the worst headspace, as far as this subject is concerned, is to become a food fanatic. To become fanatically concerned about anything throws the life out of balance; becoming fanatical about food, however, generally does vastly more harm than most anything you might eat.

I have a casual acquaintance with whom I occasionally join for lunch. She is the quintessential food fanatic. It is a trial to eat with her. She constantly worries herself half to death about food. Everything must be exactly right. She makes the wait staff crazy with her questioning about what is in every food, sending them back and forth to the kitchen to check and recheck on her various concerns. By most people's standards, she follows a healthful lifestyle when it comes to eating. Yet, she does not look healthy. She looks stressed, and indeed she is constantly stressed. I always make a point of ordering the worst junk food on the menu, topping it off with a high-carb dessert. My lame excuse for this naughty behavior is her punishment for ruining lunch. Another pay-off is that I get to eat ice cream and chocolate cake once in a while. I love her for that!

As they Say On My Local Newscasts: This Program Is Interrupted By Late-Breaking News...

Just as this book was headed for the printers, some information came to my attention that I will slip in at least in passing. I am beginning to think that I am the only person who is not aware of this huge influence on the foods that we eat everyday. The subject to which I refer is GMOs, or genetically modified organisms. The following material was taken of the Internet.

"What Are GMOs Anyway?"

"As a medical doctor, I'd like to take a moment to provide you with some background on GMOs and why they really do matter. To do this, let me first properly define exactly what genetically-modified organisms actually are. At least one of the most common GMOs -- corn, soybeans, rice, and tomatoes -- are found in nearly every food that most of us eat these days.

"Many people with whom I have "the GMO conversation" are unfortunately completely unaware of the methods used to modify formerly naturally-occurring organisms into something entirely different and hardly natural. The World Health Organization defines GMOs as "organisms in which the genetic material (DNA) has been altered in such a way that does not occur naturally." Excerpts from the American Association of Environmental Medicine's website provide a startling glimpse into the creation of today's Frankenstein GM crops:

"This technology is also referred to as 'genetic engineering,' 'biotechnology,' or 'recombinant DNA technology' and consists of randomly inserting genetic fragments of DNA from one organism to another, usually from a different species. For example, an artificial combination of genes that includes a gene to produce the pesticide Cry1Ab protein (commonly known as Bt toxin), originally found in Bacillus thuringiensis, is inserted in to the DNA of corn randomly."

"I am not sure about you, but I am not at all comfortable with the notion of bacterial DNA being inserted into my food without my knowledge or consent -- not as a medical professional or a mother.

"Are They Safe?

"An often-dismissed argument in the battle over labeling GM products is the simple, yet extremely consequential, question of whether or not these modified "Frankenfoods" are safe for human consumption. The powerful agricultural lobby will tell you that these foods are safe because of their "substantial equivalence" to the original, natural, version."

****

As I said for openers on this subject, I was aware of this subject when it came to my attention that Californians are trying to get a bill passed that GMOs must be labeled as such, which, they obviously are not now so labeled. Unfortunately, the book was halfway out the door to meet our printers' deadline, so I really don't have time to research this subject properly. Therefore, I just dipped a toe in the Internet and copied the above material. This is something that I am sure we will be hearing a lot more about. Indeed it is controversial; there are always two sides to every argument, however. I hope I have at least given those of you who are also uninformed as I am a jumping off place to find out more about this subject. I apologize for the meager treatment of what has to be a huge issue facing us re the foods on our table every day.

CHAPTER SEVEN

Let's Get Physical

We shall come to feel all the consciousness of the physical world as one with our physical consciousness, feel all the energies of the cosmic life around us as our own energies.

Patrizia Norelli-Bachelet

Let's Get Physical

There exists such a deeply entrenched mindset in Western cultures to divorce the physical from commonly held perceptions of the spiritual that it is critical to understand that the two are inseparable Siamese twins. Everything is spiritual. Is there anything that is not part of God's creation?

This disconnection from the physical body is a particularly dangerous dissociation in regard to lightbody work! Every emotion, every memory, every subconscious pattern, in other words, every *thing* is energy and possesses consciousness. Furthermore, everything resides in the body somewhere. Maybe it lives in an organ, maybe in one of the chakra centers. We are talking about hair, blood and bone here.

Body is in the word lightbody and should be taken literally. Transformations very much embrace the physical body. The core of the work that we are writing about in the TECHNOLOGY OF ASCENSCION SERIES concerns the physical body changing into the lightbody. A whole new paradigm of the physical body is being created. Religious teachings have given us this preconceived belief that we must leave the physical body to journey to a better place—a Heaven—or to some different place. Ascension can take place on the physical plane just by raising the consciousness. *We can choose to stay in the physical body and ascend.* However, it must be the *transformed* physical body.

Some people do not want to ascend if they must take their physical body with them because they think it is ugly, fat, unhealthy or otherwise repugnant. There is so much confusion about this. If you are unsure about this, maybe you should read again the material about activations. That is what the activations are all about. You will be unable to ascend to the higher frequencies unless you are in your *lightbody*, and the lightbody knows no illness. Furthermore, the process of activating additional DNA strands reverses the aging process. Maybe the best selling point I have here is that most people will take on the appearance of a youthful and vigorous 35 year old!

We need to remind ourselves that we came here to have a body experience. After an extensive study of ascension literature, I believe that the physicality of Earth is unique.

In fact, channeled messages from advanced souls often express envy that we are capable of physical experiences not available elsewhere.

In our spiritual pursuits, we have abdicated certain aspects of the physical body. Tiara Kumara, on behalf of Children of the Sun Humanitarian Foundation, channeled the following messages from Mother Gaia. Access The Children of the Sun website at info@childrenofthesun.org. This powerful organization is one of the most reliable—and exciting—sources for channeled information relating to ascension.

> "We have tried to lighten our selves for some time. This has been the spiritual teaching: to lighten up, to perhaps even to leave the body by forsaking certain foods or habits...I believe we need to move our attention from our higher chakras to the Root and Sacral chakras. This is where we begin to manifest ideas into form...to bring creation into form—to bring Heaven to Earth.
>
> "...I'm seeing now that many people, even vegans, are being called to eat meat, or at least root vegetables, just in order to ground themselves back in the body."

A Body Anybody? Georgia's Story

Georgia found my website on the Internet and contacted me. She recounted her long history of grappling with several seemingly intractable issues in her life. She and her husband were in their early retirement years. She feared that time was running out if she were ever to resolve these matters and get on with her life. I accepted her as one of my shamanic healing cases, and off we went on a journey of discovery.

Her list of insurmountable troubles included deep fears about having enough money to see her through the retirement years. Her fears were exacerbated because this was in 2008, after her stock portfolio headed south big time. She was not opposed to getting a part-time job, but complained that her energy levels were so low, it was all but an impossible option.

The next thing bugging her was the state of absolute chaos in her house. This apparently was a source of considerable consternation every day. She suffered from allergies and described her body reactions to the dust bunnies under the bed. Yet, she pleaded a lack of the energy required to tackle into the overwhelming task of setting her house in order.

The last major disappointment was that she never had a passion in life. She called it "that spark." As I proceeded to work with her, I realized that her expectation was that somehow I would use my kit bag of shamanic tricks to make it all go away. However, every time I questioned her, she always said, "Nothing has changed." I wondered just where all the healing energy was going. It was harder and harder for me to maintain a cool attitude; I wanted to tear my hair out from frustration.

Someone did appear on the scene and was willing to help her with the house and yard work. However, she was so tired she lacked the energy to utilize the helper for more than a couple of hours. Throughout this time, she asked me to investigate past lives, to do a sweeping ancestral clearing, to identify invading entities, to do yet another soul retrieval or any other psychic healing "trick."

Have You Guessed The Problem?

You may have guessed the obvious here. SHE WAS SICK. I am sharing this with you because—believe it or not—it typifies many other cases that I have dealt with over the years. In Georgia's case, there was a further little twist that revealed just how far out of touch she was with her physical body. I naturally pressured her to see a doctor. Husband Don had psychically diagnosed profound adrenal exhaustion and a laundry list of other very real ailments. There wasn't much doubt that I was on solid ground in regarding this case as one that was presenting as a physical problem.

She replied to my urgings to see a physician with, "I have spent thousands of dollars over many years on doctors. They never found anything, so I can't be sick." Here was a woman who was literally so exhausted that she could hardly lift the proverbial finger. She clearly suffered any number of troublesome physical symptoms. Yet, she was in denial that *physical* problems were the source of her troubles, regardless of the medical opinions.

Georgia did what I have observed in many clients. She beat herself up every day. She suffered from an overwhelming guilt about how she had mismanaged her life. According to her, she was a lazy, good-for-nothing failure at everything. According to her thinking, "There must be some terrible past life karma. It must be those messages from my mother."

It sometimes never occurs to people who are out of touch with the body that they are *physically* ill; that's the problem. I have also observed this more frequently now that we have ascension symptoms to deal with. It is time to seriously accept with what the physical body must cope as the frequencies change it into the lightbody. This requires more rest than usual. We can't keep our noses to the grindstone like we once did. There will be necessary time-outs, some times for days, even weeks. The transition into the lightbody produces symptoms of every sort; it ain't easy.

One last thing, allopathic doctors often completely overlook certain problems—even severe problems—especially those that respond to dietary changes, nutritional supplements and other natural and alternative modalities.

The Universe, on the other hand, is all-knowing and fully capable of sending an unmistakable message. Sometimes only the most spiritually sensitive lightworkers or shaman receive the information, however. The advice is frequently unmistakably about the physical body. I can share one example that cast me as the very reluctant protagonist. This story may well discourage those who beg me to teach them to be a shaman. Sometimes it is a very dirty business.

It was the time leading up to Harmonic Concordance.

Intestinal Cleansing Is The Next Step.

The following article is the way my newsletter readers received the news that they were to do intestinal cleanses before Harmonic Concordance. First, let me tell you how *I* found out we needed to purge. I found out the shamanic way, which is not always the most pleasant of experiences; however, you will see that the message was impossible to ignore. When the Universe wants to send me an unmistakably graphic message, for this shaman, once was enough!

You may recall that in the chapters on preparing for Harmonic Concordance, I was hit with horrific gallbladder attacks, attacks which sent messages that everybody should do cleanses in preparation for the big day. You should also recall that I requested that my guides find a less painful way in which to send this reminder. The following was their response. Not funny, guys.

My husband and I went out for Sunday brunch one sunny summer morning. I sort of needed to go to the bathroom but we were just getting ready to leave the restaurant, so I decided to wait until I got home: huge mistake. Home was twenty miles away and it turned out to be the trip from hell. You've seen the TV commercial, "You gotta go. You gotta go right now!" I screamed. I cried. I prayed to every deity in all of creation. I cursed. I beseeched every god ever known to man. I did not want to have "something nasty" happen in the car. I begged my husband to go 200 miles an hour. It was excruciating. I was barely hanging on through sheer will alone.

When we were a block from home, I screamed that I would never make it to the house. I ordered Don to rush into the garage and grab the yellow plastic bucket—fast. I suffered the ultimate humiliation over a plastic bucket in broad daylight in the middle of the driveway. (The neighbors directly across the street were throwing a backyard barbecue for their church.) That is how I received the guidance that an intestinal cleanse was part of the preparations for Harmonic Concordance. Does that qualify for giving one's all for God and country?

It took only a few days before synchronicity kicked in and confirmed that we indeed needed to do the intestinal cleanses to prepare for the new vibrations. Metaphysical sites on the Internet were awash with the news. I'll bet the messages did not come to *them* in such a compromising manner!

Other confirmations arrived shortly after I published my newsletter account of the Yellow Bucket Adventure. Letters from several other readers documented amazingly similar experiences. The only difference was: They made it to the bathroom. Does this mean that I am the "Head" shaman? (Sorry, I just couldn't resist that.) When inquiring of their guides what these particularly gross events meant, each one who wrote to me received the same answer: DO A CLEANSE! (To search on the Internet, type in "cleanses" or "intestinal or liver cleanses.")

Letters of Confirmation

I think it seems more real when I receive letters of confirmation. I just love hearing from the other lightworkers. The following letters arrived shortly after my newsletter went out, documenting the brutal way the powers-that-be alerted me in no uncertain terms that we needed to do cleanses in preparation for Harmonic Concordance.

> "I absolutely love your newsletter. I have to admit I just had one of the same episodes of needing a cleanse. Last Saturday I screamed and broke out into a sweat. My poor husband. He couldn't drive fast enough. I will be looking forward to the cleanse information. I'm on board with whatever it takes."
> J.M.

And on the heels of that one, this next one arrived:

> "As always, your newsletter was right on the money. My husband and I have been doing…work around activating the lightbody…I often find the physical symptoms you report are the ones I have been experiencing…The idea that anything we keep repeating is an addiction is brilliant. I am working with the Light Body Affirmations for cells and food daily now…The other thing is regarding intestinal cleansing. I almost fell out of my chair when I read your experience because I had something similar happen to me…My husband and I went to one of our favorite restaurants…on our way home about halfway through a 40-minute drive, I was suddenly in excruciating discomfort…Luckily I just made it into the house. When I asked my guides what that was all about, they said, "cleanse!"…just thought I would share and tell you how much I appreciate what you are doing."
>
> M.G-B.

What If There Is No Neighborhood Shaman Around?

It is all well and good if there is a local shaman around on every corner who is willing and able to tell you precisely what your body needs to stay well. That is not going to happen. So are you left in the vulnerable position in which terrible things can be occurring in your body completely outside of your awareness? I understand that colon cancer can rage through your body, but you won't feel a thing. Once diagnosed, it is often too late. There are other silent killers that can strike you down without warning; diabetes, heart attack, strokes and many others. Some may not kill you but are serious health problems requiring medical attention.

You Need To "speak body"

But maybe your body *is* talking to you. Perhaps the information *is* actually readily available at all times. I understand that medical intuitives are retrieving very specific diagnoses for their clients. We know it is out there, and it just so happens that this is a subject about which my husband and I are experts.

A simple technique accurately reveals in exquisite detail exactly what is going on in your body. Furthermore, this method also identifies with surprising accuracy just what is required to restore health. By this I mean that an entire picture of nutritional supplements for example is available, including specific ones in specific amounts. The information is out there for everyone. Traditional medicine practitioners do not utilize this technique nor do they know about it in most cases, or believe it in the first place if they do know about it. Neither do the majority of *alternative* practitioners utilize this in their practices, even though I would say that most of them are familiar with it.

Before I explain the details, allow me to dance on the table and thump my chest in unbridled enthusiasm for this information. The lack of widespread use of this technique is a flat-out crime, and the results are needless suffering and illness. Not only are we talking about needless suffering; it is indeed the difference between life and death for some people and in some cases.

What I am referring to is *kinesiology*, or muscle testing. When my husband was in practice at his chiropractic clinic, he used muscle testing with all of his patients. This will explain precisely how your body communicates with you. First, I will briefly describe the method of muscle testing that husband Don uses. Another more commonly used technique is exhaustively covered in a book by David K. Hawkins *Power vs. Force.* I recommend it. It should be in everybody's library for many other reasons as well.

Now that I have brought Hawkins's book to your attention, this reminds me of the most amazing example of synchronicity providing confirmation of some really far-out psychic information that my bother, Duane, brought through. I am referring to a very detailed description of a specific area on Arcturus, part of which includes a giant crystal in a lake, and even the dimensions of the lake were given. I mean it when I say that it was a *very* detailed picture.

Duane and I were sitting with IVs in our arms receiving chelation therapy, of all things, when Duane whispered for me to take a look at a passage in Hawkins's book, which he was reading at the time. I thought my eyes were deceiving me, honest to God. Hawkins had written *exactly the same* description of this particular locale on Arcturus down to every last detail. You'll see it if you read the book. It's not that I doubted my brother's channeling but confirmations of that order are hard to come by, and really help to reassure us that our psychic work is real. It helps keep the doubting left brain in line!

Now back to the subject at hand, but I couldn't resist that little detour. Be aware that Don uses a technique that is not really practical for laypeople. (That comes later.) Here is the protocol. His patients lie on their backs on the examining table. Don sits at their feet on a chair facing them. First, he makes certain that their heels are even. Then he introduces a toxic substance into their field by placing it on the body. This causes nearly imperceptible body-wide muscle spasming.

That is the body saying *no.* It registers in a leg-length change that is apparent to the eye. One leg actually pulls up—sometimes an inch or two—more than the other. Remove the toxic substance, and the body relaxes and the legs are even again. Understand that I am saying that the toxic substance is introduced into the energy field only by placing it on the body. It could be anything toxic like ant poison or whatever. It is not actually ingested.

This Method Is For The Pros.

This particular method is best left in the hands of the professional practitioners. There are certain protocols that exceed casual use. Then there is simply the practical matter that most people do not have an examining table at home in the first place on which others may lie to do the test. I will discuss an alternate method later that you may try at home.

I would rather focus on the astonishing information that is available literally at our fingertips. Here are some examples. When a patient required chiropractic adjustments, Don would "ask feet" about the precise position of each individual vertebra. Not only does this identify which ones are misaligned but exactly how they are misaligned. One may be tilted down and to the right and so on.

Believe me; this is profoundly more precise than what may be determined by hand palpation alone. In less than fifteen minutes, a precise picture of the spine emerges as detailed as any x-ray. From that it is obvious exactly what spinal corrections are needed. Don was a specialist in spinal adjustments, and it was largely because of this protocol. In fact, my low back owes him a debt of gratitude!

Some patients suffered from severe hormonal imbalances. You women that have endured night sweats and the urge to burn down your neighbor's house know what that is like. Any gland that is in trouble—whether under- or over-active—presents a clinical picture on which a specific therapy may be based.

By a specific therapy, this is just how specific it is. There are families of supplements designed not only to treat symptoms of say, thyroid deficiency, but rather to rebuild the gland over time. The tests determine exactly the dose for each gland. Perhaps the patient needs three tablets twice a day. Periodic testing reveals that the dose drops to less and less. Eventually the body will report that it does not need this particular treatment any longer. It is healed.

One particular protocol brings a great deal of peace of mind to me personally. The body reports whether even a single cell in the body is changing from benign to malignant. This red flags cancer at the very earliest stages. I trust this enough to put my life on the line. I no longer get pap tests or mammograms. DO NOT DO THIS YOURSELF. Only the most experienced practitioners should ever be trusted in such a serious matter as this. I am only making a point.

Not only does the body talk to you about yourself, it will also tell you about anybody else. I have many times lain on the examining table as a surrogate for another person. They do not have to be present. Sometimes the person lives in another country. Or maybe it is for a baby that is too young for ordinary testing. Take note animal lovers, oh, yes! We can test your pet. Don can do a complete examination for the other person (or animal) using my body as the surrogate, and the readings will be totally different from mine.

A Word To The Wise!

Be careful with this one. I know how to protect my energy field before Don projects the other person's energy onto mine. I got into deep trouble one time when I carelessly forgot to shield myself. I had just received a scary telephone call that my dad back in Iowa had suffered a severe heart attack. He was in intensive care.

I took off for Don's office. He did a surrogate test on me to identify what my father needed so that I could mail it to him. I left Don's office, but I got no further than a couple of blocks before I knew I was in trouble. Luckily, I was able to pull onto a grocery store parking lot. Gasping for breath, I fell over onto the front seat.

It was only by superhuman will that I was able to drive myself back to Don's office. In all of the excitement, I had recklessly taken on my dad's energy. I found out what it feels like to have a heart attack! I was not in pain, but my energy was totally drained. Don cleared me, but I was done for the rest of that day. From then on, I have never forgotten to protect myself.

You CAN Do This At Home.

The more typical method of muscle testing uses the arms rather than the feet. Have the "patient" stand up facing you. They will fully extend one arm out level with their shoulder. Their arm is not up, not down, not forward, not back. It is level with their shoulder and level to the ground. You could hang a pail on the end of their arm.

With one hand, and using just your first two fingers on top of their wrist, try to push their arm down a few inches. Gauge how strong their resistance is to prevent their arm from moving. Try it several times. Each time they will resist as hard as they can. Don't overdo it. A quick push is all that is needed. This is not a wrestling match. Do not break their arm.

Now take something like one of those little packets of real sugar like you find in restaurants. Place it at the base of their throat. You are about to find out just how bad sugar is for you. When you push on their arm again, it will drop like limp spaghetti.

Many more people are using muscle testing in many more ways than I can include here. Unfortunately, there are many more people misusing it, also. Here are some precautions. Do not use muscle testing to predict the future. It can't. The subconscious may give you an answer all right, but it is just making it up to please you.

It is also important to remember that some of your own personal hang-ups can influence the answer. To do any really serious work along these lines, you need to always keep yourself cleared and objective as in any psychic or healing activity.

How To Use The Pendulum

My experience with this sort of thing is extensive, although most of my work is with the pendulum. The principle is the same. It also has the advantage that it is a one-person show. You can do it for yourself or anybody else anytime, as long as you have the pendulum with you.

I have used the pendulum at the organic grocery store to choose the different produce that is the ripest and the best. I am usually rewarded with the ripest cantaloupes, for example. If there is questionable food left in the refrigerator perhaps a bit too long, I test before I keel over from food poisoning. In fact, this is a good way to learn how to test your proficiency utilizing the pendulum. Choose some food that you are willing to sacrifice for this test. What you want to do is purposely let a food go really bad. That is why I suggest fish over caviar. (Who has caviar in their fridge anyway?) Set out some fresh food like new crisp celery on your kitchen counter. Then set out some food that is moldy or otherwise obviously unfit for consumption. Then ask the pendulum if either one is safe or desirable to eat. These are just a couple of examples; there are many more uses for pendulum work.

You can make a pendulum using a string about eight to ten inches long tied to a nut or bolt. The nut should have some weight to it. Or you can buy a fancy pendulum. Many New Age-type stores will have them. In an emergency, I have simply used the necklace that I was wearing at the time. You Virgos may prefer the nut and string, leaving the bling to your Leo zodiac mates.

Individuals who practice as healers should make an absolute commitment to clear out their personal baggage as much as possible. Nobody must necessarily be squeaky clean, but short of that, there is plenty of fodder for the gristmill of consciousness. There are too many cases wherein healers project their own unresolved issues onto clients. I’ve heard my share of stories.

This is also something to be aware of when you learn to use the pendulum. Remember, everything comes through your own subconscious. Elsewhere in this book ("Catastrophobia"), I recount the story of Rhonda. Her pendulum provided explicit details of a proposed scheme, allegedly from her guides. The elaborate plan involved investment advice, storage of food and other lengthy preparations for the coming catastrophe. I was appalled. If she had proceeded with these plans it would have been a catastrophe all right!

Learning To Develop Psychic Skills

I have trained many students in my Huna classes how to use the pendulum. This is what you do. You will need six little boxes, all identical. I used black plastic boxes about two inches square that I found at my neighborhood pharmacy. They were pillboxes.

To begin, you will hold the string or chain tied to the pendulum between thumb and forefinger and ask it to swing one way for yes, and the other way—vertically or horizontally—for no. Stick to the same protocol every time. Start out with two boxes. Place a cotton ball in one box. Shake them in a sack so that you can’t know which is which. Then place them on a table in front of you. Hold the pendulum over each, one at a time. Ask the pendulum to identify which box holds the cotton ball. Just hold the pendulum over one box and say, "Is the cotton ball in this box?" Wait for an answer. Be patient. There is no need to rush. And don't curse if its wrong. I actually enraged my pendulum once. It's a long story. Anyway, it flung itself in circles so wildly that the trinket on the end came off and flew across the room. I have two eye witnesses. They will corroborate this story, but they never begged me to do pendulum work again.

You will continue as you use more and more boxes holding more and more items. When you progress to using all six boxes and identifying different items like buttons and paper clips in each, you will have earned your Ph.D. in pendulum.

For advanced work, start moving the little boxes farther away from you. My shamanic healing work almost exclusively deals with clients at a distance. By moving the boxes farther and farther away from you, it telegraphs the idea to the subconscious that psychic work is just as effective at a distance as it is close at hand. I eventually placed the boxes outside of my house completely out of sight.

I discovered that the subconscious is very encouraged and cooperative when rewarded for successes. Not surprisingly, Hershey's chocolate kissers did the trick for me. Again, *do not ask the pendulum (your subconscious) to predict the future.* The subconscious cannot predict the future. It *will* predict the future, but it is just making it up to please you. Used with intelligence and common sense, your psychic functioning will flourish in a safe and controlled manner.

Normally I do not encourage using psychic tools for mere parlor tricks. It is too easy to drift off course and the next thing you know, someone has gotten themselves in over their heads. However, I was introduced to a trick with the pendulum when I was about twelve years old. For the life of me, I cannot remember where I learned this. Maybe I read it somewhere, but more likely, I came across someone who demonstrated it to me.

All I know for sure is that I played the game in all innocence. I amused myself no end at the expense of my "victims," many of whom failed to appreciate an annoying kid. I certainly never suspected then just how powerful a role the pendulum would play in my life many years later.

This is how it worked. I took a hair from a cooperative person's head and tied it to a ring. For the ring, I wore a simple silver band. This procedure was limited to anyone whose hair was at least six or seven inches long. I learned to master the dexterity required to knot the hair around the ring. That's right; you have to tie one end of the hair to the ring.

The next step was to fill a glass about three-fourths full of water. Then, I held the end of the hair and lowered the ring so that it was just above, but not touching, the water. The trick was that the ring would tap out the person's age on the side of the glass. And it worked every time! For a twelve-year-old girl, this was irresistible magic for sure! However, my mother's lady friends did not particularly appreciate my public announcements that "Mildred is 52 years old," right in the middle of their Bridge game.

This trick earned me a free hamburger from time to time. Occasionally, when I was out late, I would stop by some hole-in-the-wall hamburger joint. If there were no other customers, I'd sit at the counter and schmooz with the waitress until I weaseled out a bet that I could perform my magic trick and guess her age for a free burger. When I turned out to be right, I think I got the free burger for fear I was some sort of witch with even worse tricks up my sleeve!

I do not use the pendulum anymore. My little inner self is now to the place were I communicate with it directly. It is insulted now when I resort to the pendulum. This should not be surprising after 40 years and work with hundreds of healing clients. In fact, little self (whom I call Susie Jane) really has developed an attitude about it. She is cranky now when I use the pendulum. If I press the issue, it is somehow arranged that I can't find my car keys for several days.

Muscle Testing With The Daisy Chain *O*-Ring Method

Another technique you can use for muscle testing has the advantage of allowing you to fly solo. You can employ this method by yourself wherever you are because you carry the "equipment" with you—your own two hands. I love this method. I use it for deciding what my body wants from the menu to serious medical decisions. Try it right now yourself.

First make an *O* by touching your thumb and first finger together. Make another *O* with the other hand, only this time interlock it within the first *O*. It's like an interlocking chain in a daisy chain. Or if you are old enough, remember the construction paper chains you made for the Christmas tree?

Next, ask yourself a question to which you know the answer like, "Is my name Bob?" Now pull one thumb and finger against the *O* on the other hand. Against the pressure, try to keep both *O*'s interlocked. If your name really is Bob, the fingers will stay tightly locked in place. If your name is not Bob, the fingers will go limp like they did in arm testing. You can slide the fingers of one hand easily out of the loop when the answer is negative.

It takes practice to get the feel for it. Be sure you observe a set of consistent protocols. You need to know what yes or no means. At first, experiment with questions that you know is right or wrong. If you can, check your results out with another system or another person. I caution you again; do not attempt to predict the future.

I suffer from food sensitivities. If I tangle with the wrong food, I pay the price with a couple of day's worth of increased arthritic pain. When I eat out, I can't be sure exactly what may be in any given dish. Canned foods contain additives not always listed on the label, potato starch to name one common offender. Potatoes do not like me.

On a more serious note, my doctor suspected some internal bleeding. This called for testing, including a colonoscopy and endoscopy. The tests themselves hold no particular horror for me. However, the vat of a special liquid drink that I was required to ingest the several days before, rendered me violently ill. Watch the Center for Disease Control. By the time I am through describing the evils of preparing for colonoscopies in my newsletters, the statistics for colon cancer will be off the charts. Okay, not really. The point I make is this: The tests were negative. The doctor found no sign of bleeding. This then called for another separate procedure to examine the small intestine. It also meant another prep nightmare, and that I was not about to do.

I hauled out the reliable *O*-trick and inquired of my small intestine as to whether it had a bleeding problem. I wish I had done that before the other tests. However, this provided an advantage when I asked fingers about the large intestine by already knowing the answer. It provided a good check. The fingers said there was no bleeding in the small intestine. That was good enough for me. Before anybody asks serious questions of a medical nature or otherwise, it should be after long practice and cross-checking results. Use common sense! I'm just illustrating a point.

Through the physical body lies access to the vast reservoir of information to which your subconscious is privy. Lightbeings must get out of their heads and mine the resources of the vast sea of consciousness to utilize the intuition. That is the royal road to heaven.

Dangerous Territory: The Ouija Board

Talk of the pendulum almost certainly turns to other psychic devices, one of which is the Ouija board. The answer to that is simple. Don't do it. I messed around with the Ouija board years ago. I escaped serious psychic consequences only by a lucky fluke.

The board led to automatic writing. That led to an entity that became aggressive, taking over my hand and demanding that I write. I was utterly naïve but aware that the situation was getting out of hand. About that time, I attended a lecture at the St. Louis Theosophical Society of which I was a member. It happened that Geoffrey Hodson, a famous theosophist, was the speaker. I managed to wheedle a short audience with him.

I received a short course about the pitfalls of the psychic world. I have never forgotten what he told me. It resolved my immediate circumstances as well as standing me in good stead throughout my future psychic work. I shudder to think what might have happened had it not been for his generous intervention. I certainly relate to the panic my clients feel when entities are taking over.

We may be aware of psychic material whose source is automatic writing and reject it out of hand. Two examples remind us that there are exceptions. Two that I know of are: Ruth Montgomery's books and *A Course in Miracles.* Each is generally acknowledged as valuable and legitimate contributions to spiritual/metaphysical literature. However, my advice is that you had better see wise men coming over the hills from the East before you take your automatic writing seriously.

The subject of this book is about preparing for ascension. It's best to focus on this goal when using the tools I discussed in this chapter. Consider that these helpers, used properly, grant us access to vast oceans of information and guidance far beyond the limitations of the five senses. It is nothing but foolishness to implement them for anything less.

Dowsing

Dowsing is something with which I was familiar from my very earliest recollections as a child living on a farm in Iowa. My dad was a water dowser. Dowsing was routinely used to locate where to drill a well for water on farms. It is easy to overlook the fact that in earlier times to the present, farm households don't simply turn on the tap to access city water systems. Therefore, dowsing was part of the rural culture dating from earliest pioneer days.

Dowsing traditionally used a branch cut from a tree, one shaped like a *Y.* It needed to be about a yard or so in length from one end to the other. The branch need not be more than an inch or two in circumference. We are not talking about a log. The dowser grasps the two ends of the *Y* section, wrapping the hands around from underneath. The straight stem of the *Y* is pointed *toward* the body, not away from it and at about waist kevel.

The dowser holds the intention to dowse for water, as it can be used to locate other things underground like minerals, lost items at the beach under sand, or if you are lucky, a gold mine or a genie in a jar. Joking aside, a little known fact is that dowsers are used to patrol the Alaskan oil pipeline for leaks. Dowsing would be effective finding land mines, but the problem with that is that you have to blow yourself up to do it. Seriously, we may be surprised where dowsing has been used for a variety of things, even by the government and/or in times of war.

The dowser walks back and forth across an area where there may be water. When water is located, there is no question about it. The tail end of the stick begins to pull downward. It pulls the hardest exactly where the water is. Just try to prevent the stick from pulling downward. I am not joking when I report that it literally twists the outer skin from the branch if you fight against the pull.

I was eleven years old. At the supper table, I smugly announced that the science book at school said that water dowsing was an old wives' tale. In most households, this comment probably would have passed completely unnoticed. However, my dad enjoyed a countywide reputation as a water dowser. Furthermore, the countryside was dotted with windmills located at precisely the spot on which the willow switch in Dad's hands had indicated. That included the windmill that graced the hill on our own farmstead itself!

Dad silently arose from the supper table and ambled out to one of the trees in the yard. He pulled out his jack knife and cut a forked twig. He called me out. He handed me the forked stick and pointed to our large front yard that stretched from the farmhouse to the highway. "There is an old well buried out there. Find it," he commanded. With that, he returned to his interrupted supper.

I methodically traversed the yard back and forth for a time with no action from the forked stick. A creeping paranoia brought some very dark suspicions to my mind. I could see my family standing behind the window curtains laughing their guts out at this stupid kid walking around with a forked stick looking for an old abandoned well that probably never existed in the first place. Before I was completely overwhelmed with doubt, the stick came alive. I tried to hold it steady. However, the force that tugged it downward was so powerful that it literally *did* skin the bark from the branch.

I ran screaming to the house to ask my mother if I had indeed located the old overgrown water well. I asked Mom, not Dad, because she never lied. She was incapable of pulling off a lie. It's a skill that was not in her DNA. My dad, on the other hand, was wise but wily; you were never quite sure which way the wind was blowing with him. Mom not only confirmed the location of the old well, but also nostalgically recalled how many times in the old days that my grandmother had fetched pails of water from the old well to heat on the cook stove to do the washing. (This may be a good time to genuflect before your automatic washer.)

That was the pivotal moment on which turned my curious and independent mindset, thereby setting my feet onto the road less traveled. I journeyed along all of the alternative and nontraditional information highways finding WHAT WORKED, even though sixth grade primers say it is all old wives' tales. Oh, yes, I should mention one other thing. Back in Benton County, Iowa, in the 1950s, I was recognized as a second-generation water dowser.

In recent times the forked stick has been replaced by bent coat hangars, an L-rod and other devices. It is more cumbersome, of course, but its reactions are not only to water. Skilled dowsers can secure an astonishing variety of information. Map dowsing has been used, for example, to locate missing persons and animals. The dowsers actually dowse a map of an area. Pendulums work for this purpose also. Check out the Internet if you think you may have a calling. There are books and organizations open to the budding dowser.

The Grand Daddy Of Them All.

Once one has mastered any of the techniques outlined in this chapter, any one of them can stand you in good stead when the goal is communicating with the physical body or environment. You could very well use them the rest of your life and do just fine. However, a disciplined and consistent practice with any one of these will continue to deepen your intuitive sense. The ultimate goal is to abandon all of the tools, such as the pendulum, the *O* ring method or kinesiology, and learn to communicate with any part of the body directly. It means devoting yourself to developing your innate psychic abilities.

Perhaps it is only aspiring healers and shaman who are motivated to function at this level. However, it is available to anyone for whatever reason. At this point in my shamanic work, I simply work psychically with any body part. I have mastered "body-speak," so to speak. I can dialogue with the liver specifically, or any other organ or body part with which I need to communicate. The trick is to believe your body when it speaks to you. You will remember the story of the coffee chronicles when a whole group of my newsletter readers got the message that coffee was good for them, and months before the research reports first hit the stands at that!

That is the lesson I learned in the following story:

POPCORN POWER

The little, lowly kernel that holds the secret to instant, sudden and explosive personal transformation into a different form! Betcha you can't do it.

I was born in Iowa, which is known as the corn state. Look at the auto license plates. That does not refer to a state of mind. The governor of Iowa suggested that as the slogan on the Iowa license plates one year. "A State of Mind" was just a little too esoteric for Midwesterners, who hooted it into oblivion. No, I was raised around fields of green corn stalks that I could see in every direction everywhere I went.

I was born in a little county seat town, Vinton, Iowa. The semi long-haul truckers' CB radio handle for Vinton was Popcorn City. Furthering the influence of corn in my environment was an uncle who raised popcorn, ensuring that we always had gunny sackfuls whenever my family had a yen for our favorite treat on a snowy night.

Popcorn Is In My DNA!

I never gave it much thought, except it did impress me when my mother sent me a box of popcorn balls—my absolute favorite—when I lay in my University Student Health hospital room recovering from an extracted wisdom tooth which had become infected. My roommate enjoyed them with my other dormmates. Mom's recipe was unequaled. Mom is no longer with us, God rest her soul. But my brother has kept up the tradition, and whomps up a batch once in a while. I notice that this frequency has increased now that he has a girl friend.

I may as well quit beating around the bush and tell you what all this business about popcorn is leading up to. It has nothing to do with the above stories, so just ignore them. The story that I want to share with you is one that began about two years from this writing.. Up until that time, I never ate popcorn. I did not think about popcorn. About that time, husband Don was hospitalized. I was cared for by caregivers who stayed with me around the clock. One of the girls went grocery shopping and happened to pick up some popcorn. That evening she asked me if I would like some popcorn while we watched a movie together. That was the beginning of what was to become my present addiction to popcorn.

When Don came home from the hospital, I asked him to buy some popcorn the next time he went to the grocery store, which he did. The two of us began to enjoy a popcorn treat more and more frequently. I harbored some doubts about the effects of this habit on my health, but it wasn't enough of a concern to quit. The only real objection Don raised was that the particular popcorn I was using had additives and was prepared in the microwave. He decided that if I were to continue my popcorn habit, at least we should start with uncontaminated kernels and popped in a pan on the stove. He was graciously willing to do this, and I had no objection either.

I began to hear what I thought were clear messages that my body wanted me to eat popcorn! The messages were in the firm of cravings for the little, puffy, white clouds. When I first received this message from my body to eat popcorn, synchronicity went off the charts. Every single day I saw popcorn mentioned on TV at least once in some way. Usually someone would say, "popcorn" on TV or the radio. My husband grew weary of me screaming, "popcorn," every time it was mentioned. I saw print ads for popcorn in obscure places as well. Despite doubts, I just **knew** that I was getting confirmations that I should continue eating popcorn.

But I still harbored secret doubts about whether this was such a good idea, health wise. My husband, a retired health care practitioner and recent heart surgery patient, had his doubts, but also could not overlook my many confirmations, which he has seen happen in my life for 25 years. So my popcorn addiction continued unabated. I have mentioned elsewhere that I like the medical reporter's column in The ENQUIRER. I could hardly believe my eyes when my copy arrived in the mail featuring an article about popcorn as America's most nutritious snack. It went on to report on the latest research that analyzed the various things in popcorn that were good for you. **I was triumphant!**

Not long after that, another report was printed, but sorry to say, I cannot remember the source of this particular article. The gist of it, however, mimicked The

ENQUIRER's article and even went a step further in its rave about popcorn's virtues as a nutritious snack. **I was crowing once again about my popcorn story!**

Because of a variety of health issues, my excellent doctor orders a series of blood tests every three or four months. I got my wings clipped about one month ago when I went to his office to discuss the results. I got the shock of my life. Since Don underwent heart surgery two years ago, we thought we were doing pretty well. Not so! The doctor informed me that I was pre-diabetic, and put both of us on a strict zero carb diet for 90 days. Popcorn is primarily carbohydrates, no doubt about it. **How could my body get it so wrong? And how could all those confirming coincidences about seeing popcorn at every turn be so wrong? I believe in all that synchronicity stuff.** How could this be so wrong, so misleading. I was devastated, absolutely crushed. It was like there was no God.

Vindication. I Never Doubted It.

We changed our eating habits and religiously followed the diet the doctor gave us. We put the popcorn away. He gave us a book that indicated the glycemic load of many common foods. The glycemic index ranks foods based on their ability to raise blood sugar levels. High glycemic index foods cause a rapid rise in blood sugar levels, just what I did *not* want.

One day I sat down at my computer after following the diet for about a month. I opened my email. I receive any number of health newsletters. What do I see screaming at me but an article by Emily Creasy, who holds a Master of Science degree from James Madison University. Below is the screaming headline:

IS POPCORN LOW GLYCEMIC?

Under those searing headlines was this following quote:

> "Popcorn is a low calorie snack food that can help you maintain a healthy weight ***along with healthy blood sugar levels.*** Nearly 20 percent of the carbohydrate contained in popcorn comes from fiber. Fiber is important in promoting regular bowel habits, heart health ***and balanced blood sugar levels. Popcorn is one of many low glycemic index foods <u>that can be included in both a regular and diabetic diet</u>. According to the Glycemic Index Foundation, popcorn is considered to be a low glycemic index food. Popcorn also has a low glycemic load, meaning that it contains a small amount of carbohydrate."***

I never doubted that my body was wrong. Synchronicity could not be wrong. The only reason I typed that other stuff was because my fingers were slippery from the butter on the popcorn and I hit the wrong keys. Would I lie?

Are You Contributing Positive Energy To The Collective?

In my practice both as an astrologer and a healer, it was not uncommon for clients to express deep frustration with their lives. They harbored a commitment to the spiritual life but felt that they were contributing nothing of that nature to the world. Because this feeling is so widespread, I thought some additional information from David Hawkins's book *Power vs. Force: The Hidden Determinants in Human Behavior* would dispel fears about being a non-contributing member of society. (David Hawkins is the doctor who wrote about kinesiology.)

Hawkins also set up a fascinating system of actually calibrating human consciousness. It is worth the price of the book for this enormously useful Map of Human Consciousness. The numbers on the Scale ranged from zero to infinity (1,000) on the scale). Hawkins's research findings identified 200 on the map as a critical global average for humanity as a whole if life is to be sustained on the planet. In the mid-1980s, the global average climbed above the critical 200 mark. This further confirms the growing shift in consciousness.

Hawkins was forced to resort to the logarithmic values of the numbers because the power of consciousness at higher levels is vast compared to lower levels. For example, a consciousness of 300 is not twice 150; it is 10 to the 300th power, a one with 300 zeros after it. That's a lot of zeros!

As you raise your consciousness level, you actually compensate for people living below the critical 200 mark. How much does it compensate? Let's say that you are functioning at level 300. At that level you have worked through many emotional conflicts, achieved non-judgmental consciousness and are generally optimistic. One person in the global mind operating at level 300 counterbalances 90,000 people below the critical 200 mark.

It is more amazing at the 500 level. This level is where we find unconditional love and forgiveness and an awakened spiritual consciousness. That person counterbalances an awesome 750,000 at the 200 level.. At the 600 level, it is an unbelievable 10 million people who are counterbalanced! So how can you help the world? As you raise your consciousness right where you are, you contribute to the overall quality of the collective. Paradoxically, the greatest service to humanity is the development of your own consciousness. Just imagine the wonderful service to humanity that you can bring to a world starved for spiritual enlightenment. You will change the world.

You can use muscle testing to determine where you are on the Scale of Human Consciousness. The subconscious mind can use kinesiology to answer any question. *It cannot predict the future; don't try it.* You can use it to evaluate any book, movie, person, life problem, historical event, a lecture or any teacher. Don and I tested Duane's and my book *The Lightbody Activation Manual* at 811. Enlightenment is between 700 and 1000. Only the great teachers such as the Buddha or the Christ calibrate at 1000. Our book was the measure of the consciousness of the Pleiadian Beings who gave us the information. When Duane and I lectured at the Huna conference, a guy from New York approached us to tell us that he muscle tested our book at 811!

Use your imagination. Kinesiology gives the subconscious mind a way to by-pass the conscious mind and answer any question. The more you practice it, using the same protocols, the more adept you will become in accessing all knowledge.

Here is a final quote from Hawkins's book:

> "Please note that the procedure is to use the muscle test to verify the truth or falsity of a *declarative statement.* If the question has not been put in this form, unreliable responses will be obtained. For example, 'This book is over 100, over 200, over 300 and so on until there is a negative response.' "

We muscle-tested this book at 659, associated with transcendence, self-realization and god-consciousness. Over 600 transports us to higher levels of consciousness. Hey, numbers don't lie!

To utilize the full scope of muscle testing, it is advisable to purchase Hawkins's book for yourself. He includes many uses that you probably would never think of on your own. There is much more information out there than buying a ripe pear at the fruit stand. If you don't believe that, why not try your hand at some muscle testing right now?

CHAPTER EIGHT

DNA from A to Z

An amazing revolution is coming to the world, one that is both disturbing and liberating.

Richard Zeitgeber
The Matrix (movie)

This is the chapter that nearly never was. There was so much material to organize; I played musical chairs with chapters over and over. Deep in the process of writing this book, I made a rough outline of the chapter "The Invisible Players." That is when it struck me that there was no mention of DNA in that or any other chapters. This omission dawned on me with horror. The core of the ascension process is transforming the physical body into the crystalline lightbody. The key to that process is activating the 12-strand DNA, *a process that my **very own brother** was given by our Pleiadian friends.* Not only that, I actually coauthored a book with him on this very subject and edited a second one.
My next decision was to include DNA as one section of the above-named chapter, "The Invisible Players." Since I really knew next to nothing about DNA no matter how you cut it, I figured I could get by with a nice couple of paragraphs acknowledging its critical role in the larger scheme of things. If I faked it with enough finesse, perhaps you wouldn't notice. So for starters, I consulted Wikipedia to see how to spell out what the letters *DNA* stand for, which is *deoxyribonucleac acid.* As you can see, that did not take me very far. It definitely was time to consult the writing muse.

You remember synchronicity from Alternative Metaphysics 101. Well, that is one universal force that really works for me. I worship at the feet of the god Synchronicity and for that I am rewarded by most favored status. Sure enough, information about DNA began filtering into my world. Presently, there was adequate information for my nice couple of paragraphs. It fit neatly with the other invisible players I wanted to write about.

It was pretty interesting stuff, actually. By the time the avalanche of information about DNA struck with ***g*** force, I was hooked. This was really amazing; it was earth-shattering, and it was life-changing. It also is invisible all right. It isn't invisible for the obvious reason that it can't be seen with the naked eye. The *truth* about DNA should be the story of the century. However, the real story is mostly to be found in back rooms buried in overlooked books and research reports, or yellowing on library shelves here and there. It should be headline news! I am only too thrilled to honor DNA's evolutionary journey with us for thousands of years. The question remains as to whether I am skilled enough to fit everything into the one little chapter of its own.

What with all the talk of DNA, lightbody and ascension, it is necessary to first be sure to understand this at its most elementary level. DNA is a double helix. You have probably seen pictures of it. It is in the background on the cover of this book. Human beings are born with two strands activated. However, in all, there are *12* strands in the DNA helix. What about those other 10? Scientists have labeled them "junk DNA" (more on this later). Their notion of them questions if they ever had any useful function in human beings at all; they were ancient, outdated programs no longer useful in the modern era (maybe mammoth hunting?).

Scientists can be shockingly short-sighted when they stumble over anything they can't explain. Any person who has a deep intuitive connection to Mother Nature must realize that she would never clutter up the DNA helix with junk. Or, even more so, maybe once one climbs out of the limitations of scientific thinking, a little common sense takes over. Thankfully, that is exactly what happened.

Before moving on to the new and exciting developments in recent research in the field, let's reiterate—at the expense of redundancy—the most fundamental reason that we are concerning ourselves with DNA. Fasten your seat belts once again. ***DNA is the key to ascension.***

In order to activate your lightbody, all 12 strands of DNA must be activated. Access to the next dimension is granted only to those individuals in their lightbodies. Otherwise, the higher vibrations would transform one and all into french fries. That is what the Great Shift is all about. Activating the lightbody is what the first two books in this Series were all about. My brother, Duane, will complete the Pleiadian System as he reveals the last step in the TECHNOLOGY OF ASCENSION SERIES, which is included separately as the Epilogue at the end of this book. That would be the Galactic Activation, the first time it has ever been revealed—courtesy of our Pleiadian friends.

With that said, let's move on to an unseen world that makes the ascension process more real and more believable. Whenever my brother and I have been asked to lecture on this subject, there is always one question that we can be sure will come from the audience. They want to know if the activation of the additional DNA strands are visible on the physical level. In other words, can they be seen by physical 3D sight?

Unfortunately, we had to answer that to our knowledge the change is only in the etheric body. This is not a very convincing answer for many people. Consequently, I combed the literature, year after year, hoping that there would be news of a discovery that at least one person was found to have altered DNA at the physical level.

I believe it was along about 2007 that I happened onto an interview with Drunvalo Melchizedek. In that interview, he told the interviewer that his primary interest at that time was to find evidence that an activated DNA had indeed been discovered—man after my own heart! Drunvalo Melchizedek is one of the greatest names in alternative spirituality and metaphysics. You would need to read his writings to appreciate fully who he is. For one thing, he is a person of unquestionable integrity. It goes without saying that if anyone was in a position to know about such a discovery, it would be he. I tracked all information about him, his interviews and his workshops.

From time to time, he mentioned once again his intense interest in documenting that additional activated DNA strands had manifested in the physical body, not just in the etheric body. Hints mentioned "something" going on at UCLA research labs that may be connected to this subject. I made some feeble inquiries at UCLA, but of course I got absolutely nowhere. If anybody could access what was going on, it would have to be someone of the stature of Drunvalo Melchizedek.

As I have mentioned throughout this book, I began to write it in 2006 and early 2007. To make a long story short, life got in the way, and here I was desperately trying to complete it in 2012. I told myself that there could be only one thing that would make me almost thankful that the book was delayed over and over again, and that was if positive evidence had been found to prove my quest about physical DNA soon enough to go in the book.

Absolutely Stunning Report

A baby boy was born in the United States with AIDS. He was tested at birth, again at six months of age and again at one year of age. Each time he tested positive for AIDS. They did not retest him until he was six years old. This time they were amazed when those tests indicated not even the slightest trace of AIDS, or that he ever had AIDS or was even HIV positive!

I recommend that you read a book by Gregg Braden *Walking Between the Worlds: The Science of Compassion.* Mr. Braden was the first one to report this in a popular publication. The report about the kindergarten boy who was born with HIV is from Mr. Braden's book. It also appeared in an article in the April 1995 *Science News.*

The study was also reported by Yvonne J. Bryson and her colleague in the March 30, 1996, *New England Journal of Medicine,* "The virus is not lying dormant within the body, opportunistically awaiting an external clue to become active; it is eradicated from the body!"

In an interview on May 27, 2009, Drunvalo Melchizedek reported the following, and I include an edited direct quote:

> "He (the little boy) was taken to UCLA (medical school) to see what was going on and those tests showed that he did not have normal DNA...Then they tested this kid to see how strong his immune system was. They took a

very lethal dose of AIDS in a Petri dish and mixed it with some of his cells, and his cells remained completely unaffected. Then they started testing his blood with other things like cancer and discovered that so far this kid was immune to everything.

"Then they found another kid...then another kid...then 10,000...then 100,000...at this point UCLA estimates that one percent of the world's population has this new DNA. **That breaks down to approximately 60 million people who are not human by the old criteria!"**

Getting Some DNA Facts Straight

At this point, I am going to introduce some technical material about DNA. The main concern is not the technical information about DNA, of course, but I will be referring to this in a different context later. In order for that to make sense, I'll include it here. These are only some basic facts that are easily understood by anybody.

Human DNA has four nucleic acids that combine in sets of three, producing 64 different patterns that are called *codons.* Human DNA in everyone all over the world has 20 of these codons turned on. The remainder is turned off. The exception is three, which are the stop-start codes. It is these three that science essentially throws into the scrap heap as junk DNA that I referred to earlier. The AIDS boy had 24 codons turned on. That is four more than any other human being at the present time.

Science has now stated that there are so many people on the planet that are showing up with this alien DNA that they now not only believe that *a new human race is being born,* but that they apparently can't get sick! I can totally understand that this may test one's belief system to the max.

This information, if true, has to be the most game-changing in humanity's history on this planet. Surely it would be shouted from the highest rooftops all over the world. Wouldn't it be the talk of the town in every language on Earth? Well, I advise you to get used to it. This is just the beginning of what you haven't been told; and also the beginning of the end of your dearly held beliefs that you will have to tearfully kiss good-bye.

On the other hand, I am not going to accept everything that comes down the pike either. When I report something as mind-blowing as this, I would like to absolutely confirm it if I can. Obviously, I would love to include here a signed confirmation directly from the so-called researchers at UCLA. You can understand that little old me could not get to first base in reaching any of the original researchers or the AIDS boy in question.

I can say unequivocally that I absolutely do trust this information as accurate, otherwise, I would never have included it in this book. Here are my reasons. First of all, I have been aware of Drunvalo Melchizedek for many years. I have read his astounding *Flower of Life* series, most of his other writings, and tuned into his radio and video interviews and lectures. He is well-known in the metaphysical world as a man of integrity and above reproach. I know I am probably preaching to the choir as many readers are no doubt very familiar with his name already. The same holds true for Gregg Braden.

DNA Changes Seen And Documented!

The second reason is that he is a careful researcher himself. In the May 2009 interview, he states the following: "I've been tracking this for about two years, and I've waited to say anything because I wanted to be sure that it was real." He concludes that peoples' DNA is really changing. There have been many of us who have talked about this, but none of it has been seen by science. ***Now it has been seen and it has been documented!"***

There's more. It is even more incredible. They (Braden and Melchizedek) believe that these people with the alien DNA are doing something within themselves that is a very specific emotional/mental body response, something that is causing the DNA to mutate in a certain way. Whatever it is they are doing, it is producing a wave form coming off their body. Not only is it mutating the DNA, *but **when seen on computer screens it looks almost identical to the DNA molecule!***

Drunvalo conversed with Gregg Braden, and the two men regard these people with the alien DNA as somehow fallen into a particular state of consciousness that is constant. So far they have identified three separate states. *The first is Unity.* It is a mind that sees everything as interconnected. It is not just people. Nothing is separate. When you think about it, it leads right to God.

The second thing is heart-centeredness. Everything is Love. (Where have we heard that before?) Love, however, must be understood as not a sentimental emotion but an energy that is everything. *The third thing is to step completely out of polarity,* meaning a complete absence of judgment of good or bad. It can all be summed up as stepping out of polarity completely, seeing everything as One and feeling Love. Just try to go one full day juggling all three.

Is that what is causing their immunity? Is there anything else? In the interview, Drunvalo conjectures that there may be other characteristics that we have never even dreamed of. A whole lot more research needs to happen, of course. For me, this opens up the window on something that brings December 21, 2012, a little closer to reality. I've been looking for a possibility to hang my hat on. Could that be the day that "the hundredth monkey" changes his or her DNA?*

What we should be asking ourselves is how everybody can reach this state of hyper-immunity to disease. That is exactly what Drunvalo asked himself. Apparently, it has something to do with interacting with your lightbody. At any rate, he claims to have "gone into his merkabah (lightbody) and asked his subconscious mind to change the codons the way the alien DNA people did it."

He claims to have done this over two years (from 2009) ago, and he is unable to get sick, in spite of the fact that he has been exposed to all kinds of things, sometimes even purposely exposing himself to people who are sick. If he feels something coming on, it may last an hour or so, and that's it. The last I heard, he doesn't know if he has changed the codons or not. That would require a DNA test, which has not been done. Nonetheless, he remains healthy.

After following this research for two years, he is putting it all together, and this will be the subject of his workshops. I am sure I am not as advanced as Drunvalo Melchizedek. However, I can offer you some advice that should be considered before you take it into your head to go ask your subconscious to do what those kids did to achieve total immunity. I don't want to even think about someone testing the theory by exposing themselves to AIDS. The sex may be great but the consequences?—not so much.

It seems to me that there are several components to this process that make it much more complex than a little chat with your subconscious over brandy and a cigar. First, there is the lightbody and all that implies. Then there is psychic functioning and the relationship to your subconscious. After that, it is the subconscious mind's relationship to the whole.

---

* This refers to an experience of a group of researches who were studying monkey colonies. The food the primates preferred was a type of sweet potato, which they ate, sand and all. One day, a baby monkey washed his potato in the water. They were on an island. Eventually he taught his mother to do it. One by one the monkeys learned to wash their food in the water. After the hundredth monkey (symbolically speaking, of course) switched eating habits, the most amazing thing happened. The researchers on the neighboring islands reported that all of a sudden every monkey there washed its potato before eating it. Now "the hundredth monkey" has become part of the vernacular as a symbolic number to represent when a certain percentage of a group makes a change, an entire group, no matter how large or widespread, simultaneously makes the shift to the same behavior. Rupert Sheldrake wrote about this in connection with his morphic field theories.

For the lightbody, you need to explore activating all 12 DNA strands (*The Lightbody Activation Manual).* Communicating with the subconscious requires that the conscious mind learn to function at different levels of consciousness. The Alpha level is where you are when you are asleep and dreaming, also known as REM (rapid eye movement) sleep.

When you know how to achieve the Alpha state while you are conscious, only then can you begin to communicate directly, eyes-wide-open, with your subconscious. There is no doubt that your subconscious knows the codons those kids changed. That is not the problem. We know it can be done. I'm very curious what Drunvalo will be teaching in those workshops. Before dropping the subject, let's not forget that there is more involved than manipulating different levels of consciousness. It requires dropping polarity, also.

There is a very definite mind, emotional and body response, according to Drunvalo. The body simply does not acknowledge good or bad. It sees only the higher purpose behind it all. Drunvalo goes on to say that we all know this stuff, and I bet nearly everyone reading this is shaking their heads *yes.* Yet, every day, are we making judgments and criticizing people and circumstances? Jesus and the great teachers have certainly taught about and demonstrated this for thousands of years. But just think, we now know that this is actually playing a role in changing DNA and birthing a new race of humans!

But get this–I have the entire manuscript of Drunvalo's interviews. In this discussion, he makes this one comment just sort of tossed in with everything else, "They might be immortal, who knows?" You can bet this stopped me in my tracks. Activating the 12-strand DNA and the lightbody, and moving into your next life without going through the death experience is part of ascension.

The interviewer did pick right up on his remark by saying that a lot of us have chosen immortality. She went on to ask what Drunvalo thought about some people's ideas that if everyone were immune to disease, it would upset the life/death cycle that keeps the earth in balance. He gave the perfect answer, of course. "I don't judge it."

It has been said that the little children will lead us. We all have a choice to follow the pattern they have set up. What they have to teach us is not new; all of these things have come down through the ages. (This pattern has now crossed over into the adult population, by the way.) If we trust, one of the side effects may well be immunity to disease—even immortality. If we choose to live in different ways, we may stop killing the planet. These people who don't get sick, or perhaps don't even die anymore, must be aligned with the original purpose of the Earth.

I am so grateful that this book was delayed long enough for me to confirm the information about the new human race. I think back over the years since I started this book in 2006-7. No matter how hard I tried, something delayed this book year after year, until now, early 2012. I fussed and fussed and threw a fit over each delay. I doubted myself and thought I had misunderstood my mission even to write this book in the first place. Oh, ye of little faith!

Russian DNA Discoveries

Hints of some revolutionary Russian research, unfortunately for me, was available only in German. A book, *Vernetzte Intelligenz,* by von Grazyna Fosar and Franz Bludorf supposedly reported on some tantalizing, and in-your-face evidence, disputing long-held beliefs in the scientific community concerning so-called "junk DNA." Luckily, I came into possession of an edited article translated into English, summarized and commented on by an individual who identified himself only as Baerbel.

Therefore, I will pass on the results of the Russians' conclusive research findings. I am not alone in the knowledge that our body is programmable by language, words and thought. Spiritual teachers have understood this down through the ages. Many of you reading this right now have discovered this for yourselves when involved in esoteric practices.

It is not something reserved only for the great spiritual masters. How many times have you used affirmations, remote healing or a long list of other examples that proved to yourself that this is true? How many times have groups combined their minds to focus on a single outcome—controlling weather, for example—to see it manifest in physical reality? The scientific community can finally stop laughing. This, and much more, has now been scientifically proven and explained.

The Russians concluded only what common sense should have made obvious from thc start. What about this nonsense that 90 percent of DNA is considered "junk DNA"? Western researchers are interested only in categorizing the 10 percent of our DNA that is used for building protein. The remainder was thrown into the dust bin. Russian researchers, however, concluded that Mother Nature was not dumb enough to waste her basic resources. Their willingness to go up against prevailing attitudes was rewarded by findings and conclusions that were revolutionary. Not only that, they went on to claim that their results were scientifically proven.

Some of the material included here may be redundant as far as repeating similar phenomena within a different context. *Grumbling,* for example, was defined in the chapter about negative energies. I apologize if there are other references that may seem repetitious. However, this material is set within the context of scientific research, which has been long in coming. Information about DNA is drawing increasing attention. Before long, expect to witness an explosion of information about DNA. I felt that I should at least delineate some of the most revolutionary and scientifically proven discoveries that now lie squarely within the parameters of science itself, no longer just the so-called mad claims of nut cases within the occult worlds.

First let's define the terms *syntax* and *semantics.* These two concepts, believe it or not, led to research results that are truly game-changing. First of all, syntax is the way words are put together to form phrases and sentences. Semantics is the study of meaning in language forms. I define these terms because the Russian researchers discovered that DNA did more than take responsibility for the construction of our body. DNA also serves as data storage and communication. In what I personally consider a flash of genius, the Russians joined forces with linguists and geneticists. The Russian linguists found that the genetic code—especially in the apparent "useless" 90 percent—follows the same rules as all of our human languages.

To this end they compared the rules of syntax, semantics and the basic **rules of grammar.** They found that the alkalines of our DNA follow a regular grammar, and do have set rules just like our languages. "Therefore, human languages did not appear coincidentally but are a reflection of our inherent DNA."

Bear with me here. I am trying to skip a lot of technical material and get to the bottom line of the relevance to our interests as we process the ascension experience. The vibrational behavior of DNA was also explored by Russian biophysicists. Now we are approaching the bottom line meaning, e.g., modulating certain frequency patterns (sound) onto a laser-like ray, which influenced DNA frequency, and thus the genetic information itself. One can simply use words and sentences of the human language. Living DNA substance will always react to language-modulated laser rays and even to radio waves, according to these experiments, which are proven beyond any doubt. **However, the proper frequencies must be used.**

> **"This finally and scientifically explains why affirmations, hypnosis and the like can have such strong effects on humans and their bodies.** ***It is entirely normal and natural for our DNA to react to language."***

This research absolutely and scientifically proves what has been known for centuries; the body is programmable by language, words and thought. ***To repeat: if the frequency is correct!*** That is a big *if.* Why is it that shamanic healers such as myself can consistently "read" the patterns in my healing clients regardless of their location, even those half a world away; while the ordinary inexperienced person will have little success in reading anyone, regardless of distance or location?

To quote the conclusions in the article: "The individual person must work on the inner processes and development in order to establish a conscious communication with the DNA." As you are well aware by now, I have 40 years of training and experience under my belt. I am apparently able to "tune in" as we say, and that turns out to be literally true. The Russian researchers are working on a method that is not dependent on these factors, but will *always* work, provided one uses the correct frequency. That means we are probably thinking in terms of some device. The higher developed an individual's consciousness is, the less need is there for any type of device. One can achieve these results by oneself.

Western researchers cut single genes from DNA strands and insert them elsewhere. You probably have read about it or heard about it. There is quite extensive literature on the subject. On the other hand—and this is where it gets exciting—the Russians created devices that influence cellular metabolism through modulated radio and light frequencies, thus repairing genetic defects. They successfully transformed frog embryos to salamander embryos simply by transmitting the DNA information patterns! Yes, it indeed means that the frogs come out as salamanders. This avoided all of the side effects encountered when cutting out and re-introducing single genes from the DNA.

> **"This represents an unbelievable, world-transforming revolution and sensation by simply applying vibration (sound frequencies) and language instead of the archaic cutting-out procedure."**

And the research does not stop there. The Russian scientists also found that our DNA produces magnetized wormholes. These are tunnel connections between entirely different areas in the Universe through which information can be transmitted outside of space and time. The DNA attracts these bits of information and passes them on to our consciousness. This is a process known as *hyper-communication.*

In nature, hyper-communication has been used successfully for millions of years. We observe it most dramatically in the organizing of the insect world among ants and bees. Remember Queen Ant? When a queen ant is separated from her colony, the workers fervently continue with the "building plans." The queen ant can be as far away as she wants, as long as she is alive. But if the queen ant dies, all work stops. No one knows what to do. Apparently the queen ant communicates via the group consciousness with her subjects.

In humans, however, hyper-communication is most often encountered when one suddenly gains access to information that is outside one's knowledge base. We then label it inspiration or intuition (also trance channeling). We all have heard of dramatic examples of composers, for example, suddenly writing entire pieces of music that seemed to flow from outside time and space. (Too bad they can't do the same with books called *Playing the Ascension Game!)*

Many controlled experiments showed a pattern that is now known as Phantom DNA. Irradiated DNA samples produced a typical wave pattern on screen. They removed the DNA sample, but the wave pattern did not disappear. This showed that the pattern continued to come from the removed sample whose energy field apparently remained by itself, thus the phantom DNA effect. It is surmised that energy from outside of space and time still flows through the activated wormholes after the DNA was removed. The side effects encountered most often in hyper-communication in humans are inexplicable electromagnetic fields in the vicinity of the people concerned. I have written elsewhere how these fields interrupt electronic and recording devices and the like around psychics, healers and shaman. It means that they are good at hyper-communication. Ha!

In their book, Gosar and Bludorf make another very interesting point that explains some things that have perplexed the 4Ds. The authors quote sources that describe earlier times when humans were more like the animals, very strongly connected to group consciousness. They acted as a group. I can imagine that this would be necessary for survival in many ways. In order to develop and experience a strong individuality, however, we humans had to forget hyper-communication almost completely. Now circumstances and human consciousness have changed. We are fairly stable in our individual consciousness. Following is a direct quote that falls once again under my philosophy that "if you wait long enough, you will find out."

> "...we can create a new form of group consciousness—namely one in which we attain access to all information via our DNA without being forced or remotely controlled about what to do with that information. We now know that just as we use the Internet, *our DNA can feed proper data into the network, can retrieve data from the network, and can establish contact with other participants in the network.* Remote healing, telepathy or "remote sensing" about the state of another can thus be explained. Some animals know from afar when their owners plan to return home. This can be freshly interpreted and explained via the concepts of group consciousness and hyper-communication."

First of all, I will make mention of the fact that I always know when Don will return home when he has been away from the house. My cat, Mickey, sets up a meowing fit seven or eight minutes before Don's arrival. If you are a cat lover, you know that not just any old thing is going to interfere with a cat nap. No matter how sacked out he is in one of his favorite haunts, he will spring to action when "Daddy is on the way home." Don says he always finds him parked by the door leading from the garage into the kitchen. He knows all right.

Now for an explanation that is more serious, if not as cute. If you will hark back with me to the opening chapters that talk about our preparations for Harmonic Concordance, you may recall, our Teacher, Thomas, was hellbent on establishing what he called "group mind." We even went through some kind of ceremony to tie the four of us together. Maybe we had better take a closer look at that.

From my initial hope that I could scrape together a little something on DNA, little did I ever expect that such life-changing discoveries would present themselves. Yes, DNA deserved its own little chapter all right! If you are not just blown away by the revolutionary material in this chapter, you need to re-read the entire thing. Sometimes when we are confronted by information that takes a giant leap forward, it is too much for the left brain to wrap its mind around right away. This could be a case in point. The DNA research findings prove that the brave new world is here NOW.

CHAPTER NINE

Believing is Seeing

"If you have faith as small as a mustard seed, you can say to the mountain, 'Move from here to there' and it will move. Nothing will be impossible for you."

Bible verse
Matthew 17:20

"Don't be trapped by dogma – which is living with the results of other people's thinking. Don't let the noise of others' opinions drown out your own inner voice. And most important, have the courage to follow your heart and intuition.

Steve Jobs, Apple CEO
2005 commencement address
at Stanford University

When I was a young person in my early teens, I just loved to know things. I was not interested in simply general information. What I liked was trivia, and, in particular, little tidbits that exposed urban legends—popular notions that were actually false. Whenever I encountered an especially outrageous example in print, I carefully cut it out and carried it in my billfold. Then I awaited the day when one of my juicy tidbits came up in conversation.

I remember well one example. It was about chiggers, yes, of all things, chiggers. Chiggers are tiny, invisible bugs that deliver bites that itch like crazy. I grew up on a farm in Iowa and contracting chiggers was a constant concern in an environment of timberlands, wet creek and riverbanks and the many other haunts that my companions and I frequently tramped.

It was popularly believed that chiggers burrow under the skin, and that this is the cause of the red swellings and itching. Chiggers do not burrow under the skin, nor do they feed on animal blood. They feed on the fluid in skin cells. That process is what irritates the skin causing several days of discomfort. This led to one of my most triumphant moments when this subject indeed did come up in conversation. Sure enough, someone said the magic words about the popular misconceptions concerning the habits of chiggers. I was able to whip out proof to the contrary from my billfold collection.

It was not long before I realized that whipping out printed proof that people were wrong about something was not being greeted with enthusiasm. So it was at a tender age that I experienced the great realization that most people do not want to know the truth.

A Case Of Hands-on Healing

If I had not realized this before, I certainly would have after an encounter with a woman for whom I had done some powerful healing work. In the early 80s, I enjoyed a flourishing astrological practice with an office in Portland, Oregon. I also practiced hands-on healing in those days. A woman who was a casual acquaintance showed up in the waiting room requesting a healing. Her husband was a friend of mine who shared a mutual interest in healing and other metaphysical subjects. His wife, on the other hand, was a skeptic and came only because her husband nagged her into it.

She had several benign tumors in each breast. I did my thing and each breast was free of tumors in just a couple of days. Several months later, I saw her again. This time her condition had worsened, but again I was able to clear the problem.. The condition recurred several months apart, each time worse than before. This happened three times.

I begged her to see a doctor to determine the underlying cause of her condition. I feared that one day I would find that the healing was no longer effective. Nearly a year went by before I heard from her again. This time it was an invitation to lunch. I thought this was surely a reward for my healing work with her. I was wrong. While enjoying a cocktail, she looked at me and in absolute seriousness said, "Diana, I just want you to know that I don't believe in what you do." I guess she invited me to lunch because of my sparkling personality, not because of my healing skills! At any rate, seeing in *not* believing.

There is a footnote to this story, something of a bizarre twist. I heard from her after more than 20 years of silence. She eventually developed breast cancer, which she apparently survived by conventional medical treatments. I heard through the grapevine that the tumors returned, but she was too embarrassed to contact me again.

It was her husband, my friend, who constantly, loudly and publicly, proclaimed belief in psychic healing. He complained just as bitterly about his wife's skepticism. After many years, I received one phone call from him informing me that he was in "a world of hurt" with cancer. Later, I heard that he had succumbed to the disease.

Yet, not once did he ever ask me to do some healing for him. It was not even mentioned in that last phone call. Knowing our history, it struck me as totally out of character. His wife, the skeptic, is the only one who actually came to me. Was he projecting deeply buried doubts about psychic healing onto her: he who protesteth too much? Regardless, I was shocked at these circumstances of his death and also profoundly saddened.

The Belief Game

The first thing you must remember is that in the belief game you must be very cautious about "kinda." There are certain circumstances under which, if you "kinda believe," could be very hazardous to your person or even cost you your life. No, you do not equivocate with certain beliefs. .One remarkable example in which there must be no limited beliefs concerns the firewalkers of Hawaii. In the late 1960s, I was first initiated into a deep study of the ancient Polynesian shamanic practices of the kahuna priests. The secrets of their guarded lore were very much a family affair, strictly passed down only from parent to child until recent times. Today, much of their technology is known and goes by the name, *Huna.*

When I first encountered accounts of the Hawaiian firewalkers who walked on glowing red hot lava flows without turning into cinders, I was naturally intrigued. However, at that time, this seemed a far off world that would never touch mine. That is when I think I learned to never say *never.* In the belief game, it also pays to know that there must be a certain allowance for flexibility, change and growth.

I taught Huna classes for many years. The subject of firewalking came up from time to time and, not surprisingly, was regarded as totally incredible and impossible to us. The next thing I knew, a place in Washington State opened up a firewalking training center. Anyone could go there and over a week-end, take the training. Not only that, candidates who wished to do it *actually did firewalking across about a fifty-foot fire pit!* And if that was not shocking enough, six of my Huna students actually did it before all was said and done.

Everything was well-documented with photos. What was I saying about "kinda believe"? If anyone wavered in their belief in the midst of a fire pit, they would end up with burned tootsies. Yet, none of my students suffered even the slightest ill effects from the glowing red coals. A size nine still ended up a size nine.

The film *What the Bleep Do We Know?* is one of the most popular documentaries ever made. It was produced in Portland, Oregon, where I just happened to be living at the time. It opened at the Baghdad Theater here, so I heard a lot of buzz about it. It is about spirituality and the relationship between quantum physics and consciousness.

You may still watch it on the Internet as of this writing (2012). The long list of people interviewed in this film comes from varied backgrounds including the sciences, metaphysics, physics and psychiatry. As for these people's credentials—Omygod! They didn't spare the horses. The film received several awards for best documentary for 2004.

The movie featured a story about the Peruvian Indians' inability to see the Spaniards' big ships when they dropped anchor off shore in South America. Presumably, this was because the size of the ships was too far outside of their experience. At this juncture, I would point out that the interviewees in the movie issued disclaimers stating that they did not agree with everything in the film, neither did they all totally agree with each other, quite understandable, considering the radical nature of this film. However, the story was left in the film.

A blog was put up on the Internet, and people were invited to comment on this Peruvian Indian story. I read them all, and the greater percentage was quite rabid that either the whole movie was garbage or, specifically, the Indian story was ridiculous and so on and on. However, occasionally a voice spoke up with a very well-thought-out insight about why this was believable. After my more than 40 years of experience with consciousness and belief systems, I totally agree that the story could absolutely be true. The real ironic joke is that the people who so passionately rejected the story, proved every word I have to say about convoluted belief systems.

But that is not the most outrageous example of believing is seeing. I can name one. I am not being facetious when I say it is found in our own twenty-first century medical/science model. It is what is taught in medical schools across the country and in high school biology classes. When scientists encountered anomalies, they were shunted off as just quirky and meaningless. If science couldn't explain it, science just looked the other way.

However, change is on the way. That is largely because of courageous and open-minded research by men like cellular biologist, Dr. Bruce Lipton, author of the ground-breaking book *The Biology of Belief.* He dared to pose the theory that if placebos* work so well, why aren't we researching them.

Here is a quote from the inside flyleaf cover of Lipton's book:

> "The implications of the research radically change our understanding of life. It shows that genes and DNA do not control our biology; that instead DNA is controlled by signals from *outside* the cell, including the energetic messages emanating from our positive and negative thoughts."
> Please read this paragraph twice because the implications are staggering.
> (Welcome to all this so-called New Age metaphysical fluff, gentleman.)

---

* Most people are probably aware of the *placebo* effect. In controlled research trials, one half of the recipients of a new drug is given the real thing and the other half is given sugar pills, or a placebo. No one in the trial knows who is receiving the test drug versus who is receiving the placebo, or the real McCoy.

It was long before these incidents that I came to realize that humanity must surrender beliefs as fundamental as the unquestioned pillars of biology including random evolution, survival of the fittest and the role of DNA. As I stated many times in my newsletter, "clearing negative energies, activating lightbodies, transformational experiences and the like, offer the conscious spiritual journeyman high drama." How tragic is it to falter on the path simply because one cannot recognize the truth right in front of one's eyes? If, like my friend, seeing is not believing, how much greater is the challenge for people when basic paradigms begin to crumble?

As it states in *Spontaneous Evolution:*

> "...beliefs about nature and human nature shape our politics, culture, and individual lives...by releasing the old beliefs that keep the status quo in place, and by building our lives and world on this heartening new story, we can trigger the spontaneous evolution of our species."

The handling of your belief system is not just about you and your personal journey to ascension. It is up to all of us to trigger the ascension process. As we look around at the present (August 2012) conditions of economic collapse, environmental pollution, devastating weather patterns and a host of other disturbing circumstances, one of our toughest challenges is standing tall in the face of fear.

Here is a powerful quote again from the Lipton-Bhaerman book *Spontaneous Evolution:*

> "When we recognize that we can be programmed by fear, we are less susceptible to manipulations by those who benefit from mass conflict. Nazi leader, Hermann Goering, acknowledged this quite plainly at the Nuremberg trials when he testified, 'Of course the common people don't want war...but it is the leaders of the country who determine the policy, and it is always a simple matter to drag people along, whether it is a democracy, a fascist dictatorship, or a parliament or a communist dictatorship...all you have to do is tell them they are being attacked, and denounce the peacemakers for their lack of patriotism and exposing the country to danger. It works the same in any country.' "

I have read that statement by Goering several times, and each time it makes me sick. But this makes me even sicker:

> "These words should hold particular relevance to the United States after the preemptive war on Iraq failed to accomplish its touted goal of finding weapons of mass destruction and brought the country to the brink of financial and moral bankruptcy. We can rightfully refer to the Bush-Cheney Administration

as intense fear-based educational experience for which both the U.S.A. and the world paid a very heavy tuition."

How do we address this seemingly overwhelming programming?: by making the subconscious conscious! Do the math. The subconscious runs the show 99 percent of the time. (Remember that number.)

"Making the subconscious conscious" happens to be something with which I have racked up nearly 40 years of experience through my work as an astrologer. I have developed a working model for doing just that. In fact, if I wasn't writing this book, I would be writing my astrology book *The Guidebook for Counseling Astrologers: A Nine-Step Model.* Fat notebooks bulge with case histories collected over many years, astrology charts, recordings of counseling sessions and an extensive outline. I was all ready to go. However, my guidance suggested otherwise, so here I am.

When I work with my astrology clients, I often spot the entire subconscious pattern in all of its glory within the first minutes of our conversation. It's amazing how obvious the *other guy's* problems are! I do not mean that to be a flippant remark that minimizes my contribution to astrological counseling techniques or the skill I have developed over years of experience. Of course, it involves a careful process to take my clients step-by-step through a case history, analysis of life events around the problem presented, behaviors that unconsciously communicate the pattern and finally, the subconscious belief pattern itself.

When I teach this technique in workshops for astrologers, I ask for volunteers who are willing to present a real-life problem. I work the process right on the spot. It's risky, but so far I haven't ended up with egg on my face. Impressive, yes, but that's not the point. Spotting the subconscious story frees people from really powerful energies tied up in chains around some issue in the subconscious. It makes the subconscious conscious!

In her book *Catastrophobia* Barbara Hand Clow suggests that the answer to the collective fear is to tell our story, i.e., our collective story. I consider this work with clients as telling their real story from a psychological perspective, releasing fears from one person at a time.

Once the subconscious belief is exposed on a conscious level; it's a matter of tracking down from where the person learned that belief. It is hardly surprising to anyone to discover subconscious beliefs primarily originating from early childhood. Once identified, you are on the trail of releasing it from its prison.

Now let me pose this situation. Maybe you read in books, or somehow learned that you can manifest whatever you want in life by positive thinking. Maybe you tried different techniques, but nothing ever worked like you thought it should. Maybe it worked better for other people. Perhaps you read the book *The Secret.* It created a huge sensation and made all the best-seller lists. Indeed, it was a great book for the masses just starting out with these ideas. Nonetheless, it did not quite go far enough.

I have just given you the *real* secret. The reason some of your efforts end in frustration is because they are hitting the wall of a contrary subconscious belief, and the subconscious has not been made conscious. You may rattle off affirmations, repeat mantras, visualize your head off, or whatever else you may try at the conscious level, but remember that number I asked you to remember: The subconscious calls the shots 99 percent of the time.

Anticipating the next obvious question, this is not the place for a detailed explanation about how to access the subconscious or make the subconscious conscious. What is important to understand first is that hidden beliefs in the psyche are determining critical aspects of your *outer* life experiences, in fact, most of them. (More on this subject in the chapter "Ho'oponopono")

We can't change what we can't see. Once the subconscious pattern is properly exposed to the cold light of day, the rational, conscious mind can recognize the logic of it. Once it is seen, the opportunity for a real shift in the belief system accompanies that aha! moment.

It is, nonetheless, only the *opportunity* for change. Regardless of the deep insight with which we may observe and bring to the pattern, it requires taking some action to change the behavior. Changing the behavior pattern attracts a changed life experience. Let's not kid ourselves about just how difficult that may well be. The subconscious self does not roll over and play dead without a fight.

I would like to include this quote from *Spontaneous Evolution.* It is both hopeful and scary to realize that even our biology supports radical changes in this world; however, we must each take the personal responsibility to make the choices to act.

> "Now that we understand that there is, indeed, a playing field that most definitely impacts the material world and now that we realize that the spontaneous remission of our Planet Earth involves a shift of our own mission from survival to thrival, we also see that we have the power and the responsibility to bring these changes about."

We have met the Savior and He-She is us!

Rules to live by from the Master

"Do not believe in what you have heard; do not believe in traditions because they have been handed down for many generations; do not believe anything because it is rumored and spoken of by many; do not believe merely because the written statements of some old sage are produced; do not believe in conjectures; do not believe in that as a truth to which you have become attached by habit; do not believe merely on the authority of your teachers and elders. After observation and analysis, when it agrees with reason and is conductive to the good and benefit of one and all, then accept it and live up to it."

Gautama Buddha
some 2600 years ago

Meeting at the Midpoint

This is the end of Chapter Nine—nine out of a total of nineteen chapters. This is the springboard, you might say, to the last half of this book. So far you have been exposed to an accumulation of information of the "let's breech some boundaries" kind. Maybe this is the time for a time out, a little time to contemplate your navel. This may be the shortest chapter in this book, but it is probably the mightiest. The way in which you have embraced the previous chapters will have an influence on the subtle change that occurs from here on to the end of the book.

The Universe has shown that it can reach you with any message, and no matter how preposterous, even influence you to act against what you thought you believed. Beliefs touch every area of your life: beliefs about yourself, your relationships, your food choices, and even your belief about beliefs! Yet, regardless of how all-powerful we may perceive the Universe to be, one little human may flex his or her free will muscles and block every Universal effort to convey the Truth. We also found that it is very unlikely that you can change people's beliefs no matter how much evidence you lay at their feet.

Now is the time for everyone to examine and re-examine their handling of a belief system. Do you understand the dynamics of how you do it? Maybe the most dangerous thinking in the world is to "know" that we are right. And now is the time for all lightworkers to move on and to no longer waste time trying to save anyone from a seriously flawed belief system. The Truth is out there. Anyone can find it. All you have to do is ask.

CHAPTER TEN

Preparing for Ascension

The Urgency of Transformation

"When faced with a radical crisis, when the old way of being in the world, of interacting with each other and with the realm of nature doesn't work anymore, when survival is threatened by seemingly insurmountable problems, an individual life-form—or a species—will either die or become extinct or rise above the limitations of its condition through an evolutionary leap."

A New Earth
Eckhart Tolle

Two Kinds of Ascension.

Almost everyone on the spiritual path has no doubt encountered accounts of devotees sitting in ashrams meditating for hours at a time, days at a time and yes, even years at a time. Their goal is basically a process of raising the kundalini life force energy from the base of the spine, upward through the body's psychic centers until it rises to the chakra just at the crown of the head, where Cosmic Consciousness occurs.

The successful results of this endeavor renders the initiate capable of consciously manipulating the full power of the kundalini at will. This is considered the highest form of spiritual achievement while still in a physical body. At this point, the devotee is ready for a traditional form of personal ascension.

As initiates, their physical bodies undergo a transformation giving them extraordinary mastery. This allows them to relocate at will to any location and also access multidimensional layers of consciousness. This process is mostly associated with long-standing spiritual traditions of the East. That is not to say that many of us in the West didn't take a shot at it ourselves, particularly during the wonderful-horrible Sixties.

In this chapter "Preparing for Ascension," the subject of ascension is not focused solely on the traditional form of individual transformation. It is about a rare evolutionary leap affecting all of humankind and even Earth herself. This involves a very different process from sitting in meditation in ashrams for years at a time. It is about a mass shift of all humanity into heart-centered consciousness.

No one knows when this cosmic event will take place. The best way you can serve humanity is to free yourself of fear. It is the biggest block to the Shift into conscious evolution. If you are open to the promptings of your soul, you will always be at the right place at the right time. By staying the course, you are pioneering an open pathway for others to follow.

I am beginning this chapter with a discussion about the system of doorways that opened in a planned configuration in order to admit the ever-escalating light frequencies, essential to raising our vibrations to 5th dimension consciousness.

PORTALS, STARGATES, CORRIDORS AND WORMHOLES

The metaphysical pipeline on the Internet was abuzz with information about another significant date in July 2005. Shortly after the 4th of July, as the smoke cleared from the USA Independence Day celebrations, the Higher Beings were evidently planning some fireworks of their own.

8-8 Lions' Gate Opening

Posted on-line by Brenda Tenerelli

"On August 8, we are given a rare opportunity to walk through another 'Doorway of Accelerated Awakening,' the 8:8 LIONS' GATE. This Awakening will occur within the cellular records of all beings. Each strand of DNA holds these cellular records within a crystalline code.

"In ancient times, the 'Records of Remembrance' were hidden deep within the earth physically, under, above and around sacred sites. The Mother Matrix of these encodings lives within the Great Pyramid of Egypt with the Sphinx as the Stellar Sentinel. The only way Earth can move forward is through the heart. Every tool, meditation and OM is a fruitless tree unless one moves into direct contact with the heart. Activating a doorway of love so vast one is automatically included without any effort.

"August 8 is a Natural doorway…just a natural remembering initiating our dormant light codes, lifting us up to a place where we can see the parade of light that is yet to come. 8:8: This configuration...asks you to fly to the moon and stop by the Milky Way on your way back. It is turning your nose up at earthly limitation and walking forward and upward into a place of opulence and bounty. August 8 is a celebration beyond time that escorted us home through the Sphinx Lions' Gate to the Stars.

"August 8 (8:8) has always been experienced as the Lions' Gate doorway, opening up a time portal to ancient Egyptian encodings…time coded records…held within a crystalline code in the form of a tetrahedron (3-sided pyramid) which exists within the codex and codon of each strand of DNA, within each cell of the body, as well as each cell in the Universe.

"When the ancient skies were aligned in a stellar configuration that opened a doorway, the sacred sites with these encodings would then be used to download to earth and humans new levels of truth and wisdom. In this day and time, we cannot all get up and zip across the ocean in a moment's notice to align with the incoming energies. We all carry within us every iota of every universal sacred site ever issued to existence.

"Since the Universe knows we are a hardheaded stubborn bunch, it has aligned some stars to shoot that cosmic cupid arrow our way. Not like a valentine's type of love but a doorway of love so vast one is automatically included within without one actually knowing."

New ascension energies slammed in again in rapid succession on July 17th and August 14th of 2005. These were special in that the vibrations bumped up a level and laid stronger foundations for the New Earth. July 17th marked the arrival of the Solar Goddess, setting the stage for the emergence of powerful women. Along with the August 14th ascension leap, these dates marked turning points. Portals continued to open.

I must admit that this whole thing about portals, stargates and corridors was for me, something of a frenetic scramble from one big power day to the next. Unpredictably at any minute, my email yelled, "boo!" The Something-or-Other Stargate was opening. Omygod! The 11:11:11 portal was activating. What did it mean? What was I supposed to do? Was I missing the spiritual boat?

When I first realized that I would write this book, I collected everything that came along even tangentially related to portals and stargates. I just tossed stuff in a big file. The day came when I had exhausted all other subjects. The time had come. I had to write about this. I plunged bravely into the dreaded folder.

What before had been random dates with neither rhyme nor reason for being, eventually emerged as a system of highways and byways for navigating the other dimensions. A portal by name is a doorway. A stargate * is part of any system involved with navigating the maze of pipes. It's relevance to the Ascension Game is this: How can you get out of here if you can't find the door?

Numerous high-energy dates have come and gone in the form of eclipses, solstices, equinoxes and other astrological line-ups, to name some. The significance is not

---

* *Stargates* is a term used in conjunction with the activities of the Higher Beings who aid in the evolution of humanity by manipulating cosmic energy fields to raise the vibrations of Earth. It is analogous to opening a door, or portal, to let the new frequencies flow into this dimension.

solely in the meaning of each individual date on the calendar. All of these events are part of the on-going process to raise frequencies and clear the pathways for our journey into another reality.

The process now focuses on clearing old programs and any other impediments to the transfer into our lightbody and ascension vehicle. The guidelines in this chapter should be helpful for those on many different rungs of the ladder of life. However, it presupposes that one has at least awakened and initiated a commitment to the inner life. If not, it is unlikely that you are reading this anyway unless stranded on a desert island, and it is the only book that washed ashore.

Lightbody Activations

My brother and I have written extensively about preparing the physical body for ascension into the higher frequencies. *The Lightbody Activation Manual* and *The Ascension Guidebook* give detailed, illustrated step-by-step instructions for performing lightbody activations.

This section of the book is obviously apropos for those who have worked with the lightbody activations up close and personal. But even if you have not participated in any lightbody work, you may want these questions answered before committing yourself. After all, I intended this book also for any traditional healers or counselors who wish to explore the subject not only for themselves, but also for clients. Obviously, from the very nature of any work purported to change your body at the deepest cellular levels, it only follows that we question the impact it has on all aspects of life.

The critically important distinction here is the difference between an immediate *reaction* and an actual *life change.* Those of you who have experienced the Crystal Triangle Activations can easily relate to other people's feedback about immediate body sensations, emotional responses, intuitive insights and the like. Immediate reactions, meaning those occurring at some parts throughout the activation process, vary widely. However, reactions should not be interpreted as a necessary part of the activation experience. If a participant in an activation claims to feel nothing, it does not mean that they have failed or are so spiritually dense that there is no hope for them. There is also no reason to cast doubt on the entire activation process itself. Just do it, and trust that it is right.

Some Recipient's Experiences

Two people, Reba Cain and Donna Van Duyn, partnered to give the lightbody activations. They were kind enough to send me the following report about their experiences.

- "My sister (the one who does not believe in this heegeebeegee stuff) has had two activations so far. On the first activation, she saw colors, Angel wings and a White Light."
- "My brother-in-law...on the second activation said, 'I was tingling. I have never tingled before.' He and his wife...are coming back...so they can have more activations!"
- "A friend who does not do energy work of any kind felt paralyzed by the strong energy and she asked me if I saw the white light pouring out of her third eye. When I said no, she asked if I saw (it) pouring out of her crown."
- "...my other sister...went immediately into an altered state and doesn't remember anything at all."

"We are going to teach it to as many people as possible. Thanks again to you and Duane."

If You Don't Have A Partner

This gives me the opportunity to address an issue about which many people have inquired: "What should I do if I can't find a partner to do the lightbody activations with me?" First of all, the directions for the lightbody activations, along with the illustrations, are so clear and uncomplicated that even a kid as young as 12 years old should be able to follow them.

Go to one of your local do-it-yourself printing establishments (Kinko's here in Washington) and copy *only* the directions from the book. Enlarge them if you wish. Once you have those in hand, try to find someone who is involved in energy healing, e.g., a Reiki healer. There is no need to explain the whole story, just make up something. Say you are experimenting with a new energy technique. Then ask the person to simply follow the directions. They can place the directions right on your body and just read from them while making the corresponding hand motions. As I said, even a willing kid (bribery and threats help) should be capable of doing it. Remember, this method is very forgiving; it need not be letter perfect.

If it turns out that this is not workable in your situation, then just go to the directions for "Solo Crystal Triangle" at the back of the book. After doing that several times, you may kick-start the process. Keep it up by performing it regularly. Also, set up the crystals in your bedroom permanently. If the energy gets too intense, then move them, of course. Some people call my brother, Duane Henkle, to check them out. He will be able to tell. www.duanehenkle.com. However, if you are a person who has been led to do this and you went ahead and bought the book, your consciousness may well be such that this will work for you. I've seen it often enough.

Long Term Changes

As for *life* changes, these address anything that calls for healing and transformation over time. This might range from physical illnesses to career problems, from phobias to relationship issues, or any of the other matters that spiritual seekers address as needing attention and resolution. These life changes may even call for some other supportive therapies in conjunction with the activations. Don't feel reluctant to engage other healing modalities if your inner guidance clearly prompts you to do so.

This may be particularly true of chronic illness situations. Perhaps the activations facilitate just the right doctor or treatment program coming into your awareness. Or there may be the opportunity for a successful drug intervention, whereas the addict steadfastly declined help by all earlier efforts. The energies seem to favor working within the parameters of ordinary 3D life, so don't be peeking out the window anticipating some robed figure with a magic wand. Believe me, I haven't spotted him yet!

I have to conclude at this point in time that completing the lightbody activations does, without any doubt, initiate a powerful process, the *ultimate goal of which is to prepare the physical body to tolerate the higher frequencies fundamental to the 5th dimension.* However, I do not perceive the activations in and of themselves as directly therapeutic. It will not magically wipe out your neuroses so that one day you just wake up without them. You won't be cured of your arthritis overnight, and maybe you never will be. However, *indirectly,* the lightbody activations and the clearing of negative energies will and have led to dramatic life changes.

I just recently worked with a woman with whom my brother had already done extensive lightbody work. We heard from her again a couple of years later, distraught that she was stuck in her career path. It was a long story that included some complicated early childhood circumstances and later traumatic family issues. Instead of continuing with more shamanic work, he referred her to me for some astrological counseling.

He made a good call, and here's why. This is one of the best examples of "don't just sit there, do something." How many times have we said that you must do the inner work? You can't skip steps. No lightbeing ever laid claim to an evolved consciousness without following the advice of the great philosophers of old: Know thyself. Yes, that means getting down to business, identifying what is not working in your life, and tackling the obvious problems. All of your unresolved issues need to be continuously riding at the top of the conscious mind, no matter what other things call for your attention.

In her natal chart, I spotted the subconscious patterns of the woman in question. This was straightforward, old-fashioned psychological therapy. There is a place for that, too. But sooner or later, the goal is to learn how to track down these things yourself, or learn to listen to inner guidance that tells you what will work for you, or who should work with you.

The woman's grandmother was an immigrant who amassed great wealth. Unfortunately, after living in the United States for several years, she lost everything. So what is the pattern that the subconscious is hanging onto? Answer: why work your behind off getting rich, when you lose it all in the end? After further conversation, the woman was bright enough to spot her self-sabotaging behaviors that always accompany any subconscious pattern.

The body's energy system must continually keep its feet on the gas pedal to accommodate the constant acceleration in vibrational frequencies. As the ascension process turns up the juice, old paradigms cannot exist in an elevated multi-dimensional milieu. Lesser energy patterns have only one real option, transformation. Peaceful coexistence is not in the cards. That eliminates the possibility of maintaining the various blocks listed later in the book. All of us must deal with cleaning house sooner or later.

The Pleiadians approached us at all times very matter-of-factly. There were no intoning of ancient mantras, maudlin sentimentalities, frivolous explanations or strictly personal connections. They never asked how my mother was doing. I see no contradiction whatsoever that however powerfully the activations facilitate the process, *the companion piece is our work on ourselves along with it.*

The final troublesome matter I want to discuss about activations concerns symptoms that follow directly on the heels of lightbody work. Here is something that sometimes scares the daylights out of people. They are all excited about doing the Crystal Triangle lightbody activations, only to be immediately beset with unsettling symptoms. Fortunately, this is uncommon.

For those who do experience an uncomfortable reaction, they sometimes imagine all sorts of things that have gone wrong in their energy field. Some imagine that they have been short-circuited permanently. Consequently, it takes a good bit of tender loving handholding to reel them in from Freak-Out City, and to reassure them that things have not gone terribly wrong. I need to remember that engaging in lightbody work places many people past the boundaries of their belief system comfort zones right from the beginning.

There is nothing to worry about in connection to lightbody work, I assure you. In our experience, no one ever went home without anything they came with: arms, legs, psyche, etc. On rare occasions, we kept certain individuals here for at most an hour until they were squarely back in their bodies and feeling normal. I understand that Duane has received calls from people who received an activation within the past day or two and think that they are experiencing reactions that concern them. There can be many reasons for this, too many to list here. But there are none that cannot be dealt with satisfactorily, usually right over the phone.

Some people get the jitters *before* doing the activations. Trepidations include fears that other healing work they are doing may be circumvented. We have not found that to be the case. In fact, it's just the opposite, if anything. The lightbody enhances any other healing you may be receiving. I have testimonials from healers who practice a variety of other modalities, such as massage therapy. They report that setting up the Crystal Triangle in conjunction with it, noticeably enhances their work. Simply place the programmed crystals in your work room so that your patient is well within the energies, There is no need to perform the nine steps along with your regular routine unless you think it is appropriate in individual cases.

Occasionally we encounter a practitioner who departs from the instructions for activations and concocts a sort of hybrid, intermixing their technique with the Crystal Triangle directions. We caution against this as it seriously compromises the Crystal Triangle lightbody process. However, if the two modalities are kept separate, respecting the integrity of both, each is empowered.

Some of my shamanic healing clients who have recovered from horrible entity invasion are afraid that lightbody work will open the door again to some very unpleasant energies. We never experienced activations stirring up old wounds of any kind. We do expect, rather, that there is a strengthening of the entire aura.

Another reservation, especially among supersensitive individuals, is that the lightbody activations are simply going to be too overwhelming to tolerate. Maybe we should salute the American work ethic, also. Numbers of people were actually worried that they would not be able to go to work the day after an activation!

The most common problem in my experience concerns folks who sleep inside the Crystal Triangle in their bedrooms every night. Some people are apparently just too sensitive and are over-stimulated by nightly doses. They are wired! It is easy to solve the problem. Take the crystals out of the bedroom. Then there was my personal experience. For Pele, I used a hefty, pointy amethyst geode that really meant business. I placed it at the very top of the mattress. In my sleep, I rolled over and about gave myself a brain concussion. Place the Pele crystal on the floor *under* the head of the bed.

If you are spreading the word by performing lightbody activations, it is good to reassure people that it is safe. The only cases from which we in our group back away are those troubled individuals who are highly disturbed or psychotic. Maybe it is okay, but I am not comfortable with the reactions they may experience with no professional back-up. Refer to my chapter on spiritual emergency.

On rare occasions an inappropriate client slips in under the radar. These situations have generally turned out badly. If you are a healer and misdiagnose a highly disturbed client, don't stay involved in an effort to fix it. At the first sign of recognition of what you have gotten yourself into, bail out. Duane and I have learned this the hard way. The norm is for these clients to eventually turn on us. Obviously, it can get pretty crazy. No one wins.

And Then There Are Ascension Symptoms.

After the energy portals were opened at Harmonic Concordance time, the vibrations accelerated as the ascension process kicked into high gear. It turned out to be much more difficult for most of us than we anticipated. It became increasingly obvious that we ourselves were in the trenches along with the other lightworkers, whose job it is to man the front lines to absorb the first shock waves. There is no special dispensation for lightworkers! As the mass consciousness awakens and grows more sensitive to the energies, these "spiritual sponges" forestall the utter chaos that would otherwise be the case if one of the abrupt leaps in frequencies hit the mass consciousness full bore.

Wrestling the new consciousness from the grip of the status quo told us that the old 3rd dimension was not just going to roll over and play dead simply because some hot shot lightworkers promised a brave new world. The reason it isn't going to be that easy is because we carry all the old programming right inside our own DNA and genes. It is the inner work, combined with everything else, that may in the end be our most formidable challenge!

Consider that you and others may well be suffering from any number of the plethora of ills generated by these transformational times. These can be terribly disruptive, and they are often severe. It has sent more than one lightbeing scurrying to the emergency room, only to discover that there is nothing medically wrong. If you are anything like the worried souls who contact me, you will feel much better knowing that this is not just your imagination; there is an explanation.

It is not always easy to differentiate ascension symptoms from "real" illnesses. Many readers wrote to ask me in all seriousness if they were losing their minds. I admit I was very glad to hear this. I thought maybe I was the only one headed for a rocking chair on the porch of the Home for the Bewildered.

The DNA activation focuses on the thymus gland that is situated in the chest, toward the center from the heart, and higher near the throat. During activations, the thymus is actually tapped vigorously. Many people sensitive to the ascension energies reported nearby heart and throat symptoms, sometimes alarmingly troublesome. It is scary when one of my healing clients calls to ask me if they are having a heart attack, or merely ascension symptoms. I urge common sense.

I personally suffered the "dancing heart" syndrome on more than one occasion over the past 30 years. It is one scary experience to take my pulse and realize that my heart is playing jump rope. I have consulted with specialists, and the medical people never find anything amiss. The last I checked, this has not proven fatal.

Physical symptoms are not limited to the heart or thymus by any means. There is frequently an involvement with the whole body by way of muscular and joint aches and pains. One of the most common symptoms is fatigue, yes, debilitating fatigue. Sleeplessness is another culprit, and when combined with fatigue, they are the terrible twins.

Ascension symptoms embrace much more than strictly physical complaints. There are also mental problems, including memory loss, lack of concentration, spaciness, anxiety, fear, crabbiness, mistakes in speaking and writing, crazy thoughts and just general confusion. Again, these are often severe, rendering the best of us dysfunctional for days or weeks at a time.

Solar Flare Activity Can Cause Similar Problems. Here is a sample.

> "January 16, 2012 - Today's Energy is thick and dense. It is hard to move, hard to get anything done. It would be a nice day to just hide under the covers. The Sun was busy over the weekend with a low M Class and several high C Class Flares. We are in the midst of a Solar Wind. There have been Earthquakes in South Dakota, Alaska, California, Taiwan, Sandwich Islands, Molucca Sea, Nicaragua, Indonesia, Japan, Russia, Shetland Islands and Mexico There was a 6.6 and a 6.2 Quake South of Shetland Islands on Sunday. There have been reports of headache, neck pain, loud ear noise, chest pain, heart palpitations, difficulty breathing, knee pain, foot pain, dizziness, confusion, fuzzy head, vision issues, skin burning, hot flashes, anxiety, panic attacks, depression, sadness, grief, moodiness, angry outbursts, insomnia and of course, exhaustion. Animals have been moody and needy. Be sure to drink lots of water and spend time in water if you can to put out the 'fire' of the Sun. Eat extra protein for grounding."

Whenever I was experiencing a really rotten day and was at my wit's end as to what was stirring up the problem, as a last resort I learned to check out the solar weather. It pays to remember that we live in a sea of constantly fluctuating, very real energies. It isn't always your mother's fault. I chose the sample above because of the comment he added at the end about our animal friends' reactions to the energies. Even before I thought to check out the daily "weather report," I observed that my unusually independent cat, Mickey, just could not get enough attention that day.

Sometimes it seems like we lightworkers just don't have a chance!

Use the Energetic Clearing Technique listed below: http://www.askclaudia.com/energeticclearingtechnique.htm for emotions. "Take my Higher Self and every aspect of my being to the very first incident that caused this issue to start. Analyze every aspect of it and heal it perfectly, permanently and completely."

From the Sublime to the Ridiculous

I found that the symptoms are not necessarily excluded from the outright bizarre. As the vibrations accelerate, the veil between dimensions grows thinner. I was experiencing something so strange that I was reluctant to even share it with my group of confidants. One day I blurted out, "What would you say if I told you that aliens were communicating with me through my nose?" (This is a good way to lose credibility.)

What actually was happening is that unearthly noises *were* coming from my nose. I mean literally unearthly noises right out of my nose. (Okay, go ahead and laugh.) I know that noses can snore, sniffle, snort and snuffle, but they never made any noises like these. In fact, no sounds like these ever fell on a human ear, of that I am certain. Imagine a butterfly barking or a clod of dirt singing "Ave Maria."

They were loud noises. At times, it sounded like a gale of wind blowing 90-miles-an-hour. Other times they were so loud, they startled me out of a sound sleep. I insisted that my husband look around the house for some sort of invasion, but of course, it was in vain. The only actual danger was to my husband laughing hysterically with his mouth shut and blowing out his eardrums.

One confirmation that I was not crazy came during a telephone conversation with my son. Throughout our conversation, "the noises" were having a field day. I said, "Did you hear that?" Unbelievably, he really did! We just happened to resonate to the accelerated vibrations at precisely the identical moment. These are sensory impressions from other dimensions, and it is not delusional to see and hear things.

Update January 2012. The previous few paragraphs were written several years before this update in mid-January 2012. Beginning just after the winter solstice in December 2011, once again I heard inexplicable sounds, this time resembling loud wind blowing or "white noise" and emanating from my ears rather than my nose, or so it seemed. I mentioned it to husband Don, and he too acknowledged an extreme increase in ear noise. This time I wrote it off to the "tone" that Duane described some recipients hearing after receiving lightbody activations.

In mid-January 2012, anomalous sounds were reported from various locations all over the globe. This was not the first time very loud, strange noises had been widely reported from Seattle to Norway. On January 31, 2012, I listened to an on-line interview with Alex Putney on Red Ice radio. Apparently, he was interested enough in these weird sounds that he undertook a major investigation over several years. He has a website www.humanresources.org.

He was being interviewed from Bolivia. He reaffirmed that loud unmistakable auditory events were increasingly heard and reported by people in various locations since mid-December last. The interviewer's questions, of course, concerned the validity and origin of the phenomena. Putney believes that at its core these sound anomalies are valid and indeed are very much connected to the awakening.

Apparently when the fakes, copycats and such are stripped away, there is a scientific foundation to the audio occurrences and are somehow connected to the increase in class M solar flare activity of late. There are biblical and Hopi prophecies, in fact, that such events should accompany the time of the awakening to other dimensions. I was particularly fascinated by a phrase he used, "...the Sun is playing us like a singing bowl."

What is even more interesting about Putney's investigation is that he, himself, has visited sacred sites like Machu Pichu and heard the sounds. He believes that there may be a connection to sacred sites featuring stones; for example, Stonehenge and the pyramids, and that when struck at certain times, set up an auditory communication that resonates around the world. Perhaps this sound affected the brain frequencies and DNA to facilitate the shift to a higher dimension.

I wish I were more knowledgeable on what appears to be an unshakably solid scientific foundation (it's physics, stupid), rather than something we would more likely call supernatural, but I am certain that this audio business is significant to the interdimensional shift. One last important note: On the radio interview, these sounds were recorded and played several times. Apparently, it was fairly simple to separate the authentic from the fake. I was not crazy after all; the nose knows! I was hearing those sounds; it was only my perception that it emanated from my nose. Perhaps by the time I finish this book, additional information will be virtually commonplace.

Another update September 2012: Recently, Seattle newscasts reported an unidentified noise occurring in a Seattle neighborhood. So many neighbors reported it, that the authorities launched an investigation. So far, the mystery has not been resolved. My friend, Kriss Shellman, formerly lived in that same neighborhood. Directly across the street from her home were two giant water towers. That may be a clue, considering the following article, which strikes me as a plausible explanation, all considered.

Do you hear perpetual high pitched frequencies? You're not alone!
by Christopher OV Admin on September 23, 2012 . Gregg Prescott, M.S.

"Many people are hearing high pitched frequencies which are not related to a Vitamin D deficiency or tinnitus. From my research, I've found out that these frequencies are associated with your spiritual awakening process...These high pitched sounds and frequencies may be associated with a DNA upgrade. Our bodies are mainly compromised of water. Recent studies have indicated that sounds and frequencies have an affect [sic] on water molecules...On a cellular level, these frequencies and sounds are being converted to their most concentrated form of energy, vibration.

"Past life regression hypnotherapist Dolores Cannon believes these high pitched noises are associated with your body rising in frequency as the Earth shifts into a new dimension.

"Many consider these high pitched sounds to be part of our genetic reprogramming as the entire universe is being upgraded on a galactic level. Rest assured that these sounds are beneficial to your genetic and spiritual development."

Walk-ins: Strangers Among Us

On my way to a neighborhood grocery store, I pass a beauty salon. Out front by the curb, they prominently display a sandwich board that says, “walk ins welcome.” I smile in silent amusement. They’d probably think me deranged if I told them what I think that really means.

In the early 1980s, I partnered with another healer. In those days, I did hands-on healing. My healer partner and I encountered a strange energy one day around a man’s head. He complained of a chronic headache. It did not have the usual feel of an invading entity. Yet, the energy influx through what seemed like a hole in a doughnut had an "alien" feel to it. We cleared it; the man’s headache left.

That would have been the end of it, except for one thing. My secretary arrived at that moment with a book in hand intended for us. The book *Strangers Among Us,* written by Ruth Montgomery, described a phenomenon that was totally foreign to us. It was the first time we ever heard the term "walk-in." It surely would not be the last, however.

This is how it works. Sometimes souls bite off more than they can chew in a particular incarnation. They get themselves embroiled in insurmountable difficulties, generating sort of a karmic hell for future lives. They want to end that life, but do not believe in committing suicide. A more evolved soul, who has a special mission on Earth, agrees to trade places.

The more advanced soul has reached a point in its evolutionary journey whereby there is no need to repeat the usual birth and developmental years. It wants to come in and just get to work. If my secretary had not given us that book just at that moment, and had we not immediately read the cover notes, we never would have recognized that Headache Man was in the midst of just such a transfer! Talk about serendipity. To stretch coincidence even further, remarkably enough, Ruth Montgomery herself was lecturing in town that very day, and I attended the lecture that afternoon!

In the years since that incident, my brother and I have come to specialize in the little-known art of escorting in-coming souls and facilitating the exchange. We must have done this hundreds of times. This can be a solution to a life that has become impossible to manage. On the other hand, it is not a panacea for everybody enduring a difficult life and is unable to cope. There is no negative karma or judgment if a soul exits life in this manner, however.

There is a greatly increased influx of w-in souls who are here to help with these transformational times and the ascension process. I am including this information about walk-ins because the subject is rife with misconceptions about it. Also, it is appropriate that healers are aware that this may be happening to some of their clients outside their awareness.

Whether your interest in walk-ins is from the standpoint of a healer or a candidate for exchange, the chaff needs to be sorted from the wheat. First, your soul makes the decision, not you at the personality level. It is a soul exchange. You can wish all you want, but the soul won't agree unless that serves its highest good to pull you out of the present incarnation. No other soul will ever overpower you and commandeer your soul unless all the proper papers are in order, so to speak. Then there is always the problem of a soul agreeing, but nobody wants you! Talk about the ultimate rejection. Even Ma can't kiss that boo-boo and makey well.

Why Would a Soul Take on This Mess?

You have to realize that the in-coming soul is far more mature and capable of handling Earth life than the exiting soul. The agreement is that the in-coming soul must complete all soul missions and take care of remaining unfinished business and karmic obligations of the outgoing soul. The new occupant would not be agreeing to this unless it had its own agenda for the remainder of the life. Just what those reasons are is many and varied. Just so that I am making myself absolutely clear, no one dies and then another one steps in. In fact, most walk-ins are totally unaware that an exchange has been made at the soul level.

Most people are worried about what they will be like if there is a new soul upstairs. You do not suddenly switch personalities. Your friends and family will continue to recognize you. All of the memories remain stored in the memory banks. The changes happen over time. That varies from person to person. Ruth Montgomery cites some cases where quite dramatic changes did happen. One man was a gifted pianist almost over night, for example.

In my experience, the problems that so overwhelmed the original personality is met with a new, more powerful, emotional and creative force. The increased confidence is obvious. I can't say that these are "giants among men" for the most part. They may resolve family wounds that troubled the earlier soul. It is hard to speak in generalized terms because each case is different. The important thing is to understand what it is and is not. In some rare cases, there is an agreement before birth that one soul will come in with the idea of switching after a certain point.

Another outrageous notion is one that pervaded the New Age movement in the 60s and 70s. It was somehow the really "in" thing to be a Walk-in. It was a spiritual ego trip. Don't buy into that. Each soul is of equal stature in the eyes of the Creator. Each soul has its job to do and is just where it should be at any given time.

Duane and I both walked in at the same time, unbeknownst to us, in November 1981. David walked in when he was in his twenties. Don walked in shortly after we were married. All of us were in fairly desperate straits at the time of our walk-ins. Duane and I had prior agreements with our walk-ins that they would prepare the way and then leave.

The Walk-in Agenda

Both from our personal experiences as walk-ins plus close associations with others, hindsight revealed a general agenda common to everyone. These times of the Great Shift attract walk-ins in greatly increasing numbers. Walk-ins are flooding in with soul missions primarily focused on facilitating the process, or should we say they come to play the game? Many outgoing souls contracted to prepare the way and exit at a pre-arranged time, just as Duane and I had. I recognized that this group of walk-ins followed a common agenda to prepare them for missions on Planet Earth. The process typically requires years of extremely difficult challenges.

I can clearly identify challenges and dramatic changes in four major parts of my life, post-walk-in. If you suspect that you are a walk-in, this outline may help you make sense of some challenges that have you doubting your sanity. The four things are: clearing past life memories, choices about career and money, relationship issues and physical health challenges.

Past Lives

When it came to dealing with past lives, it was very clear that somebody upstairs went to a great deal of trouble to make sure this got my attention. One day a woman with a pronounced Oriental accent called me for an astrology consultation. To prepare an accurate chart, the client's birth *time* is essential. The lady was a war orphan, and not only did she not have a birth time, she did not have an accurate birth year. I carefully explained that whereas I could not prepare a natal chart, I could use a special technique I know to discuss current and future astrological cycles.

The lady arrived as my last client on one Friday afternoon. I began to read the charts only to be interrupted with her urgent request to do "past lives." I reiterated what I told her on the phone. Without a natal chart, I could not discuss anything about her past. After two or three abortive attempts, I finally asked, "Are you talking about reincarnation and your past lives?" That was it.

Had I been in my right mind, I normally would simply apologize and send her on her way without charging her a fee. Apparently, I was not in my right mind that day. Some cosmic hypnotist saw to that because I still can hardly believe what happened next.

I thought to myself with devilish relish, "The lady wants a past life reading? A past life reading she will get." I remember staring off into space and seeing a series of pictures like movies playing on a big screen. I am not even sure how long I rattled on before I was startled back to ordinary reality by the women kneeling at my knee and sobbing, "Now I know what my life means. I can never thank you enough." I was still sitting in a daze when my husband came home from work.

You would think that was enough to get anyone's attention, but I guess the Powers-that-be decided to make sure. On two additional successive Friday afternoons, the last client of the day arrived for their astrological consultation only to announce how eagerly they awaited *their past life reading*. Was I surprised? Was I shocked? Oh, no, I proceeded with the same élan as before. One client was a man, the other a woman. What I told them in my "trance" just blew both their minds.

It blew their minds, but that was small potatoes compared to what it did to me. First of all, this was so far out of character for me to do past life readings when I did not do past life readings. And how on earth did these people call me for an astrology appointment and end up expecting a past life reading? However, the part that is hard to describe is the energy explosion that happens when there is a psychic breakthrough like this. I was absolutely reeling. I did not know what end my head was on. I buried my bare feet in soft dirt in my flower beds in a vain attempt to ground myself.

After the third client left, I was so disoriented that I called a friend of mine who is a clinical psychologist. I said I had to see him. When he said next Tuesday, I said *now.* He drove to my house and listened to the whole story. I breathlessly awaited the diagnosis and even more, I waited for the cure. I was startled when his only answer was, "Do me!" Assuming this was for professional observation and analysis, I did my past life gig for him. He did not say one word. He just yelled over his shoulder as he streaked out the door, "I have to process this!" I swear he laid down rubber pulling out of my driveway.

His past life reading was about a vision quest and initiation as a Native American. He sent me a clipping from the Sunday paper following our session, exactly describing that very same ceremony. I don't know which of us was more shocked. One thing for sure, this was here to stay.

The next thing, of course, was spontaneous recall of my own past lives. I did not realize at the time that part of my mission included a career change as a shaman, requiring clearing both my past lives as well as those of my clients. If I knew that then, I think I would have been the first walk-out!

Other chapters of this book discuss past life therapy in different contexts.

Soul Retrieval

What would happen if the Center for Disease Control were to suddenly announce that a terrible epidemic is raging out of control? Of course, there would be a public outcry demanding more information. What are the symptoms? How do you get it? Is there a cure?

Tragically, there *is* an epidemic causing great suffering and ruining lives. You will never hear about this one from the Center for Disease Control, or see it on CNN Headline News. It can strike anyone, even you, even me. However, fear and ignorance push the reality of this situation into the dark realm of myth, magic and superstition.

What is it? It is nothing you can see. You can't spot it on an x-ray or MRI. It escapes detection by the most sophisticated blood tests. You won't see it because it isn't there. That is the problem. This is a situation where a piece of the psyche splits off and departs at the time of a deeply traumatic experience.

The only way to diagnose and treat the problem is by psychic healing or special hypnotherapy techniques. The process is traditionally known as *soul retrieval.* Until recently, this was the exclusive realm of the shaman. Cutting edge psychologists now understand this to be a true phenomenon and routinely treat these cases successfully, albeit sophisticated hypnosis techniques replace the journey typical of shamanic work.

Soul in this context refers to the psyche. Western psychology would regard this as a dissociated aspect of consciousness.

Symptoms Of Soul Loss

Who are my clients, and why do they come for soul retrieval work? Some people sense that something is missing in their lives. They report low energy, lack of purpose and motivation, and no inner fire or joy. They frequently feel that they are living an empty life. Various psychological and physical disorders may develop. No mistake about it, the symptoms can be severe. Often victims have engaged in deep work to get themselves together. They can't understand why they are cut off from their Higher Selves, unable to manifest and create the life they want.

What causes a missing piece to leave? The astral body is involved in performing the basic functions of life. A significant trauma is needed for the disconnection to occur. Traumas cause a breach in your energy system, a temporary collapse in the etheric and astral defense mechanisms. A part escapes through these astral "cracks."

How do clients respond to soul retrieval healing? Well, I am reminded of a movie I saw recently on television. John Borman's *Excaliber* is a powerful telling of Camelot and the King Arthur legend. In one scene, Parsifal brings the Holy Grail to the dying king who drinks from the cup. He is miraculously revived and declares, "I didn't know how empty my soul was until it was filled!"

Psychic Healing: A Case History

A distraught and desperate sister contacts me on behalf of her brother. He has suffered from severe symptoms since the age of two or three. He is caught in the hells of severe depression and anxiety. He has terrible night terrors, and suffers from loss of sleep. He has lost a lot of weight and doesn't eat. He can't work. He is just plain miserable. Nothing helps him. He is seeing a psychiatrist and taking all kinds of medications that don't help, but only add a laundry list of side effects on top of everything else. As I speak with his sister, I feel the familiar tingling in my body, signaling that this is a case for shamanic healing. I assure her that we will take the case, and we expect that it will help him. I pray that I am right.

I work with him at a distance. I close my eyes and go to my healing place in an alternate reality. I secure permission from his Higher Self to proceed. I protect myself from negative influences, and call in my power animals, allies and helpers: Wolf, Tiger, guides, Archangel Michael, and anyone else willing to assist. I psychically bring him into view. He sits with his head in his hands in a state of utter despair.

I say my usual prayers and get down to work. I am catapulted into non-ordinary reality, and begin my journey of exploration on the man's behalf. I am taken to another time and another life. There he is, a retarded boy in his mid-teens. He has fallen under the influence of a Satanic cult in which he is abused and terrified. I follow the cords of time as he enters into the womb in this life. The cords of fear, confusion and attachment from the previous life invade the developing fetus.

A sense of outrage engulfs me. I take my sword and slash away at the cords. I bring in the power of the Light and swaddle the unborn baby in it, I return to the grown man in my healing rooms. With my Spirit Helpers, we begin the task of clearing him. We bring healing into his body at all levels. I return to ordinary reality. A half hour has passed. It is December 14, 2001, the first of three journeys, stretching over two months. (It took a lot of courage for Robert and his sister to trust non-traditional solutions to their problems!)

I call his sister and report on my adventure. His life-long night terrors cease immediately. On March 12, 2002, I receive this email from his sister:

> "Just wanted to let you know that Robert is doing well...He is having second interviews for jobs this week...hooking up with old friends...responding well to therapy...tapering off his sleep aids this week... Finally he is sleeping...He has gained 18 pounds since January. He has become such a different person in the last two months. Thank you for everything you have done for us."

The final confirmation came from his mother. She told me that when he was a baby, she was cradling him in her lap. He was a very beautiful and bright baby. All of a sudden his face changed, and she glimpsed the face of a retarded boy. That was 40 years ago, but she never forgot it because she feared he might really be retarded. It is typical and always very welcome for signs to confirm the reality of the story.

That is just one of the nearly 100 cases I worked on in year 2001. Most of them are successfully resolved, or well on their way. Hard to believe? Just hocus-pocus? Not scientifically proven? Am I crazy? Just the power of suggestion? Merely coincidence? Who gives a damn; they got well!

Dark Night Of The Soul

I remember the exact day in February 1982 that I reached the end of my rope. I was exhausted. I was so terrified about my future that I could hardly function. My home at that time featured a hot tub in my back yard. It was mercifully my escape hatch. One night I went for my routine soak before bedtime. I began to sob uncontrollably. I always felt frightened—sometimes to the brink of total panic—so I resolved to stay in that hot tub until I had cleared fear out of every last cell of my body. If that was not a dark night of the soul, I hope I never see the real thing.

Just at first light, I stood up and talked to the air. I decided that everything absolutely must be healed. I flung my arms wide and shouted, "Well, if I am to be healed, I need a doctor." At 10 o'clock that morning, I saw my first astrology client, Dr. Donald Hurd. I read his chart and told him he would leave his wife (they were already separated), and marry an Aquarian. The only thing I did not know then was that the Aquarian in question was yours truly. We were married three years later.

Relationship changes involve many tangled family problems. Learning to let go of relationships, for whatever reason, may be a difficult lesson. My son and I had an extraordinarily close relationship until his early twenties. After that, we were estranged for six years. Meanwhile, he had things to work out without me, and I accepted that "What will be, will be." When he was emotionally strong enough to accept that he was actually projecting on me what he was not ready to recognize in his evil wife, the relationship with me could heal. When he came to me asking for forgiveness, he cried (and it's a damn good thing he did!).

I was absolutely convinced that astrology was my highest calling. In the 1970s, the idea that astrology could support a full-time career had not yet taken root within the astrological community. The walk-in had different ideas. The only way out of my marriage from hell was to become financially independent. I opened an office as a professional astrologer and proceeded to work my butt off, but I paid the bills.

Walk-in Agenda Affected Career

A gnawing sense of dread settled over me as it became increasingly obvious that perhaps astrology was *not* my highest calling. Over many years, my work as a shaman increasingly began to take precedence over the astrology. For that to transpire, a long, difficult and painful training period unrelentingly propelled me forward toward another life mission that I did not anticipate or even fully understand. My image of a shaman was a jungle native squatting round a fire dining on the daily catch of monkey meat. Yes, there's that monkey meat again.

At some point, this career path hit an obstacle the size of a boxcar. I had a bag lady complex. I entertained visions of myself pushing a shopping cart on the mean streets and sleeping under a bridge at night. Walk-ins come in with a career agenda and the way to finance it. Don't think this means that your personal demons will therefore just melt away. I did years of therapy and deep inner work to exorcize the fear demon. It took two total financial wipe-outs before I manifested the financial resources I needed.

Many people no doubt share these same fears and need to deal with them. If it is part of the walk-in agenda, it is imperative that the proper career path along with the financial support is manifested. As you will read at other places in this book, you may be preparing for the role you will play *after 2012*, which is but a marker in an on-going ascension process. If these issues weren't enough to challenge me for a very long time, the granddaddy of them all had to be the health challenges. On this I am certainly not alone. The ascension symptoms include many physical changes. It was a hydra-headed monster.

In order to step into our respective roles, we needed to access the higher dimensions and adjust to other realities. To accomplish this, the physical body underwent transformation that included activating DNA. I remind you that DNA cannot change without generating a corresponding change in consciousness. This presented some problems, not the least of which was a recalcitrant belief system overwhelmed by the discovery that everything it believed began falling like dominoes.

The physical body presented a challenge to those of us who come from a home world not of human origin. Most of us never really settle comfortably in our own skin. I have struggled with health issues most of my adult life. (The chapter "The Elephant in the Room" deals with this subject.) If I were to access interdimensional travel and cross timelines, the training was necessary. It helped that Duane received the keys to activating the lightbody and the thymus. My time travel experiences occurred before the walk-in. It is titled "The Boyfriend Story" and happened when I was in high school.

The brief outline I have given requires mighty efforts over many years for most of us. At any given time in the walk-in agenda, the struggling souls may give every appearance of people who do not have a clue about what they are doing. Equally as challenging are these changes for awakening souls who are not walk-ins. I hope this encourages you, no matter where you are on the path, to just make the best effort that you can every day. As for others looking on, try not to be judgmental. I have received hundreds of well-meaning suggestions from people hoping to help me solve my physical problems. I appreciate it no end, but I am afraid that dealing with my mother complex and taking Vitamin C won't quite cut it, all considered.

This can be a very tricky subject, and I don't mean to give it short shrift. Certain supplements have worked miracles at times. I should say that they helped at a certain level. That is not to say, however, that the necessary adjustments by an ever-changing physical body that produces a broad spectrum of ascension symptoms will be wiped away by anything. It's the nature of the beast. Many lightworkers have been made to feel guilty because all of their symptoms did not subside when utilizing the latest natural remedy that seems to cure everyone but them. A good gut instinct and an awareness of your process is probably your strongest allies in picking your way through the jungle of all possible remedies.

Last Word From the Horse's Mouth

At the risk of beating a dead horse, I would like to quote a final thought before leaving the subject of walk-ins. The horse's mouth to whom I refer in this case is the person who originally brought this subject to light in her bestselling books *Aliens Among Us* and *Strangers Among Us,* Ruth Montgomery. In case there are any lingering doubts as to whether a walk-in is such a highly evolved soul that it looks upon a human experience as a WALK IN the park (Sorry, couldn't help myself), here is what the "horse herself" had to say:

> "...why it is so difficult for many Walk-ins, who come from a higher dimension, to stay on track when they come here...earth vibrations are so disruptive that they lose contact with the higher source, and many unfortunately lose their way, losing entirely the purpose for which they came back...That is why total discipline, with adherence to the impersonal, impartial, immutable laws of nature is the only way out for any spiritual seeking soul. We must be examples of the Truth...Those who falter must make every effort to maintain that balance, or they too will fall under the influence of the Dark side."

Maybe You Really *Aren't* All There.

Early in my healing work, something I encountered perplexed me. I had this simplistic view of the relationship between the soul and the personality. I envisioned each soul as lovingly watching over the personality incarnated in the body. Yet, when I psychically examined the situation in individual cases, I realized my naïveté. Their soul's interest, at best, was lackadaisical and aloof and, at worst, it just didn't give a damn.

The experiencc of clients so afflicted was no rose garden. Endless struggle marked their lives. There was this feeling that they were constantly in over their heads. An explanation came by way of Dr. Michael Newton's book *Journey of Souls.* He developed an intriguing and effective method that took deeply hypnotized clients to a place between their lives.

It caught my attention when one after another reported that they could decide before each incarnation how much of their total soul energies they would invest in any given lifetime. Sometimes they were stingy with the percentages! Once they got well along into the lifetime, there simply was not enough soul energy to support it.

I found I could assess the level of soul energy available. If it seemed diminished, I traveled to the soul level, and we had a little chat about turning up the juice. Judgment as to the ultimate efficacy of this operation is obviously deeply subjective. My clients claimed over time that they did sense a stronger helping hand. I never knew for sure if it was from my work or just a soul sugar pill. However, if soul sugar pills work, it's okay by me.

If you find yourself struggling terribly and getting nowhere, granted, there can be many reasons. If there is an accompanying sense of being cut off and isolated, maybe it is more than bad karma or lack of spiritual savvy. A deep meditation with the intention of engaging greater soul involvement in your affairs is powerfully effective in some cases.

DIMENSION TRIPPING
REALITY GLITCHES
CROSSING TIMELINES

The thinning boundaries between dimensions are growing easier to breech. That is not always a good thing. When I travel to various dimensions on purpose in my shamanic work, in the service of gaining healing information, that is one thing. When suddenly transported without warning in the midst of one's daily rounds, then that is one heck of a different story.

Let's start with the basically innocuous little reality glitches. I suspect this happens far more often than most people realize. It is rationalized away. You thought you left your teacup in the kitchen, but here it is in the living room. You just forgot. You could just swear that you paid that bill. You leave to run an errand, only to discover that you did it last week.

In the book *The Mystery of 2012,* Meg Blackburn Losy writes about these reality glitches, "As energy shifts take place, this type of occurrence seems off and on. When the veils of reality move or change in density; reality becomes questionable. Our consciousness knows what is happening, but our thinking minds begin to question our sanity." I document these experiences to make them seem more real. And in the cases that are really horrific, I hope to convince you that you are not crazy.

The following story is not only the worst-case scenario concerning dimension tripping that I ever worked with, it was the toughest healing case I ever took on. This concerns a woman I knew for many years. She was once an astrology student of mine. Later on, she often responded by email to my e-newsletter. So I knew her, and we kept in touch.

Over several years, she contacted me about a situation that was making her life a living hell. She described all of the spooky events that occurred in her apartment, namely, the disappearance of her belongings. Aside from a lengthy list of missing items, there were stories of electrical appliances that all ceased to work as well. She put up surveillance cameras, but they stopped functioning. She changed locks to no avail. She was absolutely convinced that someone was entering her place and messing with her things.

She reported this to the apartment manager and to the police several times. They regarded her as a crackpot. She moved three or four times, only to find the same state of affairs duplicated wherever she went. It got to where she performed an elaborate ritual every time she left the house for work. It took her a half hour or so to tie certain doors shut with string, intended to protect important papers and the like.

She and a friend spent nights in her car in futile efforts to observe nocturnal thievery. On top of everything else, she repeatedly lost her jobs. Money was tight. Her emotional state was total chaos. She was terrified, depressed and in despair of her life ever improving. From time to time, she called on me to do some healing work. Needless to say, it was a challenge.

I did my best with my usual tools, assuming that she was suffering from paranoia. She was always terribly grateful that I was trying to help her. I never outright said I thought she was paranoid or crazy. The best that ever came of it was but a brief respite, only for the situation to return with a vengeance.

I would not hear from her for a couple of years, after which she would contact me, again complaining about the same set of circumstances. This came and went until one time in 2009; I resolved to really pull out all the stops once and for all, one more time, in a last ditch attempt to help this woman.

It required some really gut-busting psychic work to get to the bottom of it. When I did, I was shocked. She was dimension tripping. I saw her moving between the dimensions, taking personal items with her. Sometimes various household and personal objects were on one side of the veil, and sometimes on the other. This seemed credible to me because I have sacrificed candy bars and other inconsequential items to the other side myself.

As her fears escalated, an entity decided to get in on the act also. He was a mean s.o.b. He loved to toy with her with poltergeist activity. He always left the room untouched that she sealed off with string, reinforcing her notion that her ritualistic behaviors were necessary. The first order of business was to send this guy packing, which I did.

Next, I reassured her with great confidence that she was not crazy. Finally, she complied with my suggestion that she quit all of the rituals, and simply go to work in the morning. I explained about the entity and dimension tripping. She was metaphysical, but the fact that she knew me and trusted me implicitly was the best thing I had going. And she really was not crazy.

This profoundly changed her life. I told her not to give the entity the satisfaction of toying with her. On her own, she developed some strategies to think positive and not give in to fear. She regards me as her great savior and is beyond grateful. From my point of view, total healing of this situation has a ways to go. She has trouble holding on to the idea of dimension tripping. She still believes someone like the maintenance man is taking things. She has some peace of mind, but her outer work life needs to come around.

I can't say at this writing what the eventual outcome will be. I know that she is much better off than before, and that this approach is the only one that has ever worked at all. To be convinced that she is not crazy changed everything for her. And I do not believe that she is. I trust that the healing energies eventually will free this unfortunate woman completely from her personal hell.

THE KENNEDY AIRPORT EPISODE

Kennedy Airport, Where Are You?

Dimension tripping was easier for me to accept because of my own experiences, which were only too real. The one that always leaps immediately to mind was an episode at Kennedy airport. Flight #240 heading for New York City, the plane on which I was a passenger, pitched about the midnight sky like a cork in an angry sea. The plane touched down safely at Kennedy Airport. I was shaking with relief when I disembarked and made for the baggage area. I did not suspect that my adventure was only just beginning.

I made my way down a noisy concourse, mentally reminding myself to retrieve the umbrella in my luggage before braving the storm still raging outside. By the time my familiar gray wardrobe bag negotiated the turn on the baggage conveyer belt, I was ready to put the frightening flight behind me and concentrate on checking into my hotel.

With dismay, I hoisted my bag to my side only to discover that the zipper had somehow come apart. My red terrycloth robe spilled out. I leaned down and placed the luggage on the floor, fumbling with the bag and its contents. I stood up to signal a Red Cap and went numb. *Every single, solitary soul in Kennedy Airport had vanished.* I was completely alone. It was deadly quiet.

I spotted a luggage cart, loaded my wounded wardrobe bag onto it, and set out for an outside exit. As I walked along the empty corridors, the only sound was that of my own footsteps. I spied a large poster on the wall. It was a Holiday Inn advertisement offering a free shuttle service.

I produced a note from my flight bag listing the address of my particular motel. I called. I carefully explained to the man who answered that I wished to avail myself of their shuttle service. His reply revealed that whatever strange world in which I now found myself, I was still in it. He did not just refuse my request; he reacted as though I had asked him to donate one of his kidneys! He was absolutely beyond indignant. It was like my request was so outrageous that he could barely believe he was hearing it. Undeterred, I explained that I was looking at a poster at that very moment which explicitly stated that Holiday Inn would send a shuttle from the motel to the airport. "It even lists your telephone number," I insisted. He hung up.

Considering the bizarre nature of my circumstances, I decided it was best to leave well enough alone as far as Holiday Inn's shuttle service was concerned. I smiled wryly as I walked past several more such posters, all clearly inviting passengers simply to telephone for service. "Posters from the Twilight Zone," I muttered only too obviously just to myself.

Finally, I reached a cavernous lobby area with several doors leading outside to taxi stands. By now it was very late. I found a bench and realized that it would very likely be my bed for the remainder of the night. It certainly did not appear that it was to be a bed at Holiday Inn Motel. I pushed and pulled my wardrobe bag into temporary order and lifted it off the cart. I leaned down and sat it on the floor.

I raised myself up again, and there, as though appearing out of thin air, was a man in a brown uniform with a badge pinned to it which read, "Taxi." I was in the center of a very large open area. I could not have missed seeing this man. Nor could I have failed to hear him walking toward me. Yet, there he was.

Tentatively, I inquired if he would get me a taxi. Just like the man at the motel, he reacted in utter shock, as though he could not believe his ears. He inquired if perhaps I had lost my mind to really expect taxis to be at the airport at that hour of the night. "But, isn't this Kennedy Airport? Isn't this New York City?" I pleaded. Further conversation became pointless. In resignation, I leaned down for my wardrobe bag and when I glanced up, the man was gone, vanishing as abruptly and noiselessly as he had appeared.

I dragged my bag near a bench and sat down, aware for the first time how exhausted I was. I peered absently into the black night when a lone taxi, emerging like a phantom from the fog and rain, startled me back to my senses. Suddenly, the airport exploded with people and familiar sounds.

The uniformed taxi man yelled and gestured at me, this time in typical New York fashion. "C'mon lady, do ya want a taxi or don't cha?" Out from the approaching taxi leaped a big, burly cab driver. He strode right for me, picked up my bag and loaded me inside his cab. As we drove away, I could see a long line of other passengers waiting in the rain for a taxi. A man shook his fist at the likes of this woman who dared commandeer one out of turn. I mumbled the address of my motel to the driver and shrank far back into the seat. When he asked if he could meet me after he got off work, I was only grateful that life was real again.

Okay, I know what you are thinking. Whenever I included this story in one of my lectures, I couldn't believe it. The only question anyone ever asked about it was whether I slept with the cab driver! I always answered by saying, "No, I did not sleep with *him* that night." (Figure it out.)

Most people will never confront the sudden disappearance of their fellow travelers from a major U.S. airport. Yet, pollsters reveal in recent surveys that people in increasing numbers report some kind of paranormal experience. Speculation is that this reflects not so much a growing phenomenon, but rather a greater willingness to admit to it.

The Kennedy Airport experience happened in the late 60s. I have sustained my career as a professional astrologer. However, the glitch that night in New York City, which baptized me into another reality, sent me off on a parallel track of powerful personal experiences.

The one part of this experience that impresses me the most to this day was my mindset throughout the entire episode. I was never scared. I did not think it was particularly strange at the time it was happening. In fact, I hardly reacted at all to the situation I was in. It just was what it was. Time ticked by, minute by minute, as though each one was a separate experience unto itself. I just accepted the reality of it. I think this is what it means to totally live in the Now.

After that and to this day, the whole thing does not seem real. It is as if it never happened. I don't remember it. I only remember telling the story when I got home. I had not been drinking or taking any drugs. No special spiritual practices like yoga or meditation accounted for it. I believe the terrific storm we flew through that night knocked the door ajar. Many shamanic journeys after that simultaneously coincided with wild, unusual weather.

As for the ascension process, I now know for sure that it is possible to find oneself in a completely different reality in the blink of an eye. And it can happen to any ordinary human like I was then.

Crossing Timelines?

Previous incidents such as the Kennedy airport episode, the abrupt reappearance of our Pill stash, and the disappearance of Duane's green stone, were just enough to render believable the steep increase in articles on the subject of dimension tripping and multiple timelines awash on the Internet.

The notion of multiple timelines was cause for deeper consideration all by itself. That idea morphed into claims that the timelines were *in total* heading for a mutual point where they would merge, wiping out polarity and time as we know it now in 3D. Logic would then dictate that the lines were coming ever closer and closer together. That merger point could well be the black hole in the center of our galaxy. Forgive me if I don't quite get the facts straight in the larger picture. I'm no science nerd. I could say I am a science groupie, though.

Where Did All My Other Stuff Go?

With that said, it was not surprising that weird stuff began happening to change our beliefs about what reality really is. One of these main attractions occurred while husband Don was in the hospital, recovering from spinal surgery. Since Don is my primary caregiver, I needed a caregiver to take his place around the clock. They worked in three-day shifts.

On this particular occasion, caregiver Mary was pulling the night shift. I was in my recliner working crossword puzzles. I have a little secretary that fits conveniently in my lap like a miniature desk top. It's actually just a big bean bag with a solid top for writing. It's good-sized, maybe 18 by 24 inches. The critical point as you will soon find out is that this thing is not easy to overlook.

About eleven o'clock I asked Mary to put the secretary on the dining room table because I wanted to use it first thing the next morning. The next morning I asked for the secretary. Mary went to retrieve it from the dining table only to find it missing. That did not seem possible, as I saw her put it there with my own eyes the night before. A thorough search of the entire house from top to bottom convinced us that it was missing, not only from the dining table—It was gone!

Previous to this, things had been a little weird. There were some late night loud rappings on the front door and such as that. That led me to accept that my secretary was God only knows where, but one thing we knew for sure; it wasn't in the house. I phoned my brother, Duane, to come over and travel with me to other dimensions and retrieve my missing possession. I liked that secretary, and I wanted it back.

We sat facing each other in two chairs. There was a third chair that was empty. This left the fourth chair, which was piled high with several very heavy picture frames heading for the Good Will. Duane and I closed our eyes and journeyed to points unknown. Mary was standing in the room watching us. I have no idea what she must have been thinking.

I opened my eyes and pointed to the secretary under the pile of picture frames just as Duane said, "Is that it?" There it was, squashed flat under the pile of heavy picture frames. That chair was just feet from me and in my line of sight the entire time. It wasn't there. Then it was there. Mary saw it appear also.

Mary was an older woman and small. She accepted caregiving jobs only where there was no lifting required. I say this in case anybody imagines a totally insane scenario that Mary picked up those picture frames and shoved the secretary under them. Why she would do this in the first place is unthinkable on the face of it. She did not have the physical capacity to pull off any such operation as that anyway.

Besides, I saw the secretary return and so did she. Too bad it did not have the courtesy of returning to the table where we put it the night before. Perhaps the manner in which I demanded that the secretary be returned immediately had something to do with it. When the dust of this whole episode settled down, I barely suppressed a chuckle when Mary timidly asked, "Could you and Duane come over to my house? I think I have a ghost there, and it's scaring my daughter."

The episode with the secretary reminded me of another incident that predated that one; one that I had not quite equated with a "now you see it, now you don't" situation. Once again, Don was undergoing surgery. On that occasion, I decided to check into an assisted living facility. I had my laptop set up to do some writing. I fell into the habit of sitting up most of the night so I could write undisturbed. This time, I was working on revising an earlier book, documenting some research on the U.S. horoscope.

My entire manuscript was on the computer, plus a great deal of additional material. Try to imagine if you will, what happened when I resumed work on the book, only to make the unthinkable discovery that everything connected to the book was missing– totally missing. I called my son and my computer guy, and raised hell all over the place. They were not alarmed at first, thinking it was probably easy enough to retrieve. I'm not the most computer savvy person on the planet, after all. Long story short: it was gone to the place wherever it is that these missing items hang out. Final conclusion? Too bad. It is gone forever. Not to get too hysterical or anything, but I spent three years researching and writing that book.

Now imagine how delirious with joy I was when the entire thing returned out of the blue, when I wasn't even searching for it. That's right. It returned no worse for wear. I grant you that computers can do some really weird things. Therefore, I can forgive Don for not being absolutely convinced that this was something that could be explained away somehow within the boundaries of technology glitches, rather than reality glitches. He was also casting quite a skeptical eye towards the entire missing secretary story, convinced that perhaps there was still room for a more plausible explanation. It wasn't long before the Universe set its sights on Don, and went gunning for him big time.

Let's See You Explain This One, Big Fella!

This is the story of the missing wheelchair pad. I especially like this one because I was not involved. This was Don's baby from start to finish, and there was no way out this time. A four-inch thick pad fits in the seat of my wheelchair, so you have an idea of the approximate size of the thing, not easily overlooked is the point. It turned up missing on a day when one of the caregivers was here.

It turned up missing. The search was on. It had to be in the house. This was ridiculous. Don and the caregiver looked high and low, but it was not to be found. I was in my office sitting in my desk chair. When it came time for me to be transported to the family room, I needed the pad in the wheelchair. A totally exasperated Don charged into my office several times to ransack every square inch to no avail, of course. Awhile after this scene played itself out, a chagrined Don walked into my office with pad in hand. "Where was it?" I asked.

I was delighted when it was Don himself that discovered the pad in plain sight on the ledge in front of the fireplace, a location that was totally obvious at a glance, let alone from a repeated search of the house by two people that involved passing the fireplace each time. He swore that it could not have been there just minutes earlier. It was impossible. Apparently, this did not satisfy whatever it was that was determined to make a believer out of this Doubting Thomas; only the next time involved a missing book.

I was using a book that was extra large, eight- by ten-inches and two-inches thick. This story is really quite simple and straightforward. The books I am using as reference texts for this book are kept segregated on my library shelves. I asked Don to be sure to return the book to the segregated group. As he replaced it, he said, "See? I'm putting it back right here."

When I asked for the same book again the next day, it turned up missing. Not only was it not with the special segregated group of books, it was nowhere. After searching the house and repeatedly returning to the book shelf like we do when something is missing–looking 10 times to where it should be but isn't—I announced that I would go searching other dimensions. I was successful but not until the next morning so it seemed, when Don came into the bedroom before I got up, with the book in hand. Now it was again back exactly where Don had put it the day before. And for good measure, lying on the floor just below that section of the book case, was another little book on the same subject that I had been trying to find for years.

After these experiences, I am forced to accept that there are indeed other dimensions lying very close to ours. It further appears that they are drawing closer still. Each time something goes missing, however inconsequential, we look at each other and wonder.

I don't know if it is more confounding to accept that this stuff flips into another time line, or that we are just growing older and misplacing things. At least the cat hasn't disappeared—yet.

THE BOYFRIEND STORY

The following story is one that has confounded my mind for years. If I hate to talk about it, that is nothing compared to the long-suffering family and friends themselves who wish they would never hear about this ever again.

When they read this in the book, there will be eyebrow-lifting and rolling of eyes, believe me. I included it here, because it is the most astonishing and irrefutable proof that there is a whole lot more about ultimate reality than what our limited 3rd dimensional blinders perceive.

(I warn you that this gets a bit tedious.) I am referring to a specific time period that predates all of these other experiences. It happened when I was in high school. This is the one, though, that is the most crazy-making of all. The story begins the summer before my junior year and ends during my first semester in college. It is about the boyfriends I dated and exactly when the relationships began and ended. I can tell you right now, that things just do not add up. I should know. I have been over this a million times at least, and still counting.

I did not think of this situation until about ten years ago. Why on earth it came to mind so long after the fact is a mystery to me. I began dating Jay during the summer preceding my junior year in high school. I continued to go steady with him all through my junior and senior years, and the summer following.

He was a year ahead of me in school. I remember that he delayed entering his first year in college so that we could start together. Unfortunately, I met Dean that summer after graduation and dumped Jay. Dean had already graduated from law school, but he dated me weekends at college. Unfortunately, Dean dumped me before the semester was over.

One day in my musings about this, I happened to remember Don Moody. I haven't enjoyed a moment of peace about this entire matter ever since. I played basketball all through high school. One night, Don Moody drove from a neighboring town to a ball game. Afterwards, he asked to drive me home. My brother dated his sister and besides, he was tall and good-looking, so I said yes. We started to date. I remember we went out on New Year's Eve, because the party was at Cousin Eddie's house. This is where things go absolutely haywire.

All of the time I dated Jay, I never dated any other boys. That I know for sure. So just where does Don Moody possibly fit in? If he approached me after a ball game, I had to be in high school. It also had to be my junior or senior year, trust me, it's complicated. But I was going steady with Jay all that time.

To compound the confusion, I remember corresponding with Don Moody my first year in college. That is when I supposedly had dumped Jay and dated Dean. When I was going out with Dean, I never saw any other guys. I also remember visiting another Iowa college town where Don Moody was going to school. If he was in school, then I had to have been also. We were in the same class. But if I dated Dean, how could I have been seeing Don Moody all that time? And if I dated Don Moody in high school, that could not have been, because I was going steady with Jay. (This gets worse, folks.)

The next guy to complicate an already impossible situation was Whelan Koontz. I went out with him over one summer, I remember that clearly because we tooled around in his dad's sports car. He visited me at the Green Giant Canning factory where I worked the summer before I went off to school. That was the summer, remember, when I dumped Jay and dated Dean. We already have an excessive cast of characters.

It could not have been the summer before my senior year in high school. I worked at a different job then. And besides, I did not date Whelan until I met him during our freshman year in college. Actually, I was reacquainted with him then, along with some early girlfriends from when I started primary school in a neighboring town. All of us got together at my house during that first Christmas break in our freshman year. But Whelan started coming around the summer I worked at the Green Giant. How could that be? I supposedly had not even reconnected with him yet. The time sequence was backwards and upside down. I was coming up one summer short, at least.

I went out with several other boys in high school. That adds another layer of mystery. I went steady with Theron Gordon throughout my freshman year. That leaves my sophomore year. After that, I dated Jay. How did I have time to date Dick Woods, Harrison Turner, Eldo Meyer, Raymond Cantonwine, Lefty Turner, Gene Cole, Dick Grimm, Dale Hagen, John Edwards and Darrell Dickens? If I left anyone out, I am sure you were memorable in your own way.

This is as far as I go with this inexplicable tale. I could add details, but you get the idea. Countless times, I lie awake at night going nuts over and over this impossible scenario. While patiently holding forks aloft as dinners grew cold, unwilling friends and family heard it all again and again *ad nauseum*..

Finally, at the end of his rope on this subject, my husband carefully diagrammed the timelines on a spreadsheet. He was a research chemist and engineer pre-chiropractic days. I'm saying he is a nerd for this sort of thing. He laid it all out. I have to accept it. The way things happened simply were not possible. These experiences just had to involve some other reality and/or dimension skipping, raising havoc with linear time. Do not write me about this. I'm having the last word.

Another odd thing about some of the relationships is that I have no memory about how they ended. I went out with some of these boys once and we hit it off. We parked after the movie and necked. Yet, I never went out with them again. I don't know why or what happened. It is just a blank.

Whether it's a "misplaced" teacup or inexplicable dimension tripping, it behooves us to open our imagination to embrace a much wider set of possibilities. As I discovered, some things simply cannot be rationalized. I have no problem believing that extraordinary phenomena have been a feature of human life from ancient times. Now that we are collectively in the process of an ascension shift, however, this sort of thing may not be so extraordinary anymore.

After all is said and done, I am reminded of one of Sherlock Holmes's most famous quotes, "When you have eliminated the impossible, whatever remains, however improbable, must be the truth.

Excess Baggage and Personal Demons

Some clearings involve issues more mundane than the likes of invading entities described in the chapter on clearing negative energies. I am referring to personal inner landscapes. Granted, there can be some equally grotesque denizens inhabiting our own inner space.

I have pretty much come to terms, however reluctantly, with the notion that not everyone on Planet Earth will make the Shift into the 5th dimension until long after 2012 is but a date in an old history book. Frankly, I can't imagine how anyone who snoozes his or her life away, while entertaining unresolved emotional baggage, could conceivably tolerate the higher dimensions. The same goes also for anyone dominated by hate and other equally negative energies. I could be wrong. Anything is possible.

Ascension is a process that started years ago; how many years ago depends on whose opinion one wants to accept. Some mark the beginning as far back in history as the time of the Renaissance in Europe. Frankly, I think this is as fruitless as the age-old argument about how many angels may dance on the head of a pin. It is not how long the ascension process has ignited humanity's awakening that is crucial to know. The point is that it has in all likelihood already begun, and will continue, perhaps even into succeeding generations, belying any notions that we have done it all except wait for the calendar to reach some magic date.

If there is any one thing that describes lightbeings, it is an unrelenting attention to their inner life and state of consciousness. These are the troops upon which we depend to move the collective to critical mass. Some people may not have extensive knowledge of metaphysics and spiritual matters. However, knowledge never got anyone through the gates of Heaven before a good heart.

The Great Granddaddy of Personal Change: Transformation

Personal transformation is the one time we get to talk about butterflies. Transformation has three stages: (1) death and loss, (2) transformation and change, and (3) rebirth. I have described this process many times to clients in the throes of transformation. I like to use the analogy of the caterpillar that enters a cocoon and emerges as a butterfly.

STOP! I Just HAD to Slip This Quote in SOMEWHERE, didn't I?

From *Transformers: Shamans of the 21st Century:*

> "Planets are playgrounds for the caterpillar kids of the cosmos to earn their wings. That is my *ultimate* conclusion: Life is a game that includes some very serious pain." (I do not see that the author made mention of any chrysalises. I take license to say, "Ha! to all pedants.")

To Continue:

That worked well until a client, probably a Virgo, ruined everything by reminding me that butterflies come from chrysalises, not cocoons. *Cocoons* rolls off the tongue much smoother than chrysalises, so I continue to use it. Besides, even though technically correct, I feel it sounds a bit snobbish—butterfly chrysalises. I just wanted you to be aware that I know the difference. Back to the subject of transformation, we eventually emerge as a new self. The test is whether or not we will forge ahead or retreat in fear to the old life.

There are dark nights of the soul, initiatory experiences and physical challenges thrown into the mix before we find ourselves drying our butterfly wings on a leaf in the sun. We have eaten our Cheetos, drunk our coffee, dealt with negative energies, expanded our belief systems, cut ties to toxic relationships, purged our livers, activated our DNA and much more. Now what?

Regardless of whatever high expectations and unbridled enthusiasm accompanied the beginning of your spiritual journey, the daunting task of personal transformation will not be denied. This is part of what living in the 3rd dimension is all about. You contracted to come here. Doctor, lawyer, merchant, chief—saint or sinner—you cannot skip steps and make it out of here without the house of cards tumbling down around your ears. You have to pay your dues. You have to do the work.

Stage One: Death and Loss

Whenever I discussed the process of transformation, and reported stage one to clients, I was quick to assure them that we are not necessarily talking about a trail of dead bodies littering the street. Death and loss in connection with transformation of consciousness should first be considered symbolic in its meaning. The bottom line in this case refers primarily to the *inner life.* If you are going to be a new self, you can't simultaneously hang onto the old self identity. Something's got to give. You will need to learn to let go of something, that is the loss and/or death that we are talking about.

This is not something deep and mysterious. It's what ails you! It's that simple. Do you have an anger problem? Are there sexuality and intimacy issues? The list goes on. Surprisingly, many clients over the years report cleaning out closets and dresser drawers with a vengeance!

These are the issues that must undergo death. The great forces of transformation are bubbling up from within. That is the "reward" you get for all of that work you have done on your consciousness. It is indicated in your horoscope by the planet Pluto. (We astrologers continue to treat Pluto as a planet, regardless of the current controversy among astronomers.)

Whenever there is a powerful influence of some sort operating in the psyche, it will often project onto your outer life as well. When the transformational energies are transiting stage one of death and loss, that is not to say that there may be a real life death or loss coincident with that time period. Maybe an elderly relative may cross over. There are other kinds of losses that I have observed among my astrological clientele. It usually bears some connection to financial matters, such as embezzlement by a business partner or an investment loss. Obviously, these are times when you should act conservatively in all financial affairs. It's a good time to have an astrologer keeping a weather eye on your chart.

Just how stage one will manifest in any given situation will very much depend on who you are, and where you are in your spiritual journey. If you are a very young person when this cycle hits, it is usually your parents who will experience the stage one cycle, consequently, imprinting you.

The best advice all around is to tend to the inner life without resisting the truth about yourself. Perhaps a therapy with a professional is in order. The more you contain stage one energies within, the less likely they are to project onto your outer life and bite you on the behind, or very much worse. The best thing I can say about this aspect of transformation is that it is something that you look back on and say, "I am grateful that it happened to me *back then.*" I don't hear many clients expressing that opinion, however, when they are in the throes of a difficult stage one cycle. It's value is often appreciated only in retrospect.

Stage Two: Transformation and Change

The worst is over. If stage one included a dark night of the soul, stage two definitely involves some light at the end of the tunnel. You are no longer your old flawed self. However, change is a process, and it does not happen overnight. This means that you are not your shiny new self, either. Then who the hell are you?

If we compare this to swimming across a river, you are in mid-stream in stage two, and it is a very critical time in your psychological/spiritual life. It is very scary when there is not a clear sense of identity; it can be overwhelming. One of two things will transpire at this juncture: the psyche will turn back to what may be flawed, but is familiar, or swim bravely forward toward the far shore, no matter how frightening it is. Stage two is a good time to solicit help from some supportive friends; it is a particularly vulnerable time emotionally. Again, it is obvious that these different stages are only a model. Once set within any given life experience, circumstances vary widely.

Stage Three: Rebirth

The death of one thing always implies the birth of something else. That is the way it works. Therefore, if you keep at the change business long enough, the old self "dies" and a new self is born. That is when we get to talk about butterflies. There you are, fully emerged, sitting on a leaf, drying your wings in the sun in preparation to flying off into your new life.

Memory holes

This pattern almost didn't make it into the book. Let me explain. About six months ago, certain time periods in my life began to run in the background on the mental screen of my mind. For example, during World War II, my mother left my brother and me to stay with an aunt while she visited my dad, who was stationed Stateside for a time. I began to run the movies of our time there, regardless of whatever else my mind was occupied with. I know this sounds weird, but that is the best I can explain it.

After several months' apparently exhausted whatever was to be accomplished by that, the "movies" moved to a later time, when we lived in a little community for a couple of years before returning to our home town. I began to notice that there were major memory holes in my recall of those times. I remembered some experiences that had to have been somewhat of a big deal to a 12-year-old kid. I was chosen as the cheerleader for the basketball team, for example. Yet, the experience is a total blank. I can remember not one single thing about it. As this process continued, I realized that my past seemed to be crumbling away and leaving memory holes.

Today, many people fear that they may be suffering from Alzheimer's. I admit the thought crossed my mind. At any rate, I was blessed with almost a photographic memory most of my life, so this was really a huge anomaly and grew very worrisome.

One day a favorite channeler ran an email article addressing this very same issue. She reminded readers that the physical body was crumbling away, along with many of its memories of the past, as part of the process of transforming into the lightbody. She reinforced an admonition that this not lead to fears about losing one's memory. Later that day, I mentioned to a friend my earlier worries about this, and how relieved I was to find out what was really going on. My friend let out a shriek. "The same thing has been happening to me, and I thought I was losing *my* memory. I'm so glad you told me this!" That is when I decided that this may be more of a universal problem than I realized. So just in case, there is your answer.

Preparing for Ascension

Each person's journey tells its own unique story. Some things we all have in common, however. There are times when we need help. Other chapters suggest investigating some non-traditional modalities that are more in line with surviving the roller coaster ride of processing the shift into another dimension. For starters, an extra seat belt or two may be in order.

CHAPTER ELEVEN

Clearing Negative Energies

The new NOW
must have
freedom
of movement.

It can be
no other way.

Releasing fear
and pain issues
allows you
to move forward
into the new
reality.

Clearing Negative Energies

An accumulation of negative energies from many different sources adds additional layers to this business of the ascension process. When you go for your annual physical check-up, don't expect the doctor to diagnose or treat these along with your high blood pressure.

Conventional medicine and psychiatry cling to old paradigms that preclude diagnosing the transformation that is happening on the planet now. For most people who are serious about the shift in consciousness, an assessment of the realities of traditional modalities alongside alternative solutions makes the most sense. Even at that, it is necessary to pick your way through the minefield of many confusing choices.

Many people sense that their lives are offtrack somehow. Clients sometimes insist that they are following all of the rules, yet things go very wrong for them just the same. There can be a sense of loss of control of the life. A frequent complaint is that one is simply stuck. Others can't find where they belong, especially concerning the proper career niche. It is common to hear people say that they simply have an intuition that "something" is there, blocking success and well-being.

For many others, the symptoms are far more severe. It is common that negative energies are raising absolute havoc for some and creating a life of Hell on Earth. Whether you are reading this as someone who identifies with such problems, or more from the perspective of a healer, it is helpful to familiarize yourself with the various sources of negativity.

Failure to clear the blocks that prevent us from moving on to our next life has profound implications. No longer do we choose to simply incarnate to do better next time around. This is about preparing for the leap into another reality altogether. Our choices now are unique to these extraordinary times. We are preparing for ascension.

The following material on clearing the appropriate energies in preparation for ascension makes it clear that there is far more involved than waving a magic wand that somehow magnetizes every etheric iron filing that fits the general definition of negative.

Clearing Past Lives

Troubling past life bleed-through does not fall into one broad general category, nor does it automatically clear in one fell swoop by checking that box. For example, the problem presents separate considerations. To name some, involves an analysis of specific areas of life that past lives affect, the symptoms they generate, the soul contracts involved and perhaps the place in the body and chakra system where these energy patterns are lodged.

When entering into an incarnation, the memories of previous lives in the physical body accompany us as a single thread of experiences. Ideally, this material belongs confined to the deep cellular memory banks so as not to clutter up the present. However, bleed-through may appear as innocuous as a birthmark, remembering a minor wound from a time past, to something with far more serious consequences, indeed, consequences which may seriously sidetrack the life.

For example, friends from Alaska once visited us and requested lightbody activations. We always include clearings of the aura, if needed. We psychically sensed where the woman had sustained a serious wound in a past life encounter with a spear in which, unfortunately, the spear won. It was exactly at the same place where she had recently undergone surgery to remove a kidney. Yes, these past life memories are real all right!

Our work with clients in clearing negative energies almost always includes eliminating the memories of past life wounds. However, this is by no means limited to physical wounds. Sometimes other kinds of traumas are fully as debilitating emotionally and psychologically. Earlier experiences in relationships can create perplexing problems in present day unions, for instance, and we believe this should be routinely addressed. It is common to find souls caught in a loop of repeating the same patterns over and over again.

In one of Dolores Cannon's books, she tells about fake past lives. This is not done in the spirit of deception and trickery. When volunteers agree to come to Earth at this time, they are often newcomers to a physical Earth existence. Therefore, fake past lives are provided just to make them feel at home.

There is one particular pattern that I find frequently among people on the "spiritual path." Apparently, many of us have multiple incarnations devoted to life in monasteries, temples, convents, ashrams and other places of spiritual commitment.

We took our vows embracing poverty, chastity and other disciplines very seriously, maybe a little too seriously.

This runs counter to success in a more secular setting this time around. Old vows and allegiances to another time and place, no matter how diligently we served them then, are no longer appropriate. The bugaboo here is never discovering that this may be the culprit behind some blocks in your present lifetime. It is a rare doctor or therapist who realizes that your sex life is a mess because you took past life vows of celibacy just one time too many!

When engaging in shamanic work, it may come to the attention of the healer that a past life is the reason for a problem in this life. It is not always the other way around, with the client approaching the healer for past life therapy. For healers who are psychically seeing past life problems, do take the time to explore the most effective way to set the information within the context of your client's belief system. Otherwise, different ones may well stall out and reject out of hand what you are telling them. Do not just assume that anyone's belief system embraces reincarnation, unless you know for sure already.

Why take the risk of short-circuiting the healing process on philosophical grounds? Shaman are not in the business of ramming their point of view down other people's throats, or at least they shouldn't be. Here is a protocol that I use.

I ask clients if they believe in reincarnation and past lives. If they say yes, I discuss their stories within that frame of reference. If they answer no, I am still pretty much on neutral ground with the clients who are not comfortable with past lives. I simply comment that many of my clients do believe in past lives, so I just go along with their belief. There is no need, consequently, for any awkward back tracking.

For clients who are uncomfortable with reincarnation, I simply explain that I am identifying themes in their life that are the basis for our great myths and legends and are also key elements in Jungian psychology. I go on to explain that I prefer to present their primary soul energies as myths or stories relevant to them. Then I just say the same thing as when I do a past life reading anyway. (A rose is a rose is a rose!) It takes only a minute to align your client with the way you work so as not to clash with their perception of things.

But Does Past Life Therapy *Really* Make a Difference?

If I ever had my doubts about the efficacy of past life therapy—and I did—it was quickly quelled when I worked on a woman who was seeing me in regular counseling sessions at the time. I noticed that at each visit she used the thumb of her right hand to constantly rub the palm of her other hand. After several sessions of noticing this same behavior, I quite naturally inquired if her other hand pained her, and if that was why she rubbed it all the time. She said that it was just a habit; she had done it since childhood. I wondered if there might be more to this story than that, so I asked her if she had any objections to me looking at perhaps a past life origin. She readily agreed. In fact, she was most enthusiastic at the thought of having a past life reading.

Unfortunately, this turned out to be a very sad past life story. The past life that emerged took place in New England in the United States in early colonial times. It was Christmas time. The father had a talent for carving dolls from pieces of wood. Each year, a Christmas tree was hung with the painted wooden dolls On Christmas eve, the children were delighted to see the tree ablaze with candle light.

Suddenly, there was a terrible fire that engulfed the little log house so suddenly that the entire family lost their lives, save her. She was sent to an uncle who took her in out of duty but was otherwise a cruel man. She was kept around as a servant girl.

At night, she was confined in an old shed. A rope was tied around her wrist and looped over a peg high above her head so that she could not run away. The knot in the rope dug into the palm of her left hand, as she was forced to sleep with that arm above her head. That explained the subconscious memory of that knotted rope. But that was not the end of this story.

My client was reared by a nanny in this life. Whenever the nanny put her to bed and covered her with blankets, she always pulled her left arm out from under the covers and sleep with that arm over her head!

Her nanny told her in later years that no matter how many times she put her arm back under the covers, she always found the arm over her head again. Finally she gave up. Not only that, the woman confessed that she still had that same urge as an adult. She just resisted the impulse. To prove just how strongly the past life bleed-through can be, my client also collects painted wooden dolls.

One reason that this particular past life reading still stands out in my mind is that I got the fright of my life while I was doing it. I had my eyes closed. Just as I came to the scene in which the knot in the rope was digging into the palm of her hand, my client let out a loud yelp, "It's gone!" I must have jumped a foot in my chair. But she was right. The sensation in her left hand was gone, and she had no inclination to rub it ever again. That was the fastest resolution I think I ever remember from a past life reading. It sure did make a true believer out of me!

Entity Clearing, or Things That go Bump in the Night

Careful handling is a prerequisite for myth-busting the Hollywood version of possession, featuring vomited frogs, flying furniture and lots of green stuff, obviously calculated to strike terror into the breast of most movie patrons in order to sell tickets. I have been in the exorcism business for over 35 years and have yet to see one frog or any green stuff.

Buzz words like *possession* and *exorcism* punch so many stereotypical hot buttons originating from movie land and hair-raising literary sources that we prefer to replace them in favor of the more neutral descriptions as *entity contamination, invasions* or *clearings.* It is also common practice to refer to exorcisms as *extractions.* To be absolutely accurate, absolute possession is very rare. In the shamanic world, this is regarded as multiple personality when there is a total take-over alternating with the original owner in residence.

For many complex reasons, this is a situation in which a therapist experienced in such matters ideally should be involved. I hold no formal degrees in psychology, but I have successfully treated multiple personality on my own. The circumstances of the case that led me to taking it on were atypical. It placed me in an extraordinary position in which only I could intervene for the simple reason that the client refused to be treated by anyone else.

The investment in time and energy easily accounted for nearly three years. As a case study, it would be an academy award documentary. I'll not describe the details of my strategies except to say this: The therapy was treated as a case of possession in order to be successful.

The image that most remains at the conclusion of this case is of me on the floor wrestling with my client for control, accompanied by a lot of screaming, grunting and yelling. After that, the most amazing thing happened. The woman appeared to have lost 20 pounds in an instant. It was the damnedest thing I ever saw.

But that is not all. She belonged to Alcoholics Anonymous (AA) and was due at a meeting. I told her to come back for a follow-up time immediately afterwards. When she returned, she was throwing a fit about me doing something to make others believe that she is a witch. When she calmed down, she reported that no one at the AA meeting believed that she could possibly have lost 20-30 pounds in just a couple of days. Apparently, this caused quite an uproar.

At that particular time, a popular multi-level-marketing diet product was sweeping the nation. I said, "Doris, look how much money we will make selling Cambridge at the next AA meeting." Her healing was not complete because she did not laugh, and here I thought it was really, really funny.

Seriously, this is an ideal example of just your ordinary "man in the street" intuiting that a certain something that was an integral aspect of Doris had simply vanished in the matter of a few days. I think we can pretty much assume that any so-called "man in the street" more than likely lacks the psychiatric-psychic vocabulary that would translate this subconscious awareness into a consciously articulated expression of precisely what really was missing.

You would have to imagine one of the AA members sashaying up to Doris and casually observing, "Since you got rid of those multiple personalities, you suddenly look 25 pounds lighter. Can I have the name of your therapist?"

People are more psychically attuned to their world than they realize. Other parts of the book expound on this subject in more appropriate chapters. The problem is that most people have only a very narrowly-defined range into which these psychic impressions may find expression. That range is ordinarily limited only to what can be linked to the five senses.

When Doris showed up for the AA meeting, for example, the change in her psychic field was so dramatic that the collective subconscious of the entire group was instantly hit, "What in the hell is this?" If her right arm had fallen off that would have been neat. As I said, no one was very likely to understand what had actually happened, so the next best thing was to explain it away by a nearly overnight weight loss. Even that wigged everybody out as it was. As for me, I was ecstatic. It was proof positive that something had really shifted. Also, I was very likely freed from doing mortal combat with the more aggressive of her personalities.

Shaman/healers may rightly play an adjunct role in possession cases under certain circumstances. I prefer working in conjunction with a professional psychologist. The psychiatrists and I are not normally a good match. They start throwing drugs into the patient right off the bat. That is usually extremely contra-indicated. On the other hand, sometimes the anti-psychotic drugs are a life-saver. We need to be careful with generalizations; one size does not fit all.

I cultivate relationships with open-minded therapists in my area, preferably clinical psychologists. Some cases may need hospitalization and often under emergency conditions. I have had my share of rides in an ambulance with a client in a straight jacket. Just be aware that once you get there, psych wards are going to require a professional referral. (You may refer to the information about the spiritual emergency networks elsewhere in this book.)

On one occasion, a client’s husband called me in the middle of the night. Patricia, one of the personalities, had taken over. She liked to gain control and play "I won’t drink any water for a week" game. She knew that this brought about a trip to the hospital in the ambulance. Patricia hated Meg, thereby deriving devious satisfaction when Meg "woke up" in a straight jacket, scared out of her mind.

Victims of Entity Invasion are not Sinners

People coming from a strong fundamentalist Christian orientation routinely label sufferers from entity invasion as sinners and furthermore, deserve this punishment. In their teachings, all entities are demons from Hell when it could well be just poor Aunt Martha hanging around after passing over in the confusion of Alzheimer's disease. I dissuade all my clients of this notion because I do not believe it for one minute. Moreover, it is outright cruel to add a spiritual guilt trip to anyone who may already have suffered for years from intolerable fear and a ravaged life.

Many victims mistakenly believe that entity invasion is a karmic consequence from a past life as a bad person. I don’t remember a single case in which that was true, either. If unwanted entities do not gain access to individuals from sin or karmic consequences, just how does it happen? This question nearly always comes up, and I don't blame anyone for asking.

The most important thing to remember if you are the healer is to reassure your clients that it's not their fault. Sometimes this gives as much comfort as the healing work itself. If you suspect you are afflicted by entity invasion yourself, I hope my words are enough to reassure you. While we are on the subject, I have borrowed a list from my website www.dianastone.com of possible culprits that could attract entity problems.

- Childhood abuse, probably the most common
- Difficult Childbirth
- Loss of consciousness, including anesthesia
- Drunkenness, drugs
- Severe illness
- Mediumship, automatic writing, astral travel
- Severe crises, series of deep traumas
- Rage-aholic
- Deliberate curses, black magic

Any of these things may render a victim vulnerable to easy access, entry is only possible if the energy systems are compromised. Once the door is open, other entities may be attracted to stop by for a free lunch. By the way, nearly one-fourth of the healings of Jesus were the casting out of demons and unclean spirits. Many healers, including me, invoke Archangel Michael when dealing with possession.

In many instances, it is simply a matter of "wrong place at the wrong time." I compare it to swimming in a lake and picking up a leech on your leg. The only difference is that our culture believes in leeches. In the first place, the reason it bloats into such an out-of-proportion problem is exactly because we do believe in leeches but not entities that bother people. If we left the leech on our leg, it would not be a pretty sight after a while either. Invasion problems likewise deteriorate year after year, but ignorance is the enemy, not sin or karma.

In one case, the client in therapy reported that she suffered from abuse but could supply no pertinent information. This raised some question about whether children may have felt abused because of an attached entity rather than from their own personal abuse, suggesting it was an entity that had been abused before attaching. This gives rise to false memory.

In recent years, some open-minded therapists have taken the problem of possession seriously. Lacking the tools of a shaman, they have developed some techniques of their own, e.g., deep hypnosis to successfully treat patients so afflicted. I am not sure how this is greeted by their colleagues, but a surprising number of books on the subject have been forthcoming from the field of traditional psychology. (See bibliography)

You can imagine my qualms the first time I blurted out to one of my astrology clients that her problem may be possession by an entity. I was expecting almost any other response than the one I got! "I always suspected it." In actual practice that has been my experience in almost every case. People do not "just happen" onto someone who informs them of entity invasion. That still small voice within led them to confirming something they suspected all along.

People are often more intuitive about these things than they are given credit for. However, here is the kicker. They didn't REALLY know it until I said it. It is subliminal, just barely hovering below conscious awareness, but when I say it aloud, there it is. I have to go first.

Some cases came from people who read about this in our first book. It struck an intuitive chord of recognition. Don and I successfully accomplished healings over time from a distance without ever meeting the clients in person. They have expressed undying gratitude for restoring their lives. I am waiting for them to die off to find out after the reading of the will just how grateful they really were. (Lighten up. We needed some comic relief here.)

Believe it or not, assuring people that they are targets of entities that plague them is the preliminary step for putting people at ease. Their relief at finally understanding why things are terribly wrong in their lives is palpable. It dispels many mistaken conclusions that they have drawn from their situation.

Not all entities are created equal. There are the evil doers and real dark types. Then there is the matter of Aunt Martha or grandma. There are many reasons that some folks remain earthbound and hang around you. A husband may linger until his bereaved wife is able to get on with her life. A true earthbound stays around the living in order to draw life-sustaining energy. This is not out of any malicious intent.

I worked with one client who lost her mother when the client was 17 years old. She was devoted to her mother's care for four years preceding her death. She implored her mother to never leave her, and sure enough there she was many years later when the daughter was in her thirties.

The problem came from our side of the veil in this case from someone who would not let go. The gist of this particular situation was the dramatic way in which the daughter's very troubled life turned around after we sent her mom into the Light. In fact, she eventually became a practicing professional astrologer but not without a long, difficult struggle and incessant nagging from me.

Unfortunately, not everyone dies in bed surrounded by loving family members. Instead, certain circumstances sentence the poor souls to wandering between dimensions, not even recognizing they are dead. They may have died violently as a murder victim or accidentally in a car crash. Some overdose on drugs. Some are psychotic and in mental institutions. When they attach to someone living, it absolutely raises hell in the host's chakra and energy systems.

Follow-up healing is frequently required after clearing entity contamination. I wish that were not so. The fact of the matter is, however, that simple clearing without follow-up is playing Russian roulette with your client.

Through the years, I performed clearings as a one or two shot deal. Regrettably, somewhere down the road, further work was obviously in order. After the extraction, I left some clients with an energy field all chewed up like a Swiss cheese. I might just as well send out engraved invitations to anyone "over there" looking for an easy, free lunch. I hate sloppy work—especially mine. Whenever that happened, it put my stomach right into a knot.

Here is what happens. Many healers are good at diagnosing and clearing entity invasion. They too frequently skip the critical follow-up healing; or do not know how to do it; or are not aware that it is necessary to do it, leaving the victim open to further invasions. I have completed the work of countless healers who have left the job half done. I can't count the times when a client has called, and the conversation started out the same old way. I can tell you what is coming next from a mile away. "I've been to other shaman and I'm okay for a while, but it always comes back."

It is beyond me why other healers don't figure out something that seems so obvious. To do this work requires psychic sight to tell if an entity is there in the first place. Then why can't they go on to see what horrific shape the energy field is left in as well?

Here is something else to consider. We professional shaman have the business side of our work to consider. I will give you something to think about if you make a living as a healer. I wrestled with this for years. To tell the truth, the reason I limited entity clearing to one or two times was to save my client money. I believed that if I charged what it was worth to complete the job, it would be so expensive that no one could afford it. It's a helluva poor reason.

I will leave it up to you as to how you decide to structure your fees when you do entity clearings. However you decide, just remember this: I have never seen a case where the individual's energy field was left intact after there has been an entity messing around. Sometimes it is a matter of just a little nibbling around the edges.

Nevertheless, how would you feel if you went around with just your ears chewed off? Besides, by the time most people resort to seeking help from a shaman, they are in decidedly worse shape than a bit of nibbling. As for me in my practice, I have never worked with a client who did not readily consent to however many sessions it takes to heal him-her of whatever was making life hell, once I explained what was going on.

Take precautions against the possibility of an uninvited guest sneaking in while a patient is under anesthetic. If anyone walked down hospital corridors with psychic vision, they are likely in for a shock. People die there. Some of them hang around. These facilities periodically need a good house cleaning. We always stand by in spirit whenever a friend of ours goes under the knife.

Also be aware that a patient under anesthetic is cognizant at some level of everything that is said, and will be impacted by anything negative like, "This poor devil doesn't stand a chance." Before undergoing surgery, request the surgical team to refrain from saying anything you should not hear if you were awake. I always request that any surgeries be accommodated by music of the patient's choice.

My husband and I can look back on a long and dramatic 30-year history with Ramona. I have responded to many emergency calls for help, sometimes in the midnight hour. She is an awakened lightworker, and like many others, her path has not always been easy.

One of the most terrifying experiences involved an inexplicable but no less vicious attack by her family dog. I hate to be gruesome, but he nearly tore her face off. She spent three weeks in the intensive care unit in a coma, fighting for her life. A large network of her frantic friends prayed for her day and night.

Miraculously, she pulled through. She subsequently had several surgeries on her face. I was the astrologer who chose the most propitious times for all of the surgeries. However, when after the final surgery she scheduled an update on her astrology chart, I realized I had not seen her in person all this time.

I steeled myself for her consultation in person, not really knowing if she looked like Frankenstein's monster or the attractive woman I had known throughout the years. Let's say that I must have chosen some bang-up surgery dates. If I had not known otherwise, I never would have guessed she'd been injured so horribly.

The point I want to make, however, is about an incident that happened long after her recovery. She lives in the city, but she and her husband also own a 16-acre farm in the country. She called one day to describe a feeling that plagued her only when she visited the farm—a horrible sense of dread, stemming from her stay in the hospital.

I pressed her to remember images that were more specific. She then recalled that when she was in the coma she thought that a bear on the farm had attacked her. She had a faulty memory that it had cached her body in a hollow in the ground and covered it with dirt. The subconscious picture of one's dead, decaying body lying somewhere on the property would give anybody the creeps.

We finally cleared the offending feelings, but it took a lot of clearing work before she was free of them. It was nearly a year later that she called me with what is the point of this story in the first place. She suddenly remembered hearing the doctor in the hospital saying, "Ramona is not OUT OF THE WOODS yet."

Succubus and Incubus

Even if you are into kinky sex, succubus and incubus invasion is no laughing matter for most victims. A *succubus* is, by definition, a demon in female form who seduces a man at night in his sleep. An *incubus* is a demon in male form who seeks sexual intercourse with a woman at night. Legends of both succubi and incubi stretch far back into medieval history. I have encountered this problem only rarely in my shamanic work, but it is also a phenomenon in modern times.

These types of sexual encounters are a far cry from roses, champagne and a movie. Most women are terrified of these night visits and usually describe them in a manner more resembling violent rape than consensual sex. Men also find these attacks frightening and repugnant, at least this is the profile of the few I have interviewed in connection with my shamanic interventions. I have never seen this personally, but some victims report bruise marks and even blood remaining after an attack.

In each case in which I have been involved as the healer, I have treated it as I would any other case of entity invasion, and the treatment has been successful. Nevertheless, I admit that I harbor many doubts in my mind as to the true nature of these experiences. There are a variety of psychological problems, including psychoses, which could well be misconstrued as succubus and incubus attacks. Based on my very small number of cases of this sort, I'm conflicted about whether this is best in the hands of the shaman or the psychiatrist.

So much depends on the individual circumstances of the case. One thing that each case I handled had in common was a history of behaviors that were suspect as a reason to invite such night time attacks. One woman victim in New York let herself be talked into attending a sex club with her husband. I'm not precisely sure just what this involved, but I deduced that it was some kind of partner swap for sex.

Some Christian websites that deal with this, attribute these unwanted sexual encounters to masturbatingb and "lustful thoughts." I think this has more to do with their Christian fundamentalist beliefs than anything remotely related to demon sexual attacks. If masturbation were the cause, very few individuals would be spared this frightening experience from a young age. Get real.

I'm inclined to believe that there is something legitimate about the stories that I've heard from clients. One man who confided in me was a long-time friend, and I knew his regular life was really quite normal. Therefore, I am hesitant to advise anyone suffering from this particular problem to initially visit a psychiatrist who is almost certain to diagnose it as psychosis. However, you should do something about it.

First, analyze your lifestyle and behaviors concerning fairly extreme sexual habits. Consider some of the dives you are hanging out in and the folks who are hanging in there with you, whether you know them or not. Try discontinuing this for a while, if you think you qualify for that category in some way. The problem may take care of itself.

If you continue to receive this kind of unwarranted sexual attention, perhaps seeking shamanic help is the best first line of defense. It will probably be cheaper, and you won't have any weird stuff on your records. Just be damn sure the shaman you work with know what they are doing rather than engaging some hustler you found on the Internet, charging a fee that would break the bank. If the initial shamanic intervention does not handle the problem, seek the advice of another shaman who may be more experienced. No matter what you decide to do, take this seriously and do *something*.

Toxic Relationships

Another possibility that many people do not realize is that invasion can come from people who are very much alive on this side of the veil. These are often some of the toughest cases. I do a workshop entitled, "Good People Who Tolerate Bad People." That just about says it all right there, doesn't it?

In the workshop I ask this question, "What do you do when the toxic person is your mother?" These cases are where I am tempted to restore the word "possession." Some people are under the dark influence of someone close to them—someone with whom there is an intimate relationship. Thus, they tolerate the intolerable. This sets the life careening uncontrollably on a course of endless struggling, only just barely surviving horrifically destructive forces.

It takes a lot of work to open blind eyes, and it is like pulling teeth one at a time to set them free. There is a life-long history involved when family members are the offenders, versus those who are merely random invaders. There is an entirely different dynamic at work. Severing the psychic connections is the first step. Repairing the damaged energy systems is next. The ultimate goal is retrieving the person from a living death of their true selves.

One woman, reduced to nearly a catatonic state, sat all day staring out of a deep depression, but when Dark Mother pulled her chain, she responded like a robot. Periodic healing work over several years time in this case, familiarized me with the extremely dysfunctional family relationships. Mother was the centerfold of every issue. It was nearly unbelievable how she manipulated everyone, especially my client who also happened to be a close friend.

The name of the game in this case was, "I close the door. You open the door." Even though Marjorie—not her real name—understood the dynamics of the sick relationship with her mother, the dark energies periodically sucked her in once again. I was losing my patience.

The situation reared its ugly head once again following a quiet period of several years. Marjorie was taking her mother for medical tests when the old lady slipped and broke her hip. As usual, she ripped and slashed into Marjorie, screaming about a deliberate plot to destroy her.

A near-hysterical Marjorie relayed the entire bloody episode to me from the hospital. It was time for me to go on a reign of terror. I'd had it with Mother. That night, I paid a little visit to Mom while she was asleep. I took her to one of the more undesirable astral hells. I summoned up my most menacing glare. I wished I had fangs. I raged and threatened. I promised that if she did not leave Marjorie alone, this would be her final resting place.

Marjorie was in for a shock when she visited her mother in the hospital the next day. As soon as she laid eyes on Marjorie, her mother flung her arms wide and screamed her name, "Marjorie! Marjorie! I have been to Heeeelll!" At first, Marjorie, seeing the out flung arms, thought her mom was ready to physically assault her.

Apparently, the trip through the astral hell stayed with mom and made a new woman of her. She confessed her cruelty to Marjorie. She wept and wailed how terrible Hell was and repeatedly begged for forgiveness. Mom had had enough. There was never any trouble with mother after that. I should have tried this method sooner. The trouble with Mom was that she never learned that people who play the Control Game are playing a dangerous game indeed. No matter how powerful you are, there is always a bigger son of a bitch than you, and this time that s.o.b. was none other than yours truly! No more Mrs. Nice Guy.

Another story about toxic relationships comes to mind. When I am out of town, I hire a cat sitter. Once when I returned from a trip, apparently in the grip of a guilty conscience, the sitter confessed that she borrowed a tape from my office. A tape recording of my lecture on toxic relationships was lying on my desk. After listening to it, she saw a lawyer the next day and filed for divorce. The last I heard she moved out the following week and never went back. I should have charged her a fee.

All former connections tying one individual to another call for a critical eye. Spouses from whom we have separated on less than amicable terms belong on the psychic launching pad. I have found people who are still carrying unbroken negative cords from a spouse they divorced many years ago. Every casual sexual partner leaves an imprint. Any shaman worth their salt should be able to cut all the cords that carry toxic energy. Consider it spring house cleaning and get checked out every once in a while.

Babbling, Babbling and More Babbling

If you rummaged through my file cabinets, mysterious symbols on some client's folders may catch your eye. Are these esoteric mystery codes known only to astrologers? No, they are notations to identify clients who CAN'T SHUT UP! The notations to which I refer are *CC*. Those letters are short for "Chatty Cathy" or "Chatty Chuckie." That alerts me to the fact that the entire hour consultation will be the client talking, talking, talking and me listening, listening, listening. To get them the message, I mail it in.

Please bear with me for what may seem a convoluted route to make a point. It is just that this issue turned out to be only one of the deadliest problems in Western civilization: the death of the intuitive!

First I must explain about a particular branch of astrology, horary astrology.*

---

* Horary (HOAR-air-ee) astrology involves a horoscope calculated for the date, time and place a client asks the astrologer a specific, personal question. To learn more about this powerful tool for guidance in your life, check my website www.dianastone.com. Horary astrology answers questions that exceed the level of specific details available in your personal birth chart alone. For example, a client may inquire about whether to purchase one specific house at one particular address. That is a question accessible only to the level of horary astrology to answer for certain.

This story started when the client, whom I am using as a case in point, called to ask a horary question about her private practice as a therapist. She wanted to know why her career was in the toilet despite the fact that she was especially proficient with a unique and highly effective type of therapy.

A horary question such as why one's business is not doing better may be stretching things as far as a specific answer is concerned. I must have been in a good mood that day. I relented and agreed to take a shot at it. After a first look, I wanted to call and ask her some additional questions. It is fairly routine for horary astrologers to do a follow-up call to clarify the matter at hand once the chart is cast. At the beginning of the conversation, I told her I did not have a final answer yet but needed to ask her some questions first (remember that).

I should have savored those words because they were going to be my last connected to the mission I had in mind. She launched into a non-stop, veritable storm of words, which would do a protracted Senate filibuster proud. She talked ninety-miles-an-hour. She described the inner work she had done over many years. I got a blow-by-blow account that I feared would also last many years. She shared her battle with poverty consciousness. There was a vague tale about her grandmother that I could have sold to the daytime soaps. It involved witchcraft somehow, but I failed to see that it bore any relationship to her current problem.

Then the conversation entered phase two: annoyance and frustration. It was obvious, however, that the exasperation was with ME! I was not forthcoming with details. Remember, I told her at the beginning of the conversation that I did not have a final answer and was calling for additional information only.

Phase three of the conversation revealed a hidden agenda. She launched into a philosophical diatribe about astrology in general. She suggested that astrologers believe that Saturn and other planets were "bigger than God." She was adamant that SHE certainly was not going to give up HER power. It was futile to get a word in. I was on solar plexus overload, drained of energy. I was in the dead bug position.*

This is the approximate version of what I finally said to her, "For god's sake, will you SHUT UP! I am not going to charge you for this chart. I am not going to deal with you anymore. In fact, I would pay you money to go away. After listening to you, I am absolutely drained of energy. I don't need a chart to know what your career problem

---

* Regular readers of my e-newsletter are aware that one resorts to the dead bug position following prolonged energy drain from a toxic person. Think of it as a deliberately induced coma. This is how it goes. You drag yourself to your living room floor, whereupon you lie on your back with all four limbs extended ceiling ward. You know, the dead bug position.

is. You don't listen. Your clients must leave your office on a gurney by the time they're bombarded by one hour of your incessant babbling!"

Phase four of the conversation was surprising to me and to her credit. There was a period of silence on the phone. She actually shut up. Then in the meekest little voice, she said, "I suspected that it was something like that." I'll be damned! She got it! That was a first. Sometimes it is the better part of valor to stand up and tell the truth. After all, clients pay me to tell the truth, not just give them a line of b.s. so as not to hurt their feelings.

I went on to counsel her and we, of course, found a scared little girl inside who lacked confidence in what she was doing. Subconsciously, she thought if she talked fast enough and long enough that she could hold on to clients. Sometimes the answers to horary charts come in unexpected ways! She acted it out for me.

This may be an interesting story for all of that, but what does it have to do with clearing the decks for ascension? This case turned me on to a major hindrance—perhaps THE PRINCIPLE dilemma of any you will ever read anywhere else in this book—a crisis, which not only stalls out the ascension process, but short-circuits problem-solving in your life and makes a mockery of any growth in consciousness to which one may aspire.

This annoying babbling, babbling, babbling takes on a more sinister character when you realize this: It kills the intuitive function dead, dead, dead! The left brain takes over. It is deaf to that still small voice within. It is wearing earmuffs. That is why I named it "left-brain possession."

I should not need to spell out the very serious consequences that this guarantees. You might just imagine yourself living disconnected from the inner guidance of those gut feelings—those connections to true spiritual power and wisdom that eclipses what any left-brain information-gathering could ever hope to do.

Synchronicity kicked in and several other babblers came to my attention in quick succession. However, synchronicity outdid itself when a particular book found its way into my hands. This little volume not only described left-brain possession, but took one giant leap forward by pointing out really frightening and disastrous consequences of this critical condition—both for the babblers themselves and also for those reluctant ears they bend.

The book is *The Power of I AM* by John Maxwell Taylor. He calls the babblers "talking heads." In the book, he reveals some astonishing numbers:

> *"Eleven million bits of information bombard us at various levels each minute. Yet, the conscious mind can process only 16 bits per minute. That is 16, not*

> *16 million. That leaves a lot left over with nowhere to go. Remember this astounding bit of information. It possibly may be the most significant statistics of this entire book. Key point: The subconscious CAN handle those eleven million bits coming in every minute!"* (Other chapters discuss the development of the intuitive function from different points of view.)

It is the physical body that absorbs the millions of bits of information overload not handled consciously. It creates chaos within, and consequently, without. These are the folks that race about half frantically, talking endlessly, demanding more and more information. Disconnected from their gut feelings, they are unable to differentiate true from false.

However debilitating this may be in simply dealing with day-to-day affairs, the constant adjustment to new frequencies renders this situation dangerously incapacitating. As we move collectively through the ascension process, we need our sharpest wits about us.

In both my astrological and healing practices, I deal with clients who exhibit this affliction. It is horribly draining to work with them. No answer is ever enough. No amount of explaining is ever really above suspicion. They continue questioning and questioning and questioning. They just don't get it. They are intelligent enough, yet sometimes you would swear they are actually mentally challenged.

Without any functional instinctual inner guidance system, babblers don't know whether to believe me or not. Their subconscious hope is that just maybe with enough interrogation, I will say that one thing that proves the information trustworthy beyond any doubt. They saturate me with an eternity of details when a word or two would suffice, hoping that they may stumble onto the key question. Left-brain possession is deeply ingrained and a very difficult habit to break. Actually, we diminish its malevolence by insinuating it is merely a bad habit.

I find this malady is of epidemic proportion. It is a debilitating collective disease. If you suspect you are a talking head, Taylor's book is well worth a read. Or maybe slip it under some certain someone's pillow. Or maybe you may find it under YOUR pillow. (Babblers almost never think this applies to them.) After that, you may be well-advised to run for the hills. Anytime we feel our life force ebbing from contacts with certain persons or situations, we become "temporarily dispossessed from ourselves,...vulnerable to personal invasion by the disruptive aspects of the unconscious side of human nature," to quote Taylor.

Carl Jung wrote, "The world has sold its soul for a mass of disconnected facts." And this was before the Internet, cell phones, text messaging, tweets and CNN. Once again, the solution is to get back into our bodies and reestablish a deep, organic connection to Nature. And now, it is possible to go beyond that and activate the lightbody.

Me and My Shadow

Another very special situation sheds light on a particular set of circumstances. I chased my tail in circles before I finally figured this one out. Even when one knows of this pattern, it is not always easy to differentiate. There are situations where entities are only too obvious. People see them! It scares the living daylights out of them, needless to say. What would you do if every night you were visited by someone that you didn't invite for a sleepover (and it's NOT Grandpa)?

There was a case like this once involving a woman I had known for twenty years. I knew she was not crazy. We worked and worked on this until she reported that all was well. We lost touch with her for about three years, after which time she contacted us to say that she had been waging war with the entity on her own so as not to keep bothering us. We took up the case once more, but there just seemed to be no way to stop the ghostly visits.

One day I decided to go journeying on her behalf until I found the answer. I knew the history very well as I had counseled her from the astrological chart many times. This woman was classic Super Victim, outrageously abused by her ex-husband and all seven of her grown children. She was paralyzed in any attempts to speak up and set boundaries. Consequently, a very enraged aspect of herself lurked in the deep subconscious.

Her "entity" was a shadow projection of a deeply repressed part of the psyche that had no permission to express itself. That was the first time I saw this phenomenon and am still surprised that it can create such a powerful projection. When we went down that road, she began to feel the anger. I recommended working it through with a therapist. She did, and eventually the entity disappeared into a more conscious expression of her own feelings.

Shadow projections can indeed masquerade as invading entities, and may fool the best of psychics and healers. I have since encountered this in other cases. I am not always successful in getting the person to look at it as his or her own repressed material. It happens sometimes that the shadow projection is believed to be an evolved Being, and the inflated ego does not want to acknowledge what it really is and let go of it. The troubling symptoms, therefore, continue on and on. I am forced to just cut them loose.

Clearing Ancestral Patterns

Sometimes things really are all Mom's fault-—and grandma's and great-grandma's and great-great grandma's, ad infinitum. We are speaking here of ancestral patterns traveling through generation after generation, and now it is your turn to get the hot potato. These can be every much as disruptive in the life as entities. At least, when we find entities it is obvious who the bad guys arc.

Diagnosing ancestral patterns can be very elusive. They don't have a face; they don't walk and talk. However, they are locked in the DNA, and are very much alive in our personal psychology and acted-out behaviors; however unconscious we may be of their true origins. I must say that I have found the astrology charts very helpful in confirming the validity of this culprit and even providing the first clues that ancestral contamination is the source of the difficulties. (Astrologers: Look at the Twelfth House, especially if the same sign is on the ascendant, also.)

Clearings Connected to Childbirth

Abortions, pregnancy and childbirth all provide ample fodder for the process of clearing. I remember the time I "looked" at a women's liver and was startled out of my wits to see a little face staring back at me. Just to be really clear, this is in the astral field only. I guardedly asked if she had ever undergone an abortion, and she had. She also had so-called incurable hepatitis at the time, which of course is a liver disease.

After abortions, and childbirth also for that matter, there should be a clearing because sometimes the aborted baby hangs around and, along with the life-giving placenta, needs to be cleared out of the etheric body. The case referred to above had a real Hollywood ending. The woman later wrote to me in amazement that the hepatitis completely vanished without a trace after her clearing. She's not the only one who was amazed.

Thoughtforms

There are people who target others with negative thoughts and constantly critical words. Thcy may be in our social circle, or at work or most anywhere else. My brother and I have an extensive background of study in the Huna system, the practices of the ancient Polynesian kahuna. In this system, there is a Hawaiian word, when translated into English, means *grumbling.*

Grumbling is when someone gripes and moans about someone else, over and over again, until their criticisms coalesce around an actual energy system called a *thoughtform.* Kept up long enough, the thing can take on a life of its own and psychically attack the object of the criticism. One of my clients moved her mother from a distant city, and placed the old lady in a nursing home, where she began to grumble about her daughter. She had been inclined in that direction all her life anyway, but she ratcheted it up a few notches. The daughter was indisposed in the bathroom one day when all of a sudden this funny little form with a disagreeable expression came drifting toward her in mid-air. This time it was real, apparent to real 3D eyes.

The woman picked up the plumber's helper and gave it good swat, which I regarded as very resourceful. She said she felt kind of sorry for it afterward, because it appeared to have a very hurt expression. It hung, wistfully peering at her from outside her kitchen window, for several days before it dissipated. Don't worry about disposing of thoughtforms by whacking, burning, drowning or by any other means. You are not murdering a real person.

Don't conclude from this that all thoughtforms are so innocuous and easily dissuaded. Some are hardly distinguishable from really dark entities, once one considers the source of hatred and revenge from which negative thoughtforms may spring. Knowledgeable shaman from ancient times must surely have known how to plant permanent thoughtforms, which could explain the trouble that sometimes crashes down around the ears of interlopers who invade sacred spaces or trespass ancient tombs.

The most shocking experience along these lines of sending streams of negative energy happened to me during a lecture to a group of astrologers. I had given this same lecture so many times, I could have phoned it in. Nevertheless, I found myself stumbling over my words and losing my train of thought.

I finally gathered my wits sufficiently to be aware of the most powerful beam of yucky energy aimed at me from a man sitting at one end of the front row. I used the old faithful mirror trick. Put up a mirror shield, what used to be known as the Postman Technique: Whatever is aimed at you is stamped "return to sender." I know, pretty corny, but as you will see, it works. I deliberately turned away for a moment. When I glanced back, I could barely believe my eyes. I have trouble believing it yet.

The guy was lying on the floor, out like a light! He scrambled up, his face contorted with absolute terror. He streaked out the door as if he were shot from a cannon. That's not all. What was equally weird is that no one appeared to notice anything unusual. No group flocked around him to determine whether he had a heart attack or something. It was surreal.

I lived in St. Louis then. A little clutch of groupies followed me around to every lecture. They always rushed up later to read my aura and tell me what they thought the colors meant. I saw them heading toward me that night and wondered what they would say. One girl spoke up, "We saw a beam hit your aura and then you began to stumble over your words, but you are okay now."

I later learned that this man was a professional hypnotherapist who mistakenly believed I had snubbed him during coffee break. Rumor had it that he considered himself quite the ladies man, so this apparently bruised his inflated ego. It came out later that he had been "invited" to leave several other states before moving to St. Louis. Anyway, it sure does prove that thoughts are real. Just be aware that all of our critical messages target the person about whom we speak, and kept up long enough may even do them harm.

Emotional Sponges

Negative thoughts do not always coalesce around a full-blown thoughtform. However, while on the subject of thoughts, we should consider also just how often we are surrounded by a sea of people carrying the flotsam and jetsam of *depressed emotions* in their own private worlds. Negative emotions carry a depth charge that can sink a sunny disposition as efficiently as any enemy battleship.

While we are encouraged on the one hand to develop our intuitive faculties, on the other hand, we are cautioned to shield ourselves from the sea of negative emotions that surround us everywhere we turn. Can we have it both ways? We shop at the mall; we join thousands of spectators at the ball game; and probably the most vulnerable environment of all: Who is in the cubicle next to us at work every day? Can we open and close our intuitive senses at will, depending on our circumstances at any given moment? Or once we develop a powerful psychic sense, are we just emotional sponges at the mercy of any depressed person whose energy field crosses ours?

The answer is not to simply close down whatever psychic sensitivity you possess, or limit your efforts to develop it. I have worked with clients who grew so fearful of their psychic abilities that they required a full-blown therapy to eventually come to terms with them. I think I have mentioned Edwin Steinbrecher's book *The Inner Guide Meditation* as one I recommend for safe and effective psychic opening. It has been one of the great guidebooks for students in my psychic development workshops. What concerns us here now, though, is the other side of the coin. What do you do with it after you've got it? I am speaking here about protecting yourself so as not to become an emotional sponge.

There are other places to begin before techniques like "walking in a mirrored ball" can be optimally effective. The first thing begins with staying aware when you are in a crowd of people. Don't just "dummy out" and walk around like you are half on another planet. Monitor how you are feeling and reacting. Watch for a sudden drop in energy. Maybe you started out from home in a pretty good mood, but now you are ready to kill.

Investigate Other Techniques for Protection

It is proven that thoughts are things, and, under certain circumstances, may be very harmful. However, it is not practical to live in paranoid fear about every situation that presents itself. It is true that the more you work on developing your psychic sensibilities, the more vulnerable you are to energies floating around in your vicinity. There are many techniques designed to protect your energy field. For example, simply placing your hand over your solar plexus is often all that is necessary to remain on an even keel energetically.

My best advice at this point is to learn to be cognizant of what is happening around you. Sometimes when I talk to certain individuals on the phone, I can feel my energy being drained. I take a deep breath and place my hand over my solar plexus. I visualize a shield between us. There are many, many techniques for protecting your energy field. At this point, I refer you to a proliferation of books that address this subject. Just stay aware; there is no need to be constantly fearful about it. That does more harm than any energies you are likely to encounter.

Alien Implants

The first time I ever heard about alien implants, I thought that this was just too over the top for me. I really did not think I believed it until we stumbled across one. Truthfully, I didn't want to even think about them. They present themselves as alien implants, and we have had success in removing them. Maybe it is like the saying about ducks, "If it walks like a duck, and talks like a duck, maybe it is a duck."

Additional information about implants appearing in Dolores Cannon's book *Convoluted Universe, Book One* solidified my belief that they are real, and that all implants are not created equal. Maybe we are making a mistake to go about tearing out each and every implant on sight. In her writings, Cannon claims that many humans carry implants in their bodies to act as transmitters—in a good way. They are recording knowledge and information to send home to God. Perhaps we are in trouble for intercepting postcards from the edge sent to the home office. Seriously, I doubt if we have the power to seize legitimate implants, however.

These implants exist exclusively in the etheric bodies. I don't want anyone to think that perhaps they are harboring something in their physical body that looks like little metal boxes with batteries and wires. At least I have never seen any.

Alien implants are almost always discussed in the same breath with alien abduction, implying that abductees always return home, packing something which they did not leave home with—an implant. I know someone who was an abductee at about the age of four. I know this person and her word is beyond questioning.

She lived in a small Midwestern town. Her four-hour absence had the entire town turned out looking for her. She shared her experience with her mom, who readily believed her story, amazingly enough. The fact that her mom did accept her story without question actually adds credence to its validity in a strange way. I know about Midwestern moms; I had one. You will read in another chapter in which my mom incredibly believed an unlikely experience I had. Those reactions were coming straight from the gut.

Don and I removed our first alien implant from this woman who I mentioned has been my friend for most of our adult lives. Other than that, our experience with implants has been limited. The Internet offers up a ton of information on the subject. My final conclusion on this whole matter is to have a shaman take a look and do a clearing if it is called for. Why not, while you are at it?

Soul Contracts

In a world with so many people, it seems like it is just Fate that brings us together with certain leading players in our life scripts. The truth is that these relationships are typically far from coincidental. Before we incarnate, we deliberately negotiate contracts with other souls.

One would expect that the intention is that these unions are for the good of both parties. Sometimes we enter contracts with people here on Earth, only to discover that a business partner has embezzled company funds, for example. Problems crop up with soul contracts as well. That is why I included soul contracts in this chapter on clearing negative energies.

It is obvious that some soul contracts need to be severed. They are not sacred agreements that must never be broken. For many years, I was very queasy at the thought of breaking soul contracts. I was not quite sure this was kosher in the upper realms. However, a situation presented itself that so clearly indicated that a soul contract needed to be terminated that I realized it was a mistake NOT to end it.

I have worked with clients who tell me that they are trying to "work out the karma" in a relationship. Sometimes a great deal of the life has been stalled out in vain attempts to make the unworkable work. For many of my clients, the most powerful healing was letting them know that they should have abandoned the relationship several lifetimes ago. Souls do not progress at the same rate. If we needlessly forego our own progress for a soul who lags far behind, it is not helpful to either one. We need to differentiate between true sacrifice and needless sacrifice.

I am working with a woman right now whose primary mission in this life is to "clear out the clutter." She was entangled in such a mess of relationships that they actually consumed most of her life energy. Her children are mean and critical. They bamboozle her out of money. The list goes on. She made a career of struggling to forgive everybody.

I told her I thought she had pretty good gut instincts about people. I asked her to tell me who needed to go out of her life, and who needed to stay. She identified them without hesitation. The idea of clearing soul contracts intuitively resonated so powerfully with the woman that she wasted no more time nearly killing herself trying to make impossible situations work out.

You may not know at a conscious level with whom you have soul contracts. It is important to cultivate objectivity and discernment in choosing relationships, whether based on these agreements or not. Of course, some soul contracts are positive and reinforce each party's life experience. Pre-birth agreements are not the only ones that can land us in hot water. Read this chilling letter I received from a legitimately worried mother:

> "I am a single mother. I am having trouble with my 13-year-old son. I was nosy and snooped through some saved messages from his best friend. My son said he would do anything for the girl he liked. The friend asked my son if he would give up his electronics, and my son said he would. Then he was asked if he would jump off a high building, get stabbed and several other things, all to which my son said he would. The part that has me worried sick is the last question. The boy asked my son if he would sell his soul to the devil for the girl. I am wondering if my son would do that.

Clients in my shamanic healing practice sometimes confess to making "deals with the devil." I discovered that this is not limited to simply a night out to deliberately scary movies. It is nothing to fool around with in real life, even ostensibly thinking you are just hanging out and fooling around.. The horrible consequences involved when the Dark Side takes you seriously is only too real. No scriptwriter can supply a happy ending.

The history of the human race is carried in our genes and DNA. It is the source of our instincts, and evolution sorted out the ones that were the most effective for survival. The problem is that we live in a different time from cave man days. What worked then may well work against us now. Is there now a third option besides fight or flight?

Maybe you are fighting the battle of the bulge. Remember that our primitive ancestors were instinctively programmed to eat all the food they could get hold of at any one time. That was because they could not be certain where their next meal was coming from. A layer of fat could well have spelled the difference between surviving a winter season or not back then. When we attempt to lose weight, there may be a war inside between the survival instincts versus conforming to this culture's acceptable self-images and common sense diets.

This implies dumping the programming in the cells and somehow replacing it, just as we dump spam in our computers. That is a formidable concept, needless to say. Once we recognize that consciousness rules our cells not our genes, this may open our imagination to the possibility. There is more on this subject in the chapter on the Ascension Game.

Double Trouble–The Problem with Twins

The first time in my healing work that any issue of twins causing a problem surfaced with my client, Alice. That was in the mid-80s. Since then, the problem has shown itself to have many faces, and some of them are very dark. Let's get back to Alice and remembering that I had never encountered the twin problem before.

Alice had everything going for her. Yet, she was one of the gloomiest individuals that I ever met. A dark cloud seemed to follow her wherever she went. She talked to me about it. She was aware that it was there. She agreed that some shamanic work was in order. She was almost 40 years old, yet it was as though her life had never really gotten started.

We were sitting in my counseling room in my office, so I just closed my eyes to see what I could see. The dark cloud was actually a very real thing that I could perceive as shot through her entire aura. It is what I normally see with depression. But this had more of a tinge of resigned sadness. All of a sudden, I was startled to see another Alice! I didn't get it. How could there be another Alice in the etheric body? Who is the only other person who looked exactly like Alice?—her identical twin, of course.

Alice had been, as far as anybody knew, born as a single live birth, but I could "see" that her mother had originally conceived twins. The unborn twin was hanging around, very sad and resentful that she could not live an Earth life like Alice. Alice herself, provided many behaviors, emotions and incidents that completely confirmed the twin story. It was almost as though she went through life looking through the sad eyes of her twin. Was this a form of possession?

The proof of the pudding in shamanic work is in the healing. I worked with the astral twin to send her back where she belonged, instead of infecting Alice with the gloomy, sad life to which she had resigned herself. Soon after that, Alice was accepted into law school. She also acquired a hot new boyfriend (her words) along with her degree. Most of all, it was obvious to me that the sun had come out from under the clouds.

Once again, Barbara Hand Clow's book came along many years later—and many twin stories later—as another sensational example of synchronicity. This is a quote from her book:

> "... According to mythologist Brian Clark, 'ultrasound technology has revealed that many twin pregnancies result in a single birth, and that one of the twins is either absorbed into the body of the other twin or expelled, unnoticed by the mother... *the vanishing twin syndrome.*' "

Not every case that I encountered involving twins was always about one surviving twin and one unborn twin. Sometimes both twins were very much alive. Granted, my case files on twins is very limited. For what it is worth, in each and every case of surviving twins, it was as though they were playing out mythological themes of Good versus Evil.

Before there is any misunderstanding, I don't mean to imply that this applies to all twins. These are only the cases where my shamanic assistance was requested, and it was always a third party who enlisted my aid. I am unable to provide any in-depth analysis of the situations in which live twins were involved.

The only theme that seemed typical is that one twin was dark and troubled, while the other was a very straight arrow. And the good twin always tried to help or save the bad twin, and at the expense of the good twin's well-being or ability to conduct a normal life. They seemed locked together in this horrible nightmare that just repeated over and over again. Nothing ever changed.

I never counted these relationships among my success stories. Since I worked with these situations at the request of a third party, and since that party often did not live in the same city, the data and feedback was usually pretty sketchy.

If you are reading this as a healer or counselor, there is a great deal of mythological material concerning the twin archetype. In fact, Clow includes a modest amount of background in her book. Further study of the literature would probably lend valuable insights on the subject. I just never investigated it, as the twin problem arose so infrequently. If I were to deal with this again, I think I would look at it as a symbiotic relationship first.

Curses and Black Magic

As far as I was concerned, the reality of black magic and curses dwelt only in a particular literary genre, confined to dusty shelves in obscure metaphysical bookstores. After the following experience of the ring story, I changed my mind. I guarantee that you will, too. I had a choice. I could simply assure you that my shamanic experiences have convinced me that curses are real. Instead, the ring story "rings" true enough to stand up the hairs on your head all by itself!

THE RING STORY

Don Clarkson, a professional psychic and long-time friend, was a player in the ring story. This is what he shared from one of his lectures:

> "I remember the reading because it turned out to be the most unsettling one I ever did. It exposed the true nature and power of evil and changed my life in several ways. Even the mere telling of the story often traumatized listeners. Once after recounting the story before a large group, three women left to go outside and throw up. A man in the front row leapt up, threw his arms around me and sobbed on my chest."

Are You Sure You Want to Read on?

For me, the ring story began with Don's telephone call from his friend George's house. In the course of the conversation, George, a skeptic, inquired about Don's psychic work. It piqued his curiosity, until ultimately, George talked Don into doing a psychic reading for him. Again, this is Don's recollection of it.

> "The first image was of a huge aquamarine ring mounted in an elegant gold setting. I described it in detail. The images that followed were ghastly. I saw dead babies lined up in the gutter. That is not quite what my curious friend was expecting. After hesitating to say anything at all, I finally asked if his mother, daughters or sisters had undergone abortions. He calmly confirmed that each one had aborted babies. Surprisingly, the information about the ring fascinated him the most. He said that it was lost seven years ago when he moved into his present home."

Don insisted that the ring was not lost, but was actually in the house. That is when I received a call. Don asked me what impressions I saw about the ring. I remember that I had taken the day off to give the house a good cleaning and was in no mood for this sort of thing. I impatiently confirmed that indeed the ring was in the house, and further added that it was inside something "like a metal lockbox in the bank." I assumed that this would be the end of it.

After turning the friend's house upside down, a metal box found under a bed in the guest room relinquished the ring from its hiding place. Don's feelings about the ring were so macabre that he refused to touch the thing. Further investigations convinced us that there was a curse attached to it, and it had some horrible association with dead babies. We hardly believed it ourselves, so we did not press the subject after initial warnings that it might be best to return it to the box permanently.
Privately, Don and I share a joke about the ring, although acutely aware; nonetheless, that it decidedly was not a laughing matter. Don kept asking me what he should do with the ring that was giving him the heebie-jeebies. He said I told him over the

phone, plainly impatient, "Oh, for goodness sake, Don, just do a simple exorcism." He still laughs about it.

Don's friend had his heart set on presenting the ring to his youngest daughter who was just now graduating from college. He felt that it would be an ideal time to produce the long lost ring as a graduation present. Brushing reservations aside, we decided to make an occasion of it. I agreed to entertain a group of the girl's family and friends at my house for the ceremony.

Meanwhile, there were further developments that cast a sinister tone over the entire affair. At the time of the original psychic reading, Don's friend, George, was about to become a grandpa. His daughter in another state was expecting her baby soon. Naturally, he was excited about it, and pressed Don to see what his psychic images had to say. Don remained tight-lipped about some very bad feelings about the baby's possible physical problems.

George visited the baby and all seemed to be well. Don decided that he would just ignore his negative feelings. About two weeks later, Don's fears were unfortunately about to come true. He called again to ask what I thought. I knew that the baby was in trouble, but all I saw were strange images of a scene in ancient Egypt.

After many tests, the baby was diagnosed with a rare problem called Ondine's Curse, named after an Egyptian. That was enough to stand the hairs up on the back of my neck. This situation was getting really scary. We could not know it then, but as the months and years went by, the baby never developed normally. She never did walk or talk.

Exorcism is no Party Game

On the night of the party, everyone gathered around to see George give his daughter the ring. There was some banter about a curse. In an act of total recklessness, we decided to have the daughter hold the ring while we did an exorcism. At the last minute, I came to my senses and at least took the ring to hold it myself. I laid down on the adjusting table that husband Don used at the house. I had no sooner begun than this overpowering blackness engulfed my entire being. It scared the hell out of me. I let out a blood-curdling scream. No one knew what was going on. Husband Don instinctively jumped to protect me and drained off the horrible energy. He also showed blood in his urine for four days following.

It was a huge mistake to treat this curse business with such casual disregard. Horsing around with this sort of thing as sort of a parlor trick, invited disaster. We were lucky we got off that easy. I must say, it sure sobered up the guests! In light of these developments, the girl at least agreed not to wear the ring. However, she refused to rid herself of it entirely. Over our strong objections, the cursed ring went back into the metal box once again. I feared the dire consequences if she ever decided to get pregnant and have a baby.

I am acquainted with a powerful full-blooded Indian shaman from southern Mexico, Quis. He came for the Native American Sun dances in the mountains of Oregon. Don went to the Sun dances to support one of our Native American friends. When Quis came later that year, I asked his advice about the ring. He emphatically refused to have anything to do with it himself, and he is a most powerful medicine person. He advised us to throw it in the ocean. He said only the power of Mother Ocean could wear away the curse over time.

I have never forgotten the story of the ring. To this day, it remains as a symbol and a guide. Before I begin healing work on anybody, I look for the image of the ring. It lets me know if I am in over my head. It warned me away from situations only twice. I walked away, no questions asked!

Clearing Physical Objects

After reading this, I can imagine people worriedly glancing about their house, suspiciously eyeing various objects. Where did that weird statue from the garage sale come from? By the way, I did ask George where he got the ring in the first place. This was his sinister answer, "I got it in the part of the world where children sit in a circle seeing who can make the teapot dance in the air first." True, most of us will never connect with objects tainted from places where voodoo is part of the culture. However, a variety of other physical objects besides rings can be terribly troublesome as well.

In the first book of this trilogy, *The Lightbody Activation Manual,* I wrote about a case presented by a client of mine. Her father-in-law gave her a handmade wooden cradle—handed down through generations—when her first baby was born. She had what she thought was an irrational revulsion of the gift on sight. Not wanting to cause hurt feelings in the family, she graciously accepted and kept any reservations to herself.

Nevertheless, she just could not bring herself to put the baby in it and relegated it to an old storeroom. A subsequent investigation revealed the chilling story about an unfortunate infant murdered in the cradle. The bullet hole was still visible. I don't think anybody would want that thing in their house, no matter where it was. The couple made a bonfire out of it, and threw the ashes into the Columbia River for good measure.

From other personal experiences like this, I no longer doubt that negative energies attach themselves to physical objects. Perhaps not as exotic as the ring story, or as gruesome as the baby crib incident, but that is not to say that common household items don't present more than eye candy on the fireplace mantel.

Just how seriously should you consider policing your environment for objects that may carry unwanted energy? The answer lies somewhere left of total denial and right of full-blown paranoia. It is one thing to deal with the bargain dress you bought at the flea market versus objects deliberately infected by curses.

In the former case, the dress's owner may have been a nymphomaniac. (Maybe that would spice up your sex life!) Although not life threatening, strong imprints such as grief, rage or depression can permeate clothing or articles closely associated with the owner.

Don't hesitate to call in a professional when the situation calls for it. Intervention is usually most appropriate for clearing houses and other environments, rather than individual objects. If things have reached a point in which there really is a reason to suspect that your environment has something fishy going on, don't trust that a few trips with sage is going to cut the mustard. I've never seen sage do any big time clearing. It is good for maintaining environments once they are reasonably clear, but beyond that, it is useless.

The Curse on the United States's Presidents

Undoubtedly the most famous so-called curse is the one associated with the presidents of the United States. This one cannot so easily be brushed aside as simply another urban legend because it has come true ever since the presidency of William Henry Harrison in 1840. This curse predicts the death of whoever holds the highest office in the land every twenty years. President Ronald Reagan was next in line, but as we all know, despite an assassination attempt, he survived to complete his term in office. His was widely touted as the presidency that "broke the curse."

As a long-time professional astrologer, I can tell you that there is a great deal of misinformation floating around about the presidential whammy. First, however, let's go back in history and trace the reputed origin of this curse business. The great Shawnee Indian chief, Tecumseh, was killed in a skirmish with American military forces. Whatever his beef was, he supposedly was the one who delivered the fatal curse on U.S. presidents. At least, he is the guy who is popularly connected to it.

In my estimation, if we are looking for a Native American connection, a lesser-known, but more likely candidate, was Tecumseh's half-sibling, Tenskwatawa, a medicine man also known as "The Prophet." He reportedly predicted Harrison's death, and added the 20-year hex in revenge for his half-brother's death. Convincing evidence of a curse mounted through the deaths of Lincoln, Garfield, McKinley, Harding, Roosevelt and Kennedy. Then, of course, Reagan interrupted the chain.

So to continue, one might inquire as to the two terms in office served by George Bush. He obviously survived both terms. A generous percentage of Americans believe he stole the presidency illegally, so to follow that line of reasoning, perhaps he cheated death as well. Maybe we can be grateful, at least, that perhaps he really did break the curse. I couldn't resist throwing in that juicy little political tidbit.

That pretty much summarizes the historical source of the presidential curse. Keep in mind that there are no written statements or historical records of any kind to prove that either of the Native American gentlemen had anything to do with a curse on American presidents. However, there is another side to this story, but it is known primarily within the astrological community. Nonetheless, the astrologers can make a very good case for the role of the stars in connection with the cyclical deaths of presidents.

The planets, Jupiter and Saturn, come together in the zodiac every twenty years–starting to sound suspicious? There are three signs of the zodiac that are known as earth signs—Taurus, Virgo and Capricorn. The astrologers noticed that the presidential deaths occurred only when Saturn and Jupiter joined in *earth* signs.

So what was going on in the heavens when Reagan ascended into office? The two great planetary giants came together all right, but in the *air* sign, Libra. It was close, but Reagan survived. That is the crucial missing piece that is not ordinarily included in present-day accounts of the presidential curse. In year 2000, the two planets' conjunction was in the earth sign, Taurus. But as reported, George Bush escaped the hex. How might the astrologers explain that? The astrological explanation is a bit more technical than most layman would understand. However, I'll simplify it and let it go at that. First, let's go back to the fundamental question of just *why* the deaths would occur in earth signs in the first place. Are these signs lethal?

No, it has nothing to do with the intrinsic nature of those three signs. If one happens to be your birth sign, you can relax. In analyzing the particular birth chart that I use for the United States, the earth signs were casting afflicted connections to the part of the chart that signifies death of the head of state. It would not be unusual for a sharp astrologer to actually predict these tragedies based on the current astrological cycles at the time. Indeed, it is reported that the White House received 3,000 letters from astrologers warning President Kennedy not to go to Dallas that day.

That leaves us with one dangling loose end. Why didn't those same afflicted patterns operate at the time of the Bush presidency? Even though the Saturn-Jupiter conjunction occurred in an earth sign, there are always many more cycles in play than just that one. Sometimes, these line up in such a way as to take the sting out of any afflicted combination. Astrologers must study the entire picture at any given time.

After all, the planetary picture must be very negatively reinforced to signal something as catastrophic as the death of a president. For another thing, the condition of the current astrological cycles in the president's own birth chart may be so powerfully protective that when laid side by side with the current sky patterns, he has the equivalent of a guardian angel. Regardless, we don't have to worry about it for another 600 years. It will be that long before this cycle circles around again.

Other stories of curses continue to circulate, such as the one that concerns the Red Sox baseball team. They work out with just enough accuracy in actual events to keep us wondering. The only negative energies any of us should concern ourselves with are those that I have described elsewhere throughout this chapter. Just remember that these incidents are very rare. Don't let your imaginations run away with you. Just think twice the next time you are tempted to hurl a curse in anger. Those negative energies don't just disappear. Keep it up, and you yourself may be responsible for something that you wish later you could call back.

The Fire Hose of Light

Since we are on the subject of clearing out bad energy, I will share one of my shamanic techniques that works like magic—white magic, that is. I call on the angelic kingdom for this one. Imagine an angel holding a fire hose that shoots out light. The angel goes all over the house, upstairs and down, every nook and cranny. I even aim the fire hose of light into the electrical wiring, the plumbing, all of the appliances and all around the *outside* of the house, too. I station four angels at each corner of the house for 30 days. The feedback from clients is just astounding! I give you permission to borrow the fire hose of light for your own use.

I never imagined how widespread the deliberate practice of black magic actually is. Apparently, it is not all that uncommon, if I am to believe the wild tales I hear from clients. I think we may safely assume that it sure isn't the practitioners of the black arts who are calling me. The cries for help come from their alleged victims.

Why do I say "alleged" victims? Picture this. Incredibly distraught strangers call me in the cold light of day to report a conspiracy of bad guys systematically using black magic to totally dismantle their lives. Then they violently assault me with a detailed description of hideous personal suffering as a consequence of their torturers' attacks.

The story is further complicated when they charge the town's mayor and the high school principal as part of the conspiracy. I ask you, am I talking to a hapless victim deserving my help or am I talking to a flaming paranoid schizophrenic (not that there is anything wrong with that)? I do not deal with schizoid patients. If I misjudge and they get in under the radar, it is not a good thing. How can I differentiate between the two?

The easy answer is simply to dismiss every case in which the client relates wild tales about black magic conspiracies. If you are a serious healer, however, you can bet that the Universe will eventually arrange for just the perfect situation to set you straight about what is really going on. Yes, the practice of black magic is alive and well in the living rooms across America.

The concern in this book is two-fold when it comes to dealing with negative energies. The first goal is to facilitate a heightened awareness that these things are real. The second goal is to raise a red-flag reminder that this unique time in history makes lightbeings targets from the Dark Side, desperate to stop the ascension process at any cost.

I hope this captures the attention of all healers out there. Anybody reporting black magic attacks—no matter how wild and hysterical the presentation—deserves the courtesy of a conscientious differential diagnosis. If it so happens that you are the victim, don't hesitate to ask for a second opinion besides a shrink who thinks you are crazy. (Check the resources listed in the chapter "Spiritual Emergency Room.")

The first thing I do is reassure the person that I do not think they are crazy. I encourage them to tell me the whole story. Listening depends on a perceptive ear and sensitive gut. Anyone experienced in such matters intuitively senses a certain "feel" when things are just not quite right.

Once I am fairly certain that my client is truly under attack by black magic, I proceed by cutting all the psychic cord connections. You might say I perform psychic surgery. I use the ordinary shamanic tools for restoring the energy field and chakra system. And, oh yes, I am careful to protect myself from the energies.

One thing that you must never, never do is use black magic against anyone, no matter how deserving they may be or how tempting it is to "do it just once." My spiritual beliefs require me to see everyone as part of the Whole. I regard the Dark ones as my brothers and sisters who have taken the wrong turn on their life's journey. I invoke Archangel Michael to take them into the Light. Okay, I admit that I am not above occasionally calling them dirty, stinking bastards for what they did to my client.

Husband Don and I have encountered black magicians who are highly evolved and capable of working interdimensionally just as we do. These fellows are treacherous. Their handiwork is sometimes almost impossible to spot. These are the cases where we do clearing after clearing, yet our client's symptoms continue unabated. We sometimes forget to investigate outside the 3rd dimension. If we find ourselves floundering, occasionally extraterrestrials have voluntarily rendered their superior services in the matter. You will read more about that in the chapter about working with ETs.

I address a final thought on the practice of black magic to anyone reading this book that may be toying with the idea of crossing the line. In my astrology practice, I have spoken to a handful of clients who admitted as much to me. One man told me that he was previously married to a woman who openly practiced black magic with a group of friends. The living room carpet covered a pentagram painted on the floor underneath.

What most people may not fully realize is that black magicians are often powerful enough to get results just as healers like myself on the Light side get results by what we do. This particular client described how his wife "knocked out" a competitor, so that he could get his job. The line between the Light and the Dark can be subtle.

I can share an incident that happened to me just a few days ago. I was having dinner with two friends. One lady was upset that her daughter was rushing into a marriage that Mom regarded as unsuitable to a man over twice the girl's age. Probably because they know about the work I do, the discussion led to ideas about how they could make sure that the marriage turned out badly using "woo woo," as they call it. What they were considering was actually black magic. However innocent the intention, or how clearly the bad guys may deserve it, believe me, it is the sort of energy that leaves you vulnerable to very undesirable consequences sooner or later.

Do not give even the gray areas the benefit of the doubt. I greatly admired a woman who was an astrologer, but also a powerful metaphysician and medium. Astrologers will recognize her name, Isabel Hickey. She told me a story about a young woman who came to her for the most propitious astrological timing to work a spell to get her lover back in her bed. Isabel admonished the girl that this was black magic. The girl replied, "Not when you do it for love!" I'm afraid that even love will not give its blessing for such shenanigans!

Clearing Toxic Environments

Clearly defined forces associated with different locales may heavily influence anyone living there. Intuitively, we collectively sense the distinctive character of countries and cities as well as specific "vibes" of one house on your block. For example, no one confuses gay Paree with the Big Apple. My friend and colleague, shaman Dr. Judith McLean, formerly cleared what once were WW2 Nazi concentration camp sites. Most of us, thankfully, will never deal with such frightful environments as that. But we can expect to encounter spaces holding a variety of disruptive toxic influences.
I never would have thought that a "sick house" could visit a reign of terror in the lives of its occupants until my brother worked on just such a case in California. He inherited this case from me when I threw in the towel. At the conclusion of this ordeal, we found no other explanation than to blame the house: Judge for yourself.

A Chinese man with a pronounced accent called for help because his life was straight out of a soap opera. Three bad auto accidents, losses from expensive law suits, job losses, marriage problems and financial tangles plagued him for several years. This particular gentleman called me as a last resort at the behest of his sister-in-law who knew of my shamanic work. He was not a believer! He was most difficult. He whined. He was suspicious. He was the most uninformed person when it came to psychic matters. Yet, it was impossible to explain to him in even the simplest terms. The more I tried, the more disgusted he grew with me because I did not make sense. We did not hit it off. Ours was a marriage made in Hell.

Brother Duane had better luck. I'm thinking this guy probably preferred working with a man anyway. Besides that, Duane took a very different tack from me. I routinely work directly with the individual. I look for entity interference and other things listed under clearing negative energies. It does not occur to me to check out the house and property, unless a client directly asks for that.

Duane does more work with environments in general, so he was immediately suspicious of the house and property. The problem does not always involve unwanted presences. An "oppressive, black tarry cloud" enveloped the house, according to Duane's description. Dispersing the dense force presented quite a challenge.

Bro employed a sort of last-resort technique that involved the construction of a protective matrix around the entire property. This calls for a precise combination of crystals oriented to the four directions and buried in the ground. The reason I like to use this case as an example is the unbelievable immediate turnaround in this couple's lives. Both the man and his wife markedly changed personally, along with their circumstances.

The client in question previously held a very high-powered, high paying job. This case happened at a time when the economy was in a downturn and many high-rolling CEO's got their walking papers. Nevertheless, he landed a high six-figure job almost immediately. The house enjoyed a $100,000 facelift. Talk about someone getting religion; this client is a believer now. Mr. Sour Puss transformed into Mr. Pussy Cat and attributed his dramatic change in fortunes to the shamanic intervention.

Mother Nature Takes out the Garbage, too!

Another environmental crisis comes from our terrible lack of awareness about our own Mother Earth. She is a living Being not just a pile of lifeless dirt. As such, many different systems are in operation to maintain the health of the planet. In retrospect, we fear that humanity's ignorance and disregard of nature's needs may have inflicted irreparable damage in some cases.

One system that behooves us to regard with respect is her process for eliminating negative energies herself. It is directly analogous to the condition in which the human body finds itself when elimination of wastes does not regularly occur. My psychic investigations of toxic houses revealed a sophisticated network of vortices, like a grid overlaying the planet.

At certain nodal points, I could see gushers resembling eruptions from geysers like Old Faithful. Instead of sparkling water, this stuff was like what we flush down the toilet. How would you like to live in a house built directly on top of an elimination vortex? If you figured out the four-letter word starting with s that you flush down the toilet, well, that is what life is like for people innocently residing in an outhouse.

I worked on a house in Federal Way, Washington. It was a beautiful home in a gated community. The single resident was a friend of mine who lived there with several cats. She was an animal rescuer for a local shelter. When terrible things happened with the cats, she was obviously greatly disturbed.

The house seemed to attract bizarre neighbors. People responsible for maintaining the complex made strange choices such as cutting down a beautiful stand of old trees in a green belt area. The house was constantly plagued with weird plumbing problems. Whatever was going on, I sensed that dark energies were indisputably affecting people and property in the entire area.

Powerful forces, whose job it is to maintain the balance of nature, police their own territories, great or small. Some are in charge of vast mountain ranges, but in this case I was interested in contacting the local Deva. (You will read more about the subject of unseen spirits in the chapter "The Invisible Players.")

If I expected to find some sort of a benevolent grandma baking cookies for the local trees, I was shocked out of that sensibility. I think I made the mistake of taking it for granted that she would move the elimination vortex under my client's house to another location. She acted as if I asked her to relocate the entire sewer system for New York City. She was one cranky battleaxe.

I had never dealt directly with local Devas before. I received a lesson in the proper etiquette pretty damn fast. I immediately switched to bowing and scraping and assuming the demeanor of the most subservient, undeserving wretch that God ever put on this earth. With hat in hand, I pleaded my case. I was surprised that the crotchety old crone had a heart after all. She told me that in this case, rerouting the vortex did not disrupt the system. I softened my attitude toward her when I asked myself what I would be like if I cleaned outhouses for a living.

The Deva was as good as her word. The dark neighbors up and moved suddenly. The house took on a noticeable lightness. Even her English flower garden flourished. My friend enjoyed living free of the oppressive forces that kept her locked in a permanent state of depression and hopelessness.

I screwed up my nerve five times since then to approach local Devas to adjust vortices where my clients lived. I still chuckle about a case in Beverly Hills, California. A longtime friend lived in an lavish, upscale house worthy of the 90210 zip code.

After several hundred thousand dollars worth of remodeling, she called to describe the whole property as "dead." Expensive landscaping was dying and the place felt just plain horrible. I don't know for sure if this was my imagination or not, but the California Deva was something very different from my previous encounter. This is what she said, "Sure I can move this vortex. Let's put it in Charleton Heston's backyard. I don't like his politics." When I told my friend, she told me that Mr. Heston lived just across the street from her! To this day, I wonder if she was just shining me on California-style, or whether she really did it. Whatever she did, my friend's gardens resembled an overgrown jungle immediately afterward.

In this chapter dealing with clearing negative energies, constant vigilance concerning your immediate environment needs to be a priority. Some dwellings accumulate negativity because of the history of events that occurred there over time. I encounter houses where there were particularly sad deaths or other tragic events lingering in the energy field. This no doubt accounts for some real estate problems, by either trying to sell a sick house or buying one unawares. Realtors take heed. A simple house clearing may influence the bottom line of your financial statement.

However, the deliberate targeting of a lightworker's environment concerns me the most. Nevertheless, whether the forces are benign or malicious, a powerful person brought to his or her knees by a toxic environment screams for an intervention. Although the skills of a psychic healer or shaman are customarily required to diagnose the problem of a sick house, "ordinary" people do sometimes surprise me with an amazing intuition about their troubled space.

One case I worked on proved that even if you know the house is infected, you still can't be too careful. I think this story deserves inclusion to underscore just how vigilant one must be every step of the way. I especially address healers who do this sort of work. Take heed.

A woman in another city called me and recited a litany of horrendous health problems that plagued her for over twenty years. She was adamant from the outset that her house and physical property caused the problems. She had tried just about everything before blaming her environment. It had reached the point where there was disturbing poltergeist activity almost constantly.
Don and I set about clearing the property from a distance. It surprisingly went very well. We wondered what all the fuss was about all those years. To confirm it, the woman reported that the house was free of all problems immediately. The clearing had brought about immediate positive changes, and she was thrilled. The thrill of

success was short-lived. It was not long before pandemonium reigned even worse than before.

Recalling that it historically wasn't that unusual to require another swipe or two in these situations, we were not overly concerned and took another shot. After a repeat of this scenario several times over, however; we began to wonder just what in hell was going on there. We closed the door. Things calmed down. Then "something" was just as surely opening it.

A warning to healers again: Clients do not always tell you everything! I interrogated the woman, and I mean I grilled her about every single detail of her life. I was on the hunt for anything she possibly did to negate our efforts time and time again. One of my requirements when I take on a case forbids the participation of any other healers at the same time. Otherwise, I am unable to assess the influence of our input alone.

My conversation with the woman brought to light a relationship with a male shaman who helped her with her medical problems. She saw him for several years, once a week, and for a hefty fee. It was news to me. I was immediately suspicious. It was obvious that the healer was not helping her at all. I asked her why in the world she continued to see this fellow.

Then for the clincher: She remarked that every time we did a clearing, she called him to also clear it "for good measure." When I brought this fellow into focus, he was blacker than the ace of spades. I was furious. He knew good and well what we were doing. We were acing him out of a real sweet deal , keeping this person on an income stream forever.

What remains a mystery to me to this day is how people can be so gullible as to continue paying a king's ransom to someone who never does them any good—or worse. It is not the first time I encountered the same thing with other clients. The offenders probably have a certain charismatic power to keep the suckers hooked.

It was not without a certain devilish satisfaction that Don and I took this jerk out of the picture. My close friends and family worry about the repercussions that may befall us because of the work we do. Through the years, I admit that some skirmishes came as a backlash from cases we worked on. I am no dead hero. I do take these things very seriously. (Do you hear that Mom?)

While I am on the subject, I want to emphasize that my work as a shaman is NOT the reason for my health problems, contrary to the opinions of others who have voiced their concerns about this issue. If you think I am willing to sacrifice my health for this healing work, think again! As far as I am concerned, anyone who does that is desperate for attention, severely neurotic or a total nut job who was toilet trained too early. I suggest you stop and think if I'm really that screwed up. (My physical health issues are discussed in other chapters.)

Anybody engaging in healing practices without understanding how to protect him or herself is asking for trouble and will usually find it. They certainly have no business doing healing work professionally. One reason I—and others—traditionally do not work alone in this business is for the protection of everyone. We aren't superhuman. I don't mind admitting that other members of my group have come riding to my rescue when I can't find the door.

Now back to the matter of the shaman gone bad. We had a real battle royal on our hands. This was the basis for the admonition earlier that you cannot be too careful. Stay vigilant; it is not over until it is over. I got careless and relaxed my guard a little too soon.

It started out with some doors slamming and noises such as that in my house. I heard a commotion in the garage several times, but it is easy to rationalize that something fell off of a shelf. This went on for two or three days and probably would have gone longer if it weren't for something Don said. One night I went to bed while Don stayed up to play the organ. I heard the bedroom door slam—hard!—but I figured Don had shut the door so that the music would not disturb me.

The next morning Don asked me if I was mad when I slammed the door because the music kept me awake. Now it hit me. Neither of us slammed the door! The memory of the earlier banging around suddenly came clearer, and seriously alarming, as I started to get the picture. Our shaman nemesis had sent his poltergeist buddy knocking at my door. An incident later that night sealed his doom. This was war.

When my mother died, I kept an impressive heavy three-piece cut glass set, a large pitcher, vase and candy jar. It had been in the family for over a hundred years and was of tremendous sentimental value to me. The pieces sat on a table just at the entryway to my house where I loved to see it every day.

The next day, Don walked down the hall, and as he passed the little table they sat on, the heavy glass water pitcher took flight. When it crashed to the floor, it smashed into a million pieces. You would have to see the object to understand that only from a direct blow by a big hammer could this heavy piece ever shatter like that. In addition, I think its target was probably Don's head. He should not have broken my mama's cut glass pitcher. Forgiveness is a Christian virtue, so we will just say the bastard is in rehab and let it go at that.

Postscript: I have in my files a letter from this most grateful lady whose personal health and house are doing just fine now. I have to say that this is more important than any keepsake.

Shamanic Energies Raise Havoc with Electrical and Electronic Devices

In bygone days, I thought one of the worst fates was for the electricity to go off. Now it is having the electricity go off so that I can't use the computer. Perhaps this is as annoying and crippling for you as it is for me, considering how the little machines have insinuated themselves into every aspect of life and work. Even more frightening, computers have inner demons that strike whether the electricity is on or off!

For twenty years, it never occurred to me that the constant tribulations that plagued Don's computer was anything more than buying the damn thing on a day when the Moon was constipated and Mercury was upside down and backwards. We have succeeded in manifesting two of the sharpest computer geeks in town. That part is the only miracle that keeps us in business at all.

Other people close to us just shake their heads in disbelief. Here is an example. I suffered a serious medical crisis in July of 2007. It was important to me that I notify my regular newsletter readers about what happened and alert them not to expect any newsletters for a while.

Believe this. Don was attempting to change to a different program on MY computer for handling the newsletter. *Over a year* passed by before we could publish another newsletter to my mailing list. Situations like this occurred time and again. If you want to know how to avoid this agonizing situation, I know one thing that does not work. It involves calling God dirty names.

When something goes wrong, we might as well hunker down and prepare for our computer experts to spend hours and days here, burning the midnight oil, futilely attempting to make sense of things. This refers to Don's computer woes. That is not to say that my computer is exempt, either. More than my share of hard drives have just rolled over and played crib death.

The mystery remained to bedevil us until Donna, a friend and colleague, enlisted our help. She called a couple of years ago in an agitated state to report that every single electrical and electronic device in her place had died. Even the phone was acting up. She earned a living as a writer, so this was serious business indeed with deadlines looming.

In this case, Don visited her apartment and did a clearing in person. The bad energy centered on the second bedroom that she used for her office. We knew only that the previous occupant died in that room. The results of the clearing were astonishing. The shift of energy in that apartment was almost palpable. All appliances sprang to life, including the computer.

Years before that I remembered a client who carried heavy shamanic energies. When she came to my office for astrological consultations, the tape recorder never taped us. The tape was always blank. With two shaman in the room, the frequencies were just too intense. Other shaman have reported the same thing to me.

My friend, Donna, also connects with powerful multidimensional energies, which reminded me of those earlier experiences. She is a powerhouse all by herself. In fact, she is the only other person outside of our group to whom we turn when we get our butts kicked. As it happened, we needed to clear her place every so often. Imagine then the energies that must be flying around my place!

To confirm the Evil Computer Syndrome, I received a letter from a client shortly after she read about this situation in one of my e-newsletters. She is a Reiki master. She sent me a special Reiki symbol for the express purpose of clearing infected computers exposed to high frequency blasts. Don took Reiki classes years ago, so he used it psychically to clear out the house. When we suffered computer problems, it was typical that just about every other machine died also, including microwave ovens, toasters and phones.

Most of us would never suspect this problem. It is true, nonetheless, to which the following DNA research from Russian scientists attests. (Other chapters in this book will include additional aspects of the spectacular and revolutionary research results that dispel forever long-held, but faulty, attributes of so-called "junk DNA.") Meanwhile, here is a further quote from an article apropos our discussion here, discussed previously in Chapter Eight:

> "Electronic devices, CD players and the like can be irritated and cease to function. *When the electromagnetic field slowly dissipates, the devices function normally again. Many healers and psychics know this effect from their work* (italics mine). The better the atmosphere and energy, the more frustrating it can be for recording devices as they stop functioning. Perhaps this is reassuring to read for many, as it has nothing to do with them being technically inept; it means that they are good at hyper-communication."

The ascension process has brought about the escalation of frequencies affecting us all. We certainly have struggled with the effects on our physical bodies. Apparently our machines have feelings too. Increasing numbers of the population may find that they must hold their computer's hand and lead it back to normal functioning.

What About Karma?

Many people's concept of karma is a simplistic eye-for-an-eye philosophy. You did a bad thing in a past life? That person now owes you one in this life. I personally believe that it is more complex than that, but I am not about to claim that I totally understand what runs the engines of karma.

I am interested, however, in what this may have to do with the ascension process. I did not put too much stock in the idea that some people, so heavy laden with karma, might as well kiss any thought of ascension good-bye. Subsequent reading on this subject revealed that not everyone agreed with me on this. Those someones who held opposite beliefs turned out to be heavyweight sources that I have learned to take very seriously.

I concede that there are Hitler-types who may not make it this time around. Those characters do not concern me. We ordinary mortals, who lacked the imagination for Evil on the grand scale, have likely racked up our own version of naughty things. I do lay claim to personal experience with this level of karma from clients with whom I do past life therapy. Believe me, it is an issue, but the most important consideration when clearing past life karma may surprise you.

What rears its head repeatedly where karma is concerned is the critical importance of forgiving yourself. Throughout all of my years of psychic work, not once have I ever found a judgmental God standing over anyone with a big stick and demanding that they pay penance for some past misdeed. What I do find is that through an all-too-human agency, not God, is judgment rendered and often with a heavy hand. Humans pass judgment on themselves. ***Their own self-imposed guilt is very often the magnetic energies that attract the so-called karmic consequences!***

Grace Granted from the Goddess

I can share with you a most amazing story about karma. It is a true story. It happened to my confederates and me in a motel on the Oregon Coast. This experience convinced me that there really is grace in the Universe.

It was 2004. It seemed like every time we turned around, yet another date came along requiring special observances. Some spiritual devotees gathered around Egyptian pyramids. Others made their way to other sacred spots like Mt. Shasta or Machu Pichu. Ordinarily the best I could do was light a candle in the family room and, if I went anywhere else, it was strictly through flights of imagination.

Occasionally, we received specific instructions to meet in Lincoln City, Oregon, on some cosmic special days. We stayed at the Ester Lee Motel at such times. The décor hovered somewhere between shabby and cozy. We liked it because each unit offered a suite of rooms, including a kitchen and a sweeping view of the Pacific Ocean. This time the request came from the Goddess, so we packed up and headed for the Coast, no questions asked, but many on our minds.

Once there, a catalog of unusual requests from the Goddess made up a rather long to-do list. We had The Pill with us. Each went off in different directions to acquire assigned items such as a variety of herbs, booze, specific food, sage and incense. Despite serious doubts of ever locating everything, by some miracle we fulfilled every single request down to the last straggly herb whose name we had never heard.

It was the time of year in February that Venus conjoined a new Moon. I look forward to it every year. The Moon's antlers-like outstretched arms reach for the beautiful Venus, sparkling like a diamond in the night sky. What a glorious sight hanging over the Pacific Ocean. It was the signature of the Goddess. And we were about to discover why.

We struggled through a long program of exhausting and unfamiliar rituals as we worked through the night under the guidance of the Goddess. Early in the morning hours, the place looked like it had been nuked. Empty vodka bottles littered the floor along with shoes, candy wrappers, dried herbs, half-burned sage and god knows what else. We sprawled exhausted on the various cots, couches, beds and the floor.

In all of the work we have ever done, secrecy was never mandatory. This one time it was clear that we weren't to reveal our activities of that night. Therefore, we feel honor-bound to observe the injunction, at least until a time when the Goddess Herself decides that it is purposeful to release us from this pledge. I can tell you that it pushed us all to the very limits of endurance and involved the Wounded Feminine.

I sat on the floor with my back against the wall. I stared at the ashes in the fireplace directly in front of me, remnants left from our fire earlier in the evening. We spent the day channeling the Goddess. I spoke for Her when She made this stunning announcement, "I am going to burn your karmic scripts in the fire."

At this point we were too wiped out to really understand what was happening. I had only the vaguest sense where the three guys were. I just remember some groans and grunts seemingly far, far away. For whatever inexplicable reason, Duane—wrapped tightly in a blanket on a cot against the far living room wall—kept mumbling, "Yes, my liege," over and over.

The Goddess began to read off our names, one by one. After each name, she "threw our karmic script into the fire." The fire had long since burned down. Yet, each time she threw a script into the fireplace, the thing flared up into a momentary roaring blaze. It did that four times just as each script fell on the dead ashes. At the end of the ritual, Goddess announced that She was placing a diamond in our heart center. She explained that this would always identify our special connection to the Goddess to anyone in any dimension.

At that point I must have slumped over into a deep, exhausted sleep. The next sight I saw was the next morning when I opened my eyes as David arose from the living room couch. His efforts to walk stiff-legged reminded me of Frankenstein's monster. I was too paralyzed to laugh. If I thought the room was a littered mess the night before, you should have seen it in the cold light of day.

That is the true story about how the Goddess granted us grace for services rendered in Her name. Years later, the following message appeared in my email. It was from Drunvalo Melchizedek, one of the most powerful souls on the planet:

> "Om Mani Padme Hum
> The Tibetans wrote these esoteric words:
> 'On every stone in their land to sing the Truth to all of Heaven;
> Within your heart there is a lotus, and within this lotus there is a diamond.
> This diamond is the source of Creation
> And in all of Creation, there is only One Lotus.'"

Rebirthing or Conscious Breathing

I studied Rebirthing now referred to as Conscious Breathing, with Leonard Orr, the guy who invented it. When it comes to accessing anything that dwells in the nether regions of your own psyche, conscious breathing is one powerful therapy. We shouldn't be surprised at that if we have any concept of the power of the breath and breathing. How many times when we are under stress, do we say, "Take a deep breath"?

This is one technique that I believe can be practiced safely by nonprofessionals. However, I am going to back pedal on that just a bit and add some disclaimers that need to be taken seriously. I really don't relish the thought of a bunch of overzealous wannabe healers/counselors bashing around with no notion of what they are about; what is involved; lacking any background in facilitating other people's "stuff" and worst of all; unwilling to make an effort to study up on the subject and lastly; work at first in partners with a mentor who is experienced in the process. Granted that is quite a large disclaimer!

I have used Conscious Breathing with a group of novices and a good bit of clearing was accomplished relatively easily and in a relatively short time. It is very, very powerful and extremely useful. I'm just making the point that practitioners need not be a licensed therapist as long as they work within the context I outlined.

Conscious Breathing actually healed a situation in which everything else thrown at it was totally futile. Once again this story underscores the notion that until the problem is diagnosed, it may never be healed. In this world of the psychic and metaphysical, it is even murkier than in the world of bladders and gallstones. In the fuzzy world of symptoms misconstrued as weird at best and psychosis at the worst, we are too often left with hit-or-miss flukes in hopes one will stick.

This was the case with Terry. I can still remember the haunted face befitting a person suffering as terribly as he. Terry was not in physical pain. Most observers would say that he was depressed, but his pain was so much deeper than that. He was in horrible psychic and emotional pain. He was tormented. He was a tortured soul.

When he came to see me in my office, he said that I was his last resort. After we discussed his situation for a while, I decided to do Conscious Breathing with him. Remember that this underscores my point about who should be fooling around with this. Terry stretched out on the small cot in my office. I always gave my clients the option of being covered by a light blanket. It was interesting that women said they felt safer with the blanket; men usually wanted nothing to do with any blanket.

Terry commenced the connected rhythmic breathing as instructed. I sat in my usual chair to best observe. It wasn't long before I nearly flew out of that chair when Terry let out the most horrific scream. "It's going to kill me." How would you like that to be your first foray into Conscious Breathing with a client?

I stopped the session immediately, grateful that we stayed after hours and that no one was in the other offices to hear us. I had my trepidations, but he insisted on returning for another session the following week. The same thing happened two more times. I just couldn't take hearing a man scream like that ever again. I told him that the thing—whatever it was—would just have to kill him, I was done. He begged me to keep trying. It must have been some deep intuition or guidance from on high that induced him to continue. We talked.

I told Terry to describe to me in precise detail what he was experiencing and why he was screaming. This is what he said: "I feel like two snakes are coming up my body and if they reach my throat; it will kill me. One is black, and one is white." I jumped up from my chair and ran for the phone. I told him to stay put. I called the house. It so happened I was living in community with three other healers. Two of them were home, and they both knew Terry. I told them I would be there in five minutes with Terry, and I needed their help with a healing.

I bundled a perplexed Terry into the Monte Carlo and sped home. Don was a chiropractor and had an adjustment table downstairs. I put Terry on the table and repeated what Terry had said. I was so excited; I could barely talk. "Terry said a white snake and a black snake are coiling up his body, and if they reach his throat, it will kill him." I turned to Terry and I said, "You absolutely must tell me which side the black snake is on. You can't give me the wrong answer!" He easily indicated and we three healers screamed all at once, "The positive and negative kundalini channels are reversed. And his throat chakra is blocked. If they indeed pass his throat center, this probably will kill him!"

Dr. Don did the healing work and reversed the kundalini channels to their proper locations. Terry sat up, and in the weirdest casual way, announced that he was healed and felt fine. And he felt fine forever after that. We chatted for a while, and I took him home. That has been a most powerful tool in our arsenal. We have found others whose channels were reversed. There will never be one like Terry though. Thank goodness I REALLY listened to exactly what he described and understood what the symbolism meant.

Not that every Conscious Breathing session is this dramatic, but I just have to add the time we did this with our dear friend, Helen. Helen lived in Seattle. We anticipated nothing with more excitement and enthusiasm than when Helen came for a visit over a long week-end, enthusiasm also shared by Helen herself. She was game for working with Thomas and The Pill, and indeed did a lot of deep work with us. However, we did Conscious Breathing one time, and it went just a little too deep. There will be more about Helen's story in another chapter, but it all started at our house with Conscious Breathing.

Helen had a twin brother. They did not get along at all. Helen's sun sign was Libra, and she was a total textbook Libran. To astrologers, that profiled a personality that was always socially circumspect, mild-mannered and, as the peacemakers, valued harmony and loathed scenes. Helen never raised her voice—until that day. Before she could censor it, the most unmistakable deep, ugly hatred for her brother in the womb emerged, spoken from her own lips. Don and I looked at one another in stunned disbelief.

All of a sudden she actually jumped up and off the table in the middle of the session, loudly and angrily proclaiming, "I hated Bud in the womb, so now you think that I hate all men!" and with that she stormed off to the guest room and slammed the door.

Within our rather wide circle of people committed to the spiritual path, there were incidents now and again that someone got a bit more truth about themselves than they actually wanted. There were ruffled feathers, but ordinarily by morning things were calm enough to discuss peaceably over coffee. Too my surprise, Helen's mood showed not the least sign of abating by the next morning. When she packed up to leave, the strain on the relationship was only too obvious. And it was never the same again.

You need to be aware that once you open that door to clearing negative energies on the way to ascension; it is a door that never really closes again. You have opened

Pandora's Box. The subconscious finds its voice and man, can that little turkey blab its secrets before God and country.

There is one last comment I'll add about Helen. I loved Helen. She was one of my dearest friends. But everyone that was at all close to her somehow intuited without a word ever being spoken that there were some taboo subjects, and to refer to them even once would instantly end the relationship. One of the taboo subjects was that she *did* hate men. One of her daughters confronted her about it once, and once was all it took. I don't know that she ever spoke to that daughter again.

The other taboo subject was to confront her about her diet and the fact that she lived on junk food. In another chapter, I will elaborate on what happened between this incident, and a date in June of 1991 when I visited Helen in Seattle, and she died that morning in my arms. Another event to add to 1991, *annus horribilis.*

Chakras

Metaphysicians are mostly familiar with the seven psychic centers that lie along the human spine, and number them beginning with the one at the base of the spine. These are chakras, the engines that control the most powerful energies, the life force. In her book *Bringers of the Dawn* Barbara J. Marciniak informs us that the Pleiadians indicate that five additional chakras, which are located outside of the body, are in the process of being activated.

In this frame of reference, the eighth chakra is located slightly above the head. Chakras nine through twelve are generally considered to be located well above the head. However, these extended chakras essentially transcend our time-space continuum, and thus the idea of location is not particularly meaningful. In this section, I am not going to address these out-of-body chakras to any significant degree. However, a brief example may provide a general sense of some of their functions.

Many of the lightworkers, at some point in their awakening process, begin to hear high pitched frequencies. These energies come in through the chakra which is located just above the head. Much of my own planetary energy work involves energies which come in through the two chakras beyond the chakra above the head.

You need not be especially knowledgeable about the detailed workings of the chakra system, but whenever you are dealing with negative energies, you are going to hear about them. Some basic knowledge then is helpful. First of all, there is the matter of just how the word is pronounced. *Chakra* is a Sanskrit word and, as such, the pronunciation is like this, as nearly as I can write it out: *SHUK-ruh.* In English pronunciation, it is more like this: *SHOCK-ruh* or *CHOCK-ruh.* Any one of these is equally acceptable.

Chakras, for most purposes, refer to the seven psychic centers aligned along the spine. From the base chakra and moving up towards the top of the head are the sacral, solar plexus, heart, throat, third eye and the crown chakra. Chakras are not visible except to psychic vision and resemble funnels with petal-like openings. These openings allow life force energies to support the physical body. They play vital roles in emotional, mental and spiritual functioning as well.

It is important to keep your chakras open and aligned. Energy workers can provide you with an evaluation of your chakra system. Sometimes, one or more may be blocked or completely blown out. This is not good. If the chakra system is functioning below par, it can sometimes create severe symptoms. The reason I include this here is because healing negative energies often must include a chakra balancing along with it.

Another word you may have heard in connection with the chakras is *kundalini.* That is a powerful force that lies coiled at the base of the spine, the first chakra. When initiates achieve enlightenment, the kundalini rises through all of the chakras and out through the crown chakra. This is the goal of all of the hours of meditation in ashrams. The process normally takes many years. The only safe way to achieve the rising of the kundalini and enlightenment, is under the tutelage of a teacher, or guru. This is something that should never be forced or attempted on one's own.

If we throw our back out of alignment, we think nothing about heading for the nearest chiropractor. It is just as important to keep your chakra system aligned and functioning properly. After an illness, any physical, emotional or mental trauma, it is a very good idea to visit an energy worker who can evaluate your entire chakra system. A couple of treatments should be enough unless yours is a severe and long-standing case.

Below, I have written about con artists. Of all the things that these unscrupulous operators do to scare the hell out of victims, and consequently, command exorbitant fees to save you, involve scare stories about your chakras. They realize that most people do not have a clue about what these exotic-sounding chakras are. They play on this widespread ignorance to convince people that this is a serious threat to life and limb. Don't buy into it. In the right hands, even the worst cases are fairly easy to fix.

The Death Prayer

By the time you are figuring out whether or not you are going to believe in this, we might well be ordering flowers sent to your funeral. Most of you will never encounter the Death Prayer. I did. It is the most horrendously unbearable experience that ever existed on this planet. For once, yes, I want to scare the hell out of you just in the off chance that you may need to know. On this one, make one mistake and you are dead for real. The good news?—there is about a one-in-one-million chance that you will ever need to know.

I wrestled for a good long while on whether or not to include this information about the Death Prayer in the first place . After reading different sources that claimed there really was no such thing, I decided I should set the record straight. It is something that is extremely uncommon in this era. In bygone days in the Hawaiian Islands, things were not all flower leis, summer breezes over mai tais and all of the other stereotypical images set in a background of hula dancing to romantic strumming guitars.

Various warring tribes enlisted powerful kahuna-shaman to send the Death Prayer to their enemies; the enemy often being the kahuna in their enemy's camp. Of course, the opposing forces had their own roster of "hit" men, and they faced off against each other in mortal combat of the supernatural kind. They did not need or utilize any conventional weapons. Their weapons were only of the psychic kind. At the end of this kind of battle, one or both were left for dead for real.

Extraordinarily powerful shaman, and only after years of training, are capable of successfully sending the Death Prayer to another shaman, or to anybody else who is designated as a target. In those earlier times, it was not only pitched battles that called for the use of the Death Prayer. Another sin that warranted the Death Prayer was for anyone who shared their ancient secrets with Caucasians or other outsiders.

It may be described as black magic sent deliberately with intent to kill. It is powerful focused energy with someone's name on it. The energies first hit the victim's feet. It then slowly travels up the body until it reaches the solar plexus, at which point, death is swift. It takes three days. The victim's only hope for survival is if he-she is strong enough to ward it off and return it to the sender, or enlist another kahuna who is.

You are probably wondering how it was that I was the recipient of the Death Prayer. This incident happened in 1991. I admit that the entire episode was very risky. I am not going to share all of the details for the simple reason that for ordinary readers who are not in the shaman business, and for almost all shaman for that matter, this will never be an issue. I am including this story, as I mentioned earlier, primarily to confirm that it does exist.

How did it happen?

I was interacting with a close friend who had been completely taken over by a Dark entity. Therefore, my conversation was with the entity, and I was fully aware of it. The conversation occurred just after my father's death, and the issue was a complicated family matter. I confronted the entity, and refused to be bullied by his-her (I'm not saying which) actions and demands. Later that day, I was with my husband and my son.

I began to feel bad; I mean real bad. In fact, there is no describing how bad. I lay on a couch with the two guys looking worriedly on. Finally, I screamed that my cells were exploding. Thank God, my son had the wherewithal to look psychically and realize it was the Death Prayer, and indeed I was dying. And thank God I raised a powerful shaman who was not about to let his mom check out for good. He stopped the energy in its tracks.

I repeat, the Death Prayer is real. It is also a horrific experience. Perhaps this happened to us to let us know that it is real. I like to think it is no longer used in the Islands, or anywhere else for that matter, but it very likely is practiced somewhere, here and there. Our team of healers, the 4Ds, have cleared other powerful shamanic healers of some very nasty energies ourselves. These have come from South American shaman who can be very jealous and territorial in relation to North American shaman. If you engage in this high level healing work and get into trouble, please call on us just in case. It is my opinion that if you do shamanic healing, the safest thing is to work within a group. I know that is hard in the United States. At least designate someone as back-up in case you get in over your head.

Footnote: Did David send the Death Prayer back where it came from? Not a chance! That would be black magic. We dispatched the entity, however. Sometimes there is a fine line between the Light and the Dark. I recount this incident not to scare the wit's out of you, but to remind ourselves that the 3rd dimension is still one of duality.

Don't Ever Get Overconfident.

In other parts of this book, I have spoken with confidence about the 4Ds, and my and their successes with the Dark side. Seriously, I am always only too aware of my limits. I do not rush in where angels fear to tread. It is not an ego issue with me to carve notches in my belt. That is foolishness of the highest order. Overconfidence is a good way to end up with the short stick yourself. I can't caution you strongly enough to know your limits, and never exceed those boundaries.

Con Artists are Alive and Well

Tread carefully here, too. As ascension healing and shamanism explode into greater acceptance, you have your snake oil salesman and fast buck charlatans only too willing to cash in. It pays to be very discerning. I have clients who find so-called shaman on the Internet who charge them exorbitant fees to exorcise demons, and if you are naïve enough, the first $5,000 doesn't quite do the job. Incredibly, I know clients who have paid through the nose to the tune of $10,000 on up to $35,000. I'm amazed that they have the guts to take another chance and work with me. It must be my adorable personality.

The latter situation is what I—rightly or wrongly—call the gypsy scam. It probably has been around for as long as there were suckers willing to part with their money. Many times clients call me with the same dreary saga. It is oh-so-very-alive-and-well right here in modern times. These con artists are perfectly capable of providing some accurate psychic information. That is the hook. When you stop to think about it, what good is information that you already know? Just because someone psychically retrieves a fact or two from your memory banks, a healer it does not make. That is simply psychic reading 101.

These con artists do not regard the initial fee as everything they anticipate squeezing out of you. The signature move is when more work is required to save you from demons, or curses, or to clear terrible family karma, or past life sins or anything else that they know will push your buttons. One scam that repeatedly hooks women is the promise of meeting Mr. Right. This comes to the tune of a very high additional price tag. I am shocked how willing so many people are to keep doling out money. Be wary of this age-old scam. If only I wasn't so honest, damn! I'd be a millionaire. There really is a sucker born every minute.

Here is some advice to legitimate shaman and healers, remember this: If anyone tells you that they have been told about an entity attachment, always ask who told them. Be persistent. The minute they report that there were additional services required for a wildly unreasonable jacked-up fee, do these clients a favor and tell them in no uncertain terms that they are the victims of fraud.

Also be Wary of Incompetent Healers

After I ran an article on the subject of incompetent healers, I received letters about this issue. When you deal with clearing negative energies and blocks, be discerning who works in your energy field. Sometimes it is simply a matter of good old-fashioned common sense. Following is just one of the letters dealing with the issue of incompetent healers:

> "I am so glad...you wrote about that. We recently had a young, beautiful, innocent man come in after his Reiki 1 attunement, and he was a wreck. The person who did his attunement...blew out his chakras, cut all his cords and left him flailing about. We cleared him...brought forth his guardian angel...like you, I could just cry at what this other person did...again thanks for posting the info about incompetent 'healers.'"

Soul Mates

One last thought. So many times I have been asked about soul mates in my most popular subject—relationships. I would like to put in a word about soul mates in order to correct some very misguided notions. Do not go looking for your soul mate in the hopes that if you DO find him-her that everything will come up roses. Your relationship life will reflect all of your relationship patterns and issues *exactly as they do now,* whether that be with your soul mate or someone else. My advice is to work on yourself. It is the only way to attract a workable relationship into your life. Don't ever think that your soul mate will save you from doing the inner work. Ain't gonna happen!

THE HEALING JOURNEY

It can be overwhelming to consider the abundance of ills—from the esoteric to the mundane—that may befall an unsuspecting human. Remember this, many people who have encountered any one of these challenges have lived to tell the tale. So where are you? Is there an entity enjoying you for lunch? Are past life wounds manifesting as physical problems this time around? Are you living hand-to-mouth because of your ancestors' traumas with money? Are there other things mysteriously lurking behind the scenes, secretly keeping you from moving forward to fulfill your destiny?

I remind you that the four activations described in "Books One and Two" of this trilogy, impact consciousness so as to bring your specific problems to the surface. An awakened intuition and conscious intention will lead to the right teacher, the right healer or the right book, at the right place and at the right time. Synchronicity may then lead you through the dark places to illuminate the path marked out by the footprints of those who trod the road less traveled before you.

CHAPTER TWELVE

The Spiritual Emergency Room

~ All is provided for in the time of need ~

Have faith child of the universe,
as the forms of the Earth transform,
as money dies and love is born.
We won't allow for you to be torn
by the currents of the world.

You will never be hungry nor alone

We love you.
We will always be right by you.
We will never leave you alone.
We will never let you stray.

You will always be safe
even amidst the challenge
and the lessons.
We will always be here
to light your way.

Thank you for your service…
May you always bask in the eternal light of **gentle play.**

To the divine play.

As traumatic as it is, when confronted by a medical crisis, we at least know to head for the nearest hospital emergency room. Another kind of emergency may be equally traumatic and life threatening. Yet, there are two critical problems. The first is that neither the victims—nor anybody else—may know what is wrong with them and even if they did, they may not know where to turn. I am referring to a spiritual emergency. Unfortunately, there are no spiritual emergency rooms in your local hospital.

The concept of spiritual emergency is not new nor is it original with me. Back in the 70s, I happened onto a little book by Lee J. Sanella, MD. It's title Kundalini: Psychosis or Transcendence? caught my eye because I was personally floundering through what I later learned was a spiritual emergency of my own, a dark night of the soul. That little book changed my life and maybe even saved it.

The symptoms of a spiritual emergency can be horrific. The impact on one's life is often such that even routine self-care is impossible. Usually regarded or diagnosed as a typical illness, the intervention of suppressive medications may further complicate the process. As unbelievable as this may seem for anyone observing individuals exhibiting the dramatic symptoms of spiritual emergency, these people are in reality experiencing spiritual emergence!

This life-shattering experience is not contingent on whether or not the wounded are seekers on a path of conscious spirituality. The soul is in charge of this date with destiny. The bell may toll for anybody at any given time, initiating a transformation of consciousness and opening the golden door to enlightenment. However, one may travel a rocky path before finally knocking on the entrance of that door!

The first problem concerns the enormous difficulty in putting together a support team and a safe spiritual emergency room. For many years, it was futile, and perhaps even dangerous, to count on any traditional psychiatric or medical models. More than one unfortunate soul found him- or herself in locked facilities and padded rooms.

When I look back on it now, I wonder at my guts in just such a situation. A friend of mine called me in a near panic. The police admitted her daughter to the psych ward of a local hospital during what appeared to be a very high profile psychotic episode. My friend was a battle-scarred veteran of the world of consciousness and transformation, including the pitfalls along the path.

She briefly described the daughter's experiences with what I am calling here, spiritual emergency. My own personal wounds, combined with extensive healing work with clients, have given me an intuitive nose. I can smell transformation a mile away. This was unmistakably a case in point.

My friend exhorted me to get her daughter "out of that place." The only thing I could promise was to pay the daughter a visit. I can't explain what prompted me to do what I did next. Whatever it was, it was an academy award performance.

Dressed in conservative black, I finagled a visit to the daughter's room "at the behest of the family as her spiritual advisor." I signed in as Rev. Diana Stone, and struggled to maintain a demeanor for what I believed to be appropriate for a woman of the cloth. I dared not let myself ponder the legal ramifications for impersonating the clergy in order to spring a mental patient.

The Fates smiled on me that day. I spirited her out of the hospital and returned her to the custody of her mom. Trust me, it was eventually sorted out by the fortunate intervention by a savvy psychiatrist I knew, sparing me from a chain gang. Regrettably, I can just as readily document nightmare cases with unhappy endings. Some of my clients suffering from horrendously debilitating symptoms are abandoned, misunderstood or maligned by family, friends and professionals alike.

If you were expecting me to say that the ascension process has reversed the situation and cast enlightenment upon all involved, think again. No! It is because of ascension that I am so terribly concerned about this. The higher frequencies are triggering transformational emergencies in Westerners at an alarming rate.

It was not so very many years ago that words like transformation, meditation, enlightenment, kundalini, chakras and ashrams seemed but remote exotic practices in mysterious India or Tibet. Along came the 60s, the Beatles and Maharishi Mahesh Yogi. The landscape did not just change; it exploded.

Psychic and spiritual energies took a quantum leap into a culture that had no tradition of how even to begin to manage them. The heritage of long centuries of proud spiritual traditions ended up on Haight-Ashbury* at the end of a needle.

The twenty-first century brings us to an unbelievably changed world. Eastern spiritual practices are recognizable to most people. Traditional psychiatry no longer automatically classifies spiritual crises as psychosis as it once did. An updated description is in the *Diagnostic and Statistical Manual* of mental disorders, the bible used as a diagnostic reference tool in the mental healthcare field (DSM1V-revised).

The first name to come to mind in connection with spiritual emergencies is Dr. Stanislav Grof. His book *Spiritual Emergency* outlines the symptoms, lists the various categories of spiritual emergencies, examines the problem with differential diagnosis and suggests preferred treatment modalities and resources for those in need.

Information about this subject is easily available on the Internet. Below, I have copied a review of the book and other useful information from a website.

"In his book *Spiritual Emergency* Stanislav Grof described a syndrome he termed "Spiritual Emergency." The spiritual emergency experience can feel like Heaven or Hell. Under the Hell column, you may find listed hallucinations, seizures, pain, panic attacks, mania, severe depression and euphoria--all the symptoms of physical and mental illness.

"When people suffer this way, they may feel like they're going crazy, and their doctors may agree. In many cases such a diagnosis is mistaken. Grof urges the adoption of a new category of clinical diagnosis, "spiritual emergency."

---

* Haight-Ashbury is the intersection of two streets in San Francisco and became the name for an area that drew countless numbers of street people involved in the hippie counter-culture of the 60s.

This book contains fourteen papers, many of them excellent, by doctors and other experts on the following types of spiritual crises:

1. The shamanic crisis.
2. Awakening of kundalini.
3. Episodes of unitive consciousness ("peak experiences").
4. Psychological renewal through return to the center.
5. The crisis of psychic opening.
6. Past life recalls and experiences.
7. Communications with spirit guides and "channeling."
8. Near-death experiences.
9. Experiences of close encounters with UFOs.
10. Possession states.

PLACES TO GO FOR HELP

Shared Transformations

Yes, this is the correct name to do an Internet search for kundalini problems. Much of the information is useful for ANY kind of spiritual emergency. A forum for people with on-going kundalini activity, it offers help for distressing kundalini symptoms and has superb lists of books and links.

Spiritual Emergence Network

This contact provides support and resources for individuals experiencing difficulties with their spiritual growth. Trained graduate students in the School of Professional Psychology at the California Institute for Integral Studies respond to each caller, providing assistance and educational information regarding spiritual emergence. They can also make referrals to licensed mental health professionals in the caller's area.

The Following Material in Quotation Marks is Copied From the Internet.

The following information is a sample of what is available on the Internet. Other sufferers have reached out and shared their stories of help and healing. Now that we have this amazing revolutionary tool, the Internet expands the sources of supportive information one hundred fold. Take advantage of this formidable resource. Most of the material is free to anyone with Internet access. This means that help can embrace so many more people who are looking for answers and confirmation of their particular situation. And on a bad day, well, you know what we say: Misery loves company! At any rate, I salute you lightbeings who are in pain, but who march bravely on. I know you are out there.

So Read On

"If you are feeling overwhelmed, or having doubts and fears about the dramatic upheavals a Kundalini awakening can trigger, I would recommend contacting the Spiritual Emergency Centre, or one of the Spiritual Emergence Networks in America and Canada."

"A good therapist experienced in Spiritual Emergence might be able to help you; at least they could validate your experience. Ultimately, however; it is the individual who must come to terms with this transformative spiritual process."

"For excellent guide books, get copies of *A Farther Shore* by Yvonne Kason, M.D., *Energies of Transfo*rmation by Bonnie Greenwell Ph.D., and *Living With Kundalini* by Gopi Krishna (especially recommended). I have found these books to be the most helpful with the most accurate information about Kundalini in the many books and articles I have read over the years."

"Much has been said about what you can do for kundalini problems in the Shared Transformation Newsletters and The Scandinavian Kundalini Network. You will find some of the best kundalini information on the Net at both of these sites for kundalini problems."

"Beware of people trying to sell you high-priced courses or pressuring you to join their spiritual group. While in the throes of spiritual awakening, one can be vulnerable to people who may not have a person's best interests at heart, or dispense techniques that can worsen your process."

"Warning: Once Kundalini is up and running, healing attempts may increase it and potentially wreak havoc, rather than decrease or effectively integrate it. On the other hand for some people, healers have been helpful, but for many of us, there are risks and resultant disappointments in subjecting our energy to healers."

El Collie, the highly esteemed founder of Shared Transformation, wrote: "'Whenever well-intentioned healers have given me energy treatments, in person or long distance, my kundalini goes haywire. I've had my symptoms and pain get worse, even when loving people with a lot of active kundalini have prayed for me. (This has not happened when people with dormant kundalini prayed for me.) I get overly zapped by their 'gifts' of additional energy, when I've already got more than I can handle on my own. "

"Generally, basic things are safe such as long walks, cutting back on meditation or prayer, including meat in your diet to weigh down the energy, etc. Sometimes stopping all spiritual work for a while, or permanently, is the best course of action. You may find the concentration involved in your daily activities is sufficient for growth without increasing it to uncomfortable levels."

(Diana's note: *Husband Don, Brother Duane and I have successfully aided people suffering from ascension symptoms (listed elsewhere in this book) and other spiritual symptoms as well. Healers must be careful that they don't light a match and throw it on something that is already on fire. People prone to panic and anxiety attacks need calm and lowered stimuli. It is especially critical to consider ceasing all spiritual practices, as this may add fuel to the flames. The energies can also run toward the other end of the spectrum—depression. In that case the opposite tack is appropriate; the healer seeks to bring sufferers out of a very deep, dark hole. For this, extra energy is needed to motivate the client.*

We once worked with a man who was meditating 7-8 hours a day to deliberately trigger the kundalini energy. He was fried. Dr. Don worked with him when Don still had his practice. He used homeopathics, and of course insisted that he discontinue his meditation. He urged him to add meat to his diet to ground him, even though he was a vegetarian. Nevertheless, despite all of our efforts, he eventually ended up in a mental institution as a diagnosed schizophrenic. The medical doctors took over, and he was heavily drugged. We lost track of this case, but I include it as an extreme example of what NOT to do.)

"Being in nature is wonderful for grounding Kundalini. I once read that sitting against trees to have excess energy absorbed is helpful; some Chi Kung practices work with the chi in trees as well. I don't have personal experience of trying to work with trees to balance Kundalini, but I do feel the grounding effect of being in nature."

(Diana's note: *For God's sake, do NOT hug any trees for energy when you are already on overload (including kundalini symptoms), or in a manic episode and so on. Four of my buddies and I were advised to hug a tree by a South American shaman with whom we were working. We sneaked out to hug 80-foot Douglas firs that were in front of my house, waiting until midnight so the neighbors would not see us. Those trees believed in rough love. The energetic vibrations were a marriage of domestic violence. We were shaken to pieces. The next day we were bruised and banged up as though a gang of muggers had accosted us in a dark alley! If you hug a tree, at least pick a nice little peach tree or something like that. Operative word is little!)*

Recently someone emailed me about how being near or in the ocean was helpful to his kundalini process. I can see how this would be highly effective too. I have also heard of hot baths at night being helpful; some healers advocate bathing with salt as a way to tone down anxiety attacks. The homeopathic remedies are also a mainstay in our arsenal.

"Grounding methods where you visualize the energy going into the ground are often recommended to balance kundalini and other "fiery" energies. In my experience, this does not work. When I try to direct the energy into the ground, the focusing leads to more kundalini energy flooding into my head right after the exercise. Other people have had the same problem with this, but for some it is effective. You have to experiment to see what will work for you. Remember, what works for one individual will not necessarily work for another."

"Having a support person, or persons, can be immensely beneficial. I have found this to be most effective, especially when nothing else works. Cultivating faith that the process is ultimately a blessing of the highest order is critical. I know this can be difficult to do when in the throes of a kundalini eruption, or having kundalini problems for years, but it makes a substantial difference in your process."

"I feel having a pet can be helpful too. I used to have a Labrador Retriever that I would playfully wrestle with on the floor; I always felt like this joyful abandon with my canine opponent toned down my kundalini energy. It is immensely important to strive to live an ordinary life with balance, optimism, and most importantly, a sense of humor. Try to laugh more and live your life to the fullest in spite of any kundalini-related limitations."

"I believe Gopi Krishna once wrote that there were no secret teachings that would awaken you faster; all the steps to take were already outlined in all the major religious teachings. I did not want to believe this in my earlier years of exploring everywhere for the fast lane to enlightenment. Now with the wisdom of more years, more research, and more experiences, I fully grasp his perceptive point. Usually the more complex a method is, the more it will over stimulate kundalini. I think kundalini likes the 'keep it simple' approach."

All of the quoted material above was sent to various Internet sites. I included them as suggestions you might find useful, and as examples of what help may be found when you utilize the Internet as a resource.

I am aware of cases of spontaneous kundalini in which the individuals were not forcing the experience like the man who insisted on meditating hours a day. Many others, both in Caucasian and native cultures, have reported on this same phenomenon. Yes, it may come uninvited; therefore, yet assuming it is a call from the soul. These individuals all became medicine people, shaman and healers.

Knowing When to Utilize Drug Therapy

There is a case with which I am familiar. A woman struggled for 32 years with the aftermath of a kundalini experience which left her with mild bipolar disorder. She was open to using all of the alternative therapies that were available over time, which she did. None of them reliably stabilized her symptoms. Here we have an example of considering all options: She reports that there is recently a medication that has been a "godsend" in stabilizing the moods. Do not consider any of this material as a license to abandon the possibility that drug therapy may be for you if you happen to resist the idea.

Past Life Recall Terrifies a Client: A Case History

What may seem old hat to awakened individuals sophisticated in navigating deep spiritual waters, may be the very thing that scares the living daylights out of the novice. I received a phone call from a young woman who was referred to me by a friend familiar with my healing work. The woman was nearly hysterical, so I braced myself for some horrible case of possession or something equivalent. As it turned out, she had experienced a spontaneous past life recall of her life as Billy the Kid. This is pretty tame stuff for me, but I have to remember that for the uninitiated, it can be terrifying.

Since Billy the Kid was an outlaw, I asked if she was raised under fairly strict conditions. I thought that the subconscious may be looking to "break the law." She validated my suspicions. She grew up in a military family and was educated in private Catholic schools.

I reassured her that there was an explanation for her experience and confirmed that she was not crazy. I assured her that I was experienced in such matters, so we scheduled a consultation time at my office. Linda turned out to be one of my most intriguing spiritual emergency clients. I began working with her in 1989. She has traveled a very long journey in the meantime, to say the least.

I could write about many healing clients I have worked with over the years. The reason I like to use Linda as a case study is because she is so clearly an example of spiritual emergency leading to spiritual transformation of consciousness. She undertook a deep reexamination of her life. It became increasingly obvious that her marriage was just another reflection of a lifetime pattern of excessive structure and following other people's rules. She eventually divorced her husband. Her spiritual emergency was indeed a case of spiritual *emergence.*

She became fascinated with the life of Billy the Kid. Whenever she asked if she actually was the notorious outlaw in a previous life, I told her it really did not matter if it was literally true. In any cases like this, what matters is the mythology that presents itself. If you are a healer or counselor, go ahead and work with it, even if it is the third Billy the Kid you have seen in your practice this year.

There is another little twist that gave me pause in this story. Linda knew a friend whose hobby was target shooting. He invited a few of his friends—including Linda—to accompany him to the target range to try their hands at some target practice. Linda had never handled any kind of weapon in her entire life. As her friends attempted to hit the targets, they had about the success you would expect from beginners. At least they did not kill each other. However, everyone else was just stunned when it came Linda's turn. She whipped out the pistols and was a crack shot right off the bat. Billy the Kid? Crack shot? Hmmm.

As her life progressed, I observed Linda's growing interest in shamanism. She traveled to South America several times. Her belief system was utterly transformed from that of the Catholic school girl she had been. She fell in love with a guy much younger than she. He apparently was crazy about her. Nevertheless, a siren song ever more loudly drew her to Southwestern United States, closer to Spanish influences. There were tears, but she left her son and lover behind and moved to New Mexico.

Since then, she has taken classes in herbology in both the U.S. and Mexico. There is a school in Santa Fe. She continues to stay in touch with me. I can hardly believe that the woman she is today is the same one who called me in tears back in 1989. One more thing: Anything you want to know about Billy the Kid, just ask Linda.

The Flawed Western Medical/Psychiatric Model

Mental illness has, unfortunately, taken its place alongside leading physical causes of death and disability, such as cancer and heart disease, in the Western countries. As of 2003, mental illness was the second leading cause of disability and premature mortality in the United States. We are indeed in the midst of a mental health epidemic. These, and other shocking statistics, are reflecting psychiatric treatment models that clearly are not working.

These standard therapeutic models are based on the suppression of symptoms with a wide variety of drugs that bring harmful short- and long-term side effects along with the ride. The American Psychiatric Association could more accurately be called The American Psychopharmacological Association. They have almost completely sold out to the drug companies.

It is outside the box for any practitioner in our current traditional healing community to consider that certain mental illnesses might not be strictly an illness at all! Yet, this may not be as shocking as it sounds at first. Long-held traditions around the globe subscribe to the following view. "In the shamanic tradition, mental illness signals 'the birth of a healer,'" explains Meladoma Patrice Somé (soe-MAY), Ph.D., an internationally celebrated shaman, diviner and teacher, "*thus mental disorders are spiritual emergencies* (italics mine), spiritual crises, and need to be regarded as such to aid the healer to be born."

Shamanic View of Mental Disorder

And famous psychologist and anthropologist Holger Kalweit writes:

> "If we were able to understand sickness and suffering as processes of physical and psychic transformation, as do Asian peoples and tribal cultures, we would gain a deeper and less biased view of psychosomatic and psychospiritual processes and begin to realize the many opportunities presented by suffering...."

Please note that he includes sickness and suffering as processes of *physical* transformation as well as psychic transformation! This solidly squares with one of the oft-repeated messages in this book. We must change, or transform, our physical bodies in order to ascend into the frequencies of higher dimensions. The quotes above were from a book by journalist Stephanie Marohn. The last chapter in the book is "The Shamanic View of Mental Illness."

Speaking of the indigenous view of mental illness, let's return again to the work of Dr. Somé. Dr. Somé is quite a guy. He is a member of the Dagara tribe near the Ivory Coast in Western Africa. However, he left his native roots to study in Europe and America. He holds three master's degrees and two doctorates from the Sorbonne and Brandeis University respectively. He conducts workshops and classes around the world but also maintains a close connection with his village.

When he returned to America to study, one of his friends was confined to a mental ward. When Dr. Somé went to visit him, he was shocked. Some patients were zoned out on meds and others were in strait jackets screaming and yelling. Just like other shaman all over the world, Dr. Somé could see entities swarming around the patients causing them pain.

Don, Duane and I certainly can back that up. The symptoms of many of our cases like this involve entity invasion. I have often said that if only I could get inside the mental institutions to clear out the invading entities, there would be the most remarkable remission of disorders the shrinks had ever seen. This may bring up the issue if distance healing. We heal our clients from a distance, why not these in institutions? As a matter of fact, it is possible. You will read about it in the chapter "Ho'oponopono."

As for Dr. Somé, he looked around at the stark mental ward and remarked, "So this is how the healers who are attempting to be born are treated in this culture." The people in his culture exhibited the same symptoms he had seen in his village. Yet, the patients here were treated in direct opposition to the way his culture handles such situations.

In the Dagara tradition, the community helps the person reconcile the energies of both worlds. By "both worlds," he means the outer physical world with which we are familiar, and the inner psychic worlds traversed by shaman on their healing journeys. The individual is then able to serve as a bridge between the worlds and help the living with information and healing they need. The spiritual crisis ends with another healer's "birth." When all was said and done, Dr. Somé could not tolerate the mental ward environment and had to leave.

Alex: Crazy in the USA; Healer in Africa

Dr. Somé grew increasingly curious about whether or not the shamanic view of mental illness could hold true in the Western world as well as it did in indigenous cultures, such as in his Dagara tribe. He met Alex, an 18-year-old American lad suffering from psychotic manic-depression for the previous four years. Along with dangerous ups and downs, he had hallucinations and was suicidal.

The boy was in a mental hospital where he was given a long list of a variety of drugs. Nothing was helping. His parents were at a loss about what to do next. With their permission, the doctor returned with their son to Africa. After eight months, Alex had become quite normal.

Alex went through a shamanic ritual especially designed for him. Since he had not been born into the Dagara culture, the ritual was adjusted somewhat, but the result was the same. The ritual used is called *Dupulo,* and to summarize: It is used to connect patients to their original purpose for which they planned before coming into this life.

After a few months, Alex was helping the other village healers, assisting them in their healing work with clients. Dr. Somé reported that he sat with the healers all day long. Not only that, Alex stayed in the village for four years! He stayed by choice, not because he needed more healing himself. He said he felt safer there.

The experience eventually led Alex to return to the United States. The last Dr. Somé heard was that Alex was in graduate school in psychology at Harvard. No one expected him to complete undergraduate studies, let alone an advanced degree from Harvard. There can be no question but what Dr. Somé proved his point.

Because of my own personal experiences, I just love this story as you might well imagine. However, this story does not stop here. Dr. Somé sums up what Alex's mental illness was all about:

> "He was reaching out. ***It was an emergency call.*** (Remember, emergency calls are all about spiritual **emergence.**) Alex's purpose was to be a healer. He said no one was paying attention to that...the question still remains, the answer to this problem must be found here (in the West)...There has to be a way in which a little bit of attention beyond the pathology...leads to the possibility of coming up with the proper ritual to help people."

If you are bipolar, trust that it will seek you out as well if it is a signal from the soul. The question is: Are you awake enough to hear it and do you possess the courage to follow it without question? I can tell you firsthand that in the West, make no mistake, this is a very hard road, fraught with suffering.

The Shaman and his Nature Spirit

What we did not know, and what Dr. Somé explains in his book, is that we can be accompanied by a spirit. A shaman can see the spirit and trace it back to its beginnings. He says that the spirit is usually connected to Nature, especially with mountains or big rivers.

I interrupt my story here to interject an experience I had that I did not understand until I read this part of his book. An astrological colleague from Seattle was visiting my area to lecture for our local association. He stopped by my house, and one thing led to another, until I ended up doing a psychic reading about his past lives.

I saw him as a spirit associated with a huge mountain range. I was nonplussed by it, but oddly enough, he was quite taken with the idea. He was a short guy, and he loved towering over the highest mountain. I now know that he was getting a signal, also. I can't say that I know his purpose, but by physical appearance he looks exactly like Merlin the Magician, and his star has risen in the astrological community and in a popular TV series.

Dr. Somé explains that the nature spirit—let's say it is a mountain nature spirit—is connected to the individual and requires a merger or an alignment of the two energies. The person and the mountain spirit become one. The shaman conducts a ritual to bring about this alignment. The spirit sees in us a call to something that will make life meaningful. It is a call to something that transcends materialism and possession of things, as well as success in the conventional sense.

Most of this longing is unconscious. We don't know that we are making this call. It is irrelevant to the spirit if the call is conscious or unconscious. It will answer a call. After all, it is not the spirit's plan; it is your life plan.

And now I will quote Dr. Somé:

> "As part of the ritual to merge the mountain and human energy, those who are receiving the mountain energy are sent to a mountain area of their choice, where they pick up a stone that calls to them...The presence of the stone aids in tuning the receptivity of the person. They receive a variety of tangible information from the other world about how to live their life."

It is interesting to note that the astrologer in question who was associated with the mountain spirit, lives in the great Northwest in full view of the great Pacific Ring of Fire volcanic mountains, near Mt. Rainier.

Now let me share with you the fantastic manner in which this unfolded for my brother, Duane Henkle. This is certainly a textbook case!

After graduating from the University of Iowa, Duane took a job in Chicago, eventually working in upper management for Sears in the famous Sears tower. He seemed to be driven by ambition. He was a workaholic. He made a lot of money. He was married and had four kids. He was talented and participated in sports, particularly golf and baseball. He lived in an upscale house in the suburbs. He served as a deacon in his church.

In other words, here we have the stereotypical lifestyle of a corporate executive, right down to bridge club every Wednesday night. The only problem was that this was not the real Duane. He was prescribed high blood pressure medicine and tranquilizers at age twenty-eight. He suffered his first nervous breakdown and visited his shrink four times a week.

Meanwhile, I had taken a different path. We had very little contact for many years, but he was vaguely aware of the astrology and metaphysical studies I was pursuing. He approved, but was just too busy to engage me in any meaningful interaction.

Receiving the Call

One morning driving to work on the expressway, in the mid-1980s, something bizarre happened that was engineered to grab *anyone's* attention. Writing began to continuously scroll down the windshield of his car as he drove to work, actual writing in English. When he arrived in his office, he attempted to copy down as much as he could remember.

The same thing happened again the next morning. In fact, this continued until he had a sheaf of writings that seemingly outlined a life totally different from his current one. It spoke of his role in a group as a teacher and healer, which would reach out to people all over the world, just to summarize it in a nutshell. This seemed a far cry from flying in the Sears's company jet to China to supervise the manufacture of men's shirts! It was time to contact his sister.

Meanwhile, his sister was about to experience something that, in the end, would be equally as bizarre. Yes, that would be me. I was attending an astrology conference in Seattle where I lectured every year. Another astrologer that I knew well, approached me in the hall after lunch one day. I knew that she was also a well-known medium in the Toronto area. She held out her hand and gave me two odd-looking green stones. I certainly had never seen any like them before.

As she gave the stones to me, she exhibited a good deal of annoyance over this whole affair. She said that she had gone to her room in the hotel after lunch, where her guide pressured her to give me the two green stones. She claimed that the stones had been collected from the base of the pyramid in Egypt, and since there were only a few of them, she was in a nasty temper about parting with any at all. "However, my guide will annoy the hell out of me if I don't," she said as she turned and walked away.

After parting with the stones, she stopped to explain that there was a ritual that I was to do along with the "other shaman I would train." I must have stood there looking very foolish. I had no idea what she was talking about. I was working with Thomas at the time, and that I was a shaman had not quite surfaced full-blown into my own consciousness yet. So who was this *other* shaman supposed to be? I wish I could remember exactly what the ritual was, but I do know that it had something to do with holding the green stone in the sun, and if it turned blood red, it meant that you had been "called" to the shaman's path.

Man, this stuff was growing "weirder and weirder." (If I only knew what lie ahead!) Anyway, the astrology conferences were ordinarily pretty hectic, so I raced off from this encounter in the hall of the hotel, and the last I remember at the time was tossing the green stones unceremoniously into my jewelry case.

The green stones lay mostly forgotten for quite a while. Meanwhile, my brother was navigating his way through an unbelievable change in life direction. I'm making a long story short, of course, but he divorced his wife, and began avariciously devouring box upon box of metaphysical/spiritual books, which I shipped back and forth from my own library. What took me nearly 20 years of study, he was up to snuff in about a year. He inhaled this stuff.

There were several hours-long telephone calls from Sears each week. What we must have cost that company in long distance charges! The company Controller actually approached Duane about it once, but Duane came up with some kind of sob story about family tragedies and schmoozed his way out of it. The telephone calls continued all in the name of spiritual emergence.

Somewhere along the line, I did dig out one of the green stones and held one up to the direct sunlight one day. I'll be damned if that little sucker didn't turn bright red. "Oh, well, I guess I am a shaman," was my thought. By that time, it was really all sort of a ho-hum experience. As for the other green stone, I still did not understand what it could be for.

I received a call from Duane one day. He was really agitated. When I asked him what was the matter, he said, "This guy *with the green stone in his turban,* keeps appearing to me. He acts crazy.
Now for the real kicker. Duane made plans for an exit out-package from Sears to take a job at Los Alamos Labs in Santa Fe, New Mexico. Again, not until I read about Dr. Somé's work in order to write this book, did I put it all together. Remember what Dr. Somé said about people who have the mountain spirit? They are sent to a mountain area of their choice.

Santa Fe, of course, sits at a high elevation in the mountains. After Duane stayed with us for a while to deal with his healing, I asked him why he did not move to Portland where we lived. It was obvious that we were going to be working together. This was his answer, "My soul has to live in Santa Fe."

Do you remember the remainder of the ritual? He must choose a stone that calls to him. Many people carry the stone and receive messages from the other worlds. If I have to draw you a picture at this point, then you haven't been connecting the dots. Stones? Green stones for a shaman-to-be? A ritual with a green stone? His sister's name is Stone? He receives the call from a guide who has a green stone in his turban? He turns his life upside down? How did the universal energies manage to pull that off? We did not have a clue.

In the chapter "The Invisible Players" you will read the rest of the story about our adventure with the green stone. It wasn't over yet! I will keep you in suspense until then.

One other important consideration remains when one is being called to shamanism. It was not only in Dr. Somé's work that I have read this. When one receives the call, you have free will. You may refuse it if you wish. However, if you do, you will fall back into mental illness for the rest of your life.

If you accept, you will still face a personal journey of dark nights of the soul, painful initiations, and overwhelming physical, emotional and mental transformations. In the end, however, you can potentially fulfill the mission that you chose before you ever came into this life. I am very proud of my brother. It took great courage to do what he did to change his life. He has suffered terribly along the way. Yet today, he facilitates the most powerful healing work with clients the world over, and at a unique time in history when ascension is in the air.

Duane's Dark Night of the Soul

Whereas Duane suffered through the typical dark night of the soul in his awakening of consciousness, this gives me an opportunity to discuss exactly what this means; killing two birds with one stone, as it were (Don't go there.).

No one invites a dark night of the soul. If you are experiencing a dark night of the soul, you will more likely invite it *out!* It is a very painful process. One feels that everything he-she has built up in life is now meaningless. A dark night of the soul is often triggered in advance of an awakened consciousness and a rebirth. It may appear to others as a deep depression, which it resembles. However, it is working on a much deeper, spiritual level.

If you feel that you may be experiencing a dark night of the soul, this is considered a spiritual emergency, and you are advised to cope with it just as you would a depression. You would have several options, of course, and it is up to you to explore the ones that are most helpful to you. This may be the time to contact a spiritual emergency room. However, remember this: It passes, and you have earned bragging rights to one of the great spiritual experiences known to mankind.

At this point, many years later and much water over the dam, my brother has moved to Vancouver, Washington, where Don and I live, and he has healed countless numbers of people suffering terribly themselves. And again, he answered the call without hesitation to pull up stakes and move to Hawaii. If he had not, the world would never have *Book One, The Lightbody Activation Manual* or the wonderful Crystal Triangle Lightbody Activation method so easily accessible to all.

Now my family is being challenged again. A close family member has been diagnosed with bipolar disorder. She lives a traditional life and is being treated with drugs. The question now is: Is this a signal of a healer being born, or is she one of the *general population* among which this affliction is epidemic? Is there a mountain or other ancestral nature spirit following her? Can we merge the two? At this point, only time will tell.

Before ending this material from Dr. Somé's work, I will share the last paragraph in the book. I think that you will understand that I was thunderstruck when I read it.

> "When it is the river energy, those being called go to the river, and after speaking to the river spirit, find a water stone to bring back for the same kind of ritual as for the mountain spirit. People think something extraordinary must be done in an extraordinary situation like this. That's not usually the case. Sometimes it is as simple as carrying a stone."

Elsewhere in this book, you read about "Diana's Vision" involving an encounter with the river spirit. Perhaps Duane and I didn't perform the rituals quite the same way in which one in an indigenous shamanic culture would have. Nevertheless, all steps of the ritual were honored in their own way. Perhaps I could say that they were honored American-style: We did it our way.

Disclaimer and Contraindications

I want to be clear that there is a distinction between those individuals whose emergency is a wake-up call from their soul, and the general population whose illnesses are not indicative of a healer or shaman-to-be. It is true that drugs have been used excessively, and often unwisely, by the psychiatric community. However, I have had the unenviable position of counseling patients and riding in the ambulance with them to the psychiatric hospital. Drug therapy has been a godsend for many of them, and in some cases a life-saver.

There is no test to tell if one is suffering from what is essentially a *spiritual* emergency, or if it is a spiritual *emergence* at its core. However, it is obvious that to distinguish between them is often critical when it comes to making the choice of a proper treatment modality. There may be no definitive test in the general concept of any prevailing psychiatric testing, but it is possible to tell the difference. People who are *really* crazy seem unerringly to know the ones who are not within a hospital psychiatric ward population. They will tell you so. Regardless of whether each individual there shares the identical symptoms, the others will say, "But that guy over there is not really crazy. He is the shaman."

I was privy to a research study by a group of anthropologists who were investigating the way in which native cultures traditionally handled mental illness. The research was done in the 1940s and 50s. Later information determined that the original study was flawed because the researchers never understood at the time that the native populations distinguished between the truly mentally ill and the shaman.

The shaman, or other medicine people, were afforded wide latitude for acting out any alleged "crazy behavior" versus the treatment directed at the truly mentally ill. They knew the difference. In fact, many of our own Native American tribes consider the shaman's antics, typically regarded as outside acceptable norms, as balancing the groups' energies, whereas "normal" individuals end up in the native hoosegow for the identical behaviors.

In these times when transformation is occurring at whole new levels, it is even more imperative that individuals floundering within a process foreign to Western cultures have somewhere to turn. The spiritual emergency room concept is not intended for the run-of-the-mill mental and/or emotional illness. That is not saying that these individuals aren't suffering; nor is it implying that somehow their problem doesn't merit the same level of concern.

However, we are dealing with debilitating symptoms that require a special dimension to any treatment option. Too often, this group is simply cut adrift to cope as well as it might on its own. It is a game of Russian roulette. If the treatment ameliorates the symptoms, it is more often than not just a one-time lucky "hit," and not a touted across-the-board treatment of choice for all the others who find only a chamber of horrors in their guns.

The Ultimate Solution

From the information that has been gathered together from divergent sources, it seems to me that all of the pieces of the puzzle are here. It is a matter of combining what Western medicine has to offer with what the native shamanic cultures have traditionally practiced. Perhaps someday soon people like Dr. Somé will symbolically represent successfully building a bridge that merges the two worlds.

CHAPTER THIRTEEN

The Elephant in the Room

When my son was a little tyke, we lived in a small Midwestern town. The population was predominantly white. The first time David encountered a little black kid, he pointed at him and yelled, "He's dirty." That is when we had to have "one of those" talks when we got home. Shortly after that we went out to a local restaurant for breakfast. We lived in a university town, and the University of Michigan basketball team came in for breakfast at the same time we did. We all know white guys can't jump, so there were mostly black players on the team. David confided, "Hey, Mama, I don't see those Eskimos over there." Well, my life was kinda like that if you use your imagination.

Diana Stone

After the chapters were titled, and the greater part of this book was written, I remember asking my brother, Duane, his opinion about organizing some aspects of the material. It was not unusual for me to discuss some of the finer points with him. After all, we score a double-header when it comes to shared history. He's my brother after all, so that connection through the years of working together is obvious. Also, we survived coauthoring the first book in this trilogy of which this is "Book Three." When I called him on one particular occasion, however, the conversation took an unprecedented turn that left me quite taken aback.

He commented, "I'm puzzled because you have never strategized how you will explain about your personal journey in a physical body. It would not be fair to write this book and not identify the theme that ran in the background through most of your life. There are lightbeings out there who need to hear your story for their sakes. How many readers understand why you are crippled and travel by wheelchair?" "Silence, more silence," said I.

The theme to which he referred—that thing—truly was at the very core of my life experience. What was the reason for my physical disabilities and symptoms of pain? This may be hard to believe, but I did not really discover what the reason was until I wrote the later chapters of this book when I was in my seventies! (I didn't see that Eskimo over there.) Furthermore, it is correct to say that yes, it is still a mystery to many other lightbeings why they suffer as they do, just as it was for me. I have had long conversations with lightworkers about this nigh unto 40 years. Why? Why? Why? It is the elephant in the room.

I have never had a personal session with Dolores Cannon. Nonetheless, it was in one of her books that I discovered something about who I am and what my life is about—

something that finally explained some otherwise inexplicable events that occurred, reaching as far back as my early childhood.

Cannon documented a conversation in its entirety with one of her hypnosis subjects. Even though it was not *my* experience, it triggered a stream of memories that gave me goose bumps of recognition. At first, I intended to write this chapter as a series of informational articles only, primarily about alternative healing modalities. I was locked into a mindset whereby my personal experiences only tangentially connected to a subject, and were added only to enhance credibility and interest.

The girl in Cannon's book who recounted *her* story, somehow revealed to me, *my* true story. Including some autobiographical information perhaps may shake loose some memories of *your* own, or correct some erroneous conclusions that you are using to beat yourself up. Are some of you out there struggling with a problem that just won't go away? It can be a physical problem or any other kind of problem. Maybe you are having self doubts about yourself; maybe you are doing something wrong. Or maybe you did something really terrible in the past? Or maybe there is some kind of family curse? Or maybe, maybe, maybe, maybe....

That is why I am subtitling this:

MY STORY = YOUR STORY

Because of the special times through which we are living here on Earth, and because of the tremendous changes that are required to accommodate them, the call went out to all Universes from the High Beings for volunteers. That call was answered.

Volunteers of many kinds from far and wide were attracted to come here to help the ascension process along. It was not unusual that some of the volunteers had never been to Earth before, nor had they ever worn a physical body before either. Once incarnated, most of them lost the memory of their true identity as they passed through the veil to the 3rd dimension—just as it very likely did before the doctor slapped your butt.

Dolores Cannon recognized and differentiated these volunteers from just regular Earth beings in the human family through her work with clients, people who were placed in deep hypnotic trance states. From the level of their own Higher Selves, remarkably accurate information about a particular subject's true identity and specific soul mission was given in great detail.

From hundreds of these accounts over several years' time, the larger context emerged. Cannon carefully pieced together an overall picture of voluntary soul missions that otherwise would not have been obvious from a handful of sessions alone. These were published in one of her many books *The Three Waves of Volunteers and the New Earth.*

I only recently discovered that I was one of a very specialized group of volunteers. With what special skill set, and how or where it may have been acquired to equip me for inclusion in this group, I cannot say. I was born in the 1930s (1936), and was one of the first pioneers to undertake the task of elevating my physical body frequency until it matched the level of the crystalline lightbody, capable of tolerating the rarefied energies of the 5th dimension. There, now you know something I did not all through the years.

Since there was no prototype in which the DNA of the human family had yet been altered, as would be the case later on, my physical body had no guidelines for facilitating such a profound change. It was torturous, but the purpose was to introduce a prototype into the collective. Somebody had to go first. As I look back, I just sort of flailed about, making it up as I went along. Yet, as I peep through the cracks of my life, perhaps I do see the hands of unseen helpers who probably deserve more credit than I realize.

I consulted the Internet to look up a detail about another part of this book when I "just happened" to stumble across this amazing confirmation:

> "*It seems like most people who were born before 1940 have not been able to make the shift,* **but have initiated something into the next generation that gives them the capacity to form another helix within our lifetime.** *Our immune and endocrine systems are the most evident of these changes. That is one of the reasons I work with research in immunological testing and therapy. Some adults that I have tested actually do have another DNA helix forming. Some are even getting their third."*
>
> A quote from Gregg Braden's book
> *Walking Between The Worlds*

You are now privy to the voluntary soul mission that I came here to do, he same information about which I, myself, was totally unaware until I was well into my seventies. For you, it is akin to peeking at the last page of a detective novel to find out whodunit before you even begin reading the first chapter. This way, you can track the thread of my self-doubts, and you will understand what I did not realize myself: My self doubts were completely unfounded. Time after time I was sure that I had discovered the underlying cause of my journey of pain and suffering; yet, once again, it turned out to be a false assumption. Once again, something I was doing must be wrong. I was "bad." There was an elephant in the room.

When Dolores Cannon writes of the three waves of volunteers, my group ***predated*** the first wave. Had it not been for us, the ones to come would have had a nearly impossible task of kick-starting the process. This does not imply that everyone born in the 1930s were volunteers who carried a soul mission to transform their physical vehicle into a crystalline lightbody. In fact, just the opposite is true. There were very few of us who could take on such a mission. We were Special Forces, so to speak, all with a background of experiences that equipped us for this task. I'm sure there were many casualties.

I am sure that we also lost some by their own hand, and I considered taking myself out on more than one occasion. This has been a dreadfully painful journey, and it still is at times. I don't judge any of my group for finding this mission on the physical plane just too overwhelming for them. It was set up ahead of time that there were no karmic consequences connected to a premature exit. Their physical vehicles just couldn't make the grade in those cases. Casualties were anticipated, in fact.

Some of the others did not have the support team that I managed to assemble. I considered it total madness to think I could accomplish this journey alone. Sometimes lack of confidence pays off! That was coupled with an offbeat sense of humor from which nothing was spared; absolutely nothing was sacred enough to escape my wit. I decided if that offended some folks, there was a delete button. Most of my "followers" easily read the wisdom in the wit. That is a survival tactic that trumps mollifying each and every person who may take offence. It turned out that laughter really is the best medicine. You betcha!

And So it Began

I grew up on a farm in Iowa during the middle of the Great Depression of the 1930s (1936). My brother was 21 months younger than I. I recall a scene when my brother was probably six months old, still in his high chair. That would mean that I was a very young toddler.

The family, along with our hired man, was sitting around the kitchen table. My mother was serving pancakes for breakfast. I remember that I was scooting around, acutely aware of a warm feeling of security and closeness in the household. Suddenly I pulled my consciousness up short, and thought to myself, "I had better start acting like a little kid, or I'm going to blow my cover. They may catch on that I am a grown-up."

The sun rays were streaming through the kitchen windows. You have probably noticed rays of the sun which highlight little tiny dust motes floating about. I decided I would pretend to chase them, knowing full well it was ridiculous. Sure enough, the grown-ups laughed among themselves at my childish attempts at catching a sunbeam and those little bugs. I behaved appropriately frustrated by the entire endeavor. It was enough for that day to convince everyone that I was just a little kid.

It certainly is obvious from this and other incidents that I experienced full adult awareness, which at times transcended ordinary toddler consciousness. As I grew older, these memories from a higher plane faded away, and I locked onto age-appropriate behaviors quite naturally for the most part.

The higher adult consciousness did continue to break through from time to time, however. I recall when I was about 10 years old, lying in bed at night, frequently thinking that I should get a notebook and document my belief system as it existed at the time. That way I could refer to it as I grew older and compare it to my thoughts as a kid. The beliefs to which I referred were certainly well beyond what the typical ten-year-old would have on her mind.

Regrettably, I never completed this project, so I can't say now what the specific beliefs were. I do remember that they were about God, life and deep philosophical ideas that I considered would expand and transform as I grew older. It was the sort of thing that very few adults probably ever concern themselves with throughout their entire lives, let alone a 10-year-old kid. What made this even more unusual is that I did not come from a religious family, nor were philosophical subjects fare for conversations over dinner.

Another memory that stands out very clearly was a scene in which I was looking up at my mother when she was pregnant with brother, Duane. I heard a voice tell me that I would have to be responsible for him. That later proved to be true several times throughout our lives and for very good reasons. I did not realize it at the time, of course, but I was remembering the soul contract worked out between us before incarnating into this plane.

Something else I dearly wish that I had thought to set pen to paper to record were streams of poetry. I'm referring to original verse, not simply classic writings from famous authors well-known by every school child. These apparently spontaneously surfaced only when I tramped through the timberlands native to the Iowa countryside.

However, I remember that throughout my forest jaunts, I frequently recited poetry aloud. I did not give this much thought at the time, even though it easily flowed uninterrupted for hours. A typical Sunday afternoon often found me trudging off alone to the woods. I sat and meditated on fallen logs. I counted the varieties of birds. I was mesmerized by the antics of squirrels and an occasional raccoon, woodchuck or skunk family.

I absolutely delighted in the wildflowers, presenting my mother with armfuls of bleeding hearts, violets, Dutchman's britches and jack-in-the-pulpits when I arrived home at sundown. If I really struck it rich, I would happen onto a patch of morel mushrooms. These were sacred to Midwesterners. Forays into the woods started when I was about 12 years old. I wonder to what mystical state of consciousness the power of pure Nature swept me on those magical journeys.

As you read on through this book, there were other major events that certainly were priorities, as you will easily recognize. The long physical transformation that my soul came here to accomplish was like music continuously playing somewhere in the background; sometimes pianissimo, sometimes fortissimo, but to which I was totally oblivious, nonetheless; erroneously ascribing causes of symptoms to everything else except to some special version of physical transformation. This chapter should perhaps be titled "The *Invisible* Elephant in the Room" which, of course, is what an elephant in the room is by definition anyway—so strike that redundancy. (I just wanted to be sure you got it without being too obvious.)

This, then, documents a journey that involved an invisible mission from soul about which I was totally unaware (there's that elephant again, and there is that redundancy thing again. You usually *are* unaware of invisible missions.). I did not have the advantage of understanding the true meaning behind the physical challenges that dominated my life, which turned out to be a universal theme, one way or another, among other lightworkers then and to this day.

From the perspective of my conscious self, I was just one of the regular guys trying to make sense of things. I completely bought into the popular notion extant in the so-called "spiritual community" that if one were sick or troubled, it must mean that you were doing something wrong; actually unconsciously choosing to be ill or refusing to resolve mother issues. I was not alone.

Yes indeed, I do recall the many hours talking with clients and personal friends who were squarely on the spiritual path, often working successfully as healers and counselors themselves, yet searching for the reasons as to why they remained sick and troubled. That continues with regular calls from lightworkers who are completely mystified about why they must endure such painful lives despite doing everything "right."

Physical Problems Begin

The following material that documents some of the health problems with which I was beset serves two purposes. I initially intended, as I said earlier, to include these as simply a series of articles to pass on some knowledge that I gained from using alternative therapies, which were suitable for lightworkers in particular. What I learned seemed too invaluable not to share with readers struggling with these same issues themselves. For that reason, I hope you find this enlightening and helpful in your own life. As per the title of this chapter, I most of all wanted to provide you with a front row seat right from the beginning, as I labored under false assumptions as to the true nature of my health problems over and over again. When it became apparent that the assumption du jour was erroneous, it was further compounded by a second set of assumptions: I was a failure and my spiritual mission was a bust. And with that, I had much in common with other lightworkers firsthand. Consequently, I didn't see those Eskimos over there either.

Eczema

I was plagued with a severe case of eczema as an infant. Each morning, my mother had to carefully wash off a crusty breakout on my skin, especially on my face (one only a mother could love!). One day, my dad scooped me up and promised he would be home only after he found a solution to the problem. He ended up in the medical complex in Iowa City, connected to the State University of Iowa Medical School.

Sulpha drugs had just been discovered (I'm old), and I was one of the first patients to be treated with them. The only form in which they came at that time was a yellow powder. Each morning, Mom mixed it up with lard and smeared it over me. It probably looked really hideous, but it healed. I came in with a *miasm* (MIE-az-um).

Homeopathy: A King of Healers

Miasms are one aspect of a therapy called *homeopathy.* I refer to it other places later on. All lightbeings should absolutely be aware of homeopathy. In fact, *everyone* should be aware of it and using it. I won't write a book on it, but it is worth an explanation. Someday you may kiss the ring for passing this on to you. I just could not bring myself to make mention of this powerhouse therapy without taking a little detour to explain what it is. You would write and ask anyway. I know I would.

Homeopathy, at the present time, is an alternative natural therapy and has been around for about 200 years. In fact, in the early 1900s, it was the only therapy taught in every leading medical school in the United States. Then we found...DRUGS! I tell you this—trust me—it is one of the most powerful healing modalities, bar none. Don't let its simplicity fool you. It is dy-no-myte!

Homeopathic physicians must go to school and earn a degree just like in a traditional medical school. In Portland, across the river from where I live, is the naturopathic school (NCNM, or National College of Naturopathic Medicine) which offers a full accredited course in homeopathy. Husband Don is a homeopathic physician. I don't know how I could have made it through this life without homeopathic therapy. That goes for physical, mental and emotional problems. It is especially appropriate for awakened lightworkers who deal with ascension symptoms and do not want to treat them with drugs.

Homeopathy involves the use of a wide range of individual homeopathic remedies. The remedies are actually various natural substances that have been specially prepared by homeopathic pharmacies. There are plants, minerals like calcium, even snake venoms that all undergo a process of *dilution* and *succusion* to transform them into a remedy. So they are a real physical thing.

You need not understand it any more than to say that these substances are transformed closer to pure energy by this process, and end up as liquid tinctures. These solutions are called the "mother tinctures." From these, various potentized dilutions are made. To prepare a homeopathic remedy for a patient, a few drops of a specific tincture are placed in a little bottle of sugar granules and vigorously shaken. This way, a measured dose may be taken according to your homeopath's directions. Just be aware that the little white pellets are not the homeopathic remedy; the liquid tincture that they have absorbed is the healer.

Many patients new to homeopathy cannot believe that these little bottles of sugar pellets are really heavy artillery, capable of superseding the most powerful drugs in terms of effectiveness. Also, there is not a drug for everything, and then there is the question of those nasty side effects. There are no side effects with the homeopathic remedies. Except in very rare exceptions are they contraindicated even for newborn infants and the very elderly.

I have long experience with homeopathy. For one example, I was plagued with phobias about heights. I live near the mountains. It is a beautiful drive to Mt. Hood in Oregon to admire the breathtaking scenery of the great Northwest rain forests, observe the skiers from the Mt. Hood Lodge and eat dinner in the wonderful dining room with a view. These excursions were ruined for me as I endured the winding roads that dropped off to nowhere with dry mouth, terror, white knuckles and sweaty palms. A couple of doses of *silver nitrate* and I am now completely comfortable, even standing on top of the Empire State Building—well, maybe not quite that comfortable.

I am resisting the temptation to expound at length on firsthand cases about the glories of homeopathics. That should be easy to understand given that I have observed Dr. Don manage everything from a case of schizophrenia to the morning-after hangover! It is particularly effective for treating depression without drugs, *aurum* regularly is the remedy of choice. This is especially good to know considering the profound suffering of what is fast becoming an epidemic, plus the frequent ineffectiveness and side effects of the common anti-depressants.

As an astrologer, I especially like the story of *aurum.* It is made from gold, yes, real gold. Remember, the homeopathic pharmacies process all remedies, and reduce them to a liquid tincture (dilution and succusion). In astrology, gold is symbolized by the Sun. Whenever Don prescribes *aurum* for depression, he always says, "They need a little sunshine in their lives." This remedy certainly was indispensable to me as I struggled through a major depression years ago, and a godsend for hundreds of others as well.

I can't resist the temptation to tell the story of two clients to whom I recommended homeopathic *lycopodium*. One of the symptoms of this remedy is fear of public speaking. Each remedy has an entire laundry list of symptoms, not just one. However, when we think of *lycopodium* (lie-coe-POE-dee-um), the patient's fear of public speaking is not simple nervousness, but full-blown paralyzing terror. Don's cute little tip to help remember it is that sufferers don't "like the podium."

Both women to whom I am referring are well-known in their respective fields. They received constant lecture requests from universities and other venues here in the United States and other countries as well. I felt it was a shame that the terror of public speaking held these gifted and knowledgeable women back from sharing their special knowledge with the world. I referred them to Don who administered a single dose of *lycopodium* to each lady.

From one, I receive post cards from Italy, and many other countries, as she travels about having a ball, just as though there never was a problem. She tells me that she keeps the remedy in her purse, and always takes a dose just prior to a lecture. This is a popular misunderstanding that is held by many patients. She is treating the homeopathic remedy as though it is a drug. The basic principle of homeopathy is that the remedy addresses the underlying *cause* of the problem. It is not treating symptoms only. Under most circumstances, one dose transforms the *energy* of the symptoms and over time, cures them.

Is it harmful to continue treating herself with the *lycopodium?* Generally speaking, it is not harmful, but there are some exceptions In the first place, it is a simple waste of the remedy. However, there are certain conditions under which the effectiveness of the remedy may be compromised, or antidoted. In such cases, additional doses may be required, sometimes daily, and even more frequently than that.

Complications arise when patients are on a drug regimen for other problems, such as high blood pressure, etc. Prescription drugs are notorious for antidoting homeopathic remedies. The only solution is to take the drug and the remedy as far apart as possible throughout the day. Caffeine antidotes the remedies. If you want your morning cup of java, decaffeinated is your best option until the remedy has worked its magic. For these and other reasons, it should be obvious that the wisest course is for a homeopath to manage your case, except for a handful of remedies that are considered first aid and kept around the house just like bandages for boo-boos.

The other lady to whom *lycopodium* was prescribed is also an amazing success story. I purposely withheld both their names as you may just have heard of them yourself.

The second lady has now written a script that is a TV documentary, and there is buzz around Hollywood that it will be a movie starring Sean Connery. She is in high demand as a public speaker, a role that she now relishes.

Now let's circle back to those miasms mentioned earlier. In homeopathic literature, some diseases are associated with miasms: tuberculosis, syphilis, cancer and some skin diseases to name a few. Heart disease, and most others, do not cause miasms.

A miasm is a weakness or predisposition toward a particular disease that is transmitted down the ancestral line. Imagine that great-great-grandfather goes off to war and picks up a dose of syphilis from a fetching French lass. He may be healed of the actual disease, but the *predisposition to the symptoms* will carry down the generations, likely skipping one or more. Not everyone down the line will be affected. Usually some sort of trauma is needed to activate the inherited weakness.

But one day great-great-granddaughter pays for his night of pleasure by exhibiting the mental illness and other symptoms often associated with the later stages of syphilis. The parents and the doctors are puzzled by the child's condition. However, in taking a complete case study and observing the symptoms, the homeopath would very likely recognize that a miasm has been triggered. It is almost as if a little piece of DNA has been erased by certain diseases. As far as I know, homeopathy is the only protocol that not only recognizes miasms, but successfully treats them, thereby halting their progression through future generations.

Somebody in my generational chain suffered a disease that ended up on my baby skin smeared with yellow sulpha drugs and lard! It's a miasm. The remedy for that particular miasm is *psorinim.* Too bad the doctors at The University of Iowa did not give my dad the homeopathic remedy that day.

I know my mother had the miasm for lung problems. One of her ancestors probably suffered from tuberculosis. Remember, it is not the actual "bugs" that cause any disease that is transmitted through the generations. It is only the symptoms, *as if* you have the disease. We are dealing only with energy here.

Mom never had tuberculosis; however, she was extremely susceptible to very bad colds each winter, and the colds frequently developed into bronchitis from which she required a long time to recover. She was a candidate for the tuberculosis miasm, *tuberculinum.* You can be sure that one of her ancestors really did have full-blown tuberculosis.

As her daughter, I, of course, inherited the predisposition to lung problems. It was activated when I suffered a very painful bout of pleurisy in high school. I was treated with penicillin, but how much better had it been if the miasm itself were treated along with it. Later on as an adult, I suffered two bouts of pneumonia. It's my good fortune that I learned of it and was dosed with the suitable miasm remedy in adult life. At this writing, I am 76 years old, and I never have so much as a cold.

Since I have been a practicing professional astrologer for over 40 years, I could not help but notice the profiles of many homeopathic remedies in the horoscopes of clients. There was one in particular that I recognized. It was *ignatia*, and is usually a woman's remedy. It describes people who are conflicted about intimate relationships. On the one hand, they seek close intimacy, and on the other hand, these women may even be man haters and avoid relationships like the plague.

A client of mine was divorced for many years, but I thought she fit this profile. I asked Don to send her the remedy, which he did. I know that she most likely does not associate this with the homeopathic remedy, but it was not so long after that before there was a man in her life, and he's there to this day. However, she still hangs on to some bit of independence as they maintain separate households.

If you think you may need a dose of this yourself, you can find *ignatia* on the Internet. It is better to have your homeopath prescribe the dose. It may be the case, though, that there are no homeopaths where you live. Maybe they can't even spell it, or regard it as some sort of sexual orientation. This leads me to a question about whether it is ethical to sneak a little remedy into an unsuspecting person's orange juice. If we are talking about an infant or young child, of course that is an exception. What about an adult, fully capable of making his or her own decisions? I admit that there have been circumstances under which homeopathic remedies have been secretly administered.

Keep in mind that these are not drugs, and this is not a question of harm befalling the innocent party. This is an issue that you must come to terms with yourself in each individual situation. One case involved a woman who used homeopathics for an older mentally ill brother. The brother was remarkably improved. Do the ends justify the means? I personally have agreed in many cases that secretly administering the remedies are more than justified. No harm can come from a remedy, no matter what your motive. It's not black magic, after all.

Generally, one advantage of natural therapies like homeopathics over drugs is that there are not the troublesome side effects. Yet, the process of natural healing can mimic a side effect from drugs. That has been a matter of considerable misunderstanding for patients new to homeopathy. You need to be aware of this with homeopathic therapy, or any other natural healing modality, for that matter. It may walk like a duck, and talk like a duck, but in this case it is not a duck. A healing reaction is not related to drug side effects at all. This is of critical importance for all lightworkers who are awakening and changing into their lightbodies.

Let's imagine that you take a homeopathic remedy for a troublesome skin problem that is making your life miserable. Normally, you would seek a medical doctor who would then prescribe a drug, maybe something administered topically. Drugs suppress the symptoms and drive a disease deeper into the system. Most people erroneously believe that with the symptoms gone, they have been cured of something.

They have not been cured of the *cause* of the disease, only the symptoms. That is a huge difference. But with homeopathics, the cause of an illness is addressed and the healing process works in just the opposite way from the drug. Instead of burying it deeper in the system, it brings it to the surface. And sometimes when it does, your skin problem, for example, blooms forth like a meadow in spring. "I'm worse," the patient howls to the homeopath.

Whatever the physical problems may be, if you choose the route of natural medicine, it is imperative to understand how the healing process works and how to manage it. Therefore, there may be times when the suppressed cause—physical or emotional—comes to the surface, and sometimes you will wish that you were dead for a few days. It is called *the healing crisis.*

Just remember that it is not the homeopathics that are causing you the misery if there is any. It is your own disease that is giving you the problem on its way out. The whole picture is often exacerbated by having used drugs to suppress symptoms for many years preceding the natural therapy.

Too many patients panic when the healing crisis hits, and erroneously bail out in the middle of treatment. That is absolutely the worst thing you can do. It would be better to leave sleeping dogs lie, and never stir up the healing process in the first place. You run the danger then of inviting some really difficult symptoms to manifest with no support underneath to complete the healing. When that happens, the patient will turn in desperation to allopathic medicine. Of course, all that does is drive the true cause of the disease deeper into the system once again. It can be a real mess. One mark of a competent homeopath is one who fully explains the healing process beforehand.

You Should Know What *Retracing* Is

There is another process recognized by natural healers, and it is called *retracing.* If you have ever been interviewed by a homeopath, at your initial appointment you may be surprised that he or she will take as much as an hour and a half to complete a case history. What they are doing is building a profile of your medical history since infancy.

Just imagine every illness you ever suffered, mild to serious, lying in your energy system layer upon layer. What you present to the physician is only the top layer. The physician will treat from the top down. At times, when being treated for a present-day affliction, all of a sudden all hell breaks loose as some wild symptoms from some 20 years ago comes up: retracing. This is not to scare anyone away from natural healing.

Foreknowledge allows patients to consciously deal with a healing crisis with intelligence and allow the physician to manage the symptoms.

OOOOOh. This Hurts, too

Remember that thick steak that your teeth chomp through? Well, they are easily as capable of doing the same thing—TO YOUR TONGUE. I have some misfiring in the brain where it programs the teeth to confine their chomping to food and bites my tongue instead. It hurts like the very devil. Sometimes it is the inside of my mouth that takes the hit. There is actually a homeopathic remedy for this painful affliction. It works like magic and very quickly. It is the remedy *bufo.* I couldn't resist adding this little footnote to all of you intent on eating your tongue.

Hering's Law of Cures

Dr. Constantine Hering described this *"law of order"* in his Preface to the 1845 American edition of *The Chronic Diseases* by Samuel Hahnemann, a world-renowned homeopath. Hering's Law is a tool with which to plot the progression of a cure to gauge whether movement is taking place and, if so, if that movement is in a beneficial direction. Healing starts from the top, the head, to the bottom, from the inside to the outside, from the major organs to the minor organs, and in reverse order in which they presented.

Energetically, the crown chakra, the chakra representative of one's wisdom and spiritual connectedness, is situated at the top of the head; while the base chakra, the chakra representing how at home one feels in one's physical body, and how grounded and secure one feels, is situated at the base of the spine. This also illustrates how healing would progress from a mental to a physical level. Healing ideally needs to travel down the body, thus mental healing; through the heart chakra, emotional healing; and then lastly physical healing is taking place.

An example of progression of cure from major to minor organs could be kidney problems, then bladder infection, then cystitis and burning urine and finally cure. The progression of cure would be in reverse order to that. In other words, the symptoms that appear first would heal last and vice versa. Emotions would also play a role.

The Optimum Health Institute in San Diego.

In the early 1990s I stayed for one month at the Optimum Health Institute in San Diego. This was obviously to partake of a routine to restore my health. One of the centerpieces of the regimen there was advertised as an all-raw-food diet. The first day at lunch when a plate of fenugreek sprouts, along with some other raw food items were set before me, fantasies of luscious organic mixed-vegetable salads dressed with various tempting toppings exploded like a balloon. Before the month was out, my consciousness had descended into a diabolical plot to escape the iron gates at night in search of a baked potato.

Be that as it may, I subjected myself to wheatgrass juice enemas and other staples of the natural healing culture. For the first few days, healing crises abounded. I remember one guy telling me that he had malaria during the Viet Nam war. That was many years before, of course. Yet, he broke out with symptoms just as if he had malaria for a while. It was still one of the layers in his system. He was retracing. He had reached that layer and his body was throwing it off.

Another interesting thing about that guy, demonstrated what it means to get real healing in other ways, once you commit to natural therapies. He was given little red pills for the malaria. About the third week he was at Camp O-HIGH (that's what I call it), those very same red pills began to flush out of the walls of his intestinal tract! They had been there all those years, along with other stuff, you can be sure; stuff that we don't mention in polite society. Anyway, he was being treated for cancer–not surprising.

Everything About Something You Never Wanted to Know

Now that the subject of enemas has come up, I might as well reveal that I gold medaled at the Olympics in that category. I was also granted the Platinum Enema Nozzle Award at the 1987 Convention in Vegas. It makes an attractive lapel pin, which I wear proudly next to my American flag pin. I earned this special recognition by administering two, sometimes three, coffee enemas every single day for six years (C'mon-administered to myself, you guys, to *myself!*).

It is not easy finding anything to laugh about when it comes to enemas. Actually, I am deadly serious about the subject as you will discover soon enough. But first, I want to promise you that I made up the part about the Olympics and the Platinum Enema Nozzle award. I clear this up deliberately, because I used that to introduce a lecture on this subject once, and nobody laughed. They believed me. However, the enema regimen was absolutely true, scout's honor.

I am writing my story in no particular order. Enemas came along when I was not doing well, health-wise. As I mentioned earlier, my health was an issue that I was perpetually dealing with one way or another: still unaware of the elephant in the room, background music.

Around the time I imposed the six years of the coffee enema detox regimen, I was in a lot of pain. By then I had been diagnosed with ankylosing spondylitis and rheumatoid arthritis, often found together. I was still able to get around, which is more than I can say for myself at the present time. I have been traveling by wheelchair for several years now. However, improved pain management allows me to lead a life far freer of pain than back then, thank God. For your information, ankylosing spondylitis (AS) is a condition in which the spinal vertebrae are fused.

In the world of natural healing, coffee enemas are king. The reason is that the caffeine is absorbed by the venous blood, circulating in the lower part of the body, and especially through the liver. Some people worry about it, but it is not the same as drinking the coffee, which is not a bad thing as we discovered. However, prejudices die hard.

The liver is one of our primary detox organs. When it is a stick-up by the caffeine, it gives up a load of toxins as willingly as a bank teller, the very same which is flushed out of the body when the enema is released, and before the poisons can be reabsorbed.

When patients choose to go the alternative route to deal with cancer—and many do—one of the first things they are introduced to is the enema bag. As tumors break up, it is critical that this very toxic material be immediately flushed away. I normally did two enemas a day. If the pain flared up, I would sometimes do three. Cancer patients might do coffee enemas repeatedly throughout the day and night! When I was at Camp O-High, we were handed a little pail and a rubber tube at our very first meeting. I turned to Don and said, "I sure as hell know what that is for!"

Even though Dr. Don and I both closed our offices in Portland many years ago, requests for the coffee enema instructions still come from patients. For whatever reason you yourself may choose to detox, the instructions are in the Appendix of this book.

I am usually asked why I continued the enemas for so long, so I will answer that first. As for me, I felt I was following inner guidance. However, it was not all right brain intuition. I had read extensively about the subject as well. Medical doctors had prescribed many prescription drugs when I was younger, and I didn't know any better than to take them. I took the birth control pill for eight years, just to mention one. Those were extremely high potency estrogens in those days. They were later yanked from the market because of the bad effects on the hormonal system. It was obvious to me that a major detox was in order if I were ever to restore my health.

I am not sympathetic to whining. Because it is doubtful that you will have any more of a horrendously embarrassing experience than I did on my virgin run. Everything went okay until I opened the package the enema bag came in and encountered not one, but *two* plastic nozzles that could be screwed to the end of the rubber hose. There was a long one with little pin holes all over it, and a second one that was just a short plastic tube with a hole in one end. I looked them over, and considering just where they were to be inserted, I somehow decided that the long one with the holes all over it made the most sense.

At this time, I was lying down on the bathroom floor to do the enemas. I'm afraid that I grossly overestimated the length of one's rectum. Or else I was born with a birth defect. The long tube went about half way in. I lay on the bathroom floor with water spouting like Old Faithful in every direction. That wasn't the worst of it. I continued to use the long nozzle, congratulating my cleverness at covering everything with towels so that the entire bathroom wouldn't get soaked!

How embarrassed do you think it was that through some innocent casual conversation, a smart ass pharmacist explained that the long nozzle was for a woman to use as a douche? I considered moving back to the Midwest. Instead, even though the pharmacy was just across the street from my office, I never went in there again. I was a nervous wreck until a beauty shop rented that space and I knew the guy had retired, or better still, died.

Yes, we can find some things to joke about when it comes to enemas. However, if you search the Internet, be prepared to find some very negative opinions about the efficacy of enemas, and coffee enemas in particular. Use your own common sense and consider the source. I continue to defend and recommend the positive results from enemas, which have been well-documented and should be taken seriously in conjunction with other natural therapies. They have been instrumental in helping many patients overcome chronic, even life-threatening, illnesses—including cancer as I said.

A Little Background Music

There was a long list of other health problems, most of which were painful, some excruciatingly so. That pattern follows me yet today. For now I will skip naming individual afflictions, but instead turn to some early history, some aspects to which many involved in alternate spirituality will surely relate,

At this point, I identified the elephant in the room *as ascension symptoms and the pain associated with activating my light body*. Yep, that was it!

The point to remember concerning each health episode was that I thought I was doing something wrong. Or that karma must be exacting a heavy retribution for a past I could not recall. Or that there were some terrible unresolved psychological issues buried so deep in the subconscious that no amount of therapy would ever reach them, let alone resolve them.

There was also always somebody or some book available and willing to lay a guilt trip on me. I carried a knot of fear deep in my gut most of the time. Maybe they were right. I was a healer, but I couldn't heal myself. Maybe I really *didn't* want to get well in some perverse way. There were many reasons for my health problems, and all of them made me "bad." Until the early 1990s, I never knew about ascension. There was still an elephant in the room—for me and many other lightbeings.

The Medical History

First of all, don't expect me to have anything positive to say about the medical paradigm. Individual doctors—some of them, maybe most of them—I'll be generous—may well be conscientious healers who really are motivated to cure people. When some of them wake up and see the light, they are threatened if they depart from the party line. Many doctors have seen their careers ruined by simply prescribing vitamin therapy.

No, this is not about doctor bashing. It is way beyond that. It lies with the entire medical paradigm. Doctors are pawns in a vast medical industrial complex run by "pushers," the big pharmaceutical giants. The following is a quote from a book by Bruce Lipton, Ph.D. *The Biology of Belief.* You will read more about him in other chapters.

> "...conservative estimates published in the Journal of the American Medical Association claim that iatrogenic illness, i.e. illness resulting from medical treatment, is the third leading cause of death in this country. Last year, (2004-2005) a new study, based on the results of a ten-year survey of government statistics...concludes that iatrogenic illness is actually the **leading** cause of death in the United States and that adverse reactions to prescription drugs are responsible for more than 300,000 a year."

(And what about the patients it doesn't kill, but who are left with serious illnesses? Diana) A medical profession that is killing off citizens by the hundreds of thousands is just too horrific to tolerate.

We must take personal responsibility for our, and our children's, health. More critically, we must take action ourselves to move the collective. The medical model basically treats symptom with drugs and surgery. That is the premise of the model; it never promised a cure. That is not removing the cause of disease. That's it. There is a place for traditional medicine; it is perilous not to understand exactly where that is.

The Continuing Saga

I was very active in high school. I was involved in athletics, I rode my horse and I was responsible for a large garden on our farm. I was editor of the school paper and was very involved in 4H. I was therefore shocked when I ran across one of my old diaries from my teen years. My picture of this busy girl energetically involved in endless activities was belied by the daily entries.

At the bottom of each page, I had rated my energy level each night along with a prediction about how well I could get through the next day's activities. I must have been continuously exhausted. I remembered my marathon sleep-in sessions over week-ends. My mother used to check on me to make sure I wasn't dead, especially after turning in Friday night and still not making an appearance at breakfast Sunday morning. A friend of the family's only comment was, "Doesn't that kid ever go to the bathroom?" I was constantly exhausted in college, but I worked 20 hours a week at a public radio station in addition to a full load of classes. Besides, everyone was tired all the time in college anyway.

Fast forwarding to my early twenties, I was pregnant with my first child. I had married my college sweetheart. We both had jobs with the University Photo Service in addition to a regular schedule of classes. From work one day when I was about three months into the pregnancy, I called my doctor to report that I was spotting blood. I am warning you now that this is a story about possibly the most unbelievable doctor incompetence that you have ever heard. That, however, was only the first of many similar experiences with medical doctors. I believe I have been absolutely cursed when it comes to traditional medicine.

The doctor, believe it or not, told me not to worry because many pregnant women "always see a little blood from time to time." Remember, I was a naïve girl who did not know then what I do now. I continued to work at my job, despite noticing an ever-increasing problem with bleeding. Follow-up calls to the doctor received only a repeat of his initial reassurances that this was nothing to worry about.

By the second week, I was forced to remain home from work because the bleeding was so severe. By rights, I should have gone to the nearest emergency room at the first sign of spotting. Not to be too gruesome, but by the time two weeks had passed I was literally hemorrhaging to death. Luckily for me, I suffered a miscarriage. I was so ignorant to the danger I was in that if it were not for the miscarriage; I may well have lost my life.

These were the days when doctors came to the house. When he arrived, he had the temerity to ask me if I had done anything to abort the pregnancy! There is one more mystery in connection to this incident. One of my friends was pregnant at the same time I was. She called her doctor–who was also my doctor—to report that she was seeing some spotting, and he immediately admitted her to the hospital.

I may as well tell about another incident in connection with the miscarriage that serves to illustrate the bizarre scenarios that have followed me throughout my life. I can't remember all of them, but just let me say that I can walk through life, going about the normal activities that other people do, except there is this little exit off the main freeway. Sure enough, some peculiar and totally weird event just comes in from somewhere in outer space and splices itself onto my reality.

The background to this story started when I was living in the college dorm. I occasionally received phone calls from a guy who I named my "almost obscene caller." He never really said anything outright obscene, no foul language or dirty suggestions. Yet, he would not identify himself. It had to be someone who knew me, because he would say things like, "You certainly looked beautiful in your red dress at such-and-such a restaurant last Friday night." It was mildly scary because whatever he said about observing me somewhere was always dead on. Well, maybe that is a poor choice of words.

After I was married and moved into an apartment with my new husband, the "almost obscene caller" was the furthest from my mind. I still did not have any idea who he was or how he found out, but once again there was the occasional call. So there I was, lying in bed, bleeding out so severely that I actually had heavy towels packed around me (sorry to be so graphic).

It was dusk and the phone rang. Sure enough, it was the guy. He asked my husband to tell me that a tornado was headed squarely in my direction, and that I should go to the basement immediately. I thought that this was a new low of craziness. In just a few minutes, however, we heard a sound like a roaring train rapidly approaching. Someone in another apartment yelled, "tornado!," and I could hear everyone in the building rushing for the basement, including my husband. As I found myself there alone bleeding to death, my only solace was that my almost obscene caller was the only one who cared. Weird?

We moved from that apartment, my husband took a job in another city, was drafted into the Army for two years, and then we returned to Iowa City once again. We purchased a house after about a year. The calls started up again at that house. He described the outfits I wore on various occasions. I can't recall other details of the conversations, but I do remember hanging up on him each time, so the gist of what he said must have been somewhat offensive. Since he was concerned enough to warn me about the tornado, I felt that he would never harm me. The calls eventually stopped and I never did find out who was the "almost obscene caller who cared."

When I was in my twenties, I was plagued by muscle spasms in my low back that were so dreadfully painful as to defy all description. I was in so much pain that I could barely draw a deep breath. The first time this happened, my husband had to drag me, in spite of insufferable pain, to the doctor's office who decided it must be a kidney problem. I was sent to the hospital for a barium x-ray, which showed absolutely nothing wrong. (My sacroiliac was out, you idiots!)

As usual, there had to be a bizarre incident. The guys administering the test kept sliding me around on the table. I complained loudly that I could not brace myself because of the pain and was about to slide off the table. They believed me when that is exactly what happened! Fortunately a couple of nurses broke my fall.

The doctors prescribed pain meds, tranquilizers and muscle relaxants. My mother would stay with me to help care for David, sometimes for quite long periods, until I recovered enough to get out of bed. On two occasions when I suffered one of these episodes, my husband called an ambulance to take me to the hospital. The first time, the two ambulance drivers dropped me going down the front steps. Then they took off hell-bent-for-election, jarring my teeth out when they hit every bump in the road and the railroad tracks. At the hospital they raced the gurney at top speed, missing the elevator door and ramming me into the wall. Other crazed incidents were to follow, until I wondered if I would ever make it out of there alive. However, I just don't have the energy to relive it again on paper.

I continued to live with the low back problem for many years. It ruined many occasions that I could have otherwise enjoyed, in addition to causing me a great deal of needless suffering. In fact, it wasn't until I moved to Portland, Oregon, and found a chiropractor who specialized in sacroiliac problems using a special non-force technique that I was healed at last.

In fact, I got more than I bargained for. The doctor took a set of x-rays. Afterward, he provided a written report with a diagnosis and recommendations for a treatment plan. The last line of the report said, "I recommend that you see this doctor every day for the rest of your life." This couldn't mean what I *thought* it meant...or could it? It did. We were married about three years after that. No more back problems, by God!

That was in the early 80s. There was a sinister plot to undermine chiropractic about that time. I know, this reads like some cheap detective paperback, but it is no exaggeration. I'll not take the space to retell in its entirety this long, shameful, diabolical conspiracy of the medical profession except to say that after many years of legal wrangling through the courts, the chiropractors won a judgment of money, plus a court order by a federal judge in Chicago directing the medical profession to print a full-page admission of guilt, and retraction of deliberate lies, for an entire year in the AMA's own journal.

It is not only lightbeings who need to lose any illusions about the very dark side of the medical profession, along with their insurance and pharmaceutical bedfellows. As has been predicted, information about corruption not only in the medical profession, but all major institutions, is indeed coming to light in the twenty-first century.

Whereas I would be classed as one of those "weird health food nuts" and regarded as espousing many radical ideas in the Sixties, I can now claim the right to engage in my favorite sport, "I told you so." Seriously, growing numbers of people are embracing alternative health care, metaphysical spirituality, natural foods and commitment to a lifestyle reflective of an awakening of consciousness in general.

I need to back up to a time in my early thirties to explain how I happened to get involved in holistic health care in the first place. I was still married to my first husband, had a son in the lower grades in school and still very much in the clutches of medical doctors and drug therapy. I have Rh negative blood, which in those days created problems with delivering a live baby.

After the miscarriage, I gave birth to my son, David. In the following two pregnancies, a baby boy and a baby girl survived only hours after birth. The doctors advised against further pregnancies as there were increasing complications that could threaten my own life. Therefore, when the first birth control pills appeared on the scene, I thought they were heaven sent. I was terrified of another pregnancy. There were no abortions then no matter the reason.

At first, the birth control pills sent me spiraling into a weird depression, for which I was prescribed daily diuretics. This seemed to take care of the emotional problems. However, I believe to this day that what happened after that is what caused the back problems, and consequently, the litany of drugs that followed wrecked havoc with my hormonal system until the end game was rheumatoid arthritis.

My present husband, Dr. Don, despite the positive side of the birth control pills, reluctantly and in all good conscience decided he must recommend discontinuing The Pill to his patients. The upset of the hormonal system with the debilitating fatigue, emotional mood swings and other symptoms—some so severe that the patients could not hold down a job—was not worth it. And that disregarded what was suspected as even worse long-range problems, such as in my case.

At any rate, by the time I had been on the regimen of the Pill and diuretics, thyroid medicine, and finally cortisone for pain, this found me a bedridden invalid suffering dreadfully from muscle spasms in my neck constantly. My only exercise was the painful trip from the bed to the couch, where I stayed until my husband returned home from work.

One of the strange symptoms was my craving for grape juice. If my husband did not have a tall glass by my bed each morning, I went absolutely hysterical. I was beside myself and decided I would endure this situation for three more months, and then I would seriously consider ending my own life.

Fortunately, a friend who was a psychiatric nurse called when she heard about my plight. She advised me to immediately get off the thyroid medicine. One of the side effects was cardiac arrest (what the doctor does not tell you), and I was plagued with chest pains to the extent that I feared I would check out with a heart attack. Also, I was to immediately discontinue the diuretics, which was depleting my body of potassium found liberally in...grape juice! Lack of potassium is famous for causing muscle spasms, bingo!

Another friend who learned of my desperate state of health came to my house, marched into the bathroom, searched the medicine cabinet, and I was soon greeted by the sound of the toilet flushing. She placed a sack on my bed along with Adele Davis's famous book *Eat Right to Keep Fit.* Davis was the first natural health food guru. The sack contained a starter kit of nutritional supplements for rebuilding one's health: vitamin E, potassium, and so on. On leaving, she handed me an appointment slip for a visit to a chiropractor.

I read Adele Davis's book and was an instant convert. I also abandoned the Pill. My husband got a vasectomy, and said if I got pregnant again he had better see the same angel in the Bible that arranged immaculate conceptions. I nursed a murderous glint in my eye for medical doctors for a long time. It marked the beginning of accepting personal responsibility for my own health. This was the mid-1970s. I lived in St. Louis, and the only place we could find anything other than white bread was a little hole-in-the-wall health food store—the only one of its kind we ever located in the entire city.

OOOOOOOH! That Really Hurts Really Bad: Nonsurgical Repair of Hiatal Hernia

In 1992, husband Don, my brother, Duane, and I were driving along the little gravel country roads in Iowa. My father was in a nursing home. I was taking over the management of his affairs and was on the way to his bank. I sat in the back seat with the growing realization that a nagging heartburn was growing damned uncomfortable. The stabbing pain under my left rib cage was referring pain to the upper right quadrant of my back. "I'm having a heart attack," I screamed. That got everyone's attention.

Don pulled the car into a tractor path accessing one of Iowa's famous cornfields. Luckily my husband, the chiropractor, kept a cool head unlike my brother who was screaming for him to rush me to the hospital. There among a stand of seven-foot corn stalks, he stretched me out on the back seat and poked around my left rib cage. There was a tight, excruciatingly painful knot interfering with my breathing. "You have a hiatal hernia," he pronounced and promptly pressed the heel of his hand just above the spasm and squished me really hard, as he pulled downward. After about twenty minutes the pain subsided. Don explained:

> "I saw patients in my clinic that had undergone surgery to relieve a hiatal hernia, but even at that there is no guarantee it won't return. One patient actually had undergone *five* surgeries for this problem. I fixed it in five minutes! Just be thankful I didn't take you to the hospital! If it were up to the doctors, you could well be going under the knife right now. That is, if they could even diagnose a hiatal hernia in the first place. It's better if they *don't* diagnose it if their only solution is to cut on you needlessly."

The idea that emergency room doctors probably could not diagnose a hiatal hernia if one stood up, saluted the flag and sang "Yankee Doodle Dandy," is sadly not just cynicism from an old and disillusioned reject from traditional medicine. After all, traditional medicine did save my life at a later time. However, I am including below the story of two women friends and their experiences with hiatal hernia.

Hello! Anybody Home?

A friend called me from her room in a Seattle hospital. She was experiencing pain "in the sternum." She had been given painkillers, a treadmill test for her heart, a laundry list of blood tests and a CAT scan. Still, the doctors could find nothing. I questioned her closely about her symptoms and warned her that she in all likelihood was suffering from a hiatal hernia.

I cautioned my friend that the doctors would not know to diagnose it or how treat it. I advised her to call her husband to come to her hospital room, which she did. I gave him instructions over the phone just what to do. He followed my directions precisely. The pain subsided in half an hour. She was discharged and has been fine ever since. I asked what the doctor did when she told him what it was. "He gave me a pill," she answered.

Another friend was visiting me when all of a sudden she drained ashen white and shrieked loudly in excruciating pain. These suckers can really bring you to your knees. (Hiatal hernia can exhibit a rapid onset at times.) She explained that she had suffered a similar "liver attack" a month or so before. That time, she was rushed to the emergency room and pretty much had all the tests that my Seattle friend received, to the tune of $3,000. They never could diagnose it, either.

We got her laid down and fortunately, husband Don, the chiropractor, was on hand to diagnose and treat yet another hiatal hernia. She was pain free in about an hour. It was much less expensive than her hospital tests! The doctors sent her home with nothing more than a referral to a cardiologist. You would pay one million dollars to anyone who could relieve you of that level of unbearable pain, whether in an Iowa cornfield or in your bed in the middle of the night.

So just what is a hiatal hernia and how do you fix it without surgery? This isn't the same problem associated with the popular notion of a hernia. I always thought it is a tear in the abdomen somewhere, allowing your guts to fall out. A *hiatal* hernia is an intrusion of the upper part of the stomach and esophagus into the diaphragm muscle where it gets caught or pinched. It pinches the nerves that lead down the left arm mimicking a heart attack. At first it feels like heartburn or indigestion. Pain is referred to the upper right quadrant of the back. Some of my attacks hurt worse in my back. One time the pain referred to my right jaw. I thought I was having a toothache. A spasm can usually be located by palpating the area just along the left rib cage.

To alleviate this condition, someone must manually "pull out" the stomach and esophagus trapped by the diaphragm muscle. A live demonstration would be desirable at this point, but since we are stuck with words I'll do my best. If you are right handed, it is most convenient to stand on the person's right side as they lie down on a bed, massage table or wherever they can. Their head would be to your left and feet to your right.

Poke around the edge of the rib cage on the *left side* to find where the worst knot is. It will be the most painful area. Place the heel of your left hand just *above* the spasm. Place your right hand on top of your left hand. You can push harder when you use both hands. Ask the patient to take a deep breath and expel all their air. Then push in and downward really hard with both hands. This is no job for wimps. Squish the person so hard that they grunt. You may have to repeat it two or three times in a row. If you are successful, the pain subsides in about 20 minutes. Also, the tender area below the ribs becomes softer and not so spasmed and tight.

I have seen Don treat many people suffering from this terribly uncomfortable problem. I am just appalled that most doctors not only do not know how to perform this maneuver, but also often do not diagnose the problem in the first place. Years ago when I was participating in an astrology conference in Seattle, a close friend approached Dr. Husband about a low level, chronic pain she had suffered for over 10 years. Every sort of medical test had come up with nothing. I consider this unforgivable.

Don quickly diagnosed the problem, adjusted her, and she was pain free for the first time in all those years. (I have written about this same case in which I was guided to remove the past life memory that was stuck there.) Often several adjustments are necessary over a period of time if the case has become chronic.

Another of Don's patients was a little kid. His mother said he constantly complained of pain and had missed a great deal of school over the past years. The symptoms affected his appetite, and he often refused to eat. The doctors restricted his activities, and he was not allowed to play with the other kids or participate in sports. His mother had taken him to every kind of specialist to no avail. It took five minutes to diagnose the hiatal hernia. Treatment required several sessions over some weeks. Don eventually taught the mother how to do the adjustment. The boy completely recovered, is pain-free and leading the typical life of a kid. Go figure.

You can see that the problem is not only *how* to treat the symptoms after you know what ails you. The first difficulty may be finding someone who knows *what* it is in the first place. This is where you may be pretty much on your own, considering the ignorance of many (a majority?) health care professionals where hiatal hernia is concerned. If you ever suffer from this ailment you want to know what your options are.

Final Thoughts

Again, to summarize, the symptoms mimic a heart attack. Don't be foolish. Find out for sure. But if this continues to recur, and you are not dead of a heart attack, then it is something else. It starts with heartburn; there is moderate to severe pain on the left side; pain is referred to the upper back; and there may be pain or numbness down the left arm. You feel like hell, let me tell you. There can also be headache. Breathing can be difficult if that sucker really clamps down. It scares the living daylights out of onlookers when you grab your side screaming in pain and gulping for air.

If you have these symptoms, find a chiropractor or naturopath, and tell them what you suspect it is. You may have to train them how to treat it. If you are prone to this sort of thing, it is a good precaution to have a family member around who can perform the adjustment. Severe attacks require immediate attention; otherwise most sufferers will head for the emergency room. Be certain of the diagnosis if you do that. Once I was stricken when I was home alone but was able to do some acrobatics over the back of a plain wooden chair. Position yourself on the back of the chair just above where you suspect the spasm is and really press down hard. I literally jumped onto the back of a chair just as though someone had gotten into the house with bad intentions on his mind.

I did not intend for this book to be authored by "Dr. Diana," however, this particular subject generated such huge reader response from my newsletter subscribers that I decided to treat the subject more extensively than I normally would. Who knows, it's not beyond the realm of possibility that you may very well save someone from suffering the excruciating pain and needless surgery of hiatal hernia yourself! Furthermore, that person could be you—especially since we are now playing the Mission: Impossible Game!

When all is said and done, the primary objective is to get this message to people who are suffering from the chronic pain of an undiagnosed hiatal hernia—that elephant in the room gets around—or to others who are undergoing surgery needlessly. Some following material authored by Bruce West, D.C. suggests some changes in lifestyle that may prevent this from becoming a problem in the first place.

Opting Out of Traditional Medicine

Bruce West, D.C. is associated with a company in our area that enjoys a reputation for producing the highest quality nutritional supplements, Standard Process Labs. Your own chiropractor very likely uses some of them. He is the author of *The Encyclopedia of Pragmatic Medicine.* It is a gold mine of information and belongs on everybody's bookshelf.

Dr. West routinely recommends procedures to correct hiatal hernia and also to determine if there is a lack of *adequate digestive enzymes and acids* in the stomach. Lacking them, reflux and heartburn are the norm. Acid-sopping drugs are prescribed by the millions for this condition. This is what I refer to as "television ad medicine," you know: Tums for the tummy?

Television Ad Medicine: Where is the Logic?

Proper digestion in the stomach depends on an adequate level of hydrochloric acid. As one grows older, the amount of hydrochloric acid decreases substantially, which is really the cause of reflux and heartburn. Why on earth would we take meds to further decrease necessary acids and enzymes that in turn reduce absorption of critical nutrients necessary to solve the problem?

This is one of the more insane and wrong-headed myths to come down the pike in years. It makes me wonder if doctors know anything about how the body really works. Anyone after age 40 may well consider taking extra betaine hydrochloride tablets. This is like taking more hydrochloric acid—your normal stomach digestive acid. I reach for these at the slightest hint of indigestion. Maybe I should hang out my shingle.

The Epstein-Barr Virus

The growing fatigue that increasingly overtook me was finally diagnosed as Epstein-Barr virus (Chronic Fatigue Syndrome). My condition eventually reached a point where it was impossible to continue my astrological practice. I would have closed my office for good were it not for my Spirit Teacher, Thomas, who put his foot down and would not hear of it.

It was a very rare occasion for him to lay down the law, and I'm eternally grateful that he did. It later paid the bills for many years. Another astrology colleague took over my practice for a year until I recovered enough to return to work. I healed myself with the Gerson Therapy, a well-known natural therapy primarily known for treating cancer patients. Among other things, I drank an eight-ounce glass of freshly prepared carrot juice every waking hour. I have imbibed my share of carrot juice for this lifetime. Don't talk to me about it anymore.

About all I remember about that year was sitting in a chair idly paging through the same catalog every day. For information about the Gerson therapy and diet, check the Internet. Charlotte Gerson authored a book on the use of coffee enemas. This also was the time I was formally introduced to wheatgrass juice by a guy—a real person—who called himself Mr. Green Jeans, believe it or not.

Wheatgrass juice is a potent healer. However, it must be freshly prepared. Lacking the facilities to juice the wheatgrass myself, I was fortunate to hear about Mr. Green Jeans—or so I thought. This guy grew the wheatgrass, juiced it the evening before the next morning delivery, and then immediately froze it in a glass jar inside of a paper carton filled with water. Each morning I found four ounces of wheatgrass juice frozen inside of an ice ball sitting on my front step. No one ever warned me that wheatgrass juice contained locked up energy equal to the explosive power of a nuclear bomb.

Someone should have advised me to start with one ounce or less and work up. The first time it arrived, I knocked off the ice, took a deep breath and down the hatch. I staggered to the kitchen sink, nearly passed out and probably luckily vomited it all up again. I encountered this elixir of Satan once again at Camp O-High. Seriously, however, it is a very powerful positive detox method and all-around healer when taken properly, either orally or rectally. You will understand that lingering memories make me nauseous at the sight or smell of it. Good luck.

Keep Your Gallbladder; You May Need It!

In Chapter One, I think it was clearly established that gallbladder attacks can be excruciating. (I seem to prefer the excruciating super-sized version of everything.) Many people have stones in their gallbladder. One of them may decide to exit the gallbladder into a little tube, and from there it takes a ride through the entire length of the intestinal tract. It is eliminated at the end of the line. It's when the gallstone exits out of the gallbladder that it may raise hell with the human.

If the pain is severe, most people seek medical attention. In most cases, the doctors recommend surgery before the gallbladder ruptures, scaring the daylights out of patients. There is no way I am going to advise you whether or not to have your gallbladder removed. However, I am going to suggest that you explore all of your options ahead of time just in case you are faced with the decision. It is not a given that you must go under the knife. And it is better to have a gallbladder than not to have one. Your innards never work quite right again, and that is a technical opinion.

There are treatments to stop the pain almost immediately, and then go on to dissolve the gallstones altogether afterwards. You are well-served in this regard to search the Internet and look for a product called Gallbladder Complete (www.gallbladdercomplete.com). The company also sells Liver Complete and Kidney Complete. There are, no doubt, other products along this line. I only mention these because my family has had personal experiences with these products—very successful experiences.

Some of my newsletter readers are fans of Dr. Cynthia Foster, a holistic doctor on the Internet. Find her under "Dr. Cynthia Foster's Essentials." She offers a four-day herbal gallbladder cleanse. I have never personally used her treatment or products, so evaluate it yourself. I may not personally know everything on the market, but I do wholeheartedly believe that if you choose a reputable source that these cleanses are part of a mainline defense system to optimum health.

I have suffered profoundly through four gallbladder attacks in my life. The first time, I sought help from a chiropractor. This is a very interesting story. First, he sent me for x-rays, which clearly showed the presence of gallstones. The doctor put me on a regimen to dissolve the stones. After three or four days, I passed a large number of what appeared to be bits of pea-sized soft green clay. The doctor then sent me for x-rays again, and the gallbladder was clear! So there is no arguing with me about whether these treatments work. The medics are ordinarily skeptical and dismiss the whole business of gallbladder flushes.

Even though I have lived through four gallbladder attacks, my gallbladder has never exploded. Obviously, it's better to find out why one is suffering from gallbladder disease in the first place. The culprit is nearly always diet. Now I adjust my diet to prevent recurrences. You will have to consult with a physician if you want the stones analyzed to find out what dietary changes are recommended. It is also recommended to do the gallbladder, liver and kidney flushes every so often. Consider it maintenance.

Sad to say that we pick up a heavy toxic load from several unavoidable sources: our drinking water, the air we breathe, our food and so on. It is good to always remember that there is that elephant in the room also—ascension symptoms and the additional stresses on the body to transform into the lightbody.

Systemic Candidiasis

While I am on the subject of health problems I have known, why leave out the one that brought on the worst healing crisis ever, worse than all the others rolled together? I like to claim that I have earned a Ph.D. in healing crises. Candida is a yeast normally found in the intestinal tract, but kept in a controlled balance with other yeasts and bacteria. If this balance is upset, for instance by taking antibiotics which kill off your natural intestinal flora, the Candida can grow to wild proportions, become systemic, and move from a localized area to circulate throughout the entire body, including the brain. It can be a very serious matter, even life-threatening to those with severely compromised immune systems. I am not sure that this was ever documented for sure, but many natural healers claimed that it is one of the causes of fibromyalgia, another terribly painful condition, and also chronic fatigue syndrome.

The most interesting thing about my experience with this was that at the time I had it, there was a raging controversy as to whether there really was such a thing as systemic candidiasis. This was along about the mid-80s. I'm sure it is no surprise that the lines were drawn pretty much between traditional medicine and the alternative health care providers. Once the dust settled and straight medicine was finally convinced that the anxiety, fatigue, muscle pains, mental symptoms affecting memory and a host of other seriously debilitating symptoms were actually real; their treatment of choice was limited to dietary restrictions that made no sense and never healed any patients of this particular problem.

Don and I traveled to Tijuana, Mexico, to receive treatments that were illegal, or at least nearly unobtainable in the United States at the time (more insanity). Don met with a chemist connected to the hospital. (Don has degrees in chemistry.) The hospital used a formula that knocked candidiasis in the head. For you chemists out there, it was dioxychlor, a compound similar to hydrogen peroxide, but which doesn't form free radicals as the peroxide does. Don was still treating many patients at that time, many of whom were dealing with candidiasis unsuccessfully with the medics. Fortunately, he was able to obtain the formula from the hospital. His treatment success was nearly 100 per cent . Other alternative healers were also having positive results with hydrogen peroxide therapy.

Two of the medical approaches, at that time, were: 1) to prescribe Nystatin for very long periods or, 2) impose a highly restrictive diet. As for the Nystatin—if the Candida lasted more than a week or two—the little buggers developed a resistant strain rendering it completely ineffective. Don saw patients that had been taking the drug for months or even years. Neither the dioxychlor nor the hydrogen peroxide will produce resistant strains, yet is effective in the treatment of Candida problems.

The diet approach bordered on the bizarre. The hapless patient, if they followed the prescribed regimen, were allowed no sweets, no bread products, no carbohydrates of any kind, no mushrooms, nothing with yeast in it, etc. As a healthful diet, much of it fits well in that context, but the idea was to "starve" the Candida .You would have to totally starve yourself before the Candida would be affected. You would be dead, but you would be cured.

I was exhilarated to personally start the therapy from Mexico. What happens during the healing process is that the treatment begins to kill off the bad bugs. The body must throw off the toxic material. If it is not flushed out of the body fast enough, you are going to feel real bad; I mean *real* bad. (You will willingly embrace enemas at this point.) This is known as the Herxheimer Response, or the healing crisis produced from the accumulation of dead bugs in this case. I remind you that whenever you are killing off something that's alive, or otherwise removing any other toxins from the body; the healing crisis is actually your best friend.

If a healing crisis becomes too intense, many patients bail out and quit the treatment program. This is not what you want to do. Once you have persuaded the body to begin dumping toxins, it's important to continue so that they are flushed out of the body rather than being reabsorbed. The proper course is to back off from the treatment program, but never abandon it altogether. Perhaps cut it in half. Or sometimes it's appropriate to discontinue the therapy for a couple of days. Then start up again at a lower level, and work up to the full program one step at a time.

In my case, this time the detox pathway decided to go through the lungs. I had insufferable, endless coughing fits all day. I was utterly exhausted. Don was out of town. I was finally so miserable and worried that, believe it or not, I saw a medical doctor. He was a nice young doctor who listened to my lungs, and to my relief found nothing was wrong. He said, "If I didn't know better, I would think you were allergic to something." I never tried to explain to him about the candidiasis and the treatment I was using for it. He didn't know how right he was; I give him that.

Food Sensitivities: This One is Huge

Food sensitivities are very common, and often, a serious health problem, but even more common is the general populace's complete ignorance about them. At first mention of food sensitivities, most people will automatically think "allergies," such as an allergy to the family cat, or blossoms in the spring. When one suffers the runny nose, puffy eyes and other miserable *allergy* symptoms, that is one thing. Food *sensitivities,* on the other hand, are quite another. And for a great many people suffering from a variety of what often are severe health problems—it can even be their elephant in the room.

I became intimately acquainted with the issue of food sensitivities the hard way—I had 'em. Among all of my health challenges, food sensitivities were the heavyweight champs. I battled the condition for 11 long years. Even though that was 20 years ago or more, I must keep a weather eye on the issue yet today. Treating this health problem requires eliminating every food from your diet that causes a reaction—I mean in a bad way. I mean in a specific arthritis way for me.

The following material is a quote from Dr. Ronald P. Drucker:

> "The diagnosed disease-industry term, such as arthritis, is simply a term identifying a potentially painful and damaging "condition," which is merely a consequence of the autoimmune attack on a specific area of the body. However, there are over 100 different autoimmune conditions, and hundreds of autoimmune symptoms, caused by the autoimmune attack on the various organs, systems, and tissues of the body.
>
> *"Autoimmunity* often attacks multiple systems, organs, tissues, and cells of the body simultaneously. I refer to this assault on the body as *'The Shot -Gun Effect of Autoimmunity.'* Millions suffer with *multiple autoimmune* conditions. In almost every case, the suffering person is unaware that their conditions and symptoms are all *autoimmune*-driven. The medical doctor has no motive to educate or discuss this with the patient, for the physicians are trained to treat

symptoms only and have no reason to discuss the *root-cause*. (They probably don't know this themselves nine times out of ten. Diana) They are taught by the system that the *root-cause, autoimmunity*, is incurable...."

The Bottom Line

"The modern-day medical bureaucracy will not address the *master disease, autoimmunity*. Eliminating the *master disease* via the restoration of proper *immune* and digestive function, would render an estimated 85 per cent of the current pharmaceutical drug base obsolete, thus rendering the subsequent profitable surgical consequences unnecessary as well. If you object to being merely a host for the pharmaceutical-medical matrix, and would prefer a comprehensive *root-cause* cellular healing approach...." (it is to your advantage to understand your options)

Intestinal Permeability or Leaky Gut Syndrome

The above cold medical-pharmaceutical explanation, although a necessary starting point, is a far cry from treating suffering and discouraged patients up close and personal in a clinical setting. What if it is your mother? What if it is your child? What if it is YOU? Husband, Dr. Don, has come home to dinner from his clinic, shaking his head many times in disbelief as he recounts heart-rending tales about once again treating a refugee from the wreckage of traditional medical practices. There was a day when that patient was I, and indeed I was a wreck.

The first thing to talk about is intestinal permeability, or leaky gut syndrome. (You are going to thank me for this.) Certain inflammatory conditions in the small intestine may be present that over time create damage to the delicate absorptive walls. This damage forms relatively large holes in the lining of the gut, instead of teeny-tiny (technical term) holes just big enough to absorb necessary nutrients that belong there.

One thing that does *not* belong circulating in the blood stream is large chunks of undigested proteins, and if they are; you are headed for Big Trouble. As they establish themselves through the entire blood stream, your good guy immune system goes on red alert and attacks them as foreign invaders. That tomato you ate last night may look like a monster with green stuff running out of its eyes to the immune system. A real disease is being born. Your immune system begins by attacking similar cells in your own body tissue; for instance, in your joints. This creates antibodies acting as permanent bodyguards to constantly fight the "invaders" ever after.

An inflammatory condition is created; at this point, there are hundreds of diagnostic choices that can send you to your physician. Depending on where it caused the most identifiable symptoms first, you may visit a doctor who will render a diagnosis, like arthritis if it were affecting the joints, for example. Then there is an array of really nasty drugs for whatever ails you. The side effects include even death. I know, because I saw the disclaimers on their ad on TV. But then, there are more drugs to treat the side effects, and on *ad nauseum.*

Go visit your local nursing home if you want to observe the end game of what "playing doctor" *really* means. At some point down this road to Hell, some patients will come to their senses and realize that they are actually unwitting participants in the "I am Getting Worse" game. Some of them will then find their way to salvation, and get on board some holistic healing modalities that include playing doctor for real.

Dr. Don has often found it crucial to wind down some patients from up to 10 prescription drugs. That, sadly, must frequently be the first step before any real healing can be initiated. I'm sure there are nightmare stories that top that figure, but I don't want to know about them. Fortunately, my two friends back in the 60s flushed my drugs down the toilet and set my feet on the road to real health building.

What originally sent me to Don was because I knew he facilitated a certain holistic protocol for the Big C—yes, cancer. But that is for later. The next question has to be how to heal the leaky gut syndrome that has progressed to the stage in which there are—what was that again—FOOD SENSITIVITIES! I was lucky in that Don specialized in kinesiology, or muscle testing, which he used to identify the food culprits. I was unlucky in that I was sensitive to just about everything.

The Elimination Diet

You will have to figure out for yourself how you are going to identify your own food culprits. The procedure most naturopaths or other alternative healers use is called the *elimination diet.* It works generally like this: First, choose an innocuous food that rarely troubles anybody. One doctor took me through the elimination diet. I think he started me on rice and turkey. I ate nothing else for several days. The next step is to begin adding foods, one at a time, and observe what happens for two or three days. If there is no flare-up of pain or other symptoms, move on to another food. Try to stay with foods that are most unlikely to cause a reaction.

Which are the foods most likely to be criminally involved in the food sensitivities racket? You should immediately identify the nightshade family as suspicious characters for many people, but if it is arthritis, forget about them. They are probably your favorite foods, and it breaks my heart to tell you, but nightshades are tomatoes, potatoes, green peppers and eggplant. On a cautionary note, food companies notoriously sneak potato starch into many foods, but do not list it on the label. If a "safe" canned food inexplicably causes a flare-up in your symptoms, that may be the reason.

For 11 years, I monitored every bite of food, and read every label on cans. So what happened if I ate the wrong food? Arthritis, remember? This is not an allergic reaction to the cat. Arthritis is pain in the joints. The next day I woke up paralyzed with profound pain for several hours, and this often lasted each morning for three days. It's a great motive to toe the line. As time passed, the inflammation healed as the intestinal permeability healed, and consequently, I was sensitive to fewer and fewer foods. Eventually I could again eat most foods and better yet, greatly decrease the pain in the joints. I now eat all foods, but I keep the suspicious ones to a minimum and you should, too.

Maybe your system attacked the pancreas first, and then you dealt with diabetes. If the autoimmunity settled in the thyroid, then perhaps you had to deal with Grave's disease. When the autoimmunity attacks the stomach and digestive environment in general, the industry term for defining the consequences are: gastritis, ulcers, irritable bowel syndrome, acid reflux, GERD, hiatal hernia and Barrett's esophagus, and there are hundreds more including lupus, rosacea and psoriasis.

Now What WAS That About the Big C?

When I was in my forties, I went for a Pap test used in the detection of cervical cancer. It just so happened that the office nurse once attended one of my astrology classes. She escorted me into the examining room, got me situated onto the examining table, up in stirrups and properly draped.

I can't help but be reminded about a time a male friend of mine went to the doctor. When I saw him later, he asked me what "those stirrups" were for and inquired why the doctor laughed hysterically when he entered the examining room. I laughed so hard I was unable to answer him. Several comebacks came to mind, but were a bit too colorful and best left unsaid.

This is serious, so back where I was lying there on the table. The doctor came in to do the biopsy. The nurse laid her hand on my arm and told me how much she had enjoyed my astrology classes. I fully understood her intention to put me at ease during the procedure. All of a sudden I hear this voice intoning from behind the drape that sounded like some revivalist tent show evangelist, "Astrology is the work of the devil!" Considering the circumstances at the time, I'm going to argue the point? He was the one with a weapon in his hand.

The Pap test revealed that the uterus was at the stage where the cells are just starting to turn malignant; "we caught it early" is the catch phrase. The doctor's professional recommendation was that I undergo an immediate hysterectomy. I decided that it was not a good move for me to have anyone cutting on me who believed that I was the devil's handmaiden. In fact, I was sure that I did not care to have *anyone* cutting on me. Here is an interesting footnote to our relationship. It was not more than a month or so later when I saw this guardian of the public good on the local TV news. It seems that other guardians of the public good trumped him, and his license was yanked for molesting female patients.

Persons facing cancer may know only what the traditional medical doctors recommend, which is chemotherapy, radiation and surgery. Fortunately for me, I was extremely well-versed in the other avenues of cure available to me. Not only that, I was about to stake my life on those beliefs. I knew about a cancer therapy practiced by Dr. Don Hurd. So that is what I was doing in his clinic.

In addition to that protocol—which required strict discipline combining detox, diet and nutritional supplements—I also took matters into my own hands and began a very intense private healing ritual that I had performed many times for others. I also contacted all of the fellow healers whom I knew and requested that they do their thing on my behalf. That list of powerful healers included my son, David. I was not afraid.

I held an image in my mind of having another Pap test in 30 days. At the end of that time, I envisioned myself walking out of the doctor's office, jumping in the air and clicking my heels because I was so blissed out that the cancer was gone. I worked and worked on that image; however, I could not get rid of two small spots on the uterus no matter how hard I tried. I decided to go for the test in 30 days, regardless. Needless to say, I chose another doctor this time.

Once again, the nurse settled me onto the table. The doctor came in to do the Pap test. There was a long silence. He turned to the nurse and said, "Let me see that file again." He seemed almost disgusted. Finally, he impatiently tossed the file aside and said to the nurse, "I'm not doing any Pap test here. I don't know why they did one in the first place. There's nothing wrong here. *All I see are the two spots where the biopsy was done, and if that was 30 days ago, they sure are healing fast."* That doctor never would have believed the healing energy I poured onto those two spots!

This experience in the doctor's office was a perfect example of how the Higher Creative Forces communicate with us. I trusted the experience in the doctor's office as a confirming sign from the Universe that all was well. As one increasingly accepts signs from a Higher Intelligence, the reward is eventually a veritable avalanche of further special confirmations and guidance.

Watch for those little extra sideways twists, like the doctor refusing to even do the test over again because it was a waste of time. That was practically unheard of as far as I was concerned. You have to pay attention. These are situations in which things are tilted just a little bit off center and out of the corner of your eye; God doesn't deliver a Western Union telegram via roller skates.

Yes, I would have been grateful if things had followed the normally expected protocol and yes, I would have celebrated a retest that came back negative. But it was really an extra bonus to know that someone up there likes me and influenced the doctor's behavior. And yes, I was blissed out when I left the doctor's office all right, but clicking heels was just a bit beyond the pale that day.

Taking on the personal responsibility to heal oneself of cancer, utilizing only natural therapies once you have already been diagnosed is very tricky business. In most cases, I would strongly advise against it. Something that needs to be thoroughly explored and well-understood concerns the dynamics of the disease and the healing process *before* you ever have cancer, God forbid.

I also believe that it should never be undertaken alone. A natural health care provider who is experienced in successfully treating cancer needs to be in the picture. That certainly does not include every doctor on the alternative side of the fence. They need to have one hell of a track record.

One of my best friends underwent surgery for breast cancer. As in many cases, it eventually metastasized into the lungs. She lived in San Diego. It just happened that I was lecturing at an astrology conference there. She visited me in my hotel room to break the bad news that she had been given six months to live. I spotted several tumors protruding around her neck and shoulders. She knew about my healing work and asked for my help.

I purchased a plane ticket and flew her home with me. Don did his thing and started her on his program. I referred her to Camp O-High since she lived in San Diego and could partake of their regimen as an out-patient. There never was a more rigidly disciplined person. She was motivated. She had three little kids to raise.

Kate saw her oncologist who tracked the shrinking tumors in the lungs. My friend completely recovered from her cancer, and she is doing fine nearly 30 years later. She is one of the rare exceptions. Of course, the best cure for cancer is to never get it in the first place. There are preventive measures that all but ensure that this be the case. It pays to search those out and factor them into your regular lifestyle for your own peace of mind.

Dr. Diana

I made reference earlier that I should hang out my shingle. I readily confess that in my 40 years of astrological practice I oversaw the healing of dozens—more likely hundreds—of clients that were desperately ill. They were ill from iatrogenic (doctor) causes. I was responsible for facilitating the healing of health problems that no medical doctor could or did. I usually referred them to a holistic health practitioner. After I knew Don, I sent them over to his clinic if appropriate. I have received many letters from grateful clients for literally saving their lives. What an appalling state of our medical culture when your astrologer is a better doctor than the one with the degree on the wall.

I was aware that Dr. Don successfully managed many cancer cases. Some people recovered using wholly natural therapies. Others employed a combination of traditional medicine with alternative modalities. Just so it is clear, I did not advise anyone as to their ultimate treatment choices. As for Don, he made himself available in whatever capacity the patients themselves chose.

That completes the *tour de force* through my physical and emotional afflictions. I was in the habit of keeping my newsletter subscribers abreast of my current state of health. Inquiries poured in from other lightbeings also concerned about the reasons for their own problems with which they struggled year after year. I encouraged them to understand that they were not "bad" nor doing something wrong. Apparently my own struggles encouraged them to quit beating up on themselves. However, if I did not soft pedal my symptoms somewhat, I think they pictured me as an 80-pound cripple lying on urine-soaked rags in a dark, forgotten corner of a nursing home whose license was revoked by the health department!

The Truth at Last!

Now I have come full circle to the end of my story. Several times along the way, I was convinced that I had finally discovered just why it was that my symptoms persisted unabated. However, my journey was analogous to peeling an onion, layer by layer. As each layer was repeatedly discarded as the underlying cause of my physical condition, it became increasingly difficult to maintain my spiritual equilibrium. Dark thoughts haunted the deep recesses of my mind despite my struggles to keep the faith. It required a continuous watchful eye to keep my thoughts from wondering if my problems were not some unsuspected karma of the bad kind, or an unresolved psychological issue, and on and on over territories that had been covered and resolved long ago, but yet…

Stories as Memory Triggers

Perhaps something somebody said or something you read in a book was not your identical experience; yet, it triggered a sudden memory that flashed into consciousness and explained everything! You knew it did. Perhaps my story served some purpose for you. The reason I revealed the end of my story right from the beginning was to reassure lightbeings that they, too, need not harbor doubts about their authentic spirituality, just as you could see that my doubts were unjustified all along.

It was not until a complete stranger's story somehow sparked a memory as to my true soul mission, consequently, ultimately explaining the true cause of my pain and suffering. It was not anything I was doing wrong. ***The true cause of my pain and suffering is because I am one of the first volunteers attempting to transform a physical earth body into a lightbody with no previous template to guide the process.*** I was preparing the way for the volunteers to come, by successfully placing the prototype into the collective consciousness. For me, that was the elephant in the room.

Did you find your elephant?

ADDENDUM I

Surprise! You get another chance. That elephant has a baby. Maybe it is the elephant in *your* room. This next part is something that needs to be in the book. However, as I wrote, it never found a place where it was entirely comfortable interrupting the continuity of the subject at hand. Therefore, I will give this its own dedicated space. The lightworkers who are living this deserve our recognition and thanks anyway. These are the unsung heroes, and there is an elephant in their room. I hope this helps them to see it and understand who they really are.

In the main article above in this chapter, the question is raised: If I am a lightworker, why do I have so many insurmountable challenges? What am I doing wrong? The elephant in the room for many of them is that they are one of the three waves of volunteers and/or they are one of the shock troops. Or in my case, it was finally revealed to me my special role about which I was unaware until relatively recently.

I can do it. You can do it

That leaves another outstanding group of souls that have already achieved mastery after many lifetimes of experience. They possess tremendous abilities to overcome the most difficult challenges. Yet, there are many in this category who are facing the very most difficult and painful chronic problems of all. In that regard, the same questions arises. What are they doing wrong?

In their cases, the answer is simple. They *deliberately* take on these challenges to demonstrate to those around them how to work out these issues to become empowered. More of their true selves emerge rather than less. The more the leading edge spiritual leaders are successful, the more likelihood that others are motivated to follow.

You perhaps have noticed that many of our most powerful spiritual leaders, no matter in what field of endeavor, can claim a history of triumphing over the most insurmountable odds in life. Nelson Mandela in Africa, Steven Hawking, the genius physicist, and on down the line of notables, all portraying this same inner power to emerge greater than before. In fact, they actually attribute their difficult challenges as responsible for their success.

Healing Cultural Wounds

To heal a wound in the culture, this requires a certain percentage of the total population who must first experience that same wound and then heal it by a transformation of consciousness. We are not saying that the victim is healed by exacting a terrible revenge on the persecutors. (It's tempting!) Child abuse is sadly one of our cultures' wounds. If a large enough percentage of souls are born into an environment of abuse, yet somehow rises above it to achieve some sort of extraordinary success, the culture eventually shifts and heals.

This would involve soul contracts among a rather large group for all of them to incarnate into roughly the same conditions of abuse. This sets up an entirely different emotional environment because the in-coming soul would have no awareness that he or she is part of a larger group, or its intent. The psychological damage usually gives rise to loss of self esteem and a message that one is "bad" and somehow deserves the abuse. Yet, the inner promptings are to somehow rise above the situation in such a way that the wound is healed.

Some of These May be You

The stories of success after impossible odds identifies the souls who may be setting an example that it is possible to use these challenges as motivation to greatness and to the fullest expression of the self.

I have worked with many clients who were born into situations that reflect wounds in our culture. By the time they sought help for the damage this inflicted on them at many levels, they found it difficult to believe that it was their soul mission to deliberately come into a particular environment in order to heal a cultural wound.

Is this the elephant in your room?

ADDENDUM II

One last chance! Hold on! It seems this baby pachyderm has a kid brother! Maybe he is the elephant in *your* room. Once again, a logical place in which to include the story of *yet another* group of souls never quite presented itself, either. However, they belong in this book. So once again, I feel they more than deserve their own dedicated space. The spiritual warriors who are living out this special story deserve recognition and our thanks as well. These are certainly unsung heroes as few people are even aware of their soul mission, including them! That is their elephant in the room. I hope this helps them see it just like the group in Addendum 1 and, consequently, realize who they truly are.

The question we need to be asking in this case is: Why does the Dark Side continually single out and attack highly-evolved starseeds and lightworkers, but never bother the others? Despite everything this group does in order to protect themselves, they still find that they must engage in battle with the Dark Ones. What are they doing wrong?

I undertook some deep shamanic journeys to recover information as to their soul missions in this lifetime. *Each one was exactly the same!* It is the soul mission of these particular lightworkers, or should I say "designated lightwarriors," to engage these negative forces. Let's say you can recognize them by their Army uniforms. They are obvious targets in some way.

I was gratified that I could tell the lightwarriors that it was their soul mission to experience on-going negative attacks. They were doing nothing wrong. It was not working off negative karma. It was not because they weren't love bugs. It was not because they were projecting something bad from the dark underbellies of their subconscious. In fact, they would never have committed to this mission if it weren't for a very significant reason. Likewise, it was not the job of other lightworkers to experience personal encounters with the Dark polarity. There are some complex dynamics involved with this group. There are many things that are simply beyond our 3D understanding. I don't know the reasons, but they are there and will be revealed someday.

So is that the elephant in your room?

****

During this ascension time, every person has his or her job. Not all are the same, and no one is "wrong."

CHAPTER FOURTEEN

The Invisible Players

As we progress and awaken to the soul in us and things we shall realize that there is also consciousness in the plant, in the metal, in the atom, in electricity, in everything that belongs to physical nature.

Sri Aurobindo
The Synthesis of Yoga

To summarize the purpose of this chapter: It is to confirm the reality of unseen Beings and the consciousness intrinsic to each; but more than that the cultivation of life-changing interactions with them yourself.

First, in order to grasp the largest overview of all of Nature, let's begin by imagining the great evolutionary force as a giant arc of ascending and descending energies full of life.

That's right, full of life; you may imagine it, but it certainly is not imaginary. It is all real! We may not see the life and intelligence in, say a summer breeze, but it is there. Only when we expand an awareness of the silent influences around us and further still, forge personal bonds with them, may we embrace any true notion of Oneness with all of Life. Many elements contribute to the Whole.

As a spiritual practice, we are encouraged to regard as equals all of the brothers and sisters on the planet, making One Whole. However, this embraces exclusively *the human variety,* perhaps rendering us inadvertently oblivious to the inclusion of other sparks of life—visible and invisible—sharing Nature's world with us. Recognizing the animal kingdom as an easy token membership in the exclusive Oneness Club is suspiciously akin to a sort of convoluted spiritual affirmative action. Here Spot. Here Puss Cat.

The plant world's beautiful flowers and magnificent tree forests are also capable on occasion of arousing an overwhelming sense of connecting with something larger also. "Only God can make a tree." But when reality comes face to face with the idea that *everything* has consciousness, we may well find ourselves forced to confront things decidedly alien to our idea of equality with palms, puppies, pussies and pansies. It surely was for me!

The first time I remember feeling some connection to a non-human life form was something that happened not deliberately, but quite innocently by happenstance. My kitchen was invaded by ants. A personal interest in anything considered at all metaphysical was in its infancy in my life in the mid-1960s. It was along about then that I vaguely recalled reading that one could prevail upon the ants and sort of strike a deal—leave my house or I'll kill you. I'm sure that was my simplistic, albeit grisly, interpretation of it then. However, I sometimes suspect there is some latitude for just plain beginner's luck.

Diana Versus the Ants

My automatic solution to earlier ant invasions was to set out the poison and send the little critters to ant heaven without a second thought. This time I explained that this was my kitchen and that it was off limits to ants. They could stay and be poisoned to death or march outside where I was sure they could find a good home. Actually, I was rather proud of myself for offering the ants a choice. I was sure that this signaled my first steps toward spiritual advancement. I prominently placed the bottle of poison on the kitchen counter, thinking it gave my ultimatum a bit more clout and underscored that I really meant business.

I went about my chores in other parts of the house and quickly spaced out the ant drama playing out in the kitchen. Was I ever in for a huge shock when I returned! A long, black, single-file line crossed my kitchen from the sink to the outside door. The ants were exiting like little soldiers. I was struck dumb. Whom had I spoken to, but even more unbelievable, who was listening?

No advanced metaphysical sophistication is required to conclude that it was not the little individual ant ears that heard my threats and responded to them. In the insect world, as in all other biological kingdoms in Nature as well, there exists invisible, but conscious, organized levels of life, which are hierarchical.

We can use my kitchen adventure as an example of the hierarchical ranks extant all throughout Nature. I apparently somehow stumbled onto one of the lesser Beings in charge of ants. It's inferred that one may travel further up the ranks to the One Big Being in charge of all insects (the five-star general). However, that may be considered overkill, analogous to bringing up the heavy artillery to mash a gnat.

Each level, or rank, possesses consciousness. Conventional understanding among occultists is that yes, this is conscious awareness of the human kind and even beyond, including levels *far* beyond. Could you or I communicate with and manage the evolutionary development of an entire insect species? I think not, and neither could the actual physical ants visible to the naked eye.

However, it has been known from ancient times that there are very real Beings in the *invisible* realms that do possess consciousness. In this chapter, I will consider these many other forces that impact our world. The implication of this discussion further suggests that we as humans are capable of communicating with at least some of the other levels of life.

It is important to simultaneously keep in mind that evolutionary forces have evolved through the various Nature kingdoms—mineral, plant, animal and others. As our souls participated in various life experiences throughout our earth journey, we ourselves could have very likely evolved in other forms than human. (My father the rock)

Diana the Tree

I have always had "that special feeling" for trees. In fact, many years later, I spontaneously became a tree! No, my head was not crowned with leaves nor did my toes sprout roots. Aside from that I WAS a tree. It was the damnedest thing, I assure you, to enter tree consciousness 100 per cent. I felt so immensely proud of myself as a tree.

I felt like a big closed manufacturing plant that I ran single-handedly. I knew exactly how to respond to the subtlest seasonal changes. I was conscious. I was aware. I was thinking. I was feeling. Sap flowed through my body like blood through human veins. On this one, you will have to take my word for it. It is an experience I will never, never forget. The biggest thrill was an understanding that there was a consciousness, an intelligence, inherent in the invisible realm of trees with which I could communicate.

This awareness struck out of the blue and the timing could not have been worse! My husband and I were getting settled in a room at the kah.nee.tah Indian reservation lodge in Oregon. If that was not inconvenient enough, my parents were with us. We took them to visit the Indian reservation and join us for dinner at the lodge that night. How does your husband explain that dinner is late because his wife is a tree?

Introducing Tree Devas

My home in Vancouver, Washington, is bounded along one side of my corner property by a stand of tall Scotch pine trees at least 40 years old. I love those trees! To my utter dismay a few years ago, I noticed that there were dead branches on some of the thirteen trees. I sent frantic 911 messages to the Tree Deva in my neighborhood to save them. (Patience, patience. Later there is the textbook treatise on the Devas.) When two of the trees had to be removed, my fears escalated. Fortunately, those particular ones were situated at the end of the line, a short distance from the others. Their removal did not create unsightly gaps like missing front teeth. I continued to fervently communicate with the tree Deva. At least I hoped I was!

The Northwest is famous for its great rain forests and proliferation of trees of all varieties. To protect this beloved natural resource, an extensive Forestry Service is in place at the state level to manage the great forests, creating an extraordinarily large contingent of well-educated foresters who care for trees on private property. There is somewhat of a continuous uneasy conflict of interest between environmentalists and commercial logging companies. You perhaps have heard news stories when this situation occasionally flares up into violence with protesters chaining themselves to trees and the like.

When I communicated with the Tree Deva, I suppose I expected that she would immediately heal whatever ailed my trees. The reason I share this story is to point out from the outset that interacting with invisible intelligences does not always mean that they necessarily bend to human expectations. This does not mean that our requests go unheeded or unanswered, however.

Therefore, I have learned from similar experiences to let go of expectations about *how* the Deva will solve the problem. Devas are not gods to whom we go in subservient supplication like beggars, hoping our prayers somehow will be granted this time. I understand that for most of us, the reality of actually communicating with a higher intelligence like a Tree Deva is far beyond our belief boundaries. Nonetheless, this is not the stuff of fairy tales; Devas are real.

I continued to meditate and talk to the Tree Deva. I released my frantic fears and visualized a successful outcome every day. It is also important to express gratitude for any help you wish to receive. Devas do not appreciate being ordered about or taken for granted. (Other places in the book, I mention Devas who were unmistakably cranky about my requests.) After communicating with the Deva, the logical next step was to contact some arborists to diagnose the problem and pray they had a solution.

Earlier I mentioned the extensive access to forestry services that we enjoy here in the Northwest. My husband and I agreed that we would search out an arborist sympathetic to environmental issues as a person most likely dedicated to our needs. To make a long story short, we found a young woman who is truly remarkable. Trees are her life.

She holds a masters degree in her field, and her partner is a tree guy whose diagnostic and treatment skills are one of a kind. Both of them hold special licenses as master arborists, the granting of which are given only after special training and apprenticeships. We would have lost several of the Scotch pine trees plus two additional flowering trees elsewhere on the property were it not for them. Dusty, the tree guy, claimed that he is the only arborist he knows who possesses the secret for treating the Scotch pine blight. We hire these two every year to watch over our trees. As I write this and at this very moment, they are removing worms by hand, embedded in globs of sap. If the worms are left to hatch they could eventually kill the tree. Both of my arborists are dedicated enough to climb the trees to their entire height in search of infestations.

This is how the Tree Deva chose to solve our problem—no magic wand, no supernatural instant changes before our very eyes. I've found that the Devas' solutions do not seem to favor what we would normally label as outright magical. Though no doubt capable of dramatic results when necessary, the silent unseen handiwork slips in most often within the logical framework of our physical reality.

In fact, it is easy to discount the workings of invisible forces and assume that the solution just happened coincidentally with no outside assistance. In the case of my trees, I believe that my request was answered by an unseen intelligence. Maybe it is more accurate to say that I feel it intuitively. But what revealed the hand of spirit most clearly were the energies of the two special people. I believe they were sent special delivery to me and are very likely the only ones who could solve the problem. If only you could meet them in person; they all but have "elf" tattooed on their foreheads. They are the magic.

It is always very confirming to me and my newsletter readers to hear about other people's experiences with the invisible worlds. As an example among several, I was intrigued with the following letter:

Devas, Dryads And Tree Suicide

From Julia Steffey http://www.artofstars.net

> "Some years ago there were rather large twin oak trees living in the backyard of my folks' house. These trees were clearly nearly the same age. An adult could wrap both arms around the trunks and just touch fingers. They were spaced just inches apart at the base and grew tilting a bit away from each other. Neither leaned onto or was supported by the other tree or anything else that was visible.
>
> "One of the trees died, so my folks decided to have it cut down. The tree service came and removed the dead tree. Within scant hours of this, the second living tree snapped in two about five or six feet from the ground. Remember, this was a tree with a good two and a half feet diameter! We have no other explanation—some suggested that the live tree could have been rotten in the middle, but it was not—except it appeared to have committed suicide at the sudden mutilation and loss of the remains of its companion...or possibly the "Wee Folk' were still residing there and were so upset that they demolished the living tree in their haste to move household."

Hyperboreal Haints

"Also, relating to the Devic Realm, some family members recently traveled to Iceland. My Dad had been stationed there during the Korean War. It was his first time back in 60 years. Icelandic people are very close to the 'Hidden People' and 'Invisible World' as they say. Likely this has much to do with the unspoiled ruggedness of the land, volcanic activity, the small and isolated population and the fact that their language is pure Medieval Nordic—unchanged for 1,000 years. They work hard to keep it that way.

"This is a fascinating documentary film on that topic that I think you will enjoy. Very well done with both the topic and interviewees treated respectfully.

Investigation into the Invisible World
2002 Documentary by French Filmmaker Jean-Michel Roux
http://www.youtube.com/watch?v=gRjatXe5bis

Subtitled in English (some spoken English, mostly Icelandic. About 90 minutes"

The Etheric Plane

The adventure with the ants marching out of my kitchen like little soldiers, plus personally experiencing the consciousness of a tree, had inadvertently connected me to the Devic kingdom of nature. The Devic kingdom on the etheric plane—the home of Devas, or nature spirits—is understood in esoteric literature to inhabit or rule over natural objects or environments; just a few examples being trees, rivers and even mountain ranges. Though Devas are generally invisible, people who claim clairvoyant sight can sometimes see and communicate with them, or gain intuitive access to the Devic kingdoms (yours truly included).

At this point it is imperative to comprehend that there is no activity or existence *of any sort* without some kind of consciousness or intelligence inherent within it. This is literally true. We are not playing with symbolism here. Miss this critical, most basic feature of life—seen and unseen—and it pretty much guarantees that your personal journey to enlightenment will increasingly lead you further and further down a lonely road—cut off from the Oneness of all that is.

The Full Circle of Life

It begins with the very lowest of any life form, and even that little spark of life travels the arc over perhaps tens of millions of years, progressing towards the physical plane (that's where we are), and finally awakens to experience physical life through the five senses, and hey; It's human!

So generally speaking, the life forms, or consciousnesses, *behind* us on the arc, are not as intelligent or as highly evolved as we are. That would be true of say, the

Vegetable Kingdom including carrots, but they're trying. I suppose you could say that carrots have human envy.

For the sake of simplicity—this is not intended to be a doctoral thesis—we will skip to the Elementals, or nature spirits, that are closest to human evolution. Elementals are not all necessarily evolved entities, because they are still at their *involutionary* stage, not yet visible or manifesting on thc physical plane.

As I said, they can sometimes be perceived by clairvoyant sight on the *etheric* plane. Perhaps you just learned a new word. The etheric plane is familiar territory to even the lowliest lightworkers, so if you hang out with them, just remember that the etheric plane refers to a vibratory frequency closest to the physical plane, which is where we are right now. In occult science there are seven planes in all. A *plane* refers to a specific stratum of consciousness. The term *etheric plane* is generally considered to have originated with theosophists Helena Blavatsky, Annie Besant and Alice Bailey. If anyone questions you further, quietly order another round of drinks.

Elementals of Earth

Elementals are usually divided into four main groups. Now you are on solid non-technical ground because everyone has heard of earth, air, fire and water. The Elementals of Earth are associated with the Gnomes. Remember those little guys your mom used to read to you about in the fairy-tale books? You believed it then, didn't you? But mom didn't—too bad!—because they are real and many people (humans) have seen them. Popular folklore generally pairs gnomes with the ground, the earth of course, and the world of form.

The Crystal Triangle written about in our first two books features Turtle occupying one significant point of the triangle. Turtle represents the Earth element.

Elementals of Air

The Elementals of Air oversee the air currents; you see them demonstrated on the weatherman's moving maps every night via your local TV news station. These Elementals are called Sylphs and are also in charge of cloud formations.

Don't they have an endlessly tantalizing imagination? I remember in one of the *Peanuts* cartoons in which Charlie Brown lies in the grass with Linus, studying the cloud formations in the sky. Charlie says, "I see a horsie and a ducky." To which only Linus would reply, "I see the Stoning of Steven and the signing of the Treaty of Versailles." Proving once again, it is all in the eyes of the beholder.

Here is a little game you may play to prove that humans can indeed impact the elements even at great distances in the manifested world. My mother did it, and she didn't believe in any of this stuff. Go outside on a clear sunny day when there are cumulus clouds in the sky. Cumulus clouds are the ones that look like big, white, puffy pillows. You are going to dissolve one just by commanding it to do so.

That should get your attention. It always riveted the attention of my psychic development classes. First, pick out one of the little baby cumulus clouds. For god's sake, don't start with a behemoth the size of a battleship. That is not proving anything except your capacity for punishment.

Now focus your eyes and attention on your little baby cloud. Do not take your attention away from it. Stare at it. Now begin to repeat over and over again, either to yourself or out loud, "Disperse. Disperse. Disperse." I'll trust that you try this in an appropriate place. The Inquisition never really completely died, you know. It's just that you are sent to the crazy farm now instead of the stake.

Just keep repeating it until the very last remnants of only that cloud disappear completely. It will; but it helps to cultivate some patience. Once you have convinced yourself, now is the time to graduate to a bigger, denser cloud. It will take much longer, of course, but it is that much more impressive. Give your regards to the Sylphs and leave. They don't particularly like you if you are a human.

Elementals of Fire

The Elementals of Fire are associated with the Salamanders. Salamanders are found in association with the biggest raging forest fires as well as the tiniest flickering candle flames. Obviously, fire has been one of mankind's greatest friends. It has also been one of the most destructive forces in all of nature's kingdoms. Salamanders appear as little lizard-like creatures in the visible world around us. However, in this context here, salamanders are one of the Elementals and considered real in the invisible worlds.

Psychics have reported seeing salamanders 30 feet tall within the great forest fires. In their defense, forest fires—once regarded as so terribly disastrous to our beloved national forests—were cooperating with sound environmental practices that actually preserved those same forests in the long run. In national parks like Yellowstone and Yosemite, forestry experts themselves now deliberately set controlled burns as part of long-range management of these invaluable resources. Salamanders taught us an important environmental lesson, at least in these instances.

I do not wish to be redundant, but humor me; I realize that for many readers these are new ideas. Therefore, I reiterate that when the subject at hand are the *Elementals* of fire, this refers to real living Beings of consciousness that exist at the *etheric plane* level; one closest to the physical plane in the evolutionary arc. The only reason they became known as salamanders is attributed to mythological stories about the little creatures' reputed ability to withstand fire without ending up as roasted salamanders. For the sake of the little lizards, I urge you not to disprove the myth at your next barbecue.

Elementals of Water

The Elementals of Water are the Undines, probably unfamiliar to most folks. Nevertheless, if you have ever thrilled at the sparkles dancing off flowing water, you have joined energies, however briefly, with the Undines. Regardless of their relative unfamiliarity, try to imagine a world without flowing water.

We who live in the United States should never forget that we owe our development as a world power in no small measure to the abundance of natural resources, not the least of which is our great rivers. The principle of water has given rise to the science of oceanography, for example.

Popular folklore introduced us via our fairy tales to faeries, of course, but also to the elves, goblins, trolls, pixies, leprechauns, brownies, satyrs, gnomes and others. They are real and can be seen. Generally they do not like humans. I don't think we need to look far to explain why. After realizing what we have done to the earth, to the air, to the water and even to the natural cycles of fire, is it any wonder they find us disgusting?

On the other hand, they are capable of forming relationships with humans. This occurs most frequently with simple country folk in natural environments. That is probably the reason that urban sophisticates so easily discount the folk tales of their country bumpkin cousins. That's not to say that the so-called New Agers everywhere commonly interact with these Beings as well, since that community focuses on environmental issues as an integral part of their culture.

The following article was written by a suburbanite, but who clearly falls into the category of a New Ager devoted to environmental issues. I think this is a delightful story that illustrates how we can more closely connect with Nature wherever we are, and also introduce succeeding generations to the reality of the invisible worlds.

FAERIES IN THE BACKYARD

By Kriss Shellman

I am a grandmother and a shamanic practitioner. A couple years ago I decided to call the fairy realm into my garden to help my garden grow. Sitting in the backyard during the late winter, I went into meditation and called the faeries. Using strong intention, I had a conversation with them, welcoming them into the yard and asking them to give me guidance. I sensed I needed to do everything I could to make them feel honored and welcome. At this point it was a one-way conversation. I was trusting there was actually something out there listening!
Very shortly after this on a sunny afternoon, I was standing at my backdoor looking into the backyard. Suddenly I saw a bright light dancing across the driveway—back and forth. I was transfixed. What could be causing that dancing light? I stepped outside and looked up above the roofline to see if I could see anything hanging in the tree to cause a reflection from the afternoon sun. I looked and looked. There was nothing. I went back into the house and looked outside again, and the dancing light was back! My heart leapt and suddenly I realized my prayer to the faeries had been answered. The dancing light was a sign from them. I was watching a fairy!

To make them feel as welcome as possible, I built a fairy house. I found lots of twigs with moss on them to glue onto the roof and walls, so it looked very "woodsy." I glued little glass tiles on the floor, and decorated the outside with pretty colored glass stones. Then I tucked it up next to the house under the eaves where it would stay semi-dry behind a shrub.

The granddaughters were visiting that weekend, so I decided it would be a great project for them. They were both very excited to make their own fairy houses. One granddaughter even made twig furniture to put inside! During the project we talked all about faeries.

Occasionally, I still "see" them when I put the dog out at night. I stand at that same kitchen door, peering out the window at the dog. I often see almost transparent shapes moving around. They are about knee high and dart about. I just smile and give them a wink and a nod of recognition. By the way, with their influence we enjoyed a bumper crop of green beans, strawberries, cucumbers and squash that first year—and I don't believe in "mere" coincidences!

I hope all of us can come to a place in our consciousness where we accept that the little twinkling lights that appear to us are a wink and a nod from the faeries, and not just a reflection from the gas station across the street. They are out there and just want to say, "hello." Stories have long been told in which nature spirits befriended and offered their assistance by whatever means lay within their abilities. They do differ individually as do human beings, in degrees of intelligence, consciousness and power.

Magic for Real: The Findhorn Garden

As personally enlightening as my relationships with other levels of life may have been for me, it was the truly magical events in a remote corner of Scotland that commanded the attention of the entire world. It was known as the Findhorn Garden. You may have heard about it yourself, as it has been widely publicized through books and TV documentaries. Even the agricultural university in my home state of Iowa, in Ames, got in on the act.

Peter and Eileen Caddy, along with a friend, Dorothy, and their three young sons, found themselves living in a mobile home sitting on sand between a rubbish dump and a dilapidated garage. Eileen, long practiced in trusting the inner guidance from the God within, took the leap of faith and moved her family to this inhospitable area of sand dunes. Once there, she was contacted by Devas and nature spirits and instructed to grow a garden. The soil was just sand and gravel held together by couch grass. Furthermore, it was in the midst of winter.

News of this amazing garden that was producing 40-pound cabbages and roses the size of dinner plates in the snow soon attracted horticulturists who were amazed that anything could be growing there at all. However skeptical at first, they concluded that other factors were at work besides fertilizers and mulches. Occultists regarded this as an experiment in cooperation between three kingdoms: Devic, Elemental and Human. Eileen continued to receive daily instructions from her inner guidance; Dorothy communicated directly with the Devas; and a new member of the group, Roc, could see and converse with nature spirits.

Findhorn grew into a community of several hundred people from its humble beginnings in the mid-60s. Several later arrivals worked together for seven years to produce an extraordinary game called—of all things—the Game of Life! It's an actual board game with dice and little pieces that are moved around something like in Monopoly. To participate at first, one needed to travel to Scotland, which obviously greatly limited its access to other players around the world.

However, in the early 1980s one of the original developers brought the Game of Life to the United States. Over one long Labor Day week-end in 1982, I was fortunate enough to play the Game of Life with her myself, along with four other friends as players. Considering the theme of this book, need I shout from the rooftops to validate my insane enthusiasm for this experience, or for that matter, to prove the remarkable string of amazing coincidences that wove themselves throughout my whole life, the end game sight-unseen still?

The idea was to ask the Game three questions. Throughout the course of the Game, the questions would be answered. I by-passed the usual questions about love, career and mundane concerns of the other players and went for the Really Big Questions: Who am I and what am I doing here?

The Game of Life stands out as one of my most consciousness-changing experiences; precisely at the nexus of a specific universal moment inseparably bound to reveal a personal destiny. The name itself was certainly prophetic! I'm sure it activated some subconscious shadow that would someday reflect the theme of this book. My role in life—one of my questions—was revealed to me that day as that of a shaman.

What a shock at a time when I was devoted to being a first-class professional astrologer to support myself and do what I thought was surely my mission. Only later I learned that every shaman needs a day job! I visualized myself squatting in the forest and dining on monkey meat. I seemed to be obsessed with monkey meat! I was relieved to eventually understand that twenty-first century shaman can stay in the civilized world and need not give up their wardrobes.

Findhorn continues to represent the hope that if mankind will only cooperate with Nature, even sandy deserts can spring forth with life. Oh, yes! There is real communication possible between worlds! Messages from the Tree Devas answered questions explaining the deepest mysteries about the Earth and all of Life. The beginning of this chapter introduced the concept of Oneness and Unity embracing powerful forces other than human. This quote from a book about the Findhorn experiment sums it up eloquently, "Life is a unity poured out into infinite diversity and playing into myriads of beautiful forms."

Elementals You Don't Invite to Dinner

Nevertheless, it is a huge mistake to regard all Elementals as helpful and loving, like happy little innocent children at play. Many indeed are exactly like that. Yet, consider this with caution: There are those with nasty dispositions at the very least and those who are downright evil and dangerous at the very worst.

Don't even think for a minute that since you are a Christian with only love, love, love in your heart that you may safely play kissy-face with Evil and the Dark Side. I should know; I have met some of you head-in-the-clouds-feet-off-the-ground-love everybody-to-death-airheads whom I risk my behind to save your sorry butts from the jaws of the demons. Get real.

The 3rd dimension is one of polarity. One of the polarities separates into the Light and the Dark. Refer to "The Larch Mountain Adventure" by my son, David Bills (next chapter). I didn't say that we must hold hate in our hearts; but if some bastard from the Dark Side tries to get my son; I'm taking the nice bastard out.

More About the Elemental Kingdom

There is more material about the Elemental Kingdom that is very extensive in a book by Patricia Cota-Robles *Who Am I? Why Am I Here?* I recommend it if you would like to plunge into this subject that speaks about humanity's long relationship with the Elemental Kingdom and the rift that caused them to separate from humanity for long periods of time. She describes how that rift was healed at The First Earth Summit in Rio de Janeiro, Brazil, June 1-14, 1992. There is an article in the book, "Making Peace with the Elemental Kingdom."

The Mole Story

If you are a lightworker, this is preaching to the choir. You are well aware of the multidimensionality of life. Indeed, it's very likely you've developed a comfortable relationship with other Beings in doing your own work. But for many other readers, this may well be their first introduction to other forms of life.

My next meaningful foray into "interspecies communication" after the ant episode, happened to be with what was possibly a several-generations, family group of moles who had taken up residence in the yard of the house I had just purchased in Portland, Oregon. The moles had made a terrible mess of things. There was a huge pile of dirt over an extensive area of my half-acre lot. It was terribly unsightly. It resembled a small scale model of the Matterhorn. My neighbor assured me that I would never get rid of them.

Every reader at this point should understand that the moles are merely the outer physical manifestation of a very real consciousness—a Mole Deva living on a plane of existence invisible to human sight. The next logical step would be to contact the Deva and negotiate a deal. I was brimming with confidence after my initial success with the Ant Deva.

This time I went into meditation and pictured the moles suffering horrible deaths, tortured in the metal jaws of a hideous looking trap that I had seen once in a garden catalog. But I was nice. I offered an alternative. There was a good-sized woods across the street from my house. The moles could move there and plunder the earth until the cows came home. Who cared? I made a solemn oath that the moles would be guaranteed safe passage if they vacated their residence in my yard in three days. Otherwise, they would face the dreaded death traps. Okay, so that was where my consciousness was then.

I am here to tell you that these things don't always go as planned, as I was soon to discover with horror. After a couple of days, my son came running into the house to tell me that moles by the dozens were invading Mr. Mueller's back yard and that he was "really mad." Mr. Mueller was my neighbor directly across the street, and whose back yard bordered the woods in question: the moles new home. Something was askew with their radar because the moles missed the woods by a good 50 feet! I feared for the moles safety. There was no telling what Mr. Mueller may have in mind for a mole eradication program.

I raced to my bedroom for a fast meditation, which I fervently hoped would quickly reach the ears of the Mole Deva. If Mr. Mueller whacked, trapped or poisoned a mole before I explained the situation, my neighbor's prophesy about never ridding my yard of moles could well be fulfilled.

Be it far from me to claim any appreciation of the finer points of organization in the mole kingdom, but I was less than impressed with the sloppy transfer from my yard to the woods. However, moles do travel underground and perhaps are owed a 50-foot error in latitude in the dirt highway. Anyway, in the greatest of earnest, I warned the Mole Deva to get the moles the hell out of there. I couldn't be responsible for what may happen in Mr. Mueller's yard. I was new at this after all.

This could have been the end of the mole story. Despite a little glitch, I assumed with total confidence that the Mole Deva could make the necessary adjustments; the moles would have a safe home and both Mr. Mueller's and my yards would be forever free of moles. Win, win, win.

Unfortunately, this was not the end of the story. The next chapter unfolded a couple of nights after the moles were actually spotted trekking into the woods. I was relaxing with my husband over a drink in a gazebo that was near the house, enjoying my triumph. The gazebo was in full view of the yard that included a nearby grape arbor.

What unfolded next was one of those things that happen so fast it is almost like time goes into slow motion. I glanced under the grape arbor. What did I see? a mole sticking its head above ground, a very bad decision as it turned out. Before I knew it, my husband grabbed a garden hoe that I was using earlier in the day, ran over and *chopped the mole's head off.* I was beyond horrified. I was screaming. I was hysterical. I was in trouble.

"YOU MANIAC! YOU MURDERER! YOU MONSTER!" I screamed. The really odd thing about this incident is that my husband at the time was a guy that would be the last person in the world to do such a thing. It was completely out of character. I do not know to this day what ever possessed him (note to astrologers: a Libran).

He was unaware of my deal with the Mole Deva. I wanted to tell him the whole story only after I knew it worked. I was in trouble with the Mole Deva for sure. I promised the moles safe passage, and now one of them had been murdered. I envisioned some terrible mole karma. I don't know how mole karma works, but it could have something to do with death traps and being buried alive in a dirt grave.

After all was said and done, I somehow managed to make things right and rid my yard of moles. It was complicated, but I suspect it involved Life in Mole Manor. I assume that they are still in the woods living the good life. Perhaps Mole Paradise earned me an act of grace, and I'm good to go with the Mole Deva.

Multi-level Communications

Each person chooses what their belief systems can embrace as true and believable. The theme of this chapter is not about this choice, but rather asks the question: Are there invisible forces accessible to humans? As to whispering directly into the ear of God, I leave to: 1) those who have achieved mastery, and 2) to the others, who are delusional schizophrenics. Therefore, if you are not confined to either an ashram or a mental ward, let's deal with this subject in a manner that is realistic to the likes of you and me.

Yes, we humans *can* access the evolutionary forces closest to us: 1) the Elementals just *below* the frequency of humanity, and 2) the Devas just *above* the frequency of humanity. We may stretch our consciousness wider in welcome to a great many more citizens—seen and unseen—in this Universe besides us. If there was ever any doubt about that, the following story should make a believer of anyone except the most intractable closed-minded skeptic. This may be a story about a species that does not communicate in English, but there sure is one whale of a ruckus going on outside of human earshot!

THE CLEVE BAXTER STORY

In one of my regular newsletters, I recommended David Wilcock's new book *The Source Field Investigations.* I was shaking with excitement about something in the very first chapter—something I have not read or thought about in over 40 years when Max Freedom Long reported this long-running story in his monthly newsletters. It's like something that happens and you can't wait to run home and tell your mom.

Mr. Baxter's first claim to fame was as a hypnotist. He gave demonstrations that astounded audiences. He then went on to develop the lie detector test, still used today, of course. Now I am going to share some of his other research. Before I do I want to warn you that it may make you a bit squeamish at first. It involves plants. How can you be squeamish about PLANTS? We'll see.

This is what the mystery is all about. Baxter's sister brought two plants into his apartment. He had never been a plant owner before. After one long, weary night of non-stop work, he went to his kitchen for a cup of coffee. In one of those rare moments from which genius sometimes springs out of the blue, he looked at the cane dracaena and wondered what it would do if he hooked it up to the lie detector. He was mildly surprised when it showed some rather jagged activity.

As we all know from the many TV shows, the lie detector responds when the person tells a lie. Well, you can't very well scowl at the cane dracaena and demand to know if he shot his wife. If a person feels threatened, there is a skin response. So Baxter tried to think of something that would threaten the plant. He decided to take a match and burn a leaf. (See, you are feeling squeamish already, aren't you?)

Is Your Philodendron depressed? Does your rubber plant hate you?

Here is what is really fascinating. BEFORE Baxter went to the desk to get the matches, the plant went crazy and began "screaming"—just at Baxter's thought alone. It behaved as though it could read his mind. David Wilcock goes on to document Baxter's research even further in his book. All of the eggs in the carton—unfertilized—reacted when one of their brothers and sisters hit the hot oil in your frying pan. Now don't you feel ashamed of yourself?

The sink in Baxter's lab was getting really scroungy. He used boiling water to clean it and the plants started "screaming" when the bacteria got fried. The same thing happened when brine shrimp—often used in experiments—met the same fate. One of the most interesting experiments was with human cells. Oh, yes, even these danced around the lie detector in reaction to all kinds of emotions—positive and negative. All of us animal lovers will have no trouble believing this about animals. But think about this: All forms of life are "hearing," or reacting, to even our thoughts and feelings and our emotions. The next time your favorite plant won't go to bed on time, just rip off a leaf.

I may be preaching to the choir as far as regular lightworkers reading this goes, but our most powerful spiritual guiding principle is that EVERYTHING IS ONE. I don't know where you new guys are coming from, but here is one so-called metaphysical-religious principle that tends to be confirmed through Baxter's years of experiments.

I digress for a moment to remind you folks who signed on for the Ready for Prime Time Players group—or anyone else who wishes to observe this ritual as well. (Prime Time Players and other game-players are discussed in other chapters.) You were instructed to hold your open hands, palms down, about eight inches over any food before you ate it. You repeated three times, "I raise this food to my vibration. I am the conscious master of every cell in my body. Every cell in my body is nourished by this food."

If you remember, I implored you to be discreet in restaurants; other patrons may mistake you for praying. (So hey, that's my sense of humor.) Hmmm, so that leads to praying. Perhaps I was serious after all. Where do you think that grace really originated anyway: Maybe our ancient ancestors knew something we have forgotten? People in ancient times knew this: in daily life, respect the consciousness of fire, the consciousness of your cooking pot, *of the food that you eat.* There is consciousness in everything, absolutely everything! There is consciousness in every separate animate and inanimate existence in this Universe, in this reality and every other reality. It is at base, consciousness.

In his book, Wilcock reports that whenever he lectures about this, the audience inevitably groans when finding out that "vegetables, fruit, yogurt, eggs, and the living cells in raw meat are all 'screaming' when they are cooked and/or eaten." Even vegan/vegetarian/raw foodists, who consider themselves on a cruelty-free diet, are now faced with the reality that all the food they eat go through measurable distress—at least from a human perspective. Even if you eat your veggies raw, the digestion of food goes through a burning process. But now here is the part that made the whole book worth it. I quote:

> "Baxter did tell me (Wilcock) that if you 'pray' over your food by sending it positive, loving thoughts, it then seems to accept its role in helping you stay alive—and these reactions no longer occur on the graph paper (of the lie detector). Many cultures and spiritual traditions encourage us to 'thank our food.' "

The next time your mom serves you spinach I suggest you quit saying it tastes like sh**. I am on speaking terms with the Elementals of spinach and they have received so much abuse from kids that they are very cranky. If you don't express some gratitude, I have known some people whose "bodily excretions" are bright green for the rest of their lives.

By the way, maybe your husband loves to go hunting, but you are a lightworker and are opposed to it on moral grounds. Or maybe it's your wife that is out in the woods slaughtering everything that moves. You may contact the animal spirit also, and it is happy to play its role in the food chain. The next time you sit down to venison steak, thank the animal spirit and the philodendron will quit screaming.

This just goes to demonstrate that probably all of the metaphysical/spiritual beliefs that are discussed here will NOT be given science's blessing. Just don't hold your breath. Unfortunately, that group is one of the most conservative, closed-minded groups on the planet. It usually takes them at least 20 years to catch up to the truth. Not surprisingly, many science researchers to this day regard experiments with plants as ridiculous. I'm sure all of their plants are screaming their heads off all the time. Those skeptics may wake up some morning and find ivy wrapped tightly around their necks... tighter...and tighter...and tighter...and tighter....

I decided to include this next story after Cleve Baxter's. It seemed a timely place to interject a bit of romance.

A LOVE STORY

The Story of Bogie and Bacall

By Rex Bills

I moved into a house in 1974 that included a small greenhouse attached to a dining room wall with French doors. I acquired a few plants that didn't grow in Oregon because of cold winters. One was a bougainvillea in a pot. I admired them growing all over houses in California, and later found them dazzling in the Greek Isles growing

Rex's Greenhouse with Bogie and Bacall

against pure white buildings, blue, blue skies and water. I'm not sure when I started calling the plant Bogie, but I had recently read Franklin Loehr's book *The Power of Prayer on Plants.* I was convinced that plants had feelings, so it was the start of

naming special plants in my life. Bogie rewarded me with one or two small blossomings each summer.

I have kept Bogie alive ever since, and he is still in his 12-inch pot, watered and fed occasionally. A little fertilizer in the water seemed to satisfy him. Then on a trip to Southern Oregon one summer several years ago, I found another plant like Bogie in a hanging pot and added him/her to my greenhouse. Both plants began to thrive, and I could clearly see that Bogie was recovering from loneliness. Both plants started blooming profusely, not just in the summer, but in the winter as well. I hold the greenhouse above freezing to keep the plants alive at about 40 degrees.

Last winter the greenhouse was colder than usual, and both plants went into a tailspin, losing their leaves. I thought I had killed them both, but a spring inspection showed a tiny green shoot on Bogie at the base of the plant. I cut the plant back to see what would happen. He grew a few leaves. But, alas, Bacall was totally dead. Gardeners don't offer them for sale here unless they have blooms, so I had to wait until late spring before I found a three-foot-tall floor plant ablaze with purple flowers. The new Bacall was quickly put beside Bogie on his waist-high stand. Bogie began to explode, sending out three-foot branches in all directions with double-sized leaves and profuse flowers. Bacall finally dropped all of her flowers and went into a growing spell following Bogie's sideways advances. She is now just starting to produce the beginning of little flower buds. In a month she will be spectacular, and they may just take over the greenhouse. Ain't love grand!

****

Invisible Animal Spirits

In our first book in this trilogy *The Lightbody Activation Manual,* my brother and coauthor, Duane Henkle, described a scene in which he is sitting by the oceanside when one of the wonderful big sea turtles approached him and offered its services in the lightbody activation work. I remind again that those who have done the Crystal Triangle Activation will recognize the crystal placed at one point of the triangle is dedicated to Turtle, not turtle. It wasn't the physical turtle who had a sit-down chat with Duane that day. It was the Animal Spirit of all turtles, Turtle, who spoke to Duane's inner ear.

Animal totems, animals as spirit guides, power animals or animals as allies are all associated with shamanism, the world's oldest healing tradition. Accompanying the explosion of New Age consciousness in the Sixties, animal power moved from traditional cultures into mainstream awareness.

Everyone has an animal spirit guide, often more than one. Your animal allies may change from time to time as some come and go in accordance with your current activities. I have noticed special animals temporarily coming into the life of a pregnant woman, for example. They act as teachers and guides and if you have the patience to connect with them, the experiences will enrich your life.

My shamanic healing clients from all over the world frequently asked me to identify their power animals. Rather than do it for them, I recommended a book by Edwin Steinbrecher *The Inner Guide Meditation.* The book has instructions for connecting with your guides as well. I believe also that this book offers the safest and most sure-fire way to develop your psychic skills. A big advantage is that you can practice the technique by yourself any time, any where (not while driving).

However, my husband and I have valued the *Inner Guide Meditation* for years, and find it works amazingly well with a partner, especially if each person describes aloud the images he or she is seeing. It builds confidence to take the risk to just speak out loud, rather than wandering around lost in second guessing.

If you are a virgin when it comes to psychic work, it's best to begin with a partner who will encourage you to speak. It is possible to enjoy some amazing adventures with your guides and animal powers. Go ahead and surprise yourself. You will realize after a while that this work is not just imaginary, but will have an impact on your so-called real world.

Just so there is no misunderstanding, a totem animal need not be physically present, in fact, that is typically the case. Also, your pets are probably not your totem animals. My main power animal is Tiger. I have been aware of him for many years. That does not mean that I have a real jungle cat hanging out in the back yard. Has anyone seen Spot lately? (Kidding! Kidding!)

While on the subject of pets, this reminds me of another question that I hear from worried animal lovers. Are there animals in the 5th dimension? A few clients are so attached to their pets that they are actually conflicted about ascending to a higher frequency without them.

I am not saying anywhere in this book that I personally know for certain what is going to happen as the ascension process continues to unfold right now, on December 21, 2012, or beyond. Nevertheless, I have been exposed to voluminous writings and reliable channelings for over 30 years. It is my belief at this time that humanity does not ascend as the only species to do so. I think the entire animal kingdoms rise to a higher frequency as well. It makes intuitive sense to me. Some sources describe a world in which all creatures are vegetarian, that is, if they even ingest solid food at all (See the chapter "Food for Thought."), and that peace and harmony reigns among all species of life.

Meanwhile, learn to be more acutely aware of signs from Nature's animal, bird or fish kingdoms, or any others that happen to appear in your environment. Each one means something to you personally, even bird tracks in fresh mud. The Devic and Elemental powers bring information that have relevance to specific circumstances that exist in your life at any given time.

The more seriously you invite Nature's messages, the more she rushes to communicate with you. It is not only whether the sign happens to be a soaring eagle or a spider in the corner; it is the amazing timing, or synchronicity, that provides the context of the other side of the equation of meaningful coincidence.

When my husband left the house for cataract surgery, a little snake slithered across our path. We had lived here for years without ever seeing even one snake before that morning. We always seriously regard all of Nature's signs set before us. We regularly consult Ted Andrews's book *Animal-Speak.* His book reminded us that snakes are creatures that regularly shed their skins, *even the skin over their eyes.* There was also information about Snake's association with transformation and ascension. What a great confirmation that was for us, considering the circumstances of our life at that time.

When my husband was hospitalized, I had caregivers at the house with me around the clock. As they came and went, they frequently encountered a little snake lying across the sidewalk leading to my front door. For the life of me, I could not figure out his message. I know now. I had not visited my eye doctor in four years. The last time I worked with him, I had cataracts in the earliest stages and glaucoma numbers a bit too high. This doctor was one in a million. He put me on an alternative diet and nutritional supplement plan and, consequently, each condition was completely reversed. After that, both Don and I dealt with serious health issues. All the while, however, I thought I had a home-free card as far as my eyes were concerned.

Recently I thought it was about time to have my eyes checked and get a new prescription for my glasses. I was very disappointed to find out that my eye doctor had retired. I made an appointment with the woman who replaced him, thinking she had probably apprenticed under him. Was I wrong! She gave me a perfunctory test for a glasses prescription and that was that. There was no mention made of cataracts. To make a long story short, I found out from a second doctor that I had very advanced cataracts in both eyes. I was stunned and also angry that the first doctor didn't mention it.

What I was really angry about was my four-year delay in consulting my eye doctor. I would have found out that the cataracts were returning, but at an early stage, giving me the opportunity to institute the alternative program once again. Now it is too late. The cataracts are too advanced. That is why I am undergoing cataract surgeries later this month as I write this. Poor snaky; he was trying to warn me to have my eyes checked for cataracts all that time.

Update: I underwent two successful cataract surgeries on propitious astrological dates in 2012.

Scarab Beetle

On another occasion, an ally appeared, demonstrating that they often come voluntarily in response to a problem with which one is struggling without success. Don, David and I were up against a very difficult case years ago, tearing our hair out in frustration. We were working with the client in person at the time. We were making absolutely no headway in clearing the patterns. I never encountered a problem so totally stuck.

All of us were utterly exhausted as we had been frantically trying everything for an entire night. It's not that we expected a total healing in one fell swoop. However, in our healing work, we never questioned our ability to get things started in the right direction enough to know that the condition was at least unstuck, but not this time. Along about 2:00 a.m., we reluctantly threw in the towel. I think we were in shock that we actually had to admit defeat.

Then out of the blue, a little helper appeared unbidden in our psychic vision. It was the scarab beetle. We looked on in amazement as he took over and cleared our client's intractable neurological disorder. Unmistakably pronounced and dramatic symptoms that we had been battling unsuccessfully vanished one by one. The client stood up from the healing table, looking around in puzzlement about why we seemed so surprised.

Scarab Beetle has been our power ally ever since. His area of expertise is the deep cellular memory banks, and he loves to go munching his way through all the debilitating neurological snarls there. Some of the cases he has worked on have produced spectacular results. If you invite him to dinner, maybe he will do the honors for you. However, you're the entrée, you understand.

One last story about animals again introduces the notion that there are indeed unseen forces that connect to our physical reality. When Thomas admonished us to "let it all hang out" and express our personal Truth, an outrageously amusing incident followed. Call it a confirmation if you like. We were sitting in my family room at the time of this conversation. There are sliding class doors opening onto the deck.

When David first startled me out of my wits by hollering and gesturing sans intelligent speech, I could not imagine what ailed him. Once I realized that he was not suffering a seizure, I finally understood that he was directing our attention to activity on the deck. There stood Mr. Raccoon, *for real,* upright on his hind legs, flinging outstretched "arms" to each side. The noisy commotion in the room did not spook him at all. He stood motionless on hind legs for an extraordinary length of time, his face plastered against the glass. I think he was aided by someone's assistance of the unseen kind!

Later that evening we once again consulted Ted Andrews's book *Animal-Speak* by. Not surprisingly, it echoed Thomas's uncloaking ceremony (See Chapter One) in which he spoke about taking off our coats and removing our masks. What better creature to deliver the message that night than the animal kingdom's premier masked man!

Crystals are King!

However, I surely cannot finish this chapter without a salute to the mineral kingdom, a world that boasts the inclusion of a huge variety of crystals. Obviously, I have been involved with crystals in the ascension work (the Crystal Triangle), and my last name is no accident either (more on names later). For a long time the mineral kingdom admittedly did not inspire the romance and prestige of say, the plant kingdom's grand rain forests with its crown jewel, the giant Sequoia, or the animal kingdom's captivating influence over human kind.

Well, yes, it could boast about its special place on milady's fourth finger, left hand. Nevertheless, it was not the glamorous diamond, but the crystal that rose to the evolutionary apex of the mineral world. Among other things of note, it is a main player in a world-wide revolution, the Information Age. And to do that it needed a computer!

It is hard to know where to begin when the subject of the discussion is crystals. The temptation is to go willy-wonkers in every direction and completely lose sight of the whole point of this chapter, or even this whole book. Remember you are dealing with one of the authors of the *Lightbody Activation Manual* (it says so on the cover). The lightbody activation itself utilizes three specially programmed crystals. It's called the Crystal Triangle. Our publishing company is named after it. My last name is *Stone,* do I need to draw a picture?

The purpose of this chapter is to widen human consciousness so as to recognize the spark of life in all things, to really embrace the larger meaning of Unity and Oneness in order to restore harmony and balance to our planet. Since the explosion of interest in crystals in the Sixties, most readers will likely not need reminding that crystals are connected to an energy source that is participating in the transformation of the human body into a vehicle that will transport it to another dimension of reality, its merkaba, or the crystalline lightbody itself!

I could drop the subject of crystals at that, but I receive more questions about this than any other subject. And since the other two books are so closely involved with them, I decided to answer the most frequently asked questions.

The procurement of crystals for whatever personal use is a troubling problem for many people who write in. How do you know which crystals to buy? First of all, try not to make a big deal out of it. You can't really make a mistake, and it should be fun. The only downside is its effect on your wallet. The best first step is to focus on an intention to shake hands with the crystals friendliest to your needs. Savvy crystal collectors believe that your intention will reach the "crystal ears" meant for you. Whether that is true or not, it is a good exercise in focusing your intuition and opening the door for synchronicity to work.

You are lucky if there is a rock shop in your area. Otherwise, many metaphysical book stores also carry candles, tarot decks and crystals. There is always the Internet. If you are sensitive to energies, just move your hands over some crystals and see if you get a buzz. Otherwise, just pick out the ones that appeal to you.

Crystals need not be expensive. Price does not determine their effectiveness or desirability. Clear rock quartz is inexpensive, widely available and fully as effective as more costly varieties. I have a preference for rose quartz, and have found it many times shaped into a heart. I have a heart-shaped pink quart crystal for the Dolphin point of the Crystal Triangle.

Don and I found that it has a mind of its own! We had permanently set up the Crystal Triangle in our bedroom. The pink crystal was on the table holding our TV set. One day Don and I were seated on the edge of our bed. I'm glad both of us were there to witness little pinky jump off the table onto the floor—not once—but twice, several days later.

Obviously it did not like competing with the TV, or maybe the TV energy was interfering with its own. I've been aware that crystals will indicate where they are most comfortable in your house, but I did not think it meant quite that literally! Again, don't get all uptight about it. It is one way, however, to develop your intuition to just make a game of it at first. Hold your hands over one of your crystals, ask your question, close your eyes and wait for an image to come.

Remember, you do have a say in the matter. If the image that appears in your mind's eye is really ridiculous, you are most likely dealing with your own subconscious trying to put one over on you. You don't seriously believe any crystal chooses to live in your refrigerator's veggie crisper next to the lettuce. An alternative is to carry the crystal to different places in your house and feel when you get buzzed. Crystals are great communicators. They do seem to figure out a way to "talk" to you. Play with them and see what happens.

We have a huge rock quartz crystal cluster that loves to be in the middle of things. There have been times when energy levels are high and the noise reaches the upper decibels around here. I wondered if the crystal would be happier in a quiet corner. But I never felt any vibes to that effect. On the other hand, I have crystals that like taking refuge in desk drawers or anywhere else that is not out in the open. So how do I know that crystals are talking to me? It's an intuition, a gut feeling, just something that becomes increasingly real the more I acknowledge that everything has consciousness and will interact with humans.

All of your personal crystals should be cleared—or zeroed out—and programmed with whatever information or energies you desire. Are they going to be healing crystals? Or consciousness-raising crystals? They can be whatever you like. First, clean crystals with hot, soapy water and a little brush, if necessary. Then rinse them in water to which sea salt has been added. It is best to let them dry in the sun for two or three days. That can be a problem if you live in the Northwest!

Programming the crystals for doing the lightbody activations is thoroughly explained in the *Lightbody Activation Manual.* I'll not repeat it here. Those are special crystals that must not be used for any other purpose. It is a very good idea to have several nice cleared crystals that you especially like, dispersed about the house. I say this because these are special times that we are living through right now.

As the ascension process unfolds, you should understand by now that your body is changing into your lightbody, your crystalline lightbody. The frequency of the physical body is shifting; yet, we still live in the physical density of the 3D world. I address these remarks particularly to you lightworkers who know you have awakened. The ascension symptoms are going to be increasingly physically taxing for you. Crystals can play an important role in "lightening" up the general energy levels in your house. Just program them to the light, and stash them around the house.

I prefer clear rock quartz for this purpose. They need not be very big, but not just pebbles, either. Check on them every six months or so. Don't be surprised if some of them are showing black places. That means they are absorbing negative energies. Don't worry about it. It doesn't mean your partner is evil or anything. The dark spots are just ordinary stuff that is floating around out there. I had a good-sized clear quartz crystal cluster in the counseling room in my office in Portland. After 10 years or so, I had to let it go into retirement, it got so black. It was just doing its job clearing the accumulation of intense emotional issues from many clients.

And sometimes they will take *themselves* out! Elsewhere in this book and others, I recounted my brother Duane's experience with a green stone given to me at an astrology conference.

Inanimate Objects

Don and I got the shock of the year when we stumbled across an item in Dolores Cannon's *Convoluted Universe Book Three.* A reminder that Dolores Cannon's techniques involve placing subjects in a special deep trance that she calls the *somnambulistic state.* The information comes directly from the subject's recall of their own experiences.

This is not channeling. I find Cannon's method more credible only for the reason that channeled information always passes through the channeler's subconscious. There is always the chance that strongly held beliefs or unresolved subconscious patterns of any sort may hit hot buttons and skew certain psychic material. That is why anyone involved in psychic work is ethically responsible for undertaking continual search and destroy missions to clear problem patterns. When I began working with my Spirit Teacher, Thomas, it was soon obvious that he subscribed to undertaking one's inner work big time!

One of Cannon's subjects in deep trance reported on one of her past life experiences, which was not unusual in itself. What was unusual is that the past life was described as a *little metal piece in a larger mechanical robot!* The subject, Tina, began weeping as she described an impossibly sad life—exhausting and relentless. It was total servitude. There was no choice and no hope and utter despair, without knowing if it would ever end. She repeated the same tiring job over and over.

The following is a quote from the book. This was shockingly conscious-expanding for Don and me. Her weeping turned to sobbing as she described the saddest part of all:

> "...and no gratitude, because they don't even know that we can feel. And if they would know, I don't think they would care. We are just doing their bidding continuously, continuously." And she went on to say, "It was horrible being this little thing...there was teaching in this. Even though the consciousness was mechanically installed into that robot—it's like written on my forehead—there is much more consciousness in everything, everywhere."

I prided myself in recognizing that everything has consciousness, but when I read about the little robot, a whole new awareness opened up, a whole new world of conscious inanimate objects. The little robotic creature despaired because no one ever acknowledged her or cared. The most heart wrenching, the hardest thing to bear, even beyond the loneliness was no acknowledgement, no respect. I never thought I could grow teary-eyed over a ball bearing!

I'm Sorry! I'm Sorry!

Omygod, the *computer.* There were times when the computer was addressed as $@^$*&+! *There is nothing that does not have consciousness connected to it.*

Perhaps it is time to make nice with the computer. Perhaps it's time we expressed gratitude for all of the unseen things that we ourselves have created in our technology. When creating something of metal, we unknowingly implant that small spark of life that gives it consciousness.

What we have to realize is that technology has consciousness. Every manufactured thing possesses consciousness. *Everything has consciousness,* but this time it really means it! Your morning Starbucks coffee has consciousness. Though these things are not sentient Beings as we are, consciousness is there. To acknowledge this connects us in greater harmony with all things. We may believe that we are aware of our surroundings, but I believe it is safe to say that we have a long way to go to appreciate life in all of its forms.

This insightful warning is by Ruth Montgomery's Guide, Frederick, from her book *Aliens Among Us:*

> "If we observe life we see that there is a balance between all natural elements, including bird, trees, and animals and all such elements are unconsciously in tune with the Creator's plans. Man is the only expression...created with free will...if man uses his free will...to exploit for selfish reasons, he is out of harmony with the natural order. This imbalance registers in...the astral body, and we carry it wherever we go. That is why selfishness and greed create evil and make us suffer. Nature exacts every debt."

Numerology: The Invisible Energy Around Numbers

We do not ordinarily associate the science of numerology with an invisible force that may be influencing our lives. However, every number and every letter associated with it has its own contributing impact. It exists all around you from your name, your street address and to every other article, animate or inanimate, that has a name.

Maybe this is why I have intuitively named my cars. I swear that each car does have a personality. And speaking of names, this brings up something else that impacts our life—a subject I know little about, numerology. Most of you have probably at least looked up the numerical value of your name from a basic numerology book. And like me, that was about the extent of it. However, I can titillate you with a story about numerology and intrigue, which reached all the way to Buckingham Palace! A curious combination, no?

First of all, I want to be clear that I am in no way diminishing numerology when in the hands of someone practiced in the craft. I know this is true because I met a person who is perhaps one of the most skilled numerologists in the world. He has visited me in my home several times. He made it clear that he was living here because he was "lying low," and that there was a good reason for doing so.

I barely refrained from prying. However, even from experiences with my astrological practice, there are circumstances in which a practitioner may know a little too much—at least in some people's opinions. Or maybe the man just needed a time-out and a rest, nothing more mysterious than that.

When he offered to give us a numerology analysis, everyone who was present eagerly took him up on it. I am a professional astrologer and I must say that I am no slouch when it comes to my craft as well. I can attest that his work equaled anything astrology ever offered. It was deeply impressive.

For example, one thing that has stuck in my craw my entire life is that I never completed a degree after high school. Whenever I attended university classes, I did well with the work and loved the academic world, but always stopped short of a degree. I have credentials parked here and there, but never gathered them together to represent a diploma hanging on the wall.

Surprisingly, when Mr. Numerology Guy read my numerology patterns, he implored me to avoid a higher education. My Destiny was to play a role in changing established institutions from the outside. If I were caught up in academic studies too far, there was a clear and present danger that I would derail my soul mission intended for the road less traveled. I am forever grateful for this information, which allowed me to put this matter to rest once and for all.

He could not have been more right on. The lion's portion of my knowledge is what I acquired by intense studies on my own. My career grew from these studies. That is not to say that I diminish the value of my academic work, which actually does represent a solid liberal arts foundation. Even more to the point, I have been an enthusiastic player in enlightening established professions to the alternative side of the street. I have lectured to many organizations in other fields, primarily those of a medical and psychological orientation. Even the Lions Clubs have been on the receiving end of my luncheon lectures over dessert.

Numerology Guy then shared a story about cooling his heels in a Buckingham Palace reception room. He darkly admonished us that the details were for our ears only. I'm dying to tell you and I know this is really mean, but a secret is a secret and a promise is a promise. At least this way you will remember, even words and names carry energy that you cannot see, but exert a powerful influence in your life—even if you are of royal blood! (In the chapter on DNA, even more astonishing information about language is included.)

Don't you wonder how a woman's life may be changed when she takes a spouse's last name? Instead of a marriage counselor, maybe we would be better advised to ask a numerologist how our names are affecting relationships. In researching this part of the book, I found an article that was the subject of a serious research study. People with very unusual or impossible to pronounce names generally do have a strike against them in achieving success in life; obviously there are exceptions.

I once consulted a numerologist years ago, and she cautioned that I would never make much money until I got an *o* in my name. She turned out to be right. Coincidence? At least something good came from marrying Russ Stone (my second husband). The reason I was so desperate to earn money was because I wanted to achieve financial independence in order to leave that marriage!

There is a weird story connected to my first name. When my dad was a little kid, he would every once in a while take a notion to dress up in his mother's dresses and parade around insisting he be called, "Diana." Why?–because he knew he would have a daughter some day and that was her name. I suppose I should be grateful that he didn't dress up like a chicken or something.

I originally intended to discuss the energy around names, numbers and letters in more depth until I happened onto Lee Carroll's *Kryon, Book Twelve: The Twelve Layers of DNA.* My inner circle has been interested in following Kryon's teachings for at least 15 years. Of all the channeled material out there, Kryon's information has been consistent and reliable. He introduced subjects many years before circumstances proved him prophetic.

I must admit that it was the last place that I expected to find the last word on numerology! The material is very complex, and far beyond including a simple review with a few quotes thrown in to accommodate the purpose of this chapter. If you want to delve into this very esoteric take on numerology, it's out there. I certainly recommend it, but don't expect any *personal* interpretations. The point I want to make anyway is that there is energy around numbers; just another invisible player that has an impact on our lives.

You may appreciate this one quote from the Kryon book mentioned above:

> "Numerology is a multidimensional system of old, and a conceptual system of energy developed by the far more advanced group of spiritual thinkers than we currently are experiencing. Within the pages of this book, the system I am going to speak of is simple, and right out of ancient Tibet."

What About Planetary and Galactic Beings?

Let's talk about something a bit prettier that everyone surely has heard about since childhood as well. What we are doing now is moving back to that big arc I asked you to imagine earlier, and looking to the evolutionary forces *above* humankind. These are the Beings of *ascending* order. They are also varied, and form lesser to greater ranks.

In the West, we have favored the descriptions of these *higher* beings as Devas, Angels and Archangels, which establishes their rank in ascending order.

The Earth is a sentient Being and is going through her own ascension process. The same is true for all of the planets in our solar system. As an astrologer, I feel a special kinship with the planets and have spent time meditating on each one, especially throughout the early years of my studies.
I can share an interesting story I experienced with the planet, Venus. I was trying to meditate on each planet until I really understood the essence of each one. For some reason, I was really struggling with Venus. I carried a picture of the planet stuck in the sun visor of my car. I had key words fixed with magnets to my refrigerator. I focused on it constantly.

One day I settled down with a new astrology book by Marc Edmund Jones, one of astrology's greats. All of a sudden I came to a paragraph that was just what I was looking for. It absolutely captured the core essence of Venus. I jumped up to copy it into my notebook in which I recorded such nuggets of wisdom. I quickly recorded what I could remember. Thinking that it would be advisable to copy it exactly from the book, I brought the book to the table with that in mind. When I looked for the paragraph, it was not on the page where I had found it. It wasn't on any other page either for that matter. I should know. I've looked at every page in that book every few years or so, and it has not turned up yet. Did Venus speak directly to me that day?
Let's not forget the king of our solar system, the Sun. I receive regular reports via email from Mitch Battros. He keeps us all abreast of the solar "weather." Below is a typical quote from one of the reports that underscores the key role our own Solar Being is playing in the ascension process:

> "Mitch Battros presents fascinating, and sometimes shocking, research from the world's top scientists. After years of dialogue with these experts, Mitch has been accepted into the guarded halls of NASA, NOAA, ESA, Royal Observatory, the US Naval Observatory and other highly esteemed scientific bodies. In addition to the latest research on the Sun's influence on our "weather," Mitch also presents ground-breaking evidence of how the Sun and other celestial orbs produce 'charged particles' and their impact on humanity... It is more important now than ever before to access the latest breaking news events which affect us all"... ***"I believe it will be the magnetic influence*** *produced by the Sun which will usher in what is described by our ancient ancestors as 'the transition' bringing us to a new state-of-being."*

The name of this chapter is "The Invisible Players." If I wrote a complete treatise on the occult sciences and the great religions of the world, how high up the chain of command could I travel? To whom do the Archangels look for guidance in the Administration of Nature and the carrying out of the Divine Will? Who is the ultimate CEO?

Is it logical to observe the organization in *visible* Nature on the outer realms, yet discount the possible existence of *invisible* forces at least as well organized on the inner realms? Just as it is possible to spiral downward to that little dot just beginning its journey, so, too, do conscious entities travel equally in the opposing upward direction.

In an unbroken stream, there are those who answer to ever higher and higher Intelligences, culminating in an Ultimate Intelligence, the Creator of All That Exists. Some call That God. Conceding that this is an unanswerable question for a 3rd dimension brain incapable of understanding infinity: Who is God's God?

The Higgs Boson: the God Particle

I really am not a student of advanced physics theory, but since there was apparently an historic milestone achieved in that world recently, one that is nicknamed the discovery of the God Particle, I knew that at least a passing reference was called for, anticipating the letters of inquiry. The Higgs boson is named for Peter Higgs who helped develop the theory in the 1960s. The announcement was made in Geneva, Switzerland, the location of the Large Hadron Collider. This is a 17-mile-long oval tunnel and the world's largest atom smasher. Higgs, now a gray-haired gentleman, was in the audience in tears when the announcement was made to a room packed with very excited physicists and reporters.

I certainly am not making any attempt at explaining the finer technical points from the physicists' point of view. However, it was "by coincidence" that I just happened to have the TV on in my office when the announcement was made. I jotted down some notes that were most pertinent. At first, it seemed obvious that I should toss this in with "Playing The God Game" chapter.

As I re-read it, it more and more intuitively felt like an appropriate end to this chapter. The Higgs boson is one of the final puzzle pieces required for a complete understanding of the standard model of physics—the so-far successful theory that explains how fundamental particles interact with the elementary forces of nature. According to the standard, if the Higgs field didn't exist, the Universe would be a very different place. It would be difficult to form atoms. Our orderly world where matter is made of atoms and electrons that form chemical bonds—we wouldn't have that if we did not have the Higgs field. In other words: no galaxies, no stars, no planets, no life on Earth. It explains why objects in our Universe have mass—**and in so doing why even humans have any right to exist,** consequently, the nickname the "God Particle."

Not only is this the end of this chapter, this is the last piece that I wrote for the entire book. That seems fitting since the God Particle is the glue that we could say is what holds everything together.

CHAPTER FIFTEEN

ETs, Spirit Teachers, Guides, Gurus and Psychics.

Persistent stories about little green men from Mars perhaps reflect a collective intuition that we really are not alone in the universe.

Diana Stone

Extraterrestrials

The veil between the dimensions grows ever thinner as the ascension process unfolds. The vibratory frequency to which humanity is exposed escalates at a faster and faster pace. Individuals are awakening to the new consciousness in ever greater numbers. This makes it easier and more commonplace for extraterrestrials, spirit teachers and other beings from other dimensions to make contact telepathically with humans.

Can Psychic Contacts be Trusted?

I'm convinced that there is an unmistakable increase over the past couple of years in the number of people who ask me about alleged contact from the other side. Many of these relationships with invisible beings are legitimate and potentially helpful. However, fears and doubts about this entire subject create confusion and missed opportunities. The unfortunate consequences are that some people shut down because they simply do not know how to deal with this type of unfamiliar experience.

Rather than find themselves in over their heads, many people avoid this unknown territory with a better-safe-than-sorry mindset. Without a trustworthy teacher, I can't say that I blame them. However, the first consideration is a little common sense, a quality that often seems to be inexplicably lacking from otherwise perfectly intelligent, spiritually awakened individuals.

My brother, Duane, and I have communicated with extraterrestrials, guides and spirit teachers since the early eighties. We did not grow up sitting at the feet of the masters who carefully instructed us in the fine art of communicating with invisible beings. Navigating the world of psychic communication involved its own set of difficulties, believe me! We have our days yet of flailing about, questioning if we are just making it all up. When all is said and done, the left brain will never accept information from the subconscious (intuition) as reliable or real. That is not its job. And be glad that it isn't.

Maybe this is the place to add a disclaimer. Whenever we are dealing with other entities that we consider to be separate from us, whether it is channeling or another form of psychic contact, we are connecting with energies about which we cannot totally understand. What we may interpret to be entities separate from ourselves could always be an aspect of our Higher Selves or our multidimensional selves. When I speak to Thomas, my Spirit Teacher, it may be my own High Self for all I know. To me, he is a real teacher on the other side. I can see no harm in accepting ETs, and others, at face value. I don't think it is particularly useful to spend our time attempting to sort it all out. It is more important to stay centered and focused on the relationship, however it presents itself in our lives.

Understanding Intellect Versus Intuition.

To work through the process, first understand that the left-brain, or the logical conscious self, will never abdicate its duties of checking reality against reason and logic (nor would we want it to). Whenever the psychic self "hears" an invisible something speaking to it, the rational self shifts into overdrive. No way will it roll over and play dead.

It is impossible to prove who or what may be addressing you in your mind's ear, so to speak, or even if it is real; therefore, logic dismisses it out of hand or considers the entire subject as unbelievable nonsense. It is a matter of knowing to which station you must attune at any given time—and which to tune out.

Do not underestimate this war between the intuition and the intellect if you are someone working through such issues in your spiritual life. Accept that you will very likely not be prepared right away to decide about the validity of invisible sources. Spiritual development naturally leads to an expanded intuitive function. However, what good is it if you can't accept any psychic information if and when it does come?

Just listen with an open mind. Don't be discouraged if you can't figure everything out right away. Even though information is coming through psychic channels, it does not preclude the fact that there are ways to check things against common sense as well.

Be Careful Judging Psychic Communication Godlike or Satanic

What do you do when you meet a new person? How do you know if *anything* is on the up and up? You aren't going to buy the Brooklyn Bridge. You aren't going to murder an annoying neighbor. Maybe you should make some changes in your diet, though. If it seems logical, check out the information and/or suggestions further.

Analyze everything. A rehash of what you already know is not impressive just because it comes from the other side of the looking glass. The radio and television send messages from people you cannot see and do not know. Do you believe everything you hear? Don't overreact to the extremes of regarding the psychic source as either an all-knowing God or a totally evil-intentioned Satan. I treat everyone *over there* as just regular guys, and I'm not above telling them to shove off now and then. Sorting it all out does not have to be the Mystery of the Ages.

Left Brain, I know That's You

I regularly do past life consultations for my clients. These take up to two hours and are usually by phone. Obviously, this requires sustained focus. All I need is the left-brain nattering away in the background. The beginning of every session—without fail—features this conversation in my head, "There is no such thing as past lives. You will not see any pictures in your mind. You will make a fool of yourself and disappoint your client."

I deal with this by letting things rattle on for a while. I do not take it seriously. I thank the left brain for minding its business and entertaining me. Then I patiently wait with confidence. The game is over. The stream of psychic images can then flow unimpeded.

I commonly work with people who fear that an entity will "take them over," and they won't be able to defend themselves. We don't want to be too cavalier about these matters, because there truly are bad guys and unreliable sources out there. On the other hand, paranoid fears are not realistic either. If you are a relatively stable individual, in most cases you have nothing to fear. It usually doesn't pose much of a threat to take one step at a time and test it out when approached by the other side. With enough practice that twinge in your gut will tell you. The idea of a "gut feeling" is real.

You have no business messing around with psychic involvement when you are suffering from serious mental illness, are in a terribly abusive relationship, are addicted to drugs and/or alcohol and other contraindications that should be obvious.

I sometimes marvel at how Thomas, my Spirit Teacher, put up with my doubts and constant questioning of his veracity. Since his very first appearance, I can say that he has dealt with me with total integrity. He never told me anything that did not prove to be true. We have tested and retested Thomas. Events and signs continue to authenticate the information. My shaman group shares this inside joke following unusually indulgent torrents of confirmations—proof to all but the most irreversible skeptic. "That was confirmation 187,345. We are waiting for 187,346." The left brain just never gives up!

Perhaps the most important thing to remember is that no entity is speaking to you one to one. It is not a phone call. All messages from any psychic source are coming to you via your own subconscious mind. It is always a three-party line. There is always the possibility that messages are colored by your own unresolved inner patterns, biases and prejudices. If you have never done any inner work, the more likely it is that the messages will be distorted or inaccurate. That is why Thomas's work with us focused almost exclusively on resolving our own personal issues.

The other extreme from unjustified fears are situations in which life and health are severely compromised by continued influences from invisible beings. I am referring to cases in which a person suffers horrible consequences from encounters with psychic events so crazy and dangerous that it should be glaringly obvious to anybody with a grain of sense to discontinue the contact immediately.

Even though the situation may look like a total abdication of common sense, it usually turns out that there is an investment in hanging onto the offending entities. Some people are carried away by the glamour of it all. For others, it is an ego trip. For others, it is simply the most exciting thing in an otherwise dull existence. More complicated are the ones in which the Being(s) provides a great deal of valuable information.

That was the case of one of my clients who somehow made her way to me through my shamanic healing practice. She lived in a southern state. I never met her in person. She originally presented with a physical condition. From time to time, she would require long hospitalizations because of inexplicable bleeding from the mouth, together with other bizarre symptoms.

As I worked with her, the story emerged that several years earlier she was approached by a group of entities, only one of whom actually spoke to her, a woman calling herself Mary. She announced that they were interested in channeling medical diagnoses for people.

At first, this group was true to their word. Clients came to her and not only did they receive accurate medical diagnoses, but frequently, very practical advice about healing as well. My client built up a nice little practice as word got around. She may have helped any number of people, but it soon was obvious that she herself was suffering from some alarming symptoms. She was drained of energy and when she contacted me, she had not been out of her apartment for three years, except for hospitalizations. She depended on friends to bring her groceries and attend to her affairs. She spent most of her days lying on a couch.

Over the years, the entity, Mary, grew increasingly demanding and controlling. It was obvious that my client was in way over her head and that this group exercised a very negative—even a life threatening—influence. However, despite my chagrin over the situation and vigorous admonishments to cease and desist, she was not about to let go of the relationship. "Mrs. Doctor" had a nice little practice going that earned her an income. She also enjoyed a certain prestige. Any time she would attempt a feeble protest over something that was blatantly out of line, Mary was an expert manipulator and easily brainwashed her to continue.

I worked with her over a period of months, and it was only when her health reached a really perilous state that she admitted it was life-threatening to continue. She now is in sound health mentally and physically and earns a living as a hair stylist in a salon. This case stands out as an extreme one, but there have been others where there was really no excuse for the individuals involved to trade off life and health for anything the entities might offer. That kind of obvious stupidity is obvious stupidity! It's not that the offending entities jump you in a dark alley when you least expect it after all.

Relationships with invisible beings take time to develop just as they do between your friends and acquaintances here in the 3rd dimension. I suggest you read our first book, *The Lightbody Activation Manual,* as it describes how my brother worked painstakingly step-by-step with the Pleiadian Beings. It is a powerful primer on just this subject because it demonstrates a real -life process and the outcome.

We can recognize now what would have been lost if he had not had the training to recognize the legitimacy of the information! The point is, "By their fruits, you shall know them." You can be sure that for many years preceding his work in Hawaii, Duane learned how to use tools he could trust to ascertain the validity of all interactions with extraterrestrials. Yet, it is never easy and takes guts to act on them. None of us are totally infallible; however, maintaining a stable, centered mental mindset and a dash of common sense should be enough. There is such a thing as being over-cautious to the point where you never get off dead center.

One of the primary edicts among the higher guides and teachers is to never abrogate free will. One immediate tip-off that raises a red flag is if any Being exercises controlling behavior and begins to tell you what to do. I sometimes begged Thomas at first to tell me how I should handle different situations. He never would do it. In fact, I realized, after some time, that his training was facilitating a growing consciousness in which I made better decisions by myself. However, you are the one in a physical body. If you need to have greater breathing space, then speak up.

That said, I must tell you that when Thomas first proposed that I become his charge, he warned that I must give up a little of my free will. He said that he was now responsible for me. There would be situations that for my own safety I must do exactly as he said. Thank God for that. (Other chapters tell the complete story of working with Thomas.) When he was manipulating kundalini energies and opening chakras, I would have been a dead duck by myself. I have never had any reason to regret my decision to work with him on his terms.

One incident revealed to me that there are times when Thomas will step in and take independent action. It is rare; he has done it only three times. The first incident occurred one Sunday morning when I was sleeping in. I was sound asleep, and I still am amazed that Thomas was able to get my attention. I awoke to Thomas's extremely urgent message to get out to my hot tub, and he meant NOW. I leapt out of bed and reached for my robe. "Get going," he ordered. I did not know that Don had gone out for an early soak. I got there just as he fainted and went under the water.

Another good idea is to find like-minded people you can talk to about any contacts with the other side. It is not always possible, but on the other hand there are more and more people whose consciousness is such that they can play an important role in helping you sort it all out. There is no more important reason for a group of people to come together than when dealing with relationships with the other side. It helps to keep everyone grounded.

One of the first things Thomas told me was that he was a group teacher. His efforts were directed toward bringing a group together right from the beginning. I have written about my core shamanic group earlier in the book and no need to discuss it further except to say that all of us are quick to acknowledge that there is no way any of us could have made it this far alone.

If a group of like-minded individuals is not available to you, there are professionals to whom you may turn for guidance and validation. This does not refer to your local shrink. I would be extremely cautious about telling conventional therapists that you are hearing voices. The metaphysical community and shaman would better serve you.

One of the services I provide my clients is to check out their contacts with the other side when working with supposed guides or teachers. This often requires reassurances that they are not crazy. I also urge you never to share this information with your own family if you know it is too far outside their belief system. Keep your mouth shut about it. I can't tell you the endless trouble this stirs up when your own mother thinks you are crazy or worse yet, fears that the devil has snatched you.

Each person's situation with invisible contacts of all kinds will be different. It pays to be a self-aware person who has done some inner work. Dealing with psychic contact requires a reasonably stable individual. If you are pathetically naïve and don't have the common sense to recognize gross symptoms and behaviors, I just hope someone will come along and save you from yourself.

Some books offer helpful guidance. My favorite one is one I have written about before *The Inner Guide Meditation* by Edwin Steinbrecher. I knew him as an astrologer. He has included some excellent material that relates to your astrological chart. The only criticism—and not a serious one-—is that I have talked to clients over the years that overreacted to the part of the book that alerts them to false guides. Of course, I agree that he did need to include the possibility. It may have been a bit overdone when one considers how worrisome this is for many people first starting out.

Friends in High Places

There have been two times when extraterrestrials have offered help completely out of the blue–or should I say somewhere from out in the wild blue yonder of another dimension. In the earlier years when we were heavily focused on deep personal work with The Pill, I was doing some healing work on Don one night and matters were not proceeding well. I felt as though I had stumbled in over my head and was at a loss about what to do next. That was very unusual for me. Ordinarily I had a laser-like focus with The Pill.

I got the surprise of a lifetime when six guys in full military dress uniforms—white gloves and all—appeared. They were all business, let me tell you. They operated with rapid-fire military precision without ever speaking a word. I can only surmise that they were communicating telepathically. I remind you in the very unlikely chance that anyone reading this mistakenly believes that these people do actually appear in the flesh in the 3rd dimension. I've learned to anticipate that there always may be somebody somewhere who can misunderstand.

These experiences are psychic experiences and appear in the mind's eye when in an altered state. This only serves to define the inner work and high level of psychic development that is obligatory before this psychic world appears equally as real and unquestionably dependable as the physical dimension in which we live everyday. If actual physical Beings manifested in my family room, I would not be writing this book. I would have dropped dead a long time ago.

Back to the six visitors: I saw Don lying on a table with three of the military men on either side. It is difficult to describe the lightning speed hand movements they made. They extended their arms towards each other and held their white-gloved hands palms out, facing each other. It appeared to me that each one was somehow aiming his hand to connect with another one sequentially on their opposite side. It was obvious that they were working in Don's energy field. Their eyes were staring straight ahead; they never looked at each other.

Apparently, as each one completed his part of the process, he snapped off his white gloves, tucked them under his arm, removed his hat and took one step back. When all six had stepped back, they vanished. As they left, Don groaned and reported how much better he felt. Whatever Gordian knot I had been battling in Don's field, it was apparently untied by the Team of Six, the name by which we referred to them ever after that.

Infrequently to be sure, the Team of Six put in unbidden appearances in times when we were floundering over one thing or another. Each time they came and went without a word. To this day, not one has ever even so much as glanced in my direction or spoken a single word. I have no idea who they are or where they hail from. However, we are very grateful to them for bailing us out of some very tight situations.

There came a time when we encountered one of our "situations" whereby a little help from our friends would definitely be in order! I wondered whether it was according to interdimensional etiquette to call out to them for help on our own. We timidly put out the call to the Team of Six in hopes that we were not violating star system military protocols and ending up on some sort of universal black list. Admittedly to our total disbelief, they came instantly. We are still not sure how much we should abuse the privilege, so their help is reserved for really critical circumstances. So far I have never screwed up my nerve to engage them in conversation to ask them some questions. It seems kind of like pestering the bugler guy at a military funeral. Perhaps it just isn't done.

The first time The Team of Six appeared in my family room that night, and maneuvered their hand movements in Don's energy field, it was not the first time I had seen that. I was incredulous beyond just their appearance. I once worked with another healer, and we made those very same hand movements in other people's energy fields when working on them! Our normal procedure was to seat the person with whom we were working on a chair in my office. Ed, my partner, stood behind and I stood in front. We worked with our eyes closed.

We did not realize what was happening until one day a woman casually asked us how we kept our hands moving in exactly the same positions as each other's while our eyes were closed. We looked at each other dumbfounded. Apparently, each of us was the mirror image of the other, just like Lucy did with Harpo Marx on one of her TV shows—maybe you've seen this oft-repeated episode.

However, that is still not the end of this story. Many years before working with Ed, I was living in St. Louis where I participated in a week-end course called Silva Mind Control, now called the Silva Method. I'll not elaborate except to say that Jose Silva, a friend of Max Freedom Long, developed this course along the lines of Huna, the ancient Hawaiian healing system of the kahuna practitioners about whom Long wrote extensively (in the books mentioned elsewhere in this book). By the way, I highly recommend the Silva Method to anyone interested in a safe and remarkably rapid way to advance one's psychic development. If you can find a teacher of the Silva Method, don't pass up that opportunity.

At one point in the week-end Silva course, there came a time when we were to meet our "counselors," which I recognized as our High Selves in the Huna system. When it came time for me to enter the altered state to meet my counselors, something altogether different from the ordinary method occurred. I'll just describe what I did see. There was a male and a female counselor. Their names are Seti and Aryana, and they appeared to be Egyptian.

There was a massage-type table with a person lying on it. Seti stood at the head, and Aryana stood at the feet facing him. They both had their eyes closed. They were facing each other with their hands up, palms out. It was obvious that they were engaged in a healing. *They were making the very same exact matched hand motions in the energy field that Ed and I had done, and later the Team of Six had done!* What did it all mean? This began in the 1960s when I was barely past thirty years old and just undertaking a serious practice of astrology and Huna.

More recently and after a great deal of water had passed over the dam, I found myself married to my present husband, Don. He bears an uncanny resemblance to Seti, at six feet five and a certain look across the brow. After Duane's return from Hawaii with tales of his adventures with the Pleiadians, a massage table became a permanent fixture in the living room to accommodate the Crystal Triangle Activations. The décor in my living room was Twenty-first Century Lightbody. Maybe it will catch on.

Family and friends were the first to try out the new system. We were in the habit of also clearing any negative energies along with the activation of the lightbody. I studied the energy field of the person on the table. When there was a problem, I joined him in the healing. Sure enough, there we were: Don at the head of the table, I at the foot facing him. For several years, we did activations and energy healing work together. My deep involvement in healing was being unmistakably foretold by my own High Selves on that day in the Silva class.

I mentioned earlier in this chapter if you remember that there were two unbidden visitations from extraterrestrials. The Team of Six were the first. The second ETs could not have been more different! Where the Team of Six was strictly military discipline, all spit and polish, the boys from Antares were the wild asses of outer space.

Don and I were heavily involved in shamanic work with clients all over the world for many years. It was not unusual for us, therefore, to encounter clients bothered by entities. Invading entities ranged from dear Aunt Martha just hanging around after she died to the worst of the Black Magicians. In fact, it took us awhile to catch on to the guys proficient in the black arts. The problem was that they were able to operate from the higher dimensions, rendering them invisible to 3D sight no matter how psychic.

Whenever we happened onto a situation in which there was black magic involvement, we were absolutely confounded. And let me tell you, we are not the types who appreciate playing peek-a-boo games from some other dimension. We enlisted my brother's aid. He was busy doing his own thing which, fortunately for us, included an ability to access the higher dimensions and take a look. Spotting the source of the problem did not imply that the problem was solved.

Our personal Rules of Engagement state that we do not challenge forces in which we may not end up the last man standing, so to speak. We were in the middle of just such an encounter, wondering which way to move when we heard, "This is a job for the Boooooooeeeeeeeys (Boys) from Antares." I only wish I could communicate how they sounded.

In your mind's eye you want to visualize a gang on Harleys all wearing black leather and wrap-around dark glasses. And off they roared. They were as good as their word. The poor client with whom we were working was instantly cleared of all negative energies. From what I have been able to gather, they are some sort of intergalactic vigilante police force that goes around hitting on the worst of the worst. That is why we refer to them as the Wild Asses from Outer Space. It fits.

Whenever we find we are in a very confusing situation and going in circles, we call them in and they always answer. An appearance from them is wildly chaotic, sort of like the bumper cars you've seen at carnivals. Are all of these encounters real? Are there really ETs out there who are coming to help us in our healing work? Or are we just suffering from over-active imaginations?? It is that kind of 3D left-brain thinking that can actually cut one off from this help that is obviously making a difference. It doesn't matter what it **really** is. All that matters is what it does. If that is the way it is presented to us, so be it.

Real Psychics on *This* Side of the Veil

Up to this point, relationships concerned contacts from the other side of the veil, one way or another. But what about working with a psychic that is very much hair, blood and bone? If there is potential trouble in dealing with invisible entities, at least they are not going to leave you with a much lighter wallet after their shenanigans. There are so many people who want a psychic reading, and for equally as many reasons. Some people want to entertain an old college roommate who is visiting from out of town. Gee, wouldn't it be fun to have a psychic reading! Or, my girl friend just dumped me, maybe a psychic will tell me whether I will ever get her back? Or etc., etc., and etc.

I receive any number of calls from people who are looking for a psychic. There is still widespread ignorance among the general public about what various metaphysical practitioners actually do. If they want a so-called psychic reading, call an astrologer, or astrologist as they usually say. Just try explaining over the phone what a psychic does versus what an astrologer does. Before we go on with some guidelines and suggestions, I want you to meet…

Mr. Psychic Guy

Some experienced professional psychics will wrestle every now and then with this problem of whether all this psychic stuff is real.. In my local area, a long-time friend of mine is the resident psychic for clients all over the world. His work is phenomenal. There was a time when I saw clients for weekly counseling sessions. Sometimes we were stuck and to help get unstuck, I called in Mr. Psychic Guy. I could recount his impressive assistance with numerous tough cases.

Regardless of how gifted he was, you can appreciate that it took a good bit of preparation to lay the groundwork with my clients to justify an intervention by a psychic. You can imagine my chagrin, after carefully proceeding to the point of his arrival in my counseling room, only to hear him announce, "You do realize this is all bullshit, don't you?"

That is when I invented the Bullshit Disclaimer just for him. I explained to my clients that Mr. Psychic Guy is an eccentric, and before he could proceed, he needed to go through his little ritual. I insisted that he come in, sit down and read the Bullshit Disclaimer Card. "You do know that in order to work with you, I must first say that this is all bullshit. Now I am ready." Having coached my clients ahead of time, everyone participated with an air of polite amusement, after which we proceeded without incident. I just threw that story in for a little comic relief. Beyond that, what was happening there was that we were **throwing a bone to the left brain.** Let it have its say, and then it can keep its trap shut while we proceed with the psychic work.

I have mentioned this same individual elsewhere. He is the psychic guy in the ring story. I have known him since the late 70s. In fact, I think I have told the story elsewhere about the guy whose chart I did and exclaimed that it was one of the most psychic charts I'd ever seen. And he disavowed knowledge of any such thing about himself. As months passed, I helped facilitate his career as a professional psychic, leaving a successful real estate business.

Locating a Competent Professional Psychic

I have observed close at hand how someone of integrity builds a practice and services it in a most professional manner. If only all so-called psychics could duplicate his work in every respect. All I can say is: When you are looking for a psychic; it's a jungle out there.

Here are a few guidelines. First ask yourself why you want a psychic reading in the first place. Call your local astrologer. Call the metaphysical bookstores. Check out the Internet.

How to Choose a Psychic

The thought occurred to me that one of the best ways to determine some guidelines for choosing a psychic was to ask Mr. Psychic Guy himself! Below was his response:

> "First thought is how NOT to pick one. Don't test them. Don't ask for a sample reading or 'proof' they are psychic. Do you take your doctor for a test drive? Even your doctor with his or her thousands of hours of schooling and experience can and does make mistakes, so don't expect your psychic to be infallible. I'm remembering a woman who grilled me on the phone for half an hour and then said, 'Tell me something about myself that you know already.' When I said, 'I know you're skeptical and rude,' the call ended very abruptly. The worst that can happen is you're out a few dollars if you don't like the psychic. It's not like having the wrong leg amputated.
>
> "If I was looking for a psychic, I'd ask them what their favorite kind of client is like. What is their favorite and least favorite type of question. When people ask me, I'm very willing to say my least favorite question is on romance, because it deals with such a volatile and emotional question and deals with another person. My favorite questions are medical because there can be a definite test and answer. Next I'd ask if the psychic has an explanation of the process to see if their belief system matches mine. If they said that faeries speak the information in their ears then I'd better believe in faeries. If they said Jesus gives them the answers, then I'd better be a devout Christian. If they said, 'I've never been able to answer that question,' then I'd say, 'Your hired!'
>
> "The best way to find a psychic is through referrals, of course. Let your friends do the test driving! If your friend has a belief system similar to yours and they liked the psychic and describe the process well, then take a chance with that psychic."

Thanks Mr. psychic Guy. I just "knew" that is what you were going to say!

Cults

I am sure that most of you have heard about some of the tragic consequences involving groups of people who become enamored by some charismatic leader who claims to be the mouthpiece for a higher power on the other side. These are the cults like the horrifying tragedy of Jim Jones who isolated his followers in Guyana. Nearly 1,000 men, women and children drank Kool-Aid laced with poison and perished.

This is one that was splashed across newspaper headlines and unfolded before our eyes on TV, each day growing more unbelievably horrific than before. For every one of the most sensational and tragic, there are any number of smaller groups scattered about that will never make the headlines, never lead to death or bloodshed; yet, feature a smaller group of brain-washed individuals staring glassy-eyed as they hang on every word of some so-called guru. If you find yourself participating in a group of like-minded people, just where is the line between a legitimate teacher and a dangerous, controlling cult leader?

There are some clues that mark the latter as fairly typical of all cult leaders. One of the most dangerous is when you are growing forcibly isolated from other contacts with friends and family. Another of the more extreme earmarks of a cult is when it begins to invade in your life in ways that burn bridges behind you. For example, you may be convinced to transfer your money and worldly goods to the guru. After all, you are headed for paradise, who needs money? Often, relationships, even marriages, are severed and the allegiance is only to the cult leader. This typically includes sexual favors with him or her only.

What began as the guru's claim to be the mouthpiece for a Higher Power soon transfers to the guru. He takes on the mantle of the Divine himself. As time passes, control over the group grows increasingly stronger until each aspect of daily life, down to the smallest detail, is dictated. In one such group that eventually ended tragically in the suicide of all members, the men were provided with detailed instructions about exactly how to shave each morning.

The outstanding trait of all cult leaders—be it a man or a woman—is his or her gift for oratory. That is why they are so dangerous. They have an over-developed throat chakra that has an almost unbelievable hypnotic power over listeners. The prime example of all time, of course, was Adolph Hitler. I remember an assignment that was given to me in one of my social studies classes in college. We were to go to the student library where a movie of Hitler's speeches was running all day. Our assignment was to listen to just two hours of his oratory; it was in German, of course. I freely admit that by the time two hours had passed I was strangely motivated to stand up and yell, "Heil!" As I walked out of the library, I ran into one of the kids in my class. I asked him what he thought about what we had just seen. He turned to me and said, "Shut up or I'll kill you." And I answered, "Not if I see you first!" That said it all.

What I have just described covers the most extreme examples of a cult. What may be even more dangerous are the ones where you go about your life in a fairly routine fashion, but nonetheless, become enamored of some guru who preaches his or her particular brand of extreme philosophy, a philosophy that obviously crosses the line.

You may believe that it would never happen to you. That is what I would have thought. The following story is embarrassing, but I will include it to demonstrate just how easy it is to get sucked in. If it was today, I would not have entertained it for a New York minute. We learn as we go.

A Tragic Example of a Misguided Spiritual Leader

When I was married to my ex-husband, Rex Bills, he was a tech rep for Eastman Kodak Company. We were transferred to St. Louis in 1966, one of the five largest printing centers in the U.S., as this was Rex's area of expertise. I was a professional model for the Patricia Stevens agency and a stay-at-home mom with my son, David. Those were our day jobs out of necessity to pay the mortgage and monthly bills. However, we were totally consumed with something else that occupied our hearts, minds and souls every minute. *We had awakened!*

If you do not believe me when I say we were obsessed with our new interests, some long-suffering friends who endured our fanatical ravings would readily testify to it. I blush to recall it to this day. We could have credibly argued the case for reincarnation before the Supreme Court. We read voraciously. We lived in St. Louis for seven years before we moved to Portland, Oregon. I recall those years of this adventure as one long continuous high. Our adrenaline pumped through astrology classes, Theosophist lectures, psychic readings, healing circles, spiritualist séances and anything else of a metaphysical nature that we could scare up. It was a crash course in *everything.*

Yes, we two metaphysical virgins proceeded with abandon. We were spiritual garbage cans. A series of incidents, though, shattered our rose-colored glasses and all the king's horses and all the king's men, well, you get the idea. We attended weekly sessions for over a year with a medium that turned out to be an obvious phony. Two teachers we revered as gods turned out to have feet that closely resembled clay. We were so disillusioned! I left a class that taught a bizarre philosophy which I learned later were the early Moonies, a cult that I wanted nothing to do with.

A True Life Case of a Spiritual Leader Gone Wrong, Continued

I also had a scary encounter with the Ouija board that I would just as soon forget. These painful and disillusioning brushes with the dark side of the psychic and spiritual worlds convinced me that I had endured a trial by fire and was now something of a discriminating spiritual sophisticate. However, nothing prepared my husband and me for what we were about to encounter with a man named Franklin Loehr.

I feel free to ethically share the details of our bizarre detour that veered so widely off any logical philosophy because Franklin Loehr has now passed on to his reward, and the story is quite well-documented from several other sources. Rev. Loehr started his career as an ordained minister in one of the traditional Protestant faiths. His encounter with a woman parishioner, who came to him for counseling about a personal matter, took them both down a road that neither could possibly have predicted.

As the relationship progressed, the woman discovered an ability to psychically read past lives and also connect with a guide on the other side of the veil. She ended up divorcing her husband, marrying Rev. Loehr and together they launched The Religious Research Foundation of America. There was a certain spiritual-metaphysical philosophy that they espoused, and the RRFA could boast of a creditable number of members. At least, between Franklin's book *The Power of Prayer on Plants,* Grace's past life readings at $300 a pop, several conventions a year and the cost of memberships, they supported themselves and a minimal office staff.

Enter stage left: two spiritual enthusiasts who were nearly prepared to sell their son into slavery, such was their fanatical desire to gain any scrap of information about their past lives (okay, not really). Fortunately for my son, the information was available for $300 each from the Loehrs. In the 1960s, that was a considerable strain on our budget, but as I said, we were prepared for a much greater sacrifice than that.

Our contact with the Loehrs reached well beyond the psychic past life readings they sent through the mail. I struck up a correspondence with them that included some work I did with Franklin's astrology chart. We were enthusiastic students of the RRFA correspondence course, to put it mildly.

As matters progressed, Mrs. Loehr's (Grace) Guide made an electrifying proposal, to say the very least! He, the Guide, announced his intention to materialize as Franklin's partner, and furthermore, made it abundantly clear that *he*, not Franklin, was to be the designated man in said relationship, *requiring Franklin to undergo a sex change operation.* In those years, this was extremely controversial and sex change surgery was not available in the United States. Intrepid soul that he was, Franklin Loehr actually did it! The surgery was performed in Madagascar, of all places. In fact, in those years, there were jokes that circulated about "going to Madagascar" as the cryptic code words, of course, for transsexuals desiring a sex change. At any rate: Voila! Enter Carolyn/Franklin.

I know you are wondering at this point how we could have possibly stayed on board with such ludicrous nonsense. Or perhaps I should not dignify it by even describing it as nonsense, almost as though implying it was merely an innocent child's imagination that should somehow be indulged. More to the point, this most certainly involved issues that were nothing short of seriously troubling, as far as the man himself was concerned; and potentially dangerously misleading to those around him, no matter from what angle it is examined. That is exactly why I am including this whole sorry episode in the book.

What better demonstration could there possibly be to show just how easy it was for one charismatic individual, with serious psychological problems, to actually establish what passed for an acceptable religious organization founded around what, in reality, was his own severely distorted dogma. It is true, no one drank poison-laced Kool-Aid or anything of the sort. But there is no telling how many people's search for true spirituality was interrupted by the likes of this man. And you can be sure that there is no accounting for how many situations duplicated this distorted scenario, and no doubt continues to this very day.

The first time we actually saw Carolyn/Franklin was at a weekend conference the RRFA sponsored in Chicago. My husband and I were at dinner in the hotel the night before the conference began. My eye fell on a "woman" at a table across the room. She had broad shoulders, was six feet tall with really horrid red hair. I pointed her out to my husband, and we both knew instantly that this could be none other than Carolyn/Franklin. Franklin may have had his plumbing rearranged, but he had a long way to go to achieve anything resembling a being of female persuasion. He walked like a bomber pilot shot down in the war, leaving him with one short leg, which in truth, he had.

Carolyn's regrettable appearance—I'm being kind—was the lynchpin upon which turned the fated experiences with this guy (gal?) that still laid before me. Since I was acquainted with the Loehrs, and had interacted with them before the conference, I introduced myself and struck up a conversation with Carolyn and Grace. At the time, I was a professional model and an instructor in a modeling school. Before all was said and done, I had invited the Loehrs to swing by St. Louis and stay at my house, while I attempted to whip Carolyn into shape.

Before I was finished with this caper, I rued the day that Franklin had not been born a petite blond with good legs. They arrived and we immediately set to work. This was the fastest crash course in the ways of the feminine in history. My house became a flurry of powder and paint, hair bleach and color, hairspray, foundation garments, manicure paraphernalia, piles of shoes and clothing, perms and more. There were walking lessons, sitting lessons, standing lessons, carrying a purse lessons, etc. At the end of two weeks, the transformation was truly miraculous. Carolyn, in her mid-fifties, had blossomed into a tall, elegant, tastefully sexy honey blond with a power wardrobe. God could not have been more pleased with Eve than I was with my creation of Woman.

At the beginning of this project, I promised Carolyn that after we had completed her transformation she could accompany me to one of my modeling classes, and as the *piece de resistance* we would pull out all the stops some evening and dine at one of St. Louis's swankiest restaurants. First came the modeling class. Believe me, I had no stomach for walking into my class with a guy obviously in drag. I kept my trepidations to myself. As for Carolyn, she was the soul of confidence. I briefly introduced her and went on with the class. At the break, several students actually approached me with compliments for my "elegant friend." Hurdle number one!

Next was the night on the town. I did Carolyn's hair and make-up. She wore a beautifully tailored ivory-colored evening suit accessorized with gold and pearl jewelry. She wore a lovely matching fur-trimmed cape over it. There was a party of six of us. Carolyn swept in and took a seat with all the panache of an aging star that still expects the adoration of fans. At an adjoining table sat a group of what appeared to be a group of businessmen. I was simply stunned when one gentleman came over and actually hit on Carolyn. He passed her his business card and asked to take her to dinner the following night! It was probably the highest point in her life.

As the relationship with the Loehrs unfolded, I began to entertain dark suspicions that some unresolved sexuality issues may well have muddied the waters of their spiritual judgment. When it was revealed that Franklin was a transvestite, I ordinarily would not have attached much significance to it. If he wanted to dress up in women's clothing in the privacy of his home, who cared?

I reminded myself, however, that this person indeed was living out in a major way his compulsions to cross dress. Was the sex change purely the spiritual promptings of a highly evolved Being for the good of humanity—which is pretty bizarre on the face of it—or was this an entity getting his kicks by playing off the convoluted psychology of Franklin Loehr?

My suspicions were further fueled the night Carolyn and I returned from teaching my modeling class. He initiated some very un-Christian moves toward me, and said, "Diana, I must say that the man in me is very attracted to the woman in you." I was never so grateful in my life to see my little son running into the garage to greet his mommy. That spared me from having to meet his advances with a very unladylike response.

That wasn't all. A friend of ours was also staying with us, along with the Loehrs. He did not want to miss out on this exciting adventure. One morning he took me aside to soberly inform me that he would not stay if Franklin/Carolyn made one more pass at *him.* Rex talked him out of it, but apparently the behavior continued because he finally did leave. That is the first time a male visitor made a pass both at me and my male guest!

Within the context of the Trickster archetype, it is tempting to simply write this whole incident off as some aberrant episode where everyone goes a little crazy. As I recall those events now, don't think I miss the utter absurdity of it all. The Trickster archetype is the antithesis of simplicity, however, and the meaning of that experience was a lot more far-reaching than I knew at the time. Keep in mind that Trickster is a cunning, but very wise, teacher.

Despite the wear and tear on one's psyche, personal experience is hard to rival as a teacher. It was sobering and very scary to realize just how easy it is to be sucked into accepting something that is so obviously suspect. We had to take a hard look at our own motivations in that situation.

I am much more cautious now, both in investigating what I am getting myself into and analyzing my expectations in relationship to it. It is also easy to overreact and throw the baby out with the bath water, regarding with cynicism everything that is not of the absolutely rational. In years to come, my brother and I would be confronted by our teacher and challenged to sort out if he represented truth or treachery.

Franklin Loehr, as it turned out, had deep unresolved psychological and sexual issues that tainted his judgment and exposed him to a spiritual charlatan posing as a Guide, resulting in terribly tragic consequences. In private conversations with Grace, she revealed that there were other extremely questionable behaviors that were acted out. There is no need to give any further details, except to say that these stories were really quite dark and unethical, involving other men who could not know what they were getting into.

Besides the sexual issues, he relished the role of a "messiah." The sad fact of the matter is that many of the teachings of the RRFA were basically sound and could have stood on their own. Also consider his wife, Grace, who approached him as the pastor of her church to seek his counseling on a personal matter. She certainly was betrayed, which, of course, she must take responsibility.

As you have probably guessed by now, no entity ever materialized to claim Carolyn as his bride. As the story went, once Carolyn's spirit husband manifested on the physical plane, a "husband" for Grace would follow after that. The explanation was that the Loehrs and their associates had not "progressed" adequately to pull it all off. As far as I am concerned, that's the most transparent cop-out I ever heard of in all my life

Over the years, I have encountered this same tired excuse when so-called spiritual leaders with a cult following make outrageous predictions that somehow fail to materialize. The answer is always the same. The followers had not evolved enough. It was their failure. The Loehrs accepted it, however. Years later, I learned that Franklin Loehr reverted to dressing as a man and presented himself to the world as male. I never heard the back story of his reasons for doing so. As for Grace, I don't know whatever happened to her, either. The last I heard of Franklin Loehr was that he died suddenly while attending a UFO conference.

A Real Life Experience Of Trusting Your Inner Voice

For the next part of this chapter I am going to include an experience that actually involved my son, David. It is my very strong opinion that real life experiences are in the final analysis the only way to really learn to trust this path. At some point, you will have to just jump in feet first and do it.

The name of this article is "The Larch Mountain Adventure." It is an extraordinary example of working with a teacher, including all of the elements involved: the difficulties of believing and acting on psychic communications, the synchronicities that follow, and the final confirmations of the validity of the experience. After several of these adventures, you can see how eventually one becomes a believer one step at a time. I'm just damn glad I didn't hear about this until after it was over. I'm his mom, after all.

THE LARCH MOUNTAIN ADVENTURE

By David Bills

My story takes place in a part of the country that the natives here like to call The Great Northwest. High on the list of Northwest scenic wonders is the fabulous Columbia River Gorge, carved out of the Cascade Mountain Range at the end of the Ice Age and separating two of the most beautiful of all states, Washington and Oregon. Rapidly coursing through the gorge are the waters of the mighty Columbia River.

If you ever get the opportunity to visit Portland, The City of Roses, grab a rental car and head east on Interstate 84 toward the Oregon side of the gorge. About half an hour out of town, you will encounter Multnomah Falls, the second highest in the United States, towering 621 feet. The bridge spanning the falls is a favorite for tourists, hikers, amateur photographers and newlywed couples.

Driving on Old Scenic Highway 30, you will pass in front of Multnomah Falls, climb up and out of the Columbia River Gorge and finally arrive at the Crown Point Observatory. Arriving at the observatory, you are treated to a spectacular view of the Gorge. The road from there winds its way to the top of Larch Mountain. Larch Mountain is not really a freestanding mountain in its own right. It is part of the foothills of the Cascade Mountain Range. You can drive to the top of the mountain, park your car in the lot and walk up the path to the very top of the peak.

I have hiked many trails, and I count the top of Larch Mountain as one of the most breathtaking of any view I've ever enjoyed. On a clear day, you can see all of the majestic peaks of the upper Cascade Range: Mt. Hood, Mt. St. Helens, Mt. Rainier, Mt. Adams and Mt. Jefferson. These are all part of the Pacific Ring of Fire. Of course, you are also afforded a fabulous view of the Gorge and the Columbia River. It is God's country, no doubt about it.

There is an extensive network of hiking trails running throughout the gorge, and I have hiked them all. I am a certified public accountant by trade, and hiking the gorge trails was my way to stay fit, retain my sanity and connect with nature in a very personal way. It was during this period of extensive hiking that I came to experience the darker side of this beautiful country.

Each year on July 4th I liked to challenge myself physically. I dubbed my challenge "The Annual Larch Mountain Climb." I would roll out of bed before sunrise, pack my gear for a rigorous day hike, jump in my car and arrive at the foot of Multnomah Falls at the crack of dawn. I used the forest service trail that winds eight steep miles up the gorge and continues to the very top of Larch Mountain. This is a change in elevation of about 3,500 feet and is no easy day hike. I returned to the base of Multnomah Falls at the end of the day, exhausted yet exhilarated. I was one-year older and still going strong.

Local Native American lore says that in the days before the coming of the white man, an unknown and fatal disease struck the tribe that lived in the gorge near Multnomah Falls. Distraught, the tribe tried in vain to discover a way to fend off this silent killer. It is said that the beautiful and radiant daughter of the chief dressed herself in ceremonial robes, climbed to the top of the falls and flung herself off. Her ultimate sacrifice was made to appease the evil power behind the mysterious illness. According to the legend, the illness immediately vanished and all of the members of the tribe were returned to good health. If you watch closely, the water of the Falls cascading over the rocks below, outlines the face of a woman.

Some would say that this makes a good story for the tourists, but I have a deep respect for the oral traditions of the indigenous peoples who inhabited this area for many hundreds of years. This was my first inkling that there was something clearly unfriendly at work in this land of splendor. If it had not been for the events that followed, I, too, would have chalked up this story as nothing but a fanciful legend.

One 4th of July, I was standing in the parking lot at the base of Multnomah Falls, preparing myself mentally for the challenge ahead. I recall silently looking at the Falls and remembering the legend of the chief's daughter. It was unseasonably cold and I shivered involuntarily. Although excited about my annual trek up the gorge, I had awakened that morning with a sense of foreboding. I had never felt in danger when hiking the trails, although it was possible to encounter a bear, mountain lion or some nut wandering the backcountry.

While stuffing my backpack full of gear, I spied a stout piece of wood doweling about two feet long and two inches thick lying in the trunk of my car. I grabbed it without really thinking and stuffed it inside of my pack. It had a good heft to it, kind of like a small baseball bat. The end of the doweling stuck out of my pack, allowing me to quickly grab behind my neck and haul it out should the need arise.

The parking lot was empty except for my car. Starting up the trail toward the Falls, I became aware of a man in his late twenties about 50 yards ahead. He was standing in the brush just off the trail. It immediately struck me as odd. He sported a beard and his hair was long and unkempt. He was wearing an old dirty jacket, combat fatigue pants and boots. He spelled trouble. Waves of danger emanated from him. He just looked and moved wrong.

I recalled that my car was the only one in the lot and wondered how this person had come to be here. I stood where I was, pretending to fiddle with my gear. Finally, he moved off. I headed warily up the trail. I arrived at a point where the trail passes in front of the pool at the bottom of the Falls. I stepped off the trail and walked toward the edge of the pool. The water from the Falls was deafening as it slammed into the pool. One of my rituals was to begin my hike by meditating and honoring the power of nature by standing at this particular spot. Usually it was refreshing, but my unwanted visitor had spoiled the mood.

Suddenly, I saw a movement in the corner of my eye. I turned around and realized that my strange friend had slipped up behind me. Instead of walking along the path like a normal hiker, he had scrambled up a rocky riverbed that wound up the hill toward the pool, bypassing the trail. There were signs everywhere warning hikers in no uncertain terms to stay on the trail. At that moment, I knew for certain that he was up to no good.

He jumped back onto the main path and walked swiftly in my direction. He came to the place where he could step from the trail and walk down to the edge of the pool. He put one foot off of the trail, clearly meaning to move toward me. He was about 20 yards away. There was absolutely no one else around; it was too early. Our eyes locked. He stopped dead in his tracks. My martial arts instincts taught me to slowly narrow my eyes so as not to reveal fear. I turned to face him fully. I calmly and deliberately reached back and wrapped my hand around the doweling, but I didn't pull it out of my pack.

He stood for a moment and apparently thought better about approaching me. He whirled and ran up the trail. After I was sure that he was gone, I immediately jogged back to my car and drove to another trailhead several miles away. I continued my hike by taking a completely different route. The day was cold and the hike was miserable. I am certain to this day that if I had not acted the way I did, I would not be alive to write this. I filed this experience away. It turned out to be part of a pattern of strange events that occurred in this area.

Over the years that followed, the local newspaper featured stories with troubling frequency about people losing their way off the gorge trails and succumbing from exposure to the elements. There were stories of people stuck in freak snowstorms or injuring themselves from bad falls. Almost always, these stories centered on the Larch Mountain area. The trails in the area are clearly marked, and even a novice hiker should be able to easily navigate the way back. These accounts struck me as odd and completely avoidable.

In high school, I used to play pick-up football games with the guys in my neighborhood. A number of years later, I was told that one of my football buddies had died. He fell and struck his head on a rock while hiking Larch Mountain. Several years later, my father's friends were visiting Larch Mountain and headed out for a picnic. After eating, they walked the short trail to the very top to admire the view.

The observation point at the top of the peak is ringed with a high security fence. This is to prevent people from falling off of the top to the rocks below. As my father's friends approached the top, they nervously noticed that two people had climbed over the security fence and were eating their lunch while sitting perched on the edge of a high rock cliff.

Suddenly, there was a scream. Apparently, one of them reached for something and lost his balance. He fell some 20 feet below and lay prone on a rocky ledge. Bystanders were yelling at him to stay put, but the person hit his head on the rocks and was groggy and non-responsive. He rolled over the edge and fell to his death. My father's friends left the scene, greatly shaken.

You can see why I developed a certain respect for this country over the years. As I hiked through this area, I grew aware of a certain kind of energy. It was subtle, yet powerful. It had a quality of seething anger and hatred. It was watching everything that happened in the area. It bespoke violence and death. I could tune this out with a little difficulty, but it was always there in the back of my mind.

Then I had an experience that was truly remarkable:

I was living in Portland at the time. I was in the process of looking for a new house and bunking in with my parents until I could find the right place. Christmas was approaching, my parents were traveling, and I had the house to myself. It was an opportunity to take my car in for routine maintenance. That is how I came to be driving my mother's car to work when it first started.

It was a voice in my head. And the voice said, "Go to Larch Mountain." The prospect of going to Larch Mountain was, to say the least, absolutely ridiculous. For one thing, I was on my way to work. I was the financial controller of a local electronics retailer. I managed a staff of fifteen, and we were in the heat of the Christmas season. The voice insisted, "Go to Larch Mountain."

I continued to try and put this out of my mind. After all, it was in the middle of winter. I was wearing a suit. I didn't have any hiking gear. It just didn't make sense. I didn't want to go. I wanted to get caught up on my work so that I could enjoy my Christmas vacation. It was out of the question.

The voice persisted. This time it said, "Drive to the top of Larch Mountain." I was thinking that this was crazy. The mountain roads were icy at this time of year. I was driving my mother's car. The image of her car upside down in a ditch flashed in my mind. Yet, the voice persisted.

I sat in my office until I could tolerate it no longer. The voice was relentless. I told my staff that I had to take care of a family emergency. It was like watching myself from outside of myself. I couldn't believe that I was actually going to do it. I drove home and changed into warm clothes. As if in a trance, I drove slowly up to Crown Point Observatory. I turned up the road to Larch Mountain. The road was icy and treacherous.

About halfway up the road, I encountered a closed gate. The road to Larch Mountain was closed for the winter. I pulled off of the road to decide what to do next. The voice was there. It said, "Get out....and walk." I got out of the car and started up the road. I estimated that it was about five miles to the top of Larch Mountain.

As I walked, I became acutely aware of the seething energy. It started to build. It was frightening. A fear welled up inside of me that I had never experienced. It was surreal. I felt like I was being stalked by the devil himself. I felt the energy watching and hating me. It suddenly occurred to me that I had told no one of my trip. If something happened, I might never be found. I continued on. The voice was there. It said, "Keep going and don't stop." I kept asking myself if this was really happening to me.

Finally, I reached the parking lot. Snow was on the ground in places. My feet were sore from walking on the hard pavement. I had no idea what I was doing in this place. And that is when I saw her. Coming up the mountain trail from the Gorge was a woman. She was lightly dressed in sweats and flimsy tennis shoes. She had no hat or backpack. She seemed strangely out of place. She was certainly not dressed or equipped to be hiking in this place and at this time of year.

I will never forget the timing of our meeting. We met exactly in the middle of the parking lot at the top of the mountain. It was as if we had an appointment to meet there at that exact place and time. Maybe we did. She didn't seem surprised or scared to see me. She appeared to be in her late thirties. She said that she had hiked up from the base of Multnomah Falls.

I said, "How are you getting back?" She said, "Oh, no problem. My husband is driving up here to pick me up." I told her that the road was blocked and that I had not seen any other cars at the gate. I suggested that we walk down the road together, and I would give her a ride. She thought that was a dandy idea.

What I find so perplexing to this day is that the woman never questioned why I was there. She never asked what had compelled me to walk up to Larch Mountain that day. She never questioned the truth of my statement about the road being blocked. She had absolutely no qualms about walking alone with a strange man in the middle of nowhere. I refrained from telling her what I thought about a husband that would allow his inexperienced wife to wander around in the mountains by herself and then not see that she returned home safely.

It was fairly dark by the time that we arrived at my mother's car. I drove her to the lodge where she called a friend and arranged to be picked up. I thought it was strange that the husband was nowhere to be seen. I had a gut feeling that maybe he didn't want her to be found. I will never know. I'm sure of one thing, though. She would have died that night if I hadn't arrived when I did.

Now my mom will tell the rest of the story:

When Don and David returned, the Larch Mountain adventure was riveting dinner conversation to say the least! Later, over coffee, David blurted out that he had omitted part of the story. That is when the truth came out about how terrified he was walking up that road. "Something was stalking me. I wished I had my gun, but I was pretty sure that it would have been useless against whatever this was." A chill ran down my spine. Addressing Don and David, I said, "I think maybe I should take a look at this."

I concluded from my psychic investigation that the "thing" appeared to be some sort of demonic creature. The surrounding environment was entirely bare of the usual nature spirits and Devic presences. My psychic window to the past revealed a violent crime committed around the Larch Mountain viewing platform many years ago. Was this the precipitating event that finally led to the frightening energies that existed there?

Right then and there we did a clearing of the negative energies around Larch Mountain. We restored the mountain Deva, Nature Spirits and Elementals typical of that local area and retired for the night, fairly confident that we had done a good piece of work. The confirmation of that was left in the reliable hands of the great god, Synchronicity. It was not long in coming.

It was long before any of this Larch Mountain business that a woman called me at my office to ask if I would contribute a couple of free astrological consultations to an auction sponsored by a local charity. I agreed, scheduled the two consultations and under normal circumstances, I would never have given the whole affair another thought. However, there was one little fluke that hadn't yet played its card. My name made its way to the charity's mailing list by way of the charitable donation mentioned above. One day the little newspaper that they published found its way to my mailbox.

I casually noted that this came from some obscure little environmental group. I flipped it open and the headlines screamed at me, "The Guardians of Larch

Mountain." Well, I can tell you that the hairs stood up on the back of my neck at that one!

The beauty of the area around Larch Mountain is legendary. However, the dark side there was reflected in close-by areas that were trashed. People dumped old tires and the like all over the place. Target shooters added to the disgusting mess. The environmental group had taken upon themselves to clean up the area and regularly patrol it to enforce anti-littering laws. What were the odds of me ever seeing *that particular copy* of this obscure group's newspaper only after the Larch Mountain adventure? Odds like that need a helping hand from Mr. Synchronicity. As far as any of us knows, there have been no more tragic events in that area.

Update: October 2012: Another murder on Larch Mountain was reported on my local news recently. I think the 4Ds have some tidying up to do!

Just how Many Different Folks are out There—Waaaay Out There?

Not long after my interest in extraterrestrials blossomed, I remember talking to a casual acquaintance on the phone, and she referred to the Reptilians, inquiring if I knew whether they are evil or not. I had to admit that I had never heard about any such creatures called Reptilians. That is the first time that the thought occurred to me that perhaps all of sentient life out there did not look like us! So what was all this reptilian business about? Do they crawl around on their stomachs like alligators?

Descriptions of their personality, appearance and intentions—peaceful or hostile—differ from one account to another. If we can accept that there are indeed people who have been abducted by aliens, some of the most reliable descriptions would obviously have to be from first-hand accounts by observers who have actually seen them. They supposedly stand about the same height as humans; however, we would consider their appearance as quite radically different from our own. Their eyes are slanted, green, and have a starburst design in the center. The nose is flat and snout-like. The mouth appears as just a slit. One big difference is in the texture of their skin, which is likely where the name *reptile* or *reptoid* originated. Rather than soft and smooth like human skin, theirs is covered in a scaly material, giving them the typical snake-like or lizard appearance.

Accounts vary as to their personality and intentions when it comes to relationships with humans. Most sources agree that they are a very highly-evolved race. Some suggest that they regard us in the same way that we would regard a herd of cattle. I've seen them described as totally hostile to humans. Other sources claim that there are good and bad Reptilians, just as we would categorize humans as covering a broad spectrum on the continuum of good and evil.

The only personal experience I can recall concerning reptilians was something that happened when I was off on a shamanic journey with my brother. This was something that occurred long before I had ever heard of the Reptilian race. All I know is that I did encounter a Being that resembled a reptile. In fact, I even intuitively addressed him as "reptile" when I spoke to him.

When the encounter took place, my instincts were that this fellow was up to no good. I was wearing my black leathers and carrying a riding crop, which was always my signal that something was afoot. I remember cajoling him in a most sarcastic tone, "Come on, Reptile. I won't hurt you." The encounter was short-lived. He just took off after that, apparently not desiring a confrontation with the likes of the babe in black. Whether this was actually one of the Reptilian race, I can't say for sure. Normally things are presented to me in ways that symbolize what I am dealing with. This guy was standing upright, but he was possessed of a long crocodile tail. So my guess is that it probably was one of the Reptilians.

The most common aliens have to be the Grays. They are the little guys who look like they are made of aluminum foil and their only outstanding characteristic are greatly oversized bug eyes. A great deal of controversy surrounds the Grays. Most sources are not too keen on their intentions and actions. It is even doubtful if they are conscious beings but robot-like creatures under the control of other aliens.

There is extensive literature about these and numerous other alien races from other star systems. Not surprisingly, the idea of other races of mixed appearances and intentions is fodder for the entire genre of sci-fi writers. There are cartoons, novels, TV shows and Internet sites abounding. It is hard to separate fact from fiction; that is evident very quickly.

The only thing I believe for sure is that it is ludicrous to doubt that we are alone in the Universe. I also believe that one day we humans will meet and communicate with them. First, the collective consciousness must exhibit a significant shift from where it is now before that day will come without causing total chaos. Ask yourself what YOU would do if one of them knocked on your front door. I always told myself I prayed that an alien in physical form would come calling for real. In truth, I might just as likely melt into a fetal position, calling for my mama like everyone else.

Even though the day when a UFO makes the proverbial landing on the White House lawn is not anytime soon, that does not preclude individual contacts, and I have listened to some very convincing lectures from remarkably believable people attesting to this very thing. Project Camelot and Project Disclosure hold regular interviews with any number of gentlemen whose stories are most compelling.

They talk on a wide variety of experiences with aliens, some stretching back 20 years or more. These are stories about associations with aliens in a physical body. They look like us, at least to an extent that minor differences would never be noticed. These whistleblowers, as they are now called, have very little to gain in spilling the beans about their close encounters with aliens. In fact, they have much to lose if any of this is true, including their lives. There is a very dark and ugly side to this business of aliens and our government's involvement in it. That includes the military if these stories are to be believed. You know what we say about smoke. The sheer numbers of the whistleblowers who are now speaking up attests to the fact that there is also fire somewhere.

Even though Don and I have listened to an excruciating number of hours about the dark side of aliens in relation to human beings, I have deliberately avoided any reference to this elsewhere in the book. It is very scary stuff, and I did not want to stir up any fears along these lines. Don't worry; we are not about to be invaded and eaten like steaks at a Reptilian banquet.

There is really nothing to fear. It is the frightful and unconscionable actions of our own government that you should be concerned about, if you want to be concerned about something. The reason I have made mention of this at all is because the lid is off, and even though the mainline media is tightly controlled, somebody somewhere is going to publish this where a great many people will hear about it.

Look around. The truth about corruption in every other area of life is coming to light. That is the cycle we are in. There are astrological indicators that very shocking news will blow the minds of many unsuspecting citizens. I, for one, will be only too happy to see the truth come out at last. From what I have seen, this is very much more to our advantage than any aliens we might name. I just did not want you to say that I never alerted you to this whole subject when the news hits the fan. My only warning is to use the same discernment in evaluating this information that you would in connection to anything else.

My Brother And The Pleiadians

My brother Duane's work with the Pleiadian Beings has been well-documented in our other books in this series. The Pleiadians tell us that they are human but have evolved past humanity's current level of consciousness. They experienced the Shift into a higher frequency a long time ago in their past, so they understand what is involved. They have been eager to participate in guiding our evolutionary process. Other writers have described their work with the Pleiadians; they did not work exclusively with us.

I would not be surprised if some of the Pleiadians have come to Earth in physical form and worked with certain individuals. That was not the case, however, when they worked with Duane.

When Duane was called to Hawaii to bring through the lightbody activations, the Pleiadians did not come in a physical body. Every communication was a psychic communication. There was a group of them. One of them asked permission to "walk in" to Duane's body without Duane walking out. The Being—that is what they asked us to call them—was apparently able to adjust his frequency to match Duane's fairly closely. Even at that, when the Being walked out after the work there in Hawaii was completed, Duane said that it was somewhat of a relief to be rid of his roommate.

In recent years, the rumor mill grinds out hints every so often that the extraterrestrials will either be introduced to the world by the proverbial spacecraft landing on the White House lawn, or else they will make themselves known to the world on their own. These stories often come from channeled messages and stress the notion that our brothers and sisters "out there" are growing impatient with our foot-dragging when it comes to acknowledging their existence.

As I write this, the 2012 Olympics are taking place in London. The rumor mill is buzzing once again that there will be spacecraft landings at this event. It hasn't happened yet, and I will be the most surprised of anyone if it does happen. My amazement will not be the fact of their existence. I already believe that. I don't think that they would do something of that nature because it would be so terribly disruptive and engender panic. I do plead guilty to the little devil sitting on my shoulder that loves to goad them into it just to see what would happen!

Here I am, writing this in the magic year of 2012, August of 2012 at that. One of these days, the collective consciousness must confront the reality that we are not alone in the Universe. Furthermore, we must go a step further than that and build relationships with our space family. We may be in for quite a shock one of these days if somebody doesn't get the guts to begin telling the public the truth. I can't help but seriously wonder if they indeed will do it for us one of these days.

You are aware that it has taken me several years to finish this book. Well, it is now 2012 as I said, and I am nearly finished at last. So I am probably not going to be the one who will be writing about it, unless things change pretty fast. Only a few months remain until December. Will the consciousness of humanity really be prepared for such an event in such a short time? Only time will tell, and as it turns out, I will be watching the skies along with you.

CHAPTER SIXTEEN

Waking the Twenty-First Century Shaman

So now we have an old traditional figure long lost to the West, the Shaman. The shaman has always been an agent of the unexpected, a spiritual pioneer who shatters familiar patterns of thought, and channels radical new visions into human consciousness. It is the archetype of the Teacher-Healer within us all. NOTE: Throughout I use the plural form of shaman: *shaman.* This may be used interchangeably with "shaman."

A 10,000 Year Journey in Human Consciousness

As we walk through the long corridors of pre-antiquity, we encounter the ancient wise ones who carried the traditions of vanished civilizations from 10,000 years ago and even earlier. Moses, Pythagoras, Plato, Pliny, Solon, Herodotus, Euclid, Socrates, Aristotle and many others brought us mathematics, astronomy and astrology, art, philosophy, medicine, science, government, logic, music, literature—indeed the foundation of every facet of our knowledge today.

As magnificent as these achievements were, nothing superseded their greatest achievement of all: The development of an initiate system that proved beyond question ***through personal experience*** that death is an illusion. Every one of these great initiates was born, lived, died and lived again, and the greatest initiate of them all was Jesus. The biblical Book of Revelations 11:8, clearly designates *Egypt* as the location of Jesus' crucifixion.

The location was in the secret initiation chambers in the Great Pyramid at Cheops. (There is incontrovertible evidence now that the pyramids were not tombs for the pharaohs.) A ceremonial crucifixion, known as the Initiation of the Crucifixion, faced every candidate only after long, arduous preparations. Despite the tremendous difficulties endured, the mystery schools' agendas are more appealing and certainly more intuitively credible than any gruesome tale of torture and murder on the cross.

Many other ceremonial tests at every step of the way climaxed with this initiation. Chanting and toning by twelve priests aided candidates on their three-day journey while they lay in a self-induced deathlike state of suspension of all physical processes. If this was successfully completed, the initiated became a Christed One. Christ is the name of an office, not a man. Jesus was the most successful of the many who embraced the Christ tradition.

The Great Pyramid of Cheops contains the archives of the mystery schools of antiquity. The natural laws governing the Universe and the consciousness within it are inside this temple. Proof exists of unopened chambers within the structure, and the identity of at least one entrance is known.

Shaman accessing these underground spaces via their astral bodies and their solo journey travels, erase all doubts as to the existence of secret rooms very much of the 3rd dimensional kind. My son David describes elsewhere one of his many excursions there, sometimes accompanied by my husband, Don.

It bespeaks a serious take on this work despite their uproarious "linemen for the county" routine, which is obviously a spin-off from the only too-American contemporary improv comedy theatre. Somehow I can't quite imagine the ancients in hard hats, jack hammering the streets, while imaginary neighborhood kids gather around to watch, as truly our legacy from these spiritual giants.

These teachings were left, waiting for a time when the great interlocking gears of long astrological cycles coincided to signal humankind's transcendence once again into heightened consciousness and enlightenment. It lacks only the methodology to achieve it. This was the purpose of the great Mystery Schools, to teach the methodology to access the infinite, of direct experience with God Itself. The recovery of this knowledge makes us all eligible to become Christed. To be Christed is to become an immortal mortal, consciously.

That time is now.

Ready to Deal with Immortality?

I know, ***immortality*** is a very big word. I emphasize it here to remind ourselves once again that the lightbody activation process indeed prepares us to shift into a personal reality where we live for eternity. ***Eternity is not a span of time. It is a dimension!*** We remain there until we intend to move on, which may not be for hundreds or even thousands of years.

The twenty-first century Western cultures, or any following, are unlikely ever to accommodate or duplicate the mystery schools of old. The Age of Pisces was compatible with great sages and master teachers on whom the populace as a whole depended for spiritual guidance. The advent of the new Age of Aquarius shifted focus to awakening the teacher and guide within each individual.

The Aquarian archetype departed dramatically from the dreamy mysticism of Pisces. It hailed our very own New Age heavenly body, Chiron, discovered in 1977. Naturally the discovery of a new planet stirred a good deal of excitement within astrological circles.

As time passed, astronomers began to question Chiron's true character, and the subject grew more controversial. It enjoyed a new identity as an asteroid for a time, until—final answer—it was officially designated as a comet captured by our solar system. We truly had a tiger by the tail! It features a long, elliptical orbit and at present is treated by most astrologers as another planet for all practical purposes.

Chiron was named for a centaur in Greek mythology, half horse, half human. Chiron's mythological characteristics clued us in to what was in store. He is the archetypal teacher-healer of the Olympian Greeks, specifically the Wounded Healer. His maverick nature did not fit neatly into familiar boxes, giving rise to one of the century's most overused clichés, "Think outside the box."

The astronomy profession's waffling about as to Chiron's true physical identity was the tip-off that it is obviously a shape-shifter and shamanic in nature. Chiron was not long in proving his paradigm-busting character as the dirty laundry of one institution after another made headlines. The Catholic Church sex scandals, the corruption on Wall Street, the broken American government, a healthcare system gone completely out of control and Big Pharma's suppression of life-saving natural remedies, set the psychic underpinnings of whistleblowers yet to come.

So now we have Chiron reviving an old traditional figure long lost to the West, the Shaman. The shaman has always been an agent of the unexpected, a spiritual pioneer who shatters familiar patterns of thought and channels radical new visions into human consciousness. Here we meet the fool, the gadfly, the clown, the Trickster. Look deep within your psyche. He lives somewhere within us all! To repress this archetype ensures its projection instead onto our outer world where dangerously inappropriate acting out is met with violence from an uptight, fundamentalist mentality.

In their book *Riding the Horse Backwards* Arnold and Amy Mindell describe a Native American ritual that openly embraces the unorthodox. One day each year, the medicine man dresses in women's clothing and indeed rides his mount backwards. It is not unusual for other cultures, both ancient and contemporary, to temporarily suspend acceptable social conventions and tolerate, if not outright encourage, acting out of non-conformist, silly and clownish behaviors.

Year 2012 was the year of one of the astrological community's largest and most prestigious conferences. It is held in various cities in the United States every four years, sponsored through the cooperative merger of the three largest American astrological organizations. It is an international conference in that the lecturers and workshop teachers are the leading lights among astrologers drawn from many different countries. I can't help from interjecting that yours truly was the keynote speaker at this same international conference in Orlando, Florida in 2004. I received an enthusiastic standing ovation. That was the end of my long career as a keynote speaker at such events. I went out on top! Now back to the point that I want to make concerning this year's conference that was held in New Orleans.

Since I am no longer physically able to attend conferences, my astrology buddies enjoy chatting with me post-conference and filling me in on all of the details, juicy and otherwise. This year, I was privy to many comments about the general atmosphere in New Orleans itself. It seems that there was a good deal of drunkenness abounding at all times of day and night out on the streets of the city. Consequently, many people on the streets were acting out as per expectations would dictate after a few too many swigs of John Barleycorn. Personal opinions ran the gamut about the propriety of such behaviors, of course.

New Orleans–deservedly or not——has traditionally been the city in the national psyche that represents wanton behavior, particularly during Lent; the ordinary rules are suspended and "let's party, baby." Headlines of hate crimes and violent intolerance in our own Western culture suggest that perhaps we would do well to adopt this safety valve that serves to maintain a peaceful balance in other societies. Consider an option to outright designate New Orleans as "The Nation's Playground" in which everyday behavioral conventions are suspended while society looks the other way, allowing anyone to let off steam and party for a few days. It's preferable to some of the tragic ways in which some unbalanced, uptight individuals have acted out a repressed archetype in recent times. I personally would choose to tolerate some drunks in New Orleans making a fool of themselves in place of a string of bloody bodies in a school or movie theatre.

THE THOMAS AFFAIR

In my own life, a great Master volunteered to take ordinary mortals in hand in order to reawaken the inner shaman—twentieth-century Western style—and in so doing gave life to a new archetype in the collective.

The mighty spiritual traditions of golden ages long past were the furthest thoughts from my consciousness when I, as a twelve-year-old farm girl in the Midwest, encountered a little hobo dressed all in brown. The hobo would be my Spirit Teacher, Thomas, ***here to resurrect the ancient traditions of immortality, to prepare us for a shift into another dimension and to play the Ascension Game with me.*** The curious circumstances on that hot August afternoon were such that they slept in oblivion until an extraordinary state of affairs awakened them nearly forty-five years later.

When I spotted the little man in brown walking along the road approaching our farmhouse, I was not surprised when he turned toward our long driveway. In those days—1948—it was a common sight to see hobos who lived life on the road. I was accustomed to them stopping by for a meal. I ran to the house to alert Mom. She always generously responded to any requests for food. Up to that point, everything was completely normal and familiar. The only thing slightly amiss was his lack of any knapsack or other gear hobos traditionally traveled with. Also, he appeared more nattily dressed than the usual hobo attire would dictate.

Outside the kitchen door, there was a circular concrete slab that covered a deep pit in which vegetables were wintered over in the days before refrigeration. The man accepted a plate brimming over with food and seated himself on the slab. That is when things started to go haywire. I began to behave totally out of character.

I sat myself down under a tree about twenty feet away from the hobo. At this point, he had not uttered one single word. He was directly in my line of sight. I fixed my gaze on him and STARED. I did not talk, I just stared as if transfixed. In my mind, I was reminding myself of my mother's admonitions about rudely staring at people. It simply was not done. However, my body did not respond. I just kept right on staring.

The hobo seemed unperturbed by my behavior. His eyes were like nothing I had ever seen. I can't find proper words to describe those eyes. I can only say that they were absolutely compelling. He finished his food and, without a word, stood to leave. Instead of walking back down the driveway to the road, however, he inexplicably crossed the yard toward the barn and the fields beyond. With that, the next extraordinary thing happened.

I managed to get my legs working again. I raced into the kitchen and said to Mom, "I think maybe that was Jesus." If that was not weird enough, she replied, "Yes, don't you remember the story in the Bible where Jesus appeared as a beggar to see who would give him food?" Under the circumstances and knowing my mom, that is a conversation that just could not have happened.

My family embraced strong values but was not religious. We attended church occasionally. My remarks about the man being Jesus far exceeded my twelve-year-old consciousness. Even more remarkable was my mother's reply. That was off the charts. As I said, that conversation just could not have happened within the context of our lives then.

I suddenly realized how strange it was that the hobo was not returning to the road. He turned the corner around the barn toward open fields. I raced out the door like a bat out of hell to find out what he was doing. Mind you, it took me only seconds to reach the far side of the barn. I climbed onto the fence and had an unobstructed view of...nothing. Mr. Hobo was nowhere in sight, which, of course, was utterly impossible. He literally vanished into thin air.

That was when this whole affair was just too far outside my notion of reality. By the time I returned to the front door, the subconscious became the storehouse for this entire episode, and I did not remember it again, as near as I can recall, until approximately forty-five years later under yet another set of extraordinary circumstances. Mom continued peeling potatoes for dinner.

Fast Forward to 1980.

It was a stressful time in my life dealing with a rotten marriage, health issues, career decisions and financial problems. By this time, I was living in Portland, Oregon. A friend of mine owned a funky old house on the Oregon Coast. He was aware that I was battling depression so offered to let me stay at the house, which was standing empty for a time. I gratefully accepted. There was a view of the Pacific Ocean. Walking on the beach was something that restored my soul in the past, so I eagerly anticipated the opportunity.

There was the question of the key to the front door. On the side of the house there was a little area marked off by trellises, like a little unfinished porch with only a dirt floor, covered by leaves and some odd bits of debris. On one of the corner posts was where the key to the house traditionally hung on a nail. In fact, I had used it before myself, when I stayed there. This time, it was nowhere in sight. Yes, indeed, things were about to take a turn toward the uncanny. This time, it would change my life forever.

Assuming that the key had fallen onto the ground, I was determined to sift through the rubble until I found it. I painstakingly sifted through every square inch without success. It was growing dark, so I retrieved a flashlight I carried in the car and searched again. No key.

Totally discouraged, I drove to a downtown telephone booth and called my friend to report my dilemma. Without hesitation, he insisted that I bash in one of the panes on the front door and let myself in that way. He reassured me that he could repair the window the next time he was there. With the aid of a good-sized rock, I managed to bash in the glass without losing any fingers or drawing blood. Once inside, I rounded up a pillow and wadded it into the opening to keep out any cold drafts.

By this time, it was dark. I confess that the whole business with the key had left me somewhat shaken and out of sorts. Just the sort of mindset that so often had opened doors to the sublime and ridiculous on many past occasions. I should have seen it coming! I hauled in everything I needed from my car and sorted out everything that fit into my comfort zone. I put on a pot of coffee. I had the foresight to save up three weeks of The ENQUIRER (I love the crossword puzzle.) I had a delicious new astrology book and, of course, what is life without chocolate?

I settled myself into the big easy chair, somewhat calmed by the sound of the ocean in the background and, without batting an eye, picked up a yellow pad and wrote out fourteen pages that marked the singular event that absolutely and irreversibly transformed my life. The opening sentence read, "My name is Thomas, and I am your teacher."

What impresses me most about what happened that evening was the cavalier manner with which I received dictation from a voice in my head. Furthermore, my utterly calm acceptance of the *contents* of the material was totally inexplicable. My god, here I was listening to some guy dictating how he was my teacher and that I would eventually become part of a group that would work together—fourteen pages of this stuff.

The word “channeling” at that time was not part of the New Age lexicon by any means. In fact, *Psychology Today* magazine published an article on the new phenomenon of channeling several months later. I was grateful to have a word for it! (Just try explaining channeling without knowing or using the word.)

Since you have the advantage of retrospection, you have now perhaps realized that Thomas was *voila*! one and the same as the hobo I met when I was twelve years old. This awareness did not come blasting into my consciousness until much later. It meant that I must accept the mystery of the disappearing hobo along with it. This may seen like small potatoes compared to later experiences I’ve described. However, by then I had breached the walls defining my belief system many times. By the way, the next time my friend visited the beach house, the key was hanging on the nail exactly where it always had been.

After reading Patricia Cota-Robles's book *Who Am I? Why Am I Here?* I realized that this chapter might well be one of the most significant one of the entire book! Below is a quote from page 96:

> “Many of our Ascended sisters and brothers agreed to lower their frequency of vibration to remain within the physical sight of the unawakened Children of Earth.
>
> “...As they lived their lives in their Ascended state of consciousness, we were in awe over what appeared to be miracles. ***It never occurred to us that these Beings were just demonstrating our own human potential.*** **(Italics mine.)**
>
> “We were so beaten down by our own victim consciousness we assumed that these Beings were powerful gods and goddesses who had come to save us. We started worshiping them and expecting them to do the very things they were trying to teach us that we could do for ourselves. After a period of time, it became clear to the Company of Heaven that this experiment was not working.
> "

> "The Ascended Beings were becoming a distraction for Humanity instead of an inspiration. ...With this realization, The Alpha and Omega sounded a cosmic tone, and the Ascended Beings raised their vibrations back into the frequencies of the 4th Dimension."

Throughout the nearly 13 years that I worked closely with Thomas, I was too close to the forest to see the trees. I hadn't the slightest notion then that ***he was laying down the model in the collective psyche for awakening the Twenty-first Century shaman.***

As you read the selected stories that I've included, you will have the advantage over me. You may recognize the continuous thread embedded in the background no matter how bizarre, or puzzling, or hilarious, or ludicrous, or astounding or disorganized the events in the foreground may seem. You might even feel private stirrings that evoke your own inner shaman.

Indeed Year 2012 is forever fixed in the global consciousness because of its connection to the Mayan calendar cycles and great astrological line-ups with the center of our galaxy. But time marches on. The hands of the clocks keep turning. And Year 2013 and beyond will align with its own Great Cycle written in the stars.

This model laid down by a great contemporary master will serve as an appropriate guidebook now, and throughout the continuation of this new time for Earth and on whichever dimension of reality future spiritual seekers may find themselves.

One theme unmistakably stuck out in the first message from Thomas. He insisted that he was a "group teacher," not just my teacher. But it was his prediction that I would be part of a group that kept my mind playing guessing games as I drove back to Portland. Just who was this group? And what were we supposed to do?

I enjoyed a wide circle of metaphysical friends and acquaintances. I maintained an office as a professional astrologer. I conducted a free Huna group that met once a month. I certainly was in a position to meet likely candidates. By the time the 4Ds came together, there were many years of obsessing about it as different candidates came and went.

My next concern was about how my friends would react when I told them about Thomas. Granted, I had a reputation that I was pretty outrageous, and nothing I did would surprise them. Deciding just who to tell was short-lived. Shortly after my return from the Coast, Thomas took over and "suggested" that I invite various people to lunch and then spring the Thomas adventure on them. I admit to a certain amount of foot-dragging before I actually did as he suggested.

My attempts to describe the encounter with Thomas are best described as feeble as I stammered my way through the explanation. I was absolutely shocked at everyone's reaction. *It was the same as mine had been!* Ho hum. So what else is new? They even casually struck up a conversation with him. It was about as impressive as my grocery-shopping list.

After several of these lunches, I had to believe that Thomas could somehow manipulate the consciousness with whomever he wished to communicate psychically. Some of the friends he suggested I tell did not have a psychic bone in their body. Yet, they spoke with the invisible guy quite matter-of-factly. The funniest episode concerned a close friend of mine. She was totally skeptical of this Thomas person and she told him so in no uncertain terms. In fact, they argued for a good twenty minutes while I tried not to choke on my salad! The conversation finally ended when Thomas circumvented her skepticism with the remark, "If I'm not real, who are you talking to?"

Not more than six months later, channeling exploded into the mass psyche. Suddenly, wannabe channellers, mostly young girls, were flooding my office with various tales of communicating with guides. It was soon obvious what Thomas was up to. I was learning how to counsel people about working with guides and teachers. Many people were impressed that *anybody* from the other side was communicating with them; discernment flew right out the window.

Believe me; it was like taking a baby's toy to pry the girls loose from their favorite activity with some dubious invisible characters. Many of them were channeling hours a day, giving no thought to just whom they were dealing with. My skills as a counselor in these matters were very sharp with Thomas's coaching. In fact, it formed the basis of this chapter . The Huna group to which I referred earlier was a great venue for not only introducing Thomas and lecturing about channeling but also a perfect forum for answering questions about working with guides.

You can't imagine the difficulty of capturing the essence of our experiences with an unseen teacher who, nevertheless, laid down the presence of a constant companion. However, if you truly get the message that it is all about working on yourself, you will awaken your own inner teacher and guide. You won't need a Thomas. That was his message. That is why this may be the most significant chapter in the entire book.

Don't get the wrong impression when I say that Thomas was a constant presence in our lives. That is not to imply intrusiveness or control in any negative way whatsoever. Forget any image of a stern old man cracking the whip. Thomas was the personification of the Trickster archetype. He was funny and wildly unpredictable. He could be utterly maddening. He was a cunning fox and won every encounter. He was no gentleman.

Only on extremely rare occasions did Thomas directly interfere with our lives. I have already written about the time I was suddenly awakened from sleep and ordered to the hot tub just as Don fainted and slipped under the water. I realized then that Thomas would interfere when it was a life or death situation. He also exhibited knowledge of the future. Otherwise, he could not have laid down plans to save our financial butts long before there were any red flags on the horizon.

I revealed earlier in the book that we used a consciousness-expanding drug, which I refer to as The Pill. I don't want to say what it was in case any readers are tempted to take a whirl at it no matter how much I caution against it. Also, it was legal at the time but that is no longer the case.

That Thomas engineered the whole Pill scenario wasn't ever questioned in the slightest. The way we came by it in the first place was unquestionably the workings of an unseen hand. It was synchronicity gone mad, you might say. Of course, I had no knowledge at the time that smoking and mind-altering drugs enjoyed thousands of years as an accepted tradition in native cultures. We never used it recreationally; it was always under his tutelage. At times we took rather large quantities, and I admit that every once in a while I secretly feared that I would end up as a brain-damaged vegetable.

Don and I were the first ones to work with The Pill and that is the way it remained for a long time. There were long stretches of time when we came home from our offices on Friday night, started right in and went all week-end, only to repeat it the following week. There were two aspects to the work. One was two-pronged. It involved playing therapist and patient. I was groomed as the therapist, which played into work I would do years into the future. Don was the patient.

Don was no "pretend" patient. He had deep psychological wounds from a severely troubled childhood of abuse that were far from resolved. He tried to kill himself when he was eight years old. Later on, he was in a mental hospital for a year. Unresolved issues manifested in some acted out behaviors and personality traits as one would expect. I won't spell out all of the details, but if I were in counseling training, the Universe sent me the poster child for Tough Case. However, as far as Thomas was concerned? Bring it on, baby, this was war.

Indeed, war it was. Thomas, through me, battled on, week after week, month after month and yes, year after year. Don is a very powerful customer. He had a wall around himself and was locked down like Fort Knox. He was an artist when it came to passive-aggressive behavior. However, he was no match for the wily Master Therapist.

Any attempt to accurately grasp the work Thomas did with Don is futile. One thing I can tell you, though, in answer to an obvious question, "How do I know that was Thomas and not just me working with Don?" It was all done with The Pill and since The Pill was consciousness expanding, maybe I was simply operating at an expanded level. I assure you with 100 per cent confidence that had you been there to witness one of these extended sessions, you would've been convinced. In fact, there were several other fairly savvy individuals when it came to things of this sort who did witness the Thomas-Diana Show. They agreed. Not on my best day could I ever match the Master Therapist at work.

However, I can tell you what it did do. By using the drug, I was able to let go and let Thomas work through me. It was not channeling in the sense of just repeating his words. He was able to work telepathically with me also. I perceived whole pictures and concepts. I realized when I went back to work at my office after one of these sessions that I was just a tad more psychically sensitive. I was obviously being trained as a counselor-healer by working so closely with the Master.

The second aspect of the training was work that he did with me alone. It involved meeting the archetypes up close and personal. The therapy sessions with Don were difficult but, nevertheless, they were in the world of psychology, a world with which I was familiar and comfortable. The wild and crazy world of the archetypes was something else again.

As usual, Thomas sprung this on me with no warning or introductory explanations. One week-end he calmly suggested that I take five Pills. The normal dose is one Pill of about 120 mg. We had never, ever taken even two at a time. We went around and around with howling protests for about half an hour. I asked him what I was supposed to do after calling 911 and explaining to the medics and the cops just what I had done, if I wasn't already dead, that is.

We finally negotiated two Pills. In typical Thomas style, he said, "Well then, take two, and when they take effect, you will know that it is okay to take three more." I was pretty sure that two Pills would put me in a coma. But I did it, and of course, after an hour I took three more.

I was sitting in an easy chair in our family room. Don was across the room, seated about 15 feet away, facing me. He had taken one Pill, but I could tell that he was wondering what in the devil was happening next. As Diana, I was up on the ceiling in a corner of the room. Seated in the chair, I was Zeus.

I knew something was happening by the look on Don's face. "Look at your hands. Omygod. Look at your hands. Those aren't your hands. Those are a big man's hands." About that time, Thomas told me to aim the palm of my big man's hands toward Don. "Get out of the chair," I commanded. Get out of the chair? He couldn't even move.

His face looked contoured by *g*-forces just like an astronaut going into space. He was paralyzed. I wasn't sure but what he might burst into spontaneous combustion. That gives you a clue that by this time I was never sure what in hell Thomas actually might do. But Don did not burst into flames, and I did not die in the emergency room from an overdose.

The work with the archetypes apparently was Thomas's idea of necessary training. Somehow, each time one of the archetypes was activated, this seemed to give me access to its particular brand of consciousness. Pallas Athena, the female warrior goddess, appeared when I was in a big fight with City Hall. I ended up losing my house, but I went down swinging and made the papers—twice.

I'm sure the one Don remembers most is Medusa. I was home alone one morning when Thomas suggested a little journey into Archetype Land. By this time arguing was pointless. When Don came home from lunch, he found his wife writhing naked on the bed and hissing like a snake. Fortunately, the snake-haired Medusa did not kill him with a look. He was probably Perseus in a past life. Thomas was activating the archetypes that were connected to ones I needed for my personal development (Athena) and ones that would later be used in my work (healing and shamanic soul retrieval).

The Ultimate Archetypal Journey

I will summarize by saying that over a period of a couple of years or more, I "became" many other archetypes. One time I was on a Pill trip with brother, Duane. We were engaged in some really heavy duty healing work when in the middle of the proceedings, I pulled out my Zeus gig—only, on this occasion, with a twist. I shape-shifted into Zeus, the wall behind me dissolved into a throne room. Duane was afraid that the people in the adjoining motel room could actually see us through the hole in the wall. There "Zeus" sat, very tall and regal, seated in a half slouch on a huge ornate throne. The energy in the entire room crackled with his royal authority.

He spoke to Duane. Then he stood, and with a single, seamless gesture grasped his short cape, whipped it around his arm and presented it to Duane. He was passing the torch. In describing the scene, Duane always says, "Diana could have rehearsed that gesture for the rest of her life, but she never could have duplicated it. Only the king. Only the king."

There was another that can only be described as a run-in with no less than the Trickster, Pegasus. It takes only once to hear his sinister, throaty whisper in your ear, "But horses can't fly, can they?" to carry you to the very edge of crazy. That was years ago, but the mention of Pegasus still gives my brother paranoid shakes. I don't know exactly what he experienced when I was Pegasus, and I'm not asking.

There is probably a book—at least a pamphlet—that I could write to really do justice to all of the work with archetypes. What is important is not only my personal training and whatever that may have meant for me. There is an entirely different and more universal level that Thomas introduced. It was actually the title of one of my lectures "Archetypes for a New Age." The twenty-first century shaman requires the underpinnings of a whole new set of archetypal figures. The Old Guard was powerful in its time, but this is a new time. I wanted to include enough of the archetype work to give you the flavor of our experiences with our wise but wily teacher, Thomas. Be assured, he had other tricks up his sleeve, and again they came bombing out of the blue when least expected.

LIVING IN COMMUNITY—POPULATION FOUR

After everything I had experienced with Thomas—a book in itself—I thought there was nothing that could really surprise me. I am sure the reader immediately sees the utter folly of this notion. You would be right, of course. There was something, and yes, it came bombing out of the blue, telegraphing absolutely nothing ahead of time. Yes, Thomas was just getting warmed up.

An account of the story I am about to share with you stretches my journalistic skills to the max. I have written, rewritten and rejected the opening paragraphs several times. I just cannot give it the nuclear punch it deserves. I finally had to settle for "you just had to be there."

Consequently, I'm hitting the high points without fanfare in hopes that you may read between the lines for the blast of energy from things unsaid. In the end, there are only four souls who can ever carry in sum total the memory of this most incredible experience that changed our lives forever, beginning on the night of December 18, 1983.

This story has a beginning, a middle and an end. You already know when it began. So here is the *what*. At that time, I was conducting a series of classes in my house under the auspices of The University Without Walls. During the last class of the series, Thomas told me to invite three people (who were teachers) to meet upstairs with me in my living room afterwards. We gathered there about 10 o'clock.

The mood was offhanded and relaxed. Thomas often requested time to chat, so there was no extraordinary anticipation as to what it was about. The other players were Judy, John and Don. I spoke for Thomas. He opened the conversation by nonchalantly suggesting that it would be good if the four of us worked more closely together. We casually nodded agreement.

I was not sure if I was developing into a paranoid or whether those tiny fingers of uneasiness actually were intuitions tippy-toeing over my solar plexus. It surely had nothing to do with objections to the other three people. We were all on very friendly terms. Still, there it was. I was jarred by what Thomas was saying. "I mean right away," he continued, in a tone of voice atypical of vintage Thomas.

The silence that followed seemed to last 100 years as Thomas's meaning ever so gradually soaked in. I can still remember with horror the smiling, foolishly expectant faces of my companions, futilely waiting for the rest of the instructions.

"HE MEANS RIGHT NOW—TONIGHT—YOU IDIOTS. RIGHT NOW TONIGHT. HE MEANS TO MOVE IN TOGETHER RIGHT NOW-TONIGHT. THAT'S WHAT HE MEANS BY WORKING MORE CLOSELY TOGETHER RIGHT AWAY!" I screamed.

It was my friends' turn to experience the 100 years of silence. Psychotic visions danced in our heads. The United States declared war on Canada. This could not be happening. Now I know how the passengers of the *Titanic* felt when they realized they were going down. Life was over as they knew it.

The next thing to follow was a long serious message from Thomas. He explained that if he was to be our Teacher, it meant that he must take responsibility for our lives. The four of us were given half an hour that night to decide to accept the terms that partially limited our free will, and Thomas would be the one to decide when that would be. (Remember the hot tub incident?) I was very taken aback by the seriousness of this conversation. I think now that this ritual was probably standard procedure right out of the *Spirit Teacher's Guide and Manual,* "Chapter One: Securing Student's Consent."

You never in your life saw faces more solemn than ours as we paced around the house contemplating just what it was that we were getting ourselves into. We eventually calmed down, gathered around the dining room table, reached out and joined hands as each one decided that we would make the commitment. I had the biggest house, so it was quickly decided that the only logical choice was for everyone to move in with me—that night.

John had just graduated from college and established himself in a new apartment. Don had recently divorced his wife and moved into a new apartment just days before. (Yes, this is Dr. Don whom I later married and had been dating.) Judy recently moved from Eugene, Oregon, to Portland and took an apartment just down the street from my house. The remainder of that night was mostly taken up with running around to the various apartments gathering up futons and bedding. After pushing furniture around a bit, everyone established a place to crash until morning. It was the days following this night that were *really* utter chaos. How we pulled it off I will never know.

For this to make any sense, you must understand that I lived in a magic house. It had an uncanny way of transforming itself into the needs of the moment no matter how unrelated one situation was from the other. At that time, I was living there alone since my "divorce from hell" three months earlier. I actually lived with three different husbands in that house. But there is no need to go into that any further; readers may respond the way my mom did.

I lived in a large, three story, six bedroom, three bathroom, old renovated house on a half acre property with decks, gazebo and hot tub. Don and John located a large storage unit, rented a truck and played musical chairs with furniture. My dining table swapped with Judy's, antique chairs and couches came out of the den to accommodate a bedroom for John, Don's electric organ went downstairs, an easel was set up in the front glassed-in porch for Judy's art projects. Three other apartments had to be dismantled.

There wasn't time for excessive hemming and hawing about whose coffee pot was best and the like. We had another complication to consider. Judy had three kids in school, and they were due home for Christmas break in three days. Don's remodeling skills were quickly tapped to convert my downstairs classroom into another bedroom by the time they arrived. This still left a space for a downstairs den and TV room. My upstairs bedroom and office/library were left intact, which I clung to as a sanctuary that would be my life saver.

Adding to the pain of it all was the typical Northwestern rainy winter, which showed no mercy. It was cold, and every time Don and John returned for another truckload, they looked even more wretched than the time before. It was inevitable, however, that eventually it would end. We collapsed in exhaustion around the dining room table.

Again there was the 100 years of silence. I don't remember who screamed it first, but I do know it was suddenly the collective thought. **WHO'S GOING TO DO THE COOKING? A resounding, "I'm not" made the vote unanimous—no one!** It was then I saw a vision of our aspirations for entrance into the higher spiritual realms crashing on the shores of the kitchen stove, as it were.

Psychic Cooking

Thomas didn't let us wallow in our dilemma for too long. The first step was an outline of the diet we were to follow, no, make that the diet tailored for **each** of us individually to follow. By the time this was hammered out (did you say cantaloupe or honeydew melon for breakfast?), it was too late for grocery shopping. We made do with a sack of take-out hamburgers and fries. Dinner that night resembled a wake as we silently feared that these were the last burgers we would ever see this side of the veil.

We all piled into my Monte Carlo and set out for a special health and organic foods grocery store, Nature's. I'm not so sure Nature's really existed on this plane, but let's just pretend it did. It was a little storefront place with old well-trodden wooden floors. Baskets of organic beets, potatoes, carrots or whatever else was on hand that particular day littered the floor along with the packaged ramen noodles, fruit bins, natural canned juices, teas and stuff like that.

We hit Nature's like a bunch of monkeys on speed. We were frantic. We were hysterical. We yelled. We made a lot of noise. In one hand we crashed around with a grocery cart and in the other was our own personal little list from Thomas. At that time, John and I were the only two who channeled Thomas. We were besieged by Judy and Don rushing up to ask which banana, which this or that. I noticed another guy in the store watching this pandemonium. He finally screwed up enough nerve to ask, "Are you on some sort of special diet?" "You might say that," I answered. He nodded approval. In Portland at least, the world of the health food nut granted very wide latitude when it came to personal demeanor. Nature's became our regular port of call for a very long while.

We managed to negotiate refrigerator and cupboard space to accommodate our separate stashes of food items. The problem of who was going to prepare meals was quickly solved when I heard Thomas say, "Diana, go to the kitchen and get the lettuce." Once in the kitchen, I thought I had been slapped in a strait jacket and tossed into the psych ward. Yes, that was the beginning of the adventure forever referred to as **PSYCHIC COOKING.**

Psychic cooking was frenetic, noisy and insane. John and I were the channellers; therefore, we were the cooks. We prepared the evening meals. The *cook du jour* was commanded to loudly yell the directions as they were barked by Thomas at the speed of a fast moving train.

We never quite knew just what we were preparing until the last minute. I was making a pot of soup on one occasion. I was simultaneously screaming through the process of making coffee. As soon as the coffee was perked, I was ordered to dump it in the sink and then dump the grounds in the soup along with an ice cream sandwich. The really crazy thing about these meals is that they were exquisitely delicious, the amounts for four people came out even to the last bite, and we never had the same thing twice.

I have always wished I could publish one of my recipes from psychic cooking days. I will seize that opportunity right here by giving the directions for three of my first dishes. Please remember who Thomas was working with. These weren't exactly pheasant under glass gourmet delights at a five star restaurant. After all, I'm not Julia Child.

Coconut Beef Psychic Recipe

3 rib eye steaks cubed
½ fresh coconut cubed
Fresh asparagus tips
Two whole red onions
Teriyaki sauce
Couple cloves of garlic
Couple of carrots, sliced
2 potatoes cut into cubes
Sunflower seeds
Sesame seeds,
Salt to taste

Heat oil in a wok or heavy-bottomed pan. Add sliced garlic and onion and sauté until tender. Remove from oil to separate platter. Add asparagus, carrots, potato, seeds and a dash of teriyaki. Cook on low heat until barely tender. Remove to platter. Brown meat in a little teriyaki sauce, cook to rare. Add other ingredients. Heat through. Cover and let sit for a while to blend flavors. Heat one more time before serving.

Serves four

Honey Rice

Cook rice until done.
Add honey just to coat rice.
Add English walnuts and white raisins.
You may use any nuts or dried fruit you prefer.
Also good heated and served with milk as a hot breakfast meal.
Add some cinnamon just before serving.

Cabbage Salad

Chop one head of red cabbage into bowl.
Add Mayonnaise to lightly coat cabbage.
Add about 1 tablespoon honey or to taste.
Add red cider vinegar to taste (start with two teaspoons)
Add 1 teaspoon creamy horse radish or to taste.
Add a dash of salt and celery seed.
Sprinkle dried herbs over the top (dried parsley flakes, mint flakes or what ever).
Can add carrots finely sliced and green olives with a little of the olive juice if you like.
Add thinly sliced apples for variety.

Seeing in the Dark

So far the adventures with Thomas were fairly tolerable. That was about to take a very dark turn. That dark turn was into the recesses of our own psyches. Thomas initiated nothing less than deep psychotherapy by a Master Teacher, and he was taking no prisoners. We ended up living together for six months. By then, we had been through the wringer and barely recognizable as the same four who started out.

There were hours upon hours of psychotherapy. At any given time, any one of us would need days of energy healing from the other three. There were crying spells and also physical pain as past life experiences dislodged from the body. Thomas instituted a program of opening different chakras. These were brutal and the ones I dreaded most of all. One chakra opening put me in bed for several days, and I lost my eyesight for three of them. I was terrified that I was blinded for life. Don was directed to prepare the most terrible concoctions from the juicer several times a day.

Don had his chiropractic practice, and I had an office for my astrological services, so we did the inner work nights and week-ends. Week-ends were reserved for ceremony. Thomas's version of ceremony was when one person was singled out for special healing. The remaining three followed Thomas's psychic directions for performing a variety of energy work. It was not uncommon for these ceremonies to go on for several hours. It was totally exhausting for everyone.

It could also be dangerous. During one ceremony, Judy was doing the channeling. I remember that John had gone outside to retrieve a branch that had fallen from the stand of tall Douglas fir trees in front of my house. Thomas instructed him to brush Don's energy field while Don was lying outstretched on the floor. I was to "gather" the energy and release it into Don's crown chakra. When I released it, I shot backwards. If I had not had the wits as I whirled around to raise my arms just in time, I would have bashed my brains out on the fireplace mantel.

By no stretch of the imagination were we now perfect little initiates and in need of no further personal work. All of you lightworkers out there who are reading this are laughing about now—laughing in recognition. Just like the Fool in the Tarot deck, once you step off that cliff into the unknown there is no turning back. We were—and are—grateful to Thomas for helping us along on our spiritual journey that continues to this day.

I can look back and recognize the outline and emphasis on deep inner work. You will recognize it, also. There was a special diet (more on that in other chapters.), the importance of working together in community, the psychotherapy concerning issues in this and past lives, clearing out negative energies and the clearing and opening of the chakra system.

One last thing I will mention was the weirdest of all, and that is really saying something! At the beginning of our living together, Thomas designated me as the scribe. I had a book that served as a journal to record everything that happened every day. At the end of each day, we were to gather around the dining room table as I read the day's activities aloud. Each night before retiring, I read this aloud as everyone screamed, "No! No! No way! That was last week!" And so the arguing and uproar wrangled on each and every night. Time was playing tricks on us.

Each night as I read that day's activities, I was utterly exhausted as I loudly swore above the cacophony that it was indeed just that one day's journal entry. I began to understand why Thomas made me keep the journal. Otherwise, it was not believable that so much could possibly have taken place in one day. I would not have believed it, either, if I had not documented it myself.

The sense of time was utterly whack-a-doodle. Each of us experienced one day as a week. Each week just had to be a month. Whatever occurred in the morning hours seemed at least several days earlier by nightfall. After several weeks of haggling about it over and over again I simply read the damn journal, and we went to bed. Each person was left to contemplate the impossible on their own.

So that is the end of the middle of the story of the four of us in community.

The End of the Story

Judy

Thomas felt that Judy had more work to do on her own. She moved to Rosicrucian Park in California to live for many years, following their special program in conjunction with psychotherapy. Her journey eventually led her to Pacific Grove, California where she is the matriarch of her children and grandchildren. We are still in frequent communication. She struggles with painful physical problems stemming from a childhood bout of polio. She was later joined by Maureen Callaghan, a phenomenal healer and golfer. (She would love that part about golfing.) Maureen is now very much a part of our spiritual family. I am sure that all of our soul contracts with her were activated when she joined Judy in their mutual spiritual journey.

John

John is perhaps the one to be admired most of all. He was a generation behind us other three. He blasted open psychically without warning overnight. When he moved from my house, John moved into Portland with one of his sisters. He grew very ill. He called my office one day in agonizing physical pain asking to see me. I had to help him up the stairs to my office. He explained that he never had the time to work out basic family issues like us older folks. For several good reasons, he said he was closing the door to his psychic work and go to medical school.

The reason I admire John is that he did not let his ego get in the way of an overwhelming psychic development that was going way too fast. He had no qualms in listening to his body and throwing in the towel. He shut those doors forever, and I totally agreed with him. John graduated from massage school. On a job in Montana, he met and married a girl from Switzerland. He moved there and became a Swiss citizen. As Hans he has a thriving practice as a doctor of several therapies he studied there. He calls me every few years to have his family's astrology charts updated. He is working out his family karma at his own pace and in his own space.

Don and Diana

On September 12, 1984, Don and I were married in Reno. Running concurrently with that, my divorce from hell also involved a long-running, complicated losing battle with City Hall. At the formal request of the sheriff, I moved into a rented house exactly on Christmas Day, 1984, in the pouring rain. I lost my magic house. In 1985, we bought a large condo in Lake Oswego, a suburb south of Portland. We both continued to work at our respective offices in Portland.

Not Quite The End Of The Story

My work with Thomas continued. There was another incident in which Thomas stepped in to save the day. This time it was our financial butts that were on the line. Thomas surely had a crystal ball in order to anticipate a looming financial crisis long before any red flags appeared to us. Once again I sang the same old "wrong song," I thought nothing he did could surprise me.

Year 1991 was Year *Annus Horribilus.** In January, I awoke to a body encased in terrible physical pain from head to toe. Thinking it was some exotic virus, I prepared to tough it out for a few days. Those few days turned out to be one year...and beyond.

I was a hair's breadth away from closing my office in Portland. I couldn't work, but the rent marched on. Thomas threw a cosmic fit and for that I'm forever grateful. It would have dealt a death blow to an astrological practice that I had laboriously built up since my move to Portland in 1973 and at that office location since 1981.

In those years, my astrological colleagues warned me that it was impossible to make a living as an astrologer. I silently vowed that I would be the exception because I was motivated to leave an abusive relationship. As it turned out, my astrology career continued to play a critical role in my life, financial and otherwise. By the time I met Don my astrological practice was flourishing. But this is still not the end of the story. Not by a very long shot.

As I languished in bed, my brother took ill and the only solution was for him to move in with us. We were still living in the three-story condo in Lake Oswego, just south of Portland. The place easily accommodated a long-term guest. Before this tale is told, it will be apparent that I found another magic house!

---

* "horrible year" in English

Earlier that year, brother Duane and I had the sad duty of committing our dad to a nursing home. He was suffering from severe Parkinson's disease. We made two driving trips to Iowa to supervise his affairs. The family farm crop cycles trumped any personal needs of ours for a time-out, but rather pressured us to rent it out immediately and continue its supervision from Oregon. Duane and I were barely able physically to cope with the long trips to the Midwest, one time in a blinding blizzard. Dad also owned a lovely place in South Texas, where he wintered. I luckily located another Iowa couple who were thrilled to buy it and even invited me for a visit, sight unseen. But, of course, I was an Iowan daughter.

Besides that there were dad's and our legal, medical and financial obligations to deal with at a distance by way of numerous stacks of papers covering my dining room table filing system. As time passed, the dining room table monster bloomed ever larger and was anxiously and permanently conferred the scary moniker: THE TABLE. That name strikes fear in my heart yet to recall those terrible days. The thing was alive! But there's more.

One day I was propped up in bed in my robe mindlessly watching TV as usual. I was coping with the pain by finally resorting to aspirin around the clock. Duane was sitting on the main floor couch, mostly staring into space until it was time to bring me my freshly-made carrot juice. Don flew into the house and called me into the living room. I wondered why he was home from his office so early. One look at his face and I knew that I did not want to hear the answer.

The Chiropractic Board had pulled his license to practice! If he were a lawyer; it was equivalent to getting disbarred. There is no need to describe our reactions to this shock, especially in context with our already dismal state of affairs. This turned the last calendar page of **Year *Annus Horribilis.*** *

*** By Way Of Explanation If You Care**

I did not want to clutter the text with a convoluted explanation of why Don's license was pulled. But just to satisfy readers that he did not kill or maim anyone, this was entirely one of those convoluted political situations that one gets caught up in. In Oregon at that time, in order to practice homeopathy, one must have a license if you are a chiropractor. Not wanting to repeat courses of study already covered in chiropractic school, a small group of practicing chiropractors were offered the opportunity to take a streamlined course of study in homeopathy at the Portland Naturopathic School. They were promised a license from the Naturopathic Board, and the required clinic hours could be integrated with their established practices.

Don not only completed this course, he additionally attended a one-year course in Seattle connected to John Bastyr Naturopathic School there. This earned him national certification. Meanwhile, some sort of upheaval that was never explained turned the

So what were we to do?
Was I about to lose another magic house? The answer lies in what happened in the interim between the loss of the first magic house in 1983 and again in 1991. And the answer is no, I did not lose the second house. So what transpired to save this house? There were two things: I cleared fear of loss from my psyche, and at Thomas's behest, grew income producing pot (marijuana; yes, *that* kind of pot) in my attic.

Back To The Beginning Once Again

And that explanation requires a return to the beginning of the beginning once again. Thomas presented himself as our Teacher. So just what was it that Thomas taught us? The answer to that is the one single thing that stands tall in order to prepare for ascension...and beyond!

Thomas utilized the Trickster archetype to rattle our consciousness outside of belief boundaries. Events moved and shifted so fast and so unexpectedly that we had no time to respond in old habitual ways. Even time itself went absolutely willy-wonkers. You really had to be there for that one. Many of you reading this book are the type who have already probably read in other sources that time is an illusion of the 3rd dimension. Take it from me, time is a very slippery slope.

Back to door number one: How did I clear my psyche of fear of loss, and how did that save magic house number two: by following Thomas's protocol amidst the wild and wooly antics involved in tending to one's field at all times, which is most serious business indeed! Your field in this context does not include dirt in the back forty. It is your field of consciousness.

Most people react at first that understanding what is in one's field is a simple matter. Thomas once asked us to list on a sheet of paper the contents of our field of consciousness with the understanding that we must keep track of anything that may need to be transformed. We laboriously spent several hours listing everything we could think of to impress Thomas with our willingness to really take it on.

Portland school on its head. Don went to classes one day, and his class teacher abruptly went missing along with many other teachers, and even the president of the school itself.

Meanwhile, Don was establishing quite a little practice as a homeopathic physician along with the five other doctors. The Naturopathic and Chiropractic Boards said this was practicing without a license and bam! That was it. The crazy other side of the coin was that any layperson could practice homeopathy. I, myself, could have legally practiced as a homeopath! Several years later we learned by way of the grape vine that the rules had been changed and chiropractors could practice homeopathy, blah, blah, blah.

Every so often he interjected, "Are you sure that is everything?" to the point where I really regretted that he wasn't in physical form just that once. We handed in our papers, so to speak. We failed miserably. By the time he added all of the ills of the world to our lists, it created the chapter in this book "Ho'oponopono." But first we will tackle how to tend the personal, inner items in our fields. If we finish that sometime in this lifetime, we'll move on to consider how our fields also impact large impersonal issues of the day.

Later I was experienced enough to mine the contents of my energy field of consciousness without the outer event always present. However, for beginners you start with an event. This, of course, will be different for everyone. The event is something that happens in your life that is bad. It may be a little bad or very bad. You argued with a guy at work. Your son died in a motorcycle accident. You deal with it all.

So we are talking about awareness, awareness all the time. You tend your field of consciousness all the time. That does not mean that you don't have time for your daily activities. You go about them just the same, but *with awareness.* Don't let any of the little buggers get away from you. A little scratch can become a raging infection over time if it's not cleaned out.

So there is an event, like losing your dream house, your magic house. If you knew the whole story, you would know that it was that bastard ex-husband's fault. Oh, oh, another event. There was this bastard husband in your field. He really took advantage of you. You were victimized. There is a pattern of the victim in your field. Well, how was I supposed to know he would turn out this way? (Because you saw it all before you were married.) That was called denial. That wasn't denial. I was scared. I was terrified. My first husband left me, and I was afraid.

It's the man who is supposed to earn the money. So you have the helpless woman in your field, and she went out and married an arrogant, jobless, verbally abusive raging maniac to support you. (My mom was mentally ill and she raged and raged against my dad.) So that is your picture of marriage? And on and on and on. So what is the story about the bad thing in your field? Round them all up. They are all your responsibility to change.

The point was made over and over again—it's always your story, and you had to look at yourself to find the author of that script within and do the inner work. It was never anybody else's fault. If it was, it would never change. Be glad it is your own story. That way you may empower yourself to transform it before it went out into the world and created another bad event.

I worked on my fundamental fear of loss for years. I worked on it every day. I recited mantras. I listened to self-help tapes driving in my car back and forth from work. I checked in with the knot in my stomach. I analyzed my dreams. I read books. I attended lectures. I visualized. I talked to myself a lot. Then one day it was gone. It shifted while I was driving the car. I yelled, "Yaaay," out loud. I got you, you little bitch. Now I am a real warrior, and I love you!

When Don came home and told me he could no longer practice chiropractic, meaning we essentially had no income with me out for the count as well, I calmly looked at the event. I walked upstairs and sat down on the side of the bed. I spoke out loud. Either I was talking to the air, or I was talking to God. "Okay, God," I said, "I have 100 percent faith that you will see that I do not suffer a loss here. I'm going to find out how absolute faith works because I am putting this event into Your hands."

In the following week, a young doctor wandered into Don's office and asked Don if he would sell him his practice. We negotiated a sale and received a monthly check. Meanwhile, I had dragged myself to my office, which I did once a week to see a counseling client. Coincidentally, he grew pot in his attic. On that one day, he looked around my counseling room and casually observed, "Too bad you can't grow pot in this office. This space should yield about $20,000 every few months." Thomas said, "Invite him to dinner, and we'll hammer out a little deal over brandy."

And He Wasn't Kidding

The idea that I would grow pot in my house was an idea so ludicrous, so unbelievable, so inconceivable and so terrifying that I was absolutely positive that Thomas could not possibly be serious and that we would never, ever do it. He was. And we did. And, yes, this time, unlike the Pill, it WAS illegal.

If this information wounds some readers' sensibilities to the point that they are tempted to turn the narcs onto me, I will claim literary license. This was a long time ago, and all evidence to the contrary has long since been eradicated. So forget that. What may be even more troubling is the idea that this alleged master teacher would involve us in illegal activities.

Thomas laid the foundation for growing an income-producing crop long before circumstances came to light that we were once again perilously close to losing our house. As it turned out, all three of us were without the means to generate enough income to pay the mortgage and otherwise keep us afloat. The old trickster somehow foresaw the inevitable long before the event and set the wheels in motion that would indeed save the day.

I don't want to belabor the point here, but I can tell you that I lived with a knot in my gut as long as there was a marijuana crop growing in my attic. However Thomas managed to pull this off, I can say that the guy with whom Thomas struck the deal took each crop off our hands. We never hung around school yards peddling pot to kids. I was comforted in the knowledge that our crop went to other doctors who were grateful for the anonymity, and Pot Guy was grateful for ready-made buyers.

As it turned out, we did not make a bundle on our little farming operation. We made just enough to keep the wolf from the door. As for my personal philosophy, I think it was a colossal mistake to criminalize marijuana in the first place. Thomas must have shared that philosophy as well and answered to a higher interpretation of cosmic laws. If this little adventure into criminal activity involved heroin, cocaine or any of the really BAD drugs, I would have walked away without hesitation even if it brought a million dollars into the coffers.

Interesting Update

At this writing, the 2012 elections include on my Washington State ballot a referendum to legalize marijuana.

We Made It Home Free

We obviously never got caught. By the time we shut down operations, we were left with a streak of paranoia that took a good while to clear. Pot Guy and his wife were eventually arrested and served short jail sentences. Fortunately, the entire arrangement was set up in such a way that our names never were revealed.

I lay this entire episode to the conversation with God that day, in which I handed over my trust and faith and released my fears. Nonetheless, I still can't believe we did it. We aren't the pot generation. We are the beer and cigarettes generation.

Eventually my son suggested that we try smoking a joint at least once. You guys who are into this? You would cry if you saw some of the giant colas just glistening with resin like diamonds in the sun. From the feedback we got, it had a kick like a mule. Anyway, David came over one night, and I was going to do the deed and smoke a joint for the first time. After some preliminary basic instructions, I began puffing away. David partook and patiently waited for some kind of reaction from his mother.

I smoked and smoked that cigarette, to borrow a phrase from a song by Phil Harris in the 1940s. I finally innocently inquired as to just how long it should be before I felt something. David looked at me, speechless with incredulity. He was blasted by this time. I finally answered, and that answer has become one of those on-going inside jokes in this group. "I think I may feel a slight buzzing, Butch." Now you also know how my son came to believe that I am an alien with purple blood. (Secret code: Want to identify aliens with purple blood? Get them to smoke a joint. No reaction? You got a live one!)

As for me, my work with Thomas continued until about 1993. Don and I developed our worldwide healing ministry built primarily around soul retrieval work. Parts of this book refer to other experiences with him. Actually I'm not quite sure just when he left. He unceremoniously took flight without a word, typical of the old trickster. One day I said to Don, "I haven't heard from Thomas in a while. I guess he's gone." And he was...at least for then.

What is Shamanic Healing?

"Shamanism is perhaps the oldest form of practical spirituality in the world, originating in the time of Ice Age people, going back as far as 35,000 B.C. It is also practiced virtually everywhere in the world. A shaman is someone who has gone through advanced initiation into the hidden realms. The shaman uses the information gained from the other realms for healing and for the good of the community. Shamanic healing is psychic healing, but the term delineates, in particular, indigenous healing that is rooted in traditional ritual.

Summary

After what I have experienced, especially in my work with Thomas, it is now my firm belief that each of us is potentially a modern shaman. Furthermore, I'm also coming to believe that those of us who can voluntarily enter hyper-arousal trance states are the revolutionary prototypes for a new species of human.

> **"Shamans, these old doctors of souls, or 'medicine men,' are nothing more—or less—than our new prototypes, role models for mankind to follow 'back to the future.' We are, in fact, the *Shamans of the 21st Century."***
>
> **Quote from Jon Jay Harper's book *Transformers***
> "Introduction" by Bruce H. Lipton, Ph.D.

I want to end this chapter with the story of the Drum, one of the foremost symbols of traditional shamanism for centuries. The story epitomizes the transfer of what was the voice of our ancestral legacy to a song that can be sung by individual members of the twenty-first century cultures. However, the power and traditions of our tribal heritage are available only to persons capable of awakening what is essentially the shaman within. It is they who will carry forward the centuries-long rituals that connected the group to the visible outer nature that surrounded them, to an enlightened consciousness that gives birth to a new self within the outer edges of the inner dimensions of their own heart.

NO ORDINARY DRUM

By Kriss Shellman

I had the honor of receiving a drum on my birthday 2012 from my friend and mentor, Diana Stone. This was her drum since the early 70s. This is a large eight-sided double drum which means you can play it on both sides. I was looking forward to beautiful deep tones but was surprised at how tinny it sounded when I beat it for the first time. Birthday festivities called, and I put the drum down until I could devote my full attention to it.

Hours later I was able to give the drum my full attention. First I smudged it with powerful palo santo wood smoke. As I did this, the energy in the room shifted and Diana witnessed an energy coming off the drum. I sat down, lifted the heavy drum to my lap and began beating it and was amazed at the difference in the tone!

There were the deep melodious tones I'd expected from a drum this size! Closing my eyes I felt "something" come over me, and I began to sing the Grandmother Spider Song. This is my favorite song that I've sung often for many years. That night, however, my voice sounded different. Somehow it was clearer, and I was feeling the words like never before. I found myself singing the song in a different and much stronger way. There was a power within me I'd never felt before. When I finished, there was a deep silence in the room as Diana, her husband Don, and I absorbed what we'd just heard. We all knew something had happened, but we weren't sure just what it was. We were all quite moved.

The next day, having more time to integrate the experience from the night before, I realized there was a Spirit attached to this Drum. I could feel the Spirit in the Drum pulling me to it through the days that followed. I'd sit with the Drum at least once a day feeling my connection to it strengthen. Soon I realized the Drum was a *living being,* and working with it would take me down a whole new path. I couldn't tell where this path would take me, but I sensed something far larger than I could even imagine. Because I consider the Drum a *living being* it deserves a capital *D.*

Six weeks have gone by since the Drum came into my life. During those six weeks I am drawn to connect with the Drum daily, and I've had many powerful experiences with it. I can feel the Drum waiting for my intentions to send it's Spirit out for healing, protection or manifestation, and I have followed those promptings. For the first time in my life I feel confident in my knowledge, wisdom and abilities, and I'm eager to go out into the world to expand my professional practice as a shamanic practitioner, astrologer and ascension activator. It feels very natural and easy. This is a complete reversal from my old self. My connection to my shaman self continues to get stronger and stronger, and my commitment to this new path is unwavering.

THE STORY OF THE DRUM

by Diana Stone

I want to add the history of the drum's journey that led up to Kriss's article. I know you will appreciate the rest of the story.

When I entered the little shop in Portland, Oregon, where I had recently moved in 1973, the last thing on my mind was a drum. As Fate would have it, a group of women were sitting in a circle drumming and chanting. The shop owner's drum was a work of art. Meaningful experiences in her life were translated into colorful paintings all over the surface. I bought a drum on the spot and sat in on the women's circle. I dreamed of painting my drum like hers. However, years went by and I forgot about the drum. I am an astrologer, but I never even painted on my astrological sign.

Year 2000 rolled around. I received an email from a man who was down on his luck. He was homeless, making the rounds on the couches of generous friends. He was turning to astrology as a last resort for some guidance. He came to my house, and I read his chart for him.

He was Native American. He had a dream. His dream was to have 10,000 drums constructed, and, on a certain day in the future, the drums would beat in unison all over the globe in the name of world peace. The word went out to any groups willing to make some drums. Many Native American tribes responded along with school children. Word spread to other countries. Financial donations, however small, helped buy the materials to make the simple little drum. He was encouraged by the astrology consultation. I told him he would realize his dream and that things would turn around soon. I did not charge him, of course, and he gifted me with one of the little drums.

I was happy that he stayed in touch with me. Circumstances did improve for him. I received an email that someone donated a car. At the solstices and equinoxes, Bill came by my house. I loaned him my big drum, and he did a native dance and chanted a song to celebrate the change of seasons. Yet, my drum lived in a niche in my office/library, mostly ignored.

My friend who also considers me her mentor, Kriss Shellman, shares my February 4th birthday. For years, we celebrated together. My health deteriorated for three years until 2012, when she once again drove to Vancouver where I live, to party all day to make up for lost time. We agreed that we would not bother with exchanging gifts. We both lied. In my office one day, my drum caught my eye. I still had never painted anything on it. Of course, it belonged with Kriss! It told me so.

When Kriss first played the drum, it did not sound anything like we expected. The tone was thin and tinny. Later in the evening when we were alone after other partygoers had left, we turned our attention to the drum once again. Kriss performed a special ceremony and sang a song. I have heard Kris sing her special songs before and always enjoyed them. This was different. I sat absolutely stunned as this unbelievable voice came from some other dimension. I am feeling powerful shots of energy again as I write this. We sat in silence for a long time afterwards as she began to play the drum. She had awakened the drum from its long sleep.

I told Kriss the story of the drum. First, it holds the voice of the powerful Feminine anchored by the women's circle. It holds the energies of the solstices and equinoxes to celebrate Gaia and Nature. Bill's dream was realized. So this is also the drum that is the voice of 10,000 drums for peace.

Kriss always looked to me as not only a friend but her teacher and mentor. I tried to stay in the background, hoping she would find her own way. Nevertheless, there was always an inner struggle to step confidently into her own role as teacher. However, I have now watched how the voices in the drum have led Kriss to her own voice as teacher and shaman.

Diana Stone
March 19, 2012
The Vernal Equinox

I thought I had the last word with my article about the Drum. I was mistaken. The Drum apparently had more to teach. So we close this chapter with another adventure with the Drum. (I should have kept that damned thing.)

THE REBIRTH OF THE DRUM

By Kriss Shellman

After receiving The Drum from my friend and mentor, Diana Stone, my life took a sharp turn into much deeper shamanic awareness. I began a spiritual practice each morning which included playing the drum, singing a welcome to the returning sun and calling in the directions. The Drum has changed my life in so many ways on all levels. I have clearly awakened my shamanic voice.

However, The Drum turned out to be quite temperamental. If it got too cold it wouldn't play, and a few times it required special cleansing. Sometime in early summer it lost it's voice completely. Nothing I did for it helped. It saddened me greatly as I wrapped her in a beautiful warm purple blanket and hoped for the best. I began to wonder if there was something inherently wrong with the drum's design that made it so sensitive. Why was she withholding her voice from me?

On Columbus Day I brought her out of her warm protection to see if she'd play. I tried warming her, cleansing her with sage, even giving her large amounts of energy healing. She still lay silent. What was wrong? Two days later I participated in some

Pineal Toning for the first time. It was an incredible experience that opened my throat chakra so much it felt as wide as my shoulders. I could hardly believe these tones were coming out of my mouth! My pineal gland was buzzing, and I felt an incredible sense of well-being. It had such a profound effect on me, the next day I thought maybe some Pineal Toning might help The Drum.

Before starting, I beat The Drum once to get a baseline. Imagine my shocked amazement when The Drum's beautiful voice answered back to me with that first beat, before I did any toning. SHE WAS BACK! I quickly realized the ONLY thing that had changed since I'd tried playing the drum earlier in the week was doing the Pineal Toning. And then in an instant I realized that my drum's sensitivity was *directly tied to me and my energy field.*

She was like a barometer or mirror for my own Spirit/Soul. By doing the Pineal Toning I was taking the *next step* on my Soul's evolutionary journey. The Pineal Toning was opening portals and accessing higher dimensional energies on all levels. When my body responded, The Drum responded in kind. A tear fell down my cheek, and my heart overflowed with love and gratitude as I welcomed my dear friend back.

This experience proves to me there is a Spirit within The Drum that is interconnected with my own consciousness. Shamanic traditions believe *everything* has consciousness. There is a spirit in everything. I've accepted this belief for a long time and experience it every time I do a shamanic journey, connect with my power animal, or tune into the cycles of nature. However, I've never experienced direct connection with the Spirit of an object until I received this incredible Drum. This Drum is teaching me on subtle and not-so-subtle levels all the time. All I have to do is *listen* and *pay attention.*

Kriss Shellman
Burien, WA
October 26, 2012

Not so Fast: There's more. November 2012 THE RE-REBIRTH OF THE DRUM

I have never encountered any other chapter in this book that just can't find the end. So far, there are already sizable articles about the Drum. Therefore, when Kriss called to tell me that the Drum lost its voice and had gone silent *once again,* my first inclination was that we had said enough about the Drum.

However, her story was so powerful and intriguing that it continued to haunt me. Hadn't we said enough already? Hadn't the point been made already? Yet, her experience was so incredibly revealing of the intimate relationship between Kriss and the Spirit in the Drum. If she was wounded or held blocked energies in the psyche, the Drum could not speak, either. This was definitely about a throat chakra development. It was obvious that she was not only discovering the teacher-shaman within: She was destined to fulfill her soul mission by *acting out,* or *speaking out* the role of Teacher. This is the role that I have long wanted to abdicate in favor of her taking it over! I tried to imagine myself being so united to a Spirit that I was totally responsible for whatever it was reflecting to me.

Kriss admitted that she was aware of the issue that the Drum was mirroring. It was an issue that was so huge that she pushed it to the back part of her mind and hoped never to work it through. We had a long conversation and found the pattern threading through a series of past lives. Together, we hatched a strategy for dealing with the situation step-by-sep. It seemed manageable after all.

Now I will pretend to be prophetic and report that Kriss will release this repressed energy, thus allowing the Drum to once again find its voice. Actually I don't need to be prophetic. I know Kriss. There is no question but what that repressed material is about to see its last days. Once Kriss gets on your tail, it's over. (God, am I gad I gave that damn thing away!)

Should I or Shouldn't I?

I came across some material in Jon Jay Harper's book *Transformers: Shamans of the 21st Century.* My friend, Betty Franklin, gave me this book. (I wonder why she thought of me.) This is pretty much the way most of the information I needed for this book came to me—by hook or by crook. It was just amazing. It really was. But I digress. There is a page in Harper's book under the heading: SHAMANIZING OF HUMANITY. Got your attention? Yeah, mine too! That one page captures exactly what this chapter is all about. It captures what WE are all about. So what is the problem?

It is probably pretty stupid now that I really think about it. Anyway, you don't just copy an entire page of another author's work. Usually, you take notes and write your own version of it. Well, in this case, there is just no other way to write it. It is just perfect. It is spot on. However, it is one entire page. That is lots of typing, I am ashamed to admit. No, the real reason—bottom line—it is so long I never could quite find a home for it. So I just tapped lightly on the computer keys, trying to decide whether to include it or not.

Well, this stuff about the Drum kept extending this chapter and after all is said and done I did not really like ending the chapter on that note. It's a good note, but not a good *ending* note. I hope you notice that I like to end chapters on a good *ending* note. So here goes. It goes IN. You will agree. It is one hell of an ending note all right. It says it all!

SHAMANIZING OF HUMANITY

By Jon Jay Harper

Psychologist Ken Ring coined the phrase the "shamanizing of humanity" twenty years ago to reflect what he saw coming: a world full of shamans with powers to match. In his book *The Omega Project*...he reported, 'It would appear that a new breed of mankind is about to be born, and that...our consciousness and biological structure are undergoing a radical transformation.' This 'new breed' of mankind is what he and I know to be the old *half breed* of humanity—part god, part man—the shaman. Ironically, the shaman was considered to be the 'madman' of society, the one who had one foot in the physical and one foot in the spiritual world, often confusing the two, therefore suffering a type of schizophrenia, a split between his thoughts and feelings. At least that was the verdict in the eyes of some leading anthropologists and psychiatrists in he early 20th century.

"Not so today, shamans are structural engineers of the soul—bridge builders–who use the mind's eye to span the *imaginary* gap between realms. They can 'walk between worlds' because, as we have learned, worlds are bounded only by discrete vibrational frequencies of light waves that are nothing but dense and subtle layers of consciousness. The shaman is also an educator, teaching her society to prepare themselves for what the majority of us do not yet see—the infinite worlds of the invisible. Mapping these *ghost worlds* as they soul journey into space is the skill that sets the shaman apart not the 'mask, or costume' she wears. Carlos Castaneda says in *Wheels of Time,* 'To change our idea of the world is the crux of shamanism. And stopping the internal dialogue is the only way to accomplish it.' "

"...The Universe is a magic mirror reflecting back to our mind's eye what we need to see for the growth of our soul each and every moment that we look into it."
(I *should* have kept that damn drum.)

CHAPTER SEVENTEEN

Ho'oponopono

(HOE-oh POE-noe-POE-noe)

Intention is everything.

Diana Stone *The Lightbody Activation Manual*

Intention works and brings results.

Inspiration works and brings miracles.

Which do you prefer?

Dr. Ikeakala Hew Len
"Ho'oponopono," *Zero Limits*

Yeah, I said it. My name is on it. I can't very well deny it. I not only said it; I wrote it. I wrote it in books and in numerous e-newsletters to thousands of subscribers since 2002. Not only did I say it and write it, I practiced it for many years. Okay, so I get to eat crow. Intention is NOT everything. Now can we move on? If inspiration brings miracles, then everyone who agrees that this is indeed superior to mere results, raise your hands. This chapter is about ho'oponopono, a problem-solving system—including healing—that indeed works and brings miracles.

There is no denying about the miracle part since it is well-documented and also part of my own personal experiences. Therefore, you may give up the path of intentions and instead learn to travel the path of inspiration. And you know what? You are not going to do it any easier than it was for me! In fact, you may fight it all the way. You probably don't believe that, but before you finish reading this chapter, you may predictably feel any combination of: suspicion, disillusionment, insulted, challenged, diminished, resentment, anger—even rage—sadness, outrage, fear and your entire belief system will be upside down where your feet used to be. Don't worry. I have some left-over crow in the freezer.

What is Huna? (HOO-nah)

You may relax. This is not the crazy-making, mind-bending part. Before we get to that I believe it is important to place ho'oponopono within the larger context to which it belongs. Huna is the back story, along with how Fate led me to a personal destiny that fulfilled what has turned out to be one of my soul's major life missions. It was definitely worth a little crow; it tastes like chicken, you know.

I didn't find Huna. Huna found me. It was just like magic. That is the operative word—magic—so remember it. You will soon understand just how appropriate that is! One summer day, probably about 1968, I was downtown St. Louis doing some shopping.

As I walked along, I thought I heard someone call out my name several times. I turned and recognized a friend of mine gingerly dodging traffic as he crossed the street in the middle of the block. He had one arm raised overhead, gesturing wildly. He rushed up to me and shoved two books into my hands. I think I just stood there dumbfounded. He proclaimed with utter seriousness, "I know you will want to read these books!" Then off he dashed, once again dodging cars as he crossed mid-block.

When I got home, I could hardly wait to examine the two mystery books. They were both written by Max Freedom Long *The Secret Science Behind Miracles* and *The Secret Science at Work.* They concerned an extensive prehistoric Hawaiian knowledge, which today is known as Huna. The books described the fascinating practices of *white magic*—including instant healing and fire walking—of the ancient kahuna/shaman of the Polynesian Islands. And my friend, Charlie Muench, just happened to be a *practicing professional magician* of the cut-a-girl-in-half kind. Fate apparently is a master at engineering amusing coincidences.

It was a full 35 years later, when I was preparing a keynote lecture for one of the international Huna conferences that I decided to share this story of my introduction to Huna with the audience. Only then did it finally dawn on me how Charlie could have possibly known I was in the city. and furthermore, predict where I would be at any given time. It was impossible. It was magic. I think I was gifted with a visit from one of my guides that day!

At any rate, what Charlie said to me was certainly true. I read the books all right. I couldn't put them down. I wrote to Max Freedom Long and enjoyed a correspondence with him for many years. And in 1982, I received certification from Huna International, Inc. as a teacher of Huna. Also, I maintained a worldwide healing ministry as a practicing shaman-healer myself for over 40 years.

Huna is a lifetime study and practice. I am including here only a brief outline of the basics in order that I may talk about ho'oponopono in the context of the ancient language. The secrets of the Huna system were a carefully guarded oral tradition passed down only from parent to child. There never was a written history. The only reason there is anything written to this day is because people like Max Freedom Long managed to meticulously piece together parts of the ancient lore from hints in the Hawaiian language itself. Fortunately, it is enough to serve our purposes.

It would be accurate to regard the kahuna as sophisticated early psychologists. In fact, there are still aspects of Huna that surpass the understanding in Western psychology.

Huna is described as a psycho-religious system. It really isn't a religion in the Western sense of the word, but because of certain elements, it suggests a religious component. However, it is much more powerful as a psychological system than it is as a religion. That is because the Huna theory of a personal psychology consists of three parts: the subconscious, the conscious and the superconscious, all familiar enough to Westerners. It is in the definitions of the three and the relationships among them where the differences lie.

In the Hawaiian language, the subconscious is the unihipili (oo-nee-hee-**PEE**-lee), also called the Low Self in English, meaning beLOW the conscious level. In no way does the term imply that the subconscious is lowly. The uhane (oo-**HAH**-nay) is the conscious self, or middle self. The aumakua (ow-oo-mah-**KOO**-ah) is the superconscious, or High Self. The kahuna lore was familiar with psychological complexes and blocks in the subconscious long before Freud. One of the jobs of the kahuna was to resolve these complexes for single individuals, which they often accomplished with more insight and success than western psychiatry's and psychology's drugs and psych wards do today in the twenty-first century.

It was not only individual persons but whole family groups that sometimes required the intervention of the kahuna. That shouldn't surprise anyone today! The traditional method when problem-solving was *inter*personal was known as ho'oponopono. This particular method is the one with which I was familiar for many years. I am including it here because this original traditional ho'oponopono ritual is still widely known. There are books by that name yet in print that describe the older technique. However, this method was updated and changed in the early 80s, and this is the ho'oponopono system that I will be referring to in this chapter.

The earlier version required the physical presence of all members of the family group. More along the lines of group therapy, each participant was allowed to present his or her side of the problem. Each member was required to repent to all of the others; each member was required to ask forgiveness of all the others. Also, a senior member of the group—trained in the dynamics of problem solving—mediated the session in case things got out of hand. Unfortunately, the arrival of white missionaries was bad news all around for the native Hawaiians. Ho'oponopono was altered from the original and a trained mediator rather than a kahuna was part of that change as I understand it today.

As I take you through the elements of the *updated* version, the essence of the older system is not lost. However, the difference is that everything now happens inside *individual* persons; no group is present. Remember that: Everything happens within. When one's "inner family" is aligned, he or she is at one with Divinity. Ho'oponopono helps restore balance to the individual. When one person changes with this amazing process, the collective and all of creation changes as well. Life opens up and flows. This is where anything is possible: abundance, loving relationships, career success or whatever. As one author wrote, "Do not expect it to be like a drive-through in which you get whatever you ordered." The process is simple, but not easy. It requires work, focus every day and total commitment.

Morrnah Simeona was a Hawaiian shaman and the last of one of the royal lines in Hawaii. She was, of course, privy to the secrets of the ancient kahuna passed down through countless generations. She was an amazing woman and an incredible healer. The state of Hawaii regarded her as a national treasure. She is the one who updated and taught the ho'oponopono ritual in 1982. One of the international Huna conferences was held in Honolulu that year and was honored that Morrnah was the featured speaker.

I knew that she used a prayer and had healed hundreds—probably thousands—of patients, many considered incurable. I was never able to find the prayer despite some extensive searching for it. You can imagine my surprise and utter delight when I found it in its entirety in Joe Vitales's (vih-TAL-ee) book *Zero Limits: The Secret Hawaiian System for Wealth, Health, Peace, and More.* I will quote it below. However, Morrnah Simeona's apprentice, Dr. Hew Len, begins his prayer by saying "I'm sorry. Please forgive me." This and every other element that he teaches will be explained in detail later. However, you will recognize that the essence of forgiveness, repentance and transmutation is very much alive in Dr. Hew Len's work as well.

> Morrnah Simeona's prayer: "Divine creator, father, mother, son...If I, my family, relatives, and ancestors have offended you, your family, relatives, and ancestors in thoughts, words, deeds, and actions from the beginning of our creation to the present, we ask your forgiveness...Let this cleanse, purify, release, cut all the negative memories, blocks, energies, and vibrations and transmute these unwanted energies to pure light...And it is done."

Of course, you are free to use this prayer as often as you wish. Nevertheless, you will find that the second version is streamlined, much faster and without any doubt proven powerful enough to heal even the worst of cases. The way we use it in the 4Ds group was a suggestion from my son, David, after he returned from one of the workshops. We got together, and in a meditation David read the prayer. When you work with Low Self, the subconscious, you understand that the prayer is in the memory banks forever. At the end, he gave Low Self the suggestion that whenever we said," I'm sorry. Please forgive me." that this also always triggered the entire prayer without needing to ever repeat it again.

Morrnah worked with and taught the process to her apprentice, Dr. Ihaleakala Hew Len over a period of 10 years. Dr. Hew Len holds a Ph.D. in psychology from the University of Iowa. (I weaseled my way by special permission into some advanced psychology courses when I was a journalism major at the University of Iowa. Their psychology department is outstanding.) It is Dr. Hew Len to whom I am referring as the expert in this modern-day ho'oponopono. All I can promise at this point is that you are in for quite a ride both in relation to the process and to the man.

I think this is the appropriate place to say that I will be taking a great deal of material from the book *Zero Limits: The Secret Hawaiian System for Wealth, Health, Peace and More* that Joe Vitale coauthored with Ihaleakala Hew Len, Ph.D. I will use direct quotes from the book at various times where deemed necessary to communicate exact meanings and identify authorship. However, this is not to downplay my own considerable experience with a broad-based Hawaiian shamanism over many more years than Joe Vitale's; albeit, hanging out with Dr. Hew Len directly was, of course, a unique opportunity, one which I unhesitatingly acknowledge was the trigger that led to my first complete understanding of modern-day ho'oponopono. For that, I am very grateful.

Misrepresentation of Huna and Max Freedom Long.

With that said, I feel that Joe Vitale's remarks about Huna in general, and Max Freedom Long specifically, crossed the line from merely a perplexing misunderstanding of both the Huna system and Long himself. I know that millions of people will read *Zero Limits.* Because Vitale's remarks were more than inaccurate, I feel compelled to set the record straight from this outrageous misrepresentation. That is his view of the world, and it is wrong.

He was outright demeaning of Max Freedom Long, passing him off in a few lines as an "entrepreneur, turned author;" the implication being that Long jumped on the bandwagon of the latest spiritual fad when he wrote the seminal Huna text *The Secret Science Behind Miracles.* I find it interesting that this is a complaint most often leveled at Joe Vitale himself, a marketing guru who does not hesitate to feely advertise his wares in the book.

To further quote Vitales's remarks about Max Freedom Long, "He (Long) claimed to have learned a secret tradition from Hawaiian friends while working as a school teacher in Hawaii." What an outrageous sweeping dismissal of Long's many years of patient and meticulous research as regularly published in his monthly publication *Huna Vistas.* Vitale must have been on another planet when—or if—he read Long's books. It was Long who gave the ancient Hawaiian shamanism the name Huna, which means *secret.* Long freely wrote that it was a secret no longer. It continues to totally mystify me how or why Vitale misrepresented Huna and Max Freedom Long so unfairly. Following what I know of ho'oponopono I owned, forgave, thanked and loved in order to clear any personal negativity about the matter (but it took some doing).

Do not think that I enjoy pointing this out when Vitale's book literally changed my life and the lives of others close to me. However, I not only knew Max Freedom Long through a 40-year correspondence; I facilitated the transfer of Huna International to Dr. E. Otha Wingo, Professor Emeritus of Mythology and Classical Languages at Southeast Missouri State University after Long's death. Preceding that, I introduced Dr. Wingo to Huna myself, obviously responding to some high level nudging from the Other Side. Otha remains a dear and close friend and generously agreed to write the Foreword to the first book in this lightbody trilogy *The Lightbody Activation Manual.* We still enjoy a relationship by phone and email.

To set the record straight, ho'oponopono is indeed connected to the Huna system. Were it not for Max Freedom Long's contribution via painstaking research of clues in the Hawaiian language, I believe that there would be no Huna system as we know it today, including written records. Max was a grand old gentleman, a humble man with a wry sense of humor, a master soul whose life mission was obvious to all who knew him and his work. He was unwaveringly devoted to the research that opened up a door to the West that had lost its roots to the great secrets of life. If Joe Vitale looked down, he would see his feet standing on the shoulders of a spiritual giant without whom there very likely would be no *Zero Limits* book today.

The Most Amazing Therapist you ever Heard of!

This is no urban legend. The story I am about to tell you has been fully documented. It is a most powerful example of ho'oponopono and the amazing healer who accomplished the impossible by implementing it to work miracles, Dr. Hew Len.

In Honolulu, there was a special ward for the criminally insane at the Hawaii State Hospital. It housed 30 inmates who were so dangerous that most of them were either kept shackled or isolated. Still, the staff so feared them that they walked down hallways with their backs to the wall for fear of attacks by violent patients. The turnover among staff and psychologists was on nearly a monthly basis; i.e., until Dr. Hew Len was hired as the staff psychologist where he stayed for three years. Throughout those three years Dr. Hew Len never worked with or even met one inmate; yet, all of them were completely healed. All the doctor did was work on himself. That is what ho'oponopono is. To solve all problems, you simply work on yourself.

If we had the guts to just do it, the instructions could stop right there. I could give you the key words to say right now. You could get to work immediately healing the problems in your life and in the lives of others. But we both know you won't do it. You have to ask a lot of questions first. Hi, left brain. I see you are still in control even though you are clueless. It is the unihipili, the Low Self, that has access to the vast storehouse of all knowledge that is out there, and it is the aumakua, the High Self, that can perform miracles. Remember them: the subconscious and the superconscious? So I might as well back up and start at the beginning.

Dr. Hew Len is quite a character. If he read this, he would say what I am doing is poo and probably laugh himself to tears. He would consider this as extraneous indulgence of Middle Self's (ohane) exaggerated need for the answers to everything instead of "just doing it." This is between us chickens, and I just hope to God he never reads this. Regardless of the fact that I am doing precisely what he advises not to do, I know that I would get letters asking for answers to just the questions that I am addressing. These admittedly are the same questions I asked. This preemptive strike will likely save me thousands of hours answering the mail.

So here is my story about how I came to learn about the new updated version of ho'oponopono and use it in my personal and professional life; and, furthermore, why it was so terribly difficult when the process itself is really so very simple. One day when I was more or less idly surfing around the Internet, I stumbled across some information about a new book by Joe Vitale, one of the authors of the best-seller *The Secret.* The title of this new publication was, of course *Zero Limits: The Secret Hawaiian System for Wealth, Health, Peace, and More.*

My fingers literally flew over the keys to amazon.com., the on-line booksellers. Could this possibly be about Huna or even ho'oponopono? It was! The publication date was two weeks away on June 1, 2007. I placed an order, something that causes me terrible suffering from terminal impatience. My friends tease me that when I order something by mail, I lie down by the mailbox, refusing to go in the house until it arrives. (That's a lie. I don't lie down.)

Before the book arrived, however, I was rushed by ambulance on June 7th to the nearest emergency room, gushing bedpans full of blood from the rectum at regular intervals. Sixteen blood transfusions and major surgery saved my close brush with death.

The point being that the book did arrive, but I was in the hospital fighting for life. Why my husband brought it to the hospital I can only chalk it up to the nudging of some higher power, since I was obviously in no condition to read that or any other book. Or perhaps it was because he knows that nothing lifts my spirits more than a new book. (This is a story of synchronicity at work, folks, in case you aren't getting it.)

Husband Don laid the book on the tray table that is beside all hospital beds. As it happened, my son, David, was in the room, and he has my DNA. His eyes lit up as he seized on the book. I was in no condition to wrestle him to the ground so agreed that he could take it home to read it. That proved to be a life-changing event for all of us. And I hope that it will be for you, too.

Although I knew since 1982 that ho'oponopono had been updated, there was still confusion all those years about just what it was all about. In all honesty, I never used it because I did not know what to do. So here was literally the handbook for ho'oponopono and the entire story about Dr. Hew Len including his healing of the criminally insane at the State Hospital.

We were delirious with joy. David had taken off work from his CPA practice to sit with his mom at night and read aloud. When I was released from the hospital, I was attached to a wound-vac* and anticipated a several-month recovery period. Severe rheumatoid arthritis required that I use a walker. After surgery and three weeks in the hospital, I needed physical therapy to help me get up and walk with the walker again.

David agreed to visit me at home every Sunday and read aloud in the book. So that is how we studied ho'oponopono together step-by-step. And while I absolutely do understand where Dr. Hew Len is coming from; and furthermore, agree with him that there is no need to go mental with this system. Regardless, I will share step-by-step just the way David and I studied it to answer our own questions, and that can be our secret.

Fate stepped in again and delivered a wonderful surprise. David found out that Dr. Hew Len was holding a workshop in Los Angeles very soon. It was a given that he would attend. Over the next year or so, Dr. Hew Len sponsored workshops in our area, even one right in Portland where David lives. All in all, he has attended three of Dr. Hew Len's workshops. Since I taught him Huna since he was eight years old, David had a deeper understanding and longer life experience to back up and grasp what Dr. H Len taught about ho'oponopono. Also, he never had to unlearn a previous belief system like the rest of us. As for the workshop in Portland, Oregon, it was recorded, and Don and I purchased a CD of the entire thing.

There is one more point that I want to make absolutely clear before moving on to Step One of the process. I am honoring all confidentiality agreements as is David. All participants of the workshops must actually sign confidentiality agreements before attending. Every single thing in this book is either what I knew already—which was rather extensive in itself—or what I read in Joe Vitale's book and those of other

---

* "wound vac" is short for *wound vacuum.* The name comes from battlefield medicine where many soldiers succumbed to infected wounds. This is a mechanism that involves a pump that runs 24/7 to remove fluids from a surgical incision to speed healing and prevent infection. I sported a 12-inch abdominal incision, and the entire length was packed with a bundle of wire-like hollow threads. A nurse came to the house every other day to change the packing and drain the hard plastic bag. I hated the damn thing. A 4-foot cord ran from the wound to the pump and accompanied me everywhere. Figure that out. Most patients wear it for many, many weeks, usually many months. I decided I was a healer so healed it in four weeks. The nurses and the surgeon could not believe their eyes. I feared that if I healed it any faster that some very awkward questions about witches might be raised.

authors as well or lastly, was part of the workshop CD offered for sale by Dr. Hew Len himself.

Step one: Responsibility, it ain't Whatcha Thought!

Yes, this is where the mind-blowing part begins. I promised I would warn you. The idea behind responsibility in the ho'oponopono system takes most people to a place they are not able to understand at first. It is about accepting 100 per cent responsibility and is absolutely beyond what most of us are ready to do. So get prepared to go to a place that you have never been before.

The extent to which this is taught means accepting it all. If you have chosen the spiritual path, you may be thinking with a certain amount of indignation—I know I did—that you already accept responsibility for everything that surfaces in your life. You know, the New Age mantra: You create your own reality?

Accepting 100 per cent responsibility in the ho'oponopono system means that you are 100 per cent responsible for *everything* that is in your life, *everything.* You are not to blame. It's not your fault. It is not about fault or blame. It is about responsibility. You are 100 per cent responsible for every problem that any of your acquaintances are dealing with. You are 100 per cent responsible for every crime that you hear about on the evening news. Do you hate the president of the United States? Do you think he is an idiot and his policies will drive us all to ruin? You are 100 per cent responsible. You are 100 per cent responsible for the environmental problems. You are 100 per cent responsible for *everything* in your life: everything you see, everything you experience, everything you hear, *everything!*

My husband is a retired chiropractor. He was responsible for every aching back he ever treated, 100 per cent responsible. If you are a counselor or healer, this means that for every person you ever treated, their problems were 100 per cent your problems. If you are going to take 100 per cent responsibility for *everything* in your life, then it must be your problem, also. That's it, period. No exceptions. Finito. End of story. No rationalizing. No way around it. No tricks. No loopholes.

Still with me?

This idea of taking 100 per cent responsibility for everything in your life just makes people nuts. When I watched the DVD of Dr. Hew Len's workshop, this is where some of the therapists in attendance just went insane. You wouldn't believe it. Many of them stood up and ranted. They were so angry! Some burst into tears. Others walked out. I don't know how you may be reacting as you read these words, but I can tell you this: Until you get this, you will never understand or use Ho'oponopono successfully.

I know what you are thinking. What about the other guy's responsibility? Doesn't this cut both ways? Doesn't it take two to tango? Keep thinking like that, and you might as well kiss off the ho'oponopono system. It is 100 per cent *your* responsibility, period. But don't bail out on me now. Don't you want to be a miracle worker? Once you accept it, what do you do about it? Their problem is *your* problem, remember? So how is working on *them* going to help *you*? You need the healing, not them. You have to heal yourself. Hey, where have we heard that before?

Ho'oponopono is simply a problem-solving process, but it is done entirely within yourself. It is actually a process of forgiveness, repentance and transformation but not in the way you have understood or practiced these processes in the past. The intellect, or Middle Self, can not solve problems on its own. It only thinks it can. That is why I thought it necessary to introduce some basic Huna principles earlier. Later on, you will see how the subconscious, or Low Self, must be engaged as the essential part of consciousness in this process.

When you engage ho'oponopono to solve problems or work miracles, Divinity takes over. Divinity neutralizes or purifies them. You don't purify any person, place or thing. You neutralize the energy you associate with it. So the first stage of ho'oponopono is the purification of that energy.

So now you have it—that crazy, mind-blowing, upside-down view of the world I warned you about. If you really get it, you will arrive at the place where miracles happen; and you can make of your life what you want it to be. That is what Dr. Hew Len and Joe Vitale refer to as *zero state.* Dr. Hew Len teaches that at heart we are all perfect, pure of heart, each one of us. We all have no problems, no memories, or even inspirations. That is zero state. *There are also **zero limits***!

At any given time, you are acting from what Dr. Hew Len teaches is either memory or inspiration. Memory is thinking. Inspiration is allowing. In my counseling work, I used some different language, but I will use Dr. Hew Len's words as Joe Vitale reports in his book. Most of us are living out of memories, and if I learned anything during my 40 years plus as an astrologer/shaman, that was it, replaying old memories. So let's see how this works: (1) Your High Self—the Divine—sends a message to your mind, and (2) however, your radio is dialed into the Memory Station. You don't hear it let alone act on it. Upstairs can't get a word in because Downstairs has too much going on in its head.

A memory is programming in the collective unconscious of humankind. Memories are shared. If you see something in another that you don't like, you have it in yourself as well. Again, people go really nuts when confronted with this idea. Does that mean that somewhere in the deep, dark recesses of your subconscious you are a bad guy—a rapist, a murderer, a thief or an arsonist? Remember, memories are shared. We are all

One; we are part of the Whole. We all swim in the collective unconscious of humankind. Of course we have access to it.

Our job is to clear it. Our challenge is to clear all of the programs so we are back at zero state, back where inspiration comes, back where there are no limits and where miracles can happen. Once you clear something from yourself, it also leaves the other person. Actually, it eventually leaves the world. Ah, the possibilities! Wait! You knew there had to be a catch. There is. If you think this is easy; it is not. Bad habits or those old thoughts creep in when you aren't looking. It requires conscious awareness and strict disciplined focus. But don't despair. I can say from personal experience that it is pure bliss when it works. Yippee!

Let's be Really Clear About this Before Moving on

The above material was supposed to be the end of the explanation about this 100 per cent responsibility business. However, something has come to my attention that is such an outrageous misinterpretation of the ho'oponopono system that I feel that I must set things straight. My reason for not just letting this pass is because I am referring to a passage in a book that will very likely be widely read, especially among lightworkers, healers, counselors and metaphysicians. The book is *The Source Field Investigations* by David Wilcock.

This is a name that many of you will recognize. If so, I know this will come as a shock. Let me say this. I honestly have the highest regard for David Wilcock, and it is too bad that this one thing about ho'oponopono somehow got past an editor someplace. Who knows how it happened? This does not discredit the remainder of his book, and I unhesitatingly recommend it to everyone.

I must have it in my DNA to check out the facts. Maybe it is the Virgo ascendant in my astrological chart. There will be mistakes in my book, no doubt. I just pray to God that they are the "missing period" kind of mistakes and not the "complete mis-characterization of ho'oponopono" kind of mistakes.

I really do regret having to stop and take the space to clarify this, but perhaps it is a blessing in disguise. There is so much confusion and disinformation about this subject that perhaps it is just as well to point out just how Wilcock went completely off the rails. So I am telling you ahead of time that what he wrote is basically *wrong.* I was not sure where to insert this, but decided it would be better to clarify things sooner rather than later. No use picking up any bad habits before we barely get started.

First Wilcock recounted the story about Dr. Len and his work with the criminally insane patients in the Honolulu Mental Ward. That, of course, was true. Now read this exact quote from Wilcock's book, page 96:

"What exactly was Dr. Len doing while he reviewed each patient's file? He simply took on their pains and problems as if they were his own, and worked on healing those issues within himself: 'I just kept saying: 'I'm sorry' and 'I love you' over and over again.' Dr. Len was practicing his own variation of a Hawaiian spiritual practice called Ho'oponopono. Dr. Len recommends going inside, to wherever you feel hurt by a particular person or issue, and then saying each of these four statements with as much feeling as possible–thinking through the real reasons why you genuinely feel this way: "I love you. I am sorry. Please forgive me. Thank you." That is all it takes. You heal the other person by healing yourself–and this apparently works because in the greater sense, you are both sharing the same Mind."

First of all, Dr. Len is not practicing *his own variation* of ho'oponopono. He learned ho'oponopono from Morrnah Simeona. She chose him as her apprentice in order to pass the new updated version on. This is not a variation. This is directly from the horse's mouth. Dr. Len's workshops is where you learn the true ho'oponopono. It is the real deal.

The most outrageous distortion is when the Wilcock material veers off into the part about dealing with feelings. There is no way that Dr. Len ever tells anyone to take on the pain and problems of others as if they were one's own. Neither does he EVER teach anyone to go inside to wherever they may feel hurt by another person or issue—quite the opposite! Nor would he recommend thinking through "real reasons" why you genuinely feel anything–one way or the other. If you want to deal with feelings, go to a shrink. If you are sharp, you will get the inside joke when Dr. Len says, "You can say you feel it, but if you are from L.A. you don't have to mean it."

The only place Wilcock got it right is at the end where he lists the four things that you say, and then adds, "That is all it takes." Yes, people, that IS all it takes! It appears to me that this is a direct contradiction to his earlier statements. Those four statements: "I'm sorry. Please forgive me. Thank you. I love you." are the keywords that set the process in motion. That is all it takes. "Just do it, " as Dr.Len would say.

Don and I ordered a tape of one of Dr. Hew Len's workshops with Joe Vitale. When I watched the tape again, I saw a man in the front row rise to his feet and challenge Dr. Len about whether the people there were 100 per cent responsible for the World Trade Center tragedy.

Here was the exchange that followed. I think you might find it enlightening:

Man: How can you say the Trade Center bombing was my fault?

Dr. Len: *It has nothing to do with anyone being at fault.*
I said it had to do with responsibility.

Man: How can I be responsible? I wasn't even there.

Dr. Len: *You were responsible because it was in your field.*

Man: But I had no control over that.

Dr. Len: *You don't have control over anything.*

Man: I have control over what I will take responsibility for. I have free will.

Dr. Len: *You are not in control and you do not have free will.*
You only think you do.
Only Divinity (High Self) has free will and
Divinity does everything.

I'm Sorry

Now let's look at all of the other separate elements of ho'oponopono and then fit them together. The next stage is repentance. This is where we say we are sorry. If you are 100 per cent responsible for any given situation, no matter whatever it may be, you acknowledge this by repeating the phrase to yourself, "I'm, sorry. I'm sorry. I'm sorry."

Let's say, for example, that one of my clients calls me for some shamanic work. Perhaps she says that she has been suffering from a long, deep depression. I immediately understand that there is something in me that can be cleared, or healed. When I use the ho'oponopono method to work on her case, I usually say something *to myself* like the following, "I am sorry that something in me is causing this situation in Mary Jane." Then I may repeat, "I am sorry" several times.

Please Forgive Me

As Vitale reports in the book, he did not understand how the prayer unlocked the healing within. Apparently, however, Morrnah and Dr. Len believed that it was predicated on forgiveness. So the next element in ho'oponopono is forgiveness. So you say, "Please forgive me."

You say this to acknowledge that some problem—you don't even have to know what it is—has gotten into your mind-body system. You don't need to know how it got there. This is not traditional psychotherapy where we mine the subconscious and analyze the patterns there. If you are overweight, you simply caught the program that is making you that way. To quote Vitale's review of the ho'oponopono process, "By saying 'I'm sorry' you are telling the Divine that you want forgiveness inside yourself for whatever brought it to you. You are not asking the Divine to forgive you; you are asking the Divine to forgive *yourself*." What I personally think in my mind is this, "I ask the Divine Creator to help me forgive myself. I forgive. I forgive. I forgive."

From there, you move on to "Thank you" and "I love you." By asking for forgiveness, we are clearing the way for healing. Easily the most important element is Love. What blocks our well-being is lack of love. "Forgiveness opens the door to let it back in," to quote Dr. Hew Len.

Thank You

In Vitale's book, my impression was that he used "I love you" and "Thank you" more or less interchangeably. Many people who practice ho'oponopono for a while believe that healing a problem is not some terrible ordeal but rather is one more opportunity to clear out crippling memories and negative programming. In alignment with this idea, I often repeat the following, "I thank the Divine Creator for bringing this situation to my attention so that it may be erased, cleared, healed and transmuted into the light. Clearing. Clearing. Clearing."

One of the personal demons that bugged me for a good part of my adult life was the Fear Demon. By using "Thank you" in this way when something erupts as a problem in my personal life—perhaps my husband falling ill, for example—I repeat the thank-you prayer before fear has a chance to raise its ugly head, and before I imagine Don dead and in the ground. Repeatedly turning to "I thank you" has enabled me to short-circuit nearly all my fears beyond what years of therapy failed to do. And it goes without saying that it is a very powerful mantra when dealing with my healing clients. I usually end it by chanting over and over to myself, "Clearing. Clearing. Clearing."

I Love You

The version of "I love you" that I am giving you here is the Diana Stone version. At this point it may seem like we are splitting hairs or belaboring the issues. If you stay with me, everything comes together in a very simple manner at the end. Don't be discouraged if you don't understand everything all at once. With practice you will. I don't mean to imply that you must say and do things exactly right or that one slip of the tongue may cause your healing client's arms to fall off or worse. This system is the soul of flexibility.

The more I studied and practiced ho'oponopono the more I came to regard "I love you" as the code to unlock the secrets of this system and the passage to zero limits. Saying it to the Divine cleans everything in you. This simple phrase works miracles. The key is to love everything. To quote Vitale's summary of "I love you," he says, "Love the fat. Love the addiction, the problem child, neighbor or spouse. Love it all." That's it. It's the path of least resistance. It is the most direct route to zero state, the zone of zero limits. It all begins and ends with one magical phrase, "I love you."

Inspiration is More Important than Intention

At the beginning of this chapter, you noticed the quote by Diana Stone, "Intention is everything." You have no idea the ramifications when I discovered the notion in ho'oponopono that intention is NOT everything and, furthermore, that inspiration is a directive from the Divine and where miracles are found. You will note in the other quote at the beginning of this chapter that, even though intention is not as important as inspiration; it does not say that it is without merit. It says that it brings results. Since I used that very idea in my shamanic healing work, I can testify that it not only brought results; it brought very powerful results.

I participated together with my brother, Duane, and my husband, Don, in many years of shamanic healing with clients all over the world. It is true that we got results, and we took on the toughest cases. In fact, we were often referred to as "the shaman's shaman." When other shaman got themselves into trouble, we were the ones to whom they often turned for help. We used a kit bag of different techniques.

I was known particularly for my soul retrieval work. Duane specialized in clearing environments. Don was great with ancestral curses. Of course, each one of us used any and all of our methods interchangeably, be it removing possessing entities, healing the chakra system, erasing birth memories, clearing maternal and paternal ancestral lines, tackling all manner of physical evils plus a laundry list of all of the other problems that befall human beings. Stop here for one moment, and be sure you understand what I am about to say.

I did not give you what is only the short version of our healing work to break my arm patting us on the back. I am telling you this to underscore the powerful results we accomplished. I have bulging files of testimonials from grateful clients, individuals whose lives were saved, mothers' gratitude for healing their babies, a sister's thanks for restoring her brother to the family and so on. Yes, intention brought results, very powerful results.

But what did inspiration bring? How did Dr. Hew Len heal dangerous criminally insane individuals in a mental hospital in Hawaii without ever once working with them personally? The energy was so bad in that ward that paint would not stick to the walls. No plants could grow there. Yet, the patients were completely healed and that wing of the hospital was eventually closed down.

There are testimonial letters from staff and nurses who were there when Dr. Hew Len was doing his thing. They thought he was a nut case when he first arrived. He never attended staff meetings, came in late and talked to the walls. Soon after he painted the walls. For the first time, the paint stuck and plants began to thrive.

Going back to Dr. Hew Len's work with ho'oponopono, he took each criminal patient's file one by one and *worked on himself* simply by repeating over and over, "I love you. I'm sorry. Please forgive me. Thank you." He worked diligently 20 hours a week for three years. Did I say it was easy? But if he could do that with what had to be a worst case scenario, just think what each of us could do with our comparatively smaller problems.

But What Do I Do With My Old Toys?

Here's the kicker. Am I supposed to let go of all of those neat tricks in my kit bag that has brought powerful healing to so many hundreds of clients? Instead am I supposed to simply work on myself, and the other person gets well of any problem? And I don't even have to know what the problem is? Omygod! Now do you understand the ranting from the healers and counselors attending his workshop? Using ho'oponopono, they would no longer see any clients in their counseling or healing rooms. A doctor would simply work on himself by repeating, "I love you. I'm sorry. Please forgive me. Thank you."

The answer is yes, to all of the above. I can tell you this; even on my best day, I can not heal criminally insane individuals incarcerated in correctional institutions using intention and my old tricks. However, David reported that there were individuals at the workshops he attended who were emergency room doctors. They used ho'oponopono and after a while the emergency rooms were quiet the entire night through. And I am here to tell you that when I use ho'oponopono the end game far surpasses mere results from intention only.

Believe me, it was a painful wrench for me to consider replacing the many methods of healing that had indeed brought powerful results in the past. How do you think I felt the next time a close friend called to tell me that her life was nothing but pain and problems? There was this long list of advice I was accustomed to giving as almost a knee-jerk reaction and an automatic need to help: offering solutions, recommending books, watching the movie *The Secret,* advice about picturing every day how you want your life to be, visualizing, meditating and more.

Then there were the double-barreled big guns: 1) the full range of my shamanic work and, 2) my formidable astrological knowledge that was the core of a professional practice that supported me, plus solving problems for hundreds—probably thousands—of clients. In the workshops, there was probably an understandable outcry, particularly from counselors and healers of all persuasions. Don't think it did not cross my mind as well. One participant commented, "If I serve my clientele by working on myself, I won't have enough business left to support myself." Dr. Hew Len's answer? "You will have more business and more money because you will be at zero state."

By the way, Dr. Hew Len refers to his degrees in psychology as "poo." He thinks it is completely irrelevant since his apprenticeship under Morrnah Simeona. He teaches that intention is a toy of the mind, a fool's game. Intention is trying to control life based on the limited view of the ego. Inspiration he defines as receiving a message from the Divine and then acting on it. At some point, you will surrender and start listening rather than begging and waiting.

Intention is a limp rag compared to inspiration in the sense that Dr. Hew Len teaches. As long as I continue intending to do something—whether it is to lose weight or clear out my dresser drawers—I keep fighting with what is. As soon as I give over to inspiration, life is transformed. Nothing exists at zero state, no problems, including the need for intentions. When you come from zero state, there are no limits. Expectations and intentions have no impact on Divinity. It will do whatever it will, whenever it will. You simply receive and act. And miracles happen.

Remember the definition of ho'oponopono. *It is a process of petitioning Divinity to convert error memories in the unihipili, the subconscious, to zero, to nothing.* The conscious mind is clueless. Let's picture, for example, a hypothetical situation in which you lack wealth in your life. That should not be so difficult for many people to imagine through economic hard times! You read the books, you go to the seminars, you listen to the tapes, you say the mantras, and you pray, you beg, whatever. Yet, you still do not have abundance.

What's wrong when you have done everything right? Well, you can continue to pray your head off until you are blue in the face without adding one dime to your bottom line. Why? As long as error memories, blocks and limitations are present in the subconscious, they block Divinity from giving us "our daily bread" to quote Dr. Hew Len. To open the way for the inflow of Divine wealth requires *first* canceling memories, ho'oponopono.

Here is one example: "I'm sorry for what it is in me that is creating this situation of poverty in my life. Please forgive me. Thank you for bringing this to my attention so that it may be cleared." The "I love you" transmutes the energy and connects you to the Divine. You say it to *yourself* and to the Divine. That's it. Clean. Clean. Clean. That is all there is to this simple but powerful system.

I well remember a case that came to me through my astrology practice. A woman client received two messages from her mom. One was, "There is nothing on this earth worse than being poor." And the other one was, "Every rich person is a crook." My client married a rich guy. He was a crook. He was an embezzler. He went to prison. The only way she escaped a prison sentence herself was by ratting him out in a plea bargain.

I worked with her in therapy for a long time. She married a second guy, undoubtedly unconsciously attempting to side-step the error messages this time by hooking up with someone who was scrupulously honest. He turned out to be an idiot when it came to business, however. He lost all of his *and her* money in a blighted scheme that was doomed from the start. But remember what mom said? "All rich people are crooks." He wasn't a crook so what's a girl supposed to do? Also, there was nothing worse than being poor, so she divorced him. Too bad she did not know to use the updated ho'oponopono version to clear the error messages; messages she did not even have to know were there or where they came from.

Even better, *I* could have cleared myself rather than sitting through all those hours of therapy! Come to think of it, how many more clients could I have served during those hours, at a fraction of the cost, and made tons more money? My son is a CPA; I'll have to ask him to do a projection on that someday, but it's a win-win for sure.

So what do you do for your suffering friend or client? You work on yourself to clear old programming. It is *your* problem, not *theirs.* When you clear error memories, what comes through is inspiration. Inner cleaning leads to outer results. You can't intend what the outer results will be. You can choose, but you can't decide. After using ho'oponopono in my own personal and professional life, it did work miracles. I'm not taking the space to share some of the miracles that came into my life when circumstances looked impossibly hopeless. I'm simply saying that it is true.

There is another example that I would like to share from the book. It is a problem for literally millions of Americans. It is the special project of Michelle Obama's, the present First Lady of the United States. That problem is obesity. It is particularly worrisome because of the frightening increase in obesity in young children, exposing them to diabetes in childhood and an array of health problems as adults, including heart disease.

Joe Vitale was obese most of his adult life. When he met Dr. Hew Len, he had lost 80 pounds. He was struggling to lose the last 15 pounds. He wrote Dr. Hew Len for help to lose the weight but mostly out of curiosity about how the shaman would solve his weight problem with ho'oponopono. Joe Vitale's desire to overeat was a program running in the subconscious. As it kept surfacing, he had to stay aware of his choice to overeat. This ended up being a life-long battle for him, as it is for many others.

You can over ride the tendency by saying no. Obviously this takes enormous energy. (I'm quoting him from the book here.) In time, saying no is a new habit, but what hell to go through to get there: "It's no fun" to quote him. It will keep bubbling up until it is cleared. Weight concerns are simply memories replaying, and these memories replaying displace zero. The only thing to do is to love it and forgive it, and give thanks for it. By cleaning it, you ensure that the Divine has a chance to come through with an inspiration. "I'm sorry. Please forgive me. Thank you. I love you"—that's ho'oponopono.

The following is Dr. Hew Len's actual answer to Joe Vitale's letter:

> "Talk to your body. 'I love you the way you are. Thank you for being with me. If you have felt abused by me in any way, please forgive me.' Visit with your body all through the day. The visit is all about love and thankfulness. See it as a partner in life, not your servant. Talk to it as you would a little child. Thank it for breathing. Thank it for keeping the heart beating."

I can promise that this works from my own personal experience. Fortunately, I am naturally a slim person. I was a professional model when I lived in St. Louis. I was five feet nine and kept my weight at 128 pounds. My lowest weight as an adult was 118 pounds when I stayed at Camp O-Hi. I looked like a 13-year-old boy. I'm sure some of my friends silently feared that I was dying of some terrible, wasting disease. Weight management was a constant struggle in the modeling business. Television and photography modeling added ten to twenty pound over the runway. I had to watch my weight constantly. I fasted one day each week.

I moved to Portland and eventually rheumatoid arthritis forced me to regularly take a drug for pain management. I was not able to exercise. I also was not able to step on scales to weigh myself. I did not realize that the drug I was taking had a famous side effect: weight gain! I lost track of what my weight was doing. I went to another city for chelation therapy. The amounts of chemicals needed were calculated from my height and weight. When I was eventually helped onto a scale, I just about passed out from shock: 192 pounds. I was wearing a coat and heavy boots, so I figured my actual weight was about 187 pounds.

This is what happened. I followed Dr. Hew Len's advice that he gave Joe Vitale. What happened was amazing. All of a sudden, I nearly lost my appetite altogether. I followed what my body said it wanted. Occasionally, I went an entire day eating nothing but one apple sliced thin and maybe a little cheese.

At dinner, I was hungry. To my amazement, I ate a few bites of steak, no more than four ounces or less and I was stuffed. Maybe I could eat a little salad and a couple of bites of baked potato. That was it. I surely waved good-bye to my former canine appetite. The weight just melted off. It was effortless. I hardly thought about it. The next time I was on a scale I weighed 143 pounds. For my height, that is about right.

I still eat very little compared to the past. My body seems to know how to control my weight at a certain level. I listen for any messages from my High Self, the Divine. I am very careful to never tell my body it is too fat. Sometimes I fail. My husband was famous, also, for his enormous appetite. Interestingly enough, he shifted almost over night. When I changed, he changed. It was so obvious that when we joined family for dinners out, they remarked with amazement how very little Don ate of his meal. They were even a bit concerned that he was ill. This happened years ago and the changes remain. This ho'oponopono stuff really worked!

One of the stories that I loved in Joe Vitale's book lends insight into this whole subject of food and eating that bugs the hell out of so many of us. Vitale lived in a small town. The streets rolled up early. When Dr. Hew Len was visiting Joe Vitale, it had grown late and they wanted to go out to eat. Joe realized that the only place open at that hour was a little greasy spoon-type hamburger joint. He was sure that his visitor would never appreciate the unhealthy fare of greasy hamburgers offered there. He apologetically explained, but was he ever stunned at the reply.

"A hamburger sounds great!" Dr. Hew Len enthusiastically answered. Vitale was even more shocked when Dr. Hew Len ordered a double meat, double cheeseburger on a white bun. In his opinion this was a heart attack. However, if it was good enough for the shaman, it was good enough for him, so he ordered the same thing. He asked if Dr. Hew Len was worried about the meat, the cheese and the bread.

He replied, "Not at all. I have a chili dog for breakfast every morning. I love the stuff." At this point, Vitale was incredulous. I will quote Dr. Hew Len, as it is something that everyone needs to hear. "It is not the food that is dangerous," he explained. "Before I eat anything, in my mind, I say to the food, 'I love you! I love you! If I am bringing anything into this situation that would cause me to feel ill as I am eating you, it's not you! It's not even me! It is something that it triggers that I am willing to be responsible for.' I then go on and enjoy the meal because now it is clean."

Vitale admitted that he had spent so much time reading about health issues and food warnings he had grown so paranoid that he could no longer enjoy a simple hamburger. He decided to clean on the hamburger. They both ate their hamburgers with gusto. Dr. Hew Len declared it the best hamburger he ever ate. He even asked for the cook to thank him. The cook wasn't used to receiving compliments on his deep-fried burgers, so he just stood there not knowing what to say.

Later on, Vitale was showing Dr. Hew Len his gym. There was a box of cigars in the room and Dr. Hew Len spotted them. Vitale braced himself for a lecture for sure. "I thought you were going to ridicule me for smoking," he finally blurted out. "A woman wrote me that I was putting toxins in my body when she discovered a photo of me smoking my cigar."

Vitale says that he was reminded once again that the key for Dr. Hew Len was to love everything. When you do, that thing changes. That is a huge idea; one we should not skip over lightly. Smoking is bad when you think it is bad; hamburgers are bad when you think they are bad. As in everything in the ancient Hawaiian traditions, it all begins with thought, and the great healer is Love. This emphasizes again how important it is to maintain the zero limits state.

Another interesting question that arose was, "What about war?" First of all, yes, you are 100 per cent responsible. Just remember that all cleaning helps. It will go where the Divine wants it to go. It is not up to us as individuals to decide, command or even know where the transforming energy will flow.

Not every problem that we clean on must be some huge, seemingly impossible, situation. When I write about using ho'oponopono in my e-newsletters, I encourage readers to apply this system to the everyday things and/or people that bug them. What about the annoying guy in the adjoining cubicle at work? Praying that he is transferred to the North pole means that you have grossly missed the point. It is your problem. Work on yourself. Dr. Hew Len promised himself an ice cream sundae so big it would make him sick to eat it if he could go one day without judging something. He has not enjoyed that sundae yet. I haven't made it for one hour.

One Last Comment

At the end of the day, what choices should we end up making about using ho'oponopono versus our usual way of working, whatever that may be? It is not an easy decision for most of us, even if we intellectually can agree that the ho'oponopono system is the superior one. Furthermore, it is a real challenge to the belief system for many people. Practically speaking, many people will no doubt combine the two systems. At times, we may remind ourselves when a problem comes up in our lives that it is worth taking a shot at it in a new way. Maybe there is a problem with a noisy neighbor; it couldn't hurt to try.

I have enjoyed my neighborhood for years because it has always been so quiet and peaceful. Recently, new neighbors moved in across the street from me. Their dog yapped incessantly. There were noisy kids yelling all day long. I swear to god that the most inexplicable noises emanated from their garage at all hours of the day and night. It just about drove me nuts. I began to imagine that a bunch of zombies were cutting up humans for sacrificial meals. (I said I was about nuts.) Well, today it is so quiet that I am positive that the zombies cut up the kids and they themselves all died of indigestion if you get my drift. Ho'oponopono really worked! Peace at last.

Other times, maybe there is a situation that exists in your life that appears to be absolutely hopeless. Ho'oponopono, in that case, may be the only recourse left. You may recall that I wrote about just that sort of situation in an earlier chapter in my own life. What about completely changing the way you operate as a healer or counselor? One recourse is to "just do it." More likely, this is an idea that is in transition as humanity processes through ascension and beyond. I can't decide for you. Maybe this question is the first one you address to the Divinity within. At any rate, there is no question that cleaning, cleaning, cleaning on the error messages and blocks in your own subconscious makes the world a better place for everyone.

Obviously, I can not reproduce the *Zero Limits* book, but I can do the next best thing. I have liberally quoted the main ideas of ho'oponopono, but I recommend that anyone seriously interested in understanding this system read the book yourself. If at all possible, it is worth it to make every effort to attend one of Dr. Hew Len's workshops. Joe Vitale often co-presents these workshops, which they call "Self I-Dentity through Ho'oponopono." It is the modernized, updated system, and a search of the Internet will give you the latest schedule.

At the present time, I am undertaking a renewed practice of ho'oponopono in my life. My goal is to heal myself and walk again. However, it is the Divine Creator who will make the ultimate choice about where the healing energy will flow. Despite crippling arthritis, I have received caregivers in my life exactly when I needed them. I have the financial resources I need, including funds to pay for a wonderful healer who is my doctor. I receive the most beautiful letters of gratitude from readers of my newsletter. I am surrounded by family and friends who love me. I love the arthritis. I love my body just the way it is. I love me.

This led me to thinking of some of the things I printed in my newsletter over the years. I began to worry that I had been misleading people, especially on the subjects of intentions and taking responsibility. Then I started wondering about *this* book. Maybe I should rip out all the preceding chapters and just leave this one on ho'oponopono. As I read the *Zero Limits* book, Vitale expressed the same concern. After all, his other books hit the top spot of bestseller lists and reached millions of people compared to my little newsletter. He praised the power of intention in those books. Just like me, who wished I could recall all my newsletters about intention, he wanted to recall all of his other books. He felt he was doing a disservice to the world.

When he asked Dr. Len about it, this is what he answered:

> "Your books are like stepping stones. People are at various steps along the path. Your books speak to them where they are. As they use that book to grow, they become ready for the next book. You do not need to recall any books at all. They are all perfect."

I was grateful for this message from Dr. Hew Len. My newsletters will speak to readers where they are. All I can say to all of my subscribers past, present and those to come:

"I'm sorry, please forgive me, thank you, I love you."

CHAPTER EIGHTEEN

Mommy and Daddy Dearest

We can not complete the process of ascension until we know humanity's true history.

Gregg Braden

CATASTROPHOBIA

The Chicken Little archetype:
The sky is falling! The sky is falling!

- Are you scared?
- Do you worry constantly about current events?
- Are you always preparing for the worst?
- Are you always tired?
- Do you fight lack of motivation?
- Do you see any reason to hope?
- Are your decisions based on fear?
- (and then turn out to be wrong?)

In my healing practice some clients presented a level of intractable fears that resisted every effort to dislodge them. I threw everything in my shaman kit bag at them. It was to no avail. The demons would not die.

Who were these people, and where were the irrational fears coming from? These same clients normally met other challenges very aggressively and with deep insight. They were frequently successful in their outer world affairs. Some were healers, counselors or helpers in their own right. Yet, a dip in the Dow, the latest environmental disaster and every other doom-and-gloom forecast were capable of triggering a serious attack of irrational paranoia.

The trouble, as it turned out, was that I failed to recognize the universal nature of this problem. Unlike the other negative energies discussed elsewhere, the Chicken Little Syndrome presents as a *collective* fear. That's you. That's me. That's everyone. It's buried in there.

Furthermore, the very nature of my limited perspective rendered it impossible to distinguish any overall picture that would greatly expand the timeline beyond the present. I couldn't see the forest for the trees. It began to make sense when I became aware that deeply implanted fear memories had affected entire cultures, including many, many generations past, right up to the present twenty-first century. It is an embedded racial memory. Yes, that is the clue; it is a memory! Experiences of horrific catastrophes—some that threatened extinction of the human race—are collectively bleeding through to our very own culture in our very own time.

The events surrounding Y2K brought this acutely into focus for me. You may recall the paralyzing hysteria and paranoid fears in some quarters about the computers crashing at midnight as Year 2000 rolled around. This generated widespread panic that this signaled the end of civilization as we knew it. Otherwise rational people were ready to literally run for the hills, abandoning careers and friends. Others considered converting their wealth into gold and hiding it under the mattress. There probably are still secret stashes of food left over from those days.

The depth of the reactions came acutely clearer when an urgent email warned me to include a hard hat in my preparations for the fateful day. What imagined drastic scenario could be so chaotic as to possibly require a hard hat? Was it the debris from falling buildings in darkened cities? Was it the neighbors throwing bombs at my house to steal my stored food? Only a mind overwhelmed by completely irrational fears would entertain the likelihood of such extreme conditions.

Speaking of Y2K, a hilarious incident occurred in my very own neighborhood January 1, 2000. My son and his family lived next door to me. David planned to set off some fireworks at midnight. Don and I walked out to watch the display at the appointed hour.

One big blast went off and hit an electrical transformer. It blew out all of the neighbors' lights down the street. I am sure it scared the hell out of them. The dire predictions were coming true. The interesting thing was that neither David's nor my lights went out. Our neighbors' fears were at least powerful enough to magnetize one night of darkness for themselves.

What with the impending end to the Mayan calendrical cycle in December of 2012, I wondered how long it would be before one of the naysayers would compare the meaningless Y2K madness to the hoopla surrounding the just as meaningless ascension date (according to them). I didn't have to wait long. This is comparing apples and oranges, of course, but it is likely that many people will buy into the straw man notion that "all of this talk about the end of the world is just as crazy as Y2K." Of course, reasonable people are not predicting the end of the world in the first place. If the ascension date comes and goes without fireworks, they will feel justified in poo-pooing its validity just as they predicted.

Even though I was not particularly worried about Y2K, I really did not know for sure what would happen. I turned to a source that I trusted—horary astrology. I asked the astrological question, "What should we do to prepare for Y2K?" The answer was short: Do absolutely nothing. By the way, not one astrologer or horary client ever asked me that question, even though some of them were in total panic over the impending doomsday.

I would love to wrap up this discussion by reporting the successes I had in clearing this specific brand of fears. I would love to throw in a case study or two. But no, this story was not over. I needed to read a book by Barbara Hand Clow *Catastrophobia.* I kissed synchronicity's ring when it delivered that book to me. It was a shocking revelation.

Keep in mind that I am writing this book from the perspective that humanity is on the brink of a great evolutionary advance and spiritual awakening. I totally believe that. I further believe that this is a work in progress *right now.* Consequently, I find the plethora of information to the contrary terribly troubling. It troubles me because it is not information; it's misinformation. This comes from every direction: television, movies, books, the Internet, so-called prophets and on and on.

I recently watched a series of programs on the History channel. These were unconscionable. The endless images of fires, floods, earthquakes and pestilence surely added to the terror that is already awash in the collective. It is typical of shows like these to cite a collection of prophecies about 2012. They include references to the Nostradamus quatrains, the Bible, the Mayan calendar, the Hopis and other sources that they know are universally trusted and respected.

A careful study of these predictions in their entirety clearly identifies the end dates as the end of a long cycle and the end of the calendar, not the end of the world. Read Nostradamus. *He clearly counseled humanity that a change in our collective consciousness redirected our ultimate destiny.* The Mayan calendrical system is even clearer. It tracks indisputable astrological and astronomical cycles. December 2012 features a galactic alignment that unmistakably marks the end of one long cycle. As an astrologer, I am familiar with this well-known cycle of approximately 26,000 years.

It is hard to know where to begin to describe Clow's book. It behooves anyone to read it for themselves. However, to summarize for our purposes here, you first need to realize that there have been many disasters so horrific as to threaten all life on earth, including all of humankind. Most people are familiar with the demise of the dinosaurs. That was about 16 million years ago. ***We need to understand our own story!*** Humanity experienced global trauma as recently as 9,600 years ago. That is a mere blip on the screen of time.

The great maritime civilization of Atlantis perished in a great cataclysm. This is the best known but apparently not the only time humanity suffered apocalyptic disasters. Clow documents modern archeological, mythological and scientific discoveries that prove these lesser events were real, also.

It is a safe bet that nearly everyone on the planet today carries the memories of colossal catastrophes in the past. We are all descendants of the straggling handful of humans who survived. Our DNA carries the images first witnessed by our human ancestors who literally saw their entire world crash to an end.

There are people around today who believe that the world is coming to an end. Religious fanatics who preach that the end is near are victims of catastrophobia themselves. The present-day stock market crash, recession, corporate bailouts, severe weather cycles, terrorism and every other threat to security is enough to draw many people into the collective fear. They do not realize that what they are witnessing is the death rattle of a world that is not working. The rebirth of a new world at peace will rise from its ashes. It should be a *cause celebre*!

Here is the scary part. People or groups suffering from apocalyptical fear complexes are so convinced that the end is near that they would rather end it all now. They perceive the situation as inevitable and hopeless. To quote Clow, "This collective insanity could destroy human civilization."

The meticulous research by Clow and other prominent investigators makes a well-documented case for the fact that catastrophic traumas radically altered human consciousness. Just as electroshock treatments erase personal memories, earth disturbances likewise produce cultural amnesia. Just think about it. Earth changes have functionally altered the human brain!

A series of five supernovas erupted between 15,000 to 11,500 years ago. According to D.S. Allan and J.B. Delair in their book *Cataclysm! Compelling Evidence of a Cosmic Catastrophe in 9500 B.C.,* a supernova was the likely candidate. To quote Allan and Delair:

> "The atmosphere imploded and all living things were terrified of the deafening sound. Great electromagnetic storms overwhelmed the bioelectric fields of animals, humans, plants and even rocks. It's believed that one cataclysmic event 11,500 years ago struck with such force that the earth was tilted off its vertical axis (where it remains today). On that day, fear was so deeply imprinted in human consciousness that ever since, our minds have tried to suppress and deny this memory."

Clow believes that this lost memory represents the 85 percent of our brains or the 97 percent of our DNA that scientists say we do not use, the so-called "junk" DNA. It is suspected that we are hard-wired to receive cosmic information that activates latent brain capacity and switches on junk DNA.

Here we stand, transfixed like a deer in the headlights, so crippled by a cultural malaise as to inhibit the potential of our entire species. Shocks to the earth's electromagnetic field fried the human brain. We separated from the intuitive to crown the left brain king. We became talking heads. We no longer communicate with the other kingdoms of Nature. The faerie kingdoms were lost to the lifeless pages of Aesop's fables for children. The weather gods that whispered to the animals before the great Indonesian tsunami of 2006, fell on deaf human ears.

This mind-boggling information sheds light on some personal experiences, which at the time, did not seem particularly relevant to my own healing. In the mid-1980s, Duane and I undertook our first major journey together under Thomas's guidance. It was a shamanic journey over three days and nights. The very first subject that came up was a recovery of our lives in the last days of Atlantis. We worked on it for hours and hours to the point of utter exhaustion.

The next time this same subject arose was on Harmonic Concordance in 2004. That was the date when our Pleiadian Beings gave Duane the remaining activations. I have written earlier that the first thing Thomas had on his mind was for us to deal with unresolved emotions from our Atlantean lifetimes. At first I thought, "I don't have any unresolved emotions like that."

You may remember me saying then that shortly following that thought, a stabbing pain hit my heart center and sent me doubling over, howling in pain. I thought I was having a heart attack. The whole experience was so overwhelming I actually worked it out over several months following.

We Must Remember Our Own Stories!

I asked you to remember earlier that the way to heal was to remember our own story—the real story. Now I realize that this is what Thomas was doing all along. He led us to remember our own stories. We were healing our own catastrophobia.

A Case Of Catastrophobia: Rhonda

This still is not the end of the story. Because of work with actual cases, I can add my own personal spin to this, well beyond any books on the subject. I wrote about Rhonda. She is the woman severely injured by the family dog. She also suffered from extreme catastrophobia. Long before we had that word in our vocabulary, she came to me repeatedly with elaborate plans, allegedly dictated by her guides.

In general, it involved moving to her property in the country, stocking it with tons of food, and generally preparing a place for her, her family and close friends to survive for years to come. Rhonda controlled financial resources beyond the average household. The plans included many complicated machinations with her money as well. I rejected this as utter nonsense on the face of it. She knew that. I told her often enough. However, that did not heal her obsession that a catastrophe was at hand.

However much she intellectually understood that this was paranoia, her fears were triggered by every passing threat, things like the bird flu scare, and the swine flu scare. Then came the deep recession and stock market crash in 2008. For that one, I just sat by the phone and waited for the call that was sure to come. One of Rhonda's symptoms was what she described as hyper-vigilance. She hung on the news channels, listening for anything to tip her off that the crisis was imminent. Until recently, this is about where we were left with her.

Rhonda has known me for 30 years. She trusts me. She also knows about horary astrology and trusts that as well. Whenever overtaken by her latest fear, she calls me and always says, "Okay, roll your eyes and get it over with." I always indulge her, and in all seriousness, do the astrology charts to predict if she should flee to the farm this time. At least this subverted any misguided acting out, which was to her credit. It does not cure the catastrophobia, however. For the longest time, I just accepted that this was probably the best we could ever do. Fortunately, I was wrong. I told her that if we ever healed it, she damned well better do it before I finished this book. I like happy endings.

Let me tell you about something that happened when she was in a coma in intensive care from the dog attack. This shocked me to the very core. It proved that this pattern of catastrophobia nearly cost my client her life. Rhonda's injuries were to her face. That was bad enough, of course. But read what her doctor actually told Rhonda's sister in the hospital: "*Rhonda's body is behaving as though something so absolutely, hopelessly overwhelming is happening to her that there is no use to try to fight it.* Consequently, all of her vital organs are shutting down. Her lungs have collapsed and her kidneys are beginning to shut down as well." There you have shocking proof that catastrophobia overtook her consciousness even when she was in a coma! Even more shocking to me is that it was so obvious to the doctor.

A series of synchronistic flukes somehow led me to piece together one of Rhonda's past lives that in turn provided the key to her healing. Rhonda was an oracle, a seeress in a past life with a specialized talent and a specific and narrowly defined role in an ancient culture. Her highly developed intuitive powers unerringly alerted her to natural disasters long before they actually struck. Her job was to predict such events in time to make appropriate preparations for preserving life and property.

Subconsciously, this memory remains, and she responds to it still. She fears that she won't sense nature's threats in time or perhaps not at all. The defense mechanism appears to be to "cry wolf" at everything, just in case. There is no intuitive sense there to sort out a genuine threat. Therefore, her antennae pick up everything even remotely threatening and bingo! she reflexively pushes the panic button. Once I retrieved the past life oracular consciousness, synchronicity around that just went crazy, which was extraordinarily confirming for her.

I held my breath. We told Rhonda's story. Would this heal the catastrophobia? When we started down this road, the question I had for Rhonda was this, "How would you know if it is healed or not?" Her answer was very simple. "I would quit thinking about it six to eight hours a day'" (Works for me!)

At this writing it is October 1, 2009. Just last evening, I had a long conversation with Rhonda. She called for a reality check. She no longer listens to news programs. She does not read a newspaper. She has never experienced this reality in her entire life. I thanked her for recovering in time for me to write the successful conclusion in this book. We laughed our heads off. It was not so much that it was funny. It was a release of energy after a long and terribly difficult journey.

What Do We Know Now?

In summary, we are now armed with the knowledge that an earth catastrophe delivered a knock-out punch to the electromagnetic field and, consequently, fried the connections to our intuition and to Nature. Furthermore, an intractable fear, driven deep into the collective subconscious, was finally identified as catastrophobia. Regardless that future generations did not experience the horror first-hand, the deep memory was nonetheless unwittingly carried forward by our ancestors to confound our generation still. Rhonda emerged as a singular example of this puzzling and seemingly inaccessible affliction. This beautifully illustrates that one person's story CAN cast the light into collective dark shadows.

Recovering her history–her story–freed Rhonda of this persistent pattern that proved so terribly difficult to heal. So the big question was posed: Would recovering *humanity's history* heal the entire collective subconscious of catastrophobia once and for all?

Recovering Humankind's True History On Planet Earth

There is actually an abundance of materials which are certainly likely candidates if we are to undertake the task of accurately documenting humankind's long earth journey from ape-man to *homo sapiens.* The information is well-documented by a variety of ancient scrolls in dead languages, hieroglyphics carved in hidden tombs, cuneiform clay tablets, mysterious physical artifacts in many scattered locations, biblical stories and most recently, corroborating archeological evidence, which is turning out to be the most astounding of all.

Barbara Hand Clow's book *Catastrophobia* came to my attention after the Rhonda case, confirming, and also giving a name to, the "sky is falling" syndrome. I originally intended to leave the subject of our ancient history here, confident that I had made my point: Recounting our history *would* cure cultural catastrophobia. How hard could it be with the stories already known? Point well taken: end of story.

The Most Unbelievable Road Block?

The answer to that question was inconceivable! Read on very carefully.

Was it possible that we have been led down the primrose path to a totally deliberate distortion of humankind's earth history?

This claim is so enormous, so monstrous, so seemingly impossible. Considering for the sake of argument that this is true, who would harbor a secret agenda of such magnitude that they would be willing to skew the true history of the entire human species? Furthermore, how in the world could they pull off such a preposterous scheme? Why has it never been exposed before now? How could I never have heard of this? Isn't this the Information Age? Isn't it unthinkable that such an enormous secret scenario could be shielded from prying eyes in today's atmosphere of news via portable telephones?

As it turns out, it IS absolutely true. The popularly accepted notion of humanity's story—yes, those in the history books—may as well take a place alongside tales from a child's nursery. This discussion began as a question about whether the recovery of humanity's history would cure the collective catastrophobia, just as it did in an individual case of one person recovering HER history. That question may now become, "If recovering our history doesn't do it, perhaps the shock of finding out that somehow humanity's true history has been deliberately distorted may well do it!"

It was in Barbara Hand Clow's book that I finally stumbled onto the truth of this unbelievable circumstance. Could it possibly be true? Recovering mankind's story to cure catastrophobia pales into near insignificance as we find ourselves siphoned off onto a search for the real Truth! I'll condense the issue before us by a quote most representative of this Hydra-headed monster. Here it is directly from Clow's book. Read it very, very carefully (and take two aspirin and call me in the morning):

> "Now the cataclysmic scenario is coming forth as a result of the new scientific paradigm caused by 200 years of data collecting. ...the cross-cultural global records of indigenous people are actually being verified by science...we exist in a cultural field called Social Darwinism—an intellectual elite who says that archaic people were nonverbal primitives and humanity has been ever advancing since the past...(they) are thought of as grunting hairy oafs...are described as wild hordes of vicious hunters...who roared down from Biringia to Terra del Fuego 11,500 years ago.
>
> "By being educated on such half-baked ideas, humanity has almost lost its ability to correctly reconstruct the past. As the new paradigm researchers find the evidence for highly advanced archaic cultures, more and more people wonder why modern culture is so degenerate if we've always been advancing.

> Casting aside this infantile conditioning, many are going on passionate treasure hunts to find the lost parts of our ancestry. Even if...(they) seem like excessive romantics...they are rebooting the hard drive that crashed inside our skulls. You may feel angry when you realize *we've been led by fools with superiority complexes who aim to rule the world by controlling access to the past,* ***but it is the TRUTH."***

It is not the revelations of the history itself that is at stake. No, that's not it. It's the unconscionable control of humanity by people on a power trip. They have stolen our past from us. We have been betrayed! This changes everything. They have deliberately distorted and lied about our true heritage. As unbelievable as all of this may seem, it is barely the tip of the iceberg. In science, medicine, religion, government—everywhere you turn—we are under the control of a handful of people mad with power. We live in a world of illusion that they have created for us to believe. Prepare yourselves! The old paradigms of the past are shifting and crumbling away. The death of our old world as we have known it, has progressed too far to turn back now. The evidence is in.

Is humanity ready to confirm our ancestors' experiences with visiting extraterrestrials, who may well be our true parents? Is our collective belief system flexible enough to accept the true origins of our DNA, or a nuclear war occurring thousands of years ago, plus the rise and fall of great lost civilizations, and the loss of technologies that moved great stones by thought alone, not to mention an endless stream of evidence that wipes out the teachings of religions and science of our present day? Just how ready is the collective to kick their organized religious teachings to the curb, even in the face of overwhelming evidence that so easily confirms that most everything they believe is wrong?

And that's not all!

I guess I was temporarily distracted when I encountered the idea in several books that stressed the advisability, even the necessity, of understanding humanity's history on this planet *in order to process the ascension shift.* Let's back up and rephrase that. I was not temporarily distracted. Who am I kidding? I am not that cool. How do you think I was feeling, confounded by the sudden realization that humanity's history is not humanity's history? I encountered the unthinkable! I was paralyzed, and then that gradually gave way to uncontrollable rage. Stay with me here. I did not set out to write a book about mankind's true history. Don't we already know that? I couldn't believe it. And how are you doing? Hello? Anybody there?

The idea of healing catastrophobia by recovering our history was one thing (even though it's not our history!). The utterly shocking notion that we must recover humanity's history *in order to complete the process of ascension* is quite another. This knocked the wind out of my sails completely. I had to suck my thumb, back up and do some serious investigating. Why did the spiritual leaders on the order of Barbara Hand Clow, Gregg Braden and others go out of their way to repeatedly insist that in order to complete the process of ascension, we must recover humanity's true history? Granted, it is an amazing tale all right. Furthermore, it certainly challenges our belief systems if we have contradictory cherished notions promulgated from the pulpit before which you or I happen to sit.

My first reaction was to assume that it was just too bad, but where are we to turn to corroborate humanity's "true" history? I will present some cursory examples of the enormous evidence in plain sight yet today. This is not conjecture. This is not mythology or allegory. These are not deductions from scattered archeological artifacts. These are not fakes or hoaxes.

Zecharia Sitchin is one of the translators of the ancient languages and cuneiform (CUNE-ih-form) clay tablets. I would never support Sitchin's research without corroborative evidence. I certainly do not like to make claims that I have not checked out as far as I can myself. Secondly, I certainly hate making a fool of myself! In this case, I am putting myself on the line. If it's wrong, well, I seem to remember that crow tastes like chicken.

Undoubtedly one of the most exhaustive researchers, Sitchin penned several hefty books, namely his *Earth Chronicles Series,* which the 4Ds tackled maniacally. The copies flew from one person to another while they were still warm. Brother Duane devoured all in a few days by sacrificing several nights' sleep, unable to put them down, belying what appeared to be a several months' challenge when first stacked atop one another on my coffee table. Don and I ploughed through all Sitchin books in short order also, absolutely riveted by each one, and long-faced the day when there was not another in the series awaiting us.

We wanted to discuss the books as we went along, so the most workable arrangement was for Don to read aloud for an hour each morning and evening. The evening session often stretched to the wee hours. (Sitchin's titles are listed in the bibliography.) If the entire series intimidates you, but you are willing to choose just one, we recommend his most recently published *There Were Giants Upon the Earth (2010).*

Who's Your Daddy?

Four hundred and fifty thousand years ago, in a faraway star system, there existed a planet that faced a terrible ecocrisis. The atmosphere surrounding the planet itself was deteriorating rapidly to a point at which it soon could no longer sustain sentient life of any kind. The only solution was to access a relatively inexhaustible source of gold. Treated by a particular process that reduced the gold to a nearly imperceptible mist, and injected into the atmosphere, it restored the planetary balance and maintained a habitable environment. Their technology produced a solution, but it could not increase the planet's severely limited supply of gold. The planet was called Niburu, and the Niburuans came to be known as the Anunnaki, "those who from heaven to Earth came" (actual translation of Sumerian tablets). The one question open to controversy is whether this is Niburu or any one of many other planets it could have been. If it is Niburu it raises speculations about a return visit, when that might occur, and what effect it would have as far as disruption of our solar system is concerned. We are pretty much left with a wait-and-see mind-set at this point.

The Niburuan crisis set in motion a chain of events that would eventually dramatically alter the course of history of our own planet Earth. We had gold! According to their own written records which still exist in museums all over the world, work parties mined the life-saving metal for nearly 150,000 years, until the heavy toil and isolation finally led to rebellion. They needed workers. After surveying the existing life forms on Earth at the time, ape-like creatures emerged as the most likely candidates.

Among many other recorded accounts, there was one who was an eyewitness, indeed a participant, in all of the great stories in Earth's pre-diluvian history. He was the leader of the astronauts who first splashed down on Earth's shores. He was known as Enki. He was a great scientist. It was he who jumpstarted evolution through masterminding the medical team's genetic engineering of the ape man inhabiting the area around the mines. After repeated unsuccessful experiments, it became apparent that mixing Anunnaki genes with *homo erectus* produced *homo sapiens!*

Thus did the *Adam* (literally, "He of the Earth," Earthling) come into being. As a hybrid, he could not procreate. A second genetic manipulation added the extra chromosomal genes for sexual procreation.

Homo sapiens emerged from Petrie dishes. There was an Adam and an Eve—our mommy and daddy. Archeologists can dig up every square inch of this planet, but they will never find the skeletal remains of the missing link. Evolution and natural selection were not responsible for our parentage. Darwin got it wrong. All evidence points to a sudden great leap forward, and irrefutable evidence there certainly is. A Petrie dish was our Garden of Eden, and Niburuan DNA was the missing link!

As years passed, the daughters of men appealed to the Niburuan "gods," and they ultimately married and produced children from these unions. So was unleashed the unequaled high-voltage dramas of biblical proportion that by comparison make contemporary soap operas seem as passionate as yesterday's faded roses. When the Earth-based Anunnaki gods——ETs—brought their girlfriends to dinner back home to meet Mom and Dad, all hell broke loose. If you would like to read more about the lives and loves, the wars and conquests, the laws and injustices, the jealousies and murders, the heroes and villains and the rise and fall of great civilizations of those times 300,000 years ago on this planet, read Zecharia Sitchin's multiple-book series. It's all there.

A Brief History of Archeological Work in East Iraq and Eastern Africa:

The first important archaeological finds were made in 1877 in what became known as Sumer in southern Iraq. This area started out as a large mound of a buried Sumerian urban center called Lagash, which had been settled almost continuously since 3800 BC. Besides beautiful artwork, there were more than 10,000 inscribed clay tablets in the city's library. At that time, and for more than 50 years since, artifacts from the site have gone to the Louvre Museum in Paris.

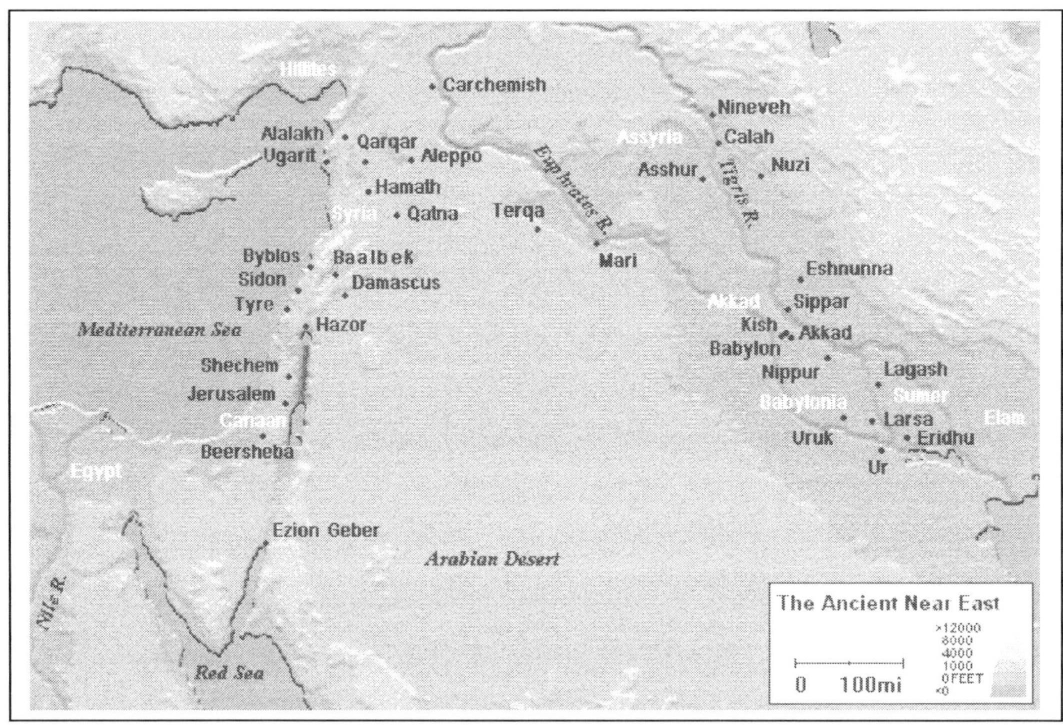

Ancient Near East showing Sumer, Akkad and some ancient cities plus archeological sites referred to in text.

An archaeological expedition from the University of Pennsylvania in Philadelphia found the city of Nippur in 1888. This very prominent ancient Sumerian city contained nearly 30,000 inscribed clay tablets in the library. Inscriptions dealing with mathematics and astronomy, and dating back to the third millennium BC, included the original Sumerian tale of the deluge (great flood) naming its "Noah" as Ziusudra (that name used in many, many accounts of the story).

It should be noted that as early as the 1850s, many tablets and inscriptions on columns, etc. showed both a strange Cuneiform script, and known Akkadian script, side by side with pronunciations (see Tablet of synonyms figure on the next page).

These clay tablets were made by pressing a stylus into wet clay, drying and finally firing the tablets. They created a veritable dictionary of these Sumerian writings. You could call them the Rosetta Stone of these ancient inscriptions.

There is no disagreement in the translated texts of these thousands of clay tablets. They contained records of all sorts: marriage contracts, commercial records and even day-to-day personal communications. Of great value were "Kings" lists of rulers and dates, plus other records of great historical significance.

Tablet containing part of the *Epic of Gilgamesh* (Tablet 11 depicting the Deluge), now part of the holdings of the British Museum

"Venus Tablet of Ammisaduqa" with astrological forecasts. British Museum reference K.160 .

Tablet of synonyms. British Museum reference K.4375 .

The Royal Library of Ashurbanipal in Nineveh was named for the last great king of the Neo-Assyrian Empire. The king was literate and known as a scholar devoted to building a great library at any cost. He established an astonishing collection of thousands of clay tablets principally written in Akkadian in the cuneiform script. Tragically, Nineveh was ravaged by fire during an attack by warring factions.

Paradoxically, the clay tablets were partially baked, preserving them for later discovery. The British Museum's database counts 30,943 tablets in the entire Nineveh collection. However, the library also included leather scrolls, wax boards and papyri that weren't so lucky. These in all likelihood contained a much broader spectrum of knowledge than that known from the surviving clay tablets alone. That notwithstanding, what has been recovered is a priceless collection, including the famous masterpiece of ancient Babylonian poetry the *Epic of Gilgamesh* and others relating to medicine, astronomy, literature and incantations to various gods.

Many archaeologists from the late 1800s to the present have worked to find the precious history of the ancient world. These artifacts and fired clay tablets, which have been preserved to this day, were obtained from all fourteen (14) of the ancient cities located in that general area. These artifacts are in the Chicago Field Museum of Natural History, Oxford's Ashmolean Museum, New York's Museums, the Louvre in Paris and numerous additional museums all over the globe.

This aerial view of the Baalbek site shows the ruins of the Temple of Jupiter, from about 3000 BC which was built upon the original megalithic flat base estimated to have been built about 9000 BC. Ancient astronaut theorists believe this huge, precisely constructed base was a landing platform for their space ships.

Consider also the abilities of precise stone carving to exactly fit these blocks that our ancestors of 8000 BC supposedly possessed.

To enhance claims that we were visited by extraterrestrials, we may visit any of the giant monuments in the Near East area. The Temple of Jupiter in Baalbek, Lebanon, for example, was built on a huge megalithic base consisting of quarried blocks, precisely carved and fitted and weighing up to 1,200 tons. They were cut and transported several miles and lifted into place. There is no equipment that can manipulate such weights today.

At the southernmost part of Sumer, where the Tigris and Euphrates rivers come together in marsh lands bordering the Persian Gulf, a site was excavated which turned out to be the oldest city in Sumer, called Eridu. This is the site where Enki says in his autobiographical account that he waded ashore when he first arrived on Earth.

As an accomplished scientist, it is recorded that he bequeathed his advanced knowledge to his sons, known to us as the Egyptian gods, Ra and Thoth. Intrigue mounts as the writings go on to say that he also shared with mankind certain aspects of his advanced knowledge, by teaching select individuals the "secrets of the gods."

View of Baalbek base platform wall with Temple of Jupiter ruins built on top.
Megalithic construction blocks shown were quarried several miles away.
These unfinished blocks are shown in the quarry pictures to the right

Such initiates were instructed to write down those divine teachings as mankind's heritage. Unfortunately, many of these books were lost, but their former existence was specifically mentioned in other texts. However, one of them was almost certainly the prototype of the biblical Enoch, the one who was taken up to Heaven after he had entrusted to his sons the book of divine secrets, and of which a version has possibly survived in the extrabiblical *Book of Enoch.*

To quote Sitchin's account from *The Lost Book of Enki:*

> "The initiation of chosen individuals into the 'secrets of the gods' had marked the beginning of Priesthood, the lineages of the mediators between the gods and the people, the transmitters of the Divine Words to the mortal Earthlings.
>
> "These developments sharpened the realization that one must distinguish between Fate and Destiny. The proclamation of ...(those Anunnaki) that used to be unquestioned were now subjected to the scrutiny of the difference between NAM–a Destiny, like the planetary orbits, whose course had been determined and was unchangeable—and NAM.TAR, literally, a destiny that could be bent, broken, changed—which was Fate. Reviewing and recalling the sequence of events, and the apparent parallelism between what had happened on Nibiru and what took place on Earth, (Enki and Enlil, brothers in the high drama) began to ponder philosophically what indeed was destined and could not have been avoided and what was just fated as a consequence of right or wrong decisions and free choice. The latter (Fate) could not be predicted, the former (Destiny) could be foreseen—***especially if all, as the planetary orbits, was cyclical; if what we shall again be, if the First Things shall also be the Last Things (bold italics mine).***
>
> "The climactic event of the nuclear desolation sharpened soul-searching among the leaders of the Anunnaki and raised the need to explain to the devastated human masses why it came to pass this way...it was Enki who stood alone in opposition to the use of the forbidden weapons. It was thus important for Enki to explain to the suffering remnants how that turning point in that saga of the extraterrestrials, who had meant well but ended as destroyers, had come to pass. And who but Enki, who was the first to come and an eyewitness to it all, was most qualified to tell the Past so that the Future could be divined? And the best way to tell it all was as a first person report by Enki himself."

That he recorded his autobiography is certain. Zecharia Sitchin used assembled materials from many sources to re-create the eyewitness account of Enki, "the autobiographical memoirs and insightful prophecies of an extraterrestrial god." The text as dictated by Enki was to be unsealed at an appropriate time.

> "In dealing with the past, Enki himself perceived the future. The notion that the Anunnaki, exercising free will, were masters of their own fate (as well as the fate of mankind) gave way, in the end, to a realization that it was Destiny that when all was said and done, determined the course of events; and therefore—as the Hebrew Prophets had recognized—the First Things shall be the Last Things.

"The record of events dictated by Enki thus becomes a foundation, and the Past becomes the Future."

Unless one is familiar with the cyclical nature of events, as externalized by the heavenly bodies in their orbits, Enki's words may be puzzling. Today's astrologers are better able to provide insight into what is meant by such phrases as, "the Past becomes the Future" and similar sentiments. You will notice in earlier paragraphs that Destiny is associated with planetary orbits and events over which we have no control, unlike Fate which can be bent or broken.

The past becomes the future because no matter what pattern exists in the sky today, its cyclical nature dictates that at some future time the same pattern will come full circle and be repeated. That was the reason that Enki was so eager to relate the history of those times and everything that happened. He knew that future generations could read it and understand that the same forces at work then, would come around again "when the time was right."

So what were the forces at work then? What history would be repeated? One thing we do know is that the "right time" is now because we have recovered the clay tablets dictated by Enki to a scribe. The ancient history has come to light once again; it is unsealed. Astrologers also observe it is the end of a cycle of the Mayan calendar system and the precession of the equinox cycle of 26,00 years.

"That our whole lifecycle is mapped by the Zodiac because time flows in a circle, not in a straight line from past to present to future. In a nutshell, what goes around comes around again and again albeit in a fresh new mixed-up way. As the sages say: 'You never dip your toe in the same river water twice.' "

Transformers: Shaman of the 21st Century
By John Jay Harper

Next, a new species was created, the Adam. Aren't we now talking once more about a population of a new race of humans on the Earth? Again, history coming full circle and repeating itself. The disharmony and discord between the righteous and evil forces are not unlike the disclosure of dark forces—the Illuminati—who have controlled mankind. In the end, it was Destiny that determined the final outcome, an outcome that therefore could not be changed. The Anunnaki, despite their doubts, actually played into the hands of Destiny in creating the human race. We assume, then, that we are once again meeting our Destiny in processing the ascension and gaining access to new dimensions.

In a sealed Attestation document left by the master scribe Endubsar to whom Enki dictated his memoirs, he leaves these final words:

> "And the voice of the lord Enki said: 'The signs will be in the heavens...and after you there will be other chosen prophets...And in the end there will be a New Earth and a New Heaven, and for prophets there will be no more need.'"

This resonates with biblical verses that also refer to a New Heaven and a New Earth (Revelations and Isaiah). The next chapter will discuss this further. Extraterrestrials came to Earth and created *homo sapiens.* Will "mommy and daddy" return again from the skies to work with the new human race?

Perhaps we cannot know for certain what the future holds for us. But from Enki's own testimony it was recorded that humankind met its Destiny in his own time. The great planetary line-up with the center of our galaxy in December of 2012 echoes a great god's prophecy from ancient times to tell us that the First shall be the Last; a time come full circle, and we once again meet our Destiny.

Biblical Stories Retold

Here is the true account of actually what happened in the Noah and the Ark biblical story. The Anunnaki "gods" were aware that the polar ice cap was melting and would soon release a huge chunk of ice because of earthquakes expected from the approach of the orbital return of their home planet, Nibiru. This would be a REALLY HUGE chunk of ice, one capable of triggering a gargantuan tsunami flood of water over much of the earth's surface. Since Big Daddy was still greatly peeved about the inter-marrying business, his uptight son Enlil decided that he would withhold this information about the impending flood and not warn the humans, and, in this way, wipe them off the map, never to break the rules and upset the Grand Design ever again.

The plan would have worked, too, were it not for one fella who felt sorry for the humans to the extent that he betrayed Big Daddy by tattling. Furthermore, it was a submarine-type boat, not an ark, that was constructed. It was Mt. Ararat that was on the highest ground and where the submarine headed for its final destination. According to the recorded stories, the Anunnaki viewed the flood from spaceships above the Earth until the flood waters subsided, then they too landed in the high area of Mt. Ararat. Enlil, who originally wanted the extinction of the humans, was convinced by Enki that they couldn't really survive without the slave help of the creatures they had created.

What about this business of a nuclear war? That's right. The United States's atom bombing of Japan was preceded by many thousands of years as the first detonation of nuclear weapons. I will skip the convoluted intrigue that generated the tragic sequence of events, one that generated an unanticipated nuclear wind around earth.

Existing evidence is available to read the *true account* of Lot and his wife, who was allegedly turned into a pillar of salt because she turned to view the final destruction of Sodom and Gomorrah. What actually happened was that Lot and his family were warned about the nuclear blast and advised to head out for underground caves pronto if they were to survive. As for Lot's wife, the blast changed her not into a pillar of salt, but vapor (another translation of the Hebrew text).

Sitchin's *Earth Chronicles Series* explained to me the true events surrounding many of the Bible stories that I learned in Sunday School as a child. All of this information, and a great deal more, exists today on tens of thousands of cuneiform carvings on clay tablets unearthed in various archeological digs. As previously mentioned, the discovery of what was essentially the Rosetta Stone of cuneiform writings enabled Sitchin and many others to translate these remarkable accounts; the equivalent of journals or diaries set down by the Anunnaki, documenting the creation of *homo sapiens,* a species that carries the extraterrestrial DNA to this day and to whom we must look as our true parents, the gods.

From the Internet

> "Around 6,000 years ago, they (the Anunnaki), probably realizing that they were going to phase off the planet, began gradually to bring humans to independence. Sumer, a human civilization, amazing in its 'sudden' mature, and highly advanced character, was set up under their tutelage in Mesopotamia. Human kings were inaugurated as go-betweens, foremen of the human populations answering to the Anunnaki. A strain of humans, genetically enhanced with more Anunnaki genes, a bloodline of rulers in a tradition of 'servants of the people' was initiated." (Gardner).

The Birth of the Mystery Schools

These designated humans were taught technology, mathematics, astronomy, advanced crafts and the ways of advanced civilized society in schools now called mystery schools, but there was no mystery about them. Gardner has brought to light the fact that there exists a robust, highly documented, genealogical, genetic history carrying all the way back to the Anunnaki, possessed by the heterodox tradition of Christianity, which is only now coming forward, no longer gun shy of the Inquisition.

This tradition, preserving the bloodline, is the one branded "heretical" and murderously persecuted by the Roman Church. There were no Dark Ages for this tradition, only for those whom the Church wanted to keep in the dark about the real nature of human history and destroy the bloodline, a direct threat to the power of the Bishops.

The Hidden Government

Nations are thought to develop through a reincarnation process. Great civilizations rise and fall along a continually higher point on the spiral of evolution. Mystery schools tell of highly evolved souls whose growth have carried them to other planes of existence. These adepts work together in Brotherhoods under the guidance of more advanced masters. They are the angels and archangels of the Christian Bible.

The occult Brotherhood functions as an inner government initiating new epochs over vast ages. The founding of races and nations conforms to the letter of natural law. That order is never violated. Nothing is abandoned to chance. All causes set into motion are in exact harmony with fundamental patterns in nature. Their purpose is to lead the human family increasingly toward self-government and freedom from the order's external control.

The first race was the Lemurian. Ancient myths tell of the continent of Lemuria, which existed millions of years ago and of which the Hawaiian Islands are the only remains. Following that race came another on the continent of Atlantis, which now lies buried beneath the waters of our Atlantic Ocean. Plato himself wrote of this fabled land.

The Spiritual Destiny of America

The people of the United States hold a position in this scheme as the seed for a coming new race. Their heritage is drawn from one of the Atlantean races. Together with Great Britain, the United States is identified with ancient Israel. Biblical promises of a "chosen people" take on wider implications in light of occult teachings.

National groups in the past have been closely guided by the invisible government. *The founding of the United States of America marked an important new departure from this necessary control. There were then men and women of great strength and initiative in the human family. The nation embarked upon an independent course this time under the guardianship of a **human** hierarchy.*

This new freedom is an inherent part of the American psyche. The urge to emancipate themselves from control was actually an undefined soul urge to break the dependence on invisible guidance. The nation has achieved a greater degree of spiritual independence than any nation before it.

Direction from within could not be withdrawn completely. In The United States of America, it is continued through the human hierarchy. Members of this group are of our own human family. Yet, they are far in advance of ordinary humanity. These elder brothers and sisters are a shadowy presence behind all important turning points in history. They ordinarily work under a concealed identity, their true mission unsuspected. They traditionally remain unrecorded in history.

In these days of crisis, *it is hard to imagine that the United States is the seed ground of a new race which eventually will establish a world government of peace and freedom*. It often appears that America is drifting away from earlier great ideals. Yet, mystics and seers have left rich prophecies foretelling the rise of a new nation bearing remarkable similarities to the United States. Sir Francis Bacon in *The New Atlantis* wrote of a future Utopia which would give birth on a higher plane to the legendary antediluvian civilization. Merlin and Virgil also left predictions bearing striking correspondence to the actual formation of the American democracy. These prophecies generally confirm occult beliefs that America marks an era of evolutionary changes ushering in a new Order of the Ages.

The forces that culminate in a vital new dimension in mankind's evolution are meticulously developed long years in advance. When the times are favorably disposed astrologically, carefully prepared eggs incarnate to implement some aspect of the divine plan. Spiritual energies at these times project from the inner planes a group of kindred souls born to a common cause. Art, science and philosophy have lurched forward periodically to new levels of excellence. The apex of these creative achievements coincides always with an entire group of extraordinary individuals.

The Golden Ages of art and philosophy in Greece, the magnificent Renaissance in Italy, the Elizabethan age of literature in England, and the great music from Bach to Wagner's time in Germany were typical epochs when souls incarnated as a body to make some exceptional contribution. In conformity with this pattern, a company of noble spirits gathered early in the eighteenth century to inaugurate a new political experiment and to lay the foundation stone for a new world order of brotherhood and peace.

On any roster of great patriots of early colonial times, one name is sure to be found. The towering Washington Monument is a fitting memorial to this remarkable statesman whose long shadow is cast across America's destiny, a destiny he often foresaw. Popular textbook accounts of Washington fail to mention his prophetic vision. Yet Washington's contemporaries recognized the great leader's attunement to inner-plane activity.

The lives of the great souls of destiny seldom follow the conventional pattern. They are born out of time. Their Uranian ideas often suffer ridicule among contemporary society. As for the personal side of life, this is frequently marred with heartbreak and unfulfillment. These disappointments temper the soul and incline toward the service of impersonal goals.

If ever there was an ambassador of the invisible government, Benjamin Franklin was one. He often is named the greatest man that this country has ever produced. Historians are amazed at his incredible psychological influence. From early childhood he bore the sure mark of an old soul returning to fulfill an important destiny. He was reading the

Bible at age five. The young boy's mind ranged far beyond the orthodox puritanical tracts in his father's library. For most of his life he steeped himself in the study of the ancient mysteries. His esoteric studies impressed him with a profound sense of Oneness with all Life. His veneration for animals was so great that he became a vegetarian in young manhood. This deep feeling of unity with nature is a common trait among disciples of the mysteries.

The Masonic Order in the new world was one of the secret societies deeply aware of the occult doctrines. Franklin eagerly promoted public acceptance of occult ideas. There is no question that he was a serious astrologer. After the American independence, Franklin was appointed minister to France. At the time, Paris was an active center for Egyptian Masonry and occultism.

The old sage was received by the most famous of all French secret orders. In their record ledger, his name is signed close to the Marquis de Lafayette. The profoundly esoteric French Apollonian Society was founded by Franklin. The light of this illustrious American genius was extinguished in 1790 when he was 84 years old. Franklin subscribed to the doctrine of reincarnation as is revealed clearly in his epitaph, which he composed himself.

Few men have approached the intellectual range and significant accomplishments of Washington and Franklin. Nonetheless, a contemporary and colleague of these men paralleled in every way their brilliance. Just as his fellow statesmen, Thomas Jefferson exhibited the characteristics of an emissary of the Brotherhood.

Like Washington he rejected the principles of the aristocracy to which he was born and zealously applied himself to founding a social democracy that guaranteed equal rights to the masses. The social class to which he was born bitterly ostracized him. Common to many dedicated agents of this cause, he was acquainted with sorrow and grief. The disciple's path is often difficult and lonely. As with other messengers of destiny, he embraced high spiritual principles outside any recognized church connections.

To list Jefferson's encyclopedic accomplishments tests the credulity of the ordinary person. As a man of science, he ranked alongside such greats as Bacon. He did extensive research on fossils, Newtonian physics and the origin of rainbows. He was an accomplished naturalist and botanist. His knowledge of calculus was advanced; he was mathematician enough to compute an eclipse. His proficiency in medicine was so skilled that he set broken bones and stitched up wounds. He classified thousands of bones of prehistoric animals.

He gathered massive collections of art, sculpture and books. The Jefferson library was so extensive that when the British burned the Capital in 1814, he sold 10,000 volumes to form the nucleus of our Library of Congress. As a landscape gardener and practical farmer he had no equal. His gardens were world famous for their remarkable beauty. He practiced contour plowing and crop rotation. His linguistic ability awed everyone who knew him. He read Cicero in Latin, Plato in Greek, Montesquieu in French, Cervantes in Spanish and poetry in Gaelic.

As an architect he takes his place among the eminent of the world. He designed the capitol building at Richmond and the campus of the University of Virginia. His own lovely Monticello is a tribute to countless hours at his drawing board. Impressive as is this partial list of his achievements, his greatness is measured in the brilliance and scope of his ideas. Lincoln himself acknowledged Jefferson as the one above all others who caught the spirit of what American democracy could become.

To produce the ideal instrument that was Thomas Jefferson, it was necessary, according to occult law, to choose an ego long under the direction of our Elder Brothers. Thomas Jefferson may be described as the most Aquarian of all American presidents. Both he and John Adams died on the Fourth of July, 50 years after the Declaration of Independence..

References have been made to the inner-plane pattern which worked through the founding fathers according to their sensitivity as the plan impressed itself upon them. The connection of Masonry to this plan was mentioned briefly. Masonry today appears to be wholly exoteric. Few members connect the rituals and symbols with occultism. I inquired of a friend, who is a high-degree Mason, whether the astrological symbols in Masonry meant that the lodge members practice astrology. I was quickly assured that I could "relieve my mind" of such a preposterous idea. There is little danger, nonetheless, that esoteric Masonry will be lost. A few souls serve as torchbearers of truth to keep alive the true inner meanings.

A 1717 merger led to the establishment in Masonry of the Rite of Three Degrees. Albert Pike, noted Masonic authority, clearly connects this with the initiation into the ancient mysteries. As the seeds of revolution were sown in the soil of early American politics, Masonic activity accelerated in the new land.

The idea of a secret organization of highly evolved Masters, guiding the spiritual development of the human race, stretches back in time to Sumeria in 6000 BC and even earlier. The high priest cults in Egypt functioned beneath the great God figure of Thoth. His symbol was the winged serpent and serves to this day as the symbol of the medical caduceus. Thoth was the lead figure in the mystery schools of Egypt. There are also many biblical references to the God-inspired magical serpent. The most famous is probably in Exodus—the story of Moses and his staff turned reptile that defeated the Pharaoh and freed the people.

Nearly every culture from earliest times embraces an occult tradition that souls of great wisdom in or out of earthly life have assumed responsibility for the cosmic destiny of the human race. The name given to this spiritual hierarchy is the Great

White Brotherhood. The use of the term "white" refers to an advanced spirituality and their pure white aura. It has absolutely no connection to race.
My first exposure to the concept of the White Brotherhood was when I joined the Theosophical Society in St. Louis in the late 60s. The head of the Theosophical Society was Mr. Charles Luntz, a preeminent astrologer, so I was attracted there at first to his astrology classes.

Helena Blavatsky was the founder of the Theosophical society. Mr. Luntz was nearly 80 when I attended his classes, and I discovered that he knew Mme. Blavatsky personally. He lectured every week from her famous tome *The Secret Doctrine.* I sat transfixed as he read aloud, adding insights and comments Blavatsky shared with him in their many private conversations. She had many references to the activities of the White Brotherhoods. I thought I was listening to God just coming from the Methodist Church as I was.

Whether in Sumeria of 6000 BC, the mystery schools of Egypt, the temples and monasteries of the East, the Theosophists of the eighteenth and nineteenth centuries or contemporary Rosicrucians, teachings have continually been interlaced with the group of sages known today as the Great White Brotherhood. Their presence was never more in evidence than in the years that eventually culminated in the Revolutionary War that created the independent nation of the United States of America. Aside from some of the references already included in this chapter, they were some of the individuals that carried the torch of our secret destiny.

Mystics for the most part live in silent dedication to the brotherhoods they serve. This was no more true than in the lives of the women who were the emissaries of the inner forces. Despite relative obscurity in history, the feminine mystique helped shape a new world in the making.

A young London woman named Leade was a disciple of the renowned mystic Jacob Boehme. The seeress was recognized for the high quality of her development. From celestial realms inaccessible to most souls, came great revelations, many concerning profound occult Masonic symbolism. Leade organized a philosophical society in London, one link in a chain that would culminate in the establishment of deep esoteric doctrines in America. A German named John Jacob Zimmerman was drawn into the developing conclave of souls. He was a Lutheran minister who cultivated an active interest in mathematics and astronomy. An illness led him to a physician who, as it turned out, was a member of a Boehme group.

Zimmerman's absorption with Boehme's teachings led to his expulsion from the church. He made his way to London where he immersed himself in study under Leade. The London Boehme group formulated the Masonic Rite of Perfection. Those who qualified for this initiation planned to assemble at Rotterdam in preparation for sailing to the American colonies.

At this point John Kelpius, in pursuit of occult studies, came under the careful tutelage of Zimmerman. Shortly before the group's departure for America, Zimmerman's sudden death unexpectedly placed his protégé, Kelpius, at the head of this party of highly advanced individuals.

The inner government long before had chosen a place where the teachings of the mysteries could be planted effectively on American soil. In the precepts of Mundane Astrology, land areas have particular astrological characteristics. So it was that the village of Germantown, Pennsylvania, came to be.

That settlement of the late 1600s established a hermitage topped by an observatory where the stars were kept under constant observation. The Brotherhood was known throughout the countryside. Many miracles of healing were reported by the sick and the troubled who visited there. The brothers could leave their bodies at will in search of missing loved ones and bring back reports of their whereabouts.

The members performed works in the outer world as well. Two famous churches were erected in accordance with their astrological calculations. Various members served these churches and others in the colonies. The community's last magister was Christopher Witt, a brilliant physician and astrologer. His close friend was the noted botanist John Bartram. The Bartram botanical gardens survived as one of Philadelphia's showplaces. William Penn also was associated closely with the mystics, working in the outer world to establish the same ideals of justice that the Brothers supported spiritually.

The inner circle of the order was celibate, which led to its eventual abandonment but not before their spiritual power was released from this inner center. (Actually the society reverted to its secret foundations and continued outside public view.) Their burial grounds were protected by magical rites in order that they would never be disturbed. Despite the ravages of war all around it, the area was never violated. It now stands in Germantown, in the heart of the city of Philadelphia beneath St. Michael's church. The chancel was positioned directly over the graves of the Brothers, leaving them intact to this day. Most of the community's occult library passed into the hands of Benjamin Franklin.

It did not take long for a young William Penn to run afoul of orthodoxy. He was thrown out of Christ Church and was arrested several times. In 1668, he was imprisoned for writings that were considered heretical. So it is not so hard to understand that Penn decided it might be better to head out to the New World to avoid future persecution.

Through an inheritance from his father, Penn was granted a large land area from King Charles II, which later became the state of Pennsylvania. William Penn has been called the father of democracy. Well ahead of the times, he was the early champion of the principles that inspired the U.S. Constitution. A bronze statue of Penn still stands at the very top of Philadelphia's City Hall. In 1884, the U.S. Congress posthumously conferred Honorary Citizen of the United States on this amazing visionary mystic.

In 1717, Anthony Jacob Henckel a Lutheran pastor brought a group of people to America in the midst of dangerous conflicts with the German Catholic Church. The intriguing aspect of this voyage is that Rev. Henckel came at the express invitation of none other than William Penn.

Henckel established the Lutheran faith in the new world. He built St. Michael's Church in Germantown, Pennsylvania. The seminary that houses his robes and communion cup can be viewed there yet today. His son wrote the catechism and many church hymns, one of which I have in my possession. I have played it on the piano, and sang it, but only when no one was listening.

Does this ring a bell? Yes, it's one and the same site of the early order associated with William Penn. The church was built directly above the burial ground of the mystical Brotherhood, thus guaranteeing that the sacred ground would never be touched! This, plus other indications, marks Rev. Henckel as an ambassador of the secret brotherhood.

It was the custom in seventeenth- and eighteenth-century Germany for the local pastor to keep all birth, death and marriage records. This was adhered to with the usual Teutonic thoroughness. In America, photostatic copies of Henckel's records show typical detail in preserving these dates. Yet, on the passage to the colonies, no passenger list was kept.

A remarkable characteristic of his descendents is their almost universal preservation of family genealogical records. It must be in their DNA! They have assembled an unbelievably extensive genealogy under the auspices of the National Anthony Jacob Henckel Family Association. I am fortunate in that I was at the right time and the right place to procure a rare limited edition in my library of the Henckel genealogy. It truly is remarkable. Furthermore, this association remarkably has always assembled a committee of trained family genealogists who enthusiastically donate nearly full-time research to the Henckel genealogy. There are still regional and national reunions at which the latest findings are compiled. Much of the genealogy is now on the Internet.

In old family papers there are references to Henckel's diary, which contained a wealth of information valuable to the early genealogy. However, the diary vanished and never was found, despite years of searching. Being "lost to history" is often the mark of the Brotherhood or recorded inaccurately, as in this case. They prefer to work behind the scenes.

Anthony Jacob Henckel himself had fallen into oblivion, and his central role in the establishment of Lutheranism in America never would have been rediscovered, except for the persistence of his ancestors. In church annals, his identity was confused with that of his eldest son, and he was listed erroneously as Rev. Gerhard Henckel.

In 1967, the Henckel family conclave of several hundred descendents gathered at Ursinas College in Collegeville, Pennsylvania, to observe the 250th anniversary of their common ancestor's arrival in America. From there the cousins departed by bus one Sunday morning to attend services at the church built by Anthony Jacob Henckel.

In 1910 his grave was discovered in a remote corner of the churchyard. The executive officers of the National Reverend Anthony Jacob Henckel Family Association moved the burial site of Anthony Jacob and his wife to a place near the main walk directly in front of the church and erected a new headstone.

Funds were raised to defray the costs of a memorial tablet to be placed in the chancel of the church. The tablet was dedicated in 1917. I was one of the family group in 1967 who viewed the white marble tablet in Pastor Henckel's original church, St. Michael's church in Germantown, Pennsylvania—directly above the burial ground of the mystical brotherhood. The German Consul came from Washington D.C. to conduct the dedication services.

As it happened, my father was also passionately driven to tracing his genealogy, true to the inexplicable obsession Rev. Henckel's ancestors carried down through the generations to seek out one another and without any suspicion that "the cousins" were very likely searching for them too. Had he not been so dedicated, my parents and I would never have been in the church in Germantown that Sunday morning, along with my young nine-year-old son.

Yes, that's right. **I am a direct bloodline descendent**, 11 generations removed, of Anthony Jacob Henckel. My maiden name is Diana Lee Henckel (Henkle).

My brother, Duane, and I are in the direct unbroken bloodline of one of the men in the White Brotherhoods. Our highest ideal is to carry forward the principles of the secret brotherhoods laid down by our ancestor who worked to prepare the foundations of America. Now at this time we are dedicated to do our part, however great or small, to fulfill America's destiny to birth a new race of humans, enlightened and ascending to a new frequency and a new dimension. It is also no accident that Destiny leads me to revise my original book *The United States Wheel of Destiny* and to be published under the new title *The Secret Destiny of America.*

It probably will remain a mystery just how deeply involved with the secret orders was this man who built his church over the Germantown Brothers' magically secured graves, but there are several features of his life that attest to his agency of the invisible forces nonetheless, evidence so extensive that it leaves no room for doubt in my mind.

If all activities of secret societies were known, many events and the changes they wrought would be rooted clearly in deep, mystical bonds between peoples and nations. However, these organizations purposely have concealed their activities which would have brought certain persecution from non-members. Esoteric orders have existed among all peoples since the beginning of recorded history.

Mystery School Symbolism

It has been claimed that the designer of the Great Seal of the United States originally drew a phoenix. In the drawing on the Seal of 1782, it is evident that the head of the bird is not an eagle, but a phoenix. The beak is shaped differently, the neck is much longer, and a small tuft of hair at the back of the head leaves no doubt of the artist's intention. Among the secret orders, the phoenix is a symbol of resurrection and immortality. Those who receive initiation are said to be "born again" into a new life.

The pyramid on the reverse side of the Seal is shown without a capstone. The pyramid is left unfinished because it represents an imperfect human society. The triangle enclosing the eye is shaped for the Greek letter D, the first letter in the name of God.

Stories of Atlantis tell of a great university on the island continent in the form of a pyramid. Did the invisible government carry a symbol of this temple of the sciences to the new Atlantis? The phrase at the base of the pyramid on the Seal reads *Novas Ordo Seclorum*—*a* new Order of the Ages. Is this meant to proclaim to all nations the purpose for which the United States was founded?

Great Seal of the United States
Original — 1882

Great Seal of the United States
Before 1912

This by no means exhausts the symbolic interpretations of the Great Seal. All this is only a superficial and greatly abbreviated assessment of the connections between United States history and an ancient Brotherhood operating from inner realms. Viewed singly, many incidents and personalities do not seem especially important. The overall picture, however, is one perfect, unbroken pattern.

All of the national mottoes, seals, emblems and flags are fertile with esoteric meanings. Yet, there is nothing in the background of a colony of farmers, shopkeepers and country gentlemen to suggest the selection of these symbols. Their origins clearly spring from the secret societies that came to this country 150 years before the Revolutionary War.

This reminds us that there is more than meets the eye in the affairs of mankind. If the bold break is made from old ways of thinking and if we pry beneath the surface of our earthly lives, there we will catch a glimpse of the marvelous intermeshing of the inner and the outer, the material and the spiritual. These two worlds exist in and through one another, linking past, present and future.

All of this leaves little doubt that secret societies, and mystery schools, have existed down through the ages, beginning with Enki handing over the "secrets of the gods," the foundations of civilization itself, to his sons. Most certainly the secret orders have evolved since then and initiations into the upper echelons have required initiates to have evolved as well.

We have seen that the mystery schools' guidance by the White Brotherhoods from the inner planes took a radical turn predating the American Revolutionary period by about 150 years. At that time, the Brotherhoods apparently decided to transfer the reins of power to highly evolved members of the *human family* in the outer world, men like Washington, Franklin, Jefferson and an entire host of brilliant statesmen with a vision of an experiment in democratic government.

Radically visionary political statesmanship, devotion to personal excellence and sacrifice was their outer life's work and particular genius. However, great initiates were expected to achieve excellence and lofty goals in the outer world equally with their esoteric contributions. Consequently, the legacy they leave in the history books was accompanied by simultaneously putting down the secret foundations for the seeding of a new race of human in the United States, a nation geographically located on soil with a special astrological signature and a special destiny.

Mystery School Symbolism And Ascension

A nation devoted to materialism, tainted by corruption in both religious and secular life and betraying many proud ideals laid down by the founding fathers seems as unlikely to relate to the esoteric symbols as were the typical colonial citizenry of yesteryear. There is every evidence to trust that the mystery schools and their torch bearers exist in unbroken succession to this present time in the United States.

Therefore, we can assume that contemporary U.S. citizens must also be confronted by an esoteric secret language that continues the long tradition of communicating the same deep mysteries of transformation and immortality. The difference is that the seeds tended by the careful hands of those great souls throughout the nation's formative years have now come into full maturity in the midst of a process of enlightenment and ascension. That leads us to questions that address unique circumstances never previously present within the human family:

What special symbolism is appropriate for a humanity preparing for life in other dimensions? What is the final step in the ascension game?

****

GOD BLESS AMERICA!

CHAPTER NINETEEN

Playing The God Game

The light of the body is the eye: if therefore thine eye be single thy whole body shall be filled with light.

American King James version Christian Bible
Luke 11: 34-36(Also Matthew 6:22)

If you can, close your eyes for just a moment and then bring your attention right to the center of your forehead. In some traditions this is called the third eye. It's the pineal gland... "I will lift up my attention to a place inside me where I can discover answers."

Mary Morrissey

Therefore, the pinecone was a symbol of the pineal gland that can be activated in order for man to achieve godhood or being in a divine status (according to the ancients of old).

Albert Mackey

The Ultimate Game?

Would you believe that the most powerful game on the planet is contained in a small pea-sized gland buried in your own brain? That is the pineal (PIN-ee-uhl) gland, often referred to in occult literature as the third eye. Yes, it is real. You can see the gland with your 3D eyes. It secretes melatonin. You have probably heard about it in connection to waking-sleeping cycles.

However, as for its role as the third eye, its pivotal in the ascension process already in motion, plus connects to revelations of history's most controversial secrets, stretching back to pre-biblical times. It is the ultimate Game.

So what do we know about the gland that roared and would be king? Would it be that it is faceted and sparkles like a diamond? Or some other gem? Or does it bear some resemblance to a gold coin of the realm? Precious gems? Solid gold? None of these? What other treasure of mankind's could be so valuable as to place its rank above ALL worldly goods together?

The pineal gland takes on the appearance of a pinecone. It obviously is not that the lowly pinecone is cherished as the most valuable of earthly treasures. It is WHERE we discover the pinecone located that we guess it must be recognized as a most sacred symbol throughout a long history. As a sacred symbol what does it mean? And who honored it in the past as such, and who does so yet today?

A massive bronze pinecone statue stands in the courtyard of The Court of the Pinecone in St. Peter's at the Vatican. It is the largest statue of a pinecone in the world. In 1608, it was moved into the position that it now enjoys.

The staff that the Pope carries has a built-in pinecone, as does several of his other staves. The Pope is supposed to be God's representative on Earth. I do know that in the ancient traditions, the Pope was required to have an awakened pineal gland.

There is no arguing the fact that the early church fathers must have held the pinecone symbol extremely significant to have placed it so prominently in the Vatican. The Bible itself holds an important clue in the verse I quoted at the beginning of this chapter.

Pinecone Symbolism at Our Own Front Door

This is my favorite depiction of the pinecone. That is because it is out in the open also, but beyond that; it is precisely WHERE it is out in the open. It is one of the biggest tourist attractions in the United States. There is a famous fresco on the ceiling of the rotunda of the Capitol building in Washington, D.C. It was painted by Constantino Brumidi and completed in 1865. The official name of this painting is the *Apotheosis of George Washington. Apotheosis* carries the meaning of one who has achieved god-like powers or an ascended state.

A search of the Internet yields many cites with interesting analyses of the various components of the painting. However interesting the outer story may be, the fresco is circular, a mandala, containing extensive secret symbolism. And don't think for a minute that Brumidi did not know what he was doing. He did! It is tempting to be sidetracked onto the whole story, but to confine this to the idea of the pinecone and its representation of the pineal gland: Exactly under the ring of stars (in the painting) there are pinecones after every second star! Just one more pineal gland symbolism which has been seen throughout history as an awakened state. It is fascinating to point out that our lawmakers pass under this symbolism every day.

Apotheosis of Washington with close-ups of pine cones.

In David Wilcock's book *The Source Field Investigation,* he cites further examples of the religious symbolism of the third eye in the Islamic tradition and the Turoe Stone in Ireland, dating back to around 200 B.C. He further cites third eye symbolism with the Buddha and nearly all Hindu gods and goddesses. Many Hindus still wear a *bindi,* or third eye, between their eyebrows to this day. A sculpture of the Mesoamerican god, Quetzalcoatl, is shaped like the pineal gland, and he wears a necklace made of pinecones.

Wilcock's research states that ancient cultures used stones to symbolize the pineal gland. In Greece, the Oracle at Delphi housed a stone shaped exactly like the pineal gland. This was an *omphalos* stone. The word *omphalos* means "the center of the earth" and "navel" in Greek. The Egyptians also had a stone that marked the center of the world. They called it the Benben. Some forms of the Benben are shaped exactly like the pineal gland.

The capstone of a pyramid is also believed to represent the Benben stone. A single eye in a triangle, floating above a pyramid, should give context for any American within the Great Seal of the United States. However significant I consider this to be for America—I spent three years of exclusive research focused on this symbolism—I will return to that later in this chapter.

To further quote David Wilcock, you will see that the pineal gland does have meaning for us in the ascension process. Follow this thread in Egyptian and Greek mythology. The Egyptian Benben stone was also associated with the Bennu bird, which was represented by various birds such as the hawk, etc.—but in Greek mythology, the Bennu bird is known as the phoenix.

> "This mythical creature experiences death by fire, followed by a spontaneous rebirth from the ashes——clearly associating the Bennu bird with a profound spiritual awakening and transformation. The words *Benben* and *Bennu* are both derived from the root syllable *Bn,* which means "ascension" or "to rise" in Egyptian. Two serpents may also be pictured with the Benben stone at times, and they appear equivalent to the 'kundalini serpents' in Hinduism—illustrating the flow of energetic currents moving up the spine and on into the pineal gland."

Master Soul: Manly Palmer Hall

I had the great good fortune to stumble onto Manly Palmer Hall's work in the 1960s and 70s while he was still alive, writing and lecturing. I was in the throes of a passion one experiences when first in the arms of a new lover, only in this case the "lovers" were astrology, spirituality and metaphysics. Mr. Hall was a prolific writer well beyond the scope of astrology alone.

I describe him as the man who knew EVERYTHING about EVERYTHING. Nonetheless, his life, death and teachings were controversial. That would not be surprising, considering anyone who wrote about astrology seriously, alongside an array of other esoteric subjects not so different from today. There has been a renaissance of interest in his body of work as well as renewed interest in this mystery man himself. He was breathtakingly handsome, possessed of the dark, brooding look of the silent movie heart throb, Rudolph Valentino.

The title of Hall's *magnum opus* makes a most convincing argument that his knowledge indeed penetrated deeply a sweeping overview of mankind's inheritance from the greatest thinkers of the distant past. It was copiously illustrated with beautiful engravings and written on an Alexandrian scale. I am the proud owner of one of the limited editions titled *An Encyclopedic Outline of Masonic, Hermetic, Qabbalistic and Rosicrucian Symbolical Philosophy: Being an Interpretation of the Secret Teachings concealed within the Rituals, Allegories and Mysteries of all Ages.*

This tongue-twister was most often referred to by its alternate title *The Secret Teachings of all Ages.* It was self-published when he was only 28 years old! It marked him as one of the metaphysical giants of the twentieth century. For this bookophile, it has been a revered addition to my library collection all through the years. It was quite a thrill to actually pull it off the shelf to consult a section on Pythagorean philosophy for this book, especially considering that it stands nearly an unwieldy 20 inches high. Manly P. Hall was undoubtedly a master soul whose mission it was to preserve and translate the ancient teachings.

This he did through the auspices of his organization, The Philosophical Research Society, Inc. in Los Angeles. There were weekly lectures open to the public for many years, plus small study groups scattered about the country. I subscribed to copies of his lectures in the form of regular monographs on many subjects, although my primary interest was astrology. It was one of the study groups that finally gave me the opportunity to speak to him on the phone. Well, even though I am not above stretching the truth just a bit on occasion, I did not actually speak to him; let's say I listened in on a conversation to be entirely accurate.

When I lived in St. Louis, a woman named Katherine Henry promised to teach me medical astrology at which she was amazingly proficient. Katherine lived in the most exclusive part of the city, Ladue. That just sounds exclusive, doesn't it? She lived in a house just a few bricks short of a mansion. However, what interested me was her fabulous library of astrology and metaphysical books to which she gave me full rein.

However, on this particular afternoon, I was not there for my astrology lesson. I was scheduled to lecture on astrology at the next Manly Hall Philosophical Research Society meeting at her home the following week so was discussing plans for my participation in the proceedings. Katherine was bustling about, rounding up the silver coffee service and supervising the household staff. In the midst of this activity, she abruptly announced that Manly Hall was telephoning at 3:30, so she must go change clothes.

My first reaction was total paralysis at the thought of Manly Hall calling her while I was there. This was like a call from God. I recovered my wits just in time to beg her permission to listen in on the conversation via the extension line. She agreed, along with stern warnings that I must just listen and not talk. As I let that sink in, the next thing was puzzlement as to the necessity for her to change clothes in order to receive the call. By the time I thought to ask, she had long left the room.

She reappeared in the library, transformed in a lovely yellow dress. The mystery was solved when I picked up the extension line to hear Mr. Hall greet Katherine, "My how lovely you look in your beautiful yellow dress today." My mouth fell open, which prompted yet another finger to her mouth in a "SHHH" warning. She needn't have worried. I was speechless. Yet, I couldn't help but wonder what he thought of my jeans and St. Louis Cardinals' t-shirt!

I think this little detour is enough to introduce Manly P. H
As per the subject of his many writings, Manley Hall was a scholar of Masonry. He claimed that Freemasonry traced back to ancient Egyptian mystery schools. He indeed referred to the pineal gland, joining many other spiritual giants in speaking of this tiny gland in the brain. Manly Hall claimed, "Each of the thirty-three degrees of Masonry corresponds to one of the vertebrae in the human spine—as the kundalini fire rises up to merge with the pineal gland."

Freemasonry and other secret societies, according to Hall, referred to the pineal gland as the Philosopher's Stone. Rudolph Steiner was also a well-known scholar of the ancient mystery schools. He argued that references to the Holy Grail was yet another reference to the pineal gland.

Edgar Cayce: America's Most Famous Psychic

Jess Stearns's book *The Sleeping Prophet* is a biography of Edgar Cayce (Cay-see), crowned America's most famous psychic. He was best known for his phenomenal body of medical readings. In 1959, I was swimming in the Atlantic Ocean on Virginia Beach with my infant son in my arms. Motherhood rather than metaphysics happily occupied my mind that summer. However, if I had walked a few blocks further down Virginia Beach, I would have found myself at the front entrance to the Center for Research and Enlightenment, the headquarters housing the Edgar Cayce readings.
Had I known it then, I would have abandoned baby David to the jellyfish and headed out for the Cayce Center. (Oh, c'mon. Just joking.) I wasn't ready for Edgar Cayce as a young girl then. As we astrologers say, "Timing is everything." But here is an interesting twist for us all. Supposedly, David Wilcock is the reincarnation of Cayce himself. At the same age, they bear a startling resemblance to one another. But I digress. Edgar Cayce spoke of the pineal gland on numerous occasions.

Helena Blavatsky, Theosophy's Mistress

Madame Helena Blavatsky is considered the mother of Theosophy and founder of the Theosophical Society. It is not for this that I make mention of this famous occultist. The written history of the pineal gland, according to Wilcock, begins with Plato and Pythagoras. Thanks to the writings of Manly Hall and Blavatsky, their references to the "secrets of the ancient mystery schools" have been handed down from ancient Egypt and continue to the present day.

The one and only astrology teacher I ever experienced in a classroom was Charles Luntz, the head of the Theosophical Society in St. Louis. As passionately interested as I was in astrology at the time (1960s), the remarkable thing about that particular experience was that Mr. Luntz—then in advanced years—knew Helena Blavatzky in person. He also gave regular weekly lectures on Blavatsky's great work *The Secret Doctrine:* lectures to which I faithfully attended, as much as to hear his personal anecdotes about his private conversations with her as to understand this complex tome by Blavatsky.

The written legends to which they refer, beginning with the works of Plato, include his statement, quoted in Wilcock's book and Hall's treatise on Plato also:

"...the study of the science of Numbers tends to awaken that organ in the brain that the ancients described as the 'eye of wisdom'—the organ now known to physiology as the pineal gland."

The Spiritual Destiny Of America

Before moving on to reveal some of the secret symbolism connected to the United States, I will have to share with you some of the back story that began in the early 70s. I never would have imagined that the project I undertook back then would figure so prominently in a completely different context over 35 years later. The idea of ascension was an unhatched egg at that time.

America was gearing up for the observance of its bi-centennial anniversary in 1976. In 1973, the editor of a national newspaper syndicate in Chicago, approached me to produce a book on astrology for the occasion. The publisher was Henry Regnery Publishing in Washington, D.C. I was living in St. Louis at the time, and as an epitome of extreme coincidences, I just happened to be shopping an idea for an astrology column and had been pestering one of the editors of the *St. Louis Post Dispatch.* I don't know whether he actually saw some merit in my sample columns or whether he simply had had just about enough of me. For whatever reason, he arranged an introduction to the syndicate editor in Chicago.

So there I was in Chicago pitching my ideas to him. When he asked me to join him for dinner at the Press Club, I let myself believe that I might have a foot in the door. (I had already sent him some 20 sample columns.) You may stop holding your breath. He turned the tables on me and pitched a proposal of his own. He asked me to write this book for Henry Regnery: right place, right time, wrong book. The problem was that I had not the least inclination to write any book of the sort that they wanted. It involved a specialized branch of astrology, *Mundane* astrology. I never studied it, I never wanted to study it, so I said NO. I continued to say NO at subsequent meetings in St. Louis.

Finally the stars, sun and moon must have been just right. I don't mean that in a good way because things turned in *his* favor. I relented and agreed to do the book, a book featuring astrology and The United States of America. Here is a teeny, tiny tidbit of information for the layperson. The book would include a birth horoscope of the United States. Well, that is easy. The birth for the United States is July 4, 1776. The accurate answer: That is when we *celebrate* our nation's birthday. Within the astrological community, however, this is a most controversial subject. What the typical layperson is not aware of is that horoscopes, in order to really zero in on anything specific, not just generalities, must include a birth *time.* Even if July 4th was the historical birth *date,* which does not enjoy a total consensus, then what *time* on July 4th was the Declaration of Independence signed? This is the gnarly part.

Since Mundane astrology deals with the fate of nations, and since I had no knowledge or interest in Mundane astrology, I really did not care what the true birth day, year or time was the correct horoscope for America. The can of worms that I was about to open with a rusty can opener made a picnic with the Hatfields and the McCoys look like a Peace Rally.

I had already chosen Portland, Oregon, as the city to which I planned to move in the summer of 1973. (I chose that city from an astrology chart, and it was the best decision I ever made!) Consequently, I was in the process of closing down my business operations in St. Louis in anticipation of that move. That gave me a couple of years to teach myself the basics of Mundane astrology and cobble together something for Regnery's. Oh, God, the naïveté.

I started out by ploughing through the biographies of the founding fathers. I lived at the library. I traveled to Washington, D.C. and looked up some rare material in the Library of Congress. I visited The National Archives for a crash course in conducting historical research. I decided there was no reason in making a fool of myself, after all. They are probably still peeing their pants—no kidding—about the dumb broad who seriously asked to see the Declaration of Independence with the original signatures. If you don't know where that document is stored, I'm not telling.

After a while, a strange phenomenon began to occur repeatedly. Please remember that when I started out I did not give a tinker's dam about any of this stuff I was supposedly trying to write about. One day I was shopping at the most obscure hole-in-the-wall health food store in all of St. Louis and its 99 suburbs. Nobody ever went there besides me. Nevertheless, on this one occasion I ran into Katherine Henry. You know, the Katherine Henry who let me listen in on Manly Hall's phone call? She reached into her shopping cart and pulled out a fat envelope of papers. She said, "I thought maybe you would want these. I have been meaning to give them to you."

What was this woman talking about? How could she know that I ever shopped at this place, let alone be there with a stack of materials she "meant to give me?" I was in for a bigger surprise than that. When I got home and sorted through it, there was extensive occult information about the United States. It wasn't anything like I was reading in the library, that's for sure.

It just so happened that there was an astrology conference in Portland in February of 1973. I decided that this would be a good opportunity to look over the city, find a realtor and maybe look at a few houses. I was heading toward my hotel room between lectures when a young man approached me with a big sheaf of papers in his hands. Right out of the blue he handed them over to me and said that if I ever wanted to come to Washington, D.C. to do some research, he could introduce me to some people at The National Archives. Besides that, he told me he was a traffic controller there, and if I gave him a heads-up when I was arriving, he would take that shift and make sure my plane landed safely.

I was dumbfounded but managed to stumble back to my hotel room. Once again, the papers were about some very occult stuff concerning the founding fathers and the early revolutionary times in this country. How in the name of God did these people know I was writing a book about this? I had not revealed to anyone that I had taken on this book project. At that time, I did not have the slightest intention of ever going to Washington, D.C. The Universe—or somebody—had different ideas.

The information coming to me in these mysterious ways spoke of occult symbolism, secret societies, hidden knowledge, ancient mystery schools with vague hints that they may exist to the present day; leading me further down the rabbit hole into uncharted territory that I had not intended to investigate. But sure enough, I did find myself on a plane for Washington, D.C. And sure enough, the guy was as good as his word. He was the airport controller when my plane landed, and he ferried me back and forth to the National Archives and the Library of Congress all week. I was beginning to uncover some very interesting information, and I wondered to myself how many other people knew about what I had in my possession.

The deadline for a book was looming larger than I ever expected it would, considering that I first decided to take it on fully *three years* prior to the bi-centennial celebration. I moved to Portland in the interim. I had stacks of reference materials to digest, organize, and somehow fit into the big picture. I was suffering the dilemma of Solomon. I was indeed a house divided against itself. How could I somehow deliver to Regnery's a book they could publish, when some mysterious force over which I had no control pulled me into the land of ancient mysteries?

Added to that was the matter of teaching myself the basics of Mundane astrology. All I can say is that I busted my butt over that book. I essentially worked on it from 8:00 a.m. until midnight seven days a week for nearly a year, which allows me to claim that I busted my butt. I was so burned out afterwards that I couldn't even think of doing astrological work of any kind for six months. Considering its problematical years' long stuttering progress, I won't know MY OWN NAME for six months after I close THIS BOOK on the last chapter.

To finally end this convoluted and painful discussion, yes, I did send the publisher a manuscript; and yes, we had a big fight over the phone; and yes, I told them what they could do with the manuscript; and yes, it was 1976, and yes, I was sitting on a manuscript that nobody wanted. (I have the rejection slips to prove it.) The name of the book was *The United States Wheel of Destiny.* That title and its unlikely author now must give us pause on several counts in relation to what has been discussed before! (The anticipated revised edition circa 2013 has been referred to elsewhere: *The Spiritual Destiny of America.)*

I finally gave the rejected manuscript to The American Federation of Astrologers, a non-profit astrological organization to which I belonged as a member. They were only too eager to publish most anything written by one of their members. The book *finally* came out in August of 1976. This is no misprint. It was 1976, more than halfway through the bi-centennial year before it saw the light of the outer world.

How about a little example of Cosmic Something-Or-Other? I had no intention of researching the correct birth chart of the United States. "Let the other astrologers duke it out," was my thinking on that. After my trips to The National Archives and my crash course in historical research, plus the mountain of mysterious information that continued to deposit itself at my feet, I experienced a growing enthusiasm for snooping under every rock.

I discovered that I had quite a nose for ferreting out obscure information. I was good at this research business! Even though it was my last priority, I determined the correct birth *date and time* of the United States as a nation, a continuing controversy in Astrology Land. Most astrologers would faint at my arrogance in making such a claim. If you think I am going to publish the co-ordinates here and now, I would have to be crazy. You have heard of "suicide by cops." Well, this would be "suicide by astrologers." Anyway, that is not the point as far as this book is concerned. Who knew that my research back then was more for *this* book than for any astrology book?

Birth Of A Nation

The founding fathers were only too aware of the symbols that made their way into prominence in reference to the new nation. The United States was founded for a secret purpose right from the beginning! Once again, I quote this mysterious passage from Masonic expert, Manly Hall:

> "Not only were many of the founders of the U.S. government Masons, but they received aid from a secret and august body existing in Europe, which

helped them establish the United States for 'a peculiar and particular purpose known only to the initiated few.' "

The "secret and august body existing in Europe" appears to have originated in Sumer, Babylon and Egypt, and ***has hidden techniques that help awaken the pineal gland.*** The pyramid is a baetyl—a symbol of the awakened pineal gland. And what was this business about the United States being set up right from the beginning for a purpose known only to a few initiates? Doesn't this smack of what we know of the ancient mystery schools? Was activating the pineal gland really the secret that they harbored? Well, if it was the mark of the enlightened human, understandably so! Was the United States carrying forward the secrets of the mystery schools by the initiated few? Was it the *spiritual destiny* of America that was really the reason for its special place in history, not just an experiment in democratic government?

Manly Hall, probably the man who knew more about the secrets of Freemasonry since ancient times, has this revelation in his book *The Occult Anatomy of Man:*

> *"The pineal gland is a spiritual organ which is later destined to become what it once was; namely, a connecting link between the human and the divine. The vibrating finger on the end of this gland is the rod of Jesse and the scepter of the high priest. Certain exercises, as given in the Eastern and Western mystery schools, cause this little finger to vibrate, resulting in a buzzing, droning sound in the brain. This is sometimes very distressing, especially when the individual who experience this phenomena, in all too many cases, knows nothing about the experiences through which he is passing."*

I must insert a reminder here that the lightbody books have mentioned hearing a continuous sound resulting from lightbody activations. In *The Lightbody Activation Manual* I wrote that "we first thought that hearing the tone was the litmus test as to whether the lightbody was activated." That turned out not to be the case; a great many of the people activated *do not* hear such sounds, including myself until recently. However, was the lightbody activation those certain exercises?

Hall continues to further comment on the significance of the pineal gland to claim that ***the biggest secret in Freemasonry is the regeneration of the human being into a Divine state—through the awakening of the pineal gland.***

An even more extensive reference from Manly Hall leaves little doubt that we are on the right track. Manly P. Hall, a well-known Masonic historian, explains the importance of the pinecone in Freemasonry and ancient civilizations:

> "Sufficient similarity exists between the Masonic CHiram and the Kundalini of Hindu mysticism to warrant the assumption that CHiram may be considered a symbol also of the Spirit Fire moving through the sixth ventricle of the spinal

> column. **THE EXACT SCIENCE OF HUMAN REGENERATION IS THE LOST KEY OF MASONRY,** *for when the Spirit Fire is lifted up through the thirty-three degrees, or segments of the spinal column, and enters into the domed chamber of the human skull, it finally passes into the pituitary body (Isis), where it invokes Ra (the pineal gland) and demands the Sacred Name.* Operative Masonry in the fullest meaning of that term signifies the process by which the Eye of Horus is opened. E. A. Wallis Budge has noted that in some of the papyri illustrating the entrance of the souls of the dead into the judgment hall of Osiris the deceased person has a pinecone attached to the crown of his head. The Greek mystics also carried a symbolic staff, the upper end being in the form of a pinecone, which was called the thyrsus of Bacchus. In the human brain there is a tiny gland called the pineal body, which is the sacred eye of the ancients, the abode of the spirit of man."

I discovered many other sources in which the pinecone symbolism appeared to figure prominently as an extremely significant sacred symbol in hundreds of religions and cultures down through the centuries. There is no question but what the pineal gland is represented by the symbolism of the pinecone and is further linked to snake symbols referring to the rise of the kundalini fire from the base chakra.

As I followed the thread of the thinking of the greatest spiritual giants of our times, this apparent homage to the pineal gland is a truly astonishing phenomenon that has never been adequately explained. Is this truly the seat of the soul, the nexus point that mediates our connection to God, or more accurately still, also to "the gods"—mommy and daddy and resides within each of us? Throughout the span of recorded human history, pinecones and the third eye have served as a symbolic representation of Human Enlightenment through the activation of the pineal gland.

Edgar Cayce in his famous psychic readings specifically mentioned that the pineal gland was a literal eye in the center of the brain stem, and that it was the anchor point where the soul joins with the body. Whether we look at ancient Babylonians, Egyptians, Greeks or Christians, the pinecone has represented the mysterious link between the physical and the spiritual worlds, which can be found in the human brain. It is taught by mystery schools to open the doors to spiritual perception once the seven Chakras are properly activated.

What were these giants of secret knowledge and ancient wisdom, stretching from the distant past to those who lived even to contemporary times, revealing about this little gland that apparently is the key to some of the most important secrets ever known?

Why Is Occultism Interested In The Pineal Gland?

The third eye, via the pineal gland, controls the attributes and functions of the sixth chakra (Ajna in Sanskrit), which includes: clairaudience, clairsentience, clairvoyance, telepathy, extra sensory perception, intuition and what the New Age calls the Christ consciousness (or cosmic consciousness).The third eye also controls the attributes and functions of the seventh chakra (called Sahasrara in Sanskrit), which includes: linkage with the Higher Self, astral projection, astral travel and ascension to the Akashic Records.

How Do You Manipulate The Pineal Gland?

The awakened pineal gland can give you a sense of well-being and an altered state of consciousness. There are different methods for doing this but the most common today is achieved through meditation, Yoga, labyrinth walking, ***accompanied by the tongue touching the roof of the mouth. This stimulates the crown chakra. When the tongue goes way back so the tip touches the soft palate, it stimulates the pineal gland.*** In the Taoist tradition, the tongue connection is used to complete the microcosmic orbit of energy [chi]. In the Tantra practice it is used primarily to quiet the mind, when you feel the Kundalini energy moving up and down the spine, you have a sense of control.

Wait Long Enough, You May Find Out

When I stumbled across that piece of information about the tip of the tongue touching the soft palate, I don't know when I was more shocked. I could hardly believe my eyes. It explained something that happened to me three or four years ago; something that I expected to never understand the reason for or its meaning. When Don and I awaken in the morning, I am a slow starter. So Don instituted a ritual that included bringing a cup of coffee to the bedroom where we talked and enjoyed "coffee break" together.

One morning I jumped up from the edge of the bed where I customarily sat and went nuclear. I felt this large lump in the back of my throat. It was like a large soft palpable marble. It moved from one side of the back of my throat to the other if I pushed it with my tongue It was unbelievably weird. It was unbelievably horrible. It was unbelievably terrifying.

Don got on the phone and managed by some miracle to get me an appointment with an ear, nose and throat doctor. (It helps when *Doctor* Hurd calls.) I was having a full-blown panic attack all the way to the doctor's office. I was positive that I had a cancerous lump in my throat. I could hardly speak. There was this terrible sensation of choking. The doctor put one of those tube things up my nose and down into my throat (not as bad as it sounds). Nothing. Absolutely nothing.

I managed to calm down and live with the monster in my throat for a couple of days. I screwed up the courage to dare very tentatively to occasionally explore the back of my throat to see if it had disappeared yet. I was forced to cancel some of my astrology clients' phone consultations because it was so weird to talk with an alien in my throat. After it went away, I never thought of it except occasionally to pray that it never happen again.

My prayers apparently fell on deaf ears. It did happen again a few months later. There is something about having a big, round lump in the back of your throat that is just intolerable—just crazy making. Once again, Doctor Hurd finagled an appointment that day with another specialist. Once again, the tube up the nose and down the throat. Again—nothing. Only this time, the doctor advised a barium x-ray. I did not like the sound of that. I did not get a good hit on it, so I did a horary chart. The chart said NO, so I never did it.

The third time it happened, I ruled out going to yet another doctor as Don was hurriedly phoning for yet a third emergency appointment. That was pointless. The Internet had all the answers anyway. I remembered that the little thingy in the back of the throat is called the *uvula.* I was not long in finding that a great many other poor souls had scared the living daylights out of themselves just as I had. There were endless letters from people describing their hysteria when they discovered the throat monster also. The articles I read said that the uvula could swell up the size of your thumb.

The cause was usually related to an allergic reaction. I know in my heart that I was having some sort of kundalini experience. As soon as I read the underlined passage above I felt goose flesh all over my body. It never happened again—so far. I instituted the *Star Trek* prime directive: Keep your tongue where it will do no harm.

When we consider all of the references to the pineal gland, there can be no question but what it holds a great secret for all humanity. There is also no question that an awakened pineal gland is the equivalent of Enlightenment. It also is the seat of the soul in the body, and the soul is connected to God. Consequently, an awakened pineal gland connects us to the Divine. Each one of us carries this gland in the center of our brain. Everyone has the independent capacity *within* to elevate our vibratory frequency and activate the doorway to other dimensions.

Now Lets Circle Back To Plato Once Again

Plato stated that it was the study of the science of numbers—a reference to Pythagoras's teachings—that tends to awaken the organ in the brain that the ancients described as the "eye of wisdom"—the organ now known to physiology as the pineal gland. I searched and searched to find out what he meant by "the science of Numbers." It did not seem reasonable that he was referring to the study of numerology. That led to a blind alley as might be expected. The clue to the answer was finally discovered hidden in this one little dynamite quote:

"The key to the whole Pythagorean system, irrespective of the particular science to which it is applied, is the general formula of *unity in multiplicity, the idea of the One evolving and pervading the many."*

It was when I read Pythagorean philosophy in Manly Hall's Great Book that I finally understood about numbers. In school, I gave math the widest birth possible. As I quoted from above "unity in multiplicity," it is saying that no matter what subject to which it is applied and no matter how great the numbers (the diversity); it is still, nevertheless, all connected, all One, Unity. Then he goes on to say that "the key to Oneness and Unity is forgiveness." By reverse engineering, he has given us a clue to activating the pineal gland and achieving enlightenment. Plato was explaining the most powerful idea in any philosophy.

It begins with forgiveness. If we hate someone or some thing, we are disconnected from Oneness. If we hold grudges and anger we are disconnected from Unity, that part of the Whole, our Self. Once the lightbody activation activates the pineal gland, the following activations are associated with unconditional love and compassion, the key to Unity.

When Duane received the activation process, maybe he was given more than we realized at first. Are the activations a process to activate the pineal gland? The clue is the tone that one hears and the activity in the throat chakra that I experienced. Did the Pleiadians indeed reveal the techniques from the mystery schools that existed from ancient times, including Atlantean and Egyptian sources, in the writings of Plato and furthermore, in the secrets that continually pulled my research into the mysteries that still existed throughout the birth pangs of the United States and assumedly to the present day?

Once I gathered these puzzle pieces together, I needed one more giant piece. I called Duane. I asked him if the activations as revealed by the Pleiadians could have any connection to the endocrine system and the activation of the pineal gland. This was his answer:

"When I do Step Eight (of the *Lightbody* activations) on prana I say, 'The chakra system is connected to the endocrine glands.' When I do the lightbody activation, I pull the energy up through the chakra system. I say, 'I am activating the endocrine system.' "

There it is!

I asked him why he started to include the part about activating the endocrine system. If you read the instructions in the *Lightbody* book, no mention is made of the endocrine system. He said that his guidance directed the insertion of that new part of the instructions. It goes with Step Eight where it talks about prana.

I hardly thought it possible that just as I was writing the last page of this book that I would discover such an amazing revelation! Yes, the Pleiadian Beings did reveal the secrets of the mystery schools and the key to ascension. It lay in those certain movements that were given to Duane. Those same activation techniques have probably been known for centuries and given only to high initiates of the secret orders. There is little doubt that Duane was once a high initiate himself, and the Pleiadians were revealing a technique already familiar to him in mystery schools that may well have stretched back to our Atlantean lifetimes. The measure of humanity's consciousness was taken at Harmonic Convergence in 1987. The High Beings concluded that we were ready and put us on the track to ascension. Now the activations are there for everyone.

Now you see them; Now you don't

Another very strange occurrence happened just as I was writing these last paragraphs of this chapter. I was referring, as I wrote, to two pages of notes that I had typed from a variety of sources. They were critically important and almost impossible to reconstruct. I had these two pages on my desk in plain sight and was referring to them off and on all day long. As I came to the final paragraphs, it was essential that I have these reference notes. However, as I turned to check out a source and look it up, the one page of notes was nowhere to be found.

Of course, I looked and looked for my notes. Mind you, they were right in front of me on my desk all day. It was as though they had vanished into thin air. Don heard me moaning and groaning and came into my office to help me. There was really no place to look as the notes were lying in plain sight all day. They were simply gone. Recalling other missing items that ended up in other dimensions, such as my secretary and wheelchair pad, this, of course, was on our minds, but neither of us wanted to suggest this out loud. We did not want to believe it.

I was so upset, and it was growing late anyway; so I decided to simply call it a day and head off for bed. While getting ready for bed, we finally discussed that perhaps the missing notes were indeed in a reality glitch or another time line, much as we did not want to deal with that possibility. Finally Don spoke out in a commanding voice that demanded the return of my notes. I suggested that he go to my office and look once again " just to see."

Within a few minutes, he investigated and found the missing notes lying in plain sight on my desk where we had both looked a dozen times earlier, Was this some sort of sign or play on words? I would love nothing better than to wrap this up with a nice tidy—even brilliant—explanation. I don't have one except to speculate that this was some sort of glitch or wrinkle in the time lines; something we might come to expect more frequently as the ascension process thins the veils between dimensional layers. If you have an explanation, write to me right away!

The God Game

In a couple of days, the God Game idea manifested when Jane McGonigal's book *Reality is Broken* arrived in the mail. (I referred to the book in the Introduction.) Sure enough, on page 297, and I quote, "There is actually a genre of computer games known as "god games"—world-and management simulations that give a single player the ability to shape the course of events on Earth in dramatic ways over lifetimes or longer."

So get this, and I quote again, "Players of god games have to consider their moment-by-moment actions in the context of a very long future: an entire simulated human life, a single civilization's rise and fall or even the entire course of human history." Of course, the operative idea here for us is that god games are those that by definition refer to events that cover long time periods, including the entire course of human history.

When synchronicity kicks itself into super gear, it's like potato chips; it can't eat just one. After Miss McGonigal's powerhouse philosophy about a god games genre, Dolores Cannon's *Convoluted Universe Book Three* weighed in with what sounded like a plan—God's plan, the big *G* God:

> "Our ultimate goal is to return to the Source, our concept of God, the Creator. When we have completed all the journeys and adventures through all the many variety of lives, we are supposed to return to the Creator with our accumulation of knowledge. It is then absorbed. In this way we are considered cells in the body of God"

Playing the God Game

Once again, just the same way as the title of this book flashed onto my mental screen, the title for an additional chapter popped into my awareness. There it was all of a sudden: "The God Game." I did not exactly stand up and cheer at the thought of yet another chapter. What was the God Game and how do we play it? Simpler childhood times, when my brother and I played Monopoly, sounded pretty appealing!

The real shocker was yet to come when the book singled out the most epic god game, *Spore.* You will recognize immediately why this resonated so profoundly when I describe further the primary feature of this remarkable game. First of all, god games can change the way players think about the world and their own powers within it, namely, *their power to change the real world.*

Spore players controlled the evolution of an entire species. Doesn't this sound familiar? If not, note the description of the five stages of evolution of the unique species they were controlling: "from single cell origins, into social, land-dwelling creatures, who form tribes, build technologically sophisticated civilizations, and ultimately venture off into intergalactic space exploration." Did we originate in a Petrie dish and are we not now exploring space? Isn't that OUR story and OUR future? ETs played the long game–a god game– with an entire species–US! Don't we carry the DNA of our extraterrestrial star gods?

The book describes players' advancement from manipulating cellular DNA all the way to "colonizing other planets and transforming them into inhabitable ecosystems. The game is meant to inspire players to adopt the kind of long-term, planetary outlook that can save the real world."

Our extraterrestrial ancestors' situation paralleled ours. They faced a severe environmental crisis as their ecosystem deteriorated to a point at which all life was threatened. Humanity's impact on Planet Earth has created an ecocrisis as well, a crisis of our own making as the result of faulty short-term thinking. ETs played the God Game. They shepherded an entire species in order to solve their crisis, and it was the result of long-term thinking. Can we play the God Game? Can we transform an uninhabitable planet into an inhabitable planet. Can we save the real world?

Revelation 21:1-27

> "Then I saw a new heaven and a new earth, for the first heaven and the first earth had passed away, and the sea was no more. And I saw the holy city, new Jerusalem, coming down out of heaven from God, prepared as a bride adorned for her husband. And I heard a loud voice from the throne saying, 'Behold, the dwelling place of God is with man. He will dwell with them, and they will be his people, and God himself will be with them as their God. He will wipe away every tear from their eyes, and death shall be no more, neither shall there be mourning, nor crying, nor pain anymore, for the former things have passed away.' And he who was seated on the throne said, 'Behold, I am making all things new.' Also he said, 'Write this down, for these words are trustworthy and true.' "

What if this biblical passage were literally true and *happening right now* (2012)? According to psychic sight, Planet Earth appears to be separating much like a single cell when it divides. A New Earth was created by many volunteers who came here in answer to a call. Acting in Unity and Oneness, they first raised their own frequency to a higher vibration and a higher dimension. Recall David Hawkins's Map of Human Consciousness? Once individuals can attain a level in the 600-700 range, they compensate for thousands, even millions, of people falling below the 200 mark. This literally stabilizes the global collective consciousness well above the merely survival levels. Many volunteers are unaware of their status and their mission; nevertheless, they are playing the long game, the God Game.

There are many people on the planet who are in the process of undergoing cellular changes and transforming their DNA. Their bodies are experiencing problems as they are shifting and adjusting. Older individuals are especially prone to aches and pains, high blood pressure, heart palpitations and other symptoms. Yet, their doctors often find nothing wrong. Therefore, it is out of necessity that the changes happen in waves that come and go. The shift to the New Earth would be intolerable unless it proceeded gradually, over years.

What about the souls who cling to negativity? They will stay with the Old Earth, which they have created. They will experience the tsunamis, the hurricanes, the unstable weather conditions and the other unfavorable environmental circumstances presently facing the human race. Eventually, they will find themselves on planets that match their level of consciousness as they work out their karmic indebtedness.

No one will be abandoned in my opinion. I know what is in the hearts of the lightworkers. They will be multidimensional Beings with a capacity for traveling the portals from one dimension to another. They will continue with the counseling and healing activities that they have always done. However, they do not have to stay behind in order to do so nor will they. Even though some of our brothers and sisters have chosen a Dark path, their souls are not without the possibility of redemption. Love conquers all, you might say. Moreover, it is not cruelty for them to reside on a planet that matches their evolutionary level. Rather it would be cruel to expose them to a vibratory level that they would find intolerable. Remember, time does not matter. God is not in a hurry. God waited for you.

The ancient Mayans seemed to have disappeared, and no one can figure out what happened to them. They are not the only tribal culture that apparently simply disappeared into thin air. These other cultures raised their mutual frequencies to match the higher dimensions. They left in bodies transformed into light. They left all at once. However, we must continue to go in steps for now, because it is the first time that a *planet* is also ascending in partnership with a *species* who awakened to the higher dimensions.

> "*Spore* has *a supergoal that represents the ultimate achievement in a game…to develop a civilization into such a successful galactic space-faring civilization that it eventually reaches one galactic destination in particular: a super massive black hole at the center of the galaxy.*

Coming Full Circle

Playing the Ascension Game was one step along the way in the God Game, the long game that sanctified the United States as the seed ground for a population that was transforming its DNA to become a new race of human. Yet, as the frequencies of consciousness increased, a parallel condition raced dangerously toward the creation of an uninhabitable planet for the new humanity. The players' goal was to create a habitable planet and reach the black hole at the center of the galaxy. Earth will align with the black hole at the center of our galaxy on December 21, 2012. Only in a game is the impossible possible. We are creating a New Heaven and a New Earth. The long game is for players who understand that we can save the real world together.

Where are we now?

I have repeatedly said throughout this book that I do not know what will happen on December 21, 2012. Perhaps we will not recognize its full significance only in retrospect long afterward. All I believe for certain is that this date is significant as part of the process of ascension. The clue is in the *Spore* game, which I described in detail above as: 1) reaching the center of the galaxy as its end game and, 2) convincing players that they can change the *real* world.

The reason that I accept this as true and accurate is because this follows the process that has led me throughout the writing of this book from the beginning. Synchronicity has unfailingly operated to bring me exactly the information I needed just when I needed it, no matter how obscure or off the wall. All information that so miraculously appeared at just the proper time never made a sudden giant leap forward. It was always little baby steps at a time. Why would I distrust it now?

Therefore, I feel safe in predicting that the next step is disclosure. We are going to be introduced to our galactic family at some time after we connect or align with the center of our own galaxy. We are not alone in the Universe. In fact, our star brothers and sisters have been with us since they created us in a Petrie dish. They are human. We look like them.

The entire world has been under the control of governments and religions whose only goals were to maintain this control at the suppression of anything that would transform and benefit the human race, including the eradication of disease, poverty and all else of human ills. They work hand-in-glove with a controlled media that lack the guts to stand up and be counted. But we—you and I together—can stand up and be counted.

We might ask why the star beings have not interfered to eradicate these corrupt forces. They will never violate our free will. However, they HAVE aided us in many unseen ways. In fact, much of our technology has come directly from them. They live among us. Humans have told stories of boarding their craft. They have left signs in the authentic crop circles. We have no reason to doubt our fellow citizens who have reported spotting UFOs in the skies. All of this is real, of course. Why doubt our neighbors who have nothing to gain, yet believe those who suppress the truth who have everything to lose?

There have been visions of the New Earth separating from the Old Earth. Sources fully as reliable see this as a merging rather than a separation. I believe that both are symbolic of a New Earth, regardless. I further believe that the New Earth will be achieved by humanity working together with our space friends in loving cooperation.

The time when disclosure occurs will surely be a great day for Earth! However, it does not necessarily follow that this is met with joyful acceptance by everyone. I don't mean to imply that they meet with armed resistance so much as with fear, shock and disbelief. You have read in earlier chapters that some people cannot accept what is before their very eyes if this challenges deep core beliefs. There may still be work for lightworkers to do through a period of transition, however long.

So may the games continue. Allow the *Spore* game to play out to its ultimate conclusion!

And after all, isn't it only fitting that this book ends with a Game?

EPILOGUE

The Galactic Activations

Channeled by Duane Henkle

Duane Henkle

One day I received a phone call from a man who was searching for someone who might help him with an unusual condition of the nervous system. If he stubbed his toe, for example, the pain lingered for months, instead of going away in an hour or two. This led to a life of constant pain. Not knowing where to turn next, he called a college in Santa Fe, New Mexico, from Florida, and inquired if there was a shaman-type in town who might help him. The person on the line had been a client of mine, so she gave him my name and number. The man struck me as elderly, enlightened and humble. I suggested we do a healing session by phone every week for a month at no charge. We completed the work and I wished him well.

Several weeks later, he called again. Yes, his condition was better, but that was not the reason for the call. He felt obliged to repay me, and being a past-life regressionist of some repute, offered to lead me through a past life regression over the telephone at no charge. I thanked him for his generous offer, and "if I felt so inclined one of these days," I'd give him a call. I wasn't overly impressed with the offer, simply because I was skeptical of past life regressions when the subject wasn't under hypnosis, but was rather led through a guided visualization when lo and behold!--a past life reached out and grabbed him. Based on feedback from friends, too often the past life event resembled more the product of a lively imagination and a hungry ego.

However, my curiosity won out, and we ended up doing a past life session by phone. I reclined on my bed, the telephone receiver cradled against my ear, feeling relaxed and calm. He led me through a guided visualization for a good 30 to 45 minutes. I must have been under more than I realized because few specifics stick in my mind.

I do remember images at the very end of the session:

> I was walking down a solitary country road, approaching a building. I walked up the steps and paused before large wooden double doors. I was instructed to open them and walk into my past life.
>
> I was inside a temple in Atlantis. The day outside was sunny, but inside the temperature was cool, as the temple was made of marble stone blocks. The sounds of my footsteps echoed off the hard walls. I ranked high in the central

> government. It would not be advisable if the others in power realized that I was in secret partnership with the priestess in charge of this place. The priestess was Diana, my sister in this life.
>
> There was a subterranean level under this temple, one floor below. In the center of this lower area was a large amethyst crystal, projectile shaped, and weighing easily a ton. A holographic geometric image flowed from this crystal. About 20 massage tables encircled the crystal like spokes of a wheel. The foot of each table pointed toward the center. People lay on the tables, absorbing the holographic image into their chakras. After two hours, the image became permanent. Consequently, those individuals became carriers of "Atlantis Ascended." If critical mass were reached of 10,000 people carrying the frequency of Atlantis ascending into the 5th dimension, then the probable future of Atlantis sinking into the sea could be prevented.
>
> But there was one catch. The only individuals who could hold the high vibration of Atlantis Ascended were the Law of One believers, and these individuals were harder and harder to find because the consciousness of Atlantis was sinking lower and lower. It was my job to supply the temple with the Law of One believers, and it was the job of the priestess and her helpers to transform them into "Holders of the Hologram."
>
> The priestess was growing desperate as was I. The needed number was 10,000, and we were bogged down at 8,000 with time running short. The images of Atlantis sinking into the sea were more and more vivid. I promised the priestess I would maximize efforts to secure subjects, and secretly returned to my post. Two months later, Atlantis went down and all of us with her, but not before I promised to return at a later life to successfully complete the job. I set the alarm clock in my soul.

That alarm clock had already rung some years earlier in this present life, prompting wholesale transformational changes. I had divorced my wife and quit my corporate job. I moved from the suburbs of Chicago to the high desert of New Mexico. I experienced financial meltdown and a long health crisis from which I eventually recovered. Following that Dark Night of the Soul, I rekindled an old relationship with a lady friend, and after a handful of dates, we felt that guidance directed us to move together to the Big Island of Hawaii.

After a few months there, I was psychically contacted by the Pleiadians. They expressed their desire to teach me the secrets of lightbody activation in preparation for the coming shift to the 5th dimension. They trained me for three years, after which I left my partner and returned to the mainland. Two years later, my sister Diana and I coauthored our book, *The Lightbody Activation Manual*, documenting the Pleiadian Method of lightbody activation and related shamanic healing practices.

The Pleiadians continued their teachings while I established a private healing practice utilizing their methods. These were later summarized in *The Ascension Guidebook*, the second book of The Technology of Ascension Series. That successfully completed all four ascension activations revealed by the Pleiadians up to that point:

1. The 5th dimension lightbody activation
2. The 6th dimension Venus activation
3. The 7th dimension Christ activation
4. The 12-Strand DNA activation.

Step-by-step instructions for these activations are given in the above-mentioned two books. The first four activations are summarized for your convenience in the Prologue of this book.

The Chakra System

For simplicity, in all the directions to follow, we primarily refer to the Sanskrit chakra energy points by their numbers. The chakra numbers are defined as follows:

1. **Base** chakra located at the base of the spine - the seat of the kundalini energy Psychological grounding, security, sensuality and courage — Earth element Adrenal glands
2. **Sacral** chakra (also referred to as the spleen chakra or sexual chakra) Psychological seat of creativity, excitement and sexual energy — Water element — spleen, kidneys, urinary and sexual organs
3. **Solar plexus** chakra (also known as the naval chakra) — Psychological emotion center, personal power, will — Fire element — pancreas and liver organs
4. **Heart** chakra — Psychological feelings of love, compassion, peace — Air element — thymus gland, lungs, endocrine system
5. **Throat** chakra — Psychological communication, wisdom, self expression, healing — Sound element— thyroid and parathyroid glands
6. **Third Eye** or Brow chakra — Psychological intuition, psychic abilities, memory, clairvoyance — Light element — pineal gland (the etheric organ of psychic perception)
7. **Crown** chakra — Psychological knowingness, self awareness, higher self, cosmic consciousness, bliss — Thought element — pituitary gland, central nervous system, cerebral cortex

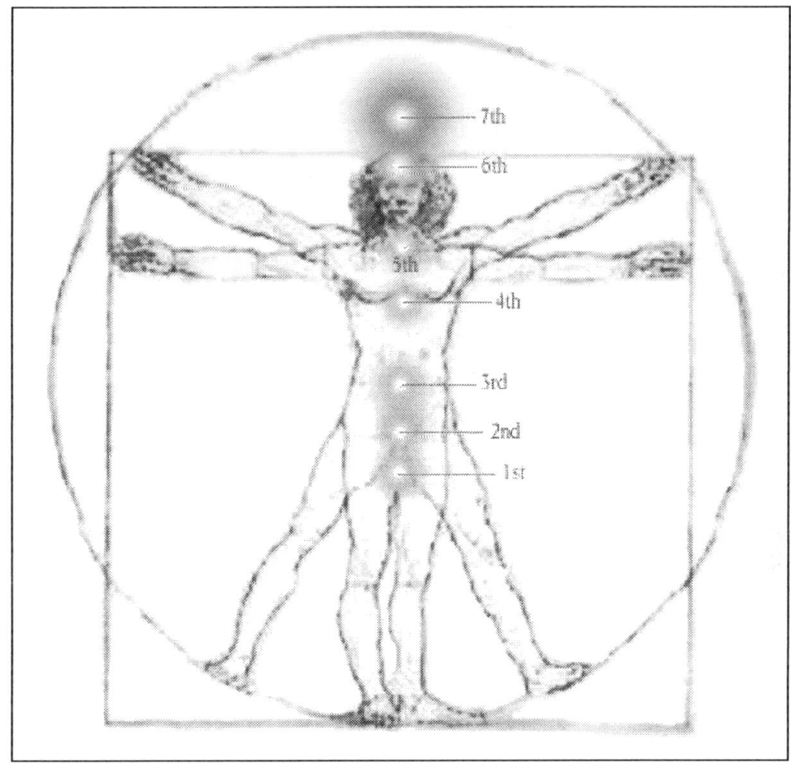

GALACTIC ACTIVATIONS

In 2006, when I authored *The Ascension Guidebook* explaining how to perform those four activations, I assumed that that was the end of it. However, the Pleiadians had something else in mind! They initiated communications about Galactic Activations. Their instructions were clear that these were to follow *only after completion of the first four ascension activations mentioned above.* The reason given was because the Galactic Activations are only for those who have completed, or are nearing completion, of their karmic obligations.

The Galactic Activations are done—no surprise—using the Pleiadian Method. This is a *non-meditation* method suited to western-culture people like me who are bored with any meditation lasting over 60 seconds. The Pleiadian Method has these four characteristics:

1) Utilizes two people: the *facilitator,* or the one doing the activation, and the *subject,* or the one receiving the activation.

2) Crystals are placed on or around the body of the subject.

3) The facilitator does patterned movements in the energy field of the subject.

4) The facilitator leads the subject in speaking a series of short affirmations.

Because of the elegant simplicity of The Pleiadian Method, an activation can be accomplished in 20 or 30 minutes.

You'll need eight clear quartz crystals—irregular shaped is fine—diameter need be no larger that a quarter. In addition, obtain a crystal wand, pointed on one end; the size need not be larger than a four-inch piece of chalk. Also, you must have access to a massage table, bed or other flat surface, as it is preferable to lie down while getting an activation.

Allow from one week to one month between activations, as these energies need some time to settle in. I emphasize the one week minimum for all you spiritual eager-beavers out there who want to do all four activations at one time. I consider one week to be the ideal spacing although longer is certainly OK.

The Pleiadians explained:

The etheric blueprint body surrounds the physical body in energetic, unmanifested form. This etheric blueprint carries the template of the physical body in perfection—totally balanced, dis-ease free and no longer subject to the reincarnation cycle of death and rebirth. When one's frequency reaches a certain level (as a result of the first four activations or other similar methods), then it is possible to download and merge the etheric blueprint body into the physical body.

This new body is activated not by earth energy, not by solar energy, but by *galactic* energy—the energy of Oneness, the energy of Unity Consciousness, the energy that pours from the center of the Milky Way Galaxy. The result is a "new" physical body, programmed not for death, but rather for life, unity, harmony and oneness. That's how you and I become Galactic Humans and members of the Galactic Federation of Planets. For the first time in 26,000 years, on December 21, 2012, earth is directly aligned with the center of the Milky Way Galaxy.

REMINDER: This is all about activating your *Galactic* body. In order to do the Galactic Activation, you must *complete the first four activations—your lightbody must be activated.*

THE FIRST GALACTIC ACTIVATION

Step 1–Connect to the 14th Chakra

When you entered this galaxy, you came in through the galactic center and left a part of yourself there at home—your 14th chakra. So now we tell the subject that we are running a cord of light from their crown chakra to their 14th chakra and—bingo—we've made a connection to the galactic center.

To do this step, place a clear quartz crystal at the subject's crown chakra and

- Guide them in saying this affirmation three times:
  "I desire the connection to my 14th chakra and to the full expression of my divine mission at this time on Earth."
- Allow five minutes for the connection to complete.
- Maintain sacred silence during this time.
- Remove the crystal at the end.

Step 2–Upgrade the Chakras

Upgrading the seven body chakras involves changing the sacred geometries of the chakras from processing 3rd dimension energy to processing 5th dimension energy. Said another way, we are upgrading the chakra system to process galactic energy.

1. Place a small clear quartz crystal on the person's 1st chakra and
   - Guide them in saying this affirmation once:
     "I welcome the 5th dimension upgrade in my 1st chakra."
   - Allow two minutes for the upgrade to complete.
2. Place another small clear quartz crystal on the person's 2nd chakra and guide them in saying this affirmation once:
   "I welcome the 5th dimension upgrade in my 2nd chakra."
   - Allow two minutes for the upgrade to complete.
3. Place another small clear quartz crystal on the person's 3rd chakra and guide them in saying this affirmation once:
   "I welcome the 5th dimension upgrade in my 3rd chakra."
   - Allow two minutes for the upgrade to complete.
4. Place another small clear quartz crystal on the person's 4th chakra and guide them in saying this affirmation once:
   "I welcome the 5th dimension upgrade in my 4th chakra."
   - Allow two minutes for the upgrade to complete.
5. Place another small clear quartz crystal on the person's 5th chakra and guide them in saying this affirmation once:
   "I welcome the 5th dimension upgrade in my 5th chakra."

- Allow two minutes for the upgrade to complete.

6. Place another small clear quartz crystal on the person's 6th chakra and guide them in saying this affirmation once:
   "I welcome the 5th dimension upgrade in my 6th chakra."
   - Allow two minutes for the upgrade to complete.
7. Place another small clear quartz crystal on the person's 7th chakra and guide them in saying this affirmation once:
   "I welcome the 5th dimension upgrade in my 7th chakra."
   - Allow two minutes for the upgrade to complete.

Remove the seven crystals at the end.

Step 3–Activate the Subtle Bodies

This step activates subtle bodies 4, 5, 6, 7, 8 and 9. These bodies form concentric envelopes around the physical body. Subtle body number 9 is the farthest out and is called the Electron Body or the Christ Body. According to J. J. Hurtak's *The Keys of Enoch,* Christ's subtle bodies were activated by initiation at the Great Pyramid in Egypt. The veil is so thin these days, we can do the same activating sans pyramid. If you are wondering about bodies 1, 2 and 3—the emotional, mental and spiritual bodies—they were already activated by the initial four activations.

- To do this step, place a clear quartz crystal on the person's 3rd eye chakra.
- Guide the person in saying this affirmation three times:
  "I welcome the expansion of my energy field into full love and power."
- Allow ten minutes for subtle bodies 4, 5, 6, 7, 8 and 9 to activate.
- Maintain sacred silence during this time.

At the end, remove the crystal from your subject's 3rd eye chakra.

THE SECOND GALACTIC ACTIVATION

Step 1–The Heart Transplant

The etheric blueprint surrounding the physical body carries the template of the physical body in perfection, totally balanced and dis-ease free. We begin the process of downloading the etheric-blueprint body into the physical body. But it cannot be done all at once. In this step, just the etheric-blueprint heart is transplanted into the heart of the physical body.

- Place a clear quartz crystal on the person's heart chakra.
- Guide the person in saying this affirmation three times:
  "I welcome the transplant of my etheric blueprint heart into the heart of my physical body."
- It takes eight minutes for the transplant, or download, to complete.
- Maintain sacred silence during this time.

At the end, remove the crystal from your subject's heart chakra.

Step 2–Connect to the Galactic Heart

The person's "new" transplanted heart consists of eight energetic chambers. These chambers are connected to the Galactic heart (at the galactic center), one chamber at a time. To do this step, eight small clear quartz crystals are used. Leave all the crystals in place until the end of the process.

1. Place one clear quartz crystal on the person's heart chakra.
   - Guide the person in saying this affirmation once:
     "I desire the connection of my 1st heart chamber to the Galactic Heart."
   - Maintain sacred silence for two minutes while connection takes place.
2. Place a second clear quartz crystal on the person's heart chakra.
   - Guide the person in saying this affirmation once:
     "I desire the connection of my 2nd heart chamber to the Galactic Heart."
   - Maintain sacred silence for two minutes while connection takes place.
3. Place a third clear quartz crystal on the person's heart chakra.
   - Guide the person in saying this affirmation once:
     "I desire the connection of my 3rd heart chamber to the Galactic Heart."
   - Maintain sacred silence for two minutes while connection takes place.
4. Place a fourth clear quartz crystal on the person's heart chakra.
   - Guide the person in saying this affirmation once:
     "I desire the connection of my 4th heart chamber to the Galactic Heart."
   - Maintain sacred silence for two minutes while connection takes place.

5. Place a fifth clear quartz crystal on the person's heart chakra.
   - Guide the person in saying this affirmation once:
     "I desire the connection of my 5th heart chamber to the Galactic Heart."
   - Maintain sacred silence for two minutes while connection takes place.
6. Place a sixth clear quartz crystal on the person's heart chakra.
   - Guide the person in saying this affirmation once:
     "I desire the connection of my 6th heart chamber to the Galactic Heart."
   - Maintain sacred silence for two minutes while connection takes place.
7. Place a seventh clear quartz crystal on the person's heart chakra.
   - Guide the person in saying this affirmation once:
     "I desire the connection of my 7th heart chamber to the Galactic Heart."
   - Maintain sacred silence for two minutes while connection takes place.
8. Place an eighth clear quartz crystal on the person's heart chakra.
   - Guide the person in saying this affirmation once:
     "I desire the connection of my 8th heart chamber to the Galactic Heart."
   - Maintain sacred silence for two minutes while connection takes place.

At the end, remove all eight clear quartz crystals.

Step 3 – Activate the "New" Heart

This step initiates a flow of energy from the Galactic Heart the subject's new heart. Once the flow starts, it keeps on flowing and continuously energizes the new heart with galactic love energy.

- place a clear quartz crystal on the person's heart chakra.
- Guide the person in saying this affirmation three times:
  "I accept the love of the Galactic Mother into my own heart."

Now, with the tip of your finger just above the chest and over the heart chakra, trace a figure eight pattern by going up and around the person's left breast and returning to center, and then by going up and around the person's right breast and returning to center, completing one figure eight pattern.

- Do this eight times.

THE THIRD GALACTIC ACTIVATION

The etheric blueprint heart was transplanted into the physical body in the previous activation, which initiated the process of transplanting the entire etheric blueprint body into the physical body. Now the process is completed as the remainder of the etheric blueprint body is transplanted into the physical body through the body chakras, using a clear quartz crystal on each chakra. Leave crystals in place throughout this activation and remove all of them at the end.

Step 1–Complete the Transplant of the Etheric Blueprint Body into Physical Body

1. Place a clear quartz crystal on the person's 1st chakra.
   - Guide the person in saying this affirmation once:
     "I welcome the transplant of my entire etheric body into my physical body so I can become a Galactic Human."
   - Allow two minutes for the download to complete.
2. Place a second clear quartz crystal on the person's 2nd chakra.
   - Guide the person in saying this affirmation once:
     "I welcome the transplant of my entire etheric body into my physical body so I can become a Galactic Human."
   - Allow two minutes for the download to complete.
3. Place a third clear quartz crystal on the person's 3rd chakra.
   - Guide the person in saying this affirmation once:
     "I welcome the transplant of my entire etheric body into my physical body so I can become a Galactic Human."
   - Allow two minutes for the download to complete.
4. Place a fourth clear quartz crystal on the person's 4th chakra.
   Even though the heart was previously transplanted, we include it here for additional emphasis on this key chakra.
   - Guide the person in saying this affirmation once:
     "I welcome the transplant of my entire etheric body into my physical body so I can become a Galactic Human."
   - Allow two minutes for the download to complete.
5. Place a fifth clear quartz crystal on the person's 5th chakra.
   - Guide the person in saying this affirmation once:
     "I welcome the transplant of my entire etheric body into my physical body so I can become a Galactic Human."
   - Allow two minutes for the download to complete.
6. Place a sixth clear quartz crystal on the person's 6th chakra.
   - Guide the person in saying this affirmation once:

"I welcome the transplant of my entire etheric body into my physical body so I can become a Galactic Human."

- Allow two minutes for the download to complete.

7. Place a seventh clear quartz crystal on the person's 7th chakra.
   - Guide the person in saying this affirmation once:
     "I welcome the transplant of my entire etheric body into my physical body so I can become a Galactic Human."
   - Allow two minutes for the download to complete.

Remove the seven crystals at the end.

Step 2–Connect the New Physical Body to the Galactic Body

In this step, the chakras in the person's new body are connected to the Galactic Body.

1. For the 1st chakra, guide the person in saying this affirmation once:
   "I desire the connection of my new body to the Galactic Body through the 1st chakra."
   - Do a figure-8 movement eight times just above the person's body at the 1st chakra. The figure eight should be about a foot wide and crosswise to the body, not up and down with the length of the body.
2. For the 2nd chakra, guide the person in saying this affirmation once:
   "I desire the connection of my new body to the Galactic Body through the 2nd chakra."
   - Do the figure eight movement eight times just above the person's body at the 2nd chakra.
3. For the 3rd chakra, guide the person in saying this affirmation once:
   "I desire the connection of my new body to the Galactic Body through the 3rd chakra."
   - Do the figure eight movement eight times just above the person's body at the 3rd chakra.
4. For the 4th chakra, guide the person in saying this affirmation once:
   "I desire the connection of my new body to the Galactic Body through the 4th chakra."
   - Do the figure eight movement eight times just above the person's body at the 4th chakra.
5. For the 5th chakra, guide the person in saying this affirmation once:
   "I desire the connection of my new body to the Galactic Body through the 5th chakra."

- Do the figure eight movement eight times just above the person's body at the 5th chakra.

6. For the 6th chakra, guide the person in saying this affirmation once:
   "I desire the connection of my new body to the Galactic Body through the 6th chakra."
   - Do the figure eight movement eight times just above the person's body at the 6th chakra.

For the 7th chakra, guide the person in saying this affirmation once:
"I desire the connection of my new body to the Galactic Body through the 7th chakra."

- Do the figure eight movement eight times just above the person's body at the 7th chakra.

Leave crystals in place for the next step.

Step 3–Activate the New Physical Body

This step initiates a flow of energy from the Galactic Body into the person's new body. Once the flow starts, it keeps on flowing and energizes the person's new body with the love energy of the Milky Way Galaxy, a vast living being.

- Do a figure eight movement eight times just above the person's body, over the entire length of their body from head to toe.
- Guide the person in saying this affirmation 3 times:
  "Let the energy of the Galactic Mother bathe me in light and love."

This initiates the infinite, continuous flow of energy from the Galactic Body into the person's new body.

- Allow the flow to continue for eight minutes.
- Maintain sacred silence during this time.

Remove crystals at the end

THE FOURTH GALACTIC ACTIVATION

It has been said that we view the world in duality because of the duality of the brain—the separation of our brain into right and left hemispheres.

There is a spiritual body membrane separating the two brain halves and obstructing total Galactic Oneness.

By means of this activation, this membrane is energetically removed (not surgically sliced out) so that the hemispheres may move into Oneness and Unity, and no longer view the world in duality.

Step 1–Imprinting the Star of David

In this step, a Star of David pattern–a six-pointed star–is imprinted on the crown chakra (directly over the hemispheres of the brain).

- You will need a *clear quartz crystal wand, pointed on one end, to do the job.*
- With your crystal wand in hand, lightly press the top of the head in ***three*** places, forming a triangle.

The apex of the triangle lies on the left hemisphere and the two base points lie on the right hemisphere. Apex to base, the triangle runs sideways from ear to ear, not front to back.

- Again, take the crystal wand in hand and press the top of the head in ***three*** places, forming a second triangle.

This triangle is positioned opposite the first one. The apex of this triangle lies on the right hemisphere and its two base points lie on the left hemisphere. Again, apex to base, the triangle runs sideways from ear to ear, not front to back.

Step 2–Activating the Star of David

- Now trace around the first triangle from point to point using the crystal wand and a gentle pressure against the top of the head.
- Then trace around the second triangle the same way.

What you have formed on the person's crown chakra, directly over the brain hemispheres, is a Star of David pattern formed of two triangles, each of which overlaps both sides of the brain and begins moving the person's brain into Galactic Oneness and Unity.

- This Star of David energy grid now begins to "dissolve" this membrane of separation.
- Finally, guide the person in saying this affirmation three times:

"The veil of separation is dissolved from my perception. I can now become a Galactic Human."

RE-ACTIVATION EXERCISE

To maintain your new Galactic Body so that your journey toward Oneness and Unity moves as fast as possible, it is desirable to do a simple 30 minute re-activation meditation at least once a month. *The re-activation exercise can be done by oneself; a partner is not needed.*

Step 1, Set up Star of David Pattern

Using six clear quartz crystals, make a 6-foot-diameter circle on the floor, placing a crystal every 60^0 around the circle. Sit down in the center of the circle, assuming a comfortable meditative position. Now, in your mind's eye, form a Star of David pattern out of 2 triangles overlapping in opposite directions, just as you did in the Fourth Activation, Step 2 (above).

Step 2, Meditate for 30 Minutes

Say this affirmation aloud 3 times:

"Let the energy of the Galactic Mother bathe me in light and love."

- Meditate in the Galactic Flow for at least 30 minutes.

GALACTIC ACTIVATIONS SUMMARY

The purpose of having a fully divine and galactic human is to merge the physical with the spiritual—and to reconnect the left and right hemispheres of the brain so that the human biology operates within the context of the spiritual blueprint. This blueprint, which is the roadmap for our human incarnation, contains the information required for a soul to live a human life.

This switch is subtle, but powerful; it clicks our soul plan into place, reorients all of our desires from head to heart and adjusts our internal compass to follow the path of our highest good. Learn to trust your process.

Contact Duane Henkle

Duane does all activations, including the Galactic Activations, either in person or at a distance by telephone consultation, including for international clientele. He is also available for other spiritual work for reasonable fees, including clearings, healings, extractions, breaking soul contracts, and many other of the psychic afflictions that can primarily be addressed only by shamanic healing. He can be reached in Vancouver, WA at 360-571-5748 or by e-mail at duane@cybermesa.com. Also see his Web site at www.duanehenkle.com.

APPENDIX

Enema Instructions

OR

EVERYTHING YOU EVER WANTED TO KNOW ABOUT TAKING AN ENEMA... BUT WERE AFRAID TO ASK!

By Donald Hurd, D.C.

I know that title may be just a bit on the corny side, but it is not easy to treat this subject on the light side. We understand that to most people, having to give yourself an enema on a regular basis is no laughing matter. However, the very serious chronic diseases—even life-threatening conditions—that can and do result from colon and body toxicity is something I am very serious about. Enemas are recommended for good reasons, so try to bear with it and you will discover as other patients have that even enemas can be introduced into your routine with a minimum of fuss. I may prescribe salt-water enemas, coffee enemas and occasionally certain other types.

MATERIALS

Table salt or coffee (see instructions to follow) plus enema bag and equipment. Purchase a "Combination Set." This consists of a standard hot water bottle (with screw-in plug), a long tube with an enema nozzle (about 2" long which opens only on the end) and a vaginal douching nozzle (about 4" long with holes in the sides). DO NOT purchase an enema bag that stays open on top without the screw-in top.

PREPARATION OF BAG AND SOLUTION

SALT WATER ENEMAS

Add two teaspoons of regular table salt to the bag (holds about two quarts of water). Run tap water and adjust temperature to be very warm, almost hot on the hands, but not so that you cannot keep your hands in it. The body is very warm inside. If the water is too cool, it may cause cramping. Fill the hot water bottle. Clamp the hose shut (near the nozzle end) and screw into the hot water bottle. Gently shake the bottle a few times to dissolve the salt. This saline solution is very close to many body fluids. For comfort, you want to get all air bubbles out of the system. The best way to do this is to hold the bag upright next to your chest. Release the clamp. Press the bag against your chest to squeeze some fluid up out of the bag, through the tube and into a sink, clearing the air out. Clamp the tube shut again.

COFFEE ENEMAS

The caffeine in coffee enemas is used to stimulate the liver to release toxins and also create a stronger detox reaction in the colon. Some purists prefer to use regular brewed coffee (not decaffeinated). Using this method, add one quart of the brewed coffee to one quart of water (makes half-strength coffee). Be sure it's not too hot. Just as for salt-water enemas (above), the coffee solution should be very warm, almost hot on the hands but not so that you can't keep your fingers in it. A satisfactory and much easier method allows the use of two tablespoons (not teaspoons) of crystal, or instant, coffee (not decaffeinated!) per bag of hot water. Use the same directions as for salt-water enema preparation.

TAKING THE ENEMA

Lie on the bed with a soft towel under you (just in case). It should not be necessary to "lie on the bathroom floor" or in the tub or on the toilet as some people imagine. To insert the nozzle more comfortably, you can moisten it with water or Vaseline. Insert it all the way to the shank and unclamp the tube. Lie on your back and hold the bag about 18" above the bed level; i.e., hold it in the air with your hand with your elbow bent and lying on the bed relaxed, not high in the air. When you feel the water flowing, roll over on your left side and let about one third of the contents enter. As the solution flows into the left side of your abdomen (on the bottom), knead that area with your hand to help the washing action and to free any trapped air bubbles within the colon. Such air bubbles can cause a feeling of colic or cramping; releasing them will stop or relieve the cramps. Next, roll over on your back to allow another one-third of the bag to enter. When in this position, concentrate your rubbing and kneading efforts across the top of the abdomen. Finally, roll onto your right side for the remaining one-third bag and concentrate your kneading on the right and lower parts of your abdomen. This far area deserves the most attention because this is the area of the appendix, the area where the small intestine joins the large intestine (colon) and the area most prone to buildup of toxic materials. This should take only about 10 minutes.

Since all of the solution is now inside, clamp the tube and remove the nozzle. Knead the entire abdominal area with special emphasis on the right side to help break up built-up toxic wastes on intestinal walls. Do this for an additional 10 minutes (or 20 minutes all together). If you have difficulty in holding for the full time due to gas or cramping, get up and go sit on the toilet. You will be able to do better the next time. As you become more cleared out, any problems should disappear. If the colon is inflamed at first, colic (gas pains) is more likely. When you are finished, get out of bed, sit on the toilet and just let the fluid and material expel in a relaxed way. Do not try to force it. Sit there long enough to expel it all. It exits in waves. You may feel finished and everything may stop for even 2-3 minutes, then expel a lot more. This is due to natural peristaltic (wave like) action in the colon (the way the body moves material forward in the colon.

NOTES

When toxins begin to be dumped from the liver into your bloodstream (to be processed out of the system by the kidneys into the urine) some people may feel "icky" for a few minutes or even a few days. Toxins are being released just like stirring sediment on the bottom of a glass of water. Slight headaches, nausea and fatigue are the most common occasional symptoms. If these are your symptoms, whatever you do, don't stop the enemas. They are not making you sick. It is even more important to keep the toxins flushed out when you are having a reaction. This may be the time to take two or three enemas to flush the system. You may want to discontinue coffee enemas for a time or two, however, and substitute a plain salt water enema instead. If symptoms are more severe than outlined, you may be either unusually toxic or unusually sensitive. Stay in touch with your health care practitioner. He or she will suggest ways to ease you through those initial toxic reactions (if you have any), or cut back the enemas for a day or two. Once the body has been cleansed and helped in initial healing, any such symptoms should disappear. Believe it or not, enemas usually become comforting very shortly. A lighter diet of raw fruits and vegetables and lots of fluids is also a good idea for a few days.

- This detoxification program you are doing is part of the larger picture of regenerating the body and restoring health naturally. There can be ups and downs as the body struggles to restore balance. Don't expect miracles overnight. Commit yourself to your program of healing and see it through. You won't regret it. Hundreds of patients have reversed even serious chronic problems. You may wonder "Why coffee for an enema? Isn't that bad for you? When coffee is taken rectally:
- the coffee stimulates cleansing of the bowel;
- it <u>opens</u> the bile ducts; and
- it is absorbed into a special blood system that goes directly to the liver for processing before joining the regular blood supply.
- Most importantly, it stimulates the liver to much greater activity as a blood-cleansing organ, and causes stored toxins to be dumped into the bloodstream for processing out of the body.

Now you know the best thing to do with your next cup of coffee.

A final postscript to patients who freak out at the mere mention of an enema: We don't know what happened to you in your life to produce a fixation about this particular body part. We'll leave that to Sigmund Freud. No one will force you to do anything, or ridicule you, if you need help or encouragement from your doctor. There may be homeopathic remedies that will further aid anyone who suffers from unusual resistance. If done properly, there should be little or no cramping—in fact, the warm water can be very soothing. The results, of course, can give great relief of symptoms plus renewed health.

THE AUTHORS

Diana Stone

Diana Stone is a shaman woman of power. Yet you do not see her name on the bestseller lists. Oprah has not called. That is because she is not visible walking the deep murky trenches of ascension, focusing her light on the psycho-physiological transformation process of light-workers in her worldwide healing ministry. She sends postcards from the edge to readers of her free newsletter.

Astrology exploded into Diana's consciousness in the 1960s. She was convinced she had found her passion and her destiny. Her vision became a reality when she established her private practice as a professional astrologer. She traveled, lectured and contributed to the astrological literature via books and articles.

A magician friend introduced her to the study of Huna. This is a psycho-religious system practiced by ancient kahuna-shaman in the Polynesian Islands. Her studies led to a deep involvement in healing and psychic development. In 1982 Huna Research, Inc. certified her as a teacher of the ancient lore.

In 1980 a visit from her Spirit Teacher revealed that her true destiny was to establish a new paradigm: the twenty-first century shaman. Her teacher, Thomas, worked with her for twelve years. Their work together re-introduced a distinctly Western-style shamanism.

Diana continues with her astrological practice in Vancouver, Washington. She also has a busy international practice as a shaman specializing in soul retrieval She also participates as part of the 4Ds, a family group of shaman. The 4D's include Diana; her husband, Don, her brother, Duane, and her son, David, in the ceremonial opening of key portals connected to the ascension process.

Diana is a voice in the ascension process, coauthoring with her brother, Duane Henkle, the TECHNOLOGY OF ASCENSION SERIES. Books One, Two and Three.

To contact Diana Stone:
PHONE (Pacific time): 360-546-2497
E-MAIL: dianas@spiritone.com

Check out her website at www.dianastone.com for information on ordering books, requesting horary charts or signing up for her free newsletter.

David Bills

David Bills is Diana Stone's son. He is a CPA by day, managing a thriving private practice in Portland, Oregon. He is otherwise occupied participating as one of the 4Ds mentioned in the book. His father is Rex Bills, famous in astrological circles as author of the standard reference text, *The Rulership Book,* since the early 70s.

David is the one of the 4Ds who has been deeply involved in gaming along with his father. He was introduced to the study and practice of Huna as a young boy. He has studied with Dr. Hew Len in many of his workshops on the ancient Hawaiian system of ho'oponopono. David is on intimate speaking terms with the Goddess. He also does a vastly amusing impersonation of Elmer Fudd singing the Beatles song "Yesterday" to entertain his mother.

David may be contacted by e-mail at:
David Bills (david@davidbillscpa.com) .

The
Lightbody Activation
Manual

DUANE HENKLE & DIANA STONE

Foreword by Otha Wingo, Ph.D.

THE LIGHTBODY ACTIVATION MANUAL

By Duane Henkle and Diana Stone

Authors' Introduction

This book is about activating the lightbody for the ascension into the fifth dimension. Humanity is in the dawn of a mass awakening of consciousness. Mother Earth is increasing her vibratory frequency. Darkness is merging into the Light. During this preparatory period both the Light and the Dark are intensified. We need not be troubled by the apparent proliferation of violence and evil. It is only within the context of acute polarities that a true choice can be made between the right or left-hand path.

The material presented here is oriented toward a direct experience designed to realign the physical body and surrounding energy field with the new frequencies. If readers avail themselves of the lightbody activation method given in this book they will resonate and respond to the initiation of a physiological process that mutates the very DNA itself.

Many readers may be moved into uncharted intellectual territory. That need not be a problem. The detailed nine-step energy method carefully explained and illustrated in this book is not primarily directed toward the intellect. There are many other levels that do respond. It really makes no difference if readers understand or even believe everything written. The method we give in this book addresses the heart and the soul. All that is necessary is an open mind and an adventurous spirit.

Duane is Called to Hawaii

Spirit called Duane, coauthor of this book, to move from his home in Santa Fe, NM to Hawaii. The first chapters chronicle the story of Duane's three-year hiatus on the Big Island. Once in Hawaii, Duane connected with Pleiadian energies in a powerful way. First, a Pleiadian Being actually merged with Duane. This merger enabled Duane to form a deep psychic link with a small group of Pleiadian entities identifying themselves only as "The Beings." This group then communicated the lightbody activation method Duane and his partner, Betty Sherman, used to activate each other's lightbody by following their step-by-step instructions. Duane recounts their struggle to anchor into their physical bodies these powerful fifth-dimensional energies. The lightbody is the vehicle that takes us through the fifth-dimensional shift.

Directions and Illustrations

The sixth chapter of the book features a step-by-step description of the lightbody activation method. One person moves through the nine-step process within the energy field of a second person lying on a massage table or bed. The directions tell you exactly what to say and exactly what to do. There are illustrations that accompany each step. The entire process in a single session normally takes about twenty minutes.

Pele, Dolphin and Sea Turtle: The Crystal Triangle

Duane and Betty were guided to connect with three energies: the goddess Pele and two power animals, Dolphin and Sea Turtle. They visited various power spots in Hawaii bonding with these powerful forces, then were directed to purchase three magical crystals which would channel the energies of Pele, Dolphin and Sea Turtle. These crystals were set out around the massage table to form an energy triangle in which one lies as the nine steps are performed directly within the recipient's aura. The book gives detailed instructions about choosing your own set of crystals and programming them. Special shaped crystals (like the ones shown below) are attractive if you like but any crystals of modest size, etc. are just as powerful

Carved green turtle crystals

Unlike earlier lightbody activation methods, no special knowledge is required. No special training is required to do the Crystal Triangle method. No special psychic abilities are required. There is no meditation or other spiritual practices involved. The Crystal Triangle work over a period of time will activate the lightbody all on its own.

All You Need are the Instructions in this Book

When Duane returned to the Mainland, it was Diana Stone and her husband, Don Hurd, who then received instructions to "field-test" the Crystal Triangle method. Three years of hands-on experience with the energies preceded the publication of this book. Chapter seven documents the early volunteers' experiences with the method.

Mass consciousness is the soup that is created when we take every person's individual consciousness and put it into one pot. The mass consciousness is the driving force behind world and national events, the stock market, wars, political fortunes and the general ebb and flow of our collective histories. It is the planetary consciousness that is due for a shift into the fifth dimension. The only way for that to happen is for a given percentage of the population to shift its consciousness until critical mass kick-starts the whole.

Awakened individuals along with the help from our friends in high places have already considerably shifted the mass consciousness in recent years. The Pleiadian Beings explained that this elevation of collective vibratory levels and the subsequent opening of "cosmic doorways" are the reasons that the Crystal Triangle's direct access to human energy fields is now possible. Consequently, we may now safely connect our higher-dimensional selves directly to our physical bodies. That is the ascension process.

Crystal Triangle Healing

Many individuals will need supportive therapies to take them through the many changes that often accompany the transformation of consciousness and mutations in the physical body at the cellular level. Psychiatry and medicine function within models that are not designed for proper diagnosis or treatment of many symptoms resulting from the physiological changes triggered by the lightbody activation process.

In the last chapter, "Crystal Triangle Healing," the authors share some of the alternative tools they use in their shamanic healing work. Some are appropriate for the layperson to clear negative energies from people and places, to balance emotional and mental energies, to enhance psychic functioning, to use the pendulum to evaluate the chakra system, to clear energies after giving birth and much more. Healing therapies are enhanced when paired with the Crystal Triangle process. There is a special section for professional healers and how they can incorporate the lightbody work into their own therapies.

The critically important thing to remember when all is said and done is that we are embarking on one of the greatest adventures in the history of the planet. It is not dependent on a few great masters as has been the case in times past. This is a time of testing and choice for every person. Evil is pulling out all the stops in these final days. Stand up and be counted for the Light.

The Ascension Guidebook

Pleiadian Guides Reveal the Four Energy Activations that Prepare Earth Beings for Ascension in 2012

Duane Henkle

Coauthor of
The Lightbody Activation Manual

THE ASCENSION GUIDEBOOK

By Duane Henkle

Introduction by Diana Stone

Duane Henkle is one of the high-profile voices in the ascension movement. This book, *The Ascension Guidebook*, is the second in the series: THE TECHNOLOGY OF ASCENSION. His first book, *The Lightbody Activation Manual,* was published in 2003, in collaboration with his sister, Diana Stone.

Heightened awareness of ascension has exploded into the mass consciousness since the publication of the first book. Information about the subject is awash on the Internet. A proliferation of recently published books and articles increasingly include material about ascension from many points of view. Individuals and groups all over the world are using the Lightbody Activation method described in Book One. (For the convenience of readers, the nine-step Fifth Dimension Lightbody Activation method from that book is reproduced in this volume.)

Harmonic Concordance Day

A significant date in the ascension process was Harmonic Concordance Day observed by people all over the globe on November 8-9, 2003. On that date, which featured a rare Star of David planetary line-up, Pleiadian extraterrestrials once again transmitted information directly to Duane. These were the very same Beings—the name is their preference—that taught Duane the Lightbody Activation method in Hawaii. Readers who are new to this subject are strongly urged to read the first book for the entire background story.

After months of working with clients worldwide after Harmonic Concordance, three activations were added to the original Fifth-Dimension Lightbody Activation to become the four activations that are the basis for this present book. The four activations now include the Fifth, Sixth and Seventh Dimensions plus the very critically important 12-strand DNA Activation. These processes are the ones used to construct an ascension vehicle in which one ascends into the Fifth Dimension. This vehicle is not the foreign import kind with four wheels.

The enthusiastic responses from clients to these additions to the original lightbody work made it clear that the Pleiadian Beings once again repeated the successes that have become so obvious from the Fifth Dimension method by itself. This book includes some case studies and testimonials which represent people from all walks of life and varying levels of awareness.

The Lightbody Activation Manual (Book One) described the participation of helpers from the special consciousness of the crystal kingdom. Some readers may be aware of the power of crystals. *The Lightbody Activation Manual* described a method that incorporated the use of specially programmed crystals. The new methods in this book once again utilize specific crystals with detailed instructions and illustrations in how to use them every step of the way to do the four activations by yourself at home. Duane also described in the first book his amazing relationship with power animals that came to him to volunteer their services throughout the ascension period, i.e., Sea Turtle and Dolphin. These remain the two power animals participating in aiding humanity through this time of evolutionary change.

Anyone Can Do It

THE TECHNOLOGY OF ASCENSION SERIES is not exclusively for those individuals who are sophisticated in their knowledge and experience of the ascension process. It is for virtually everybody. The author is aware that this is a paradigm shift that is confusing and unbelievable for many readers. The material in this book was designed by the Pleiadians in order to extend the opportunity of the coming Shift to individuals who have no special knowledge of ascension by providing simple tools. The method combines crystals along with programmed movements in a receiving partner's energy field. By temporarily allowing oneself to ignore the intellectual need for detailed understanding and by just following the precise directions in this book, you will be convinced by the self-evident results.

Most people are aware of the evolutionary process. It is usually thought of only in terms of changes in *physical* forms. However, consciousness also evolves. At whatever level changes occur, the forces of evolution build up energies over long periods of time until they reach critical mass. That is exactly what is happening at the present time. Humanity is headed for a leap in consciousness into another Dimension, the Fifth. This is a unique evolutionary step in that the Earth is also preparing to make the change along with us.

The date that is most often given for this event is December 2012. This date should be significant in the ongoing evolutionary process of mankind. There are multiple sources for this date and this information; the Mayan calendar, the Hopi Indians, reliable contemporary channels and many others.

The transition into the Fifth Dimension includes preparing the physical body to tolerate the higher frequencies. That is why it is essential to activate the lightbody and construct an ascension vehicle. Too often, people participating in the ascension process lose sight of the fact that **this very much requires a physical change.**

Over the past years there have been other lightbody activation systems and other 12-strand DNA activation methods. The Pleiadians have revealed the way to accomplish changes in a uniquely different and simplified way.

It is no longer required to work with complicated meditations and spiritual practices over years that are difficult for most people to complete. These systems are not wrong. The Beings explained that this is simply the first time that the conditions are right to activate the body from only an energetic level. This energetic 12-strand DNA Activation is an ascension DNA activation and different from other methods.

One of the most remarkable sections of the book is the material in Chapter 9 when the Pleiadian guides define each additional DNA strand (three through twelve) and the etheric changes which take place upon activation. For example, the third DNA strand Activation decommissions the death programming in the body. There is no longer a need to physically die to be reborn. The Shift into the next life is seamless as we change dimensions.

The meanings of all the ten additional DNA strands end with the twelfth. That is the one that activates the personal ascension vehicle.

We should gratefully acknowledge the Pleiadian Beings for this astounding roadmap to ascension. Their skill at placing complex technology within a context of such power, clarity and simplicity bespeaks a consciousness evolved well beyond our own.

The instructions in this book teach you how to do this important activation on your own. It is simple and straightforward. You need not understand the finer points of any metaphysical system or ascension in particular. You need not be psychic. You really need not even be sure that any of this is true or that it works. It is easy to check it out for yourself.

Be sure to understand that the completed Shift is a move into a very different reality from our present Third Dimension life. There will be peace. There will be an enhancement of psychic abilities. Most communication will likely be telepathic. Other profound changes will be commonplace. It is outside the subject of this book to give a lengthy description of the Fifth Dimension. It is mentioned in passing to underscore what is at stake. It holds out the real opportunity to leave behind the world of duality, of light and dark. It has taken millions of years for Earth and all of humanity to step into this brave new world where we can join the galactic community free of the dark things that have made life here a very tough struggle.

Book Three in this series is *Playing the Ascension Game* by Diana Stone, Duane's sister and coauthor of their first book. Diana serves an international clientele as a shaman healer and professional astrologer. When this brother-sister team first learned the Fifth Dimension Lightbody Activation method, the big question was: What happens after lightbody? Will everybody be instantly healed of everything? Maybe absolutely nothing will happen. Will some people walk on water? Diana and her husband, Don, field tested the activation for three years before the book was first published to answer this very question.

The answer is that something definitely happens. Logically it is not the same experience for everyone. The most compelling awareness, however, is that it is necessary to focus on one's inner work more rather than less. All of the activations for that matter bring out the issues that need to be dealt with in both one's inner and outer life.

It is obvious that Duane and Diana are bringing together both sides of a very complex process. Based on Duane's relationship with the Pleiadians, he brings through the technology aspect of ascension, the actual techniques. Now that it is apparent that personal transition does not "just happen." Diana draws on long experience to describe in *Playing the Ascension Game* how to map out your personal journey to the dimensional Shift when it occurs.

Many guidelines for healing within the context of the crystal triangle are successfully used by professional healers and beginners alike. These include dealing with toxic relationships, invading dark entities, past life influences, body memories of past wounds, ancestral patterns and the like. ***When Duane does the Four Activations, an invaluable aspect of his work is the clearing of blocks along with them.*** Some of his cases are included in this book.

Where Are We Now?

A significant shift in the Mayan calendar marked the beginning of one of the most important cycles in history. This came to be known as the Breakthrough Ceremony and was observed May 27-28, 2006. Duane journeyed with his shamanic troupe with whom he has worked for over 25 years and was surprised to get the early pieces of what appears to be the beginnings of yet another book in this series.

At this point the new information is clearly associated with the heart and heart chakra. The alignments extend beyond Planet Earth to line up with our Sun, our Galactic Center in the Milky Way galaxy and even beyond to the Great Central Sun of the Creator. At this very early stage of working out this new system, there are already four pieces to the Heart Activation. Duane has experimented using this new protocol with several clients and they reported extremely powerful reactions. It is difficult to jump to conclusions at this point; however, there are clues that a powerful new healing system may be in progress. Watch the Web sites (www.dianastone.com and www.duanehenkle.com) or subscribe to Diana's free newsletters to keep abreast of exciting new developments.

July 10, 2006

BIBLIOGRAPHY

Anderson, Don. *Musings of an Old Soul: A Cosmic Paradigm*: Self Published, 2010.

Arguelles, Jose, Ph.D. *The Mayan Factor: Path Beyond Technology*. Santa Fe NM: Bear & Company, 1987.

Baer, Randall N. and Vicki Vittitow Baer. *The Crystal Connection: A Guidebook for Personal and Planetary Ascension*. San Francisco CA: Harper & Row, 1987.

Baer, Randall. *Windows of Light: Using Quartz Crystals as Tools for Self-Transformation*. San Francisco CA: Harper & Row, 1984.

Baldwin, William J. *Spirit Releasement Therapy: A Technique Manual*. Terra Alta WV: Headline Books Inc., 1992.

Beaconsfield, Hannah. *Welcome To Planet Earth: A Guide For Walk-Ins And Starseeds*. Sedona AZ: Light Technology Publications, 1997.

Berney, Charlotte. *Fundamentals of Hawaiian Mysticism*. Freedom CA: The Crossing Press, 2000.

Bishop, Karen. *The Ascension Primer*. Bangor ME: Booklocker.com, 2006.

Bishop, Karen. *Stepping Into the New Reality*. Bangor ME: Booklocker.com, 2008.

Bishop, Karen. *Heart In The Night: From Death To Rebirth*. Pisgah Forest NC: Gama Books, Inc., 2011.

Bolen, Jean. *Crossing To Avalon: A Woman's Midlife Pilgrimage*. San Francisco CA: Harper San Francisco, 1994.

Braden, Gregg. *The Divine Matrix: Bridging Time Space Miracles and Belief*. Carlsbad CA: Hay House, 2007.

Braden, Gregg et al. *The Mystery of 2012: Predictions Prophecies & Possibilities*. Boulder CO: Enfield: Sounds True, 2007.

Brock, Rita. *Saving Paradise: How Christianity Traded Love of This World for Crucifixion and Empire*. Boston MA: Beacon Press, 2008.

Calleman, Carl. *Solving The Greatest Mystery Of Our Times: The Mayan Calendar*. Coral Springs FL: Garev Pub International, 2001.

Calleman, Carl. *The Mayan Calendar and the Transformation of Consciousness*. Rochester VT: Bear & Co, 2004.

Calleman, Carl. *The Purposeful Universe: How Quantum Theory And Mayan Cosmology Explain The Origin And Evolution Of Life*. Rochester VT: Bear & Co, 2009

Cannon,, Dolores. *Conversations With Nostradamus: Volume One: His Prophecies Explained*. Huntsville AR: Ozark Mountain Pub, 1992.

Cannon, Dolores. *Conversations with A Spirit: Between Death and Life*. Huntsville AR: Ozark Mountain Pub, 1993.

Cannon, Dolores. *The Custodians: Beyond Abduction*. Huntsville AR: Ozark Mountain Pub, 1999.

Cannon, Dolores. *The Convoluted Universe: Book One*. Huntsville. Huntsville AR: Ozark Mountain Pub, 2001.

Cannon, Dolores. *The Convoluted Universe: Book Two*. Huntsville AR: Ozark Mountain Pub, 2007.

Cannon, Dolores. *The Convoluted Universe: Book Three.* Huntsville AR: Ozark Mountain Pub, 2008.

Cannon, Dolores. *The Three Waves of Volunteers and the New Earth.* Huntsville AR: Ozark Mountain Pub, 2011.

Cannon, Dolores. *The Convoluted Universe: Book Four.* Huntsville AR: Ozark Mountain Pub, 2012.

Carroll, Lee. The *End Times: New Information for Personal Peace: Kryon Book I.* Del Mar CA: The Kryon Writings Inc., 1993.

Carroll, Lee. *Don't Think Like A Human! (Channeled Answers To Basic Questions): Kryon Book II.* Del Mar CA: The Kryon Writings Inc., 1994.

Carroll, Lee. *Alchemy Of The Human Spirit (A Guide To Human Transition Into The New Age): Kryon Book III.* Del Mar CA: The Kryon Writings Inc., 1995.

Carroll, Lee. *Partnering With God (Practical Information for the New Millennium): Kryon Book VI.* Del Mar CA: The Kryon Writings Inc., 1997.

Carroll, Lee. *Letters From Home (Loving Messages From The Family): Kryon Book VII.* Del Mar CA: The Kryon Writings Inc., 1999.

Carroll, Lee. *The New Beginning: Kryon Book IX.* Del Mar CA: The Kryon Writings Inc., 2002.

Carroll, Lee. *The New Dispensation: Kryon Book X.* Del Mar CA: The Kryon Writings Inc., 2004.

Carroll, Lee. *The Twelve Layers Of DNA: An Esoteric Study of the Mastery Within: Kryon Book XII.* Sedona AZ: Platinum Pub House, 2010.

Cayce, Edgar Evans. *Edgar Cayce on Atlantis.* New York NY: Paperback Library, Inc., 1968.

Clow, Barbara. *The Mayan Code: Time Acceleration and Awakening the World Mind.* Rochester VT: Bear & Co, 2007.

Clow, Barbara. *Alchemy of Nine Dimensions: Decoding the Vertical Axis Crop Circles and the Mayan Calendar.* Charlottesville VA: Hampton Roads Pub Co., 2004.

Clow, Barbara. Catastrophobia*: The Truth behind Earth Changes in the Coming Age of Light.* Rochester VT: Bear & Co, 2001.

Cori, Patricia. *The Starseed Dialogues: Soul Searching the Universe.* Berkeley CA: North Atlantic Books, 2009.

Cori, Patricia. *Atlantis Rising: The Struggle of Darkness and Light.* Berkeley CA: North Atlantic Books, 2008.

Cori, Patricia. *No More Secrets No More Lies: A Handbook To Starseed Awakening.* Berkeley CA: North Atlantic Books, 2008.

Cori, Patricia. *The Cosmos Of Soul: A Wake-Up Call For Humanity.* Berkeley CA: North Atlantic Books, 2008.

Eades, Michael. *Protein Power.* New York NY: Bantam Books, 1998.

Essene, Virginia and Sheldon Nidle. *You Are Becoming A Galactic Human.* Santa Clara CA: S.E.E. Publishing Company, 1994.

Fallon, Sally. *Nourishing Traditions: The Cookbook That Challenges Politically Correct Nutrition And The Diet Dictocrats.* Washington DC: New Trends Pub, 2001.

Ferguson, Marilyn. *The Aquarian Conspiracy: Personal and Social Transformation in the 1980s*. Los Angeles New York: Martin's Press, 1980.

Fickes, Bob. *Ascension The Time Has Come: An Enlightening View From Masters Who Have Ascended*. Mount Shasta CA: Council of Light, 1991.

Franz, . *On Divination And Synchronicity: The Psychology Of Meaningful Chance*. Toronto: Inner City Books, 1980.

Free, Wynn. *The Reincarnation Of Edgar Cayce?: Interdimensional Communication & Global Transformation*. Berkeley CA: Frog Ltd., 2004.

Gerard, Robert. *Change Your DNA Change Your Life!: Self-Empowerment Healings*. Coarsegold CA: Oughten House Pub, 2000.

Goodman, Saul. *Light Body Activation: Science Dialogue & Non-Practices for Interactive Evolution*. Buckingham PA: Infi-Tech Publications, 1997.

Hall, Manley P. *The Secret Destiny of America*. Los Angeles CA: Philoso. Research Soc., 1958.

Hall, Manley P. *An Encyclopedic Outline of Masonic, Hermetic, Cabbalistic And Rosicrucian Symbolical Philosophy*. Los Angeles CA: Philosophical Research Soc., 1972.

Hancock, Graham. *Fingerprints Of The Gods*. New York NY: Crown publishers, 1995.

Harner, Michael. *The Way of The Shaman: A Guide To Power And Healing*. New York NY: Bantum Books, 1980.

Harper, John. *Transformers: Shamans Of The 21st Century*. Foresthill CA: Reality Press, 2006.

Hawken, Paul. The *Magic of Findhorn: An Eyewitness Account*. New York NY: Bantum Books, 1975.

Hawkins, David R., M.D., Ph.D. *Power vs. Force: the Hidden Determinants of Human Behavior*. Carlsbad CA: Hay House, 2002.

Henkel, Elon. *The Henckel Family Records: 1635-1939*. New Market VA: Henkel Press, Inc., 1926.

Henkle, Duane and Diana Stone. *The Lightbody Activation Manual*. Vancouver WA: Crystal Triangle Publishing, 2002.

Henkle, Duane. *The Ascension Guidebook*. Vancouver WA: Crystal Triangle Publishing, 2006.

Hoagland, Richard. *The Monuments On Mars*. Berkeley CA: North Atlantic Books, 1990.

Hofstadter, Douglas. *Godel Escher Bach: An Eternal Golden Braid*. New York NY: Vintage Books, 1980.

Ingerman, Sandra. Soul *Retrieval: Mending The Fragmented Self*. New York NY: Harper San Francisco, 1991.

Joseph, Frank. *The Destruction Of Atlantis: Compelling Evidence Of The Sudden Fall Of The Legendary Civilization*. Rochester VT: Bear & Co, 2004.

Joseph, Frank. *Survivors of Atlantis*. Rochester VT: Bear & Co, 2004.

Kalb, Ken. *Lightshift 2000: Let's Turn On The Light Of The World*. Santa Barbara CA: Lucky Star Research Institute, 1998.

Klein, Eric. *The Inner Door: Channeled Discourses From The Ascended Masters On Self-Mastery And Ascension.* Livermore CA: Oughten House Pub, 1993.

Laszlo, Ervin. *Worldshift 2012: Making Green Business New Politics And Higher Consciousness Work Together.* Rochester VT: Inner Traditions, 2009.

LaViolette, Paul. Genesis *of the Cosmos: The Ancient Science of Continuous Creation.* Rochester VT: Bear & Co, 2004.

Lipton, Bruce. *Spontaneous Evolution: Our Positive Future (And A Way to Get There From Here).* Carlsbad CA: Hay House, 2009.

Lipton, Bruce. *The Biology of Belief: Unleashing the Power of Consciousness Matter and Miracles.* Santa Rosa CA: Mountain of Love-Elite Books, 2005.

Long, Max Freedom. *The Secret Science Behind Miracles.* Marina del Rey CA: DeVorss & Co., 1954.

Long, Max Freedom. *The Secret Science At Work: New Light On Prayer* (Now Subtitled As: *The Huna Method As A Way Of Life.*). Marina del Rey CA: DeVorss & Co., 1953.

Lowary, Sheila Petersen. *The 5Th Dimension: Channels to a New Reality.* New York NY: Fireside Simon & Schuster Inc., 1988.

Marohn, Stephanie. *The Natural Medicine Guide to Bipolar Disorder.* Charlottesville VA: Hampton Roads Pub, 2003.

Matthews, Caitlin. *Psychic Shield: A Personal Handbook Of Psychic Protection.* Berkeley CA: Ulysses Press, 2006.

Maynard, Sharon. *The Ancient Ones: The Mission Remembered.* Seattle WA: Lemon Tree Press, 1995.

McGonigal, Jane. *Reality Is Broken: Why Games Make Us Better And How They Can Change The World.* New York NY: Penguin Books, 2011.

Melchizedek, Drunvalo. The *Ancient Secret Of The Flower Of Life: Vol. 1.* Flagstaff AZ: Light Technology Publishing, 1998.

Melchizedek, Drunvalo. *The Ancient Secret Of The Flower Of Life: Vol. 2.* Flagstaff AZ: Light Technology Publishing, 2000.

Milanovich, Dr. Norma J. *We the Arcturians (A True Experience).* Albuquerque NM: Athena Publishing, 1990.

Miller, David K.. *Connecting With the Arcturians.* Pine AZ: Planetary Heart Publications, 1998.

Modi, Shakuntala, M.D. *Remarkable Healings: A Psychiatrist Discovers Unsuspected Roots Of Mental And Physical Illness.* Charlottesville VA: Hampton Roads Publishing, 1997.

Montgomery, Ruth. *Strangers Among Us: Enlightened Beings From A World To Come.* New York NY: Coward McCann & Geoghegan, 1979.

Myss, Caroline. *Sacred Contracts: Awakening Your Divine Potential.* New York NY: Three Rivers Press, 2003.

Newton, Michael. Ph.D. *Journey of Souls: Case Studies Of Life Between Lives.* St. Paul MN: Llewellyn Publications, 1994.

Newton, Michael. Ph.D. *Life Between Lives: Hypnotherapy For Spiritual Regression.* St. Paul MN: Llewellyn Publications, 2004.

Newton, Michael. *Journey Of Souls: Case Studies Of Life Between Lives.* St. Paul MN: Llewellyn Publications, 1994.

Nørretranders, Tor. *The User Illusion: Cutting Consciousness Down To Size.* New York NY: Penguin Books, 1999.

Null, Ghary Ph.D. *The Complete Encyclopedia of Natural Healing.* Stamford CT: Bottom Line Books, 2004.

Paddison, Sara. *The Hidden Power of the Heart.* Boulder Creek CA: Planetary Publications, 1995.

Phylos, Orpheus and Virginia Essene. *Earth The Cosmos And You: Revelations By Archangel Michael.* Santa Clara CA: S.E.E. Publishing Company, 1999.

Pila of Hawaii, *The Secrets And Mysteries Of Hawaii.* Honolulu HI: Health Communications, 1995.

Pinchbeck, Daniel. *2012: The Return of Quetzalcoatl.* New York NY: Jeremy Tarcher-Penguin, 2006.

Roberts, Jane. *Seth Speaks: The Eternal Validity Of The Soul.* Englewood Cliffs NJ: Prentice-Hall, 1972.

Roberts, Jane. *The Seth Material.* Englewood Cliffs NJ: Prentice-Hall, 1970.

Robles, Patricia. *Who Am I? Why Am I Here.* Tucson AZ: New Age Study of Humanity's Purpose, 2010.

Sannella, Lee. *Kundalini: Psychosis Or Transcendence.* San Francisco CA: HS Dakin Co, 1981.

Santillana, Giorgio. *Hamlet's Mill: an Essay on Myth and the Frame of Time.* Boston MA: Godine, 1977.

Shook, E. Ho'oponopono*: Contemporary Uses of a Hawaiian Problem-Solving Process.* Honolulu HI: East-West Center-Univ. of Hawaii Press, 1985.

Sitchin, Zecharia. *The 12Th Planet: Book I.* New York NY: Harper, 2007.

Sitchin, Zecharia. *The Stairway to Heaven: Book II.* New York NY: Harper, 2007.

Sitchin, Zecharia. *The Wars of Gods and Men: Book III.* New York NY: Harper, 2007.

Sitchin, Zecharia. *The Lost Realms: Book IV.* New York NY: Harper, 2007.

Sitchin, Zecharia. *When Time Began: Book V.* New York NY: Harper, 2007.

Sitchin, Zecharia. *The Cosmic Code: Book VI.* New York NY: Avon Books, 1998.

Sitchin, Zecharia. The *End of Days: Armageddon and Prophecies of the Return: Book VII.* New York NY: William Morrow, 2007.

Sitchin, Zecharia. *Genesis Revisited: Is Modern Science Catching Up With Ancient Knowledge?.* New York NY: Avon Books, 1990.

Sitchin, Zecharia. The *Lost Book of Enki: Memoirs and Prophecies of an Extraterrestrial God.* Rochester VT: Bear & Co, 2002.

Sitchin, Zecharia. Divine *Encounters: A Guide to Visions Angels and Other Emissaries.* Rochester VT: Bear & Co, 2002.

Sitchin, Zecharia. *The Earth Chronicles Expeditions.* Rochester VT: Bear & Co, 2007.

Sitchin, Zecharia. *The Earth Chronicles Handbook: A Comprehensive Guide to the Seven Books of The Earth Chronicles.* Rochester VT: Bear & Co, 2009.

Sitchin, Zecharia. *There Were Giants upon the Earth: Gods Demigods and Human Ancestry: The Evidence Of Alien DNA*. Rochester VT: Bear & Co, 2010.

Stearn, Jess. *The Power of Alpha Thinking: Miracle of the Mind.* New York NY: Signet Books, 1976.

Stearn, Jess. Edgar Cayce. *The Sleeping Prophet.* New York NY: Doubleday, 1067.

Steinbrecher, Edwin C. *The Inner Guide Meditation.* York Beach ME: Samuel Weiser Inc., 1988.

Stone, Duane Henkle and Diana. *The Lightbody Activation Manual.* Vancouver WA: Crystal Triangle Publishing, 2002.

Stone, Diana. *Remarkable Healings: A Psychiatrist Discovers Unsuspected Roots Of Mental And Physical Illness.* Tempe AZ: American Fed. of Astrologers, 1976.

Stone, Diana. "The Artistry of Imagination" in Exploring *Consciousness In The Horoscope.* St.Paul MN: Llewellyn Publications, 1993.

Stone, Diana. "Root Causes of Mental Illness" in How *to Manage the Astrology of Crisis.* St.Paul MN: Llewellyn Publications, 1993.

Stubbs, Tony. *An Ascension Handbook.* Lithia GA: New Leaf Distributing, 1999.

Sugrue, Thomas. *There Is A River: The Story Of Edgar Cayce.* New York NY: Dell Publishing, 1942.

Sutphen, Dick. *Past Lives, Future Loves.* New York NY: Pocket Books, 1978.

Tachi-ren, Tashira.. *What Is Lightbody?* Lithia GA: New Leaf Distributing, 1999.

Talbot, Michael. *The Holographic Universe.* New York NY: Harper Perennial, 1991.

Thomas, Chris. *The Annunaki Plan? Or The Human Plan?* Llandysul: Fortynine Publishers, 2010.

Thomas, Chris. *The Journey Home.* Chieveley: Capall Bann, 1998.

Thomas, Chris. *The Human Soul 2.* City: Capall Bann Pub. Chieveley: Capall Bann, 2007.

Thomas, Chris. *Planet Earth: The Universe's Experiment..* Milverton: Capall Bann, 2003.

Thomas, Chris. Project *Human Extinction: The Ultimate Conspiracy.* Somerset: Capall Bann, 2009.

Thomas, Chris. The *Fool's First Steps: The True Nature of Reality.* Chieveley: Capall Bann, 1999.

Thomas, Chris. The Universal *Soul.* Somerset: Capall Bann, 2005.

Villoldo, Alberto, Ph.D. *Mending the Past and Healing the Future with Soul Retrieval.* Carlsbad CA: Hay House Inc., 2005.

Villoldo, Alberto, Ph.D. *Shaman Healer Sage.* New York NY: Harmony Books, 2000.

Villoldo, Alberto, Ph.D. *Courageous Dreaming: How Shamans Dream The World Into Being.* Carlsbad CA: Hay House, 2008.

Vitale, Joe. Zero Limits: *The Secret Hawaiian System for Wealth Health Peace and More.* Hoboken NJ: John Wiley & Sons, 2007.

Vitale, Joe. The Key: *The Missing Secret For Attracting Anything You Want.* Hoboken NJ: John Wiley & Sons, 2008.

Vithoulkas, George. *Homeopathy: Medicine of the New Man.* New York NY: Prentice Hall; Press, 1979.

Ward, Suzanne. *My Conversations with Animals.* Camas WA: Matthew Books, 2009.

Waters, Owen. *The Shift: The Revolution in Human Consciousness.* Delaware: Infinite Being Pub, 2006.

Waya, Ai Gvhdi. *Soul Recovery and Extraction.* Cottonwood AZ: Blue Turtle Pub, 1993.

Weeks, Nora. *The Medical Discoveries of Edward Bach, Physician.* New Canaan CT: Keats Publishing, 1973.

West, Bruce, D.C. *The Encyclopedia of Pragmatic Medicine.* Monterey CA: Health Alert, 2012

Wilcock, David. *The Shift of the Ages.* http://www.ascension2000.com.

Wilcock, David. *The Science of Oneness.* http://www.ascension2000.com.

Wilcock, David. *The Divine Cosmos.* www.ascension.2000.com.

Wilcock, David. *The Source Field Investigations: The Hidden Science and Lost Civilizations Behind The 2012 Prophecies.* New York NY: Dutton, 2011.

Wing, R.L. *The I Ching Workbook.* Main Street Books: Doubleday, 1979.

Wurmbrand, Richard. *Tortured For Christ.* Bartlesville OK: Living Sacrifice Book Co, 2007.

INDEX

E

F

G

O

P

Q

R

Made in the USA
Charleston, SC
08 December 2012